SUSAN WEISSMAN is a Professor of Politics at Saint Mary's College in Moraga, California. She is an award-winning broadcast journalist, sits on the editorial boards of *Critique* and *Against the Current*, and is the editor of *Victor Serge: Russia Twenty Years After* and *The Ideas of Victor Serge*.

VICTOR SERGE

The course is set on hope

◆

Susan Weissman

VERSO

London · New York

This updated paperback edition first published by Verso 2013
First published by Verso 2001
© Susan Weissman 2001, 2013

Verso
UK: 6 Meard Street, London W1F 0EG
US: 20 Jay Street, Suite 1010, Brooklyn, NY 11201

www.versobooks.com

Verso is the imprint of New Left Books

ISBN-13: 978-1-84467-887-7

British Library Catologuing in Publication Data
A catalogue record for this book is available from the British Library

Library of Congress Cataloging-in-Publication Data
A catalog record for this book is available from the Library of Congress

Typeset by The Running Head Limited, www.therunninghead.com
Printed in the US by Maple Vail

To the memory of Roberto Naduris
whose bright smile is on every
page of this book,
to Eli and Natalia,
and to the memory of my parents,
Perle and Maurice Weissman

Contents

List of illustrations

Preface to the Paperback Edition

This book aims to bring back to life the extraordinary commitment and hope of one of the great writer-thinker-activists of the twentieth century. Victor Serge is remembered for the intellectual richness and moral insight he brought to our understanding of the significant historical struggles of our time, as well as for the principled revolutionary life he exemplified. The journalist Daniel Singer wrote that 'Victor Serge devoted his life and brilliant pen to the revolution which for him knew no frontiers. An anarchist turned Bolshevik, he was unorthodox by nature, often a heretic but never a renegade.'[1] Serge lived in the maelstrom of the first half of the twentieth century, but his ideas are germane to current debates in our post-Soviet, post-Cold War world. His contribution is especially attractive today because Serge never compromised his commitment to the creation of a society that defends human freedom, enhances human dignity and improves the human condition. He belongs to our future.

Some readers may wonder how, more than a decade into the twenty-first century, the work of this almost forgotten revolutionary could have contemporary relevance. As the last century drew to a close, the Soviet Union collapsed, and with its demise the colossal battle of ideas it had provoked nearly disappeared from public discourse. How could the ideas and struggles that Serge represented, emerging from the titanic debates over the Russian Revolution and the society to which it gave birth, continue to resonate?

In fact, interest in Serge's work experienced a stunning revival just as the Soviet Union was disintegrating, and is today in virtual renaissance – his books are being published or re-published in many languages.[2] With the end of Stalinism, the victors of the Cold War have proclaimed there is no alternative to Western-style capitalist democracy, even as inequalities have continued to deepen, everyday life and culture have been crassly commercialized, and democracy has been hollowed out. In response, a new generation has taken to the streets demanding a better world, and what is more, insisting that it is possible. As one sorts through the intellectual and political disputes of the disastrous Soviet experience, one is struck by the voice and testimony of Victor Serge. His works address the paramount and still unresolved issues of the day, as if he were speaking directly to this generation. Serge worried about how human beings could secure liberty, autonomy and dignity, and he belonged to a revolutionary generation that sought to create a society sufficient to realize these goals. They failed, but Serge spent the rest of his life elucidating the attempt, analysing the defeat and seeking better ways to the same ends. For that reason his life and work merits republication, analysis, interpretation and, above all, *rescue*.

Why rescue? The history of the Soviet experience is being rewritten by Cold Warriors and free-market dogmatists West and East who see early Bolshevism as no different from mature Stalinism. Both sides in the Cold War – in a rather strange symbiosis – thrived on this deliberate dishonesty in defining the nature and character of Communism, in theory and horrible practice. Both sides had an interest in distorting the ideas of the Soviet Left Opposition, who are once again being airbrushed from the platform of history. This book was written to rescue Serge from the margins and to redeem his reputation and his ideas, as well as to contribute in some small measure to correcting the historical record. Serge wasn't the only one nearly erased from historical memory, but he stands in this rendition as a clear representative of the ideas behind the October Revolution, ideas that fell by the wayside with the rise of Stalin.

The new editions of Victor Serge's writings have been well received by leading contemporary intellectuals who recognize Serge as an important figure for the present. The American historian Walter Lacqueur finds the present Serge revival well deserved. 'Serge's political recollections are very important because they reflect so well the mood of this lost generation [the small group of revolutionaries who were survivors of World War I]. His writings will find readers now because they help grant an understanding of the aftermath of the Russian Revolution and its impact on militants and intellectuals' from what Lacqueur calls 'a world of yesterday almost as distant from subsequent generations as the Napoleonic wars'.[3] No longer invisible, Serge's articles and books speak for themselves, and as Lacqueur concludes, 'we would be poorer without them'.

So contemporary a writer as Antonio Negri has appreciated the power of Serge's contribution, commenting that Serge 'joyfully, ironically and light-heartedly strove to build the world soviet republic … never gave up hope, despite betrayal and defeat, prison and exile … [and was] a member of that race of giants, a gargantuan in the fight for freedom and collective happiness'. Adam Hochschild calls Serge one of the 'unsung heroes of a corrupt century', and Mike Davis considers Serge the 'Revolution's most ardent lover and indestructible conscience'.

Readers needn't share Serge's views, nor the optimism that he retained despite the defeats he witnessed and lived through, though it is hard not to be impressed, as Christopher Hitchens wrote, 'by the difference that may be made by an intransigent individual'.[4] Serge stands as a persistent reminder of the political decay of the twentieth century's great revolution. He believed the revolution's death was self-inflicted by the reactionary tyranny it let loose on itself, a process Serge relentlessly strove to understand. For the Russian poet Yevgeny Yevtushenko, Serge 'permitted himself a very dangerous luxury – to be ashamed by the inhuman face of his beloved revolution, and he was punished for it'. Serge's shame and punishment were for his insistent hope and attention to the irrepressible vitality of individual human nature. As Yevtushenko wrote,

> In 1968 when I was preparing for a poetry reading in Mexico, my Mexican friends loaned me Victor Serge's typewriter. My fingers almost froze as each touch of the keyboard woke up so many ghosts of the past … This is … a unique man, Victor Serge … one of the first fighters for socialism with a human face forty years before the Prague Spring was trumped into mud by Brezhnev's tanks.[5]

Between 1919 and 1936 Serge lived mostly in the Soviet Union, his 'homeland', though as with his son Vlady, it could be argued that 'revolution' was his home. But Serge's perceptions differed in important ways from those of his Soviet comrades. He came to the Soviet Union from Western Europe, where he was raised in the Russian anarcho-populist exile community, and was connected to anarchist, syndicalist, artistic and literary circles, and he continued to associate with non-Party artists and writers in revolutionary Russia. He did not spend his entire political life in the Bolshevik Party, nor did he share the 'Party patriotism' of many of his comrades. Serge's critical sensibilities were a product of his experiences as both an outsider and an insider, a Russian raised in Western Europe with experience across a broad spectrum of leftist thought and practice. He was with the Bolsheviks because they managed actually to function as revolutionaries at a time of revolution. He shared their democratic goals and was critical of their authoritarian practices.

For Serge, democracy was a defining component of socialism: he didn't think of it as an 'accessory of the revolutionary process' but as integral to it, indeed at the heart of the socialist project. The workers in Tsarist Russia created soviets, or councils – profoundly democratic organizational forms whose existence marked the health of a revolutionary process. These institutions were key to the success of the revolution and the transition, and were to be the governing institutions of socialist society. Revolutionaries like Serge from around the globe understood the power of soviets and saw in them 'the realization of our deepest hopes' for a libertarian, democratic, truly tolerant and egalitarian form without the 'hypocrisy and flabbiness of bourgeois democracies'.[6] Yet these organs of genuine democratic control from below did not survive the measures forced by the dire conditions of the besieged revolution in the civil war. It is also fair to say that the Bolshevik leadership had an underdeveloped commitment to them. Serge called for the revitalization of the soviets in substance, not just form.

The conditions that left the Bolsheviks isolated in power as well as in the world led to their developing party power rather than soviet power. Not long after Lenin died, Stalin came to power and killed what remained of any hope for soviet socialist democracy. Serge's critique of this process of political degeneration was at the core of his activities and his writings, and that critique made Serge suspect in some quarters, misunderstood and maligned in others. Social democrats and anarchists distanced themselves from him, as did the apologists for Stalinism. Although Serge had stood with Trotsky and the Left Opposition since 1923, and was the best-known Trotskyist among circles of intellectuals in the West, he was criticized by Trotsky and Trotskyists in the late 1930s for his differences over political issues and organizational practices. Though Serge argued with Trotsky from within the anti-Stalinist left, and was an unrepentant revolutionary Marxist, his perceptions also put him at odds with his co-thinkers in the West, causing him much grief and isolating him from the very movement – the Left Opposition – that he had devoted so many years to and at such risk.

Reading through the record of these debates, arguments and accusations gives us a sense of the desperate atmosphere of the time as well as the anguish Serge felt as he witnessed Stalin's campaign of assassinations that stretched from Moscow to Madrid. The small group of Trotskyist exiles in Western Europe were free to work and free to meet, yet there were agents in their midst, assassins marking their movements, and bitter denunciations and infighting among the increasingly isolated sectors of this far left opposition. Pressed into Stalin's intelligence service were accomplished members of the creative intelligentsia, poets, writers, psychoanalysts and anthropologists, making anyone and everyone suspect, even Serge. Though Serge was now out of the USSR, he wasn't free from Stalin's reach, and life in exile was very difficult. He was in constant peril, vilified in the Communist Party press, suspected at times by his own comrades, caring for his sick wife, campaigning to refute the fantastic charges of the Moscow Trials, writing and translating, and always broke.

Misinformation, deliberate distortions and outright lies about what was happening in the Soviet Union were pervasive in the West. Concrete information was very hard to obtain, especially about those who opposed Stalin's rule back in the USSR. For this reason we ransack Serge's novels for information about how the Oppositionists coped, and read between the lines of the messages passed among them. The form may be fiction, but Serge was a revolutionary *witness* who regularly and conscientiously recorded his memories. His testimony and ideas are not simply a time capsule from the front lines of history: his writings give us a real sense of the human and political dramas unfolding in those years in a way that is directly comprehensible.

It may seem surprising that Stalin concentrated such fury and zeal in hunting down the rather small number of Trotskyists and oppositionists who challenged his rule in organizations and far left journals in the West in the late 1930s and early 1940s. The mighty effort to extinguish the small flames of defiance seems disproportionate in view of such enormous tasks at hand as preparing for war. Yet Marxist critics like Trotsky and Serge were not just a thorn in Stalin's side, but a moral reproach to his rule. Better to silence them, to prevent their voices from finding large audiences. Trotsky was assassinated in August 1940. Serge survived and continued to wage the battle of the pen, his thinking now directed toward analysing the features of the postwar period. Looking forward from the defeats inflicted by Stalinism, which threatened the ideas of socialism itself, and by Fascism, which had deeply damaged the working-class movement, Serge called for a renewal of socialism if it were to remain relevant.

Reviewing the issues that preoccupied Serge in these dark years yields much to reclaim for the present day, even though the context of his time is radically different from the present we inhabit. Serge was writing during World War II and in the immediate postwar period, before the Cold War began in earnest. He was deeply troubled by what he saw – efficient bureaucratic machines with collectivist tendencies that completely choked democratic participation from below.[7] His writings about these developments reflect a world that is long gone. Yet the tendencies he noted and the questions he asked are surely relevant. Serge indeed proved prescient: if an historically conscious democratic collectivism did not successfully challenge the totalitarian collectivism of Stalinism and fascism, it would mean the end of socialism on a world scale for a whole era.

Serge held that the assumptions derived from the days of the Russian Revolution were no longer adequate. Writing in 1945, he observed that everything – science, production, social movements and intellectual currents – had changed. History permitted apparent stability only to religious dogmas. An intellectual rearmament was necessary, and for that a creative investigatory effort was required. As Serge noted, 'the poverty of traditional socialism coincides in reality with the immense revolutionary crisis of the modern world that puts unavoidably on the order of the day for all of humanity – independently of the action of socialism – the problem of a social reorganization oriented toward the rational and the just'.[8] Serge couldn't emphasize strongly enough that the socialist movement had to break free from its fossilized thinking, and that the terrible new conditions demanded a fresh approach – dialectical thought combined with political action, a form of active humanism. Serge was fully justified in warning that continued adherence to the old patterns and formulas would bear grave consequences for the socialist movement. Sadly, he was proved right.

Much had changed in the years since 1917. The actuality of the revolution had emboldened workers in the West, radicalized by war, revolution and the deepening capitalist crisis. Labour movements in the West were active and Communist Parties grew in membership, supported financially by the USSR. In the inter-war period, the threat to capitalism's very survival was so great that Germany and Italy resorted to fascism. The New Deal in the United States was capitalism's response to a militant labour movement, using concessions to incorporate the working class rather than try to crush it. After World War II the welfare-state reforms, including capitalist nationalization of key sectors of industry, were accommodations to the threat represented by a radicalized working class and the continued existence of the Soviet Union.

Stalinism – in the guise of Russian socialism – was degenerate and intolerant, according to Serge. European socialists, tainted by Stalinism, could not see the roots of racism and anti-Semitism, nor the appeal of fascist reactionary nationalism – and they were weakened by their inattention to the changes brought about in the state and the economy by technological innovation.[9] It was undeniable that the Soviet regime, fascism, Nazism and the New Deal shared common traits that reflected the collectivist tendencies of the modern economy. Trotsky, writing in 1939, also noted these similarities. The socialist movement needed intellectual rigour, an understanding of political economy, a living philosophy – which could point the way for workers to transcend bureaucratic statism if they were to achieve democratic control of society, organize a rational economy and realize a higher dignity.[10]

In essence, socialist thought needed updating to keep current with developments in the economy, discoveries in science and advances in the understanding of human psychology. Stalinism had retarded intellectual development with its state dogma, directed thought and 'ownership' of philosophical truth. The Marxist method of analysis and interpretation of history had been degraded as a consequence. Even on its own *terra firma* of political economy, European socialists had ignored the changes wrought by advances in technology that increased productivity but reduced the importance of manual labour. The developments in industry upset the traditional class proportions and relations, giving increased importance to governing bureaucracies as well as intermediary layers of administrators, technicians, managers and an intelligentsia of sociologists, economists and psychologists. The existing analysis of the class struggle was too schematic, Serge wrote, in that it did not take into account the role of the shareholders and tycoons, or the civil employees of the totalitarian state.[11]

The USSR represented a new, negative force in the world, influencing and altering the nature of current struggles. It was now an obstacle to socialism – and this made the question of democracy even more important. Much of what Serge was writing at this time is the product of his efforts to come to grips with a world where totalitarian collectivism, as he called it, dominated both the Soviet Union and, during the war and its immediate aftermath, appeared to be increasingly influential in Western Europe as well. For Serge this foreboded a dark future, where the economy would be subject not to the democratic control of workers and their organizations, but run by technocrats and totalitarians who strangle democracy, even as they organize production ever more efficiently.

It was sobering to realize that collectivism was not synonymous with socialism (as Serge and his comrades had previously thought) and could in fact be anti-socialist, manifesting new forms of exploitation. For Serge this revealed the extreme weakness of socialist movements and socialist thought. The defeats suffered in Europe were partly due to this theoretical as well as organizational debility. Lacking energy and foresight, the European social-ists were 'brutally overtaken by events'. Serge added that 'the subjective factor was not equal to the objective circumstances', that the socialists were not clearly aware of the dangers they faced nor of the opportunities offered to them. Likewise, the Bolsheviks were responsible in part for the march toward totalitarianism in the Soviet Union: Serge blamed their psychology, their ignorance of democratic values and the methods they employed. The Bolsheviks compensated for their ideological insufficiency with will and authority – and also terror.[12]

American socialists (Sidney Hook, Dwight Macdonald, James Burnham et al.) and liberals were more concerned with freedom and liberty than their European counterparts, but Serge noted their ideas were based on the ideals of bourgeois liberal humanism and the traditions of parliamentary democracy – honourable but out of date, Serge warned, because the role of the state and its executive had increased so radically in the era of national-ized economies. On the other hand, the extended functions of the modern state, Serge believed, made obsolete the notion of the abolition of the state. The libertarian commune state of the Bolsheviks in 1917, theorized in Lenin's *State and Revolution*, went bankrupt, and the withering away of the state died during Lenin's lifetime.[13] The Stalinist scourge nearly eradicated the notion that socialism is full democracy and rendered it equivalent in the popular mind with anti-democracy. For Serge it was crucial to realize that 'Wherever totalitarian communism prevails, nothing progressive will be able to be done. On the contrary, we will see the stifling of thought and strangulation of oppositions.'[14]

There were grounds for optimism, according to Serge: the rebuilding of the European economy after the war would strengthen the working class, and the interdependence of nations could result in an internationaliza-tion of societies that Serge believed would promote the growth of socialist struggle. At the same time, the totalitarian regimes spawned a vigorous and deeply anti-totalitarian reaction, and no matter how tragically difficult the immediate situation was, socialism might still have a great future in front of it. But the intellectual weakness of the socialist movement (sapped of its energies by the formidable Stalinist machine) could only be remedied by an 'epoch of uprising'.[15]

Serge misjudged the tendencies he noted, believing the world was in transition away from capitalism towards some form of statist bureaucracy. He was trying to define the characteristics of a world still in the process of becoming, and he couldn't see past the period he lived in. Unlike other thinkers of the time, Serge did not proclaim socialism a failure, but called for its rebirth. Democracy must mean democracy at work and in the economy as a whole; liberty must mean personal and political freedom.

What then may be salvaged from his writings, given so much has changed? The fact that the revolution took place, despite what it turned into, changed the nature of the world, and the influence of the revolution's promise was felt in the industrialized capitalist democracies. Important elements of a more advanced political democracy, such as universal franchise, representative democracy, free speech and other basic rights, were won and conceded to in response to the existence of the Soviet Union and to contain radicalism at home. After 1918 and again after 1945 the radicalized working class demanded and gained social protections and democratic advances. The concessions provided a springboard for further demands. The democratic gains of the second half of the twentieth century, brought by the labour, civil rights and women's movements, significantly deepened democracy leading to substantial changes in advanced industrial democracies without appreciably deepening the struggle for 'economic democracy' or workers' rights.[16] These reforms strengthened democracy, and democracy in turn brought the welfare state. Yet the latter cut into the profitability of capitalism at a time – after 1973 – when capitalism seemed increasingly stagnant. With the disintegration of the Soviet Union and Eastern Europe, the concessions to social democracy became less necessary, and increasingly difficult to deliver in the age of finance capital. It is no surprise, then, that the collapse of the Soviet Union hastened the decline of social democracy. At the same time, we are seeing the hollowing out of bourgeois democracy, perhaps nowhere more pronounced than in the United States itself, and caricatured in the so-called new democracies of the former Soviet bloc. The decline of bourgeois democracy is directly tied to the weakened labour and socialist movements.

The fine principles of liberal democracy are not enough – their forms of democratic governance cannot solve economic crisis, nor can elections halt the downward slide in the standard of living, much less empower workers. Still, the promise of democracy is potent and even risky, as more and more people demand the genuine article, not managed electoral shams.[17]

Today the struggle for democracy is a direct fight for new forms of democratic decision-making, exercised from below. Authentic democracy – control from below – requires a sufficient level of understanding and education, and is impossible if money has influence in the process. In many ways the struggle for this bottom-up democracy is a revolutionary struggle that involves coming up with better forms than the soviets promised. We can't presume in advance what they will look like, as the political form will be determined by the struggle itself, though without a high level of participation and control from below, substantive democracy remains but a dream.

The world faces a bleak landscape brought about by economic collapse and careless disregard of the environment (both natural and human). Preliminary responses came from the right in religious, nationalist, terrorist and populist forms. One decade into the new century the discontent and disillusion with dysfunctional or deceptive democratic forms has not led to despair, but to massive mobilizations of profoundly democratic social movements toppling dictators in the Arab Middle East, protesting and striking against an unjust economic system throughout Europe, and occupying cities and towns across the US by the '99%' against the financial elites who were blamed for drowning the population in debt while destroying their chances for a decent economic future. Disaffected by a politics that only serves the rich and the powerful, people are reclaiming democracy and revitalizing political protest against the ravages of capitalism. Their demands may not constitute a call for socialism, but the protestors have given the elites notice that they refuse to continue with the status quo. Repression has been swift, but has not suppressed the workers, students, unemployed and foreclosed, who invent new forms, fighting to reclaim their autonomy and be heard. They lack the intellectual armour of the revolutionary generation a century ago, but they share their hope that the economy and society can be organized to serve humanity and the community. The human impulse for freedom, dignity and self-organization emerges over and over again – and is cause for great hope. Serge's epoch of uprising may be upon us.

*　　*　　*

Since the publication of this book, both Vlady (2005) and Jeannine Kibalchich (2012), Serge's son and daughter, have left us, as did his wife Laurette Séjourné in 2003. This new edition contains an extensive biographical glossary at the end, identifying some of the many characters and organizations Serge encountered or mentioned in his writings, and publications that carried his articles. The sources for these entries were too numerous to cite. It should also be noted that a new edition of Serge's *Memoirs of a Revolutionary* was published in 2012 by the *New York Review of Books*, containing the complete, unexpurgated text, which had been cut by an eighth as a condition of publication by Oxford University Press in 1963. The references in this work pertain to the earlier edition.

I am grateful to the late Clara Heyworth for helping bring about this Verso paperback edition, and to Verso's Jacob Stevens, Audrea Lim and Mark Martin. Thanks are also due to translators Michel Vale, Patrick Silberstein, Patrick Le Tréhondat and Francisco Sobrino for their conscientiousness and commitment. There aren't adequate words to express my gratitude for the gift of Robert Brenner's probing questions, editorial refinements, steadfast support and love.

Preface

Julian Gorkín called his friend Victor Serge an 'eternal vagabond in search of the ideal'. Serge's life's journey was rather in search of justice, for a higher dignity for humanity than either Soviet Stalinism or capitalism could allow. In setting 'the course on hope' he pursued truth, struggled against privilege, and sought social justice and dignity. He chose to participate in the making of history by involving himself in the daily struggles of ordinary people. In Serge's time, these struggles were heroic.

Nearly invisible to history, Serge stood on the side of the defeated, with those who refused to compromise with capitalism or surrender to Stalinism. Neither was acceptable. The cost was high: Serge's eloquent voice and mighty pen could not prevent him from being sidelined by history. The general ignorance of this man – in all but the smallest circles of the far left and among Soviet specialists – is at once perplexing and frustrating.

This aura of invisibility made my own discovery of Serge all the more remarkable. One of my professors in graduate school at Glasgow University's Institute of Soviet and East European Studies hinted to me as I walked out of his room that I must read Serge's *Memoirs*. His hushed tone intrigued me, and that weekend I took the train to London, with Serge's *Memoirs* as company. The six-hour, bumpy journey passed in a moment and when I arrived I simply moved from the bench on the train to a bench in the station, where I sat until I finished the book. I never looked back.

The trail from there to here has been long and interrupted, and the research has taken me from Scotland to California, New York, Mexico, France, Belgium and the then Soviet Union. Along the way there were too many frustrating misses because I had started this project nearly forty years after Serge's death. Many who knew him were also now dead. Some died just months or weeks before I found them. One was murdered just days before our appointment!

Serge's son Vlady and his wife Isabel welcomed me into their Mexico City home as if it were my own, and I left exhilarated after finding so many file cabinets and boxes filled with Serge's unpublished writings. It was clear that his unpublished *œuvre* was easily as large as what had been published, and there was much to discover.

I returned to Mexico City the following year to give a talk on Serge and Trotsky at a conference. Afterwards a woman in the audience approached and hugged me – then whispered in my ear that she was Serge's daughter Jeannine. She bears an uncanny resemblance to her father.

Political passions drew me to Serge, and it was his political sense that sustained what some might call a mission to rescue from the margins of history a voice important to the twenty-first century. Familiar with the political milieu from which Serge had broken, I shared his scepticism about organizations certain they alone possessed 'the truth'. It perplexed me that the mere mention of Serge's name could arouse hostility. It made me curious to get at the heart of the controversies, to find out what, exactly, Serge stood for.

Once into the work, my original questions seemed less important, yet whenever I mentioned I was working on Serge I faced these queries: did Serge, at the end of his life, support de Gaulle and renege on revolution?*

---

* In the appendix to the English version of Serge's *Memoirs* (London, Oxford University Press, 1963 and Writers and Readers, 1984), Peter Sedgwick, the translator, included an excerpt of a letter Serge had written to André Malraux six days before he died. The American FBI had the letter as well, and a translated excerpt is quoted in Serge's file. (FBI Memo 100–72924–833, 5/27/48, translated from *Demokratisches Post*, vol. V, no. 14, 1 March 1948, Mexico DF, in a section entitled 'Treason and Traitors' – Serge apparently being the traitor.) It appeared, in the excerpted lines, that Serge expressed something approaching support for Malraux's collaboration with the Rassemblement du Peuple Français (RAP). Serge wrote: 'I should like to assure you that I consider the decision made by you regarding your political attitude as courageous and logical. If I were in France I should surely belong to the socialists, who are cooperating with the movement to which you belong. I consider the election of your movement the most decisive step in the direction of the necessary salvation of France.' I have not spent space on this incident in this study, largely because I think it unimportant to understanding his life and his views, and because I am in full accord with Peter Sedgwick's explanation, that Serge nowhere supported Gaullism in his entire body of work, and indeed criticized it in print. I could add to Sedgwick's examples a letter Serge wrote to Podoliak (Hryhory Kostiuk) in the same month he wrote to Malraux, in which he proclaimed his unwavering and intransigent commitment to socialism. Vlady, Serge's son, explained that he urged Serge, nearly destitute and without any way of making a living in Mexico as a French writer, to write to Malraux to see if Serge could return to France. Serge, Vlady continued, did not want to write the letter, but at Vlady's insistence, did so. There can be no doubt that the extracted lines, which the RAP published in January 1948 in *Le Rassemblement*, were written by Serge. There is no record of Serge's reasoning when he wrote the letter. One could say Serge was flattering Malraux and that it was an act of opportunism. As Sedgwick wrote, if Serge had

Did Serge veer toward the right wing Menshevism of the original Cold-War liberals? The questions revealed much more about the axes those asking had to grind than about Serge.

Victor Serge was one of the few Bolsheviks from the revolutionary generation who refused to surrender and who struggled so that their ideas would survive Stalin's attempt to exterminate them. Serge let his literary voice speak for those Stalin silenced. Amazingly Serge did not succumb to pessimism, despite the horrors of the period. He was alert to the danger Stalin represented throughout the world. In Mexico, Serge cautioned the 'fossilized dogmatists' who believed that European revolution was inevitable at the end of the war:

> A dark age is opening up before Europe and the world. The best revolutionaries have been destroyed by past defeats and the war. Time will have to elapse before new cadres are formed. The old socialist programmes and routines have been superseded and must be renewed. Stalinism, victorious thanks to the unconditional support and concessions made by the Allies, will be more dangerous than ever. If we want to save Europe we have to start by bringing together all free democratic forces in order simply to practice the art of not dying away.

The world has changed in unimaginable ways since Serge wrote those lines. The Soviet Union disintegrated, and its satellite states fell like a row of dominoes. Stalinism is dead, and the anti-Stalinist Left Serge knew is tiny and nowhere capable of influence. Serge's star is rising nonetheless: his ideas are read and discussed in the former Soviet Union, where a library has been founded in his name. In the West, his work is receiving new attention. The aura of invisibility seems to be disintegrating.

Serge scholarship began to get off the ground in 1991. Several international conferences marked the centenary of his birth, new editions of his work were printed, critical articles appeared in journals devoting special issues to Serge, and Bill Marshall's analytical study of Serge and the uses of dissent was published. It is my hope that this modest first examination of Serge's political, social, literary and economic writings on the Soviet Union

---

any idea the lines would be published, he would no doubt have written something else. Further, weighed against a lifetime body of work that ceaselessly promoted socialist ideas and action, like Sedgwick, I dismissed these lines as insignificant. Rummaging through the archive in Vlady's home I found one, just one, further essay that could be quoted and seemed to indicate a pessimistic surrender to the *status quo*. It was, significantly, written in English, and left behind unpublished. In it Serge despaired that the only way the Soviet people could be saved from Stalinism was through outside intervention. That raised all manner of questions – intervention by whom? Under what banner? Have we not all had thoughts we did not later defend? Is it telling that Serge made no apparent attempt to publish these thoughts?

will inspire others to mine the riches contained in Serge's life and voluminous writings.

Primary sources for this work have been Serge's published and unpublished writings plus extensive interviews and correspondence with surviving comrades and relatives in several countries. Vlady Kibalchich – Mexico's well-known artist and Serge's son who shared most of Serge's experiences with him, including deportation in Orenburg – has been a valuable and treasured resource. I have also conducted interviews with his daughter Jeannine Kibalchich, his third wife Laurette Séjourné, and with surviving Left Oppositionist comrades in Mexico, Russia and the United States. Serge's archive left in Mexico has been the richest source of material.[1] I have also had access to the thick FBI and Military Intelligence files on Serge obtained through the Freedom of Information Act (FOIA);[2] and the Hoover Institution's Trotsky collection within the Boris Nicolaevsky Papers. Additional primary source material came from the enormous quantity of journalism Serge produced in more than twenty publications in France, Belgium, Spain, the United States, Ukraine, Mexico and Chile. Serge's articles are written mainly in French, but also in Russian, Spanish and English. Secondary sources include the works of Serge's contemporaries, much of the vast memoir literature, and the important secondary literature on the Soviet Union and Comintern for the years covered.

Acknowledgments

A precious group of people have inspired, encouraged and supported me during the years this project has occupied in my life. Hillel Ticktin, my friend and teacher, has provided intellectual reflection and provocative analysis for many years. The wisdom and comradery of Mike Davis has been invaluable. Jon Amsden and Lee Smith have cheer-led, coddled and cajoled as necessary throughout. Marc Cooper's sound advice and steady support spurred me to the finish, and Daniel Singer was a constant source of inspiration, not simply for his ideas, but for his elegant life.

Vlady Kibalchich has shared his time, his home, and Serge's archive, enlightened me with his personal reminiscences of his father and provoked my undeveloped artistic sensibilities. Thanks to his wife Isabel Diaz for her elegant recollections of Serge, and her repeated hospitality in Mexico City and Cuernavaca. Thanks to Jeannine Kibalchich for her poignant childhood memories of her father and photos from the family album. Jeannine took me to Laurette Séjourné, Serge's third wife, who consented to answering my questions, despite her frail health. Thanks to Wilebaldo Solano (leader of the 1930s' POUM youth) for his enthusiastic recollections of meeting with Serge, and Hryhory Kostiuk for his personal correspondence with Serge. In Moscow, Sergei Zavarotnyi took Vlady and me to meet Irina Gogua, Serge's niece, who spent twenty-one years in Vorkuta and Ukhta. She graciously allowed me to tape and photograph her first reunion with Vlady in fifty-seven years, and vividly related her memories of Serge, his family and the travails of the time. She died just months after we left. I am grateful to Sieva Volkov, Trotsky's grandson, for his encouragement, and Manuel Alvarado, Left Oppositionist and friend of Serge's who recounted sharp political discussions he had with Serge in Mexico.

Many scholars have generously shared Serge documents in their possession, sent me their own unpublished writings or taped interviews, and provided me with lively discussions over the years. These include Alan Wald, Pierre Sauvage and Richard Greeman in the US, Pierre Broué, Loic Damilaville, Jean Jacques Marie, Jean Rière in France, David Cotterill,

John Eden, Bill Marshall, Paul Flewers, Richard Kuper in Britain, Alejandro Galvez Cancino and Paco Taibo II in Mexico. In Moscow I was delighted to find eager interest, warmth and intellectual challenge to my ideas. Thanks to Alexander Pantsov and to Alexei Gusev, whose own archival work on the Left Opposition provided for many stimulating discussions, along with Kirill Buketov, Alexander Buzgalin, Yulia Guseva, Boris Kagarlitsky and Vladimir Yevstratov. I am especially grateful to Mikhail Voyeikov of the Institute of Economics of the Russian Academy of Sciences in Moscow, and its Institute of Trotsky Studies for inviting me to inaugurate the Trotsky Institute with a seminar on Serge and the Fourth International which provoked keen interest and critical commentary.

I could not have done this research without the Serge papers in private and institutional collections. A special thanks to archivists Elena Danielson, and Carole Leadenham of the Hoover Archive at Stanford University for remembering my research when they spotted Serge material, and for giving me first preview of the Serge–Sedov correspondence found in the Boris Nicolaevsky collection. Thanks to Yuri Tutochkin for his kind and generous assistance at RGASPI, the Russian State Archive of Socio-Political History in Moscow.[3] Additional material was found at the Archives of the Prefecture of Police in Paris, the Houghton Library's Trotsky Archive at Harvard and the Sterling Library's Dwight and Nancy Macdonald Papers at Yale.

I received research assistance from Saint Mary's College of California Faculty Development Fund. I am eternally grateful to my friend Alex Buchman (one of Trotsky's guards at Coyoacán), whose continued moral, material and intellectual support made many of my research trips possible.

Thanks to the following for helping me decipher, transcribe and translate Serge's Russian and French handwritten letters and papers, written on the cheapest paper, often photocopied poorly: Michel Vale, Robert Wahl, Tanya Yampolsky, Carl Barrelet, Claudette Begin, Michel Bolsey, Greg Jacks and Joanna Misnik.

I want to thank Martin Jenkins, Jane Hindle, Colin Robinson, Annie Jackson, Michelle Ticktin and others who helped in the editing process. I enjoyed the considerable editorial expertise of Lee Smith and Dave Blake.

Many thanks for much needed encouragement, intellectual and moral support and enlightening arguments to Bob Arnot, Emilio Brodziak (died October 1999), Michael Cox, Sam Farber, Don Filtzer, Frank Fried, Olivia Gall, Adolfo Gilly, Al Glotzer (died February 1999), Rosa Kischinevzky, Patricio Sepulveda, Zorya Serebriakova, Mark Sharron (died September 1998), Jeanne Singer-Kerel, Daniel Singer (died 2 December 2000), Clare Spark, Edward Taylor and Jimmy White. I'd like to say *no thanks* to the late Marc Zborowski, who successfully rebuffed my every request for information and clarification by hanging up on me and shutting the door in my face.

A large debt of gratitude goes to my close and supportive immediate family, including my mother Perle Weissman and late father Maurice Weissman, my brothers Jerry and Irv Weissman, my sister Lauren Weissman and brother-in-law Michael Lauer.

Finally my late husband Roberto Naduris provided me with critical encouragement, political wisdom and loving support, sorely missed. My son and daughter, Eli and Natalia Naduris Weissman, suffered with me and supported me in ways they will never imagine. Their childhood included hearing Serge bedtime stories and accompanying me on research trips, and neither dampened their impulses to struggle for a better world. They belong to a special generation of thoughtful, intelligent youth whose activity confirms Serge's course set on hope.

Our apparent error was to be neither devious nor skeptical . . . Our mistakes were honorable. And even from a point of view less absurdly exalted, we were not so wrong. There is more falsification of ideas now than real confusion, and it is our own discoveries that are falsified. I feel humiliated only for the people who despair because we have been defeated. What is more natural and inevitable than to be beaten, to fail a hundred times, a thousand times, before succeeding? How many times does a child fall before he learns to walk? . . . The main thing is to have strong nerves, everything depends on that. And lucidity . . .

Human destiny will brighten.

The Long Dusk by Victor Serge

Part I

In the orbit of revolution

Introduction

From the detritus of the disintegrated Soviet Union there seems little worth salvaging for a possible future. Sifting through the ruins, we find a voice that merits rescue – the voice of Victor Serge, a political witness, committed participant, and literary historian. Serge's personal experiences mirror the history of Soviet political development and are richly documented in his writings. Though Serge wrote in French for an international audience, his novels and his histories reflect the Russian tradition of telling the story in history, linking historiography and literature in powerful, evocative prose. His fertile mind strove to understand the past in order to see the future, which he believed would be organized by a healthy and profoundly democratic collectivism. Serge belonged to a critically minded and intelligent group of old Bolsheviks who resolutely resisted totalitarianism, a large group he insisted was right at the heart of Bolshevism.[1]

Committed to a non-doctrinaire, non-sectarian approach to political questions, Serge criticized not only Stalin, but also Bukharin, Lenin and Trotsky. He later wrote that the Left Opposition, to which Serge belonged, succumbed to Party patriotism at a time when the Party paralysed politics, leaving them to struggle in the one place they had no chance of winning – the Party. They fought a losing battle because of Stalin's stranglehold on all forms of political and organizational expression. Serge believed the solution lay in pushing for a revival of the soviets as an arena of free political activity. Instead, the entire current of old Bolsheviks was wiped out, and any hope of socialist revival died with them.

This experience of defeat informed all of Serge's thinking, writing and activity. He warned all along of the inherent dangers of a 'totalitarian way of thinking' – based not on looking for truth, but on conducting a political fight. This method, Serge reminded us, developed under the weight of the Stalinist machine which engaged in a distortion of thought, fraud and massacres so monstrous as to be unimaginable.

Serge himself has left perceptive and eloquent testimony of what he witnessed. New social histories have now been written that confirm Serge's earlier view from the ground up of these historical processes.[2] This book analyses Serge as a political writer and activist whose views reflect the significant struggles of our time. If Preobrazhensky was the economist of the Left Opposition, then we can say that Victor Serge was its historian.

But who was Victor Serge? A worker, a militant, an intellectual, an internationalist by experience and conviction, an inveterate optimist, and always poor, Victor Serge lived from 1890 to 1947. He took part in three revolutions, spent a decade in captivity, published more than thirty books and left behind thousands of pages of unpublished manuscripts, correspondence and articles. He was born into one political exile, died in another, and was politically active in seven countries. His life was spent in permanent political opposition. Serge opposed capitalism – first as an anarchist, then as a Bolshevik. He opposed Bolshevism's undemocratic practices and then opposed Stalin as a Left Oppositionist. He argued with Trotsky from within the anti-Stalinist left; and he opposed fascism and capitalism's Cold War as an unrepentant revolutionary Marxist.

Victor Serge's life and writings challenged political and academic orthodoxy about the Soviet Union. His refusal to surrender to either the Soviet state or the capitalist West assured his marginality and consigned him to a life of persecution and poverty. Despite living in the shadows, Serge's work and his life amount to a corrective to Stalinism, and an alternative to the market. Serge wrote about the early years of the Soviet Union as an insider, from the perspective of a Left Oppositionist with an anarchist past. The Soviet experience did not lead Serge to renounce socialism but rather to enrich socialist goals with a declaration of the rights of man. He opposed one-Party rule in 1918, and declared in 1923 that a coalition government, although fraught with risks, would be less dangerous than Stalin's secret police state. Serge criticized Lenin's New Economic Policy (NEP) because it restored inequality and failed to revitalize democracy. Serge proposed reforms, including workers' democracy and a 'communism of associations' instead of rigid, top-down 'plans'. At the end of his life he wrote:

> We want to participate in the construction of a socialism restored to its dignity and real aims, which can only be through an organization of free men. We want honest and clear ideas within a healthy workers' movement invigorated by fraternal competition and free debate. From the heart of threatened democracy, of socialism and the workers' movement, above all we defend freedom of opinion and the human dignity of the militant, the rights of minorities and a critical spirit. We fight relentlessly, and we will not cease to fight, against controlled thought, the cult of the leader, passive obedience and the despicable ploys of parties subject to blind discipline as well as the systematic use of lies, slander and assassinations.[3]

Such a passionate and honest reappraisal is characteristic of Serge's writings, which powerfully evoke the atmosphere in the USSR and the

Communist movement during the 1920s and 1930s, reflecting the dynamism of the revolutionary generation of Bolsheviks.

If nothing else, this is of great historical value, especially since the entire Soviet enterprise is now looked upon with disdain, even ridicule. History is rarely kind to losers, and Serge comes from the defeated side *within* the revolution. Despite an enormous literary legacy, he has been, like the other Left Oppositionists, airbrushed from the platform of Soviet history. The tide began to turn with the demise of the Soviet Union, and more of Serge's work as well as critical studies of Serge are now appearing in print.[4] It is hoped that this book contributes to a fresh examination of Serge's ideas, and that new interpretations, debates and clarification will follow.

Victor Serge, a Belgian-born Russian, was twenty-eight when he first set foot in his homeland in January 1919. He began his political odyssey in the USSR as a seasoned revolutionary anarchist who had already served two prison terms and fought in the failed Spanish insurrection of 1917. In May 1919 he joined the Bolsheviks, working on the first administrative staff of the Executive Committee of the Communist International. He participated in the first three Congresses of the Comintern, fought in the siege of Petrograd during the civil war, served as Commissar of the archives of the Okhrana (the Tsarist secret police), and mixed freely in Bolshevik, anarchist and literary circles in Petrograd and Moscow. Sent on a Comintern assignment to Berlin to help prepare the German revolution of 1923, Serge edited the French edition of *Inprekorr*, the Comintern's main journal. With the defeat of the German October Serge moved to Vienna, where he continued Comintern work. In 1925, Serge returned to the Soviet Union to stand with the Left Opposition.

Back in the USSR Serge again mingled in diverse political, social and literary milieux. He earned his living translating the works of Lenin, Zinoviev, Trotsky and others. He openly supported the Left Opposition as one of its main spokespersons in the Leningrad Party Organization. Serge was expelled from the Party just after the Fifteenth Party Congress in December 1927. Three months later he was arrested and held for eight weeks. He nearly died of an intestinal occlusion just after he was released.

His brush with death marked a turning point for Serge, who now began to write in profusion 'about these unforgettable times'. During the next five years of precarious liberty in the USSR Serge wrote and published abroad five books, including three novels and the historical *Year One of the Russian Revolution*. Not one line of his works was published in the USSR until 1989.

In 1933, Serge was again arrested and deported to Orenburg where, for three years, he and his son nearly starved to death. Serge wrote four books there, all of which were confiscated by the GPU when he was expelled from the country in April 1936. An international defence campaign by prominent French intellectuals resulted in Serge narrowly escaping with his life, just four months before the first Moscow Trial initiated the 'Great Terror'.

Once Serge was in the West, Stalin stripped him of his nationality and passport. European Communists slandered him, and Moscow used its considerable influence to prevent him from publishing in the mainstream press. Nevertheless, Serge began to 'unravel the labyrinth of madness' (the purges) and to analyse the nature of the social organism emerging in the USSR. This became his life's work. Despite enormous personal and economic hardship – his wife was driven insane by the relentless persecutions – Serge engaged in a daily struggle to feed himself and his family while writing to expose what he saw as Stalin's betrayal of everything socialist.

Serge remained in Paris until the Wehrmacht arrived in June 1940. Fleeing with his family on foot, he spent a frantic year in Marseilles waiting for a visa out of Vichy France, hounded by Hitler's Gestapo and Stalin's NKVD. In frightful danger, Serge channelled all his efforts into writing. Finally he was admitted to Mexico where he spent the rest of his life, writing 'only for the drawer' in the face of an almost total publishers' boycott. Filled with plans for future projects, Serge died in poverty in November 1947. He knew real hunger almost all his life, ten years of which were spent in various forms of captivity.

His works include more than thirty books and pamphlets of history and politics; seven novels, two volumes of poetry, three novellas and a collection of short stories; hundreds of articles and essays, biographies of Lenin, Stalin and Trotsky, a diary, his own memoirs, and translations of the works of Lenin, Trotsky, Zinoviev, Figner, Gladkov and Mayakovsky. One of his books was published under Panaït Istrati's name, and he was the ghostwriter for Alexander Barmine's memoir. It is a prodigious published record – largely unknown and mostly out of print. And Serge left an enormous archive of unpublished work including correspondence, polemics and essays.

This book analyses Serge's work while describing his life, tracing his views and their evolution through his writings. An intellectual and political biography, it aims to bring to light the importance of this relatively unknown and forgotten figure. Serge's ideas – born in the tumultuous struggles of the first half of the twentieth century – address dilemmas that still confront the world as we enter the twenty-first century. Rediscovering the revolutionary but resolutely independent thought of Victor Serge contributes to the reconstitution of a usable past for a radically different future. The relevance of Serge is perhaps best measured by the emergence in the former Soviet Union of a new generation of scholars and activists who are at work discovering the buried Soviet past. A dedicated group of enthusiasts have established a Victor Serge Memorial Library in Moscow and Serge's work is slowly being published in Russia, while new editions of out-of-print Serge works are appearing all over the West.

This study does not presume to be a full-scale biography of Serge. There is ample room for Serge studies, and other scholars are investigating his anarchism, his role as a revolutionary novelist, his political practice in

Belgium, France, Spain and Mexico. These aspects of Serge's life and work are examined here mainly through the prism of his Soviet experience and his wrestling with the vexing questions raised by Soviet development. How was the revolutionary promise destroyed? Was the rise of the social group headed by Stalin inevitable? How did the new system crush and erase the original revolutionary vision and politics? What impact did it have on socialist politics and practice around the globe? How did the Soviet experience shape Serge's mature reflections on the USSR, Stalinism, socialism and the possibilities for the future?

Biographies can be a useful vehicle for examining social history, but they more often fall into the genre of exposé. There is no attempt in this work to reveal an imagined inner life, nor is there any speculation about emotional affairs designed to titillate the reader. As a writer Serge had a talent for summoning up the multifaceted character of revolutionaries he knew by means of a quote, or a simple, physical detail: 'the beard gone white, but the eyes are clear'. A sense of intimacy is rendered with little detail, and the effect is to portray personal characteristics which form a part of political motivation. The portrait thus evoked rounds out our knowledge of the political figure described. By drawing out character traits while delineating political alignment Serge evoked the whole person, refracted through his lens. The sum adds to a heightened understanding of the actors in the Russian Revolution and hence the process itself. Yet when it came to himself, Serge protected his privacy and revealed little. Those who knew Serge insist he was man of quiet integrity. He spent his life poor and hungry, but rich in intellectual and political experience. He maintained his dignity even in imprisonment and exile. He clearly suffered from the difficulties he faced, made more arduous by the consequences of his political commitment. Like the Bolsheviks of his generation, Serge thought it more important to discuss ideas than his personal life, except when they intersected. These ideas and the quality of his commitment to them provide more fertile and attractive areas for research than speculation about the unexpressed and unrecorded feelings they provoked.

As an independent thinker, Serge often challenged revolutionary orthodoxy. The health of the Russian Revolution began to deteriorate quickly and Serge argued that it died a 'self-inflicted death in 1918 with the establishment of the Cheka'. Yet Serge worked with the Bolsheviks and supported their policies, including the demoralizing suppression of the Kronstadt rebellion. He joined the Opposition in 1923. Serge's concerns were always with the life and conditions of the masses of people affected by policy. Serge viewed Stalin's accession to power as one of the bloodiest counter-revolutions in history — a betrayal of everything the revolution stood for. Serge argued that 'socialism in one country' had inevitable disastrous consequences, which he demonstrated, step by step: forced collectivization, crash industrialization, super-exploitation, famine, sabotage, terror. The purges, proceeding from an internal dynamic set in motion by

Stalin's methods of industrialization and rule created new social relations and a new, unstable society based on coercion and terror. None of the basic problems of society was resolved by the purges, but millions of people paid with their lives. A costly and wasteful industrial infrastructure was constructed with the help of slave labour. All forms of collective resistance were broken as the weary population concerned itself with survival. Stalin wiped out the entire revolutionary generation of Bolsheviks, Serge's comrades. Serge dubbed the new society a 'concentration-camp universe' – fundamentally anti-socialist, anti-democratic and anti-human.

On the eve of his final arrest in the Soviet Union Serge managed to smuggle a letter to his friends in Paris, thinking he would not survive. The letter is his last testament and the ideas in it remained with him the rest of his life. The testament amounts to a declaration of the rights of man, and a defence of truth and unfettered thought, without which the socialist project is 'false, bankrupt and spoiled'. Serge's defence of all human beings, including 'class enemies', was a response to the Stalinist system of terror and murder.

Serge's analysis of Stalinism was dynamic and non-dogmatic: neither the ideological clarion call of the later Cold Warriors nor the sterile slogan of a Left sect. He simply tried to understand the processes at work and to point to the consequences for human progress. Stalin's rule was chaotic and improvised, but it followed a course consistent with protecting the concentration of power in the bureaucracy and himself. Once the bureaucracy usurped power from the working class, an inexorable logic generated the terror to protect the concentration of power against any and all challenges. This 'bureaucracy' acted almost in reflex and proved incapable of controlling the forces of terror it unleashed. The absence of control resulted in extravagant abuses. Industrialization, collectivization and purges led to the formation of a new working class and a new ruling elite, with a particular relationship between the two. Serge spent the rest of his life trying to analyse and characterize the new social formation, to define its nature.

Serge finally defined the Soviet state as 'bureaucratic totalitarian with collectivist leanings'. His use of the term totalitarian was different from the later totalitarian school of analysis just as his usage of the words bureaucratic and collectivist differed from the 'bureaucratic collectivist' school.[5] For Serge, who believed he was the first to employ the term to describe the emerging Stalinist system, the Soviet Union was neither capitalist nor socialist, operated out of fear of independent thought and was in permanent conflict with its own people. His analysis of the system was not limited to political decision-making, which often characterized the approach of the 'totalitarian school' identified with the works of Carl Friederich, Zbigniew Brzezinski and Leonard Schapiro, but was a fuller social analysis which studied the relationship between the economic form, how power was exercised, and the way the population adapted. Serge tended to use the term 'totalitarian collectivist' to identify a new form that grew from both Soviet

Stalinism and Hitler's fascism and threatened the development of the post-war democracies. He worried that the post-war nationalizations of key industries could combine with the growth of a technocratic elite and create a fearfully anti-democratic outcome.

Serge's ideas were drawn from his own experience in the Soviet Union and European exile after the defeats of the 1930s. He perceived in the twin total-itarianisms of Stalinism and fascism the essential 'collectivist' tendencies of the modern world. Opposing these tendencies, in Serge's view, was the his-torically conscious collectivism which would emerge from decomposing capitalism and enfeebled Stalinism.

New research by so-called 'revisionist' scholars has challenged the older totalitarian model of analysis, contending the Stalin period was one of chaos and lack of control and claiming the loss of life caused by Stalin's policies has been inflated.[6] Serge took up questions at issue in the debate decades earlier, grappling with contradictions that could not satisfactorily be resolved. The Soviet state was totalitarian *and* it was incapable of totally controlling economic and political events. His treatment of this dilemma reflects the discussions that raged in Left Oppositionist and Left Menshevik circles – discussions that reverberated in the Gorbachev years in the debate of 'plan versus market'.

Later, working in isolation, Serge played out his ideas on the nature of socialist planning, which required workers' democracy, against the totali-tarian bureaucratic administration that existed in the Soviet Union. Again, Serge was only able to state, not reconcile, the contradictions. While he ran into difficulties when he tried to generalize the tendencies he saw at work in both capitalism and the Soviet Union, his work reflects the enormous pressures Marxists faced during and immediately after World War II.

Serge also addressed the question: was Stalinism the inevitable conse-quence of Bolshevism? Serge argued that it was not. He saw Stalinism as the corruption of Bolshevism. In a letter to Sidney Hook Serge wrote that the 'authoritarian centralization of the Party contained the seeds of Stalin-ism as a whole', but 'revolution and Bolshevism also contained other seeds, notably that of a new democracy that Lenin and the others endeavoured to establish with good will and passion in 1917–18'.[7]

Serge's critique of Stalinism was the core of his life and his work. His life, Serge wrote in the *Memoirs*, was 'integrated into history; we were inter-changeable'. He added that 'the only meaning in life lies in conscious par-ticipation in the making of history'. Serge was both social analyst and social activist, and his contribution to our understanding comes from his ability to see social reality clearly and honestly and to write about it poetic-ally.

His writings reflect his experiences, his commitment and the vision which enabled him to survive the twentieth century's worst cataclysms without recourse to pessimism. Serge described terrible suffering while explaining how Stalinism came about and what the Opposition would have done in its place. Consequently even his bleakest descriptions contain an irrepressible optimism and hope for a socialist future.

Serge spoke up for those who could not speak for themselves. He fails to conform to any recognized political or literary tendency. His writing 'style' is a literary-autobiographical-political one that transcends the boundaries of conventional literature and traditional social science. His discussion of the nature of the Stalinist system was one that avoided the slogans that have characterized debate within the Left for sixty years: one can look in vain through his writings to find the terms 'degenerated workers' state' or 'state capitalist'. He did use the term bureaucratic collectivist (twice) but in referring to a World-War-II Europe that included both the Stalinist totalitarian Soviet Union and the Nazi totalitarian fascist Germany. Instead of catchwords, Serge preferred to describe the Soviet Union, to explain how policies affected ordinary people and examine how their reactions affected the formulation and execution of policy. When Serge turned to literary forms, he did not avoid political-economic debate but brought to it new expressive language. He valued lucidity above all, and his lifelong, often lonely struggle was waged to overcome isolation and help create a collective future that enriched human progress. He was, in his own words, a 'curiously disturbing figure', this 'vagabond' who never stopped his search for justice.

1

In the service of the Revolution: 1917–21

On the way to Petrograd

The Russian Revolution of October 1917 ushered in a new epoch. A large country had broken from world capitalism and socialists from all over the world, whose attention had been on the 'epoch of the cannon'[1] watched the development of the first society beginning its transition to socialism with hope and enthusiasm. For Europe, 1917 was the fourth year of the World War in which

> The flower of the youth of a continent, an entire generation of young men were mowed down . . . along blood-soaked frontiers, thousands of combatants died each day . . . [This was] the fourth year of the war for the partitioning of the globe among the financial imperialists.[2]

The events of October caught the imagination of revolutionaries everywhere; those who could began to flock to Russia,

> Leaving the void and entering the kingdom of will . . . where life is beginning anew, where conscious will, intelligence, and an inexorable love of mankind are in action. Behind us, all Europe is ablaze, having choked almost to death in the fog of its own massacres. Barcelona's flame smoulders on. Germany is in the thick of revolution, Austro-Hungary is splitting into free nations. Italy is spread with red flags . . . This is only the beginning.[3]

Leaving the void, and entering his never-seen homeland, was Victor Serge.

Evoking the images of war-torn and war-weary Europe, Serge recalled stopping with a group of his prisoner-comrades in a tavern filled with British soldiers. Serge had been released from fifteen months incarceration in a French prison camp whose regime was notable for the lack of food and the Spanish flu epidemic that killed one quarter of the camp population. Serge was in a group of forty 'Bolshevik suspects' to be exchanged for French military officers held by the Russians. The shabby appearance of

Serge and his group attracted the attention of the soldiers, who approached them. 'Who are you?' Serge answered their questioning faces: 'Bolsheviks. Prisoners. We are going to Russia'.[4] His message was understood: we are revolutionary internationalists on our way to begin the construction of socialism. The soldiers' response surprised Serge: 'Us too! We are too! Later you will see!'[5] From his prison isolation, Serge had not understood the depth of inspiration produced by the successful October Revolution which was evident on these tired soldiers' faces.

Serge reached his homeland expecting to enter the first phase of the world revolution. It was 26 January 1919 when Serge set off, the first days of February when he arrived. The revolution was in its second year. It had taken Serge eighteen months to make the trip.

Serge had gone to Spain in February 1917 on his release from prison and his expulsion from France. In the middle of the insurrectionist street fighting of July 1917 Serge left, drawn like a magnet to the distant revolutionary beacon of Russia. He was not only 'leaving the void', he was leaving behind him his anarchist past. Serge was disillusioned with the anarchists' inability to confront the question of power,* and impressed by this very characteristic of the Bolsheviks. He tried to reach Russia via France, was arrested for violating his expulsion order, and thrown into a French prison camp in October 1917 as a Bolshevik suspect.

Serge encounters Bolshevism and Marxism

Serge was not yet a Bolshevik, but he was on his way. His commitment was strengthened by his fifteen months at Precigne,[6] where Serge joined the other Russian and Jewish revolutionaries to form a discussion group. Here Serge studied Marxism for the first time. While arguing with the only real Bolshevik at Precigne (the rest were, like Serge, suspected Bolsheviks), Serge put forward the idea of a libertarian, democratic revolution, while the Bolshevik favoured a merciless dictatorship and an authoritarian revolution. Serge admitted that, theoretically, he stated his point of view badly, worse than the Bolshevik, though 'from the human standpoint, we were infinitely nearer the truth'.[7] According to the *Memoirs* and *Birth of Our Power*, the prisoners studied Marx's *Civil War in France*, kept abreast of events in Russia and discussed all the questions facing the Bolsheviks. This second prison experience taught Serge the importance of group solidarity

---

* Serge did not stay for the final insurrection in Barcelona in August 1917. He had seen enough in July: the anarchists would not hear any talk of seizure of power. Only his friend, the syndicalist leader Salvadore Segui, seemed aware that they had no plan beyond the street fighting. Serge said they went into battle 'as it were, in the dark' (Victor Serge, *Memoirs of a Revolutionary*, London, Oxford University Press, 1963, p. 56).

and was a 'university' of revolutionary study.* It was at Precigne that Serge began to acquire the Marxist method of analysis which was to remain with him until his death.

What Serge already had in common with the Bolsheviks was his praxis: Serge was a man of revolutionary practice, who translated his words into deeds time and again throughout his life. Revolutionary theory put into practice: this is what impressed Serge about the Bolsheviks. In his retrospective on the thirtieth anniversary of the Russian Revolution, Serge wrote that 'the unity between thought and action' was one of the characteristics of the Bolsheviks which gave them an innate superiority over the rival parties with which they shared a common outlook.[8]

What did Serge find in the land of will which expressed the suppressed aspirations of all humankind in struggle? 'A world frozen to death . . . a metropolis of Cold, of Hunger, of Hatred, of Endurance.'[9] Year Two: Serge managed to arrive in the midst of counter-revolution, white terror answered by red terror, famine and disease, to a city expectant of a world revolution which would save them. His romantic hopes were met with a harsh reality, which Serge did not hesitate to describe. The first shock was not the cold, nor what seemed to Serge the worst food any of them had ever eaten. It was the first newspaper filled not with 'popular ferment, bubbling ideas, rivalry of clubs [and] parties',[10] but with an article signed by G. Zinoviev on 'The Monopoly of Power'. Serge quoted from memory: 'Our Party rules alone . . . It will not allow anyone . . . the false democratic liberties demanded by the counter-revolution'. The newspaper, *Severnaya Kommuna*, was dated January 1919.

Serge was hit in the face with the basic dilemmas which were to concern him for the rest of his life: how to defend the revolution without sacrificing freedom, and how to prevent acts that are justified by a state of siege and 'mortal perils' – based on the extinction of freedom – from being elevated into a theory.†

---

* The Spanish flu epidemic nearly wiped out the prisoners, and informers kept the warden apprised of activities. The solidarity of Serge's revolutionary study group kept them better fed, and stronger in body, mind and will.

† Serge's use of the word 'freedom' here and elsewhere is vague. Although he cites examples of popular ferment and free political expression from the French Revolution, Paris Commune and Revolution of 1905, he does not define himself in relation to either the Marxist or anarchist conception of freedom. For Marxists, freedom is indistinguishable from institutions of popular democracy, usually in the form of councils. Anarchists, on the other hand, favour participatory democracy and community control but are wary of democratic *institutions* – even workers' councils – and tend to describe freedom in less concrete terms.

In Revolutionary Russia

Serge's first impressions of Petrograd tell us a lot about the early days of the revolution.* The Finland Station, where Lenin had delivered his famous 'April Theses' was deserted; the city, covered in snow and ice, looked abandoned. The people Serge and his group did see looked frozen and hungry ('a gaunt soldier' . . . ' a woman freezing under her shawls'). In the one year since the seizure of power, the population of Petrograd had fallen from a million to 'scarcely 700,000 souls'. But the people Serge met were open and curious about the political situation in Europe: 'All they asked us was whether Europe would soon be kindled: "What is the French proletariat waiting for before it seizes power?"'[11] Serge found the same attitude everywhere; nurtured by the knowledge that the Russian Revolution was but the first – Lenin often said it was 'a terrible misfortune that the honour of beginning the first Socialist revolution should have befallen the most backward people in Europe' – they all knew they were doomed without an international extension of the revolution.

In Serge's opinion they were too optimistic about the imminence of European revolution. Serge had just come from the West, where thirteen years of political activity had filled him with disgust for the parliamentary opportunism of the social democratic misleaders, and impatience with the ultimate irresponsibility of the anarchists who abdicated on the question of power. Indeed, most of the European socialist leaders had supported World War I. Serge saw no revolutionary Party able to lead the European masses to revolution. Moreover, he could not help but wonder if leading Bolsheviks, including Trotsky and Lenin, who had also lived abroad between the two Russian Revolutions, based their optimism more on hope than concrete analysis. After all, they also knew the weaknesses of the socialist leaders who could hardly be expected to ride the wave of revolutionary upsurge to a successful conclusion. Perhaps Lenin and Trotsky hoped that the ripening objective conditions would produce cleavages and form new

---

* Serge was at his best when evoking the atmosphere of the new revolution in the midst of peril and ice in the final chapter of *Birth of Our Power*. He related the story of being housed with a family in Petrograd in an abandoned apartment of a former Counsellor of the Empire. The rooms were large and there was no fuel for heat. They congregated in the nursery, the smallest room. For warmth, they burned the massive tomes of the *Collection of the Laws of the Empire*. The scene works as literature, politics, history and irony. Richard Greeman has subjected the scene to an insightful analysis in his article '"The laws are burning" – Literary and Revolutionary Realism in Victor Serge', *Yale French Studies*, no. 39, 1967, pp. 146–59. Serge confirmed in his *Memoirs* (p. 116) that the scene actually took place, and that he took great pleasure in burning the now obsolete statutes of imperial repression.

leaders.* Despite Serge's misgivings about what he saw as the Bolsheviks' overestimation of Europe's readiness for revolution, he embraced the Bolsheviks' goals.

Serge told Grigori Zinoviev, then President of the Soviet, that the unfolding revolutionary process in the West was sluggish, especially in France, where Serge believed no revolutionary upheaval could be expected for a long time. Zinoviev replied: 'It's easy to tell that you are no Marxist. History cannot stop halfway.'[12]

Zinoviev's wife Lilina, People's Commissar for Social Planning in the Northern Commune, told Serge to go with his family to Moscow where conditions were better. He did not take her advice, deciding to stay in Petrograd, the revolution's front-line city. He immediately set about to talk with everyone, to mix in all the social and political milieux to get a political grounding. Of the democratic intellectuals, Serge said:

> If the Bolshevik insurrection had not taken power . . . the cabal of the old generals, supported by the officers' organizations, would have certainly done so instead. Russia would have avoided the Red Terror only to endure the White, and a proletarian dictatorship only to undergo a reactionary one. In consequence, the most outraged observations of the anti-Bolshevik intellectuals only revealed to me how necessary Bolshevism was.[13]

From anarchism . . .

Serge decided that he was neither against the Bolsheviks nor neutral; he was with them. He wrote in one of his first letters from Russia that he would not make 'a career out of the revolution, and, once the mortal danger has passed, [he would] . . . join again with those who will fight the evils of the new regime'.[14]

Serge arrived in Russia as a seasoned revolutionary armed with 'a critical method, doubt and assurance' and thirteen years' experience as a socialist, anarchist and syndicalist. In his youth Serge had joined the Belgian Young Socialists but had soon become disgusted with their electoralism, corruption and opportunism. His political and geographical journey went from Belgian second international socialism to French anarchist individualism, from Spanish anarcho-syndicalism to Bolshevik revolutionary Marxism.

At the age of fifteen the young Kibalchich (he did not adopt the name Serge until 1917) gave his first public speech as a member of the Jeunes

---

* Deutscher intimates that had the Bolsheviks known the real situation, they may not have founded the International which was 'fathered by wish, mothered by confusion, and assisted by accident'. He also suggests they assumed that in real revolutionary situations the small European Marxist sects would rise rapidly to influence and leadership, just as the Bolsheviks did. Isaac Deutscher, *The Prophet Armed, Trotsky 1879–1921* (Oxford, Oxford University Press, 1970), pp. 451–3.

Gardes Socialistes, the youth group of the Belgian Socialist Party. It was 1905, and Kibalchich's speech was about the revolutionary process under way in Russia.[15] Together with his earliest friend from his boyhood, Raymond Callemin, Serge immersed himself in a mélange of ideas, reading Zola, Bebel, Blanc, Kropotkin, and later Nietzsche, Stirner and Elisée Recluse, a Bakuninist and veteran of the Paris Commune. They protested the horrific activities of Belgian imperialism in the Congo, supported a commitment to revolution, both personal and social. The Belgian Socialist movement's reformism could not match the revolutionary passions of Kibalchich and his group of friends, 'closer than brothers'.[16] Disillusioned with the leaders and the masses, Kibalchich and his friends turned to anarcho-individualism, and illegalism. Anarchism attracted them because it offered a lifestyle that matched its principles.[17]

Serge's early anarchist experience was an extension of his boyhood friendships, his profound disappointment in his parliamentary socialist experience in Belgium, and youthful experimentation with avant-garde lifestyles. Seeking a commitment to liberty and action, and an escape from capitalism, Kibalchich and Callemin entered into their first anarchist commune while still in Belgium. In 1908, Serge noted that 'above all, our work was our writing'.[18] Expelled from Belgium in 1909, Kibalchich moved to France, living first in Lille and later Paris. He learned the print trade and later translated (from Russian to French) for a living. He also began living with his lover Rirette Maîtrejean and her two young daughters in a succession of anarchist communes. Kibalchich wrote that anarchism 'demanded everything of us and offered everything to us'. This included vegetarianism, and participating in 'illegalist' activity, as it was known among anarchist-individualists. For Kibalchich/Serge, 'the anarchist is always illegal – theoretically. The sole word "anarchist" means rebellion in every sense.'[19]

Kibalchich became something of a street orator, speaking regularly in Libertad's 'Informal Lecture Series' (Les Causeries Populaires), encouraging others to 'make your own revolution by being free men and living in comradeship'* and wrote pensive articles in Anarchy (L'Anarchie) where he signed his articles Le Rétif – the stubborn one. Although Kibalchich/Serge and Maîtrejean were part of the infamous Bonnot gang, the social bandits of pre-war France who were ruthlessly repressed, they were propagandists rather than bandits. The Bonnot gang, subject of films, books, romantic revelry and even cults, has been compared to Bonnie and Clyde, Robin Hood and his merry men, and alternately called tragic bandits and dashing revolutionaries.

Writing first in the Belgian Le Communiste (The Communist) and then in Le

---

* This was the credo of Albert Libertad, their hero who so rejected bourgeois conventions that no one knew his real name, nor did he give names to his children, since it would require state registration! Libertad died in 1908.

Révolté (*The Rebel*) Kibalchich assumed editorship of *L'Anarchie* in 1911. In the *Memoirs* Serge explained that his multiple political commitments of the time demonstrated his growing ambivalence with individualism and his attraction to the developing revolutionary ferment in Russia. He made the argument that he was moving from individualism to social action. As early as 1908 Serge wrote in *Le Communiste* that solidarizing with the rebels 'does not mean to advocate theft or to elevate it to the level of a tactic'.[20] He had no respect for private property, but theft and killing were ill-advised, even mad. Three years later Kibalchich/Serge came into conflict with his friends over the question of violence, and he used his pen to express his growing impatience with the futility of the tactics and ideals of the Bonnot bandits.* In the *Memoirs* Serge described their descent into violence as 'a kind of madness' and 'like a collective suicide'.†

The Bonnot gang, made up of some twenty French and Belgian anarchists, were involved in bank robberies and shoot-outs. Public sympathy was with the tragic bandits at first, but then turned. In December 1911 one robbery turned deadly when they shot a bank messenger, and other deadly attacks followed. Raymond Callemin and another 'bandit', Octave Garnier, hid out for a few days at Kibalchich/Serge's place. Overpowered and desperate, the outlaw anarchists were doomed. The police came to the offices of *L'Anarchie* and found two revolvers that came from a break-in at an armoury.[21] Both Victor and Rirette were arrested. The rest of the gang were also arrested, while others were rounded up simply for 'association'.[22] Garnier and Valet were killed resisting arrest. The others stood trial in February 1913 in what became a sensational political trial.

In the dock, Kibalchich/Serge had the difficult task of keeping solidarity while drawing the distinction between anarchism and 'illegalism', and at the same time protecting Rirette – who had admitted getting the two Brownings found at their residence in rue Fessart.[23] When the verdicts

---

* Richard Parry, in his book *The Bonnot Gang* (London, Rebel Press, 1987) disputes that Kibalchich in fact turned from individualism to social action. Rather, he insists Serge was consistent in his defence of the actions of his anarchist comrades, though he himself never participated except as an intellectual. Parry attributes the developing hostility with his comrade bandits to more banal disagreements over science and diet, noting Victor and Rirette continued to drink coffee and tea and grew irritated at the salt- and pepperless diet. Thus an 'unscientific diet' was the root of hostility, not strategy and tactics! (Parry, pp. 57–60). Serge's account in the *Memoirs* mentions the difference over 'scientific individualism' and their 'algebraic formulae' and dietary discipline, but emphasized political differences and the futility of their political practice, even while affirming his solidarity with his comrades.

† Serge, *Memoirs*, p. 34. Serge wrote a novel about the pre-war anarchist movement in France, *Les Hommes perdus*, which was confiscated in the Soviet Union. It has never been recovered.

came in, Rirette Maîtrejean was acquitted, Raymond Callemin was sent to the guillotine. Edouard Carouy committed suicide in jail with a sachet of potassium cyanide secretly passed to him during the trial. Kibalchich was singled out as the intellectual author of the Bonnot band's crimes, and sentenced to five terrible years in prison, spent in solitary from 1913 to 1917. In the *Memoirs* Serge acknowledged that he believed he too would be acquitted, but realized how impossible that would be for a young Russian militant. Odd then, that he dressed in a Russian peasant-style blouse at the trial, while the others wore their Sunday best.[24] Much later he wrote that he could only free himself from the nightmare of those incarcerated years by writing his first novel, *Men in Prison*. In a telling passage he admitted that 'we wanted to be revolutionaries; we were only rebels'.[25]

In prison Serge had ample time to reflect, and for the first time to study seriously.[26] Outside the prison walls, the world war was waging, drenching the countryside in blood. Serge understood the nature of the war which incited 'fratricidal patriotism' and killed at an astonishing rate. He was resolutely opposed to the war, but saw a gleam of light in it – the Russian Revolution – which heralded a 'purifying tempest'.[27]

Serge was released on 31 January 1917. Expelled from France, he had just two weeks in Paris before boarding the Barcelona express. Serge had contacts there, and events in Spain had played an important part in Serge's political formation, especially the execution of Spanish anarcho-syndicalist Francisco Ferrer in 1909. As an independent thinker, the schoolteacher Ferrer had challenged Spanish parochialism, and the state responded by blaming Ferrer for a popular uprising at Montjuic. His execution sparked a wave of international revulsion and protest. Serge remarked in the *Memoirs* that going to the spontaneous demonstration that erupted in Paris on the news of Ferrer's execution was a cardinal moment for him, one that heightened his growing collective awareness, and at the same time highlighted the seriousness of the impasse for the whole revolutionary movement.[28] Now, eight years later, Spain was again in ferment. Not only Spain. The February Revolution in Russia, which brought down Tsar Nicholas II, had an enormous influence on Spanish events, which culminated in street fighting in July and a failed insurrection in August.

In Spain, Serge dispelled the wretched years of prison from his psyche, and in the process left behind anarcho-individualism. He worked in print shops and joined the printers' union, gravitated toward the CNT (The National Confederation of Workers), and participated in the Spanish syndicalist uprising of 1917. He wrote in *Tierra y Libertad* where he began to sign his name 'Victor Serge'. His experience in Spain, where power was lost, is memorialized in his novel *Birth of Our Power*. The masses had burst on to the scene at both ends of Europe, and Serge headed to his Russian homeland, just before the Spanish insurrection was crushed.

Serge made the mistake of passing through France on the way to Russia, where he was banned following his expulsion earlier that year. He managed to spend two months studying art history in Paris, before he was rearrested in October 1917, this time as a Bolshevik sympathizer, just as the October Revolution in Russia loomed. And so Serge began his second sojourn in captivity, this time for fifteen months. With the end of World War I in November 1918, negotiations took place between France and Russia, and Serge became part of a prisoner exchange, allowing him to be repatriated to a land he had never seen. It was January 1919 when Serge and the other 'Bolshevik prisoners' set sail from Dunkirk. Arriving at the Finnish border in February 1919, Serge met the British tommies who opened this chapter.

. . . to Bolshevism

The emergence of the Russian proletariat on the stage of history melted away Serge's disillusionment with the masses, and he embraced Bolshevism. Serge based his allegiance to the Bolsheviks on a sober assessment of a grave situation; he decided that the Bolsheviks had the vision and the will needed to carry the revolution forward. He believed their political positions were correct. Yet Serge was already critical of their authoritarian excesses. His criticism was not of curbs on freedom, which he understood to be justified by the revolution's mortal peril; he objected to the stultifying structures – the committees on top of councils, managements on top of commissions. He saw a breeding ground for 'a multitude of bureaucrats who were responsible for more fuss than honest work'.[29] They were the 'smart set', decorated in 'chic uniforms' who sent people from office to office.

Serge joined the Bolshevik Party in May 1919.[30] That did not stop him from keeping company with poets, writers, anarchists and social revolutionaries. He belonged to the Free Philosophic Society, *Volfila*, led by the symbolist novelist Andrei Bely. Serge called it the 'last free thought society' and admitted he was probably their 'only Communist member'.[31]

Serge's Marxism was fused with an anarchist's spirit and a primary commitment to socialism's international character. His Marxism was deeply humanistic, preoccupied with questions of personal development and individual freedom. In his earlier anarcho-individualist years, Serge was impatient and disappointed in the masses. Now they were his central concern. This preoccupation with the condition of life of the masses meant that Serge always saw democracy as an integral component of socialist development. These aspects of Serge's Marxism did not come only from his earlier anarchism; Marxism is not devoid of humanism. Serge became a Marxist because the Bolsheviks knew what to do next, and also because he shared their ultimate vision of socialism as the means to liberate humanity.

Serge had begun to see anarchism as a dead end as early as 1913, when the goals of the anarchist bandits of the Bonnot gang had led them to violent acts of murder and robbery. Serge was repulsed by these acts, but sympathized with their goals.[32] He ended up in jail when the French judicial system failed to recognize this subtle distinction. The violence of the

Bolsheviks, however, served a purpose. The anarchists seemed better at pontificating than at moving forward. Serge saw the anarchists' failure to support the Bolsheviks as objective support for the counter-revolution.[33] He viewed anarchism more as a way of conducting one's life, but Bolshevism was the embodiment of a technique of revolution that fitted its theory of social emancipation.[34]

What Serge retained from his anarchism was a healthy opposition to authoritarianism. While recognizing that even the anarchist movement was populated with authoritarian figures, from Bakunin to Makhno, Serge saw the essence of anarchism as the absence of authority; but authoritarianism can exist among those who oppose authority.[35] One scholar has charged that Serge's early writings, for an anarchist turned Bolshevik, seem remarkably devoid of public criticism of the authoritarian side of Bolshevik rule.[36] In Serge's later writings of this period, particularly the civil-war novel *Conquered City*, he was 'alert to the authoritarian worm in the bud of revolution'.[37] Yet in his writings of the early twenties there is no such criticism. While evidence suggests that in the USSR Serge was privately critical of emerging authoritarian practices, his writings published abroad did not contain that criticism. Was Serge acting as a Bolshevik propagandist, as Sedgwick intimates?[38] Vlady Kibalchich, Serge's son, dismisses the criticism stating that these were 'early days' for the Bolsheviks, too soon to make definite pronouncements about the character of the society being formed.[39] It was impossible to tell what would happen once the immediate danger of foreign intervention and civil war passed.

Serge did not try some impossible mix of anarchism and Bolshevism; he became a Bolshevik, and subsequently a Left Oppositionist, and never returned to anarchism. His later opposition was not to Bolshevism, but to its corruption, Stalinism. His preoccupation with the masses, with democracy, with the question of freedom, was shared by other Left Oppositionists, particularly Trotsky.

The view that Marxists and Bolsheviks in particular are manipulative and authoritarian, even if sometimes true, is a part of the Stalinist legacy that distorts Marxism. Serge admitted that authoritarian seeds existed in Bolshevik thought which grew to full blown weeds under Stalin, but he also held that there were many other seeds that could have flowered into a full-blown democracy had circumstances existed for their germination.[40]

Serge tried to win the anarchists over to Bolshevism, to get them to draw the same conclusions as he had. He wrote a pamphlet for the purpose, called *Les Anarchistes et l'expérience de la révolution russe*. This booklet was written in the summer of 1920 and published in Paris in 1921.[41] In 1937 and 1938 Serge published 'Méditation sur l'anarchie', and 'La Pensée anarchiste'. One further essay, 'L'Anarchisme', written from his exile in Mexico was left among his unpublished papers. In the first three Serge discusses the relative merits of anarchism and Marxism, looking for a point of synthesis. Serge was aware of both the pluses and minuses of the two theories. Marxism was superior analytically and organizationally but would be enhanced by the spirit of humanistic idealism of the anarchists. This idealism of the anarchist tradition, which was a sort of morality, would serve as a corrective to the tendency in Bolshevism to subordinate their revolutionary, democratic principles to expediency, or the force of circumstances. Anarchism was better as a way of conducting one's life, but not as a theory of change. Serge wrote in the last-mentioned essay that anarchism was well suited to the terrain of pre-industrialized countries among artisans and petty-producers; but in the heart of industrial countries, Marxism had largely surpassed and eliminated anarchism.[42]

Serge's point of synthesis was more of a plea for humanity and liberty within Bolshevik practice, neither of which are qualities alien to Marxism. Serge's writings show more how he had matured and rejected anarchism, but found Bolshevik practice wanting and looked back to anarchism for the qualities he would have wished present in Bolshevik practice. Serge pointed out the problem with the individualist anarchists: they reduced everything to the self. Marxists, however, had an understanding of class, of individuals consciously acting in collectivities in the process of history. This became a Bolshevik theory of struggle enabling individuals acting in solidarity to accomplish profound social change. Class action actually enhanced the importance of the individual.[43]

In his balance sheet *The Anarchists and the Experience of the Russian Revolution*, Serge suggested that the Russian anarchists had failed as revolutionaries by remaining outside the revolution. Although many fought in the civil war, they had presented no alternative libertarian programme to the Bolsheviks. Worse, some took up arms against the new workers' state and became objectively counter-revolutionary.*

Serge thought the Bolsheviks proved themselves superior in method, programme and practice. Their failures resulted not from flaws in their theory, but from obstacles imposed by real circumstances. 'The proletarian dictatorship has, in Russia, had to introduce an increasingly authoritarian centralism. One may perhaps deplore it. Unfortunately I do not believe that it could have been avoided.'[44]

The anarchists lacked the Bolsheviks' will and unity of thought and deed. At essential moments anarchism proved politically bankrupt: in

---

* Serge had considered the betrayal of the 'blacks' under Makhno, who had tried to build an anarchist federation while defending themselves against both Whites and Reds, a terrible crime of the Bolsheviks with a demoralizing effect that was one of the basic causes of the Kronstadt rebellion (Serge, *Memoirs*, p. 123). But he also said the anarchists had abdicated in the face of their duty to the revolution (*Les Anarchistes et l'expérience de la révolution russe*, pp. 17–26). Serge's views have earned him the epithet 'The Bolsheviks' pet anarchist' in an unsigned article of the same name which appeared in *Red & Black Revolution*, no. 4, 1998.

Spain (1917) the anarchists abnegated power, and in Russia they fought against it. The anarchists, Serge said in his *Memoirs*, 'had an essentially emotional approach to theory, were ignorant of political economy and had never faced the problem of power' and 'found it practically impossible to achieve any theoretical understanding of what was going on'.[45] Serge agreed with Lenin and Trotsky that it was important to win the support of the best among the anarchists and Serge also thought they could play a creative role within the revolution as the guardians of its idealism, working for greater freedom by insisting that the masses exert control over revolutionary institutions.[46] 'Their [the anarchists turned communists] clear-sightedness will make them the enemies of the ambitious, of budding political careerists and commissars, of formalists, Party dogmatists and intriguers.'[47]

Serge the Bolshevik in Comintern and civil war

Serge joined the Bolsheviks after months of discussions with various political tendencies. He found most of them sincere, honest and possessed of bitterly clear vision. Zinoviev was an exception; he affected Serge as flabby, a man of puffed confidence, comfortable at the pinnacle of power.[48] Serge befriended Maxim Gorky, who had been a friend of his mother's family at Nizhni-Novgorod. Gorky was a non-Bolshevik critical intellectual whom Serge admired as 'the supreme, the righteous, the relentless witness of the Revolution'.[49]

Gorky offered Serge work in his publishing house 'Universal Literature' but Serge declined. He felt his duty was to work within the revolution while retaining his critical sense. Serge decided to eschew posts of importance and responsibility, to remain at the ground level of the revolution.* This attitude demonstrated both Serge's independence and his lack of personal opportunism. Serge did not wish to be cast into the limelight of leadership, but would not decline such positions if he deemed it necessary. Personal wishes and political tasks often came into conflict. Revolutionaries of the Bolshevik mould were sometimes called upon to put Party needs before their own.

In Victor Serge's case working for the revolution meant working in its propagandistic organs, putting his talents to good use. Ironically his first job was as a journalist for the newspaper of the Petrograd Soviet, *Severnaya Kommuna* (Northern Commune), the same newspaper he had read with such horror on first crossing the Finnish border into Russia. Like most other

---

* This desire to remain at the rank-and-file level may account for the absence of Serge's name in any of the histories of the early Comintern, with the exception of *The Forming of the Communist International*, by James Hulse (Stanford, Calif., Stanford University Press, 1964). But although Serge may have functioned at 'ground level' he was also an intimate of the top Bolshevik leadership, a colleague of Zinoviev, Lenin, Trotsky and others.

Bolsheviks at the time, Serge worked at many jobs: he was a teacher in public education clubs, an organizing inspector for schools and a lecturing assistant to the Petrograd militia. These many jobs brought him 'the means of bare existence from one day to the next, in a chaos that was oddly organized'.[50] Serge was married by now to Liuba Russakova whose family had travelled with Serge to Petrograd.

The Communist International was formed in March 1919, and although Serge was not yet a member of the Bolshevik Party Zinoviev asked him to organize the administration of the Executive Committee in Petrograd.[51] Serge's political experience in Europe meant he was ideally suited to Comintern work. The Russian Revolution, for the Bolsheviks and for Serge himself, was but the beginning. At the top of their historical agenda was the world socialist revolution. They believed only the world revolution would establish a socialist commonwealth which must comprise all advanced nations. Serge and the Bolsheviks were Russian *and* world revolutionists. They saw no essential separation between their revolution and the world struggle for socialism; the two were inextricably linked. The founding of the Third International, or Communist International (Comintern), was the concretization of this political principle. Ironically, its founding came upon the heels of defeat in Germany and the executions of Rosa Luxemburg and Karl Liebknecht. The initial manifesto of the Communist International, written by Trotsky, extended Marx's historic statement in the *Communist Manifesto*. Trotsky wrote:

> Proletarians of all countries! In the struggle against imperialist barbarism, against monarchy, against the privileged classes, against the bourgeois state and bourgeois property, against national oppression and the tyranny of classes in any shape or form – unite!
>   Proletarians of all countries, round the banner of workmen's councils, round the banner of the revolutionary struggle for power and the dictatorship of the proletariat, round the banner of the Third International – unite![52]

Serge took part in the first three Congresses of the Comintern, used his offices to intercede when he could on behalf of victims of the Cheka, met the leaders of the international revolutionary movements (of whom he drew thumbnail portraits in his *Memoirs*), and like all his comrades performed a host of functions: he ran the Romance-language section and publications of the International, met the foreign delegates who arrived 'by adventurous routes through the blockade's barbed-wire barrier',[53] became a trooper in the Communist battalion of the Second District during the civil war, engaged in smuggling arms between Russia and Finland, and became a commissar in charge of the archives of the old Ministry of the Interior, the Okhrana.

The early Comintern was made up of men and women like Serge: they shared Serge's disgust for the spineless and opportunist parliamentary social democratic leaders of the European workers' movement; their revolutionary internationalism and political vision matched his own. People such as the Russo-Italian socialist and first Secretary Angelica Balabanova, the Canadian anarchist Bill Shatov, the American revolutionary journalist John Reed, the Spanish syndicalist Angel Pestaña, the Italian maximalist Amadeo Bordiga,* the French syndicalist Alfred Rosmer and many others. Serge confessed that in these first meetings the 'superiority of the Russians, compared with the foreign revolutionaries amazed me'.[54] Serge befriended Vladimir Mazin, his assistant and comrade whose revolutionary record was at least as long as his own.

Serge clearly had a deep affection for Mazin, and named his son Vlady after him.[55] When the civil war threatened the revolution, Mazin did as he had written:

> He renounced his command, picked up a rifle, collected a little band of Communists and tried to stop the rout and the enemy simultaneously . . . [For Mazin, there was] no point in doing jobs of organization, publishing, etcetera, which were fruitless from now on; and at an hour when so many men were dying quite uselessly out in the wilds, he felt a horror of Smolny offices, committees, printed matter and the Hotel Astoria.[56]

Zinoviev had him appointed political commissar, but Mazin demanded to be given a private's rifle. He died at the hands of the Whites.

Mazin, who had begun as a Menshevik and had become a Bolshevik, shared Serge's view that the only way to fight for democratic and libertarian ideals was in action, within the revolution. Serge and Mazin stayed at the Hotel Astoria and worked in the Comintern Headquarters in the Smolny Institute of Petrograd. Although Balabanova was nominally the first Secretary of the Executive Committee and Zinoviev the first President, she lived in Moscow and he stayed in Petrograd as head of the Petrograd Soviet, where the real power resided. Thus Serge and Mazin, both critical communists, were at the seat of power in the Comintern, creating the organization from scratch.[57] That was the extent of the staff of the organization which would coordinate the activities of the world revolution: two people! After Mazin's death, Serge continued alone.[58]

Serge's knowledge of languages and his experience as an editor were put to good use as a propagandist in the Comintern.[59] He wrote dozens of articles in the various Comintern journals, and described his activities as

---

* Bordiga was a founder of the Italian Communist Party who broke with the Comintern because he refused to recognize the tactic of the united front. He also disagreed with Lenin on questions of perspective and organization. He doubted that peasant Russia could lead the international working-class movement, and worried about the temptations of compromise and corruption. The Bordigists worked for some years with the Left Opposition.

emissary, functionary, secretary, editor, translator, printer, organizer, director, 'member of the collegium' and more.[60]

This frenetic activity in the Comintern took place at the height of the civil war, in Petrograd, which was threatened by British troops and the White General Yudenich. The battle of Petrograd was the subject of two of Serge's books: *Pendant la guerre civile: Petrograd, mai–juin 1919*; and *La Ville en danger: Petrograd, l'an II de la révolution*.* Serge's activities in the Comintern were frequently interrupted by the immediate needs of the city's peril. He was worried that if the city fell the archives of the Okhrana would fall again into the hands of reactionaries, providing 'precious weapons for tomorrow's hangmen and firing-squads'.[61] Serge saw to it that the archives were packed in boxes and ready to be smuggled out or burned at the last moment. He returned to these archives later, in 1920, when he wrote articles published in the French journal *Bulletin Communiste*, nos 50, 51 and 52, November 1921. These articles became the book *Les Coulisses d'une sûreté générale. Ce que tout révolutionnaire devrait savoir sur la répression*. The English edition was titled *What Everyone Should Know about State Repression*, and it is one of Serge's best-known works.[62]

But in 1919 Serge's concern was with the survival of Petrograd and the revolution: 'It seemed, quite plainly', he said, 'to be our death-agony'.[63] Children were evacuated, known militants tried to change their appearance; Serge spent his nights with Communist troops, and his pregnant wife slept in the back of an ambulance.

The siege of Petrograd tested the endurance of the hungry, frozen and choking revolution. The victory over the Whites at Petrograd was organized by Trotsky, described by Serge as a real leader, whose energy, organization and confidence saved the city, by convincing the workers that fifteen thousand Whites could not possibly 'master a working class capital of seven hundred thousand inhabitants'.[64] It was Trotsky's appearance at the Tauride and his role in saving Petrograd from Yudenich that began Serge's three-decade-long devotion to Trotsky. Serge was attracted by Trotsky's concrete and decisive action in defence of the revolution.

---

* These short books, unlike his history of the first year, *Year One of the Russian Revolution*, are eyewitness accounts with all the immediacy of a participant with inside knowledge. They are more anecdotal and passionate but no less honest or revelatory. The frailties of individuals are highlighted, as in Serge's depiction of the anarchist in charge of taking captured White guards to jail: out of softness and remembrance of a not-so-distant time when the anarchist himself was imprisoned, he let the Whites go. Serge calls this 'libertarian craziness', an act of 'generosity which if it had been repeated, would have meant the suicide of the revolution'. The whole story, recounted in Victor Serge, *Lenin: 1917: La Defensa del Petrogrado, año segundo de la revolución rusa*, Mexico, Ediciones Transición, 1977, pp. 118–20, is worth reading for its style and its underlying point, which is to show the problems anarchists faced when their ideas confronted reality.

Fighting for the revolution in the civil war was clearly a seminal experience for Serge. Politically it meant that he saw the real choices open to the Bolsheviks, and the heroic sacrifices demanded of them. Serge held the civil-war generation of revolutionary fighters in the highest esteem; later he criticized others, like the Yugoslav Left Oppositionist Anton Ciliga, who were quick to judge the Bolsheviks without understanding the perils they faced when the revolution was at death's door.[65] Serge recognized the hard choices made by Lenin and Trotsky in this period as drastic but necessary measures, and supported them wholeheartedly. It was only in looking back later that Serge was able to see that cardinal errors were made – the gravest being the creation of the Cheka.

Documenting a country at war

When Serge took the conscious decision to be a writer in 1928, he already was one. His voluminous civil-war writings were written both close to the events themselves, and years later upon reflection. His articles on the civil war were published in *La Vie Ouvrière* (March 1921 to July 1926), *Bulletin Communiste* (April 1921 to October 1924), *La Correspondance Internationale* (1922–25), *Clarté* (1920–26). His books include *Year One of the Russian Revolution* (1925–28), *La Ville en danger: Petrograd, l'an II de la révolution* (November–December 1919), *Pendant la guerre civile: Petrograd, mai–juin 1919* (January 1920), *Vie des révolutionnaires* (published in 1930 with a preface dated 1929), *Ville conquise*, the novel about the civil war and Red terror, written in 1930–31 and published in English as *Conquered City*, 1967, as well as the aforementioned *Les Anarchistes et l'éxpérience de la révolution russe*.

Serge's writings reveal his public priorities as he saw them at the time: this is the first socialist revolution, and revolutionaries must be within it; the White terror threatens to destroy the revolution, so revolutionaries must defend it; look what happened in Finland: the workers thought they could have a peaceful transition to socialism and were drowned in blood by the Whites; the Cheka, instrument of Red terror, the Bolsheviks' worst creation, was formed as a defence against the mortal threat posed by the White terror, made clear in attempts to assassinate Lenin and Trotsky.

When Serge undertook the writing of a history of the Revolution he began with the first year. This is not an eyewitness account, and differs considerably from his participatory accounts of the civil war. The latter works, based on direct experience, are much more impressionistic, anecdotal and evocative. *Year One of the Russian Revolution*, on the other hand, deals with events that took place before Serge arrived on Russian soil. It is a revolutionary, partisan and uncompromising history, revealing the limited choices the Bolsheviks faced.

His sources were official documents, speeches, memoirs, notes, reports and fragmentary studies.[66] In this work as in his others, Serge was writing to correct the record and to draw lessons for revolutionaries. The book, pretending no 'objectivity', expresses 'no other point of view but that held by the proletarian revolutionaries',[67] but does strive to present the facts accurately.

In trying to revive the early history of Bolshevism, and distinguish it from what followed, Serge turned to the first Bolshevik controversies, beginning with the insurrection itself, the role of the urban middle classes, the Constituent Assembly, the first flames of the civil war and the treaty of Brest-Litovsk. Serge declared himself with Lenin and Trotsky on the seizure of power, against those Bolsheviks (including Zinoviev, Kamenev and Stalin) who hesitated at the moment of revolution. Serge compared Lenin's *On the Road to Insurrection* with Marx's *The Communist Manifesto*. He confirmed Trotsky's complete accord with Lenin, judging them both correct on the timing of the insurrection.[68]

Taking on the notion of a Bolshevik *coup d'état*, Serge concentrated on the role of the 'Party of the proletariat' which 'expresses at a conscious level, what the masses want and carry it out'.[69] He embraced Lenin's conception of the Party as 'the nervous system of the working class', 'its brain', which 'reveals what they [the working class] have been thinking'.[70] The Party is the majority Party of the working class; 'It is all one multitude'. Serge also said the Party in 1917 suffered not the slightest bureaucratic deformation.*

This view of the Revolution was repeated in Serge's 1920 article 'La Révolution d'octobre à Moscou',[71] in his biography of Lenin, *Lenine 1917* (1925), in *From Lenin to Stalin* (1936) and his article 'Trente ans après la révolution russe' (1947) among other works. Serge saw the Revolution as a genuine expression of the mass sentiment of the overwhelming majority of workers and peasants, and 'the Bolshevik Party was the political organization which best expressed the popular sentiment. From this fact came its popularity and the effectiveness of its activity.'[72] Moreover, the superior capabilities of Lenin, the 'most hated and the most loved man on earth'[73] were of supreme importance. His genius, Serge wrote, lay in his consistency as a revolutionist.[74] Trotsky, 'the second head of the revolution' was also indispensable to its realization.†

---

* Serge noted in *From Lenin to Stalin* (New York, Monad Press, 1973): 'the Party discussed, tendencies appeared and disappeared, and opposition elements, which must not be confused with counter-revolutionists, agitated unceasingly in broad daylight during the whole civil war – until 1921. They were not to disappear completely until 1925–26, when in consequence all internal life disappeared from the Party . . . Men fought and died for a new kind of freedom' (pp. 22–3).

† Serge described Trotsky's role in *From Lenin to Stalin*, pp. 16–19. Serge also drew a portrait of the two leaders of the Revolution, nameless but instantly recognizable, in his civil war novel, *Conquered City*, written in 1930–31, published in Paris in 1932. In *From Lenin to Stalin*, Serge quoted from his portrait of the two, explaining that although he wrote it in 1919 (to be incorporated into his novel eleven years later) he was in Leningrad when writing the novel: if he had used the names in 1930 'the Black Chamber would not have passed my manuscript' (p. 22n).

As to the idea that October was the work of a small conspiracy,[75] Serge urged that the words of eyewitnesses such as John Reed and Jacques Sadoul be read to see how 'the Bolshevik "conspiracy" was literally carried into power by a colossal and rising wave of public sentiment'.[76]

Serge's basic attitudes on the early tasks and decisions facing the Bolsheviks were the same as those of Lenin and Trotsky. If anything Serge criticized the Bolsheviks for their leniency toward their White enemies. Citing instances where White officers were allowed to escape instead of being shot on the spot, Serge called this lack of firmness 'foolish clemency'. He added, 'the greatest humanity lies in the utmost rigour: magnanimity costs too much'.[77]

Conforming with his newly acquired Bolshevism, Serge praised the 'Party patriotism' of the Bolsheviks, a patriotism of 'inestimable value in the class war, a patriotism of class and Party: better to be wrong with the Party of the proletariat than right against it. There is no greater revolutionary wisdom than this.'[78] By 1928 Serge had completely reversed his position: the Opposition, he said, was defeated by 'Party patriotism'.

> The Party that was excommunicating, imprisoning and beginning to murder us, remained our Party, and we still owed everything to it; we must live only for it since only through it could we serve the Revolution. We were defeated by Party patriotism: it both provoked us to rebel and turned us against ourselves.[79]

Serge's frank portrayal of the besieged revolution in 1918, when the question of 'liberty' fell victim to the 'avalanche of all the other problems which were . . . threatening to engulf it',[80] seems contrary to his later preoccupation. At the end of his life he wrote that 'the only problem which revolutionary Russia, in all the years from 1917 to 1923, utterly failed to consider was the problem of liberty'.[81] Serge never succeeded in reconciling these contradictory stands. He clearly demonstrated the revolution was hemmed in from all sides: from within the anarchists,* Socialist Revolutionaries (SRs), Mensheviks and Kadets† all opposed the Bolsheviks and formed part of the counter-revolution, and famine and epidemic took hold; from without, the White armies of Kolchak, Denikin, Yudenich and later Wrangel were joined by the armies of fourteen capitalist powers[82] to blockade and strangle the Revolution. With all these forces determined to destroy the Bolsheviks, the miracle is that they survived at all. Serge argued with convincing examples that the measures taken were not only necessary but too lenient. Later Serge examined the measures taken out of necessity

---

* Makhno's Black Guard fought the Whites while opposing the Bolsheviks.

† The Socialist Revolutionaries were a moderate, neo-populist Party. The Mensheviks were moderate Social Democrats. Each of these had left wings: the Left SRs and the Menshevik Internationalists. The Kadets or Constitutional Democrats were the main Russian liberal Party.

and theorized that certain of them formed the foundation of Stalinist totalitarianism.

From treaty to trial

Despite the life-threatening difficulties the Revolution faced from the very
beginning, its history was one of a developing socialist democracy.[83] The
minutes of the Central Committee from August 1917 to February 1918
attest to the lively atmosphere of free-wheeling and intense debate which
went on within the Bolshevik Party and between the various parties. In the
early months the Revolution exhibited the 'popular ferment, bubbling
ideas, rivalry of clubs, parties and publications' which were so noticeably
absent when Serge crossed the border from Finland in February 1919.
Serge's critical spirit would have met kindred souls had he been able to
make it to Russia in time for those first heady months. When Serge arrived
the Revolution was only fifteen months old, but events had already forced
the Bolsheviks to retreat on matters of principle.

One of the tendentious myths of the Russian Revolution's historiography which Serge demolished in his retrospective on the Revolution's thirtieth birthday was that the Bolsheviks' immediate goal was to establish a
monopoly on state power.[84] Serge showed that the truth was just the opposite: the Bolsheviks were most afraid of being *isolated* in power. The Left
Social Revolutionaries participated in the government with the Bolsheviks
from November until July 1918. On 6 July they began an insurrectional
revolt in Moscow, proclaiming their intention to govern alone and to
'reopen the war against German imperialism'. They were defeated and from
then it was left to the Bolsheviks to rule alone. Marcel Liebman noted, 'The
Leninists . . . against their will, concentrated the whole state power in their
own hands, with no share held by other socialist parties'.[85] And Serge commented, 'as their responsibilities increased, their mentality changed'.[86]

This 'change of mentality' meant that the Bolsheviks moved to suppress
their socialist and anarchist opponents, a move which, it is now apparent,
had irreversible consequences for the further development of socialist
democracy. At the time, however, what was apparent was that the SRs had
launched a series of terrorist attacks, killing first Voludarsky, then Uritsky,
and had attempted to kill Lenin.

The SRs were not the only early critics from within the revolution:
arguing against the 'peace of shame',* Preobrazhensky and Bukharin, later
to stand on opposite sides of the industrialization debates, joined with
others to put out the 'Theses of the Left Communists' in 1918. Although
the debate began on the question of war or peace, it soon turned to industrial policy.[87]

---

* As the Treaty of Brest-Litovsk was called by many Bolsheviks, including Serge.

The debates over the Treaty of Brest-Litovsk show Bolshevism at its best; democratic, principled and yet maintaining a balance between flexibility and firmness. Serge called this period 'The Great Years'. The debates were passionate and committed. The minutes of the Central Committee of the Bolshevik Party show how deeply divided the Bolsheviks were on nearly every major issue – with members lining up on different sides of every question.[88] The debates with the other socialist parties at this juncture were equally lively and creative.

Although Serge was not in Russia to take part in this debate, he devoted a chapter to it in his *Year One*. Serge sided with Lenin's realistic approach to the negotiations because they were based on hard facts, not Left sentiments. It was impossible to conduct a revolutionary war against imperialism – the old army did not exist, and the new one was just forming. Serge said 'The phrases with which the Lefts were so lavish expressed pure sentiment. The reasoning they invoked was simply pitiful.'[89] Moreover, Serge found Lenin's realism even 'more impressive in that he displays no *basic* tendency to overestimate the forces of the enemy'.[90] Serge had points of agreement with Trotsky in this controversy as well, acknowledging that Trotsky's desire to hold out gave strength to the Western proletariat, who saw a separate peace as a capitulation to German imperialism and as prolonging the war.* Serge's overall agreement was with Lenin, however,† on the need for surrender; yet from the vantage point of 1928[91] Serge reflected that the weakness of German imperialism at that time would have prevented it from destroying the Russian Revolution – saying that even a German occupation would *not* have meant the collapse of the Soviet regime.‡

---

* E.H. Carr suggests that the differences between Lenin and Trotsky on Brest-Litovsk were concerned with emphasis: 'In the Brest-Litovsk controversy, though Trotsky was the most eloquent and ingenious advocate of world revolution, he was also the champion of the policy of playing off one group of capitalists against the other; he was at the opposite pole to those who stood on the ground of pure revolutionary principle unsullied by compromise or expediency . . . On the other hand, Lenin, while insisting on the needs of national defence, was so far from abandoning world revolution that he constantly stressed it as the supreme goal of his policy'. See E.H. Carr, *The Bolshevik Revolution 1917–1923*, vol. 3, London, Macmillan, 1953, pp. 55–6.

† Trotsky came to side with Lenin as well.

‡ Victor Serge, *Year One of the Russian Revolution*, New York, Holt Rinehart and Winston, and London, Allen Lane, 1972, pp. 172–3. Upon reflection Serge appreciated better Trotsky's line at the time, which was to exhaust all revolutionary possibilities and to convince the proletariat of the West of the intransigence of the Bolsheviks before Austro-German imperialism. Yet Serge personally remembered the attitude of French soldiers who believed that in conducting a separate peace with Germany, the Bolsheviks were prolonging a hated war. Trotsky's tactic during the negotiations helped dissipate this attitude shared by many in the West.

Serge sided with Lenin after carefully examining the position of all the opposing tendencies inside and outside of the Party. Although he sympathized with the anti-bureaucratic stance of the Left Communists, he did not agree with them on the question of the peace treaty. The Bolsheviks were forced into accepting the terms of the peace by the advancing German front. 'Proletarian realism' demanded recognition of this fact, not adherence to abstract, romantic or dogmatic conceptions. 'Revolutionary honour', Serge wrote, 'is not put in question when, without abandoning the struggle, one submits to an unavoidable defeat.'[92]

Serge examined the Left Communist economic policies and Lenin's response in *Year One of the Russian Revolution*. Here one would expect to find a larger measure of sympathy for the positions of the Left than Serge actually demonstrated. Instead Serge criticized the Left Communists for their emotionalism and zeal, and their lack of a grasp of the real and desperate state of the Revolution – what Serge described as the country 'at its last gasp'. Lenin had grasped the real situation and was not trapped by any 'revolutionary subjectivism to which intellectuals of middle-class origins are prone' according to Serge, echoing Lenin and using his phraseology.[93] Clearly the situation was drastic and demanded far-sighted and rational policies; Serge decided Lenin possessed the clarity and foresight necessary. Serge also wrote that Lenin's handling of the Left Communists was a model of revolutionary politics, and saved the Bolshevik Party from suffering a split.[94]

Although the terms of the peace of Brest-Litovsk were disastrous – revolutionary Russia lost Poland and the Baltic regions, huge tracts of the Ukraine, 27 per cent of her own sown area, 26 per cent of her population, a third of her average crops, three-quarters of her iron and steel and 26 per cent of her railway network[95] – Serge weighed the pluses as well as the minuses. One of the pluses was that the conduct of the discussion showed the health of the Party which was able to strike a balance between authority and democracy, discipline and lenience; the minuses were described forcefully by Serge, particularly the sacrifice of the Finnish Revolution, which was drowned in blood in 1918. Serge has the almost singular merit among historians of the Russian Revolution of not letting the tragic events in Finland get lost.

Potential destroyed: Finland

Serge had passed through Finland on his way to Petrograd in January 1919. His description:

> Finland received us as foes, for the White Terror was only just over . . . The cold air was heavy with chilled violence. Without ever leaving the train, we crossed this huge land of sleepy woods, snow-covered lakes, tracts of whiteness, and pretty painted cottages lost in the wilderness. We went through towns so tidy and silent that they reminded us of children's toys. We had a moment of panic

when, as evening fell, the train stopped in a clearing and soldiers lined up alongside the tracks: we were invited to get down. The women murmured, 'They're going to shoot us'. We refused to leave the train, but it was only to give us a breath of air while we waited for the carriages to be cleaned and the engine to be fuelled with wood. The sentries ignored their instructions [they were ordered to shoot at the first attempt of anyone to leave the train] and started to be pleasant to the children.[96]

The trip through Finland was also recounted in Serge's novel *Birth of Our Power*, where Serge saw in the hostile eyes of the Finnish guards the bitter defeat of the Finnish workers. What had happened?

The Treaty of Brest-Litovsk had sealed the fate of the Finnish proletariat, in whom the Russian Revolutionaries had placed great hopes.* Finland had been a largely autonomous part of the Russian empire since 1809. The Finnish bourgeoisie was determined to gain independence. After the October Revolution in Russia, the Finns pressed their claim on the Soviet government, citing the Bolshevik principle of self-determination. Without a favourable decision from Russia, Finland could not get recognition from Western countries like Sweden, Denmark, Norway, Germany, France, Great Britain and the US.[97] Although the Bolshevik policy of self-determination had allowed for nations to secede, they had hoped that the 'freedom to break away' would encourage these small sister-nations to freely join the Russian Socialist Federation.[98] On 18/31 December 1917,† the resolution recognizing national independence of Finland was adopted by the Sovnarkom (Council of People's Commissars). But this independence gave freedom not to the Finnish workers but the bourgeoisie.[99]

The Russian Revolution had polarized Finland, and independence highlighted the class divide. Lenin and Trotsky had hoped the Finnish workers would join them in revolution, as the first in the Revolution's spread westward. Instead, the leadership of the Finnish Social Democrats supported the Finnish bourgeoisie's quest for independence and failed to make a revolution. The Soviets were then forced to recognize the Finnish bourgeois Senate instead of a Finnish workers' government.[100] Forty-two thousand Russian troops were still posted on the Finnish border.

Like the Scandinavian and German workers' movements, the Finnish labour movement was political from its inception. The Federation of Labour

---

* Serge, *Year One*, p. 182. Lenin had written, in his *Third Letter from Afar*, before returning to Russia, that 'The Finnish workers are better organizers than us and will help us in this field; *in their own fashion* they will form a vanguard pressing towards a foundation of the Socialist Republic.'

† December 18 (Old Style), December 31 (New Style) calendar. The Finns mark 6 December as their day of independence, reflecting the date the Finnish Parliament, the Eduskunta, debated the question. Seppo Hentilä, 'Finland Becomes Independent', in O. Jussila, S. Hentilä and J. Nevakivi (eds), *From Grand Duchy to a Modern State*, London, Hurst, 1995, p. 103.

was proposed at the inaugural convention of the labour Party in 1899, and finally came into existence in 1907 with a class struggle orientation.[101] While its leaders looked to Sweden, Finnish workers, who did not have the franchise, often took temporary jobs in St Petersburg. The Finnish workers' movement paralleled the Russian one. There was a Finnish general strike in 1905, an offshoot of the strikes rocking Russia throughout that year. Like the Russian strike, all classes participated in the Finnish strike, demanding primary civil rights, freedoms of speech and association, and reform in the system of popular representation. In 1906 Finnish workers won the franchise and immediately had the most democratic of European elections.[102]

The Finnish Social Democrats, formed in the German Social Democratic mould, had gained a majority in the Finnish Parliament in 1916. They voted in the eight-hour day and other social legislation, raising the question of whether socialism could be achieved through the ballot box.

Tensions mounted, and a highly political general strike was proclaimed on 14/27 November 1917 – under the banner of class struggle – just weeks after the Russian October Revolution, only a few miles away.* The Social Democrats, fearing repression, defensively took over the largest towns, including Åbo, Tampere and Viipuri – and the whole of southern Finland. They vacillated between parliamentary and extra-parliamentary means. Following the example of the Bolsheviks, they introduced workers' control over industry and took over the banks. Bloody clashes ensued between Reds and Whites. Serge called it a revolution aborted. He blamed the Finnish Social Democratic leaders, who were indecisive. O.W. Kuusinen, one of the principal leaders of Finnish Social Democracy, later wrote: 'Wishing not to risk our democratic conquests, and hoping to manoeuvre round this turning-point of history by our parliamentary skill, we decided to evade the revolution.'†

The situation continued to escalate until January when it became clear that the parliamentary road had reached a dead end. The Finnish Social Democrats then attempted to seize power: they not only introduced workers' control over industry as mentioned above, they debated whether it was now possible to 'establish, without the expropriation of the rich or the dictatorship of labour, a parliamentary democracy in which the proletariat

---

* At the Finnish Social-Democratic Congress in November, Stalin, representing the Council of Commissars, appealed to the Finnish comrades to seize power, and promised them the fraternal assistance of the Russian proletariat. The Social-Democrats did make a bid for power, but the promised aid was not forthcoming because of the provisions of Brest-Litovsk. See Carr, *The Bolshevik Revolution* and Boris Souvarine, *Stalin: A Critical Survey of Bolshevism*, translated by C.L.R. James, New York, Longmans Green, 1939, p. 100.

† Quoted in Serge, *Year One*, p. 184. The passage evokes the situation in Chile 1970–73, when the Popular Unity Coalition came to governmental power and attempted a parliamentary road to socialism.

[would be] the leading class'.[103] The leaders of 'Red Finland' were not Bolsheviks, and they had hoped, in social democratic style, to create a parliamentary democracy that could introduce socialism through reforms.* The 'Finnish Commune' lasted just a few months but passed revolutionary legislation, attempting, in Serge's words, 'a workers' revolution conducted in the name of an ideal democracy'. They were rapidly defeated by the 'greater realism of the bourgeoisie' and General Mannerheim's troops, beefed up by a brigade of Swedish volunteers and the German Schutzkorps. The White terror followed. Soviet troops had to retire under the provisions of Brest-Litovsk, giving a whole new perspective to the consequences of that 'shameful treaty'.

Finland had neither an army nor a police force, so the bourgeoisie formed 'civil guards' sometimes known as 'fire brigades'. Mannerheim used these forces – the Whites – along with outside help (mainly German) to crush the Red Guards, formed by labour organizations to fight the Whites. The Whites' aim was to free Finland from Russian power and defend the bourgeoisie from the increasingly radical labour movement. For their part, the Reds had hoped for aid from their Bolshevik 'brothers' which did not materialize. Although some Russians fought with the Reds, their numbers were small. To match Mannerheim's forces of Finns, Germans and Swedes, the Reds needed Soviet troops, but they were forced to withdraw under the terms of the Brest-Litovsk treaty. Lenin promised rifles and cannons, but they did not arrive until after hostilities began.

The 1918 war between Reds and Whites was short and bloody.† Helsinki was captured in early April after Mannerheim's troops organized a massacre whose main victims were women and children.‡ There was fierce fighting in Tampere on 6 April, with the Whites finally taking it in Easter week.

---

* Hentilä, 'Finland Becomes Independent', pp. 109–10. Their programme, presented on 29 Jan. 1918, appealed for 'democratic methods' to be used to introduce social reforms, and socialism. The draft constitution was a mixture of the American Declaration of Independence and the ideas of the French Revolution. In this way the revolutionary attempt of the Finnish labour movement differed from the other revolutions of 1919 inspired by the successful Bolshevik revolution: the Berlin Spartacist revolt, the Bavarian Soviet republic and the Hungarian Commune under Béla Kun.

† The Finns refer to the war between the Reds and Whites as a 'war of liberation', 'revolution', 'class war', 'revolt', 'civil war' and 'internal war.' The various terms reflect the opposing interpretations of the war in 1918. According to Seppo Hentilä, it was not until the 1960s that bourgeois Finland admitted that the struggle of the Reds was justified (Hentilä, 'Finland Becomes Independent', pp. 113–15).

‡ General Mannerheim, a Finn of Swedish origin, was a former general of the Russian army, who returned to Finland after the October Revolution. One of Helsinki's main thoroughfares is named after this butcher of the Finnish

Workers were rounded up and taken to concentration camps, where many were shot. Some eighty thousand Reds were put in these camps, where conditions were such that 12,000 died from hunger and disease. The terror which followed resulted in more than 30,000 deaths, 25,000 of which were Reds.[104] The bloodbath, which Serge noted had only been matched by the Paris Commune massacre, killed one in four Finnish workers.*

Serge drew theoretical conclusions from the White terror in Finland, which he said could not be

> explained by the frenzy of battle . . . The psychosis of civil war plays a purely secondary role . . . The terror is in reality the result of a calculation and a historical necessity. The victorious propertied classes are perfectly aware that they can only ensure their own domination in the aftermath of a social battle by inflicting on the working class a bloodbath savage enough to enfeeble it for tens of years afterwards. And since the class in question is far more numerous than the wealthy classes, the number of victims *must* be very great.
>
> The *total extermination* of all the advanced and conscious elements of the proletariat is, in short, the rational objective of the White Terror. In this sense, *a vanquished revolution – regardless of its tendency – will always cost the proletariat far more than a victorious revolution, no matter what sacrifices and rigours the latter may demand.*†

Serge made a final observation: the butcheries in Finland took place in April 1918. The Russian Revolution had, until that moment, been very lenient towards its enemies, and had not used terror. 'The victorious bourgeoisie of a small nation which ranks among the most enlightened societies of Europe' had reminded the Russian proletariat of the 'first law of social war'.[105]

The defeat in Finland had multiple consequences for the Russian Revolution: the Bolsheviks were prevented from aiding the extension of the revolution to a Western capitalist country by the terms of the Brest-Litovsk treaty; the savagery of the bourgeois response demonstrated the high social cost for failed revolutions, forcing the Bolsheviks to abandon clemency and use terror to meet terror; and Finland presaged the successive defeats in Germany, Hungary and Poland. As a consequence, the Bolshevik quest for the extension of the Russian Revolution turned eastward with the convening of the Congress of the Oppressed Nationalities and Toilers of the East in

---

working class. Mannerheim remained an anti-Soviet 'patriot'; he was Chairman of the Defence Council, then Commander-in-Chief during the wars of the 1940s, and extricated Finland from the war in 1944 as Finland's President.

* The Chilean experiment with the peaceful transition to socialism (1970–73), strikingly similar to that of the 'People's Republic of Finland', suffered a comparable bloody ending.

† Serge quoted a group of Finnish communists who wrote that 'all organized workers have either been shot or imprisoned'. *Year One*, p. 190.

Baku.* The failed Bavarian, Baku and Hungarian communes brought home the lessons of Finland.

Serge's treatment of the Finnish defeat, mentioned in precious few other histories, is an extraordinary account for revolutionaries.[106]

Civil war: Cheka, terror and revolutionary repression

Although Serge was cognizant of the need to match terror with terror, he nevertheless was critical and fearful of its use. The civil war was full of horrors which Serge made no attempt to hide or idealize. His writings make the case for understanding what the stakes were: defeat of the Revolution would have brought greater bloodshed and a reactionary dictatorship. The victory was a victory for the world, for culture, for humanity.[107]

Serge wrote in his *Portrait de Staline* (1939) that the gravest error committed by the Bolsheviks was the establishment of the Cheka (Extraordinary Commission for the Repression of Counter-Revolution, Speculation, Espionage and Desertion),† the security force formed to protect the revolution from counter-revolutionaries. He called it an inquisition. The Cheka judged those accused or merely suspected without hearing or seeing them. There was no defence. Arrests and executions were ordered and carried out in secret. In later years this preoccupied Serge; he wrote about the significance of the Cheka – in almost identical terms – in his *Portrait de Staline* (1939), *Memoirs of a Revolutionary* (1942–3), and 'Trente ans après la révolution russe' (1947). Despite the extraordinary measures made necessary by a bitter civil war, Serge asked how socialists could forget that public trials were 'the only guarantee against arbitrary and corrupt actions'.[108] Although Serge said that Dzerzhinsky was 'incorruptible' and a 'sincere idealist' the personnel gradually selected for the Cheka had 'psychological inclinations' that

---

* Aimed at India and China, the Congress was more anti-imperialist than socialist and laid some of the seeds which were later sown in the debacle of the Chinese revolution of 1927 – due to Stalin's Comintern policies. See Serge, *Memoirs*, pp. 107–9, and the review by Michael Cox in *Critique 1* of *The First Congress of the Toilers of the East* documents, pp. 101–2.

† The Cheka was originally created at the suggestion of Dzerzhinsky as an administrative organ with limited powers of investigation of cases. It was subordinated to the Sovnarkom. A decree of 5 Sept. 1918 conferred sweeping powers on the Cheka which it never in practice lost. This extension of power became known as the 'Red Terror'. By the end of 1922 it was estimated that the Cheka had imprisoned approximately 60,000; the Cheka was also responsible for 140,000 deaths by direct execution and a further 140,000 deaths while suppressing insurrections in the same four years. The figures were arrived at by the historian G.H. Leggett, and quoted in Leonard Schapiro, *The Russian Revolution of 1917: The Origins of Modern Communism*, New York, Basic Books, 1984, pp. 183–7.

prepared them to devote themselves tenaciously to the task of 'internal defence': suspicion, embitterment, harshness and sadism.

> Long-standing social inferiority complexes and memories of humiliations and suffering in the Tsar's jails rendered them intractable, and since professional degeneration has rapid effects, the Cheka inevitably consisted of perverted men tending to see conspiracy everywhere and to live in the midst of perpetual conspiracy themselves.[109]

Serge insisted that Dzerzhinsky 'judged them to be "half-rotten" and saw no solution to the evil except in shooting the worst Chekists and abolishing the death-penalty as quickly as possible'.*

To be fair to Lenin's Central Committee, Serge pointed to the extenuating circumstances which led to this unpardonable terror. The leaders knew the Party would be massacred in the event of defeat, and they knew defeat was a real possibility. Previous experiences cited by Serge from the Paris Commune and Finnish White terror made clear what the consequence of defeat would be: 'mass extermination of the vanquished proletarians'. The Cheka had innocent beginnings, changing only after counter-revolutionary uprisings, the assassinations of Volodarski and Uritsky and the attempts on Lenin.[110] Nevertheless Serge would say later in his life that the Bolshevik Revolution died a self-inflicted death with the creation of the Cheka.

But from 1919 to 1921 Serge was not publicly critical of the Cheka. Under the conditions of civil war it appeared to be a tragic necessity. Privately, Serge interceded frequently on behalf of its victims, but his writings of the period contain no public condemnation.† Serge in fact made the case for the need for repression given the opportunism of 'petty-bourgeois individualism . . . unleashed in chaotic struggles . . . The Cheka was no less indispensable than the Red Army and the Commissariat for Supplies'.[111]

One question which has perplexed Serge scholars and historians of revolution is that of revolutionary repression: how to control it, when to end it, how

---

* Serge, *Memoirs*, p. 81. The death penalty was abolished, at the recommendation of Dzerzhinsky with the approval of Lenin and Trotsky, by the decree of 17 Jan. 1920. Serge recounts that he was told that the night the Petrograd newspapers were printing the decree the Petrograd Chekas were liquidating their stock! In Petrograd and Moscow, that night, as many as 500 suspects were shot. The Chekists responsible later justified their horrendous massacre: 'If the People's Commissars were getting converted to humanitarianism, that was their business. Our business was to crush the counter-revolution forever, and they could shoot us afterwards if they felt like it!' Serge, *Memoirs*, pp. 98–9. The epilogue to this affair is that the death penalty was reintroduced after the Polish invasion in the spring of 1920.

† Later, in his dispute with Trotsky over Kronstadt, which appeared in the pages of the *New International* and elsewhere in 1938, Serge argued that the establishment of the Cheka was fatal for the future course of the Revolution.

to return to democratic practices. The reservations which Serge frequently expressed in his later works and in his polemic with Trotsky were not aired in his discussion of the problem of revolutionary repression (*What Everyone Should Know about State Repression*) in 1925, written for a French readership.

Serge painstakingly pointed out the events which brought the Bolsheviks to their position of monopoly of power. The opposition parties themselves went from competition with the Bolsheviks to harsh opposition to them and the Revolution. Serge noted in the *Memoirs* that political life could not be separated from the reality of civil war and War Communism. Discontent turned into hardened opposition and as such increased the regime's authoritarianism: from the Bolshevik leadership's point of view, discontent turned into enemy activity.[112] Serge himself found the dissenters, excepting the Workers Opposition, to be politically bankrupt. The Bolsheviks were unwilling to allow counter-revolutionary opposition to exist, and increasingly, as the civil war, famine and War Communism continued, the opposition became counter-revolutionary.

Although Serge's private activities and later writings attest to some misgivings, he remained committed to the Bolsheviks because they were the best of the existing alternatives. Serge named four characteristics which gave the Bolshevik Party the edge: its Marxist conviction; its view of the hegemony of the proletariat in the revolutionary process; its intransigent internationalism; and the unity between thought and action.[113] What was *missing* in the period in which political pluralism was terminated, first in the society at large and then within the Party itself, were *institutions* that could guarantee that democratic freedoms, suspended for a specific timeframe for specific political reasons, would later be restored. The tragedy of what actually happened is that a virtue was made of historical necessities: authoritarian anti-democratic practices were institutionalized. The tragedy turned to bitter farce as subsequent revolutions imitated the Bolshevik experience, perversely arguing that autocratic policies represent some sort of higher form of political governance.[114]

Serge never satisfactorily resolved the problem of repression and the restoration of democracy. The combined effects of economic crisis, civil war and internal counter-revolution meant that any alternative to Bolshevik dictatorship would be chaos or worse. No democratic institutions yet existed in reality; the Soviets after 1918 were merely auxiliary organs of the Party, *de facto* Party committees. The Party itself had been invaded by careerist and bureaucratic elements. In this period Serge thought the only hope for controlling bureaucratization and for returning to democratic practices lay in 'the discreet dictatorship of the old, honest and incorruptible members . . . the Old Guard'.* Serge could not resolve the dilemma into which history

---

* Serge, *Memoirs*, p. 119. This wishful thinking on Serge's part was quite uncharacteristic of an author who had described how power changed the Bolshevik mentality.

had forced the Bolsheviks, but he was able to express the tragedy in his novel *Conquered City*, where the bitter fruits of victory under siege turn into a defeat for revolutionary ideals.[115]

Poland and Stalin's march on Lvov

Capital punishment was abolished in January 1920 because the civil war was ending. Serge later wrote that he had 'the feeling that everyone in the Party expected a normalization of the regime, the ending of the state of siege, a return to Soviet democracy and the limitation of the powers of the Cheka, if not its abolition'.* Although the country was exhausted, there were still great reserves of 'faith and enthusiasm'. Serge saw the fatal moment for the future of the Revolution in the summer of 1920, when Pilsudski's Polish army invaded Ukraine. Pilsudski's aggression against the Revolution coincided with France and Britain recognizing General Baron Wrangel, who was entrenched in the Crimea with the remnants of Denikin's army.

Pilsudski was turned back at Kiev, but Lenin and the Central Committee took the opportunity to try to provoke a Soviet revolution in Poland. They undertook a march on Warsaw, which they imagined would be victorious, thereby creating an ally and scrapping the Treaty of Versailles. Lenin, with information more than a year out of date, believed the Polish workers and peasants would greet the invaders as liberators.[116] To the Bolsheviks Poland represented the bridge between Russia and Germany – where revolutionary ferment was still kindling after defeat. Tukhachevsky's army was sent to Warsaw. Serge described Lenin, in high spirits, pointing to a map of the Polish front while discussing the progress of Tukhachevsky's march at the Comintern's Second Congress. His speeches, Serge recalled, were 'confident of victory'.[117]

Trotsky had serious misgivings of the risks involved in the venture, and Tukhachevsky complained of his troops' exhaustion. Stalin, who at Tsaritsyn had carried out his own version of revolutionary terror and intrigue against Trotsky,[118] was ordered to provide support to Tukhachevsky. Instead Stalin, Budyenny and Voroshilov decided to march on Lvov (Lemberg)† to assure themselves of a personal victory. Stalin was defeated at Lvov, and

---

* Victor Serge, 'Thirty Years after the Russian Revolution', in Susan Weissman (ed.), *Russia Twenty Years After*, Atlantic Highlands, NJ, Humanities Press, 1996, pp. 311–12. Deutscher confirms that Trotsky also looked forward to the curtailment of the powers of the Cheka and the abolition of the death penalty as steps in the direction of a domestic truce which would allow the parties of at least the socialist opposition to resume open activity. These hopes were overshadowed by the 'horrors of war' which 'had not yet receded into the past'. Deutscher, *The Prophet Armed*, p. 447.

† Before World War I the Austro-Hungarian city went by the name Lemberg. After 1918 it became the Polish city Lvov.

never forgot the people who criticized his actions there: Tukhachevsky and Trotsky (who also criticized his methods at Tsaritsyn).

Serge described Stalin's intrigues at Tsaritsyn in his *Portrait de Staline*. Stalin, jealous of Trotsky's successes in the civil war, supported the opposition to Trotsky's use of conscription, discipline and old military specialists in the Red Army. The nucleus of this opposition was at Voroshilov's headquarters at Tsaritsyn. Stalin's opportunistic support of the opposition's democratic concerns for the army did not extend to his administration of Tsaritsyn, where he organized the local Cheka, instituted repression, discovered numerous 'plots' and resolved any doubts about suspected conspiracies with the simple order to shoot all suspects.

The Red Army was defeated at the gates of Warsaw when the Polish workers and peasants failed to rise. Serge conjectured that the defeat at Warsaw would probably not have come had Stalin followed orders to provide support to Tukhachevsky.[119] Had it won, the Red Army would have acted as a substitute for the Polish working class, and a dictatorship of the proletariat would have been established without the participation of the Polish proletariat. Practising revolution by conquest, although contrary to Marxist principles, was a product of the Bolsheviks' fear of being isolated; the rout at Warsaw resulted from a desperate attempt to break out of that isolation. Serge drew the lesson: 'Revolution cannot be brought into a foreign country at the point of a gun. Pilsudski . . . wins the battle of Warsaw. Russia loses a common border with Germany, and Germany loses its chance of revolution'.[120] And in the *Memoirs*, Serge concluded: 'This point marked a kind of boundary for us. The failure of the attack on Warsaw meant the defeat of the Russian Revolution in Central Europe . . . Once more the westward expansion of the revolution had failed. There was no alternative for the Bolsheviks but to turn east. Hastily, the Congress of the Oppressed Nationalities of the East was convened at Baku.'[121]

It was at this point that Serge 'began to feel . . . this sense of danger from inside, a danger within ourselves, in the very temper and character of victorious Bolshevism'.[122] The growth of privilege, intolerance, and the widening gap between stated theory and reality alarmed Serge. He was amazed that Zinoviev could still believe in the *imminence* of proletarian revolution in Western Europe, that Lenin could believe in the prospects of insurrection in the East.[123] Serge remarked, 'The wonderful lucidity of these great Marxists was beginning to be fuddled with a theoretical intoxication bordering on delusion; and they began to be enclosed within all the tricks and tomfooleries of servility'.[124] Yet Serge still saw Bolshevism as 'tremendously and visibly right', marking 'a new point of departure in history'. The problem was that the revolutionary state was now better as a weapon of war than as a means of organizing production. More than ever, Serge witnessed the young state, in the process of disowning its former promises, becoming a danger to itself. As the civil war drew to a close the country was drained, exhausted and paralysed by a moribund economic regime which was intolerable to the population: the regime of War Communism.[125]

War Communism and the Kronstadt tragedy

War Communism, as the social and economic system of the civil war years came to be known, was, according to Lenin, 'thrust upon us by war and ruin. It was not, nor could it be, a policy that corresponded to the economic tasks of the proletariat. It was a temporary measure.'[126]

Serge began his description of War Communism by attacking Bukharin's ideas, which he characterized as schematic Marxism, in his book *The Economy in the Period of Transition*. Bukharin contended that War Communism was to be final.[127] Yet as Serge pointed out, no one could live under it; it was the reign of the black market, which everyone, even communists, had to use in order to eat. Instead of working in production workers spent their time making goods for the black market. Industrial production fell to less than 30 per cent of the 1913 figure.

The winter of 1920–21 was particularly torturous. Without fuel for heat, pipes froze and sanitary conditions deteriorated. Famine was everywhere and typhus set in. Serge described a mansion that had once belonged to the society beauty Morskaya in which rooms were plastered with frozen excrement. The toilets would not flush so soldiers stationed there had installed field latrines on the floor. Excrement overflowed and froze, ready to thaw and spread disease in the spring.[128] The situation was critical, and Serge recalled seeing a veteran revolutionary who told him the only way to put an end to speculation and to restore order was to resort to force. Serge, writing in the *Memoirs* some twenty years later, indicated that force 'only made matters worse'.[129] He left no written record of his thinking about War Communism at the time.*

Serge defined the elements of the system as requisitioning in the countryside, strict rationing in the town, wholesale nationalization of production, suppression of dissent, Bolshevik monopoly of power, a state of siege and the Cheka. The state of production was so catastrophic that drastic measures were needed to restore the nation's productive capacity and return to a normal working environment.

---

* Except for the already mentioned civil-war novel *Conquered City* and two books about the siege of Petrograd, his journalistic output in this period concentrated on an analysis of the revolution ('La Révolution d'octobre à Moscou', *Bulletin Communiste*, Sept. 1921), an analysis of the middle classes in the revolution ('Les Classes moyennes dans la révolution russe', *Clarté*, 1922), an article on Russian writers and the revolution 'Les Ecrivains russes et la révolution', *Clarté*, 1922, an article on the four French Comintern delegates who perished at sea on their return; and articles on Mazin, Korolenko, the confession of Bakunin and Raymond Lefebvre.

Serge was critical of War Communism in his *Memoirs*, written in 1941 and 1942, describing its non-viability, sympathizing with its opponents, but also critical of NEP, its solution. But in the chapter he devoted to War Communism in *Year One of the Russian Revolution*, Serge was far less critical. He first called 'War Communism' a misnomer, agreeing with Lev Kritsman* that the system represented 'the organization of the natural economy of the proletariat'.[130] Serge said the system was a *'project for the organization of the socialist society*, undertaken in the most difficult circumstances'.[131] He said further that

> The Factory Committees were increasingly assuming managerial functions in production: in this process the direct management of production by the producers was beginning to be realized, and the organization of production began to be merged with the organization of the working class.[132]

Serge was writing about the system in 1918 and 1919, not during the later, more disastrous period of 1920 to 1921. It was understandable that he saw War Communism as an attempt to shore up the economy against a complete breakdown of production and exchange. Serge defended the Bolsheviks' dictatorship of the Party in the circumstances of working-class decomposition due to the ravages of civil war and famine, because he saw *no alternative*. The Bolsheviks were right, in this 'epoch of social war' to promote policies that would rapidly develop a 'proletarian class consciousness'.[133] Serge's reasoning made sense in theory; but it took him two years' experience of War Communism to see the gaps between theory and reality.

The system provoked general discontent and organized opposition. Serge was well placed to follow the discussion as practically the only member of governing circles in Petrograd to be on good terms with Mensheviks, Left SRs and anarchists. He had many long discussions with Shliapnikov of the Workers Opposition, the only oppositional grouping Serge did not consider bankrupt.[134] The Workers Opposition believed the revolution was doomed unless the Party restored genuine freedom and authority to the trade unions, workers' control of production and true Soviet democracy. Serge listened with sympathy, but was unconvinced.

The painful and bloody civil war drew to a close, leaving a drained and exhausted country and a frustrated, discontented population. Anarchists gained support and prepared their Congress until the Cheka suddenly arrested them *en masse*.† Serge was horrified. He said this 'fantastic attitude

---

* Lev N. Kritsman was a Bolshevik economist and one of the first leaders of VSNKh (Vysshyi Sovet Narodnovo Khozyaistva) or Supreme Council of National Economy. Serge wrote in 'The Worst Counter-Revolution', *Inprecorr*, vol. 2, no. 108, Dec. 1922, of the play on words of VSNKh: 'Steal without fear, there is no master'.
† Serge, *Memoirs*, p. 122. What made this even worse was that anarchists like Makhno had successfully fought the White army only to be betrayed by the Reds.

of the Bolshevik authorities' had a terribly demoralizing effect and contributed directly to the revolt at Kronstadt.

Kronstadt

Serge wrote profusely about the significance of the suppression of the Kronstadt uprising, and it became a serious point of contention with Trotsky in
1938. Serge's description of the Kronstadt events, written in the *Memoirs*,
have been published separately as a pamphlet by the anarchist group Solidarity in London, and his work is widely cited by students of the Kronstadt
controversy.[135]

For Serge, the errors and mistakes of power were exposed with the
handling of the Kronstadt rebellion of February–March 1921. He believed
the Bolsheviks could have reached a compromise with the sailors, but the
danger the rebellion represented for a country exhausted by four years of
revolution and civil war was real. In Serge's view the Bolsheviks gave in to
panic, rather than listening to the Kronstadt sailors' grievances and negotiating with them.

The sailors were protesting against the economic regime of War Communism and the dictatorship of the Party. They saw the Bolsheviks as
usurpers, bureaucrats and Cheka executioners.[136] The revolt in many ways
heralded the transition from the unlivable War Communism to the relaxation under Lenin's New Economic Policy. The demands of the sailors
reflected their denunciation of the authoritarian direction of the Central
Committee more than their own specific grievances. The ideas they
expressed were the same ideas the Bolsheviks themselves had championed
in revolution. But as the terrible civil war that had killed large numbers of
the revolution's main constituency – the working class – neared its end, the
nature of these demands changed. Acceding to them now would threaten
the survival of the Bolsheviks in power. Among their demands were the
abolition of the militia's barricades which stopped the population from
looking for provisions in the countryside on their own, and, even more
threatening, 'freely elected soviets'.[137]

The navy base at Kronstadt was a strategic outpost, guarding the western
approaches to Petrograd.[138] From the point of view of the Party, the mutiny
could incite another anti-Soviet invasion, or ignite the anger of the peasants,
which Serge admitted would 'destroy everything'. There was evidence that
White émigrés were using the Kronstadters to their own advantage, and
there is no doubt this added to the sense of urgency and panic of the government. It is also true that the government exaggerated the rumours of White
Guard involvement to discredit the Kronstadt rebellion.[139] Behind the
larger issues of the deteriorating relations between the Party and the masses,
the unethical and brutal response marked a watershed for the Revolution
and its ideals.

The drastic economic situation of the country had isolated the Party in power. Serge wrote that the intentions and virtues of the Party were practically irrelevant since it could not govern a starving nation and maintain its popularity. The masses had lost their enthusiasm and the continuing sacrifices demanded by difficult circumstances were wearing down the remaining revolutionary activists. Petrograd workers were on strike, and the Kronstadt mutiny began as a movement of solidarity with the Petrograd workers. Lack of food, ferocious winters, sickness and constant requisitions 'spread bitterness' everywhere. Serge said,

> This despair left people open to confusing bread with counter-revolution. If in this situation, the Bolsheviks had let go the reigns of power, who would have taken their place? Was not it their duty to hold on? They were right to hold on. Their mistake was to panic at the Kronstadt revolt which they could have handled in any number of ways, as we who were there, in Petrograd, know well.[140]

Serge lived in the Hotel Astoria at the time, as did the Petrograd leadership and the Cheka. Working in the Smolny, he was fully aware of events. Serge was uniquely placed as a Bolshevik with access both to the leadership circles of the Party and to the opposition groups outside the Party. He met with the anarchists, including the Americans Emma Goldman and Alexander Berkman who tried to mediate the conflict as important members of the international working class.*

Serge's version of events indicates a mess of fabrications, cover-ups and bungling. Where persuasion and understanding were needed, the President of the Executive Committee of the Soviets used only threats and insults.

---

* Serge met with the American anarchists nightly, but at the crucial meeting where the mediation attempt was discussed, held at the house of Serge's father-in-law, Alexander Russakov, Serge did not attend as it had been decided that only the American anarchists would undertake this initiative because of their prestige and the influence they held with the Kronstadt soviet. Serge was on the verge of leaving the Party over Kronstadt, but was won over by his comrades who said to him 'Where would you go? You have to face it, there is no one but us.' Apparently Serge's ambivalence earned him the mistrust of both sides in this affair: Sedgwick notes that Marcel Body (*Un piano en bouleau de Carélie: mes années de Russie 1919–1927*, Paris 1981) told of Emma Goldman and Alexander Berkman's hostility to Serge (Peter Sedgwick, 'The Unhappy Elitist: Victor Serge's Early Bolshevism', *History Workshop Journal*, vol. 17, spring 1984, p. 126, note 15). After the failure of the mediation attempt the Russian mediators were arrested and Zinoviev offered the Americans the chance to tour the whole of Russia by special train to 'Observe . . . and understand'. Serge was spared because of his reputation and the 'kindness of Zinoviev, Zorin, and others', Serge, *Memoirs*, pp. 127–8. See also Victor Serge to Angelica Balabanova, 23 Oct. 1941.

Instead of being fraternally received, the Kronstadt delegation to the Petrograd soviet was arrested by the Cheka. The truth about the conflict was hidden from the Party and from the country as a whole by the press, which for the first time, lied shamelessly, saying that a White general, Koslovski, was in charge in Kronstadt.[141]

The well-intentioned mediation efforts of Goldman and Berkman were inexplicably refused and instead of mediation, the cannons opened up a 'fratricidal battle and the Cheka later shot its prisoners'. Serge agreed with Trotsky that the sailors had changed since the revolutionary days of 1917 when they were in the vanguard of the Revolution. But calling them 'petty-bourgeois' glossed over a more complex reality. It was true that the sailors now tended to reflect more the aspirations of peasants, but 'these were men of the Russian people, backward perhaps, but who belonged to the masses of the revolution itself'.[142] And it was not just the Kronstadters who had changed – so had ruling circles. Rather than pointing to who had changed more, Serge asked: 'Which of the two contending forces better represented the higher interests of the toilers?'[143]

Kronstadt was a tragedy, more so because of the insidious role played by rumour-mongering. Serge blamed Kalinin and Kuzmin* whose 'brutal bungling had provoked the rebellion'. The uprising of the sailors had been non-violent and according to Serge the majority of Communists had rallied to their cause, proving the instability of the Party's base. Kalinin and Kuzmin had shown no intention from the first moment of using 'anything but forcible methods'.

The whole affair was shrouded in lies. The campaign of slander – begun by sectors of the Party and the Cheka and picked up by the press – had the effect of stifling any discussion of the issues raised by the sailors. The sailors' programme, which Serge called 'a programme for the Renewal of the Revolution' included: new elections to the soviets, freedom of speech and press for all revolutionary groups, free trade unions, freedom of action for the peasants, release of political prisoners, abolition of road-blocks, and an end to requisitioning in the countryside. Yet as Serge himself admitted, the political conjuncture was one of a life-or-death struggle in which defeat would mean a massive spilling of proletarian blood. Abstract demands

---

* Kuzmin was the commissar in charge of the fleet and the army. Rumour had it that he had been brutally handled during his captivity at Kronstadt, and had been earmarked for execution with orders written by counter-revolutionaries. When Serge saw him at Smolny following his 'escape from Kronstadt', Serge expressed incredulity that the sailors would shoot him. Kuzmin admitted it had been an exaggeration, that the so-called counter-revolutionary 'execution order' was but 'some little sheet written in threatening terms'. Nor had he been handled brutally, but 'had a warm time of it, nothing more'. Serge, *Memoirs*, pp. 126–7.

which were politically correct did not address the issue of the counter-revolution of the peasants and the Whites. The demands did point however to the danger the abuse of power posed for the health of the revolution.

Worst of all for Serge – worse than the abuses of authority – was the realization that the Party had lied; a barrier had been broken. The press 'was positively berserk with lies . . . and this was our own Press, the Press of our revolution, the first socialist Press, and hence the first incorruptible and unbiased Press in the world!'[144]

Yet Serge, after 'many hesitations and with unutterable anguish' declared himself with the Party on the issue of Kronstadt. He explained his position: either support the Party reluctantly or unleash the counter-revolution, which already had the embryonic form of a black fascism. There was no choice.

Kronstadt had right on its side. Kronstadt was the beginning of a fresh, liberating revolution for popular democracy: 'The Third Revolution!' it was called by certain anarchists whose heads were stuffed with infantile illusions. However, the country was absolutely exhausted, and production practically at a standstill; there were no reserves of any kind, not even reserves of stamina in the hearts of the masses. The working class elite that had been moulded in the struggle against the old regime was nearly obliterated. The Party, swollen by the influx of power-seekers, inspired little confidence. Of the other parties only minute nuclei existed, whose character was highly questionable. It seemed clear that these groupings could come back to life in a matter of weeks, but only by incorporating embittered, malcontent and inflammatory elements in their thousands, no longer, as in 1917, enthusiasts for the young revolution. Soviet democracy lacked leadership, institutions and inspiration; at its back there were only masses of starving and desperate men.

The popular counter-revolution translated the demand for freely-elected Soviets into one for 'Soviets without Communists'. If the Bolshevik dictatorship fell, it was only a short step to chaos, and through chaos to a peasant rising, the massacre of the Communists, the return of the émigrés, and in the end, through the sheer force of events, another dictatorship, this time anti-proletarian. Dispatches from Stockholm and Tallinn testified that the émigrés had these very perspectives in mind; dispatches which, incidentally, strengthened the Bolshevik leaders' intention of subduing Kronstadt speedily and at whatever cost. We were not reasoning in the abstract. We knew that in European Russia alone there were at least fifty centres of peasant insurrection. To the south of Moscow, in the region of Tambov, Antonov, the Right Social-Revolutionary school-teacher, who proclaimed the abolition of the Soviet system and the re-establishment of the Constituent Assembly, had under his command a superbly organized peasant army numbering several tens of thousands. He had conducted negotiations with the Whites. (Tukhachevsky suppressed this *Vendée* around the middle of 1921.)

In these circumstances it was the Party's duty to make concessions recognizing that the economic regime was intolerable, *but not to abdicate from power* [my emphasis]. 'Despite its mistakes and abuses', I wrote, 'the Bolshevik Party is at present the supremely organized, intelligent and stable force which, despite everything, deserves our confidence. The Revolution has no other mainstay, and is no longer capable of any thoroughgoing regeneration.'[145]

Serge the Bolshevik, brutally honest and rooted in concrete conditions, was not alone; other dissident Communists joined him in supporting the Bolsheviks, since there really was no other organized force. But Serge was demoralized by the whole affair. The Tenth Party Congress, which convened in Moscow at the same time as the Red Army was attacking the Kronstadt fleet, ironically abolished requisitioning, the system of War Communism, and proclaimed NEP. As the demands of the Kronstadt sailors were being met, they were being massacred.

NEP, according to Serge, was a response to Lenin's realization that the regime had become untenable and uncompromising. Just the year before Trotsky had denounced the situation as dangerous and in need of the changes Lenin had just proclaimed. NEP abolished requisitions in the countryside, re-established the freedom of commerce and small-scale business and made concessions on attractive terms to foreign capital. 'In a word, it [NEP] loosened the mortal grip on the country of the complete state control over production and exchange.'[146] It amounted to a partial restoration of capitalism but did not bring with it any relaxation of authority or political tolerance.

Instead a purge was directed toward the Party while the other parties were effectively outlawed. Serge lamented that disciplinary measures were directed at those 'with a critical outlook' rather than against 'the unprincipled careerists and conformist late-comers'.[147] As far as the other parties were concerned, Serge sympathized with Raphael Abramovich's criticism of the Bolshevik Central Committee in 1921 for not being more tolerant to those who 'accepted the parameters of the Soviet constitution'. A policy directed toward reconciliation would have been more desirable. Serge admitted that had 'a coalition government . . . been formed at this time, it would have internalized certain dangers, but, and this is well-proven, they would have been less than the danger of this monopoly of power'.[148]

Emergent totalitarianism

1921 was a crossroads for the revolution, though Serge did not consider it Thermidor.[149] Interestingly, at the height of the Kronstadt assault Serge quoted Lenin as saying to one of his friends: 'This is Thermidor'.[150] It was a turning point for the Party, for Soviet democracy and for the Comintern as well, signalling a shift from the offensive to the defensive.

March 18 was a day of ironies: Kronstadt sailors met their death while shouting 'Long live the world revolution!' On the fiftieth anniversary of the Paris Commune, Communists in Berlin were going down to defeat. Serge described the atmosphere in Smolny as tense and sombre, with conversation generally being avoided 'except with . . . closest friends, and among close friends what was said was full of bitterness'.[151]

According to Serge, although the term 'totalitarianism' did not yet exist, it was on its way to crushing the Revolution. The monopoly of political power, the Cheka and the Red Army had turned the dream of the 'commune-state' into a far-off theoretical myth. War Communism, famine (with its bureaucratic rationing-apparatus), civil war and counter-revolution had killed Soviet democracy. Serge said he belonged to 'the pitifully small minority' that realized what was happening. There had been hope that the conditions of peace would bring about a spontaneous resurgence of Soviet democracy, but no one had any conception of how this would happen. Serge concluded that renewal from within was not possible, that only the extension of the Russian Revolution would bring fresh energy and the resources for industrialization. But world revolution was not at hand.

Serge began to question certain aspects of Marxism in light of subsequent events and to look especially at this period as the beginning of what he called Soviet totalitarianism. He believed he was the first to coin this term, in 1921. While the totalitarian school of analysis is well known, Serge believed he was the first to coin the term in describing the Stalinist system, which he saw as 'emergent' as early as 1921 during the period of War Communism. Abbott Gleason, in his *Totalitarianism: An Inner History of the Cold War* (1995) states the term was first used in May 1923 in Italy, in an article by Giovanni Amendola in *Il Mondo* (Gleason, p. 14). Serge could have been acquainted with this new term through his contact with Gramsci and others in Vienna from 1923–25. The term was later taken up by Trotsky and subsequently by anti-communist and liberal critics of the Soviet Union. The important point is that the first analysis of the USSR as a totalitarian state came from the *left*, not the anti-communist right. Later in Serge's life he extended his analysis to the first socialist utopian experiments.[152]

What Serge was questioning was the *totality* of the socialist goal. Capitalism in its advanced industrial form was a world system which dominated every aspect of life – making everything conform to its overt and covert organization of social, economic and political existence. Marxism, therefore, had as its response and its goal to renew and transform everything from property and social relations to the world map and the inner life of man. The physical world would be changed through the abolition of national boundaries and man's inner life would be transformed by liberating the mind from religious thought. Thus Serge concluded that the project itself, insofar as it aspired to total transformation, was etymologically totalitarian.*

---

* Serge discussed his views of emergent totalitarianism on pp. 133–4 of the *Memoirs*. He differs significantly from the later 'totalitarian school of Sovietology': Serge's analysis was not static but rather looked at the society through the dynamic of conflict; nor did he see the Soviet Union as classless, as do the Totalitarians of the Friedrich, Brzezinski, Kornhauser school. Using Serge's analysis, one could also argue that capitalism is totalitarian: the system is totalizing, one cannot opt out, capitalist ideology is pervasive and ubiquitous, and capitalist political power does not tolerate any opposition which in a real sense threatens its integrity.

Serge went on to point out the dual nature of socialism ascendant in its democratic and authoritarian aspects. The duality Serge analysed was fraught with contradictions of which he, and the Bolsheviks in general, were only too aware. Serge looked to the source of the Party's intolerance in its conviction that the Party 'is the repository of truth'. This conviction gave the Party both moral energy and simultaneously a 'clerical mentality . . . quick to become Inquisitorial'.[153]

The Bolsheviks could see the contradiction between their democratic goals and their authoritarian methods, which they justified by the all-too-real danger of reaction. Serge said they could often only surmount their contradictions through demagoguery. He never criticized Lenin for not being sincere in his goal of the 'broadest possible workers' democracy'. Yet Serge asked rhetorically what the meaning of 'rule' was, referring to ubiquitous posters announcing that 'the rule of workers will never cease'.[154] At that time Serge had raised but not resolved this theoretical problem.

Bureaucratic centralism and NEP, or 'communism of associations'?

Serge was dismayed by the new kingdom of the market. Other civil war veterans were equally confused: why had they spilled so much blood, to see a return of the market?[155] Serge was distressed that democracy had been obliterated, yet glad that War Communism was over.

Serge was opposed to even a limited revival of the capitalist market, and instead proposed an alternative which would bring about a degree of prosperity without giving rise to speculation, greed and corruption. He began to argue for a 'communism of associations' as opposed to the 'communism of the State'. Knowing the Bolshevik leadership was committed to the NEP solution, Serge offered his theoretical vision to visiting Comintern delegates and international revolutionaries in casual meetings at the Hotel Lux, consciously restricting his ideas to the level of theoretical interest.[156]

In Serge's view economic recovery could have been achieved without a return to the market – by freeing the state-strangled cooperatives to initiative from below in the form of associations which would take over the management of different branches of the economy. Using shoe-making as his example, Serge explained that there was a shortage of both shoes and leather, yet the rural areas had plenty of leather. In Serge's vision, the unfettered shoemakers' cooperatives could easily have obtained the necessary leather and made the shoes if left to themselves. They would likely charge high prices for these shoes, but less than the exorbitant prices encountered in the black market. The state would regulate price and could assist this form of workers' control by exercising a downward pressure on prices.

Workers in other branches of production would similarly spontaneously organize cooperatives to fill collective needs. Serge's view of the state and planning would be 'not something dictated by the State from on high but rather resulting from the harmonizing, by congresses and specialized assemblies, of initiatives from below'.[157] Serge did not elaborate on the state's role in distribution in this cooperative form of worker-controlled production. But production in this manner could avoid both the exploitation and anarchy of the capitalist market and the 'muddle and paralysis' of 'stringent bureaucratic centralism'. In Serge's view economic relations represent basic, objective forms of spontaneous cooperation, what Ernest Mandel, more than sixty years later, would call 'articulated workers' self-management'.[158] Combined with democratic planning at the macro level, this economic form would constitute the ideal for the transition period that is moving toward socialism, while still containing money and some market forms. Serge was vague on the role of planning in his early critique (seeing the plan as harmonizing initiatives from below), but elaborated more fully after evaluating the experience of Stalin's industrialization and the nature of the Soviet economy.[159] Clearly Serge's view is more than a syndicalist reprise:* it is much closer to the Marxist notion of socialism as the planned self-rule of the associated producers.†

Disillusionment and romantic retreat

Serge was disgusted by the growing bureaucratization of the Bolshevik Party and the self-serving opportunists entering its ranks, stunned by the Kronstadt events and psychologically exhausted. He was active in two Communist sections, the French language Communist group and the Petrograd Russian Communists; after Kronstadt he wondered with many of them how they could usefully serve the revolution 'without closing their eyes'. Serge had no interest in bureaucratic sinecures; he was offered a diplomatic post in the Orient but declined. The Orient interested him but not diplomacy.[160]

---

* Sedgwick intimates in his introduction to the *Memoirs* that Serge's vision represents an advanced syndicalism. Robert Daniels in *Conscience of the Revolution* (New York, Simon and Schuster, 1960) also refers to the anarcho-syndicalist side of Leninism; Philip Spencer calls it 'libertarian Leninism' in his article 'On the Leninist Tradition', in Susan Weissman (ed.), *The Ideas of Victor Serge: A Life as a Work of Art*, 1997, Glasgow, Critique Books, p. 155. Unfortunately Stalinism has distorted Marxism to such a degree that when democratic, workers' control is put forward, it is immediately attributed to a syndicalist or anarchist throwback. As argued in this work, Serge's influences after 1917 were Marxist, and it was his lifelong project to rescue Marxism from its Stalinist deformation and restore in the public perception the synonymity of Marxian socialism and democracy.

† Serge was not alone in his preoccupation about the direction of the economy, seemingly destined toward either blind market forces or authoritarian bureaucratic centralism. These issues are the same ones which surface in 1923 with the Left Opposition of the New Course. Serge here predates their concerns by two years.

Serge participated in the Third Congress of the Comintern in Moscow (June and July 1921) which he found utterly lacking in inspiration. The foreign delegates in their desire to approve had abdicated all responsibility for critical thinking, and did not seem to notice the discrepancy between the lavish privileges they enjoyed and the condition of the starving populace. Serge found them 'quick to adulate and reluctant to think'.[161] Almost immediately after the Congress, Serge retired to the countryside.

Serge thought he had found a way out. He and his father-in-law Russakov, a group of his French Communist friends, and some Hungarian prisoners-of-war founded 'the French Commune of Novaya-Ladoga' on an abandoned estate north of Petrograd. Demoralized by the petty greed, corruption and speculation revived under NEP and the lack of political liberty, Serge and his comrades retreated to the countryside to live off the land.

The harsh realities soon hit these revolutionary romantics. They were boycotted by the local anti-Semitic peasants who went so far as to steal their corn and tools while refusing to sell to them. The peasants viewed Serge's group with hostility and hatred, calling them 'Jews' and 'anti-Christs'. After three months of hunger and exhaustion the commune was abandoned.

Serge returned to Petrograd and continued frequenting literary and humanist circles. He belonged to *Volfila* or the 'Free Philosophic Society' whose guiding light was the symbolist poet Andrei Bely. Serge was the only Communist member.[162]

Although Serge was not as optimistic as the Bolshevik leadership about the prospect of successful revolution in the West he agreed that Russia's only chance for survival was pinned on the international extension of the Revolution. Serge was convinced that revolutionary Russia, in the throes of hunger, isolation and defeat, would collapse if left to itself. He decided to go to Central Europe, 'the focus of events to come' to work toward building a 'Western working-class movement capable of supporting the Russians and, one day, superseding them'.[163] His own anxiety over the turn of events and the precarious mental and physical health of his wife Liuba after all the privations also propelled him to leave. A change of scenery and new activity would be welcome. He accepted a Comintern post in Berlin in late 1921, editing the French edition of the Comintern journal *Inprekorr*, or *La Correspondance Internationale*.[164]

The revolutionary stance Serge took in late 1921, to rigorously analyse the political conjuncture and determine the necessities and possibilities of the moment took him on his illegal European assignment. The same logic would bring him back to Russia four years later to take his stand with the Left Opposition, the only hope Serge saw for revolutionary renewal after internal and external defeat, corruption and decay.

2

Blockaded in Berlin; neutralized in Vienna; and into the Soviet fray

Berlin impressions

The contrast provided by a simple journey to another country could not have been more dramatic. Serge stopped with his family in Tallinn, Estonia.[1] Serge was overcome with emotion when he saw some bricklayers building houses. After witnessing so much destruction, this simple act of building moved him deeply.[2] The streets lined with shops made Serge recall the Volga territories where 'the children of Russia were turning into living skeletons'. Serge said he now understood the theory and politics of the self-determination of nationalities, 'raised as it was to perfection by the blockade of the Revolution'.[3]

Serge travelled to Berlin 'illegally' with a dozen other agents of the International. Although Serge was vague about the date, his articles datelined Berlin, began to appear in *Inprekorr* in November 1921.[4]

Once in Berlin Serge was instantly struck by the collapse of post-Versailles Germany. Capitalism was rampant amidst insolvency. According to Serge the capitalists lived in fear of revolution; only the Social-Democrats believed in capitalism's future![5] Serge placed the blame for Germany's state of collapse on the industrial bourgeoisie who were completing the ruin of the German economy which the war had begun. The bourgeoisie, driven now to speculation and no longer capable of sustaining the arts, sciences, universities, libraries and other hallmarks of civilization, had become the enemy of German culture as it had developed since 1848.[6]

The German Social Democrats had the misfortune to preside over this societal disintegration (and, in taking on the responsibility, shared some of the blame), although they did so with a very democratic constitution. Serge viewed these social democratic leaders with their enlightened, optimistic attitudes[7] as the standard-bearers of the liberal bourgeoisie of 1848. Yet Weimar Germany gave the impression of a society in the process of self-destructing: everything appeared for sale, including 'the daughters of the bourgeoisie in the bars, [and] the daughters of the people in the streets'.[8]

The decadence that characterized Germany in the period of 1922 and 1923 had the effect of making the 'spartan' conditions of the proletarian revolution in the Soviet Union appear to Serge as clean, pure and healthy by comparison. Even Russia's authoritarian excesses could be put into philosophical perspective from this standpoint. The chance to see Germany had the effect of reanimating Serge, taking the edge off his disappointment with the Soviet Union. His colleagues in the Comintern struck Serge the same way: he remarked that the editorial staff of *Inprekorr*, the 'intellectual and political mentor of the world Communist movement, was of an outstanding mediocrity'.[9]

Berlin bound

Serge set to work in his new duties as Comintern agent and editor of *La Correspondance Internationale* (*LCI*), the French edition of *Inprekorr*, or *International Press Correspondence*. *Inprekorr* was published simultaneously in three languages with the German edition being the fullest.[10] Serge wrote under various pseudonyms, often writing whole issues of the magazine.[11] He most often used the name 'R. Albert' writing the section entitled 'Notes d'Allemagne' of *LCI*, usually datelining his articles Berlin.[12] In the *Memoirs* Serge said his articles signed Victor Serge were datelined Kiev, a city Serge had never visited.[13] These articles mostly dealt with the Soviet Union.

Since Serge's activities took on the character of clandestine political life he was known first as Siegfried and then Gottlieb at his office at the *Rote Fahne* (Communist Party [KPD] daily), Dr Albert in town and in his articles, Victor Klein on his papers and Alexei Berlovsky in his travels to Russia.[14] Serge functioned as an underground agent. When he passed Karl Radek, the Comintern emissary to Germany in the street, they exchanged knowing glances but did not speak.

Changing identity and nationality as required, Serge bought a Polish identity card for ten dollars, but it turned out to be useless. Anti-Polish feeling in Germany was reinforced by the Polish annexation of Upper Silesia, making Serge's life nearly impossible until he traded his Polish nationality card for a Lithuanian one.[15]

Serge's analysis of the world situation which had partially propelled him to move to Central Europe to help build 'a Western working-class movement capable of supporting the Russian and, one day, superseding them' was not altered by his sojourn in Germany. Although he was only too aware of the weakness of German revolutionary leadership he still viewed socialist revolution in Europe as the key to the salvation of civilization. Serge was also alert to the danger of fascism, which was gaining ground.* This perspective

---

* Serge had followed the progress of fascism closely and opposed the leadership of the International on this question. They underestimated the threat of reaction,

guided his articles of the period which essentially promoted the Comintern line on Germany. Serge intimated that he was sometimes obliged to print things he knew were wrong, and he watched the growing careerism and corruption of the Comintern with alarm. Filling the Comintern ranks were unthinking yes-men such as Gyula Alperi and Franz Dahlem. With such human material staffing the Comintern, its utter domination by the Russian leadership was accelerated.

Serge kept abreast of events in the Soviet Union and he travelled to Moscow to attend Comintern Executive meetings. In his capacity as a journalist he attended the historic meeting of the Three Internationals on 22 April 1922 at the Reichstag building in Berlin. Representatives of the Socialist International, the Two-and-a Half International[16] and the Third International met to lay the basis for cooperation between socialists. The meeting ended in failure after representatives of the Second International attacked political persecution in Russia, particularly the impending Moscow trial of the Socialist Revolutionary Party leadership (the Party of the 'middle peasantry' as Serge called them in *Year One*). While he tended to sympathize with the Social Democrats' criticism of the trial, Serge at the same time agreed with Bukharin's judgment of the Socialist International: 'These people are determined never to fight for socialism'. Serge noted that Bukharin added as though 'by way of a directive, "Our Press must attack them mercilessly"'.*

Watching the proceedings of the trial against the SRs from Berlin greatly distressed Serge. Now that the civil war was over, he wrote, 'Were we going to shed the blood of a defeated Party which, in the old days, had furnished the Revolution with so many of its heroes?' What worried Serge most was that he heard the Politburo's decision to 'behead this peasant Party of significance' was taken in the belief the revolution was 'moving towards an inevitable crisis with the peasantry'.[17] Serge moved into action to prevent this 'calamity' along with Clara Zetkin, Jacques Sadoul and Boris Souvarine. Gorky also wrote to Lenin. In the end no one was killed. The Serge who had privately interceded on behalf of victims of the Cheka during the civil war was continuing on the same path, from Berlin.

Serge wrote about the 1918 defeat of the German workers in his *Year One*

---

but Serge said this 'new variety of counter-revolution had taken the Russian Revolution as its schoolmaster in matters of repression and mass-manipulation through propaganda . . . [and] had succeeded in recruiting a host of disillusioned, power-hungry ex-revolutionaries; consequently, its rule would last for years.' Victor Serge, *Memoirs of a Revolutionary*, London, Oxford University Press, 1963, pp. 160–63.

* Ibid., pp. 163–4. Serge certainly agreed with Bukharin that these Second Internationalists would never fight for socialism: he had amply noted how in Germany they believed in capitalism more than the bourgeoisie and were responsible, as power-holders, for the murder of Liebknecht and Luxemburg.

of the Russian Revolution.[18] He saw the German Communist Party as too young and inexperienced and without the cadres or the leadership capable of daring initiative. On the other hand, Serge saw the German proletariat as too subservient to the Social Democrats, who had become the defenders of capitalism. Liebknecht was too impatient and made a grave error in signing the manifesto calling for the deposing of Ebert and Scheidemann without consulting the Central Committee, and in so doing initiated an untimely insurrection which he was unable to guide. Luxemburg initially opposed Liebknecht and then supported him. She was, as Serge noted, clear-sighted but powerless.[19]

The consequences of the failed Spartacist uprising in Berlin in January 1919 were catastrophic. Directed against the policies of Ebert's Social Democratic government, the uprising ended with the arrest and murder on 15 January of Germany's most capable revolutionary leaders, Rosa Luxemburg and Karl Liebknecht. War Minister Gustav Noske, charged with the suppression of the Spartacist uprising, ordered the assassination of the two revolutionaries.[20] Two months later Leo Jogiches (Tyszko) was murdered for similar reasons, followed later by the death of Franz Mehring and the assassination of Eugen Levine. Germany's young Communist Party had been effectively decapitated. The leadership of the KPD was left in the hands of the young intellectual Paul Levi, who had been Rosa Luxemburg's lawyer. Radek took an active leadership role. There is no evidence of Serge's role, other than his journalistic output as a propagandist for the Comintern, in any of the sources consulted except Serge's own *Memoirs*.

The defeats of 1919 were not the end of the revolutionary crisis. The Kapp Putsch and the General Strike of March 1920 followed in short order. The young and inexperienced KPD tried to unleash a general offensive before the majority of the workers was ready to accept its lead.

The defeats in 1920 revealed the crisis of revolutionary leadership and the contradictions in Comintern policy. Bukharin, Zinoviev and Radek believed that in light of the developing revolutionary potential the European parties were too inactive and had to assume the offensive. At home Lenin was calling for a revolutionary breathing spell and peaceful coexistence: NEP had supplanted War Communism. The contradictions between the revolutionary breathing spell and the revolutionary offensive were reflected in the German Party. The Kapp Putsch, led by German generals and put down by the general strike of German workers presented a moment of choice for the KPD. The leadership of the Party vacillated – first opposing the strike and then reversing its stand. The revolutionaries had missed a rare opportunity to attempt to take power following the general strike. As a result the KPD was mangled. Comintern leaders differed in their analysis of the Kapp Putsch and the opportunistic approach of the KPD, but roundly attacked Levi. Events had moved quickly and the Bolsheviks watched from a distance; those closer to the ground had a more nuanced understanding of the difficulties of the situation.

The occupation of the Ruhr by the French in January 1923 led to a disastrous devaluation of the mark, and economic decay befell the country. Protests against the Versailles Treaty and its consequences grew, sparked by the French occupation. The KPD's ranks grew rapidly as the economic crisis further polarized German society.

Serge's articles from Germany concentrated on the conditions of decay. He used statistics to show the impoverishment of even the German middle classes, reduced along with the workers to destitution by massive unemployment and galloping inflation. Characteristically, Serge evoked the ambience by describing what happened to one person, in this case 'an old lady with a black lace neckband' paying for her purchases at a store with hundred mark notes from the previous year, during the 'age of Walter Rathenau'.[21] When she was told the money was worthless she became confused. Events, Serge explained, needed to be followed hourly, as they hurried along at a dizzying pace. Inflation was catastrophic, accompanied by widespread speculation in currency; the rate of exchange with the dollar often changed twice a day, causing utter chaos in commerce. There was rioting outside grocers and bakeries. Since there was no rationing the shops could be stripped of their wares by panicked shoppers with money every time the exchange rate changed. Hunger and begging became epidemic.

Politically Serge's articles reflect the general line of Comintern policy toward Germany and, more specifically, of the emerging Left Opposition within the Bolshevik Party. Serge's assessment of conditions in Germany was more guarded and cautious than that of the Bolsheviks because he was there to see the actual state of revolutionary leadership. Much of German revolutionary policy was decided in Moscow. Radek travelled back and forth frequently. Serge also travelled to Moscow on Comintern business.

To Russia, with relief

Serge returned to Moscow to attend an enlarged session of the Comintern Executive. The date in the *Memoirs* for this trip was the end of 1922, precisely the time of the Fourth Congress of the International. But Serge did not attend the Congress, which in any case was held in Petrograd.[22] Rosmer gave 12 June 1923 as the date of the Executive meeting, which he also attended.[23]

NEP had already brought relative prosperity to Russia, which pleasantly surprised Serge. Yet Serge saw NEP as a regression, reintroducing disparities in wealth, promoting greed, and encouraging all the vices they had hoped the Revolution would eliminate. The return of the market, it seemed to Serge, meant that all the blood and suffering of the civil war had been wasted.

But NEP was a response to famine and the standstill in industry – insupportable conditions. As opposed as Serge was to market solutions, he was glad of any change which would revive industry.[24]

While Serge despaired of the gambling, corruption, theft and the growing chasm between 'the prosperity of the few and the misery of the many',[25] he admitted that conditions had improved, which was nowhere more apparent than in the arts. New writers, previously unknown, were now considered seriously, among them Boris Pilniak, Vsevolod Ivanov and Konstantin Fedin.[26] Serge was very encouraged by the fact that these writers, none of whom were Communist Party members, and all 'intense, impetuous, saturated with virile humanism and a critical spirit',[27] were allowed to publish and were greatly loved. Russian literature was being reborn after the years of revolution and civil war. The state of the arts was one of the signs of health that Serge observed in other spheres as well. The collapse which had seemed imminent on Serge's departure a year earlier had not occurred, and although there were still signs of poverty people were not dying of hunger. The Cheka terror had faded into memory.

The corruption of the Comintern Executive, it seemed, had proceeded apace. Servility and bureaucratism were rampant. As to the meeting itself Serge observed the degeneration of the Comintern, though he paid little attention to the discussion, stating in the *Memoirs* that he could not recall the nature of the deliberations. This is rather surprising, as it was here that Radek delivered his famous 'Schlageter Speech', confusing the International delegates[28] by appealing to rank-and-file Germans on the basis of nationalism.[29]

Back to Berlin: the Comintern and the German revolution of 1923

Serge returned to Berlin in the summer of 1923 in time for the July–August mobilizations and strikes. Germany was in the midst of the crisis provoked by the French occupation of the Ruhr. Serge remained in Germany until the defeat of the revolution in October made the situation too dangerous. Serge's analysis and account of events in Germany are virtually the same in his *Memoirs* of 1941 as in his articles written between 1923 and 1926, more than fifteen years earlier. His *LCI* articles are journalistic and expose the machinations of German Social Democracy during the 1923 revolutionary crisis. There is also a great deal of information on the disintegration of the German economy and its effects on the deteriorating situation of the German working class. Serge's later articles put forward the line of the Left Opposition but are nuanced by his personal observations.

The conditions imposed by the Treaty of Versailles were, in Serge's words, 'a noose around the German nation's neck',[30] destroying the economy with the social and economic costs of heavy reparations payments. The rich became 'self-seeking' speculators and the masses became increasingly destitute. Inflation was such that workers' salaries, fixed at the beginning of the week, were worthless by payday.[31] By the summer of 1923, the country was bankrupt and the Cuno government announced it could no longer pay reparations.

As the political and economic disintegration caused widespread misery and hunger German workers fled the democratic parties and the ranks of the Communists and the fascists swelled. The German people, known for their orderliness, began to riot, albeit in a disciplined fashion, and loitered in the streets. Serge described rioting in front of bakery shops, yet observed proletarian discipline in the looting of a shoe shop, where the workers waiting in line for their turn to steal came out 'scrupulously empty-handed' if there were no shoes to fit them.[32]

The working class mobilized in response to the disintegrating economy. 'Each day brought its windfall of strikes, and every night the sinister silence echoed with revolver shots'.[33] The workers' movement was on the march again. In a series of articles entitled 'Au Seuil d'une révolution',[34] Serge described the mood of the masses of Communists and nationalist students as one of 'strike now' – *Losschlagen*. Most of the political preconditions of a revolutionary situation were present in July and August 1923.

It was in this context that Radek pushed through his 'Schlageter line' appealing to the rank-and-file nationalists to join the Communists.* Curiously, Serge did not oppose the political content of Radek's Schlageter line. Was the appeal to the fascist rank-and-file a concession to nationalism? Serge apparently did not see the line as a move to the right but as a tactical manoeuvre, and as such as part of the Left's revolutionary action. Serge said of the Schlageter tactic: 'It's playing with fire – all right let's play with fire! . . . *Losschlagen!* – Strike now!'[35]

The German crisis was exacerbated by events playing out in the Comintern in Russia.† From May until August 1923 all actions of the KPD and the Comintern were initiated by Radek.[36] Yet the strikes of August 1923 caught the German Party and the Comintern politically unprepared. The

---

* Albert Schlageter was a young nationalist agitator who was shot by the French troops on the Ruhr on 26 May 1923. According to E.H. Carr (*The Interregnum 1923–1924*, London, Macmillan, 1954), Schlageter became a martyr and symbol to the nationalists; his name became a symbol of the revival of German national honour and a battle-cry to 'spur . . . fresh deeds of violence against the French aggressor' (pp. 170–77). Radek's speech to the enlarged session of the Comintern Executive stated: 'Today National Bolshevism means that everyone is penetrated with the feeling that salvation can be found only with the communists. We are today the only way out. The strong emphasis on the nation in Germany is a revolutionary act, like the emphasis on the nation in the colonies.' *International Presse-Korrespondenz*, no. 103, 21 June 1923, p. 869, quoted in Carr, p. 177.

† The events in Germany in 1923 pointed to the crisis within the KPD, the Comintern and the Soviet Party, who were already embroiled in factional disputes brought about by NEP, the industrialization debates, the ebb of international revolution, and Lenin's illness and the succession of leadership, with the triumvirate of Zinoviev, Kamenev and Stalin organizing against Trotsky and indirectly against Lenin.

workers' movement had been ascendant throughout the summer, culminating in the August strikes. The Comintern shifted into action at the high point and tried to escalate events when they were beginning to ebb. Brandler, the KPD leader, was called to Moscow to prepare the German revolution, and was kept there in endless debates until early October while the KPD underwent a transformation from mass work to military preparations.

The Bolsheviks and the Comintern now went on the offensive, determining KPD policy from Moscow. The German revolution's proposed date was set by the Bolsheviks to coincide with the sixth anniversary of the Russian October Revolution. Trotsky defended this policy in an article entitled 'Is It Possible to Fix a Definite Schedule for a Counter-Revolution or a Revolution?'[37]

Serge became alarmed when the date of the insurrection was fixed from Moscow, while in Germany he witnessed stocks of arms being seized every day and the mood of the masses passing from urgent expectation and 'insurgent enthusiasm' to 'weary resignation'. Serge wrote to Souvarine in Moscow in order to convey to the Executive Committee of the International that 'unless the Party's initiative joins with the spontaneous movement of the masses, it is doomed beforehand'.[38]

Radek had also wired Moscow saying that the German masses were not ready. Zinoviev and Bukharin spurred the Germans on. At first Trotsky said he needed more information, but then went along and proposed planning the insurrection in advance.*

The 'aborted' German October

The plan decided on was artificial, trying to force events from the outside. Although Trotsky and Radek had some misgivings† they nevertheless believed the revolution in Germany had to be directed with bold and decisive action.[39]

Uncertainty in the Comintern gave way to a plan of action. KPD members

---

* Isaac Deutscher, *The Prophet Unarmed, Trotsky 1921–1929*, Oxford, Oxford University Press, 1959, pp. 142–5. Deutscher notes that Brandler balked, feeling, as he put it, that he was not the German Lenin, and asked the Politburo to assign Trotsky to lead the insurrection. Instead of Trotsky the Politburo assigned Radek and Piatakov. Serge was part of their entourage. Had Trotsky gone and led a successful revolution he would have been the leader of both the Russian and German revolutions and consequently too powerful for Stalin. On the other hand had Trotsky been killed leading an unsuccessful German revolution he would have become a martyr like Che Guevara. It was better for Stalin to keep Trotsky in the Soviet Union.

† Trotsky and Radek worried about the divisions within the KPD between Brandler (whom Trotsky supported) and Maslow and Fischer over whether or not the moment for the seizure of power was at hand.

Brandler, Heckert and Böttcher were to enter the Social Democratic Dresden cabinet which, according to Comintern directives, was to be the springboard for revolution.[40] The Communists were to use their influence from within the government to arm the workers. Red Saxony and Thuringia were to lead the insurrection. Serge lived with the workers and youth who prepared to fight; some were veterans of November 1918 and January 1919, old Spartacists who lived through 'the murder of . . . Karl and Rosa, the dictatorship of the man of blood, Gustav Noske'. He noted these men were ready to do anything they were asked.[41]

The Comintern's plan was clumsy and based on insufficient and outdated information. Haste, indecision and amateurish preparations combined in a disastrous mixture. Serge had agreed with Trotsky that the crisis of revolutionary leadership was decisive, but added there was also a 'crisis of popular consciousness' not to mention an already bureaucratized International.[42]

The Comintern analysis of the German situation had been outstripped by events. Conditions in October were not as favourable as they had been in July; the social crisis was less acute, and the stabilization of the mark had eased the economic situation. The political situation was thus calmer, according to Deutscher's interpretation, or anything but calm according Borkenau, who blamed the Communists for not realizing they lacked support. In his view the drift of disaffected social democratic workers was more to the right than to the left; he cited a decline in trade union membership as proof that workers were withdrawing from politics. According to Gruber, the KPD should have known the situation better, especially with regard to the strength and inclinations of the fascists, and he criticized the Russians for seeing too many 'homologues to their October Revolution'. Carr noted that the underlying political conviction of the revolutionary social forces was more illusory than real, though the situation in Germany 'had lost none of its tenseness'.[43]

The KPD Central Committee had failed to arouse the masses and prepare them for insurrection. The arsenals were empty. The Russian military experts called off the insurrection at the last moment but word did not get to Hamburg where 300 disciplined and courageous Communists took over the city and found themselves isolated and doomed.* In a bloody sequel the Communists rose and fought for four days.[44] Serge said there were 'few of us who realized the full extent of the defeat in the first moments'.[45]

Hitler staged his abortive coup in Munich on 9 November. Although the putsch failed Serge did not underestimate Hitler's potential. In fact one

---

* Because, as Carr wrote, of an inexplicable, tragic blunder in which Thälmann and Remmele, two members of the KPD Central Committee under the impression that the insurrection's success was assured, left the conference of workers' organizations at Chemnitz before it ended and gave the order in Hamburg for the rising to begin. Had they stayed to the end of the conference they would have received word that the insurrection had been called off. *Interregnum*, pp. 221–2.

salient feature of Serge's articles in 1923 in *La Correspondance International* and *Bulletin Communiste* was his appreciation of, and attention to the significance of, the fascist danger.[46] In his later article in *La Vie Ouvrière*,[47] Serge explained that German capitalists did not yet need Hitler as they had been able to stabilize the situation, but they would keep him in reserve should the crisis flare up again.

The defeat of the German revolution paved the way for Stalin's triumph.[48] It also removed an obstacle to Hitler's march to power. The failure of another revolution in Europe left the Bolsheviks isolated and in turmoil. The Russian Party crisis entirely dominated the German debate. Its effects were felt throughout the Comintern. The evaluation of the KPD in the post-mortem of the German 'fiasco', as Carr termed it, became a battleground in the struggle within the Russian Politburo between Trotsky, Radek and Piatakov on one side and Stalin, Zinoviev and Kamenev on the other. Trotsky wrote seven years later,

> The internal discussion in the Russian Communist Party did not lead to a system of groups until the events in Germany in the fall of 1923. The economic and political processes in the USSR were molecular in character and had a comparatively slow tempo. The events of 1923 in Germany gave the measure of the differences on the scale of that gigantic class struggle. It was then and on that basis that the Russian Opposition was formed.[49]

The deliberations on the German question marked the first time Stalin had participated in the life of the Comintern. His attitude was revealed six years later when Brandler (expelled from the International) sought to clear himself by publishing Stalin's letter to Zinoviev and Bukharin opposing the insurrection: 'It is in our interests that the fascists should attack first . . . Moreover, according to all information, the fascists are weak in Germany'.[50] Zinoviev hesitated but tended to favour the insurrection. Brandler was opposed but was forced to assume leadership of the action. Later Stalin and Zinoviev blamed Brandler in an attempt to clear the International of responsibility.

In the wake of defeat, recriminations and scapegoating went on among the KPD, the Comintern and the Bolsheviks. Ruth Fischer and Maslow lined up opportunistically with Stalin and Zinoviev, Trotsky supported Brandler, and everyone agreed that the revolutionary leadership had been woefully inadequate.* Serge concurred, but begged the question of the working class: were *they* revolutionary? Serge's account is loaded with quotes telling us they were not: they were too 'respectable', too moderate.

---

* Peter Sedgwick, in 'Victor Serge and Socialism', *International Socialism* no. 14, 1963, noted 'everybody . . . demonstrated the crying inadequacy of the leadership of everybody else' (p. 20). Reprinted in Susan Weissman (ed.), *The Ideas of Victor Serge: A Life as a Work of Art*, Glasgow, Critique Books, 1977, p. 190.

Characteristically Serge's analysis begins and ends with the actual condition and political consciousness of the working class.

In Serge's view the Weimar Republic survived the October and November crises of 1923 due to the weight of inertia of the masses. The bulk of the masses were uninvolved; the unemployed sold themselves for a crust of bread to the Nazis; the Social Democratic leaders were too invested in a crumbling social system, while its rank and file were frightened of revolution. In the ensuing search for scapegoats Serge noted that from defeat came 'the lying, the suppression, the demoralizing discipline that ruins consciences. Nobody talked about the basic fault. The whole Party lived on the involuntary bluff of functionaries whose first concern was not to contradict their superiors.'[51] Misinformation had accumulated, passing through a hierarchy of functionaries and secretaries until the KPD Central Committee could say to the International that they were prepared, while in reality they were only prepared on paper.[52] Part of the problem resulted from the chain of command which went from the Russian Politburo through the Comintern to the German Party. The consequence was further bureaucratization. Serge argued in his article in *Clarté* that the disease of bureaucratization had its hand in the inept bungling of the German fiasco. The KPD had not only allowed all initiative to come from Moscow but remained passive while a revolutionary situation developed under their noses. When they should have been developing connections with the mass struggle the German Communists concentrated on gathering arms – and this they did more on paper than in fact.* Accepting a date for the insurrection in this situation was a further indication of the bureaucratic isolation from reality which defeated them in the end.

The German events coincided with the beginning of sharp factional strife in the Bolshevik Party. The Platform of the Forty-Six† appeared in

---

* The inflation of arms-gathering on paper, performed by bureaucratized militants who wished to look good to their superiors, was then covered by the superiors to look good to their superiors, until it looked on paper as if the Party was ready for insurrection when in fact they were not. R. Albert, 'Au Seuil d'une révolution', *Clarté*, 15 Feb. 1924, p. 97. Serge's analysis of the crippling behaviour of bureaucratism and the consequent effects of acting with inaccurate information in the German events were to find their reflection in the subsequent developments in the Soviet Union.

† A Manifesto signed by Preobrazhensky, Serebryakov, Breslav and forty-three other leading members of the Party, issued on 15 Oct. 1923. The Manifesto attacked the gulf separating the 'secretarial hierarchy' and the 'quiet folk' or 'general mass of the Party' and complained about the ossification of the Party leadership; and declared that the 'casual, unconsidered and unsystematic character of the decisions of the central committee' had brought the country into a 'grave economic crisis'. The Manifesto, or 'Platform of the 46' is reproduced in full in Carr, *The Interregnum*, pp. 367–73.

the month of the German defeat, as did Trotsky's two letters which opened the period of debate and factional struggle within the Russian Party. The German affair was intimately bound up with the crisis in the Russian Party and the Comintern. Radek, a Left Oppositionist (with Trotsky), came up against Zinoviev's power in the Comintern. Members of Comintern sections took positions in the debate to the growing alarm of Stalin, Zinoviev and Kamenev, who worried that foreign leaders might side with the Left Opposition. In fact Radek reminded the Politburo that he was responsible for his actions in Germany not to the Politburo of the Russian Party but to the World Congress of the Comintern, of which the Russian Party was a section like the others.[53] The question of dominance of the Stalin faction in the Comintern was thus acutely posed.

The well-documented debate in the Comintern on the German revolution offered two opposing assessments of the defeat. One took the view that the German proletariat had not been ready to seize power when the call was made; the other maintained that conditions had been ripe for revolution but the moment had been lost because of the crisis of revolutionary leadership. Serge's assessment fell somewhere between the two; he saw a crisis both in revolutionary leadership and in popular consciousness.* He did not side with Zinoviev or Stalin. Now that another opportunity for world revolution had failed, the inward-looking faction ('socialism in one country') came to the fore. Serge was well aware of the consequences for the Comintern and the Russian Revolution, and he alluded to them in his *Clarté* articles and *Memoirs*.

Serge left Berlin for Vienna by way of Prague with his wife Liuba and son Vlady on the same day (9 November 1923) that General von Seekt took power to restore order. At the last moment the Soviet Embassy left them to fend for themselves. Serge had lived in difficult circumstances without money or proper papers for two years.

Watching and waiting in Vienna: 1923–25

From Vienna Serge followed events in the Soviet Union, the Comintern and the turbulent Balkans. These included the death of Lenin, Zinoviev's Estonian fiasco,† the Georgian affair,‡ and Bulgaria, still 'pregnant with revolution'.

---

* The crisis of popular consciousness and the bureaucratization of the International were both expressions of what Trotsky called the crisis of revolutionary leadership. Thus Serge's view was a more nuanced version of Trotsky's.

† Refusing to accept the German defeat, Zinoviev initiated attacks on Tallinn with the objective of seizing power. Serge admitted that they used to say Zinoviev was 'Lenin's biggest mistake'. Serge, *Memoirs*, p. 177.

‡ Stalin had shown his hand in Georgia using Ordzhonikidze, whom Serge called 'an honest and scrupulous man tormented by recurrent crises of conscience'.

Austria itself was a peaceful country governed by enlightened social democrats who were engaged in building workers' housing and biding time in the knowledge that their powerful neighbours' influence (Germany, Italy and Hungary) would decide their future. Serge arrived with his diplomatic passport and occupied himself with international questions while enjoying Vienna's sweet music.

The years of Serge's sojourn in Vienna, from 1923 to 1925, coincided with the years of watching and waiting throughout the Comintern and within the Soviet Union itself. Vienna had become the crossroads of the International, where leading international revolutionaries were either living or spending time. Serge had the opportunity to get to know many of them, and through his writings reveal what they were thinking – thoughts they would not express publicly. Once again, Serge found himself in a nerve centre of political activity.

From Vienna, Serge watched the bureaucratic cancer spread in the Soviet Party and Comintern.[54] He associated with some of the finest revolutionary minds of the day and sketched portraits of them in the *Memoirs*. He studied Freud and Marx, befriended Lukacs* and Gramsci.† Of his life at that point, Serge wrote:

---

* Serge described Lukacs: 'Lukacs was a philosopher steeped in the works of Hegel, Marx, and Freud, and possessing a free-ranging and rigorous mind. He was engaged in writing a number of outstanding books which were never to see the light of day. In him I saw a first-class brain which could have endowed communism with a true intellectual greatness if it had developed as a social movement instead of degenerating into a movement in solidarity with an authoritarian power. Lukacs' thinking led him to a totalitarian vision of Marxism within which he united all aspects of human life; his theory of the Party could be taken as either superb or disastrous, depending on the circumstances. For example, he considered that since history could not be divorced from politics, it should be written by historians in the service of the Central Committee.' Serge, *Memoirs*, p. 187.

† Antonio Gramsci had known of Serge before they met in Vienna. He had translated Serge's *Lenin 1917* and some of his *Clarté* articles and published them in his paper *L'Ordine Nuovo*. Serge's relations with Gramsci are discussed by the editors of the Italian edition of Gramsci's prison letters. Gramsci also alludes to Serge in a letter dated 13 Sept. 1931. See Antonio Gramsci, *Lettere del carcere*, edited by Sergio Caprioglio and Elsa Fubini, Turin, 1965, p. 487n. (cited in Richard Greeman, 'Victor Serge: The Making of a Novelist, 1890–1928', unpublished Ph.D. dissertation, Columbia University, 1968, p. 344). In his *Memoirs*, Serge described Gramsci as 'an industrious and Bohemian exile, late to bed and late to rise . . . Gramsci fitted awkwardly into the humdrum of day-to-day existence, losing his way at night in familiar streets, taking the wrong train, indifferent to the comfort of his lodgings and the quality of his meals; but intellectually he was absolutely alive. Trained intuitively in the dialectic, quick to uncover falsehood and transfix it with the sting of irony, he viewed the world

All we lived for was activity integrated into history; we were interchangeable; we could immediately see the repercussions of affairs in Russia upon affairs in Germany and the Balkans; we felt linked with our comrades who, in pursuit of the same ends as we, perished or else scored some success at the other end of Europe. None of us had, in the bourgeois sense of the word, any personal existence: we changed our names, our posting and our work at the Party's need; we had just enough to live on without real material discomfort, and we were not interested in making money, or following a career, or producing a literary heritage, or leaving a name behind us; we were interested solely in the difficult business of reaching socialism.[55]

Rarely has the life of a revolutionary been so evoked. Serge had the unique ability to capture the authentic mood of daily life or a person's real presence in his remarkable thumbnail sketches. He documented reality in a creative literary style. Above all, he never forgot that politics and history are forged out of individual lives, and that these individuals' *characters* shape their public actions. How else could a paragraph describing the lack of personal existence of a revolutionary be so immediately personal?

The Russians Serge knew in Vienna managed to 'keep their plain integrity and abundant optimism'.[56] These revolutionaries, whose usefulness to the Party had been exhausted, had been given sinecures abroad, where they could observe the decay of the bourgeois world and where their voices would not be heard. Among them was Adolf Abramovich Joffe, just back from China and Japan, who appeared to Serge as a 'wise physician, almost affluent in his appearance and almost comical in his gravity, who had been summoned to the bedside of a dying patient'.[57] Others were Dr Goldstein, 'old' Kozlovsky and Yuri Kotziubinsky, with whom Serge shared confidences. Kotziubinsky had been a hero in the civil war, along with Yuri Piatakov and Evgenia Bogdanova Bosch, one of Bolshevism's greatest personalities, about whom he had written in *Year One*.[58] Serge also met Angelica Balabanova again, and Béla Kun – 'a remarkably odious figure . . . the incarnation of intellectual inadequacy, uncertainty of will, and authoritarian corruption'.[59]

They had almost no contact with the Austrian Social Democrats and the Communist Party, which had split and only had 100 members in each group. Although Austro-Marxism had produced fine minds and organized one million proletarians, it had failed to take power three times in ten years because of 'its sobriety, prudence, and bourgeois moderation'.[60]

---

with an exceptional clarity . . . When the crisis in Russia began to worsen Gramsci did not want to be broken in the process, so he had himself sent back to Italy by his Party . . . a fascist jail kept him outside the operation of those factional struggles whose consequence nearly everywhere was the elimination of the militants of his generation. Our years of darkness were his years of stubborn resistance.' Serge, *Memoirs*, pp. 186–7.

Serge spent his time discussing the Russian Revolution, the Comintern and the world situation with his friends, and writing.* He noted that he and Gramsci had agreed that the quarter million new militants recently recruited to the Bolshevik Party could not have been worth much if they had waited for the death of Lenin to enter the Party.[61] With Lukacs, he had discussed whether or not revolutionaries who had been condemned to death should commit suicide.†

Serge wrote of the impending fascist menace in Austria in the French *La Vie ouvrière* in 1925, which became 'an ineffectual pamphlet' in Russia. He wrote that the Austrian working class could survive only so long as Weimar Germany existed: its collapse spelled Austria's doom.[62] Serge's journalism in this period took up questions like the campaign against the terror in Spain – waged against Serge's old comrades – and against the White terror in 'Bulgaria ruled by the knife'.[63]

Writings from Vienna

Disillusioned with the bureaucratic character and nationalist focus of both the Soviet Party and the subservient Comintern, Serge had already signed up with the Left Opposition. Serge's political doubts were reflected in his writings in this period, albeit in an Aesopian fashion. In his writings Serge avoided direct political questions as that would have called into question his loyalty to the Bolshevik Party, of which he was still a member.[64]

Serge wrote a study of Lenin in 1917, just after his death in 1924. On the surface it looks like a typical product of the cult of Lenin which followed his death. If it was a Comintern assignment, Serge was well suited to the task of recommending Lenin's politics in 1917 to the French left; he had translated Lenin's *State and Revolution* into French and had worked in the Lenin Institute translating *Lenin: Collected Works*.[65] He had known Lenin personally and his wife had been Lenin's stenographer in 1921.[66] At the news of Lenin's death, Serge reflected on the sweep of Lenin's remarkable achievements.[67] He remembered Andrés Nin had predicted Lenin's death would provoke a riot. Nin added 'the unity of the Party' depended on this 'shadow of a man, no more than that'.[68]

The significance of Serge's study of Lenin is not so much its content but its context: it was written from Vienna, after the defeat of the world revolution in Germany. Stalin had begun to stand out as the primary leader, ascending above the Triumvirs by means alien to the vision that had

---

* He began his first novel, *Men in Prison*, wrote a biography of Lenin, *Lenine 1917*, wrote on culture and revolution in a series of articles in *Clarté*, which later formed the backbone of a small book Serge produced called *Literature and Revolution*, published in 1932.

† Lukacs had decided when he was imprisoned that he had no right to suicide as a Central Committee member, charged with setting an example. Ibid., p. 188.

inspired the Russian Revolution; means foreshadowing the more terrible methods to be used in the near future. Superficially, the book appears a rather uninspired official account.[69] Yet underneath the apparently unimaginative propaganda, Serge analysed Lenin's role in such a way as to implicitly criticize Stalin's leadership.

Describing Lenin in the year of the revolution Serge stressed two points: Lenin's internationalism and his view of the Russian Revolution as but 'a strong impulse to the international socialist movement';[70] and Lenin's commitment to the role of the masses in the revolutionary process. Considering Stalin's policy of socialism in one country, the book is a veiled attack on the direction of the Party in 1924 and 1925.

Serge followed the events of the year 1917, demonstrating Lenin's decisive role. To Serge, Lenin was the embodiment of 'thought as action' and the 'absolute harmony between intelligence and will'.[71] Serge underscored Lenin's understanding of the role of workers in taking power and constructing socialism, and in this sense the whole book is an attack on Stalin and the troika, who ruled by dictatorial fiat. By emphasizing Lenin's understanding of the role of the organs of workers' democracy in advancing the mass struggle and without referring at all to the struggles following Lenin's death, Serge was able to accentuate the democratic side of Lenin, making the book an oppositional text.

Lenin 1917 attacked Comintern and KPD policy in the 1923 German revolution without mentioning Germany or the Comintern; Serge invoked Lenin to condemn the pre-planned insurrection. Under the heading 'Marxism and Insurrection', Serge quoted Lenin on the 'art of insurrection': if a revolution was to be successful it could not rely on a conspiracy nor a Party, but on the advanced class, and a revolutionary upsurge of the people. 'The insurrection must rely upon that *turning point* in the history of the growing revolution when the activity of the advanced ranks of the people is at its height, and when the *vacillations* in the ranks of the enemy and *in the ranks of the weak, half-hearted and irresolute friends of the revolution* are strongest.'[72]

Literature and revolution

In what was to become a pattern for Serge during periods of imprisonment or restriction from political activity (political censorship due to Party discipline this time), Serge shifted his attention to literary questions. Serge was first and foremost a political animal, and it was only when barred from political action that he turned to literary activity. The Vienna period was one of watching and waiting, because the real centre of political activity was within the Soviet Party. Serge's attention returned to literature again after 1928, when he became a novelist after being expelled from the Bolshevik Party and later imprisoned.

Serge's articles on Russian cultural and artistic life, which were published in *Clarté* and *La Correspondance Internationale*, mark his entry into the field of literary criticism, to which he would return in 1932 when he published a little book called *Littérature et révolution*.

Serge wrote some twenty-five articles in the period from 1922 to 1926, chronicling culture in the Soviet Union. He profiled the leading Soviet artists and by way of their work, discussed the trends and conditions of culture in post-revolution Soviet society. These articles document Serge's impressions and analyses of the brief cultural renaissance during the civil war and under NEP. Serge was no stranger to the Soviet literary scene. Although not yet a novelist himself, Serge had associated with literary artists during the civil war and had belonged to the *Volfila* group.[73] He kept up with their work, and their fate, marking many of their suicides in the post-1925 period. Serge had interpreted the works of these early Soviet artists for the French reading public, and had translated Andrei Bely's 'Christ est ressuscité'[74] and Fyodor Gladkov's *Le Ciment*.

Serge did not limit his associations to revolutionary writers, but mingled with Christians and symbolists as well. He appreciated creative genius, whether it was revolutionary or reactionary, materialist or mystic. Writers and artists were in a special category and Serge believed that the rights of artistic self-expression were above the political struggle.

In his chronicle of literary trends in the Soviet Union Serge traced the continuity of pre-revolution literary traditions in the current cultural scene. He examined the role of literature in the revolution and vice versa. The ending of capitalist exploitation was never simply an end in itself for Serge; it was the means to allow the flowering of creative expression. It was a necessary beginning. Serge wrote,

> Revolutionaries need to understand and to love. For the question that it poses denotes eternal dissatisfaction, the disdain of mediocre happiness, the aspiration to escape from the cycle of the vegetative, purely animal life of so many slaves and so many masters, to rise finally to human life, whose justification can only reside in the affirmations of superior energies: love, intelligence and the will to create.[75]

The revolution was to be measured in human, spiritual and cultural terms, not just in economic ones. Artists would be evaluated by their ability to place themselves and their art within a revolutionary context. Having defined his position on art and revolution Serge examined novelists and poets. He wrote that Vladimir Mayakovsky had created a unique revolutionary work with his poem '150,000,000' which was new in both form and content. Serge lauded Mayakovsky, the Futurist, and the Christian poets, saving his lesser praise for the Communist poets. He discussed the limits of *proletcult*,* anticipating the literary debates of the late twenties and early

---

* The *proletcults* had emerged at the height of the civil-war years of 1918–21, battling for a proletarian culture, founding circles in small towns, covering city walls with posters, putting on plays, producing poets, setting up courses,

thirties about whether or not a proletarian culture could exist. In the end creativity was strangled under Stalin and Soviet socialist realism was born.

Serge wrote a series for *Clarté* on 'La Vie intellectuelle en Russie des Soviets' describing Russian cultural conditions and trends and the question of 'revolutionary culture'. He noted that the weight of the older, pre-revolutionary artists and their ideas still dominated the newer revolutionary artists struggling to establish new movements. A parallel existed between the new revolutionary artists and the new nationalized industries, both struggling against older established ways. The new artists had absorbed the dynamism of the revolution but were impressionable and unformed. Serge did not consider these artists revolutionary yet because they had not developed an 'architecture of ideas' about the revolution, and although they were imbued with the creative energy unleashed by the revolution, their understanding of the revolutionary process lacked depth. 'They observed the smallest aspects, but were unable to penetrate the underlying law.'[76]

These writers were in fact closer to populism than to proletarian culture; they spoke of 'the people', an imprecise term used more by liberals than revolutionary Marxists. Serge explained that the revolutionary Marxist intellectuals had been too busy to write fiction, and those who wrote showed the influence of NEP. Writers did not stand above society and its movement; they developed with the revolution and its stresses and strains.[77] There was no time to develop a proletarian culture in the space of a few short years, especially when considered in light of the time it had taken to generate bourgeois culture. Within this theoretical framework Serge turned his attention to individual writers, including Pilniak, Libedinsky, Ivanov, Tikhonov, Serafimovich and Mayakovsky.[78]

Serge's examination of Mayakovsky celebrated the young futurist poet's form and style, and the vigour brought to his work by the Bolshevik revolution. Serge criticized Mayakovsky[79] because he lacked equilibrium, used too much hyperbole and was excessively individualistic, too iconoclastic, and futuristic only in a superficial way.* Mayakovsky was still influenced by the decadence of pre-revolutionary poetry and had not succeeded in expressing his individuality without depending on old myths. Serge said

---

elaborating theories, and founding an international committee. See Victor Serge, 'Is a Proletarian Literature Possible?', a translation of *Clarté*, no. 72, 1 March 1925, in *Yale French Studies*, no. 39, 1967, p. 137.

* Mayakovsky was very annoyed by Serge's *Clarté* article, asking him, 'Why do you say that my futurism is no more than Past-ism?' Serge answered, 'Because your hyperboles and shouts, and even your boldest images, are all saturated with the past in its most wearisome aspects. And you write "In men's souls / Vapor and electricity". Do you really think that's good enough? Surely this is materialism of a peculiarly antiquated variety?' Serge said they parted cordially, but Mayakovsky became so official that Serge never met him again, and most of the friends Mayakovsky had in his youth also dropped him. Serge, *Memoirs*, pp. 267–8.

Walt Whitman had succeeded lyrically where Mayakovsky failed. Serge decided Mayakovsky had an inevitable stamp of the old in him because the new culture could not be created overnight. A new culture would come only after creative individuals had assimilated the consciousness, beliefs and ideology of the new society. Serge concluded that in order to support the conditions necessary for the germination of a new culture in this transition period, rigorous Marxist criticism must develop alongside total freedom for artistic expression.

In the penultimate article Serge wrote in the *Clarté* series, 'Une Littérature prolétarienne est-elle possible?' Serge discussed some of the new literary groups and their journals. He considered *Na postu* the best and most characteristic example of the new reviews: it was rigorous yet easy to read, clear and consistent ideologically, a journal of 'demolition and savage attack' as well as of criticism. Citing examples of its criticism and style, Serge quoted Sosnovsky, who had attacked Gorky's bitterness and defence of old intellectuals as 'the ex-falcon turned hedgehog'. The review criticized Voloshin ('the poetic counter-revolution'), Pilniak, Ehrenburg and Nikitin as calumniators of the Revolution. The State library directors were criticized for clumsy editing, Kollantai for her books on free love; even Lunarcharsky's theatre came under fire, as did Mayakovsky's claims of a proletarian Futurism. Serge said the 'mutual attacks by Bolsheviks' were a joy to read.[80]

Nikolai Bukharin's ideas were the most sensible, wrote Serge. Since the country was 95 per cent peasant Bukharin proposed the literature should be peasant, and above all should not be restricted nor regulated by the state. Proletarian writers had to 'win literary authority for themselves' by freely competing with other creative movements.[81] Bukharin was the only Politburo sponsor of the idea of a separate proletarian culture, but vigorously opposed 'methods of mechanical coercion' in achieving the new literature. Writers' organizations should not be modelled on the Party or army, and only a multiplicity of writers' organizations would allow artists the latitude they needed for artistic creation. Bukharin declared: 'Let there be one thousand organizations, two thousand organizations; let there be alongside MAPP and VAPP as many circles and organizations as you like'.[82] The literary dispute did not yet relate to the political tensions and divisions within the Party.

Serge criticized the boring works of gifted young writers who were so 'theory-obsessed' and 'hamstrung by their preconceptions' that their literature failed altogether. He attacked the Association of Proletarian Writers for asking writers to 'not imitate bourgeois art forms, but to surpass them to create new forms' and to write only monumental works on proletarian life. These pronouncements lacked insight and a grounding in concrete reality. Serge asked, how could a young writer from a workshop *surpass* the expertise of bourgeois art methods?[83]

Serge based his ideas on Trotsky's *Literature and Revolution* (Serge called

Trotsky's work 'definitive'[84]), in which Trotsky denied that a proletarian literature could exist: the new culture would be universal, not proletarian, since the proletarian dictatorship would give birth to a classless society. During the transition period of the proletarian dictatorship there would not be time for a genuine culture to develop, since the conditions for the development of intellectual culture – normal production, high technology, well-being, leisure and time – would be more appropriate to the Communist society that would supplant the proletarian dictatorship. Even the term 'proletarian culture' could be dangerous since it anticipated future culture within the framework of the present. Serge concluded that the state of culture mirrored the crossroads of the revolution, and its future was intimately connected to the future of the revolution. Serge's analysis of culture (as of politics in general) was deeply influenced by Trotsky, who provided the theoretical germ.

Serge put aside the question of culture when he returned to the Soviet Union to stand with the Left Opposition but returned again to these questions after his arrest and expulsion. Many of the ideas he had expressed when criticizing or admiring other Russian writers, ideas about style and structure, were incorporated into his own novels, which were ideological at their core. The literary legacy of the Russian writers from this period survived in Serge's work.

Serge and the Left Opposition

Critical of the use of terror, the bureaucratization of the Party and the state, the growing privileges which distanced the bureaucracy from the population and the aims of the Revolution, the Left Opposition of Trotsky and others characterized the bureaucracy as rooted in the new conditions of Soviet rule. Given that the original revolutionary working class had been largely destroyed by civil war and foreign intervention and that the new working class was drawn mostly from a semi-literate peasantry, the Left Opposition argued that it was necessary for the Soviet state to promote an early and gradual industrialization as a precondition for the regeneration of class consciousness within the newly formed proletariat, who had just one foot out of the countryside.

Industrial expansion would ensure that an increasing portion of the population would be exposed to collective production relations, which would serve to generate a proletarian consciousness among the mass of the population as opposed to the petty-bourgeois consciousness of the peasantry.[85] As the working class grew the bureaucracy would need to cede to it increasing control over the political administration of the society. The logic of this position also pointed to a dilemma which was not addressed: given the inevitable rise of bureaucracy in the terrible conditions in Russia, the new bureaucracy would be called upon to reform itself, to carry out policies which would lead to its own loss of power in favour of the new working class it was being called upon to nurture.[86] Theoretically the new working class would serve as a check against bureaucratic excesses and anti-democratic measures.

Serge was anxious about the increasing power of the rich peasant and the self-serving bureaucrat and about the weakness of industry under NEP conditions;[87] a crisis was developing that demanded immediate attention. Without the hoped-for success of the world socialist revolution the Soviet Union would be forced to industrialize on its own.

Preobrazhensky, the economist of the Left Opposition, argued that the 'primitive socialist accumulation' had to come from the private peasant sector, but had to result from a *reciprocal* relationship; higher productivity in industry would provide goods for the peasants, and an increase in agricultural production, possible with a revolution in technique, would better feed the working class which must supply the machinery required for higher productivity. Finally the Left Opposition argued, the problem could only be solved by material assistance from victorious revolutions in the advanced capitalist countries.

Bukharin came up with the opposite programme, developing Stalin's notion of 'socialism in one country': profit incentives for the peasant to stimulate growth. Stalin was suspicious of Trotsky's potential influence and wanted to undermine his authority and so supported Bukharin's programme largely as a way to weaken Trotsky's political influence. Consequently the critical need for industrial accumulation was postponed while NEP proceeded apace. The political and economic situation hurtled toward disaster, sped by the continued neglect of industry.

During the period from 1923 to 1926 Stalin, in charge of Party organization, packed the Party bureaux with people whose loyalty to him was well compensated, predetermining the outcome of Party debates.[88] To find an audience for his alternative political programme, Trotsky would have to go outside the Party. He was not prepared to do so.

Serge joined the Left Opposition in 1923 while in Vienna. He wrote that Trotsky's works *The New Course* and *The Lessons of October* stood as 'flashes of daylight' in the 'spiritual impoverishment of recent years'.[89] Serge met discreetly with other Oppositionists in Vienna to discuss these 'pulsating pages'.

> Then, bound by discipline, prisoners to our daily bread, we went on endlessly printing our news-sheets, with the same insipid, nauseating condemnations of everything that we knew to be true. Was it really worthwhile being revolutionaries if we had to ply this trade?[90]

Jargon filled the pages of the International's publications, making life difficult for Serge. He said the Oppositionists called it 'Agitprop Pidgin' – the stifling air of monolithism and 'three hundred per cent approval'. He refused to carry out a dishonest directive from Béla Kun dealing with the

French Party. Monatte, Rosmer and Souvarine were being hounded out of the French Party for showing political courage in criticizing Stalin. Everything Serge observed strengthened his view that the Comintern was rotting from within and the only way to save it was to go back to Russia to fight for the regeneration of the Bolshevik Party. Serge could have remained in Europe in relative comfort, but his revolutionary spirit compelled him to return to the Soviet Union to fight against the corruption of the Party in the front ranks of the Left Opposition. Lukacs had told him

> Do not be silly and get yourself deported for nothing, just for the pleasure of voting defiantly. Believe me, insults are not very important to us. Marxist revolutionaries need patience and courage; they do not need pride. The times are bad, and we are at a dark cross-roads. Let us reserve our strength: history will summon us in its time.[91]

Serge did not heed Lukacs' warning.* Instead he told Lukacs that if Moscow and Leningrad proved to be unbearable he would ask for an assignment in Siberia, where he would 'write the books now maturing in my head and wait for better days'.[92]

---

* Lukacs fell into disfavour over his book *History and Class Consciousness*, and was expelled from the Party. He later recanted, followed Stalin through the worst years, producing 'spiritless works'. He was 'summoned by history' again in 1956, this time to oppose Soviet tanks invading his native Hungary, where he was now Minister of Culture. He was deported to Romania, but later was allowed to return to Hungary.

3

Back in the USSR –
the Left Opposition struggles
1926–28

Signs of suffocation

Serge returned to the USSR to stand with the Left Opposition in its battle for the soul of Bolshevism. He arrived in 1925, before the Fourteenth Party Congress which broke up the ruling triumvirate of Stalin, Kamenev and Zinoviev.

Serge travelled by way of Berlin. Again he was struck by contrasts: Berlin had suffered – it cost a 'trillion for a postage stamp' – but the city lit up the night sky; Leningrad* was dark and depopulated; its inflation and unemployment were much worse than Berlin's.[1] The cost of returning to the market revealed itself everywhere: beggars and abandoned children roamed the streets. Young girls, the daughters of 'famine and chaos' with nothing but their youth to sell, sidled up to managers and bureaucrats. A morbid alternative to such degradation was evident in the swelling suicide lists Serge checked daily as an editor.[2] But five years of NEP had ended famine and, for those who could afford it, the grocers' displays were abundant and sumptuous.

Disturbing incidents pointed to a moral crisis in NEP Soviet society, which Serge called a 'social inferno'. Evoking the ugly atmosphere in 1926 of what he called the 'obscure early stages of a psychosis', Serge cited the 'epidemic' of gang-rapes. He tried to explain this in terms of conflict between a resurgent sexuality and its suppression, first by revolutionary asceticism, then by poverty and famine. Soviet youth had neither the inhibitions of bourgeois religious training nor the moral values of the revolutionary generation. Their culture was of the streets, where sexual

---

* Petrograd's name was changed to Leningrad after Lenin's death. Lenin would never have stood for it during his lifetime, although while he was alive Stalin had changed the name of Tsaritsyn to Stalingrad, Elizvetgrad was changed to Zinovievsk, and factories, ships and schools also bore the name of Central Committee members. With Lenin's death Stalin initiated the cult of Lenin and then his own cult. See Boris Souvarine, *Stalin: A Critical Survey of Bolshevism*, translated by C.L.R. James, New York, Longmans, Green, 1939, pp. 303–4.

exploitation and promiscuity thrived on misery.[3] In place of their parents' sexual mores, the notions of the new generation echoed the 'oversimplified' theories of Alexandra Kollantai, who said 'You make love just as you drink a glass of water'. Serge quoted a discussion among university students in 1926 about Enchmen's theory on the disappearance of morals in the future communist society. Without offering his own ideas, Serge simply lamented, 'How difficult is social transformation!'*

Serge returned to a country plagued by a mood of surrender to desperation and death, in which the creative and the revolutionary alike were driven to suicide. Serge named some well-known victims, while reminding the reader that Leningrad had ten to fifteen suicides per day, mainly among those under thirty.[4]

Serge wrote about the suicides of oppositionists such as Lutovinov (of the Workers Opposition) in May 1924, Glazman, Trotsky's young secretary, and Evgenia Bosch, who was given neither a national funeral nor a burial place in the Kremlin wall because her suicide was seen officially as an act of indiscipline, proof of her oppositional politics and disloyalty. When Preobrazhensky objected to the mean, small-minded treatment of Bosch's memory and remains, he was told to 'hold his tongue'.[5]

Poets killed themselves, a significant phenomenon for Serge who saw in these acts a signpost for the revolution, no longer able to hold onto its artists – first Yesinin, and later Mayakovsky, the two giants of Russian poetry. Yesinin hanged himself in his hotel room after writing his last lines in blood for lack of ink. Serge, called to his room in the Hotel International, said farewell to 'our greatest lyrical poet . . . of the Revolution's singing Bohemians . . . Thirty years old, at his peak of glory, eight times married.'[6]

Serge returned to a Soviet Russia in the throes of a crisis different from the one which had racked the country he had left four years before. The threat of civil war and foreign intervention had given way to a new, internal threat: budding class antagonisms wrought by market forces, presided over by a single Party in power. Within that Party the normal democratic dynamic was being suffocated by bureaucratic manoeuvring.

The Revolution self-destructs

Looking back at the NEP period (1921–28) twenty years later, Serge affirmed that NEP ought to have been accompanied by a coalition government. Sharing power would have been dangerous for the Bolsheviks, but the dangers would have likely proven less terrible than what actually resulted

---

* Victor Serge, *Memoirs of a Revolutionary*, London, Oxford University Press, 1963, pp. 205–7. Serge alluded to a problem which would surface decades later: a spiritual and moral vacuousness endemic to alienated and apathetic Soviet youth lacking political, social or religious purpose. Serge could detect in 1926 the crisis of ideology which would result from the conditions of Soviet rule.

from the monopoly of power.[7] In fact, discontent and opposition within the Party and working class forced the Central Committee to adopt a 'state of siege' stance (albeit mild compared to what came later), rather than a policy of reconciliation and tolerance towards other socialist elements, principally left Mensheviks and anarchists (both of whom accepted the Soviet constitution). Serge wrote that deeper reasons for the strengthening of the monopoly of power had to be examined. After the trauma of Kronstadt, the Central Committee was afraid to open the political arena to competition.

Serge offered another explanation for the Bolsheviks' unwillingness to trust anyone else in power* – the Bolsheviks' commitment to world revolution. A coalition government in Russia would have weakened the Comintern, whose task was to guide and direct the coming revolutions. Serge considered the role of the Russian Party in the Comintern paramount because of the European revolutionary leaders' political inferiority to the Bolsheviks.

Here Serge touched on what he considered the 'greatest and gravest error of the Party of Lenin and Trotsky' and posed the question of whether the Bolsheviks' enthusiasm for European revolution was justified. Conceding that a satisfactory answer was not possible, he nevertheless maintained the question needed to be asked and 'delimited'.[8] Serge agreed that capitalism was finished as a stable force and the Bolsheviks were right to warn that if socialism did not succeed capitalism then barbarism would follow. Writing after World War II, Serge counted the cost to humanity of having failed to to establish world socialism.

The Bolsheviks had hoped that social transformations would take place in Europe through the awakening of the masses, who would reorganize society on a rational and equitable basis. Their mistake, wrote Serge, was not to see clearly that the transformation was taking place amidst a 'terrible confusion of institutions, movements and beliefs'.[9] The clarity of vision the Bolsheviks possessed was absent in Europe. Yet they were right to see the German revolution as the salvation of both Russia and Germany. Serge insisted that the German revolution would have spared history the 'hellish machinery of Hitlerism and Stalinism'.

Serge's argument contains a characteristic tension. He often posed essential questions perceptively, but then failed to resolve them. In the case of the German revolution Serge contradicted himself. The Bolsheviks, Serge argued, committed their 'gravest error'† in overestimating the revolutionary

---

* Though Serge often conceded that by this juncture all the revolutionaries were already *inside* the Bolshevik Party.

† Although Serge uses the superlative, he elsewhere proclaims their most 'incomprehensible error' to have been the establishment of the Cheka; the handling of the Kronstadt rebellion was for Serge the culmination of the 'errors and mistakes of power'. Victor Serge, 'Thirty Years After the Russian Revolution', in Susan Weissman (ed.), *Victor Serge: Russia Twenty Years After*, Atlantic Highlands, NJ, Humanities Press, 1996, pp. 313–15.

mood of the West European masses; yet they correctly analysed the vital necessity of European revolution to the success of socialism in Russia.

The Bolsheviks' mistake, according to Serge, was misinterpreting the political understanding and energy of the working classes in the West, Germany in particular. The Bolsheviks' militant idealism, not to say desperate hope, caused them to fail to connect with the working classes in the West. The Soviet-led Comintern issued orders but did not listen to its non-Russian members. John Reed's struggle with Zinoviev was a case in point.* Especially so was the German tragedy. But for Serge these mistakes did not eclipse the revolutionary vision which at bottom motivated the Comintern's failed attempt to extend the revolution:

> In fighting for revolution the German Spartacists, the Russian Bolsheviks, and all their worldwide comrades were struggling to prevent the global cataclysm which we have just lived through. They understood what was approaching. They were moved by a great will to liberation. Anyone who ever rubbed shoulders with them will never forget it. Few men in history have ever been so devoted to the cause of men as a whole.[10]

Inside the Bolshevik Party

Stalin began to concentrate organizational power in his hands in 1922 when he became General Secretary – a post considered relatively unimportant at the time. Stalin became known as 'Comrade Card Index' (Tovarishch Kartotekov).[11] He paid close attention to organizational details, skilfully using this 'administrative' post to accumulate power by placing people loyal to him in key positions throughout the apparatus. As Serge put it, Stalin had long been boring from within; his 'tireless activity consisted in placing his creatures everywhere. His political flair lay in translating with great practical skill the aspirations of the parvenus of the revolution.'† He carefully prepared the Fourteenth Party Congress which ousted Zinoviev and Kamenev – Serge wrote in his biography of Stalin that Zinoviev and Kamenev had lost power without realizing it. The Party's voting had ceased to be important some time ago; its role had shrunk to approving the secretaries designated

---

* Reed and Lewis Corey represented two organizations vying for the franchise as the American section of the Comintern. Reed tried to argue the case of American specificity, but Zinoviev insisted they patch up their differences, unify into one section, and end the discussion.

† *Victor Serge: Russia Twenty Years After*, edited by Susan Weissman, New York, Humanities Press, 1996, p. 153. Documents from the 1920s that have been released support Serge's analysis. In an article in *Argumenti i Fakti*, no. 27, 1990, Alexander Podshchekoldin, using CPSU archives, shows that Stalin, in the first nine months of his job as General Secretary, bought the loyalty of Party functionaries by granting them wide pay differentials and extravagant privileges.

by the Central Committee (in reality, by Stalin).[12] Souvarine called this five-year process Stalin's 'molecular coup d'état'.*

In contrast to Stalin's attention to detail Trotsky, although described by Lenin as a zealous administrator, concerned himself with policy and theory. Lenin called Trotsky the most 'capable' man on the Central Committee. Echoing Lenin, Serge stated that only Trotsky had the stature needed to lead the Party. Serge considered Trotsky the 'most lucid of the inheritors of the "heroic times"',† armed with a programme which, in Serge's view, correctly addressed the key problems facing the young Soviet state. But Trotsky – a latecomer with a Menshevik past who did not belong to the old 'coterie' of Bolshevik militants – was unacceptable to them.

When Lenin fell gravely ill a struggle broke out over who would 'succeed' him. On his deathbed Lenin proposed an alliance with Trotsky. His last letter called for Stalin's removal. Lenin's 'Testament', as it became known, showed that Lenin had been preoccupied in his last months with the growth of bureaucratism. Serge quoted Souvarine, who said that the dictatorship of the proletariat was being replaced by the dictatorship of the secretariat.[13]

Lenin had also feared a split in the Party. Souvarine thought Lenin's attitude much more ambivalent than Trotsky's version in My Life, often cited by Serge. Souvarine believed Lenin was so worried about a split that he sought to counterbalance Stalin with Trotsky. Despite Lenin's concern, within a year of his death the Party divided into Left, Centre and Right tendencies, holding different perspectives on industrialization, collectivization, bureaucratization and 'permanent revolution' versus 'socialism in one country'.

During the last year of Lenin's illness and the year following his death (1923 to 1924) Zinoviev, Kamenev and Stalin launched a vicious campaign against Trotsky and the Left Opposition. At the Thirteenth Party Confer-

---

* Serge, *Russia Twenty Years After*, p. 154, and Souvarine, *Stalin*, chapters VIII and IX. Serge read Souvarine very closely and agreed with many of his formulations. His own work is peppered with quotations from Souvarine. When Serge disagreed with Souvarine, he would do so in long footnotes, such as on page 162 in *Russia Twenty Years After*. Here Serge criticized Souvarine's easy characterization of the Opposition's defeat as the result of its own mistakes. Serge objected to Souvarine accusing the Oppositionists of lacking practical sense. Serge wrote: 'the practical sense of revolutionists who deem it necessary to fling themselves under the chariot wheels because it is in the higher interests of the proletariat, is just as different from that of the parvenus to whom the morrows of the great defeats of the working class offer invaluable opportunities for better installing themselves in power. Souvarine ought to know this, after all, for he, too, was a "doctrinary" vanquished by the "empiricists" because of his devotion to the International of the great years.'

† Serge, 'Thirty Years After', p. 320. Serge always distinguished the civil war revolutionary generation of Bolsheviks from the 'parvenus' who followed.

ence in January 1924, the first of a long line of completely stage-managed gatherings,[14] the Triumvirs denounced Trotsky and the 46 for a 'petty-bourgeois deviation from Leninism'.[15]

The Troika and the anti-Trotsky campaign

Once Lenin was too ill to participate actively in Party life the 'old' Party members, who had vacillated on the October Revolution – Zinoviev, Kamenev, Bukharin and Stalin – began to organize against Trotsky. Rewriting history and attacking Trotsky's independence from the Bolshevik Party before 1917, Zinoviev, Kamenev and Stalin formed the Triumvirate, or Troika, which effectively ruled the Party and campaigned against Trotsky and Trotskyism.* The aim was to prevent Trotsky from garnering a majority in the Party and replacing Lenin.[16] The Troika began a campaign of lies to attack Trotsky. They used the press to promulgate anti-Trotsky slanders, but libraries were also supplied with what Serge called 'dishonest books'. Kamenev (Trotsky's brother-in-law) had the distasteful job of directing this falsification of history and ideas and later spoke to Trotsky about it 'with unrestrained cynicism'.[17] In this same period (throughout 1924) the Comintern grew monolithic, and the international sections were instructed to condemn Trotskyism. Those who dared question or oppose the line were expelled. The French Party eliminated Rosmer, Souvarine† and Monatte. This process was called 'Bolshevization' of the Comintern.‡

The Troika feared Trotsky as the most capable revolutionary leader of the masses. A magnificent orator and brilliant theoretician, Trotsky had organized the military victory in the civil war. But Trotsky was ill-suited to the struggle for the apparatus. Superior in character to other members of the new ruling group,[18] Trotsky had no taste for gossip, intrigue, slander or treachery. His presence made others uncomfortable.[19] He was a 'revolutionary to

---

* Trotsky called the Troika's anti-Trotsky campaign 'a fight against the ideological legacy of Lenin'. Leon Trotsky, *My Life*, Harmondsworth, Pelican Books, 1975, p. 508.

† Souvarine was expelled for translating and publishing Trotsky's *New Course*.

‡ The 'Bolshevization' of the parties of the Communist International was the thesis of Béla Kun at the Fifth Congress of the International in June 1924. Zinoviev saw the Comintern as the 'single world Party'. Ruth Fischer, the leader of the German Party, echoed Zinoviev, calling for a monolithic International. The parties imitated the internal structure of the Bolshevik Party, banishing dissent, demanding 100% approval of the leaders' positions. Serge called it the perfection of the bureaucratic machine. See *Russia Twenty Years After*, pp. 153–4. See also Isaac Deutscher, *The Prophet Unarmed, Trotsky 1921–1929*, Oxford, Oxford University Press, 1959, pp. 146–7, and 'Theses and Resolutions of the Communist International', in Jane Degras (ed.), *The Communist International 1919–1943: Documents*, vol. 2, *1923–1928*, London, Cass, 1971, pp. 98–107.

his bones'[20] whose concern was class struggle, both national and global. He measured human personality on 'the Marx scale', that is, he judged men by their ability to serve the demands of historical necessity.[21]

Trotsky remained silent during the campaign against Trotskyism. He came down with a fever of unknown origin that kept him in bed and out of the struggle. Trotsky confessed that it was then that he realized, 'with absolute clarity the problem of the Thermidor – with, I might even say, a sort of physical conviction'.[22] Lying in bed, Trotsky analysed the historical curve of development which created such a large demand for slander and which allowed such a degradation of the theoretical level of argument.

This was the political atmosphere to which Serge returned from his years abroad. He considered the Party to be in a state of slumber. The universities had been purged, the public was apathetic, and the youth had turned in on itself. Serge wrote that the Oppositionists remained optimistic despite the situation. Their optimism was based on the conviction that their ideas were correct, rather than the actual state of the struggle.

Serge recalled a directive brought to him by Victor Eltsin from 'the Old Man' (Trotsky) which said: 'For the moment we must not act at all: no showing ourselves in public but keep our contacts, preserve our cadres of 1923, and wait for Zinoviev to exhaust himself'.[23] Serge interpreted this to mean restricting his role to literary activity. The Opposition remained under Party discipline and kept their political and organizational activity to a minimum. Their theoretical output in this period, however, was prodigious.

The waiting period was difficult for the militants of the Left Opposition. Trotsky laid low and refused to go outside the Party to fight. Keeping the struggle for their ideas within the Party made it hopeless – Stalin had packed the Party with his minions who shouted down the Oppositionists.

Once the Triumvirs had defeated Trotsky and removed him from the Commissariat of War, the bonds of their solidarity snapped.[24] A year of growing political divergence within the Politburo ensued, accompanied by petty manoeuvring between Stalin, Zinoviev, Kamenev and Bukharin. The Leningrad and Moscow organizations of the Party were in conflict; Zinoviev headed the Leningrad organization, while Stalin controlled Moscow. Zinoviev denounced the kulak danger and the bureaucratic regime which he himself had created.* But it was not until April 1925 that political differences within the Triumvirs clearly emerged. Zinoviev was

---

* Panaït Istrati, *Soviets 1929*, Paris, Les Editions Rieder, 1929, p. 115. This book was actually written by Serge. His authorship has been cited in several sources, among them the introduction to the first volume of Istrati's trilogy *Vers l'autre flamme*, republished in Paris in 1980, by the Fondation Panaït Istrati, Union Générale d'Editions, with an introduction by Marcel Mermoz, pp. 29–30. The second volume of the trilogy was *Soviets 1929* and the third was penned by Boris Souvarine, although published with Istrati listed as author.

opposed to 'socialism in one country' and entered into conflict with both Stalin and Bukharin. Throughout the summer of 1925 the dissension was kept out of view. Zinoviev and the Leningrad organization attacked Bukharin and Rykov, which Deutscher said inadvertently helped Stalin to consolidate his position at the helm.[25] The Stalin–Zinoviev–Kamenev Troika split at the Fourteenth Party Congress in December 1925, where the conflict openly erupted. This ended the Opposition's period of laying low and waiting. Zinoviev and Kamenev, manoeuvred out of power, now went over to the Opposition's side. Bureaucrats of the worst order themselves, Zinoviev and Kamenev now attacked bureaucracy. In 1926 they joined Trotsky to form the United Opposition to Stalin.

With hindsight it is easy to say that an open fight should have been waged from 1923 to 1925. But why did Trotsky refrain from taking the battle to the workers? He probably could have staged a successful coup early in the conflict. He had widespread support among the masses and in the army. But he was opposed to palace coups. Such a 'victory', for Trotsky, would not be victory.

Trotsky still believed that the Party, though degenerated, was 'the only historic instrument which the working class possessed for the solution of its fundamental tasks'.[26] He believed that if there were even a remote possibility to rectify the Party, it had to be tried. Serge agreed that failing to struggle against the bureaucratic degeneration of the Soviet regime would have meant a further demoralization in the international labour movement.[27] But Trotsky confined his terrain of battle to the Party, where he stood the least chance of victory.*

Confining the battle to the Party ranks left the masses of workers with no arena for political activity. Caught in the dilemma of trying to promote democracy while remaining loyal to an organization that prohibited opposition, the Left Opposition undermined its own struggle. Serge's postmortem on Soviet democracy maintained that it had been killed long before by civil war, War Communism, Kronstadt and the dilution of the Party.

From vanguard Party to a rearguard with bureaucracy

The Lenin levy in the spring of 1924 brought a mass of inexperienced workers into the Party, strengthening Stalin's position. Serge wondered about the worth of Communists who waited until Lenin died to join the Party.[28] The quarter-million new recruits (later to be 500,000[29]), Serge remarked, changed the Bolsheviks from a Party of the vanguard to one of the

---

* Moreover Anton Ciliga maintained Trotsky was more popular than Stalin in the country at large, and that all he had to do was show himself at the factories in the three major cities to ensure his victory. But, Ciliga continued, Trotsky wanted to avoid an open break in the Party. Anton Ciliga, *The Russian Enigma*, London, The Labour Book Service, 1940, p. 86.

rearguard. He defined it as 'a mass Party of backward workers led by parvenu bureaucrats'.[30] The Oppositionists, effectively isolated, were also organizationally hamstrung by the ban on factions in force since 1921. Party patriotism ran deep, and the idea of going over the head of the Party to the masses was not considered. Serge wrote to his friend Jacques Mesnil in 1928:

> Basically what is happening – leaving aside the economic roots of the problem . . . boils down to this: the elimination of one generation by another. Those who made the revolution are removed by those who are rising. The new generation did not know the class struggle in its clear and direct forms, nor the yoke of the old regime. On the contrary, it has been told time and again that it was victorious and it ends by believing it . . . Nor did it go through the Civil War . . . Everything we went through before, the difficult and perilous working out of convictions, the tempering of the militant by devotion and individual effort, the courage of being in a minority, scrupulous theoretical intelligence, revolutionary lyricism – all these things are alien to it. It is fed an official science, it has an oversimplified, avid and practical mentality of the parvenu on the make. It naturally distorts the clearest ideas as its interests dictate, ready to retain the old prestige-labels so long as they cover something new. Since heredity weighs down, since the country is one of small peasant property, since the pressure of the capitalist encirclement is enormous . . . you now have a whole new potential bourgeoisism, latent but already pushing upward and even flourishing in places, and infinitely skilful in disguises. I am intimately acquainted with writers, with intellectuals, who are, at bottom, our mortal enemies, whose anti-socialist convictions have the firmness of rock: their professions are made in Marxian terms, they remove heretics from editorial staffs . . . And they understand quite well what they are doing. Their whole problem lies in staying on for a few years and then the game is theirs . . . This process has overtaken the Party. Here is the membership proportion of a cell that I know well: Four hundred members, twenty of whom go back to August 1921, and three or four to August 1917. Consequently, three hundred eighty against twenty came over not to the militant or the painful revolution, but to the power, and after the NEP.[31]

Serge's analysis of conditions in the Party made it plain that it was being taken over by NEP men, former bourgeois and opportunists of every stripe who recognized power and wanted part of it. The Opposition had no hope of winning within such a Party. Serge explained why the Opposition did not take their programme outside the Party, responding to those who criticized Trotsky for not resorting to a coup which would probably have been successful. Serge wrote that would mean 'forgetting that socialism and workers' democracy cannot be born out of pronunciamentos. It is to the merit of the revolutionist that he refuses to take this road, so tempting to all the ambitious.'[32] Serge also cautioned that a Marxist must look deeper than whether or why Trotsky did or did not fight during this period. The Marxist, wrote Serge, understood that the socialist revolution which unfolded in Russia could never be considered apart from the international labour movement.[33] Although by 1923 both the Russian Party and the

International were 'dulled' and 'stiffened at the joints', the Russian proletariat still hoped boundlessly for a successful outcome in Germany and actively worked toward that end. The bureaucratization of the International compromised everything, wrote Serge.[34] The bureaucratic conquest in the Soviet Union could be explained above all else, he continued, by the defeat of the workers' revolution in Central Europe.

Finally, in relation to the process of bureaucratization, Serge found it necessary to clarify the situation again in a 'Reply to Ciliga' written in October 1938, many years and experiences later:

> In reality, a little direct contact with the people was enough to get an idea of the drama which, in the revolution, separated the communist Party (and with it the dust of the other revolutionary groups) from the masses. At no time did the revolutionary workers form more than a trifling percentage of the masses themselves. In 1920–21, all that was energetic, militant, ever-so-little socialistic in the labour population and among the advanced elements of the countryside had already been drained by the communist Party, which did not, for four years of civil war, stop its constant mobilization of the willing – down to the most vacillating. Such things came to pass: a factory numbering a thousand workers, giving as much as half its personnel to the various mobilizations of the Party and ending by working only at low capacity with the five hundred left behind for the social battle, one hundred of them former shopkeepers . . . And since, in order to continue the revolution, it is necessary to continue the sacrifices, it comes about that the Party enters into conflict with that rank and file. It is not the conflict of the bureaucracy and the revolutionary workers, it is the conflict of the organization of the revolutionists – and the backward ones, the laggards, the least conscious elements of the toiling masses. Under cover of this conflict and of the danger, the bureaucracy fortifies itself, no doubt. But the healthy remittances that it encounters – I mean those not based upon demoralization or the spirit of reaction – come from within the Party and the other revolutionary groups. It is within the Bolshevik Party that a conflict arises in 1920, not between the rank and file – which is itself already very backward – but between the cadres of the active militants and the bureaucratic leadership of the Central Committee. In 1921, everybody who aspires to socialism is inside the Party; what remains outside isn't worth much for the social transformation. Eloquence of chronology: it is the non-Party workers of this epoch, joining the Party to the number of two million in 1924, upon the death of Lenin, who assure the victory of its bureaucracy. I assure you, Ciliga, that these people never thought of the Third International. Many of the insurgents of Kronstadt did think of it; but they constituted an undeniable elite and, duped by their own passion, they opened in spite of themselves the doors to a frightful counter-revolution. The firmness of the Bolshevik Party, on the other hand, sick as it was, delayed Thermidor by five to ten years.[35]

The economic roots of the problem and the issues at stake: the debates of the 1920s

The issues which embroiled the Party and the Opposition in both political and literary activity revolved around the questions of industrialization, internationalism and bureaucracy. These debates were rich, yet increasingly dangerous: discussion was stifled, silenced or falsified.

Serge wrote that from 1924 to 1925 it would have been possible to 'curb the formation of a rural bourgeoisie without leaving the framework of NEP'. Failure to do so led to a civil war with the peasantry in the form of forced collectivization.[36] Had it begun at the right time, industrialization would have improved relations between town and country. Trotsky advocated such a policy. According to Serge, Preobrazhensky, Sokolnikov[37] and Piatakov took these ideas up numerous times before they became the programme of the Opposition.*

The civil war had almost wiped out the working class. In place of the fallen workers came semi-literate peasants without class consciousness, class traditions, and revolutionary consciousness. The surviving working class and the newly formed workers laboured under conditions remote from socialist goals: without any say in factory management and without voice in political decision-making.[38]

In response to the Revolution's isolation Stalin concocted the doctrine of Socialism in One Country which Bukharin developed into a theory. The doctrine emerged from the political reality of isolation. Stalin reacted pragmatically to events, improvising theories to fit circumstances and his own objectives, rather than proceeding from any theoretical vision. Socialism in one country was a product of pessimism and fantasy: pessimism about world revolution, and the fantasy that a classless communist society could be built in a single, backward and beleaguered country, enveloped by the capitalist world market. The idea was not entirely new: the utopian socialists and nationalists had advocated a similar isolated socialism. The concept was completely alien to Marx and Engels, to Lenin, and even to Stalin himself, before he became demoralized with the world struggle and power hungry in the domestic one.†

---

* Serge, *Russia Twenty Years After*, p. 279. Serge's writing here, in the conclusion to *Russia Twenty Years After*, was done hastily to get the book out quickly; nevertheless his lumping together of Sokolnikov with Preobrazhensky and Piatakov in the context of Oppositionist economic policy is highly misleading and can only be considered as historical sloppiness. Sokolnikov defined the Soviet state as 'state capitalist', with the major shortcoming of the leadership (apart from its anti-democratic and bureaucratic tendencies) its inability to make the system function efficiently. He favoured the expansion of agricultural production before the expansion of industry – in direct conflict with Preobrazhensky's economic prescriptions – and coincided with the Opposition on political questions, such as bureaucracy and on the need for Party democracy.

† Stalin was compelled to admit that Marx and Engels never entertained the idea, and said the idea was 'first formulated by Lenin in 1915'. This reference to Lenin is entirely unfounded as the overwhelming bulk of his work states precisely the opposite, that 'For the final victory of socialism, for the organization of socialist

The Opposition argued against Stalin's 'reactionary utopia',* counterposing to it Marxist economic theory. To try to maintain the proletarian revolution within the boundaries of the Soviet Union, the Trotskyists argued, would inevitably lead to submission to its own internal and external contradictions. Trotsky wrote in *Permanent Revolution*, 'internationalism is no abstract principle but a theoretical and political reflection of the character of world economy, of the world development of productive forces, and the world scale of the class struggle'. The debate between the nationalist conception of socialism and socialist internationalism was opened in 1925 but it assumed greater importance in 1927 in the wake of the Chinese revolution. While the theoretical debate continued the crisis in the country deepened.

Bukharin's conversion from Left Communist and 'proletarianist' to theorist of the Right Opposition arguing for a pro-market, nationalist socialism in one country, was facilitated by the defeat of world revolution.† Recognizing that Soviet Russia was left with the Russian peasantry, Bukharin turned to them with new enthusiasm. But instead of improving conditions, Bukharin's policy of encouraging the kulaks to enrich themselves made things worse. 'There was talk of broadening the rights of inheritance', Serge wrote, and 'Stalin proposed in a barely veiled form the restoration of landed property for the rich peasants. There was squalid, heartbreaking poverty, an ulcer in our young society, while wealth was arrogant and self-satisfied.'[39] Serge's anxiety – shared by the Left Opposition – was deeply felt but based on a rational appreciation of economic truth: the society was being degraded and becoming bourgeoisified.

What were the facts? In an article published in *Clarté* in 1927 Serge discussed the social structure of the countryside, quoting an inquiry done in 1925 by the Communist Academy of the Caucasus, the Ukraine, the Urals and the region of NovoSizirsk.[40] The study found that the peasantry was accordingly divided: poor peasants (with only a few machines) consisted of 25 to 40 per cent of all families; middle peasants 40 to 50 per cent, and kulaks, or rich peasants (with most of the machinery) were between 15 and 25 per cent of all families – not a negligible fraction. Beyond that the poor

---

construction, the efforts of one country, particularly of such a peasant country as Russia, are insufficient. For this the efforts of the proletarians of several advanced countries are necessary.' Many other similar citations of Lenin's show his understanding of the international character of socialism. See Max Shachtman, *Genesis of Trotskyism: The First Ten Years of the Left Opposition*, London, IMG Publications, 1973, pp. 18–19.

* The phrase comes from Trotsky's *The Permanent Revolution*, New York, Pathfinder Press, 1969, p. ix.

† Bukharin had come a long way from his days as an early Left Communist of 1918, and an enthusiastic supporter of War Communism in 1919–20 in which he proclaimed the mode of organization under War Communism to be 'final'. See chapter 1, pp. 29, 42.

peasants often cultivated their plots with tools rented from kulaks. Moreover the poor and middle peasant together held only 35 to 65 per cent of
arable land, the rest belonged to the kulaks. These findings led the Commission of the State Plan to declare 'small circles of rural capitalists hold a
considerable part of the wealth in the countryside'.[41] Still more wealth was
held by the merchants and traders (NEP men) who benefited from the
market, at the expense of the workers and poor peasants. Serge found it
threatening that the 'kulak, the merchant, the intellectual bourgeois are
becoming one, with many links to the bureaucracy of the State and the
Party . . . laying down the basis of a duality of powers which menaces the
dictatorship of the proletariat'.[42]

Serge saw the country approaching 'a crisis which might arouse a
hundred-and-twenty million peasants against the socialist power and place
it at the mercy of foreign capital by forcing it to import (on credit? and
under what conditions?) great quantities of manufactured goods'.[43]

Both Preobrazhensky and Bukharin sought to increase national wealth,
but while Bukharin thought this was only possible through private accumulation Preobrazhensky argued in his New Economics that 'primitive socialist accumulation' must be accomplished by taking more out of the private
sector than was put into it. There was no alternative, given their isolation, to
hardships and restricted consumption. Had a socialist revolution occurred
in an advanced capitalist country with an industrial base, as Marx had envisioned, the problems would have been different. Given the actual situation
there had to be sacrifices, but in Preobrazhensky's view the decision to
impose hardships should be a conscious one made by the proletariat.*

Preobrazhensky's programme was based on a thoroughgoing workers'
democracy, and although it meant the peasantry would be squeezed, he
never favoured forced collectivization or forced grain requisitions. He also
postulated growth in the private peasant sector. Yet Preobrazhensky
realized that without an extension of the revolution to the West the Soviet
Union was doomed.

---

* Preobrazhensky discussed the difference between what he called 'primitive
socialist accumulation' and capitalist accumulation in The New Economics. Capitalist accumulation takes a 'ruthless, barbarous, spendthrift attitude to labour
power, which it attempts to treat like any other purchased commodity which
forms one of the elements of production. The limits of exploitation and oppression in this sphere are the purely physiological limits (the worker has to sleep
and eat) or else the resistance of the working class.' But 'from the moment of its
victory the working class is transformed from being merely the object of exploitation into
being also the subject of it [my emphasis]. It cannot have the same attitude to its
own labour power, health, work and conditions as the capitalist has. This constitutes a definite barrier to the tempo of socialist accumulation, a barrier . . .'
Evgeny Preobrazhensky, The New Economics, Oxford, Oxford University Press,
1965, p. 122.

Trotsky had certain disagreements with some of Preobrazhensky's formulations, but not fundamental ones.* Both Trotsky and Preobrazhensky advocated the necessity of systematically taking up industrial accumulation, and neither held any brief for 'socialism in one country'.[44]

By the middle of the 1920s the battle lines were drawn: the bureaucracy was with Stalin, the opposition gathered behind Trotsky.

Serge entered the battle in 1927, just before the Fifteenth Party Congress in which the Opposition was expelled, by publishing 'Vers l'industrialisation' in two parts in the French review *Clarté*. The article put forward the platform of the Opposition with Serge's own nuances. The article clearly employed caution in its style of argument – Serge was still under Party discipline – but was nevertheless fundamentally at odds with 'official' policy. The novel points Serge introduced concern the financial resources for industrialization, the pivotal point of contention between the Left and Right Oppositions. Serge noted that even the policy of allowing the peasant to accumulate was being undermined during the NEP by the NEP men themselves. Private capital dominated the retail trade in NEP Soviet Union, buying wholesale in the cities to sell retail in the provinces. The private traders, not the state, thus reaped the profit of squeezing the peasantry.[45] Admitting that statistics were difficult to obtain, Serge quoted from the Kutler inquiry carried out by the Institute of Economic Research of the Commissariat of Finance, which showed that private capital in 1926 had reached one-fourteenth of its pre-war level.[46] Serge estimated that private commerce in 1925 to 1926 had attained 7.5 billion rubles per year out of a total GNP of 31 billion. Given that even these figures were deceptive, Serge concluded that a mixed economy was impossible because private capital gouges the profits from state production. A vivacious new bourgeoisie was blossoming, obtaining its capital exclusively from the 'pillage of state goods and by speculation'.[47] Serge conceded that this was made possible by the weakness of Soviet industry and distribution. His solution was the same as the Left Opposition's: industrialization on a large scale. How to finance the industrialization?

> To industrialize, we need capital. The capitalists won't give us credit. Where will we get the money? We have just seen that the peasants accumulate wheat and money; we have seen that private commerce rakes in big profits; we have seen the bureaucracy levy a parasitical amount that Stalin and Rykov evaluated last year at more than three hundred million rubles per year. The necessary

---

* Preobrazhensky's ideas could be interpreted to mean that it was possible to accomplish primitive socialist accumulation within the Soviet Union alone, or in association with other underdeveloped countries. Trotsky not only thought this unrealistic, but saw that it opened the door for a theoretical accommodation to socialism in one country. Trotsky also differed with Preobrazhensky on the pace of industrialization.

capital for industrialization circulates, therefore if the dictatorship of the proletariat could seize this capital for the growing new bourgeoisie the industrial
development of the Soviet Union could be undertaken with unprecedented
vigour.[48]

Like the Left Opposition Serge saw the only way out of the economic
impasse in large-scale industrialization, financed through the elimination
of NEP speculation and profiteering. (The role of the international proletariat, Serge added, was to aid this process.) Industrialization might be
undertaken in a single country, but Serge nowhere indicated that this could
be construed as building socialism in one country. Serge's article did not
pose the problem as ultimately insoluble in socialist terms, as both Preobrazhensky and Trotsky finally did.

Victor Serge: Left Opposition activist

Serge did not come to Oppositionist ideas suddenly. He had been critical of
anti-democratic and bureaucratic tendencies that surfaced in the revolution's first months. The trends between 1923 and 1927 would probably
have placed even Lenin in the Opposition. Krupskaya said she would have
expected Stalin to imprison Lenin.

By the time Serge joined the Left Opposition in Vienna in 1923–24 he
had already been in agreement with oppositional views for several years.
Serge, like the others, felt obliged to rescue the revolution from those who
were destroying it from within, to revive its essence and vision – to create a
democratically planned economy controlled by the associated producers,
which could serve as an example to the international working class.[49] The
Oppositionists fought against Stalin's narrowly nationalist and bureaucratic conception of Soviet development, crudely 'legitimized' by a single
phrase of Lenin's taken out of context.*

Serge's activities within the Left Opposition had three dimensions:
domestic, international and literary. Trotsky called him one of the Opposition's most capable members.[50] The French historian Pierre Broué identified Serge as 'marginal' within the Left Opposition,[51] because Serge was not
one of its theoretical leaders and did not totally agree with all its politics.
Serge wrote no theoretical treatises such as Preobrazhensky's *New Economics*,
or Rakovsky's analysis 'The First Five Year Plan in Crisis'. As a spokesman,
historian, pamphleteer and revolutionary novelist, however, no one else in

---

* In 1915, Lenin remarked about the fits and starts in the unfolding of the world
revolution: 'The victory of socialism is possible at first in a few capitalist countries or even in one taken separately.' Lenin was *not* referring to Russia – yet
Stalin leaped to the conclusion that 'socialism in one country is entirely possible
and probable'. See Robert V. Daniels, *The Conscience of the Revolution*, New York,
Simon and Schuster, 1960, p. 252.

the Left Opposition was more valuable than Serge. Serge was an unorthodox member but the Left Opposition was not monolithic. Serge was an
excellent example of its capable militants.

Serge's unique qualities made him valuable to the Opposition: his
knowledge of languages, his international revolutionary experience (by
now in three revolutions) and his stature as a well-known intellectual in
France. Serge was a regular contributor to the press of the international
communist movement, mainly in France but also in German- and English-
speaking countries. His articles in *Inprekorr*, *Bulletin Communiste*, *Clarté* and
La Vie Ouvrière helped spread the Opposition platform and gathered political support. As a member of the Leningrad cell of the Soviet Party Serge
was a public spokesman for the Opposition, and as a member of the clandestine Leningrad Opposition Serge helped recruit more Party members to
the Opposition. Serge also played a role in the Opposition leadership, con-
ferring with Trotsky, Preobrazhensky, Radek and others on Opposition
policy.

The Opposition sought out Serge immediately on his return to Russia at
the end of 1925. The Piatakov Circle in Moscow designated the password
'Taras' for Serge to use to contact the clandestine Opposition in Leningrad.[52] Although the Trotskyists had been playing a waiting game since
1923, they met regularly and Serge was invited to join their circle.

The group met in the Astoria in the agronomist N.I. Karpov's room. The
group usually consisted of Karpov, Serge, two or three students of working-
class origin, two old Bolshevik workers who had been 'in every revolution
in Petrograd for the last twenty years', the worker Feodorov who was later
executed as a member of the Zinoviev tendency, and two Marxist theoreticians 'of genuine worth' (Grigori Yakovlevich Yakovin and Feodor Dingelstedt).* Alexandra Lvovna Bronstein – known as 'Babushka' – usually
chaired the meetings. She had more than thirty-five years' revolutionary
experience, and it was she who brought Trotsky into the Marxist circle she
ran in Nikolayev in the 1890s.[53] Alexandra Lvovna became Trotsky's first
wife and was the mother of his two ill-fated daughters Zinaida (Zina) and
Nina. She herself was deported and disappeared during Stalin's Terror.
Serge said he had known few Marxists 'as free in their basic outlook as
Alexandra Lvovna'.[54] There was also Nikolai Pavlovich Baskakov, who

---

* Yakovin had been in Germany and wrote what Serge described as an excellent
book on Germany. He spent many years in Oppositional activity, making the
rounds of the prisons, and disappeared in 1937. Dingelstedt was one of the Bolshevik agitators behind the mutiny of the Baltic fleet in 1917. He published a
book *The Agrarian Question in India* and was described by Serge as representing
an extreme-left tendency which, like Sapronov, considered the regime's deterioration now complete. Serge said that Dinglestedt, like Yakovin, was never
broken. Serge, *Memoirs*, pp. 207–8.

questioned whether the system could be reformed. Chadayev,* who raised the question of the collectivization of agriculture long before the Party leadership, was the only one in the Opposition to privately put the question of a second Party. He predicted the 'great trials of deception'. These outstanding characters rounded out the group with Serge, who specialized in international questions. Serge emphasized that this was the sum total of the roll-call of the Leningrad Opposition circle, and that there was never any other Centre of the Left Opposition in Leningrad.[55] Serge's insistence (written in 1941) must have been a response to later charges by the GPU of 'Trotskyite' centres in Leningrad.

Moscow's Opposition circle numbered more than 500 according to Victor Eltsin.† The Party was 'in a state of slumber' and the Opposition kept up its morale by writing and publishing Trotsky's Collected Works. All this was to change when the inner-Party struggle came alive with the ousting of Zinoviev and Kamenev from the Troika at the Fourteenth Party Congress in December 1925.

Serge mentions in his *Memoirs* that he passed through Moscow in the spring of 1925 and learned that Zinoviev and Kamenev were about to be overthrown at the upcoming Party Congress.‡ Yet he expressed surprise when they were outmanoeuvred by Stalin at the Congress. The action confused the Left momentarily: Serge thought the bureaucratic regime organized by Zinoviev could not get any worse. It seemed to him any change 'must offer some opportunity for purification. I was very much

---

* Chadayev, who became Serge's friend and collaborator in the Opposition and member of the same Party cell at the *Krasnaya Gazeta*, was the first of their circle to be killed. After spending six months in prison in 1928 Chadayev was sent on assignment by *Krasnaya Gazeta* to investigate *kolkhozes* (collective farms) in the Kuban. Once there he wrote of corruption and rackets in building, industry and agriculture. He had obviously stepped on too many toes and asked too many questions. On 26 August 1928 the local authorities insisted he take a carriage to another town; the carriage was accompanied by a militiaman, but he made himself scarce when only Chadayev's carriage was stopped by 'bandits'. Chadayev was shot in the face and chest with sawn-off shotguns. His murderers were never discovered, the Leningrad Committee prevented a public funeral for him (he had fought in the Revolution) and his headstone was smashed into pieces. See Serge, *Memoirs*, pp. 214–15, and 242–3.

† Trotsky's secretary and son of Boris Mikhailovich Eltsin, an old Bolshevik and Opposition leader who spent time with Serge in Orenburg and became a character in his novel *Midnight in the Century*. Victor Borisovich Eltsin, who had the 'cool temperament of a tactician' spent five years in prison and was then deported to Archangel. Deutscher called him one of Trotsky's 'gifted secretaries'. See Deutscher, *The Prophet Unarmed*, p. 431, and Serge, *Memoirs*, pp. 209, 307.

‡ This trip of Serge's, while he was on assignment for the Comintern in Vienna, most likely was on Comintern business. It was probably upon his return to Vienna that he put in his explicit request to return to the Soviet Union.

mistaken'.* In fact the victory of the Stalin–Bukharin–Rykov coalition over the Zinoviev group gave Stalin the opportunity to shift the blame for everything onto his erstwhile colleagues Zinoviev and Kamenev.

As much as Serge detested Zinoviev and his style of politics he admitted Zinoviev's internationalism was sincere. Zinoviev's own bureaucratic practices in the period up to 1925 were now used against him. Zinoviev and Kamenev were forced to realize that their own policies had enabled the growth of a nascent bourgeoisie and allowed bureaucratic manoeuvring to destroy the Bolshevik Party.

Stalin soon attacked the Leningrad machine, which Zinoviev apparently thought was impregnable. Serge said the machine Zinoviev had forged since 1918 crumbled within a week under the 'hammer-blows' of Gusev, sent by the Central Committee to install new committees. Serge's Opposition circle had first abstained and then walked out in the Leningrad faction fight. They were shocked, shortly thereafter, when Trotsky concluded an agreement with Zinoviev. 'How could we sit at the same table with the bureaucrats who had hunted and slandered us – who had murdered the principles and ideas of the Party?'[56]

Zinoviev and Kamenev signed a declaration which recognized Trotsky's position of 1923 on the internal Party regime as correct. Serge's view of the 'overnight' change in his comrades in the Leningrad Party was magnanimous: he reflected that they must have been tremendously relieved not to have to fabricate lies anymore. Whereas they had attacked Trotsky just days before, they now spoke of him admiringly.[57] Zinoviev and Kamenev presented Trotsky with letters as evidence of their conspiracy with Stalin, Rykov and Bukharin in the smear campaign against him.

Serge's Leningrad Centre numbered some twenty militants. The Zinoviev tendency in Leningrad numbered more than 500. When the Zinovievists demanded the immediate fusion of the two groups and asked for the Left Opposition's membership lists Serge's group balked. 'What would they be up to tomorrow?' Serge, Chadayev and others immediately set up clandestine meetings with a view to recruiting as many as possible to the Left Opposition for the time of the merger of the two oppositions. Afraid of being swamped, they wanted the two tendencies to face each other with organizations of equal size. Serge reported they were successful, with more than 400 organized on the day of the merger.[58]

While they were recruiting to the Trotskyist tendency Serge followed Chadayev and Nechayev to Moscow to brief Trotsky. Trotsky was 'shivering with fever; his lips were violet-coloured, but his shoulders were still set

---

* Ibid., p. 210. This error of Serge's seems strange given his earlier political insights. Serge quoted Mrachkovsky who opposed uniting with Zinoviev, who 'would end by deserting us and Stalin would trick us'. Serge's position in December 1925 reflects the situation within the Party – alliances had not yet solidified into more permanent tendencies.

firmly and the cast of his face displayed intelligence and will'.[59] Trotsky justified the amalgamation of the two tendencies on the basis that the salvation of the revolution depended on it. Serge noted that visitors to Trotsky's house were being photographed by the GPU. They were instructed to pretend to blow their noses as they left.

The unification of the two Leningrad oppositions was brought about by Preobrazhensky and Smilga, sent to Leningrad to sort out their differences. Serge gave his impressions of these men in 1926:

> Preobrazhensky had the broad features and short auburn beard that befitted a man of the people. He had driven himself so hard that during the meetings it seemed that he might at any moment drop off to sleep; but his brain was still fresh and crammed with statistics on the agrarian problem.
>
> Smilga, an economist and former army leader who in 1917 had been Lenin's confidential agent in the Baltic fleet, was a fair-haired intellectual in his forties with spectacles, a chin-beard, and thinning front hair, ordinary to look at and distinctly the armchair sort. He spoke for a whole evening in a little room to about fifty workers who could not move at all, so closely were they squeezed together. A Latvian giant with gingerish hair and an impassive face scrutinized all who came in. Smilga, sitting on a stool in the middle of the room, spoke in an expert's tone and without one agitational phrase of production, unemployment, grain and budgetary figures, and of the Plan that we were hotly advocating. Not since the first days of the Revolution had the Party's leadership been seen in an atmosphere of poverty and simplicity like this, face to face with the militants of the rank and file.[60]

Serge's recollections of meetings provide us with much more than just an account of how and when the Opposition met. Serge's eye for penetrating detail, his descriptive depth, and his ability to sum up a figure's character through a physical description add flesh and blood to our knowledge of the life and death struggle of those years in the Bolshevik Party.

The fight to be heard . . . for five minutes

Serge's account of the activities of the Left Opposition in the years 1926 to 1928 is even more intimate than Trotsky's *My Life*. Serge wrote that the battle of ideas took place on three issues: Soviet agriculture, Party democracy, and the Chinese Revolution.[61] Party discussions consisted of long monologues by Party hacks justifying 'socialism in one country' and denouncing the Opposition. According to Serge everything said about China was dictated by the bureaucracy and was completely falsified.

Crude manoeuvres such as padding speaker lists were used to prevent Oppositionists from speaking. Serge and Chadayev were effectively clandestine and thus able to get on the list. Because Oppositionists were given just five minutes they adopted a style that got as much as possible out in five minutes before the shouts overwhelmed them.

Serge was able to score a few points in these five-minute bursts; but to have to argue in this way was profoundly demoralizing. As their Party 'comrades' kept up their shouts of 'Slanderers! Traitors!', Serge wrote, they suddenly felt, 'that the enemy was in front of us and prison was a step away'.[62] The points Serge was able to score were meagre: on the occasion of Adolf Abramovich Joffe's suicide,* Serge was able to render homage and closed by demanding details on how and why Joffe died from the cell secretary. But the cell secretary was able to bury Joffe under a mound of memoranda. Demoralized, Serge and Chadayev despaired of even trying to speak. Then after one such meeting when they had kept quiet they scored a moral victory: the normally apathetic audience cried for the two of them to answer the 'activists'. Serge and Chadayev won an extra vote that evening and discovered that forty workers supported them discreetly, with an equal amount of sympathizers around them. From other sources they discovered that this reflected the general situation throughout the Party.

Serge described another meeting they held with Zinoviev and Trotsky in a small room packed with fifty people. When a woman worker asked Trotsky what would happen if the Opposition were expelled from the Party Trotsky explained that 'Nothing can really cut us off from our Party'.[63] Serge commented that what was reassuring about this meeting was watching the 'men of the proletarian dictatorship' returning to the poor districts to gain support 'from man to man'. Despite the courage, simplicity and humanity exhibited by the former leaders, which Serge so aptly conveyed (and which he excelled at describing in his novels), the sense of tragedy was already present. Serge accompanied Trotsky home from the meeting and reported:

> In the street Leon Davidovich put up his overcoat collar and lowered the peak of his cap so as not to be recognized. He looked like an old intellectual in the underground of long ago, true as ever after twenty years of grind and a few dazzling victories. We approached a cabman and bargained for the fare, for we had little money. The cabman, a bearded peasant straight out of old Russia, leaned down and said, 'For you, the fare is nothing. Get inside, comrade. You are Trotsky, surely?' The cap was not enough of a disguise for the man of the Revolution. The Old Man had a slight smile of amusement: 'Do not tell any one that this happened. Everybody knows that cabmen belong to the petty-bourgeoisie, whose favour can only discredit us.'[64]

---

* Adolf Abramovich Joffe, 'an outstanding figure' (Serge, *Memoirs*, p. 136) of the Russian Revolution, killed himself, leaving a political testament addressed to Trotsky, which was first stolen by the GPU and later released to him. Joffe's experience included prisons, exile, the revolutions of 1905 and 1917, Brest-Litovsk, the German Revolution, the Chinese Revolution and posts at embassies in Tokyo and Vienna. He was forty-seven. See Nadezhda Ioffe, *Moi Otetz: Adol'f Abramovich Ioffe*, Vospominania, Dokumentui i Materialui, Moscow, Isdatel'stvo Vozvrashchenie, 1997.

Serge's description is amusing, tender and tragic. The attractiveness of the Opposition to Serge is obvious, and affects the reader as well. Serge's talent as a writer and spokesman for the Opposition presenting the human element of the Opposition, as well as the distillation of its overall political stance, wins sympathy.

Serge wrote of another Opposition meeting which took place in his apartment around the kitchen table. On this occasion Karl Radek was present, and gave 'an impression of extreme intelligence, which was, at first encounter, disagreeable because of a certain flippancy; but beneath the sarcastic retailer of anecdotes, the man of principle shone through'.[65] The meeting was cut short at midnight by a telephone call warning them that the GPU was on its way to arrest them all.

Political life had deteriorated greatly by this point. It was difficult to maintain morale. The Central Committee had gangs of 'activist' thugs out breaking up 'illegal meetings' by force. The situation was grim and Serge was certain that they would be defeated since the mass of workers were indifferent to their struggle. He confided this to Trotsky, who told him: 'There is always some risk to be run. Sometimes you finish like Liebknecht and sometimes like Lenin.'[66] Serge summed up his own feeling:

> Even if there were only one chance in a hundred for the regeneracy of the Revolution and its workers' democracy, that chance had to be taken at all costs. I was unable to confess these sentiments openly to any one. To the comrades who, under the firs in the cemetery, or on a waste plot near a hospital, or in poverty-stricken houses, demanded some promise of victory from me, I would answer that the struggle would be prolonged and harsh. So long as I confined this way of talking to personal conversations with a few people, it worked, it made their faces harden; but if it was used against a more numerous audience, it cast a chill. 'You behave too much like an intellectual', I was told by one of my friends in our Centre. Other agitators were lavish with promises of victory and I think that they themselves lived on such hopes.[67]

We learn from Serge that the Programme of the Opposition was a collective effort, with Zinoviev writing the chapters on agriculture and the International with Kamenev; Trotsky wrote the chapter on industrialization; and Smilga and Piatakov edited the draft. The Programme served not only to demonstrate that the Opposition's ideas represented the way forward, but also to expose the absence of ideas put forward by the Party. Serge noted that the combined effort of drawing up the Opposition Programme was the last time collective thinking was allowed in the Party, and even that was cut short by GPU raids.[68]

With all legal means of expression closed not only to the Party Opposition, but also to the anarchists, syndicalists and maximalists, the Central Committee controlled absolutely the dissemination of the printed word. Nonetheless the *Platform of the Opposition* appeared clandestinely.

The Programme attacked the growth under NEP of the kulak, trader and bureaucrat as anti-socialist forces. Also under fire were low wages, high unemployment, and high indirect taxation which increased the misery of the masses. Calling for the development of *kolkhozes* (collective farms), a progressive tax-system, the creation of new industry (attacking the 'pitifully weak version of the Five Year Plan'), and the abolition of the state alcohol trade, the Opposition also demanded restoration of the Soviets, self-determination for nationalities, and revitalization of the trade unions and the Party. The Comintern was also heavily criticized, especially for the policies in China, which led to a bloody disaster.

The Revolution's tenth anniversary

Serge saw the tenth anniversary of the Russian Revolution as the point at which the 'exhausted Revolution had turned full circle against itself'.[69] Elsewhere Serge had characterized the anniversary as the realization of Soviet Thermidor, finishing the cycle of the Revolution's first ten exultant years.[70] Serge described Trotsky's and Zinoviev's speeches on this occasion as barely audible under the torrent of abuse, which included the throwing of books. Trotsky countered sarcastically: 'Your books are unreadable nowadays, but they are still useful for knocking people down.' This suggests that the rage expressed by the Party faithful came from what they saw as treasonable conduct – after all the Opposition was also part of the ruling bureaucracy.

One of the last hurrahs of the Opposition took place on 7 November 1927, the tenth anniversary of the Revolution. The Opposition had decided to take part in the anniversary parade. According to Isaac Deutscher, who uses Serge's description of the Leningrad demonstration as a reference, this public manifestation of the Opposition was more an appeal to the Party than an attempt to go around the Party directly to the masses. Carrying banners proclaiming the slogans of the Opposition as well as placards with Zinoviev's and Trotsky's names, the Oppositionists were attacked by Party activists and charged by mounted militiamen, then beaten and dispersed. Deutscher wrote that the Opposition was defeated in this demonstration not only by Stalin's readiness and repressive response, but by the underlying contradiction in the Opposition's action: a public demonstration of opposition to the conduct and policies of the Party, while maintaining loyalty and self-discipline within its ranks.[71]

Serge's description of the brawl, though nearly quoted in full by Deutscher, imparts a different meaning. Deutscher describes Serge's brush with an angry crowd, stressing Serge's physical and, by implication, political isolation. Deutscher translates the workers' silence following the Party activist's threat as ominous. In Serge's description, after shouting the names of Trotsky and Zinoviev to an astonished crowd an

> organizer, roused from his sluggishness, answered in a spiteful tone: '– to the dustbin!' No one echoed him, but all at once I had the very distinct impression

that I was about to be cut to ribbons. Burly characters sprang up from nowhere and eyed me up and down, a little hesitant because after all I might be some high functionary. A student walked across the clear space that had arisen all around me and came to whisper in my ear, 'Let's be off, it might take a turn for the worse. I'll go with you so that you won't be hit from behind'.[72]

Deutscher's translation imbues Serge's sluggish organizer's shout with 'threat and fury' and elides the lack of 'echo' – the workers remaining silent. The difference here is that Serge leaves the impression that although the crowd was astonished to hear the names of the Opposition leaders shouted, their lack of response to the organizer was not complicity with him but refusal to take up the action against Serge. Deutscher's rendering of the episode leaves the impression that the crowd, though probably intimidated, was with the Party. Serge on the other hand describes a non-complicit and shocked crowd, that although intimidated would not go against the Opposition – thus the need for the 'burly' thugs who made Serge fear for his safety. The Party used the press to accuse the Opposition of a mini-insurrection that day. In fact Serge described battles between hundreds of Oppositionists and the militia on horseback.[73]

Louis Fischer was in Moscow and described the scene as tense. Rumours had circulated that the Red Army would make a bid for power against the Stalin regime, but nothing happened. The demonstrations in Moscow and Leningrad differed only by degree of violence. According to Fischer the Chinese students of Moscow's Sun Yat-Sen University 'threw Trotzkyist slogans in the air'[74] and the GPU moved in to make arrests. Later pictures of Trotsky were torn down from buildings, and when Trotsky and Zinoviev appeared they were not allowed to speak.

The subtle difference between Serge's and Deutscher's accounts leaves intact a common judgment – that the Opposition was defeated, that Thermidor had arrived. Both accounts agree that the Opposition could not rouse the crowd or masses to engage in action against the Stalinist regime, against the Party. Serge understood the reason; the Opposition had been too loyal, had allowed Party discipline to choke off its ability to command a platform for its ideas in society at large. Trotsky had reacted to the repeated charge he was an 'outsider' to the Bolsheviks by striving to prove his loyalty. Ironically, this contributed to his own undoing. Trotsky could not have acted without the other Oppositionists, who were perhaps even more loyal to the Party than Trotsky, judging by the lengths to which they later went to remain within its ranks. Serge concluded that one had to have been in the Party to understand its psychology.[75]

Expulsion

On 14 November 1927, one week after the demonstration, the Opposition was expelled from the Party. Two days later the expulsions were published. The ousters ensured that the Opposition would have no voice in the upcoming Fifteenth Party Congress. Once out of the Party the former Central Committee members had to move out of their residences in the Kremlin. Trotsky had already vacated the Kremlin, and Serge went to see Zinoviev as he was moving. Serge found Zinoviev and Radek amidst their belongings. Zinoviev 'feigned a supreme tranquillity',[76] taking with him only a poignant death mask of Lenin. Kamenev dropped by, and Serge noted that his beard had turned completely white, though his eyes remained 'unclouded'. That was the last time Serge saw Kamenev.[77] Serge's impression of Radek, in the process of sorting and destroying papers, surrounded by books, is very revealing: Radek confided that he deplored the fact that the Opposition had followed Trotsky's advice and broken with the Group of Fifteen (Sapronov and V. Smirnov). The Fifteen had called the ruling group a bureaucratic police regime which had replaced the dictatorship of the proletariat. Radek also bemoaned that

> 'We've been absolute idiots! We haven't a halfpenny, when we could have kept back some pretty spoils of war for ourselves! Today we are being killed off through lack of money. We with our celebrated revolutionary honesty, we've just been over-scrupulous sods of intellectuals.' Then without a pause, as though it were about the most commonplace matter: 'Joffe killed himself tonight.'

Joffe's funeral, exile of Oppositionists . . . the issue of capitulation

Joffe's suicide was a landmark in the inner-Party struggles. Louis Fischer had gone to see Joffe a week before his suicide. He described him as extremely ill, racked with pain, but curious about the revolutionary consciousness of the European proletariat. Joffe asked Fischer whether he believed revolution was imminent in Germany, China, England and America. Fischer's negative replies distressed Joffe whose body was already tortured with pain.[78] Joffe wrote in his last testament that his death was 'a gesture of protest against those who have reduced the Party to such a condition that it is totally incapable of reacting against this disgrace' (the expulsion of Trotsky and Zinoviev from the Central Committee). His funeral was the Opposition's last public demonstration and Trotsky's last public appearance.

The GPU had tried to prevent the funeral from becoming a show of strength of the Opposition. Both Trotsky and Rakovsky spoke, and the crowd protected Trotsky, who told them:

> Joffe left us, not because he did not wish to fight, but because he lacked the physical strength for fighting. He feared to become a burden on those engaged in the struggle. His life, not his suicide, should serve as a model to those who are left behind. The struggle goes on. Everyone remains at his post. Let nobody leave.[79]

Serge was also at the funeral. It reminded him of another demonstration by different persecuted Oppositionists at the same cemetery just six years before: Kropotkin's funeral. Serge remarked that there was a secret justice in the persecution that was now descending on 'us' – who had persecuted the anarchists in the Revolution's early years.

The Fifteenth Party Congress saw the Centre and Right congratulating themselves for successes in all fields. One of these important 'successes' was the expunging of the 'Menshevik or Social Democratic deviation' on its way to becoming a 'Second Party'. This was the language typically used to characterize criticism. Bukharin took the floor at the Congress to denounce the crimes of Trotskyism. He explained that Trotskyism was preparing to establish a new Party which would rally behind it all the disaffected and those who hated the regime: in this way a split would undermine the dictatorship of the proletariat and the Opposition would thus spearhead the hidden 'third-force reaction'.[80]

Bukharin's argument resonated within the Opposition, which was divided on the question of capitulation. Serge was caustic about certain Oppositionists' desire to capitulate in order to prove their loyalty in the face of the purges, and wrote that the 'third force' was 'already organized in the heart of the bureaucracy'.[81] Zinoviev and the other capitulationists from Leningrad could not see that the transformation had already begun in the Party and signalled the end of all vital initiative in the Party.

The expulsion of the Opposition marked the death of the Party. Without any discussion or dissent it could not function as a political Party in a real sense. Yet the Zinovievites were certain that there was no political life outside the bureaucratic machine they had helped to build, that no humiliation was too great if it provided a way back in. Serge described an exchange of notes between Zinoviev and Trotsky: 'Leon Davidovich, the hour has come when we should have the courage to capitulate . . .' Trotsky: 'If that kind of courage were enough, the revolution would have been won all over the world by now . . .'[82] Zinoviev and Kamenev recanted, which Serge said was seen by the Trotskyist Opposition as political suicide. Yet the blow was deep. The psychology of being a Bolshevik Party member meant that finding oneself cut off from the Party was akin to religious excommunication. That psychology prevented the Opposition from taking their ideas to the masses at large, in a sense representing a kind of contempt for the masses; the notion that thoughts must be filtered through the Party smacks of elitism and distrust of the ability of the ordinary workers to judge which policies were correct. Although Serge suffered less than some from this elitism, not even he advocated such broad democratic ideas in 1927. Trotsky's writings about democratization in this period were all about inner-Party democracy. Serge challenged the decision to ban political parties, not just the ban on factions in the Party. By the time Trotsky wrote *The Revolution Betrayed* (1936) he was calling for a multi-Party system, but nine years earlier the struggle was to cleanse the Party.

Trotsky affirmed his belief that even if it were impossible to regenerate the Party from within, that impossibility must be demonstrated by trying and failing. Trotsky shared with most other Oppositionists and the

capitulators an acceptance of one-Party rule. Serge was more evasive on the
question. Serge wrote of the dangers of totalitarianism, of the consequences
of Party patriotism, of the blind loyalty which prevented his comrade
Oppositionists from taking their fight to the society at large. Serge was still
in the Party which is probably the reason for his elusive approach to the
question. After 1928 Serge stated his position more clearly.

Once the Opposition had been expelled the Soviet press overflowed with
fantastic charges against them. Although no 'insurrectionary plots' had
been contemplated in 1927, Serge wrote that the question of a Trotskyist
coup had been discussed at the end of 1925 and beginning of 1926, because
it was plainly obvious that Trotsky would have had the support of the army
and even the GPU. According to Serge, Trotsky dismissed out of hand the
possibility of a seizure of power

> out of respect for an unwritten law that forbade any recourse to military mutiny
> within a Socialist regime; for it was all too likely that power won in this way,
> even with the noblest intentions, would eventually finish in military and police
> dictatorship, which was anti-Socialist by definition.[83]

Serge agreed with Trotsky on the question of ends and means, because the
end 'commands its own means'. Trotsky himself admitted that a coup
against the leadership would have been relatively easy and bloodless, 'but
its consequence would have been a speedier triumph for the very bureaucracy and Bonapartism against which the Left Opposition took its stand'.[84]
Trotsky and Serge's arguments were powerful and command respect for
their adherence to rigorous revolutionary principles.

The capitulators were offered posts far from the nerve centres of
Leningrad and Moscow. Rakovsky was sent to Astrakhan, Radek and
Smilga to Siberia, Preobrazhensky to the Urals. Trotsky refused to agree to
such a posting and was forcibly removed from Moscow and sent to Alma-
Ata. Natalia Sedova's account of their 'removal' is poignant.[85]

A few days before Trotsky was forcibly removed Serge went to say
goodbye to the Old Man at Beloborodov's residence in the House of the
Soviets in Granovsky. Comrade Oppositionists kept a constant watch on
Trotsky while they themselves were being watched by the GPU. Serge
described 'the Bolshevik from the Urals who in 1918 had the task of deciding the lot of the Romanov dynasty and had even lately been People's Commissar of the Interior'[86] as still majestic: 'his hair standing nearly white on
his head . . . he exhaled a fierce, caged energy'. Arrest for everyone was
around the corner, and they all knew it. Serge and Trotsky discussed the
Opposition abroad. Serge's Oppositional work was to take on an even more
urgent significance since outside support must now, more than ever, be
built in the face of enforced political inactivity within the USSR. Serge had
collaborated with Magdeleine and Maurice Paz in Paris on the publication
of the journal *Contre le Courant*.[87] Trotsky had read and approved of the
journal, and told Serge he must immediately go to France to work on the

spot. Trotsky added, 'We have begun a fight to the finish, which may last for years and require many sacrifices. I am leaving for Central Asia: you try and leave for Europe. Good luck!'[88]

Serge's work with the French comrades was not simply literary. He had been the political guide of visiting French revolutionaries and had belonged to the French group of Bolsheviks in Russia. Rosmer had written of Serge earlier, in 1920,[89] describing him as the best possible guide in Russia because of his astute political sense and intimate knowledge of Russian and international affairs. When Gérard Rosenthal and Pierre Naville, two French surrealists who later became prominent Trotskyists,[90] were selected French Communist Party delegates to the Tenth Anniversary Celebration, Serge took them around Moscow. They accompanied Serge to keep watch over Joffe's body prior to the funeral, and Serge took them to visit both Zinoviev and Trotsky.

The French comrades questioned Zinoviev on the prospects for the Opposition in the International. His crude approach shocked Serge, Rosenthal and Naville: 'We are starting the Zimmerwald Movement all over again . . . we are already stronger than they were. We have cadres practically everywhere. In our time, history moves faster.'[91] Zinoviev's statement left Naville and Rosenthal incredulous: but Serge assured them that Zinoviev was serious.

Serge began to concentrate his Opposition activity on literary work in France. His relationship to the French political and literary scene was of critical importance for several reasons: it allowed him to earn a living in the years 1927 through 1936 by publishing in France (he was prevented from publishing a single word in the Soviet Union); he was provided with a platform for the ideas of the Left Opposition in Europe, making it possible to win the allegiance of comrades in France, Belgium and Spain, and to create a public for the novels he was to write in the next five years; and he was able to build a reputation for himself as a revolutionary writer and serious novelist. That public was mobilized in his defence when Serge was arrested.

Serge's writings on the Chinese revolution

The journals *Clarté*, *Contre le Courant* and *La Lutte des classes* provided Serge with his platform for disseminating the politics of the Opposition. The Opposition disagreed with Stalin on both domestic and foreign policy: the industrialization debate at home, and Comintern conduct abroad, principally in China. Accordingly, Serge's most important articles in *Clarté* were 'Vers l'industrialization'[92] and a five-part series on the Chinese revolution called 'La Lutte des classes dans la révolution chinoise'.[93]

Serge's articles on China are important not only for his rigorous analysis but because their appearance in *Clarté* turned the attention of the French-speaking Communist movement to the Chinese revolution and the debate it had provoked within the CPSU and Comintern. Thus Serge exerted strong influence on political debates in France.[94] The articles were the immediate cause of his expulsion from the Russian Communist Party. The five-part series, plus two additional articles, have now been published together as a full-length book in several languages.[95] Serge's work on China remains relatively unknown. The richness of information and the perspectives and analyses Serge developed were later to appear in the classic studies of the Chinese revolution, such as Harold Isaac's *The Tragedy of the Chinese Revolution*, and Trotsky's *Problems of the Chinese Revolution*.

Pierre Naville, who visited Serge in the Soviet Union in 1927, found Serge very preoccupied with the Chinese question.[96] Serge himself said he lectured on China to clandestine meetings of Oppositionists, discussing the problems with the official line on China, and examining Mao Tse-tung's articles, which Serge found noteworthy.[97]

Serge was well informed on events by comrades who had returned from China, including Joffe, Radek (the Rector of the Chinese University in Moscow), Zinoviev and Trotsky. The only Western sources available to Serge were *Le Temps*, the conservative French newspaper, *Deutscher Allgemeine Zeitung*, the historian René Grousset, the libertarian novelist Paul Morand, the reactionary Catholic Henri Massis, and Romain Rolland.[98]

In order to write his analysis of China Serge immersed himself in Chinese history from 1911 to 1927, relying on a rigorous Marxist analysis and above all on clear concepts of revolution. Amidst all the confusing arguments about the special class conditions in China, Serge stressed key requirements of revolution that the revolutionary Party must develop. These include the independence of the proletarian Party even if in embryo, and the hegemony of the proletariat.[99] Serge emphasized the primary, essential role of class struggle in history in China as in Russia, a fact apparently lost on Stalin's Comintern.[100] On the 'sacred union' with the national petty-bourgeoisie against the foreign imperialists, Serge quoted Lenin, reminding the reader that political power rests on economic power and in class-divided society the government can only represent the possessing classes. The 'sacred union' in practice meant the abdication of the proletariat. The bloc of four classes, Serge wrote, was a regression from Marxism to liberalism,[101] reminiscent of Menshevik confusion in 1905. Serge added that the revolutionary vanguard must be wary of adventurism and premature insurrections and most importantly, must stress the absolute necessity of creating Soviets, organs of dual power, without which the Communist Party substitutes itself for the action of the masses and must necessarily become a bureaucratic political apparatus.

Serge also urged the Chinese comrades to pay attention to China's specific social structure, and not to mechanically apply the Russian model.*

---

* In fact Serge pointed out that the Kuomintang adopted the rigid, monolithic internal structure of the Communist Party of the Soviet Union and was supported in this move by the Comintern. The opportunistic adoption of the centralized, non-democratic internal apparatus was directed *against* the Chinese Communists. Serge, 'La Revolución China', *Clarté* no. 13, 15 Sept. 1927, pp. 125–7.

The proletariat was a tiny minority in China. It would need the support of its natural allies, the peasants, but the revolutionary vanguard would have to liberate itself from the petty-bourgeois intellectual prejudices and liberalism of Sun Yat-Sen. It would also have to free itself from idealist doctrines and nationalism, and must break with the past; intellectual liberation would be necessary to have a clear communist conscience.[102]

Serge suggested that it would be impossible to go forward without a rigorous balance sheet of past errors and successes. The horrible errors of the Soviet Party and the Comintern had never been subjected to self-examination. The Kuomintang remained the Chinese section of the Comintern even after the massacres.

The tone of Serge's articles may seem didactic, but it expressed the utter frustration of the Opposition in the face of the beheading of the Chinese revolution for the sake of power plays within the Soviet Party. Serge's articles were meant to persuade and convince, to reach out and explain an alternative political point of view to the international Communist community. Although his tone was urgent, Serge's analysis was clear, rooted in empirical fact, and not in the least dogmatic. The style of argument which he adopted was similar to all Serge's political-historical works: not polemical demagoguery but careful attention to detail, the scrupulous compilation of important data which lead to clear theoretical conclusions.

Serge's Chinese articles are remarkable for their perspicacity. Twenty-two years before Mao Tse-tung led the Chinese revolution to victory (in 1949) Serge recognized the clear-sightedness of an 'unknown young communist militant' named Mao Tse-tung. Referring to two works by Mao,[103] Serge wrote that he had read many works on China, but did not encounter such clarity as Mao's anywhere else. Serge said Mao's formulations reminded him of Lenin in 1917 and 1918. He then quoted Mao:

> The leadership of the revolutionary movement must belong to the poor. Without the poor there is no revolution. Distrust of the poor is distrust of the revolution; attack them and you attack the revolution. Their revolutionary measures have been an infallible justice . . . If the completion of the democratic revolution is represented by the number ten, the part of the cities and the army must be represented by three and that of the peasants that have made the revolution in the countryside a seven.[104]

To this Serge added: 'If the leaders of the revolution had been inspired by such a clear conception, complete victory would have been possible.'[105]

What Serge saw in Mao was an uncompromising commitment to the poor, which seemed refreshing in the morass of class collaboration and kowtowing to nationalist generals. Serge's study was an application of Trotsky's theory of 'permanent revolution'. The criminal policies of the Soviet Communist Party and the Comintern had aimed at inhibiting the socialist character of the Chinese revolution, subordinating it to the interests of the bourgeois democratic nationalists.

Serge and Mao coincided in that both recognized China's particular social structure in promoting an indigenous revolution, as opposed to imposing the 'model' the Russian Party in the Comintern put forward. The tragedy of the Chinese revolution was that in the world communist movement it took a back seat to the internal struggle in the Russian Party.

The Left Opposition and the Chinese revolution

The accuracy of his study on China in predicting defeat surprised even Serge. The Left Opposition had effectively propagandized about the regime's disastrous policies in China throughout 1926 and 1927. Serge had said that 'China galvanized us all'.[106] China's ascendant revolution in 1927 represented for the Opposition the next vital struggle for the international extension of the revolution, an affirmation of Lenin's theses on the national and colonial question.

The Opposition's arguments on China proved embarrassing for the regime which desperately sought a victory to use as a showpiece at the Fifteenth Party Congress. Chinese masses had advanced from victory to victory in 1927; Hong Kong was blockaded by Canton, a revolutionary republic had been proclaimed in the south of China, and Soviet advisors were sent in.[107] This coincided with the defeat of the Opposition in the USSR and the consummation of Stalin and the bureaucracy in power. Serge explained the thrust of Chinese policy as defined by a new social stratum,[108] which had driven the workers from power in the USSR, leaving only the name 'proletariat' in its dictatorship.[109] Serge dared to suggest that the new functionaries in power feared victory in China more than they desired it.* Stalin's policy commanding entry into the Kuomintang by the Chinese Communist Party (CCP) 'first paralyses it, then compromises and strangles it'.[110] The Opposition's warnings were ignored. In fact they were not even heard. The Comintern proscribed the Chinese revolutionists from forming Soviets, arming themselves, or encouraging peasant revolts. The Chinese workers and peasants were led from one ambush to another. Stalin's 'bloc of four classes' policy,† wrote Serge, was a travesty of Lenin's revolutionary policy.

---

* Trotsky would later say this assessment was too radical.

† Stalin's policy viewed the Kuomintang as the embodiment of a 'bloc of four classes' – bourgeoisie, petty-bourgeoisie, peasantry and proletariat – and therefore could be a government located above social classes. Stalin, inspired by Bukharin, claimed this policy would encourage a socialist revolution in China by means of penetration into the Kuomintang. Instead it sealed the revolutionaries' fate. Their blood flowed freely, largely due to Stalin's consideration of China's insignificant national bourgeoisie, his fight with the Opposition, and his disastrous leadership of the Comintern. See Souvarine, *Stalin*, pp. 440–43, Deutscher, *The Prophet Unarmed*, pp. 323–7, Serge, 'La Revolución China', *From Lenin to Stalin*, pp. 45–9, *Russia Twenty Years After*, pp. 255–7.

With the debacle in Shanghai, protest mounted in the Soviet Union. Serge, filled with despair, took his five minutes to speak out in his branch meeting. He shouted 'The prestige of the General Secretary is infinitely more precious to him than the blood of the Chinese proletariat!' Serge wrote that a 'paroxysm of hatred' swelled up, and the hysterical audience was on the brink of lynching the Oppositionists.[111]

Stalin, needing a victory to counterbalance the bloody defeats, sent his cousin Lominadze along with Heinz Neumann to foment an uprising in Canton to coincide with the opening of the Fifteenth Party Congress in December 1927. After forcing the CCP against their will into the bourgeois Kuomintang, forbidding the creation of Soviets, holding the agrarian revolution in check and preventing the CCP from arming the workers, Stalin switched course. Now he urged the CCP to immediately bid for power by staging an insurrection. C.L.R. James, in a discussion of the history of the Left Opposition with Leon Trotsky in April 1939, quoted Victor Serge on Stalin's zig-zag, saying the Commune was necessary 'if only for a quarter of an hour' for the sake of the Sixth World Congress of the Comintern.[112] Souvarine wrote in his biography of Stalin that Stalin needed 'a victory bulletin as an argument against the "pessimism of the Opposition". The result is a revolutionary rearguard action, isolated, artificial and doomed to failure.'[113]

Canton blazed in glory just long enough for the Soviet press to print rapturous proclamations of triumph. Their short-lived victory bathed Stalin in adulation through the first two days of the Congress. The next day the Cantonese Commune was drowned in blood.* While Chinese revolutionaries were murdered *en masse*, the Congress pronounced the expulsion of the Opposition. Serge said this was the first time the bureaucratic regime

> stubbornly sabotaged a prodigious revolutionary movement because its own (national) interests, contrary to those of the proletariat, forced it to . . . The Comintern untiringly approved everything, without having to overcome the slightest nausea when it stood before the deepest pools of blood, the most enormous or the most pettifogging knavery.[114]

Trotsky's discussion with C.L.R. James mentioned above presents a different slant on this issue. The thrust of the argument of Serge and Souvarine (and James) is that the bureaucracy, acting in its own interests, sabotaged the Chinese revolution. Trotsky wrote in *My Life* that the 'epigones'

---

* Serge noted that the 'subalterns' Lominadze and Neumann were not treated kindly for their services in China. Lominadze became an Oppositionist after the Chinese events and committed suicide in Sverdlovsk in 1935 on the eve of his arrest; Neumann disappeared in the purges of 1937, having taken refuge in the USSR from the Nazis. His wife was turned over to the Gestapo after the Nazi–Soviet Pact. Serge, *From Lenin to Stalin*, p. 49, and *Memoirs*, p. 173.

leadership in China trampled on all the traditions of Bolshevism'[115] but that they were anxious for the success of the revolution. Trotsky affirmed that Voroshilov, Chicherin and others, all Stalinists, sat on a committee with Trotsky and considered Trotsky's attitude too pessimistic. Yet the crux of the difference, as Trotsky enunciated it to James in 1939, was that Stalin and the others genuinely wanted to push a dictatorship of the proletariat and peasantry* onto what they believed was a bourgeois democratic revolution in China. In other words, Serge's position, shared by James, led to the conclusion that the bureaucracy could not support a proletarian revolution because it was a bureaucracy, whereas Trotsky, while agreeing that bureaucrats acquired 'bureaucratic habits in thinking' and thus 'proposed to restrain the peasants . . . so as not to frighten the generals',[116] nevertheless saw Stalin's position as one of misunderstanding the dynamic of both the Russian and the Chinese revolutions. He said Stalin and Bukharin were overwhelmed by events in China just as they were in Russia in 1917 until Lenin came. Trotsky continued:

> In different writings of theirs you will see passages that show that they never understood . . . their bureaucratic habits affected their thinking and they reverted to their previous position. They even enshrined it in the programme of the Comintern: proletarian revolution for Germany, dictatorship of the proletariat and peasantry for semicolonial countries, etc.[117]

In 1939 Trotsky wished to stress that in 1927 the degeneration of the revolution was still in process, not yet completed. Stalin acted not just out of embryonic class antagonism, but out of a crude understanding of Marxism, which had earlier, in March 1917, caused him to miss the boat in the thick of rapidly unfolding revolutionary events. Trotsky believed Bukharin was likewise equally confused (a point Serge often suggested as well), and this was clearly apparent in his wide swings – from dialectician to pragmatist, from Left Communist, to Right Oppositionist.

As for the effect of the Chinese defeat on the inner Party struggle, Trotsky recalled scores of Oppositionists visiting him in the offices of the Chief Concessions Committee in the wake of the Chinese bloodbath. He wrote that the younger comrades were certain that the bankruptcy of Stalin's policy was bound to bring victory to the Opposition. Trotsky wrote:

> I was obliged to pour many a bucket of cold water over the hot heads of my young friends – and over some not so young. I tried to show them that the opposition could not rise on the defeat of the Chinese revolution. The fact that our forecast had proved correct might attract one thousand, five thousand, or even ten thousand new supporters to us. But for the millions the significant thing

---

* This formulation is not accidental; the clear conception of the hegemony of the proletariat, put forward by Serge and the Opposition, is muddled in Stalin's 'twin dictatorship'.

was not our forecast, but the fact of the crushing of the Chinese proletariat. After the defeat of the German revolution in 1923, after the break-down of the English general strike in 1925 [sic], the new disaster in China would only intensify the disappointment of the masses in the international revolution. And it was this same disappointment that served as the chief psychological source for Stalin's policy of national-reformism.[118]

The Opposition vanquished

Serge explained that the defeat of the Opposition (and hence the working class) by the 'parvenus' could only be understood by taking account of the twin defeats of the revolution – Germany in 1923, China in 1927. Souvarine gave more weight to the Opposition's own mistakes.[119] Serge, admitting that the Opposition had 'committed a number of secondary mistakes', considered Souvarine's viewpoint too detached. In particular Serge wrote it was unjust to compare Trotsky's attitude to the Party with Robespierre's deference to the Convention of Thermidor. Souvarine had written: 'In both cases, the actual power of empirical politicians triumphed, by a cynical combination of force and astuteness, over doctrinaires poorly equipped with a practical sense'.[120] Although Serge would later agree that Party patriotism clouded the sense of the Opposition, in 1936 he answered Souvarine:

> Isn't it plain that the practical sense of revolutionists is basically different from that of the empirical politicians *who represent other social formations?* The practical sense of Liebknecht has little in common with that of Noske. The practical sense of revolutionists who deem it necessary to fling themselves under the chariot wheels because it is in the higher interests of the proletariat, is just as different from that of the parvenus to whom the morrows of the great defeats of the working class offer invaluable opportunities for better installing themselves in power. Souvarine ought to know this, after all, for he, too, was a 'doctrinary' vanquished by the 'empiricists' because of his devotion to the International of the great years.[121]

Arrest

Preobrazhensky met with Serge and warned him to stop publication of his article on Canton or risk years in jail.[122] Serge was convinced he would be deported anyway and went ahead, although as a precaution he let a Parisian comrade put his signature to the article devoted to the Canton Commune.[123]

Preobrazhensky was right, and Serge was soon called up before the Party's Control Commission. He was expelled from the Party, ostensibly for calling the decision of the Fifteenth Congress to expel the Opposition a 'grave error'. The astonished Control Commission of the Leningrad Central District, headed by the tired old worker Karol, expelled Serge forthwith: the Party Congress was not capable of error![124]

Serge was arrested three months later. In the interim the killings began.

The first Oppositionist to be killed was Albert Heinrichsen, a worker in the Putilov factory in the Leningrad suburb of Narva and the former commissar of a Red battalion at the front. When the GPU came to arrest him he flew into a rage and said 'Ah, you have come to the point of locking up the Leninists! And you aren't ashamed of yourselves! Thermidorians!' He was taken by force and the next day his wife was informed he had committed suicide. She insisted on seeing his body, and when she finally found it the bruises and mutilation made it clear that he had been savagely beaten. Serge and others pressed for an official investigation to no avail. This was in December 1927 or January 1928. Serge's comrade and good friend Vassily Chadayev followed in August 1928, assassinated on the highway near Kuban with the complicity of the authorities. Chadayev had written on the agrarian problem, advocating efforts toward collectivization. After six months in prison, he was sent on assignment to Kuban by *Krasnaya Gazeta*. His dispatches exposed racketeering and corruption. His reward for his honesty was a hail of dum-dum bullets.[125] At about the same time Trotsky's secretary George Valentinovich Butov died after carrying on a hunger strike for fifty days. Serge noted that when the Lord Mayor of Cork died from hunger strike the civilized world was shocked. Butov's fate remained unremarked.[126]

Serge was arrested in March 1928.[127] Two agents came to his door at midnight and made a beeline for his translations of Lenin. Serge ironically commented on the seizure of Lenin's writings to which the soldier replied: 'Don't joke, we are Leninists too, you know.' Serge remarked: 'Perfect: we were all Leninists together.' After an all-night search Serge was taken to jail. Serge commented in the *Memoirs* that his seven-year-old son Vlady wept not in fear but anger. Vlady recalled the event as his first 'Trotskyist act': he rescued a portrait of Trotsky from under the heels of the GPU agents ransacking the apartment.[128]

Serge's first Soviet arrest was to last seven to eight weeks. He was held in the old House of Arrest. His warder had 'taken Trotsky out for his walks after the 1905 Revolution'.[129] Serge was held without charge in a tiny cell meant for solitary confinement but crammed with four prisoners. Serge wrote that the prison was packed with victims targeted by the 'hated functionaries who were obsessives, maniacs, and torturers by profession'. Serge passed the time rereading Dostoevsky. Serge determined that he would not take part in any 'recantation', and he was soon released with the proviso he not take part in 'anti-Soviet activity'.

Serge owed his release to the efforts of his Parisian friends who had caused enough commotion to embarrass 'high circles'. *Clarté*, now published under the title *Lutte de Classes*, published an editorial protesting his arrest and the persecution of Oppositionists, and attacking the bureaucratic regime. The editorial outlined Serge's political past, the many articles he had contributed to a wide variety of French journals and his years of service to the revolution now bent on persecuting the Opposition for its opinions.[130]

Not all French Communist intellectuals mobilized on his behalf, however. Once he was released Serge's erstwhile comrade Vaillant-Couterior reported in *L'Humanité* that Serge had been treated well. Barbusse let him know that during his imprisonment he had removed Serge's name from the masthead of *Monde*.

Although Serge admired some of Barbusse's prose, he found him a slippery character. After meeting Barbusse in the Hotel Metropole at the Tenth Anniversary celebrations, just prior to Serge's arrest, Serge commented:

> Right from the first I saw him as a quite different kind of person; concerned above all not to be involved, not to see anything . . . all with the aim of making himself the accomplice of the winning side! Since it was not yet known whether the struggle had been definitively settled, he had just dedicated a book, at great length, to Trotsky . . . When I told him about the persecution, he pretended to have a headache or not to hear . . . My jaws shuddered as I realized that I was face to face with hypocrisy itself.[131]

Nonetheless Serge felt compelled to answer Barbusse's opportunistic action. He carried on a correspondence with Barbusse, which was later published in 1937 in *Les Humbles* as 'Trois lettres de Victor Serge à Henri Barbusse'. The letters recount Serge's experience of arrest, interrogation and release, and defend his Oppositional views. Barbusse's letters suggested that the campaigns for Serge's release had harmed the Soviet Union and that Serge was somehow responsible. Serge diligently answered Barbusse's barbs, blaming the regime for its treatment of the Opposition.

The treatment that Barbusse and other French 'comrades' had meted out to Serge – out of cowardice, complicity and slippery opportunism – contrasted sharply with the lonely and courageous struggle of the vanquished Opposition. The dark period was just beginning, and the men with whom Serge had shared struggles for the last decade were one by one disappearing secretly to the far corners of the USSR. The stage of struggle just commencing would be especially bitter. While prison and exile were nothing new to these seasoned revolutionaries, those now persecuting them were their former comrades, using the state which they had helped to create.

4

Stalinization 1928–33: the bureaucratic counter-revolution, solitary struggles in precarious freedom

'Our intellectual activity is prodigious, our political action nil'

If the years 1926 to 1928 represented the 'deadlock of the revolution' for Serge, the years 1928 to 1933 comprised his 'years of resistance' followed by three years (1933–36) of captivity. His personal experience in those years illuminates the struggle of the Opposition against the Party as well as the struggle of the individual against the 'relentless, overwhelming pressure of a totalitarian system'.[1]

The year 1928 was a watershed in Soviet political development and a turning point in Serge's life. He was expelled from the Bolshevik Party, though he remained a Left Oppositionist, and was arrested that spring. The arrest was short and inconsequential compared to his other periods of captivity but clearly marked a new period in Serge's life. The sort of open political activity which had occupied him for years was now denied him. Ten years in the Bolshevik Party had followed thirteen years in Europe, six of them spent in prison, as an anarchist, syndicalist and socialist.

Another significant event marked this period of Serge's life: he suffered an attack of intestinal occlusion just days after his release from prison. His physical condition had never been strong, probably due to a life of privation from childhood.* Serge felt he had narrowly escaped death. Not only did Serge suffer a 'political death' in 1928 but he nearly expired as well. Having had so close a brush with death, Serge determined to devote the rest of his life to writing. He sketched out in his mind a series of documentary novels about these 'unforgettable times'.[2]

---

* His childhood was extremely poor; Serge described meals of stale bread dunked in coffee; his younger brother did not survive the Spartan regime, dying of starvation at the age of nine. Victor Serge, *Memoirs of a Revolutionary*, London, Oxford University Press, 1963, p. 5. Serge's five years in a French prison also contributed to his weakened physical condition, as did his years in Orenburg, later.

Serge's decision to become a serious writer was deliberate, and supported by those around him. Trotsky and Serge had discussed Serge's literary intervention in the French Left. Vlady, Serge's son, recalled Nikos Kazantzakis' words to Serge when he stayed with the family in Leningrad six months before Serge's arrest: he insisted that Serge was a *writer*, a novelist, first and foremost. Vlady felt Kazantzakis' words were well taken by Serge.* Serge wrote of his decision, taken in a moment of 'rich and tranquil inner lucidity' at death's door.[3] Guided by political considerations, Serge decided to bear witness to the Bolshevik experience.

Serge explained how he had given up writing literature when he entered the Russian Revolution. Serge believed the needs of the revolution precluded 'serious writing'. As editor of the French *Inprekorr*, and a frequent contributor to various French journals Serge chronicled and analysed the heady years of revolution, civil war and the German revolution. Yet he considered that this work contained 'nothing of value' since 'there was such a striking discrepancy between my sensibility and my opinions'.† Party journalism was not serious writing in Serge's estimation – a harsh self-critique.

Now, ten years later, Serge anticipated a long reactionary phase. He concluded that since he was 'refused the right to join the work of industrialization except at the price of my freedom of opinion, I could provide a serviceable testimony on these times'.[4]

Writing, for Serge, was something to do only when one was unable to fight actively. He had renounced writing when he joined the revolution, only returning to it when open political action was proscribed. Serge always produced political journalism as part of the political struggle. Writing literature, however, took a back seat to his 'duty' as 'dictated by history itself'.[5] Serge would now bring the political maturity gained during his years of struggle to his writing. No longer bound by Party discipline Serge was freed from caution, Aesopian language and the 'striking discrepancy between my sensibility and my opinions'. He set to work on *Year One of the Russian Revolution*, gathered material for *Year Two* and finished *Men in Prison*, his first novel.

Serge wrote with a mission: to expose and analyse the significance of the rise of Stalinism. He worked continually until he died, churning out novels,

---

* In private conversation, 17 May 1987, Mexico City. Ironically, Kazantzakis returned from Russia feeling sorry he and Serge had not enjoyed a closer rapport. In her biography of Nikos Kazantzakis, Helen Kazantzakis (his wife) wrote that Kazantzakis thought Serge 'a tried and tested revolutionary . . . [who] had translated Trotsky . . . had known Lenin intimately from the early days, and all of Lenin's comrades. You could have confidence in him.' Helen Kazantzakis, *Nikos Kazantzakis, a Biography Based on His Letters*, Berkeley, Calif., Creative Arts Book, 1983, pp. 222–3.

† Serge *Memoirs*, p. 262. Serge's articles in *Inprekorr* during the German revolutionary process are a good example of this 'discrepancy'.

histories, pamphlets and polemics. In the years 1928 to 1936, while still in the Soviet Union, Serge wrote four novels, two short stories, one volume of poetry, and six works of history, politics and literary theory; he translated novels and poems and seven volumes of history, politics, theory and memoirs. Considering the difficult circumstances under which Serge laboured, his prodigious output is extraordinary.

Serge resolved to write a certain way. He eschewed the personal and sentimental; he wrote about great historical events, in which the actions of the masses, not a single character, drove the plot. Serge's historical and political works are partisan yet scholarly, coherent and analytical. They rest on first-hand knowledge as well as immersion in source material. Confessing that historical work did not satisfy him entirely and demanded time and access to resources he could not afford, Serge searched for a literary form which allowed a larger 'scope for showing men as they really live, dismantling their inner workings and penetrating deep into their souls'.[6] He turned to literature but not for its fame or fortune. His writing had a 'mightier justification':

> as a means of expressing to men what most of them live inwardly without being able to express, as a means of communion, a testimony to the vast flow of life through us, whose essential aspects we must try to fix for the benefit of those who will come after us.[7]

During the five years Serge spent in precarious liberty in Moscow and Leningrad the fate of his literary writings in Western Europe paralleled his own life. The Left in the West boycotted his work, finding it too critical; bourgeois critics found it too revolutionary and withheld public comment. Within the Soviet Union Serge was told point-blank: 'You can produce a masterpiece every year, but so long as you are not back in the line of the Party, not a line of yours will see the light!'[8] Not one of Serge's books was printed in the Soviet Union before it disintegrated in 1991.[9]

Serge was not singled out for boycott. Only Soviet writers who could conform to Stalinist strictures were published. Serge agreed with Max Eastman that these were 'writers in uniform'. Censorship mutilated creative expression.*

The history of annihilation of non-conformist writers in the years of the Great Terror has yet to be written. Some writers were resurrected during Gorbachev's *glasnost*, but there is so far no published account of their collective fate. Serge sketched what happened to some in *La Tragédie des écrivains soviétiques* (*Conscience de l'écrivain*) published in Paris in January 1947 and reprinted in English in *Now*, no. 7 (1947). In it Serge mentioned the fate of certain 'master-writers' of Soviet literature such as Boris Pilniak, Isaac Babel, Voronski, Ivanov-Razumnik and Osip Mandelstam. How hundreds

---

* Serge himself translated Maria Shaginyan's novel *Hydrocentral*, a product of bureaucratic conformity.

of lesser-known writers vanished is known only to the secret service of the political police. Serge added that *perhaps* they knew and only perhaps as 'the police chiefs who made the purges have themselves disappeared. The rule is that once the man is suppressed, his works are eliminated, his name is no longer pronounced; it is erased from the past and even from history'.[10]

Serge characterized the atmosphere for writers in this period as one of 'overpowering, sickening absurdity'. Writers were 'compelled to fanatical obedience' in their 'prestigious' meetings of the writers' union. Serge recalled the confused reaction of the great Bavarian anarchist poet and playwright Ernst Toller, when 'Young men of letters, who were none the less practically unlettered, suggested the formation of "mopping-up squads" to go to the second-hand bookshops and remove from them historical works which the Leader had just attacked'.[11]

Serge was entirely out of place among such *literati* and his presence both compromised and reproached them. He made his living working for the Lenin Institute as a translator of Lenin's collected works into French, although as an Oppositionist his name was kept out of the published volumes. His translations were 'checked, line by line, by experts charged with the task of uncovering possible sabotage in the disposition of semicolons'.[12]

The 'inner counter-revolution': from NEP to nightmare

By 1928 the combination of the lack of industrial policy and the growth of the private sector in agriculture led to a grain crisis.[13] The low prices peasants were offered for their grain coupled with the high prices charged for scarce industrial goods were a powerful disincentive to produce more than the peasant needed for himself and his family. Then a series of poor harvests threatened both the state's export plans and food supplies. The peasants boycotted grain requisitions and Stalin responded by ordering extraordinary measures to collect the grain. Red Army soldiers began to take the grain from the peasants at gunpoint.

Serge wrote in *Soviets 1929* that there were five real causes of the crisis: first, the general poverty of the Russian peasants and the backward state of agriculture; second, the population growth from 135 million in 1914 to 145 million in 1926,* third, the weakness of industry, which meant scarcity of quality goods and high prices for manufactured goods compared to low prices offered for the peasant's grain; fourth, the effects of the bureaucratic regime in the countryside which allowed the real kulaks to conceal their wealth; and fifth, the conscious resistance of the rich peasants, sustained by the majority of cultivators, because 'All peasants are at ease . . . who dream unconsciously of becoming a little capitalist'.[14]

---

* In times of peace growth would be two to three million per year; this period included world war, revolution, civil war and famine.

The grain crisis predicted by the Left Opposition broke out less than three months after the expulsion of the Opposition. *Pravda* declared in February 1928 that the peasants refused to deliver their grain to the state because the price was too low.[15]

Stalin's Central Committee responded with Article 107 of the Penal Code on concealment of stocks.[16] Requisitioning began and fields were stripped of their crops. Reminiscent of the civil-war period and War Communism, 'Communists were found at the roadsides with their skulls split open. The stacks of confiscated grain were set on fire. There was no fodder at all.'*

Serge used both the terms 'requisitioning' and 'confiscated grain' to discuss the *razverstka*, or forced procurement of grain. Moshe Lewin called the *razverstka* an 'emergency measure', 'the allocation by administrative order of quantities of produce to be delivered by households, irrespective of the views of the latter'.[17]

Stalin's brutal bureaucratic response to the grain crisis set a precedent, leading his regime from one adventure to another, each one increasing human and social costs. The issue of power remained paramount. Opposition was settled first by deportation, later by prison or death. Serge noted that Stalin was caught in a blind alley with no policy, but was 'dominated by the instinct of preservation'.[18]

As Stalin was ridding himself of Party opposition, he suddenly faced massive peasant resistance – more than 300 centres of peasant insurrection flaring up simultaneously in Soviet Eurasia[19] – and declared war on the peasantry, designating them as kulaks to be wiped out as a class.

Serge devoted a chapter to the grain crisis and the kulaks in his *Soviets 1929*, as well as a chapter on collectivization and industrialization in his *Destiny of a Revolution* of 1936–37. In the 1929 work, Serge explained the background to the crisis and restated the solutions offered by the Left, Right and Centre of the Party.

To break the considerable resistance of the peasants, Stalin embarked on a war against the class enemy and began mass deportation of the so-called kulaks and their families to the icy north. In a brilliant little book, *From Lenin to Stalin*, Serge demonstrated cause and effect in the Soviet experience, showing how the regime could not escape the consequences of a policy, or of not having a policy. Serge stated that it is

> a hundred times untrue that the end justifies the means . . . Every end requires its own means, and an end is only obtained by the appropriate means . . . More personal well-being, more liberty, fewer lies, more dignity, more respect for

---

* Serge, *Memoirs*, p. 246. Lars Lih, in 'Bolshevik *Razverstka* and War Communism', *Slavic Review*, winter 1986, discussed how the 'quota assessment' – his preferred translation of *razverstka* – was carried out during War Communism, and how the term has been misinterpreted by many historians as requisitioning or confiscation, the terms Serge employed.

humanity. The socialism which proceeds otherwise gives in to a sort of inner counter-revolution, discredits itself and risks suicide.[20]

Economic factors plus bad leadership led to the crisis of 1928 and to the terrible solutions which destroyed the soul of socialism. Stalin spent years defeating Trotsky while industry stagnated, and NEP men and rich peasants grew comfortable. By 1928 the peasant lost his incentive to sell grain or even sow, since his crops were likely to be stolen. The political struggle within the Party overshadowed everything for Stalin. Because the Opposition was a threat to his power, he rejected Opposition policy and ignored the dangers that policy addressed.

As Serge noted in his 1936 study, *Russia Twenty Years After*, requisitioning met with fierce resistance, especially since the requisitions were illegal and ran counter to the often-repeated promises the Party had made to the peasants. Stalin's response to the resistance was to dispossess the peasant and force him onto the collective farm.

Serge maintained that no one could have predicted wholesale, forced collectivization. The idea was madness, especially since the collective farms were not prepared. The very idea of collectivizing agriculture had been to make it advantageous to the peasants and increase agricultural production. The plan, in discussion since 1926, envisioned collectivizing only as much crop area as could be supplied with agricultural machinery. The whole purpose was to industrialize agricultural production, providing an attractive alternative to the small, primitive farms of the peasantry. The *kolkhoz* without tractors made no sense. Indeed, Serge referred to collective farm activity as 'large-scale motoculture'.[21] He argued that 'this would have been the only, the genuine socialist policy and the peasants would have promptly convinced themselves of the benefits of the new mode of production over small-scale and primitive cultivation'.[22]

Stalin's actions, Serge pointed out, were not dictated by the interests of the 'community' but by those of the emerging bureaucracy. Stalin declared war on the resisters, 'designated as enemies of the people . . . [to] be "liquidated as a class"'. Those now labelled kulaks included many peasants, Serge observed, who had fought well for the Soviets. Now they were suddenly driven from their homes

> packed together in cattle carts and sent in trainloads to the subarctic tundras, the forests of Siberia, the marshes of Narym, the sandy wastes of Kazakhstan. All the deserts of the vast Russia are going to swarm with little white crosses. Several million peasants will undergo this fate. It will be the greatest transplantation of populations that history has ever known and its concrete details are atrocious.[23]

Quoting the Russian scholar Prokopovich, who used admittedly unreliable official statistics (at the time Prokopovich was making his study the statisticians were being imprisoned and shot) Serge estimated that by the time collectivization was completed in 1936, five million peasant families had disappeared.* The bureaucratic policy had terrible consequences for millions; Serge described how people had resisted. He recounted the story a comrade had told him about some women in a Kuban Cossack village:

> They had undressed, thinking that nobody would dare to take them, nude, from their dwellings and lead them to the train by force. The young communists, the Party and GPU men, surrounded the village in which all the men had previously been arrested, dragged from their homes the dishevelled women and their kids, crazed with fear and rage, and brutally drove this naked flock to the station . . . The children, the old folk, and the feeble succumbed en masse. The newspapers, however, overflowed with copy on the collectivist enthusiasm of the agrarians. In *Monde* I read the shocking prose of Barbusse on the miracle of the collectivization.†

The resulting devastation of agriculture is by now well known. Peasants slaughtered their livestock and burnt their grain. The country went from poverty to famine. There was no bread for workers in the cities nor for soldiers in the army. Bread-cards were issued, wages dropped, the black market grew and industry was affected. Total collectivization threatened utter disaster, so that even Stalin had to call a halt when it had reached 68 per cent in March 1930, at the height of frenzy. His famous article 'Dizzy with Success'[24] called a temporary retreat.‡ As entire populations were

---

* Serge, *Memoirs*, p. 247. Serge's suggested figure that five million peasant families were deported was confirmed by Moshe Lewin in his study on Soviet peasants. Lewin affirmed that five million households and ten million peasants were affected, although this figure indicates that peasant households only contained on average two people. Moshe Lewin, *Russian Peasants and Soviet Power, A Study of Collectivization*, Evanston, Northwestern University Press, 1968, pp. 507–8. More recent scholarship on collectivization both in the West (Robert Conquest's study on the artificially created famine, *The Harvest of Sorrow*, New York and Oxford, Oxford University Press, 1986) and within the former Soviet Union suggests even greater numbers. In a Soviet study reported in 1988, Soviet sources indicate some ten million peasant *families* (more than two people) were affected. See for example, Dr Igor Bestuzhev-Lada, 'Pravda I Tol'ko Pravdu', *Nedelya* 1–7 Feb. 1988, pp. 14–15.

† *Victor Serge: Russia Twenty Years After*, edited by Susan Weissman, New York, Humanities Press, 1996, pp. 168–9. As a footnote to this barbarous episode, the Central Committee member in charge of beating naked women with rifle-butts as they were driven to be loaded in cattle-cars – comrade Sheboldayev – was shot in 1937 for his enthusiasm. Serge, *Memoirs*, p. 247.

‡ Igor Vasilyevich Bestuzhev-Lada (doctor of history, head of a sector of the Russian Academy of Sciences' Institute of Sociological Research, and Professor at Moscow State University) wrote in *Nedelya*, 11–17 April 1988 (pp. 10–11): 'It is clear that the article "Dizzy with Success" (2 March 1930) was simply a tactical manoeuvre.' He questioned, therefore, why the policy was continued once its disastrous, 'catastrophic' nature had become clear. Later in the same

deported, Serge noted that peasants rushed toward the borders of China, Poland and Romania, risking machine-gun fire to cross. 'In a message to the Government, the Abkhazes of the Southern Caucasus offer it all their possessions; with oriental politeness, they thank the government for all the benefits it has heaped upon them and ask only one favour: permission to emigrate to Turkey.'[25]

With the publication of Stalin's reproach to forced collectivization in March 1930, permission had effectively been given to leave the *kolkhoz*. The peasants left *en masse*: between March and June 1930 half of the newly 'collectivized' peasants abandoned the collective farms. Had the collectivization drive not been halted there would have been no spring planting. Once the crops were harvested in the autumn, the collectivization campaign was renewed with vigour, although the *artel* (allowing a private plot, cow and chickens) was now made the basic unit. Scarcity resulting from the peasants' dislocation turned to famine by 1932. The problem of reduced harvests resulting from peasant resistance and dislocation was exacerbated by the state confiscation of grain for the cities, the army and export.

Such were the results of Stalin's attempt to destroy an enemy class. Trotsky had noted that an entire class could not be eliminated by administrative methods, but 'only by a change in technology and the mode of production . . . It was no more possible to create large-scale mechanized agriculture out of wooden ploughs and kulak horses than it was to create a ship by adding up fishing boats'.* Serge agreed with Trotsky. Stalin and Bukharin, following the logic of 'socialism in one country', had sought to overcome the urban–rural contradiction through the mechanism of trade

---

article, Dr Bestuzhev-Lada wondered whether Stalin's shooting of Yagoda and Yezhov was not again 'diversionary manoeuvres' in the spirit of the article 'Dizzy with Success', suggesting that both were attempts to 'adjust the process' rather than any real retreat.

* Leon Trotsky, *Byulleten' Oppozitsii*, IX (1930), p. 3. Quoted in Richard Day's article 'Leon Trotsky on the Problems of the Smychka and Forced Collectivization', in *Critique* 13, 1981, pp. 55–68. In an interesting variation of Trotsky's quote, Anton Ciliga cited Trotsky as having said: 'By putting together the poor hoes and the poor nags of the *mujiks* one no more creates large agricultural estates than one creates a large steamer by putting together a lot of fishing boats'. Anton Ciliga, *The Russian Enigma*, London, The Labour Book Service, 1940, p. 270 (first published in Paris in 1938 as *Au Pays du grand mensonge*). Finally, Serge quotes Trotsky in *From Lenin to Stalin*, p. 66: 'From his exile in Constantinople, Trotsky never ceased to protest severely against what he considered a "fatal economic adventure". No more than you can build a transatlantic liner by assembling hundreds or thousands of fishing smacks – he wrote with bitter irony – can you create modern, large-scale agriculture by forcing small farmers to pool together their ploughs, their oxen, and their chickens . . . True socialist collectivization must be brought to the farmer by showing him the unquestionable advantage of its mechanization and planning.'

and finance between the sectors. Serge understood, like Trotsky, that the industrialization of agriculture was the key to resolving the urban–rural contradiction.

Serge bemoaned the absence of socialist spirit and the disregard of the Marxist classics, especially Engels' ideas on the socialist attitude to small-peasant property. Serge recalled Lenin's recommendations: make an ally of the middle peasant, fight the rich peasant who is becoming a small capitalist, but do not coerce the peasant masses.[26] Lenin's policy towards the peasants during the civil war, despite mistakes and abuse, led to victory; Stalin's crude parody in 1930–31 led to disaster.

Understanding the interrelation of industry and agriculture was fundamental to the formulation of policy. Stalin's dictatorial reactive agricultural policy led to distortions in industry. Total collectivization, unforeseen and unplanned, created a need for giant factories to produce agricultural machinery. This used up resources intended for other sectors. As Serge observed, collectivization produced a shortage of raw materials, hostility, a ruined agriculture, and destroyed the plan for industry. As hostile peasants hoarded grain and destroyed their livestock, agricultural output dwindled;* Stalin demanded higher quotas and extracted every last grain in Ukraine for the cities and export. This state-organized famine killed seven million peasants in 1932 and 1933.[27] Serge wrote about this atrocity while it was being widely denied in the West.† He noted wryly that collectivization had produced anarchy rather than a plan, quoting Souvarine's expression, 'the anarchy of the plan'. Serge wrote: 'Instead of applying a political pattern, Stalin is reduced to improvisations'.[28]

The period of forcible collectivization is being re-evaluated by scholars both in the West and in the former USSR. Serge's writings on the beginning of the Stalinist system are the work of a revolutionary documentarian, analyst, witness and participant. He analysed Stalin's effects on ordinary

---

* Trotsky had predicted that all-round collectivization would destroy incentives and lead to 'all-round weeds in the fields'. *Byulleten' Oppozitsii*, XXXI (1932), p. 6, quoted in Day, *Leon Trotsky*, p. 67.

† On the fiftieth anniversary of the famine in 1983, the whole story of the suppression of the facts by prominent Western journalists such as Walter Duranty of the *New York Times* and Louis Fischer of the *New Republic* came out. Few correspondents reported the truth about the famine, although it was thought that Duranty had sold out or the Soviets had something on him. One of the exceptions was the reporting by Malcolm Muggeridge of the *Manchester Guardian* who wrote a series of articles describing the horrors of the famine in Ukraine and the North Caucasus. Andrew Smith, in his memoir, *I Was a Soviet Worker* (New York, E.P. Dutton Inc., 1936) wrote of a boat trip on the Volga which passed through the starving hamlets of the countryside, described in grisly detail. The Western coverage of the famine is discussed in Conquest, *Harvest of Sorrow*, pp. 308–21.

Soviet citizens. In Serge's analysis, collectivization and forced industrial development were part of the attack arsenal used against the whole of Soviet society by the emerging Stalinist elite. Serge's writings on industrialization are extremely penetrating. As early as 1929 Serge pointed out that the Soviets were creating useless factories, wasting tremendous human and social resources. His analysis is contradictory – not just because reality itself was contradictory, but because of internal contradictions in the Left Opposition's analysis which they could not have seen at the time.

Defeated revolutionists in precarious liberty

At the beginning of 1928 Serge remained alone with Alexandra Bronstein, Trotsky's first wife, in the Leningrad branch of the Opposition. There had already been many arrests, thanks in large measure to effective GPU infiltration.* Serge believed that the only way to survive would be to work openly, intransigently, in a loyal opposition to the Party which was strangling itself. Trotsky was in exile in Alma-Ata, writing that the state and Party were still proletarian, to be defended. Serge's thoughts were filled with bitter irony; in the *Memoirs* he noted that nobody was willing to admit that the bureaucratic state 'had emerged from our own hands to crush us' and that the idea held throughout the Party and the Opposition – that the only way to serve the Revolution was through the Party – consigned the Opposition to 'rebel and turn us against ourselves . . . We were defeated by Party patriotism.'[29] Serge wrote these lines in 1941, and it is not possible to know if he was projecting his thoughts from 1941 backward to 1928, but if it is true that he advocated an open, loyal opposition to the Bolshevik Party in 1928 (albeit without an organization) Serge was indeed a maverick; other Oppositionists wavered between capitulation and clandestinity, with a view to being reintegrated into the Party.

The Stalinist counter-revolution made the question academic. Open political agitation was simply not possible. Serge wrote that the leaders of the defeated Opposition discussed setting up a strong clandestine organization which would later 'achieve rehabilitation in the Party . . . with freedom of speech and propaganda'.[30] Serge opposed the idea, calling it an illusion in the face of a powerful and ubiquitous secret police dedicated to seeking out

---

* One of the agents, Tverskoy, cleaned up the Moscow Opposition, including the old Bolshevik Boris Mikhailovich Eltsin, who was to appear in many of Serge's novels as 'Elkin'. After Tverskoy successfully led the Oppositional sympathizers in Moscow factories into arrest, he offered his services to the Leningrad Opposition – ostensibly to help them 'reorganize'. Alexandra Bronstein and Serge refused his 'help' but he nevertheless organized 'fifty or so workers, only to have it [the shadow organization] rally noisily to the "general line" within two months, while those who resisted were thrown into jail. This police manoeuvre was repeated in all the working-class centres.' Serge, *Memoirs*, p. 245.

and crushing opposition, and moreover because 'our own ideological and sentimental loyalty to the Party made us vulnerable both to political man-oeuvrings, and even more, to police provocation'. Serge again reiterated that open activity was preferable to being bundled into illegality, that the Opposition must defend its right to exist, write, think, speak openly. The hopelessness of the clandestine project also contained an irony: the vanquished Opposition had not fought for freedom of expression and propaganda within the society at large. Would they now demand something for themselves which they had denied their previous opponents? Preobrazhensky and Trotsky had much to say about inner-Party democracy in the 1920s: it was not until the second half of the 1930s that Trotsky wrote of political pluralism and a multi-party system in the USSR. Serge consistently defended broad democratic rights both inside and outside the Party, and had even suggested in 1923–24 that a coalition government was preferable to the bureaucratic rule on its way to becoming the 'dictatorship of the secretariat and secret police'.

During the next two years Stalin turned on the Right Opposition, initiated dekulakization and collectivization and began his programme of crash industrialization. By appearing to adopt in crude caricature the Left Opposition platform, Stalin confused the Opposition, making unity among them difficult. Worse, they were scattered to the far reaches of the Soviet Union.* Serge wrote that 'the vocation of defeated revolutionists in a totalitarian state is a hard one. Many abandon you when they see the game is lost. Others, whose personal courage and devotion are above question, think it best to manoeuvre to adapt themselves to the circumstances.'[31]

Serge recognized that Stalin had taken elements of the Opposition programme, emptied of their democratic content, and ruthlessly implemented them. The Opposition had proposed a tax on the rich kulak – Stalin had eliminated him. The Opposition had proposed limiting NEP – Stalin had abolished it. The Opposition had favoured industrialization – Stalin initiated it late, on a grandiose scale, at enormous human and social cost. The Opposition's programme had featured working-class democracy – one platform plank that Stalin made no attempt to appropriate.

Still, some Oppositionists rallied to Stalin because he had adopted elements of their programme. Perhaps they preferred capitulation to political immobility. The Party was still the 'only game in town' and for life-long revolutionaries to be cut off from political activity was virtually to live without meaning. In this manner Piatakov, Krestinsky, Sokolnikov,

---

* In fact, by 1929 only three well-known Oppositionists in the entire USSR remained at liberty, albeit precarious: Andrés Nin in Moscow and Alexandra Bronstein and Victor Serge in Leningrad. They were under surveillance, as were the wives of Oppositionist deportees. See Victor Serge and Natalia Sedova Trotsky, *The Life and Death of Leon Trotsky*, London, Wildwood House, 1975, p. 161.

Antonov-Ovseenko, Ivan Smirnov and Smilga all capitulated.* Zinoviev and Kamenev made capitulation a way of life. They gave many reasons but they boiled down to these: the Opposition programme was being implemented; the USSR was in danger; or it was better to take part in *building* than to cling to ideological purity and be inactive. Trotsky, in a letter to Rakovsky in July 1928, wrote that the capitulationists imagined that 'the Stalinist faction, having moved leftwards, had only a "rightist tail" behind it and should be persuaded to rid itself of it'. Doubting the truth of this, Trotsky remarked, 'an ape freed of its tail is not yet a human being'.[32] Anton Ciliga saw the capitulators as:

> intellectuals [who] cared very little about the fate of the working class. That was not the factor that decided their political attitude, it was the speeded-up industrialization and the offensive against the kulaks. Their attitude towards the horrible oppression and exploitation under which the workers suffered was exactly the same as that of the Stalinists and Bukharinists.[33]

In fact Ciliga admitted that many of them saw Stalin as necessary, saw Russia as Asiatic and backward, in need of a dictatorship to save the revolution, and dismissed Ciliga's protestations as 'Western illusions'.†

Serge was both more profound and more kind. Though not cut from the

---

* Isaac Deutscher, in the second volume of his Trotsky biography, suggests that Stalin lured these Oppositionists to his side with his 'left turn' as he needed their assistance to defeat the Bukharinists and take on the kulaks, but he feared that a reconciliation with Trotsky would mean Trotsky's triumph. His secret appeals to the confused Oppositionists centred on the futility of their Opposition now that he was implementing elements of their programme. Indeed, Trotsky had called for critical support for Stalin against Bukharin, the kulak and the NEP men. The persecuted and exiled Oppositionists, whose morale was at a low point, saw the reasons for their Opposition disappear as their 'cause' was partly taken up by their persecutor. Their battle became purposeless according to Deutscher, who attempted to unravel their thought processes. See Deutscher, *The Prophet Unarmed*, pp. 407–11. The recantations and capitulations did not affect all Oppositionists: Serge belonged to the group of 'irreconcilables' who were in general younger, less tied to the old Party and attracted to the revolution by the principles of proletarian democracy which were paramount. The Left course of Stalin, devoid of any democratic content, had no appeal to this group.

† A Soviet diplomat had told Ciliga that 'the way of Genghis Khan and Stalin' suited Asiatic Russia better than 'the European civilization of Leon Davidovich' (*The Russian Enigma*, p. 85). The Genghis Khan reference comes from Bukharin, who compared Stalin to Genghis Khan – neither of whom had any scruples. Another Oppositionist said: 'A workers' democracy is out of the question in Russia. Here the working class is so feeble and demoralized that to give it liberty would be to ruin the revolution once and for all. What may save it is an educated minority dictatorship.' Ibid.

same cloth as the old Bolsheviks who debased themselves by capitulating, he did not see them as opportunists. In Serge's view,

> These old Bolsheviks have no private life outside of their political activity; they attach little importance to what the bourgeoisie calls position, or even to happiness. Are they cowards? Ahead of them are nearly ten years of the most intolerable life, leading up to the most frightful end. Their attitude combines a great courage, an absolute devotion without phrases or gestures – a courage which does not hesitate to cloak itself as pusillanimity, a devotion which does not shrink before the worst humiliations – with a very real intellectual and moral deficiency. Too much attached to the Party, they fear to see reality as it is. The Party is finished. They shrink back before this final realization. They do not sense that in debasing themselves, they debase the Revolution; that it is better to remain erect and proud in error than to give an example of such abasement even for the best of causes. They aim to manoeuvre, in the belief that the main thing is to remain within the Party until the day when spontaneously the decisive struggles break out which will make Party reform possible.[34]

Even comrades who understood the dynamic of capitulation later succumbed to it. This has been difficult for scholars and activists outside the Soviet Union to understand.

Soviets 1929

In Leningrad in 1927 Serge had met Panaït Istrati,* the Romanian novelist, and Nicos Kazantzakis, the Greek writer, who were touring the Soviet Union. Serge was their political guide, and they made his flat their home base in the USSR.[35] After Serge was released from his first Soviet arrest he and Istrati went to stay in a little dacha in the depths of the Bykovo woods (about forty kilometres from Moscow), where their friendship and collaboration grew. They spent three months in picturesque solitude in the fresh air, with plenty of time for discussion and reflection.[36]

Istrati had worked politically with Christian Rakovsky and was in the Soviet Union at Rakovsky's invitation. Istrati and Serge had visited a model prison colony in which the prisoners – hardened criminals – worked in freedom under their own supervision. Istrati commented ironically that in the Soviet Union one had to murder at least three people to live in comfort

---

* Istrati, a man who came to writing after diverse experiences, was what Serge considered a true poet, 'incapable of theoretical reasoning, and so could not fall into the trap of convenient sophistry'. Serge heard people tell Panaït: 'Panaït, one cannot make an omelette without breaking eggs. Our revolution . . . ' He exclaimed, 'All right, I can see the broken eggs. Where's this omelette of yours?' The phrase became famous as a description of the course of the Soviet Union. See Serge, *Memoirs*, p. 278.

and under such a wonderful work system.[37] Serge recalled that Istrati keenly observed and commented on many such ironies and injustices.

Istrati subsequently returned to France,[38] heartbroken by his experiences in the Soviet Union and resolved to write about them. Still free in Leningrad, Serge wrote the second volume of Istrati's trilogy on the Soviet Union, *Vers l'autre flamme*. In fact, Istrati wrote only the first volume, Serge wrote the second, and Boris Souvarine the third. As Victor Alba explains:

> After long discussions with Souvarine, Istrati signed his own name to a second volume titled *Soviets 1929* and actually written by Victor Serge, then in Leningrad at liberty but still subject to harassment. Finally *La Russie Nue* [Naked Russia], a book of factual documentation, appeared signed by Istrati but written by Souvarine. Istrati signed the books with his name to aid their publicity: 'I want the voices of my friends to be heard as widely as possible, to at least provoke the debate now prohibited in the USSR, and to try to save the Communist International'.[39]

In the introduction to the 1980 edition of Panaït Istrati's *Vers l'autre flamme*, Marcel Mermoz recounts how Serge, in Leningrad, managed to smuggle out the second volume of Istrati's trilogy. Istrati's companion Bilili got past the police with the manuscript hidden in her blouse. Mermoz confirms that Souvarine indeed wrote the well-documented third volume of the trilogy.[40]

More so than *Year One of the Russian Revolution* or *Destiny of a Revolution*, *Soviets 1929* resembles *Portrait de Staline*, directed to a mass audience. Written as the impressions of a visitor from the West, the book clearly means to engage sympathy for the politics of Trotsky's Left Opposition.* Analysing the situation in 1929, the year Stalin proclaimed 'the Year of Great Change',[41] Serge's book renders the programme of the Left Opposition, detailing the crisis in industry, agriculture, within the Party, and society as a whole. The book follows the debates of the 1920s in clear, simple prose. It lays out the society created by Stalin's 'socialism in one country'.

The work takes the side of the Left Opposition while explaining the other currents. Following the point of view of the Left Opposition, Serge said: 'We are, in the country of workers and peasants, reformists, not revolutionaries'.[42] Trotsky shared his view. What was necessary, they argued,

---

* Clearly Serge was never fooled by nor attracted, as were other erstwhile Oppositionists, to Stalin's apparent adoption of some of the Oppositions' programme in 1928–29 during the grain crisis and subsequent collectivization and industrialization. Serge wrote in 1929 that Stalin's policies were *'une application caricaturale vouée à l'échec. Remarquez qu'il ne pose sérieusement, ni la question ouvrière, ni celle du régime intérieur du parti.'* Panaït Istrati, *Soviets 1929*, Paris, Les Editions Rieder, 1929, p. 35.

was not revolution, but reform, uprooting the parasitic bureaucracy which had usurped control.*

The last chapter is a call to action to the proletariat of the West and the Soviet Union: 'Everything is in your hands.'[43] Serge declares that the future health of the proletarian dictatorship depends entirely on the vigour with which the revolutionary proletariat will fight against the 'fossilization of Marxism', using Marxist method as a guide to action. 'Comrades . . . You are again the masters of your destiny.'[44] Serge outlined the ideas and 'spirit' of a programme of reform for the Soviet Union, to include:

- a return of internal democracy in the Party;
- profound reform of the press, guaranteeing the right of response (without reprisal) and the right of expression of all nuances of Soviet and Communist opinion;
- scientific, literary and theoretical freedom;
- a judicial system that would defend the workers' and peasants' state, not be a tool of the counter-revolution. The accused must have the right of defence and security. The Cheka must account for its acts in front of the regular justice of the workers' state.
- stimulation of the individual interests of the workers and a maximum of workers' democracy in production.[45]

Serge called for a return to democracy within the *Party*, not society at large, in order to demonstrate the Opposition's loyalty to the Party. The Stalinist faction had accused the Opposition of trying to form a second Party, which it steadfastly refused to do. The Opposition wanted to challenge the power of the bureaucrats *from within*. It was a loyal opposition to reform the party-state. Trotsky thought a second Party would rally the 'malcontents and . . . become an unconscious tool of reaction'.[46] He changed his view as the Soviet Union degenerated further, and by 1938 Trotsky and his followers founded a new International, with the aim of replacing the Comintern.

---

* It must be remembered that Serge was writing in 1929, as events unfolded. The Left Opposition argued that the nationalized means of production provided the base for socialized production, but that a new privileged stratum, thirsty for power and determined to rule, had strangled the proletarian state. Rakovsky, in his 'Letter to Valentinov' had described the Soviet state as 'a bureaucratic state with working-class remains' and was deeply anxious about working-class apathy. Trotsky stuck closer to Lenin's formulation of a 'workers' state with bureaucratic distortions' and thought the indifference of the masses was temporary. The Opposition's programme of 'Soviet reform' and a return to revolutionary methods could be accomplished, they thought, by a secret ballot first in the Party, then in the trade unions, and finally in the Soviets, ensuring that the leadership of all three was elected by a truly democratic poll. Serge and Sedova Trotsky, *The Life and Death of Leon Trotsky*, pp. 167–9.

In the chapter 'Le Gaspillage bureaucratique dans l'industrie', Serge's method of exposition is typical. He does not begin with abstraction, but rather by piling detail upon detail and example upon example to demonstrate how the human and financial resources for the development of industry existed in the Soviet Union, but would be squandered if the bureaucracy was not overturned.[47] It is instructive to see in this 1929 work that the wasteful nature of Soviet production, about which so much has been written since the thirties, made itself evident right from the beginning. The enormous waste was obvious to those living in the Soviet Union at the time; it is mentioned in nearly every memoir of the period. However, few attempted to explain its cause.

Serge's method was to amass empirical detail, intersperse it with pregnant observations, and suggest the consequences of Stalinist coercion. To develop his point, Serge painted the whole picture: industry, agriculture, political superstructure, political currents, society at large and the rising bureaucracy. Serge's examination leads the reader to the simple conclusion that the bureaucratic system had compromised the future of the USSR.[48]

Serge's political analysis suggests itself in his organization of the material. In this particular chapter Serge catalogued examples of waste: he discussed the construction in metallurgy that proceeded entirely without plans, squandering immense resources and years of effort to build an unusable factory. The factory, in Kertch, in the Crimea, began with an estimated cost of twenty million rubles and four years later had cost sixty-six million, '*sans plans ni devis*'; the problem at the end was how to get fuel to Kertch from Donetz. Serge laid the responsibility with the bureau of Glavmetal and the trust Yugostal. This example was reported in the *Pravda*, 8 September 1928, but Serge insists it was typical.[49] Factories were produced but could not function because there were no power stations to feed them. In other areas power stations were constructed where there were no factories. Stalinist planning, or anti-planning, resulted in waste.*

While waste mounted, in a number of instances, 'The bureaucrats of the socialist state had a business understanding with the NEPmen who found it easy to enrich themselves'.[50] Serge presented the reader with the important contrasts: the construction of beautiful public palaces for postal and telegraphic services and the famous Moscow subway – which with all its glorious marble splendour, failed to provide even a single bench for a tired working woman waiting to go home to her 'other job'.† These 'monuments' of the 'workers' state' presented an attractive façade, masking incredible

---

* See chapter 7 for a fuller discussion of this theme in Serge's later writings on his perceptions of the Soviet version of a 'planned economy'.

† As Serge ironically commented in the *Memoirs* (p. 321): 'We know how to build subterranean palaces but we forget that a working-class woman coming home from work would love to be able to sit down beneath all these rich-hued stones.'

waste of resources. Serge asked: would it not have been better to spend some money to improve workers' lodgings, which were a terrible disgrace? Serge demonstrated how the parvenus not only ignored workers' needs, but also because they owed their plum positions to political loyalty, not technical expertise, were responsible for the staggering waste.

Serge used another example to illustrate the way the bureaucratic system 'passed the buck'. Long lists of signatures made it easy to add one more rubber-stamp to even the most outrageous adventure, without anyone taking the blame. Privately, these bureaucrats would acknowledge the horrible waste, but publicly they adopted the rule *'pas d'histoires'*.[51] The example Serge used involved the importation and manufacture of tractors:

> Tractors were imported from abroad and even produced in Russia. Agriculture had the greatest shortage, but replacement parts were not produced, so that thousands of tractors could be out of service a good part of the year due to the lack of a little part hardly important in itself. This scandal was made public by *Pravda* on last January 29th: 'For two and a half years,' wrote the journal, 'claims, demands, official inquiries and conference reports have swollen the dossier without anything effective being done to increase the output of necessary parts for tractor repair. The Putilov works produces replacement parts but can satisfy only fifteen per cent of the demand.'[52]

Serge has taken us inside the bureaucratic machine to try to comprehend its workings. As for the individual worker, what happens, Serge asked, when an energetic individual with innovative talent comes along? How does he fit into this system? According to Serge, his potential contributions will never surface because what gets rewarded is not critical initiative, but conformity to the Party and the bureaucracy. Zeal for the Party is all that counts. The leaders of industry never had to prove themselves. They rose through the ranks by demonstrating their aptitude for political adaptation, not their ability in industry. Anyone who disagreed with what was going on was relieved of his post, and usually arrested later.

What makes this work remarkable is not that its subject is unique,* but that Serge's keen powers of perception and description provide a vivid picture of the bureaucratic system on a grand scale. It is also unusual in the degree of detail. Others joined Serge in attacking this subject at that time. Rakovsky was grappling with the same theoretical questions.[53] So was Trotsky. The value of Serge's work lies in his skilful use of examples to portray how economic events in this period occurred reactively, not according to any carefully developed plans. We can identify Serge's sympathy with

---

* In fact, later memoirs and studies are more precise and factual; for example, Anton Antonov-Ovseenko's work *The Time of Stalin: Portrait of a Tyranny*, New York, Harper/Colophon Books, 1981. Reading Ovseenko is like filling in the basic outline Serge provided in 1929, even though the two authors do not hold similar political stances.

Trotsky and Rakovsky, whose work he complemented and popularized, as well as with certain exiled left-wing Mensheviks writing in *Sotsialistichesky vestnik*. Repression in the late 1920s and early 1930s made collaboration impossible, yet working independently and apart, these separate observers formed a unified current of thought criticizing the nature of economic growth and the chaos of planning, or more accurately, the lack of socialist planning.[54] They called it *besplannovost* (planlessness), and Serge's work in 1929 and later clearly identifies his sympathy with this current.

'Build, build, build, export, shoot, build': the first five-year plan

While Stalin held the political superstructure in a choke-hold, he unleashed his forced collectivization and the five-year plan. His policies created a system, flowing from the logic of socialism in one country, which the Left Opposition opposed at every turn. Stalin's system was characterized by a nationalist foreign policy, a centralized 'plan', vast corruption, an elaborate hierarchy, and atomization of the overworked and undernourished workforce. The system was rigidly controlled from the centre and maintained by terror.

In production, Stalin's political decisions were all-important; in 1929 when he called for a higher rate of growth he was responding to the desperate need for capital goods and exports. He did not base his commands on actual economic resources or the needs of the population. Stalin exhorted the working class to work harder and harder, without any apparent concern about how realistic his goals were or what they would cost in human terms. He appeared to have no policy, shifting from 'right' to 'left'. Stalin incorporated hierarchical trends manifested earlier during War Communism, and then NEP, into Soviet society after 1929. The result was what was later called an 'administrative command system' or an 'administered nationalized economy with an hierarchical structure'.[55]

Serge's descriptions of this system evoke a sense of a rigidly regulated society that paradoxically was out of control. Commands issued from the top were often impossible to fulfil, but could not be questioned, so the impossible was attempted. The result was usually quite different from what was planned. Serge presents a picture of unrelenting gloom, with inhuman production-line speeds and working conditions, and severe penalties for a careless word or perceived sabotage (which could mean anything). Conditions were 'dismally, onerously primitive'.[56] Although Serge's descriptions and analyses remain undeveloped, they contain a hard kernel of truth. More often than not, Serge's views are apparent in his questions. After carefully analysing working conditions and comparing them to those in the West, Serge wrote:

> The management of the enterprises is in the hands of communists who merely carry out the instructions of the central organisms. Do these instructions prove to be inexecutable? Do they have unforeseen and vexatious consequences? Do

low wages adversely affect the productivity of labour? Has the plan been discredited? Finally has the engineer permitted himself to formulate objections? Did he keep still, out of prudent complacency, on the eve of an experiment that turned out badly? In all these cases and in many others, the technical personnel, accused of incompetence, of negligence, of bad faith, even of the counter-revolutionary spirit or of conspiracy, is the object of mass punishments which always mean arrests and all too often end in executions.[57]

Industrialization was carried out at the expense of both worker and peasant who survived at the very brink of starvation and exhaustion. When workers were asked (in 1936) if they lived better before the revolution, Serge wrote that those aged forty and over answered unanimously in the affirmative. Mothers complained, he added, that no matter how poor they had been before the revolution, at least then they enjoyed occasional good times during old religious festivals when children could taste creams, preserves and pastries, things no one could obtain now.[58] Andrew Smith made a similar point in his *I Was a Soviet Worker*.

Serge, in describing the way the Soviet Union developed, presents history dramatically as a dynamic process full of conflict and contradiction. He transforms empirical data about economy and society into a compelling chronicle. 'Industrialization is directed like a march through conquered territory.'[59] During the first five-year plan, production was beset with bottlenecks, including constant breakdowns. Quotas had to be met because Stalin demanded the five-year plan be fulfilled in four or even three years. Precious resources, needed elsewhere, had to be used increasingly to repair machinery exhausted by improper usage. Spare parts, in short supply to begin with, often got lost in delivery. Stalin's answer to every problem was the same: squeeze the workers, make them work harder, consume less, hold up their pay, cut their wages.[60]

Stalin's commands had to be obeyed without question, but they did not result from any clear or consistent plans. He made each economic move in response to events, which followed their own course, beyond the reach of the centre. Conscious regulation of the economy by and in the interests of the associated producers was replaced by political exhortation and coercion. Balance and proportion gave way to a race to fulfil – and overfulfil – targets regardless of dislocations or hardships. This was the first five-year plan.

One of the conditions produced by Stalin's policies was spontaneous labour turnover. Serge, quoting official statistics, pointed out such turnover was so widespread that in the Ukraine, whole factories were turned over in three months as workers moved on looking for food, housing and better working conditions.[61] Serge noted that mainly 'You travel because wherever you are you feel bad'. Putting this in human terms, Serge quipped that travel exceeded the forecasts of transportation, as more workers were on the move than during the California gold rush. At the same time as workers returned en masse to the countryside, Stalin was introducing all manner of schemes to increase productivity.

Shock work brigades (*udarnichestvo*) and Stakhanovism were among Stalin's schemes to speed up production. Serge pointed out they were doomed because they were a fraud, rigged by opportunist managers and workers in collusion to win bonuses for themselves.[62] Selected workers, working in special conditions, produced very high quotas which were then established as norms. The 'ordinary' workers, working in normal conditions, could not possibly match this output. However, in the process of trying, they did manage to produce defective goods, exhaust expensive machinery, and wear themselves down from exposure to perpetually intolerable conditions without proper nutrition, rest or shelter.* The workers were treated worse than the machines. Production, at any cost, was the only consideration. The cost was terrible.

Stalin introduced draconian labour laws, along with productivity schemes, to impose control over a workforce on the move. Internal passports and severe penalties for violating work rules aimed to reduce the high turnover by controlling the individual worker, jailing him at his work-bench.

Resistance

Workers resisted Stalin's labour policy individually and collectively. They reacted sharply to Stakhanovism and the creation of a 'numerically small, well-paid labour aristocracy'.

> Stakhanovists had their heads smashed. Some were killed. The young communist who, in order to get a bonus or to quit the plant later on tried to beat the record was considered a traitor by his shopmates. This resistance was broken by means of repression, and Stakhanovism was attenuated by generalizing it. The name was speedily worn down, in a few months, amidst abuse and even ridicule. The Party were forced to react against the exaggerations of Stakhanovism.[63]

Serge conveyed the regime's contradictory response to resistance, showing graphically what happened to those who dared to protest collectively. Workers struck, and the youth were often the most militant.† Serge

---

* Andrew Smith, a black-listed American Communist worker who left the depression-ridden USA in 1929 to join the 'workers' paradise' in the Soviet Union, wrote a remarkable memoir, *I Was a Soviet Worker*, upon his return in 1936. It is replete with examples demonstrating how the forced tempos and conditions of production wasted both human and material resources in the Soviet Union, and produced defective products as well.

† Serge pointed out that the youth in general were 'evolving towards a succinct realism. Smitten with technique, thirsting for well-being, supple in adaptation, hardened against pain and hunger. The word "Americanism" still best expresses its spirit. Few general ideas, no formulated ethics, no conscious idealism, an aversion to politics' (*Russia Twenty Years After*, p. 34). The militant youth were the non-conformists and, Serge said, 'set the tone' in the struggles, camps and prisons.

described a strike at the textile plant in Ivanovo-Voznessensk in April 1931, where the workers had but one slogan to express their demands: 'We are hungry!' The authorities yielded, blaming the local leadership. Food was sent in; work was resumed. Then the purge began quietly.* The Trotskyists (among the strikers) were shot without a word.[64]

The regime also had to cope with the results of its policy, while preparing for war. The result was absenteeism, alcoholism, high turnover, and general disruption of labour discipline, making it impossible to fulfil planned targets. Collectivization had created a situation of extreme scarcity. Serge made the point simply and forcefully: an underfed and malnourished workforce, living a joyless existence, could not be depended on to work well. What capitalist society had learned about slavery was a lesson lost on the Stalinists.†

Much of the revolutionary working class was killed fighting the civil war, famine and foreign intervention, leaving a raw mass of politically unschooled peasants. Exploitation of workers and peasants was accomplished by force, and opposition was eliminated with terror. Serge summed up Stalin's policy: 'Build, build, build, export, shoot, build. This is what is called the epopee of the great plan.'[65] The best of what the workers produced was exported, while they laboured under cruel conditions, threatened with arrest, labour camp and death if they resisted or even failed to push themselves to the extremes demanded of them.

Meanwhile, as peasants became workers overnight, the Party absorbed the most opportunist, careerist elements, the parvenus we meet in Serge's novels. His portraits of this parasitic caste, crudely adopting the worst traits of privilege, border on the absurd. Serge's descriptions of the functionaries, and of the former bourgeois women who flocked around them, conjures up the sleaze and slime of an underworld suddenly thrust into power. Rakovsky's discussion of the decomposition of the French Jacobin Party, drunk with power, uncannily matches Serge's description of the Soviet parvenus.[66]

Trying to meet the urgent needs of the economy, Stalin attempted to force rapid growth which was costly and wasteful. Serge's writings implicitly recognize the emerging social relations engendered by Stalin's system. His novels do particular justice to the temperament and behaviour of those in different sectors of Soviet society. His discussion of the bureaucracy's consciousness, forged both by origin and function, is especially insightful in *The Case of Comrade Tulayev*.

---

* This became the standard pattern of response to workers' resistance throughout the Soviet period.

† In fact Serge was reminded of the pages of *Capital* where Marx described the 'relentless mechanism of primitive capitalist accumulation'. The present accumulation, Serge noted, was just as cruel, and 'anti-socialist in its methods and in the treatment inflicted upon man' (*Russia Twenty Years After*, p. 177).

The trials begin – even silence is suspect

'So long as the man is in your hands, there is always a way of framing him.'
'So long as you have the neck, the rope will be found somewhere.'*

Serge commended the brave agricultural technicians and experts who dared to denounce 'the blunders and excesses; they were arrested in thousands and made to appear in huge sabotage-trials so that responsibility might be unloaded on somebody'.[67] This was the beginning of the hunt for enemies, which climaxed in the mighty crescendo of the Great Terror of 1936–38. The search for scapegoats would become even more desperate and frenzied as Stalin's 'blunders and excesses' multiplied and grew worse.

Stalin's rule by edicts and commands, backed by ruthless force, devoured real and imagined opponents, conveniently blaming them for the chaos and misery his breakneck policies created. The accusation of sabotage was directed, Serge noted, 'at thousands, or rather tens of thousands of technicians' which 'was in general a monstrous slander justified solely by the need to find culprits for an economic situation that was now insupportable'.[68] By 1930 those who hoarded silver coins were shot as the ruble disappeared; a crisis in the coal industry led to the execution of five Shakhty engineers;† the meat shortage caused by the peasants killing their livestock led to the execution of Professor Karatygin (of the Department of Meat and Canned Goods) and his forty-seven co-defendants, for sabotage of the meat supply. Serge noted that on the day these forty-eight men were massacred, Stalin gave Rabindranath Tagore a splendid reception replete with speeches about the new humanism and abundance.[69]

From 1928 to 1931 a series of sensational and well-publicized trials of specialists featured confessions to extravagant charges. The presiding judge was Andrei Ia. Vyshinsky.‡ In November 1930 the so-called 'Industrial

---

* Well-known sayings in Russian Revolutionary circles, quoted by Serge in *Russia Twenty Years After*, p. 64.

† In the Donbass region in May 1928, fifty-three engineers were accused of wrecking equipment, organizing accidents and having links with the former bourgeois owners of the coal mines. The misuse of equipment, due to the inexperience of the new workforce and the intolerable tempo of production, led to fire and explosions in the mines, giving the regime a pretext to repress technicians, using them as scapegoats to threaten others.

‡ Serge wrote an unpublished sketch of Vyshinsky which he titled 'El Ciudano Vichinsky' (The Citizen Vyshinsky). Serge recounted how in the Lubianka in 1933 his cellmate Nesterov told him how Vyshinsky had organized strikes in the Ukraine to paralyse the workings of the Soviets, and that Vychinsky was known as a counter-revolutionary. The paradox was that now Vyshinsky presided over the courts which sent revolutionaries to their death, though this time at the behest of the Party and the regime of the Soviets! 'El Ciudano

Party' was on trial, and its leader Ramzin confessed to plotting military intervention from foreign capitals. Serge called it 'raving madness'. Desperate to escape execution, the accused confessed to 'infinitely more than can be believed', but their confessions rarely saved them. Those who did not confess simply disappeared. Serge commented: 'They are strange trials, in which the accused accuse each other more than they are themselves accused, going to the point of flagrant enormities in their self-flagellatory zeal'.[70]

The so-called 'Toiling Peasant Party', whose leaders Kondratiev and Makarov opposed total collectivization, was 'liquidated off-stage' in 1930. They were accused of conspiring with kulaks to revive the Socialist Revolutionary Party and overthrow the Soviet system. There was a secret trial of bacteriologists charged with organizing a horse epidemic in August 1930.[71] Thirty-five leading figures in the Commissariat of Agriculture, many of them old Communists, were executed in 1930. Secret trials of historians (Tarle,[72] Platonov and Kareyev) took place in 1931. There were similar trials of geologists,* physicists, and others.† Shortages and dislocations were now claimed to be the result of criminal sabotage – allowing the regime a fantastic but convenient explanation for its own ineptitude. Shooting 'saboteurs' also gave the regime an excuse to get rid of an unreliable elite drawn from the revolutionary generation of Communists and former bourgeois specialists (whose capacity and inclination to think critically made them troublesome).

The planners came under extreme political pressure, as they predicted the disastrous consequences of the government's decisions. Groman, the old socialist and former Menshevik, was the principal exponent of equilibrium planning for optimum economic development. He and his whole working

---

Vichinsky' (in Spanish), 1947, 3 pages, Serge archives, Mexico. Also: Gen MSS 238 Box 3, Folder 129, Victor Serge Papers, Beinecke Rare Book and Manuscript Library, Yale University.

* The geologists were imprisoned for 'having interpreted subsoil qualities differently from what was wanted in high places: ignorance of the natural wealth of the country, hence sabotage, hence treason', Serge, *Russia Twenty Years After*, p. 53. In this work, Serge also described in detail what happened to Soviet literature, when intellectual freedom was completely extinguished, and to the masterful authors who were censored, banned and purged.

† Roy Medvedev, in his *Let History Judge* (New York, Vintage Books, 1973), describes these trials in detail, quoting verbatim testimony and defendants' depositions. Medvedev shows that not only were the charges 'ridiculous' but gave the impression that the first five-year plan could not have been discussed in any detail at the Sixteenth Party Conference in April 1929, and that the people's commissariats were 'not headed by communists, [but] that wreckers were in complete control of the economic and state machinery' (pp. 111–39). See also pp. 248–89 of Medvedev's revised and expanded edition, 1989.

group were accused in a public show trial in March 1931 of the crime of deliberately retarding the country's industrial development. Serge wrote that Groman was arrested after quarrelling with Miliutin at the Planning Commission. The very idea of balance between different sectors of the economy began to be politically suspect,[73] and Groman's exasperation under pressure led him to shout to Miliutin that the country was being led to the abyss.[74] The example made of the Groman group directly influenced the development of Soviet planning. Planners preferred, as the statistician Strumilin said, 'to stand for high growth rates rather than to [be imprisoned] for low ones'.[75] Original plan figures gave way to fantasy about what could be achieved, causing the chaos and imbalance which have become permanent features of the Soviet economy.

Serge wrote in the *Memoirs* that the slander heaped on these specialists could not withstand close scrutiny, although in *Russia Twenty Years After* he admits that in some cases there was perhaps a grain of truth at the core of the fantastic claims:

> Some, honest men, contest the value of hastily recast and militarily applied plans. They foresee disastrous results and sometimes they even refuse to comply with demands which they consider absurd but which are in reality only demagogic, whether it be for the purpose of bluffing foreign opinion, of duping domestic opinion, or in the case of zealous administrators, of pulling the wool over the eyes of the government; others follow the course of the-worse-the-better, thinking that 'this cannot last'. Some of them sabotage, thinking that the hour has finally struck for the long-awaited catastrophe of Bolshevism. And, indeed, never has the situation been so bad since the worst moments of the civil war and the blockade. Some engineers are subsidized by émigrés whom they keep informed or by spies who flatter them. Above all, scapegoats are needed.[76]

The last line is the most significant, because it set a pattern of response for decades to come: when things go badly, never take responsibility, always blame someone else, someone less powerful, usually local officials. Serge noted another harbinger of things to come: the way 'the patriotism of the technicians was constantly appealed to in the course of wringing confessions out of them'.[77]

Serge pointed out that industrialization proceeded amid 'such chaos and under an authoritarian system of such rigidity, that it was possible to find "sabotage" in any place, at any moment'.[78] Serge added that in his own experience he had observed the 'whole mentality of the technician is quite antagonistic to sabotage, dominated as it is by love of technique and a job well done . . . All that there was in fact was a fairly widespread "technocratic mentality". Technicians saw themselves as indispensable and as distinctly superior to the men in the Government.'[79]

Serge thought the trials were only used to manipulate public opinion, at home and abroad: the sentences, prescribed by the Politburo itself, were often rescinded, seemingly arbitrarily.* During the Menshevik Centre Trial Serge met with people every day who were connected with the accused. Thus he was in a position to 'trace, line by line, the progression of the lie in their evidence'. Later, when the old historian Sukhanov was incarcerated in the Isolator of Verkhne-Uralsk, Serge wrote that he had documents circulated among political prisoners detailing the methods used by the GPU to extract confessions. Serge told how a combination of death threats and appeals to patriotism were used. Medvedev's citation of Yakubovich and I.I. Rubin's† deposition leaves no doubt that confessions were also extracted under physical and mental torture.‡

Isaac Rubin was described by Serge as a protégé of David Borisovich Ryazanov, whom Serge met a number of times. Ryazanov had created a 'scientific establishment of noteworthy quality' at the Marx-Engels Institute. Ryazanov, Sukhanov, Groman, Rubin and Ginsberg had a sort of *salon* in the Planning Commission where they freely discussed the 'utterly catastrophic' situation in the country in 1930.[80] Serge greatly respected Ryazanov for his steadfast honour and independence: he had never failed to denounce the death penalty, and demanded strict limits on the activities of the GPU, as he had with its predecessor, the Cheka. Ryazanov provided an intellectual haven at his Institute for 'heretics of all kinds' so long as they had a 'love of knowledge'. During the trial of the Menshevik Centre, Ryazanov went to each member of the Politburo to express his rage at such fabrications and monstrosities. After a violent exchange with Stalin, in which Ryazanov accused the General Secretary of concocting incriminating evidence against old socialists, he was arrested and deported. His books were removed from the libraries, although he had just been officially recognized in a celebration of his sixtieth birthday. Serge noted that he died 'alone and captive, nobody knows where' sometime around 1940.[81]

These tumultuous events which affected the lives of millions of people

---

* So that some of the accused, e.g. physicist Lazarev, were rehabilitated, while others (the 'pretended' Mensheviks) disappeared. Serge commented that he had dinner with one expert in energetics who had been condemned to death, pardoned, sent to a concentration camp, rehabilitated, and decorated, all in the space of twenty months. Serge, *Memoirs*, pp. 249–50.

† Isaac Rubin's interpretive works on Marx's *Capital* and the history of the labour theory of value remain among the outstanding theoretical contributions of the 1920s. See I.I. Rubin, *The History of Economic Thought*, edited and translated by Donald A. Filtzer, London, Ink Links, 1979.

‡ Medvedev, *Let History Judge*, pp. 125–37 (pp. 274–84 in the revised and expanded edition). Yakubovich's deposition was written in May 1967, while the account of Rubin's years in solitary confinement and horrible torture was written by his sister B.I. Rubina. Of these men, Sukhanov was rearrested and shot in 1937, Ryazanov perished in 1938. The place and time of death of Rubin is still unknown, and Yakubovich survived until 1980.

coincided with fierce inner-Party struggle. After the Left and United Opposition were beaten by the 'hierarchy of secretaries, in a kind of inter-locking directorate with the commissars of the GPU under the guidance of the General Secretary, the so-recently obscure Georgian',[82] Stalin turned his attention to defeating the Right. Bukharin, Tomsky and Rykov opposed Stalin's policy of forced collectivization and what they saw as premature industrialization. Serge called the Right Opposition 'more of a state of mind than an organization; at certain junctures it included the great major-ity of officials, and enjoyed the sympathy of the whole nation'.* Henry Grigorievich Yagoda sympathized with the Right, as did Kalinin and Voroshilov, but, as Serge noted, for 'personal motives whose nature is still obscure' they gave a majority to Stalin and Molotov. In actual fact, the so-called Right never created a clear-cut faction, as Stalin himself admitted[83] but remained loyal members of the Party who disagreed with Stalin's line.

The Right fought to save itself from expulsion, while the Zinoviev ten-dency was reinstated. Bukharin, the theoretician of 'socialism in one country', told Kamenev in a secret meeting, organized by Sokolnikov in the summer of 1928: '*He* will slay us . . . *he* is the new Genghis Khan'.† And, Bukharin added, 'If the country perishes, we all [i.e. the Party] perish. If the country manages to recover, he twists around in time and we still perish.' Serge's Opposition centre published the account of this secret meeting, and wrote that 'Our centre [B.M. Eltsin] may very well have much to answer for in publishing these documents'.[84] Yet as Stalin defeated the Right, they followed in Zinoviev and Kamenev's footsteps, recognizing the 'errors of their ideas' and capitulating to stay within the Party.

---

* Serge, *Memoirs*, p. 253. The widespread support the Right Opposition enjoyed owed much to the improved situation following War Communism in agricul-ture and the arts. This was attributed to the NEP, widely identified with Bukharin.

† Kamenev summarized the conversation which the Moscow Trotskyists then leaked abroad. Deutscher gives a full account in *The Prophet Unarmed*, pp. 440–42. This meeting took place as Bukharin attempted to block with the Left to defeat Stalin. Serge recounted how Trotsky wrote to the Oppositionists from Alma-Ata that since the Right represented the danger of a slide toward capital-ism, they should support the Centre – Stalin – against it. While this may seem incredible, it follows because the Trotskyists refused to engage in 'unprincipled combinationism', that is, blocking with groupings whose politics are dissimilar with the purpose of getting rid of a leadership. Serge wrote that Stalin at this time sounded out the leaders of the imprisoned Left Opposition, promising rehabilitation if they supported him against the Right. Serge said his Opposi-tion group discussed the issue 'with uncertainty' and Boris Mikhailovich Eltsin, from his prison cell in Suzdal, demanded a conference of the Oppositionists (including Trotsky) to come to a resolution. The conference never took place. Serge, *Memoirs*, p. 253.

As Stalin easily defeated the Right, Serge commented on the essential, 'overwhelming fact' of what had happened.

By means of a *coup de force* within the Party, the revolutionary Party-State becomes a bureaucratic police state, a state which is reactionary in every important way with respect to the ideals of the revolution . . . A Marxism of dead slogans born in offices takes the place of a critical Marxism of thinking men. The cult of the leader begins. 'Socialism in one country' becomes the password of parvenus who intend no more than the protection of their new privileges. What opponents of the regime see with a kind of anguished myopia is the profile of a new, emerging state, a totalitarian regime. The majority of the old-Bolshevik opponents of Trotsky – the Bukharins, Rykovs, Tomskis and Riutins – are horrified at the sight, and pass over to the resistance. Too late.[85]

Before his capitulation, Bukharin commented to Kamenev, illustrating the way Stalin's totalitarian regime was able to use the old Bolsheviks against one another, because 'it had a hold on their souls' through Party patriotism. Stalin was thus able to confuse, humiliate and wear out any opposition.[86] A natural consequence of the crushing of freedom of opinion within the Party was that duplicity prevailed. Serge said the 'capitulator comrades' still kept their ideas and met clandestinely.* In 1929 he met Smilga, who summarized the thinking of these men. 'The Opposition is all astray with its sterile bitterness. One's duty is to work with and in the Party . . . What do our petty deportations amount to? Oughtn't we all to be walking around by now with our heads tucked underneath our arms?'[87]

In the remaining years of the first five-year plan, Stalin continually uncovered 'plots' in the Party. The alleged 'rightist–leftist' bloc of Syrtsov and Lominadze was attacked by the press. Their so-called group also included Yan Sten, the philosopher. Also known as the 'Young Stalinist Left', they were arrested and accused of opposition in 1930.†

The Ryutin group, imprisoned in late 1932, was a more real threat to Stalin than the scapegoats and dissatisfied who were framed in the years after the defeat of the Right. Ryutin, who Serge remembered for having organized 'gangs of thugs against us', was close to intellectuals in the Bukharin tendency, all 'Red Professors'. His supporters in Moscow included the old Bolshevik worker Kayurov, and the Red Professors Slepkov, Maretsky and others. Ryutin, former Secretary of the Moscow Committee, drew up a document of nearly 200 pages[88] which amounted to a programme

---

* Later, Andrew Smith recounted in his book *I Was a Soviet Worker* that in 1934 the clandestine Oppositionists in the factories were the most vociferous pro-Stalinists, railing against the Opposition to divert attention from themselves and their work (p. 268).

† In reality, Syrtsov *et al.* had expressed doubts about the excessive growth targets (Stalin often doubled suggested targets) and the regime's disregard for the livestock disaster.

of reform for the Party and the nation. According to Serge, he distributed the document to Zinoviev, Kamenev and 'several of us'. The document called for 'peace with the peasants' in much the same vein as the politics of the Bukharinists (an end to forced collectivization and a slowing of the pace of industrialization). Placing blame squarely on Stalin, Ryutin's document called for the reinstatement of Trotsky and all the Opposition-ists and for a 'fresh start'. An entire chapter was devoted to Stalin, 'the evil genius of the Party and the revolution'.[89] Zinoviev was kicked out of the Party (again) for reading the document without informing on its authors.

The Ryutin affair posed a serious threat to the regime and became a test of loyalty in the Politburo. The GPU and Stalin recommended the death penalty. This would have been the first execution of a Central Committee member. A majority in the Politburo, led by Sergei Kirov, refused to go along with the death penalty and Ryutin was exiled, rather than killed. The Ryutin affair demonstrated that Stalin was still unable to control the Party in late 1932, years after the defeat of the Left and Right Oppositions. Kirov's obvious popularity as Party Chief in Leningrad (Zinoviev's old power base) and his ability to go against Stalin's wishes made him as a serious threat in the General Secretary's eyes.

The remaining Left Oppositionists purged

By 1929 the core of the Opposition was reduced to three comrades not yet jailed or exiled: Serge and Alexandra Bronstein in Leningrad, and Andrés Nin in Moscow. Leon Sosnovsky, Eleazer Solnstsev, Vassily Pankratov and Grigory Yakovin were all in jail; Maria Mikhailovna Joffe* was exiled in Central Asia; Fyodor Dingelstedt in Central Siberia; Muralov on the Irtysh in the Tara forests; Rakovsky in Central Siberia; and Trotsky in Alma-Ata. The rest, numbering up to a thousand according to Serge, were in prison or deported, engaging in hunger strikes, and other forms of resistance. Serge wrote: 'Our intellectual activity is prodigious, our political action nil.'[90] There was no contact between the remaining Left Oppositionists and the capitulators. The times were very difficult but would only get worse. Trotsky's secretary Georgi Butov died after a long hunger strike, during which he was tortured. Yakov Grigorievich Blumkin was killed. Accord-ing to Serge, Blumkin had been sent to Constantinople to spy on the Old Man, as Trotsky was called, but instead acted as a courier, bringing a message from Trotsky to Serge and the other Oppositionists. Blumkin was arrested and sentenced to death. Serge noted that between arrest and

---

* Adolf Joffe's second wife, who miraculously survived decades of hard labour and constant interrogation in the far north. See her memoir, *One Long Night*, London, New Park Publications, 1977.

execution, Blumkin won a fortnight's reprieve to write his memoirs, which 'made a first-rate book'.[91] Blumkin's execution marked the first time a Party member was executed for being in contact with Trotsky.[92] Alexander Orlov wrote that Blumkin shouted 'Long live Trotsky' as the fatal bullets were fired. Serge recalled how it was still possible then for the few survivors to assemble in the gardens of the Marx-Engels Institute and exchange scraps of information or lament the loss of comrades such as Blumkin.

One of the questions they discussed was whether to publish abroad information about the struggle. Serge was in favour of sending everything to their comrades in the West, beginning with the letters of Zinoviev and Kamenev in 1924 which describe Stalin's suggestion that they get rid of Trotsky 'by a Florentine technique'. Others opposed washing dirty linen in public.

In 1929 Serge managed to smuggle out to Trotsky a voluminous correspondence from the Verkhne-Uralsk Isolator written in microscopic characters on strips of paper – the last communication Trotsky received from his comrades inside the Soviet Union.[93] Trotsky's *Bulletin of the Opposition* reached Serge and his comrades in bits and pieces for a while, then not at all. Ironically Serge wrote that the one place people still talked freely of Trotsky's thoughts was in the prison yards.

Serge said they were upset to learn that Trotsky defended in principle the death penalty, recently applied to Blumkin; and that he accepted the sabotage charges against the Mensheviks and technicians. Since the charges against the Mensheviks – that the conspiracy was directed in agreement with the French General Staff – was outrageous at face value, how could Trotsky make such a mistake? What did it say about his attitude to opponents? Deutscher explained that Trotsky later regretted his mistake, that the element of truth in the charges, that Groman had sought to obstruct the first five-year plan, explained, although it did not justify, Trotsky's mistake.[94] Serge proved more magnanimous: although clearly distressed with the implications of Trotsky's position, Serge longed to inform him of the truth. Whereas Serge admitted that Trotsky 'was grossly mistaken' and 'under the unfortunate influence of his Party patriotism', he conceded that the monstrous lies of the press seemed 'sensible' and that Trotsky would have been 'unable to imagine the state of inhumanity, cynicism, and mania that our police-apparatus had sunk to'.[95] One can only imagine the surviving Oppositionists' frustration – cut off, unable to tell the truth even to their own members.

Because he and his writings survived, Serge was able to make an important contribution to our understanding of the mechanism of repression, the advent of the bureaucratic totalitarian state, and the fate of the repressed. Serge's concern with the nameless and faceless victims lost to Stalinism was singular. His writings, in a sense, served as their voices.

Serge wrote pages and pages, simply giving names and telling stories.

The *Memoirs, From Lenin to Stalin*, and especially *Destin d'une révolution* (*Russia Twenty Years After*) are testaments to the men and women who resisted the crushing of the revolution and its ideals by Stalin and his faction. Serge's books contain thumbnail sketches of many of the men and women who devoted their lives to the struggle for socialism:[96] many turn to his *Memoirs* precisely for these accounts of what so-and-so said, how he looked, what became of him.

From Lenin to Stalin contains many sketches, as well as long quotes from Serge's personal correspondence with leading Bolsheviks and ordinary citizens. *Russia Twenty Years After* devotes six chapters to outlining who filled what prisons, what individual and collective resistance took place there. It tells us in great detail the fate of workers, youth, peasants, scientists, writers, teachers, the anarchists, the socialists, the Communists, the Oppositionists, the capitulators, and even of Stalin's coterie. The book is a memorial to the makers and victims of the revolution. Every scholar should have recourse to this book. Although it was out of print for fifty-five years, it was republished in 1996.[97] There is no room here to repeat Serge's histories and thumbnail sketches. However, any student of the fate of Stalin's opponents who does not consult Serge is missing a vital source. By naming names and telling what happened to so many otherwise nameless and faceless victims, Serge in effect cast the first bricks for the national memorial to Stalin's dead the Soviets agreed, in 1988, to build.* Serge's artist son, Vlady, drew up a proposal to build a monument in the USSR† featuring a sculpture of Stalin standing on a heap of cadavers, surrounded by bricks with victims' names engraved on them (see Plate 9).[98]

Persecution comes home

Like all Oppositionists still at large, Serge was kept under police surveillance. He lived in a communal apartment in Leningrad with his wife, son and nine others,[99] among them three GPU agents who kept track of his comings and goings, opened his mail, and reported his conversations. Two more 'guardian angels' followed his every step outside his apartment. The agents made no attempt to hide their spying on Serge. Sometimes Serge

---

* Nineteenth Party Conference Decision, 28 June 1988. The initiative was animated by the group 'Memoryal', a band of scholars, lawyers and amateur historians who took to the streets with a petition which earned them detention, fines, harassment and threats. The group demanded a monument attached to a museum, an archive of repression that would allow people to trace a victim's arrest, the name of his interrogator, and the time and manner of his fate, or as much of this as is known. *New York Times*, 2 July 1988.

† Serge told his son Vlady shortly before he died that although he would not live to see it, Vlady probably would – monuments to Trotsky and to Stalin in the public squares of Russian cities. Serge, *Memoirs*, p. xxii.

was warned that he was about to be charged with treason for his foreign correspondence, that he should be more discreet. On his frequent trips to Moscow, Serge found he could not stay with friends, relatives or anyone without compromising them, so he often squatted in houses made empty by recent GPU roundups. Serge noticed that his friends and acquaintances, including Bukharin, avoided him in the street. The Italian Angelo Tasca, on the Comintern Executive, warned Serge that every time there were 'three of you together, one of you is an *agent provocateur*'.[100] Serge commented that his crime, the Opposition's crime, was simply that he existed.

The torment went on for five years. His entire family suffered. Serge's father-in-law, the old revolutionary Russakov,* was driven from his factory and union, indicted along with his wife and daughter, Serge's wife, as suspected anti-Semites (they were Jewish), counter-revolutionaries, capitalists and terrorists; whole factories demanded they be put to death. Party faithful and GPU agents came to the communal apartment which Serge shared with his in-laws to taunt him, once even slapping Serge's wife in her face. Serge was with Panaït Istrati in the Bykovo woods while this went on, and Serge intimated that the GPU only went ahead with this persecution because they had lost sight of Serge. After two trials, and the intervention of Serge and Panaït Istrati (they went to see Kalinin and others), the inquiry fizzled out. But in 1932 the persecution was resumed. Russakov, out of work, was denied a bread-card and an internal passport.† He died from the privations. The affair devastated Panaït Istrati, who subsequently returned to France and wrote about it.[101]

Serge's wife was driven mad by the persecution. Liuba Russakova endured nine years of incessant harassment against her entire family, bore a daughter while her husband and son were deported, and even after expulsion to Western Europe continued to be hounded by the GPU, and also live in constant fear of the Gestapo. Serge took her from clinic to clinic in the Soviet Union, but found them full of GPU agents. Liuba's nerves could not

---

* Russakov had fought in the 1905 revolution in Rostov, had been Secretary to the Russian Seamen's Union in Marseilles and was expelled from France in 1918 for organizing a strike on ships loaded with munitions for the Whites. Serge was on the same boat bound for Russia in 1918 as the Russakovs. He married Russakov's daughter Liuba, and Pierre Pascal, the French Left Oppositionist, married Russakov's daughter Jenny. In the Soviet Union Russakov was a dye-worker.

† The only semi-bright spot in this sordid affair was when the Workers' and Peasants' Inspectorate held their own trial and had Russakov reinstated in the union, although they could not find him a job. The investigator for the Inspectorate was a young man 'who displayed a singular honesty' named Nikolayev. Serge never found out if it was the same Nikolayev who shot Kirov in 1934. Serge, *Memoirs*, p. 278.

stand the strain and she withdrew to the world of insanity. In exile, after many difficulties, she entered into a mental institution in the south of France, where she remained until her death in 1985.

The Oppositionists' families all suffered similarly, the most devastated being Trotsky's, which was almost entirely wiped out.* Serge survived the tension through work, deriving great satisfaction from translating the works of Vera Figner, who organized the attempts on the life of Tsar Alexander II that led to Serge's parents' exile. In this terrible atmosphere, Serge wrote: 'The ring closes in relentlessly. The value of human life continuously declines, the lie in the heart of all social relationships becomes even fouler, and oppression ever heavier.'[102]

Serge believed there was a high probability that he would disappear. He petitioned Stalin for a passport. By way of response, Serge was demoted from Deputy Commander of the Front Intelligence Service, a high rank he was surprised to still hold. (This later showed up in the intelligence files of the American FBI, released to this writer through the Freedom of Information Act.) The arrests of Oppositionists and their families continued as the economic and political situation deteriorated. Stalin's wife Nadezhda Alliluyeva committed suicide.† Serge only dared see other Oppositionists at great risk. He managed to see Alexandra Bronstein and Preobrazhensky.‡

---

* His grandchild Vsevolod (Sieva) Volkov, the only one of his children to leave the USSR, survives. Trotsky's son Seryozha had a daughter who survived, and Sieva's half-sister surfaced in 1988, only to die three months later. Thirty-six members of the close family perished.

† Alexander Orlov, former Soviet diplomat and counter-intelligence chief, wrote that Alliluyeva was shocked by the conditions her husband's policies had provoked in the country, especially the situation in Ukraine, where famine had caused people to revert to cannibalism. She fought with Stalin over this, and he accused her of 'collecting Trotskyite rumours'. He treated her with abuse, obscenities and torment, according to Pauker, the chief of Stalin's bodyguard. Orlov wrote that 'death was for her the only deliverance from the vulgarity and caddishness . . . and from the rude blows [Stalin] inflicted to her human dignity'. Alexander Orlov, *The Secret History of Stalin's Crimes*, New York, Random House, 1953, pp. 314–26. Serge discussed the circumstances of Nadezhda Alliluyeva's suicide (told to him by his relatives Julia and Kalistrat Gogua, intimates of Nadezhda Alliluyeva) in his diary entry of 10 Aug. 1944. Victor Serge, *Carnets*, Paris, Julliard, 1952, Avignon, Actes Sud, 1985, p. 128.

‡ Serge said of his encounter with Preobrazhensky: 'We opened our hearts for a moment in a dark little yard beneath leafless trees. "I do not know where we are going," he said. "They are stopping me from breathing, I expect anything to happen." Symptoms of moral treason were being uncovered in his economic works on the world crisis. Hands in his pockets, melancholy and hunched against the cold night air, he was, as I inexplicably sensed, a doomed man.' Preobrazhensky subsequently disappeared. Serge, *Memoirs*, p. 281.

Serge's last testament

After many close calls,* Serge saw in the eyes of the GPU agents in his apartment that arrest was near. Feeling alone and in danger, Serge managed to smuggle a letter to his friends in Paris, Magdeleine and Maurice Paz, Jacques Mesnil and Marcel Martinet. He asked them to publish the letter in case he disappeared. Serge considered the letter his last testament. The letter was datelined 1 February 1933, Moscow. Six weeks later Serge was arrested. The testament, titled '1933 – Everything is put into question' was published in *La Révolution prolétarienne*, 25 May 1933, with the headline 'Victor-Serge Arreté'.[103]

Fearing his own demise, Serge wrote openly to his friends, asking them to fight for his release and to take care of Liuba and his son Vlady should he be killed. More importantly, Serge poured out his thoughts and feelings about the way in which life under totalitarian surveillance was choking him and indeed everyone else. It is in this document that Serge first identified the Soviet Union as a totalitarian state, before Trotsky and well before the 'totalitarian school'.

He also used the opportunity to put forward what he considered essential points that must be guaranteed as intrinsic to the socialist project. These three conditions were: *Defence of man*: respect for the rights of every man, even 'class enemies'. Every man has certain rights, including the right to a secure existence, without which there can be no socialism. Serge spoke in particular against the use of the death penalty, and against the practice of depriving men and women of liberty for mere suspected dissent. *Defence of truth:* Serge was horrified by the falsification of history already under way and the censorship of news. He said, 'I hold truth to be a precondition of intellectual and moral health. To speak of truth is to speak of honesty. Both are the right of men.' *Defence of thought:* Serge denounced the regime's embezzlement of Marxist theory, which it was replacing with empty slogans. He explained:

> I hold that Socialism cannot develop in the intellectual sense except by the rivalry, scrutiny and struggle of ideas; that we should fear not error, which is mended in time by life itself, but rather stagnation and reaction; that respect for man implies his right to know everything and his freedom to think. It is not against freedom of thought and against man that Socialism can triumph, but on the contrary, through freedom of thought, and by improving man's condition.

Questioning the scope of the regime's fear – it had gone to great lengths to prevent Serge from leaving – Serge concluded that Stalin was terrified of

---

* Serge had missed the call inviting him to a party at which all the guests were arrested; twice Serge managed to escape from comrades' houses just as the GPU were raiding. Serge, *Memoirs*, p. 275.

witnesses, of ideological opponents, and what they would say. Stalin was bitter that Trotsky was out of his reach, and was afraid of another voice against him abroad.

Serge compared Stalin's behaviour with that of Ivan the Terrible: 'the same intolerance, the same incapacity to evolve, the same horror of freedom, the same governmental fanaticism and bureaucracy, the same arbitrariness . . . the same implacable and gloomy coercion'. Serge concluded that the revolution was in a phase of reaction, that the concentration of economic and political power in the hands of the regime had resulted in 'the individual being kept on a leash by bread, clothing, lodging, and work, and totally at the discretion of the machine, which neglects man and only counts large numbers in a line'.[104]

The regime, Serge asserted, was in absolute contradiction with everything stated, proclaimed, thought and intended by the Revolution itself. Everything had changed since 1926: now, in 1933, a member of the Party would not even dream of asking a simple political question; internal passports would have been thought crazy even two years earlier, according to Serge.

How did this happen? Beyond the objective conditions of backwardness and isolation, Serge insisted that the bureaucracy obstinately chose the wrong path every time, paralysing intelligent initiative.

> The extreme concentration of power, in the presence of a profoundly embittered and disenchanted population who passively adapt and manage without illusions, increase to a large degree the importance of a handful of men who exercise . . . an uncontrolled dictatorship, without even the ability to recognize public opinion.

Serge asked the unavoidable question about the future: when the new men who are developing today put their hands on the levers of totalitarian power tomorrow, where will they take it? Reaction is accumulating, Serge pointed out. When men must fight each other for bread-cards and information on scarce lodgings, when civic courage is not tolerated, when the official ideology is so at odds with harsh daily reality that it can only be scoffed at, what kind of social consciousness can emerge? Serge observed with sadness that the youth were already sceptical of ideas and in love with material things, wanting 'Americanization'. 'The reaction at the heart of the revolution puts everything in question, compromising the future, the principles . . . creating an internal danger much more real in the present hour than the external danger.' These are not the words of a discouraged liberal, but of a genuine socialist who saw the future clearly.

Serge claimed that he was not a pessimist, but he realized that the socialist project's name would be soiled because its first experiment was so diseased. Serge wrote that socialism can only win

> not through imposing itself, but by showing itself superior to capitalism; not in the fabrication of tanks but in the organization of social life; if it offers to man a

condition better than capitalism: more material well-being, more justice, more liberty and a higher dignity.

The revolutionist's obligation in these conditions, Serge concluded, 'is a double duty: exterior defence, interior defence'. To serve the revolution, one must keep one's eyes open and resist, even when the resistance is only within one's self. To shut one's eyes 'to the bad' is to be an accomplice. The double duty then, is also to preserve one's ideas and refuse to succumb to corruption of the revolution.

Serge wrote of the Opposition's proposal for reform that 'it is impossible and cannot be carried out except with time – long years – at the price of long and painful struggles. And nothing is less certain than its success. EVERYTHING IS IN QUESTION.'

By 1933 Serge had made a definitive break with the politics of Party patriotism, and understood that the Party was finished as a vehicle of revolution and reform. Open to new collaborations, Serge wrote to his friends,

> I sympathize with all who go against the current, looking to preserve the ideas, principles, and the spirit of the October Revolution. I think that to do that it is a must to review everything, so that we can begin to institute among comrades of the most diverse tendencies a really fraternal collaboration in discussion and in action.

Serge's last testament, defining three inalienable rights of man, is not the document of a libertarian anarchist, nor of a liberal reformist. Serge explicitly wrote 'And I am not making here an apology of liberalism'. Serge's testament, penned from deep within the bowels of totalitarianism, is a rich expression of socialist goals. The need for institutional guarantees of what are basic human rights has been amply demonstrated in the years since Serge wrote these lines. Serge's testament is that of an authentic revolutionary whose life was devoted to the belief that socialism without liberty and democracy is not and cannot be socialism.

5

Orenburg 1933–36, interrogation and deportation: digging the graves of the Revolution

Crimes of existence

Serge wrote his last testament letter to his friends in France on 1 February 1933. That same month Sergei Kirov, speaking to Party activists in Leningrad, said:

> We shall be pitiless, and not only against the communists who engage in counter-revolutionary activity [that is to say, Oppositionists], but also those lacking in firmness in the factory and the villages and who fail to carry out the plan.

In early March 1933 the People's Vice-Commissar for Agriculture, Konor, and Wolfe and Kovarsky of the Council of the Commissariat, along with thirty-two other agronomists and functionaries, were executed without trial, accused of having had relations with Ukrainian nationalists in Poland.[1]

The mechanism of repression had swung into high gear. Between 1928 and 1930 by Serge's estimate some four to five thousand Oppositionists were arrested.* Socialists, anarchists, syndicalists and communists were

---

* The data Serge quoted was 3,000 to 4,000 arrested in early 1928; 1,000 more arrested in October 1929; 300 arrested in Moscow in January 1930; another 400 to 500 arrested on the occasion of the Sixteenth Party Congress in Moscow in May 1930; in August 1930 'several hundreds' more arrested. Those arrested in 1928 ended their five-year sentences in 1933–34 at which time their sentences were automatically doubled, usually after being rearrested and charged in connection with the Kirov affair. No more Oppositionists were at large after 1931–32, with the exception of Serge, Alexandra Bronstein and Andrés Nin. 1932 marked the resumption of repression in the wake of famine and terror, and with the assassination of Kirov in 1934 the terror escalated dramatically. *Victor Serge: Russia Twenty Years After*, edited by Susan Weissman, New York, Humanities Press, 1996, pp. 105–15.

imprisoned or deported. At this point nothing could save a suspect: not even silence.

In March 1933, Serge was rearrested. Although arrests were still selective, the sweep of the Opposition was thorough. Rather than the customary 'knock on the door', the GPU met Serge on the street while he was trying to buy medicine for his ailing wife. He was taken to the new GPU headquarters, a 'spacious, stern and magnificent' building.

Serge was immediately taken to the investigating magistrate responsible for Party cases, 'Comrade' Karpovich. Karpovich interrogated Serge for more than twelve hours, using the fact that they were Party comrades to get Serge to understand what was required of him. Serge noted that during the 'interview' he was able to get information surreptitiously from Karpovich about the fate of Christian Rakovsky, who had reputedly died in deportation.* The interview covered Serge's views on everything: agrarian policy, industrialization, Comintern, inner-Party regime.† The transcript of Serge's interrogation shows how Serge complied without compromising his politics. Following the interrogation, Serge was taken to the same House of Arrest he had visited in 1928. Noting that prisons are 'so durable as to prevail over revolutions and the fall of empires',[2] Serge began his fourth captivity in the same way as all the others: 'Formalities of entry, a registration-office, and a series of partitions through which a man passes like a grain on its way into some intricate milling mechanism'.[3]

Serge's first cellmate was another writer who had been cooped up in freezing solitary for months. Their cell was underground and very cold. Serge was soon transferred to the infamous Lubianka in Moscow. Disturbed and frightened, Serge 'determined to resist unyieldingly', with dignity. He was put in a tiny six by six feet windowless waiting cell for prisoners about to be executed. There were ten prisoners, two beds, constant bright light,

---

* In fact Rakovsky was sick, not dead. Without any means of effective communication, however, rumours circulated freely. Serge wrote in *Russia Twenty Years After* (p. 104) that for months comrades could not learn whether or not this particular rumour was true. It is also possible that rumours were deliberately planted to demoralize the surviving Oppositionists. This seems to be the case with Rakovsky.

† In 1992, the British film-maker and Serge enthusiast, John Eden, obtained Serge's Orenburg KGB (NKVD at the time) file. The file contains Serge's written deposition structured around questions that outline Serge's political biography. The interrogating officer is listed as V.R. Karpovich. While Serge seems to make every attempt to answer fully there is a subtle subtext of critical views. For example, Serge states that his disagreements are not with the programme of the Party but with everyday existence. He hedges on the question of socialism in one country, trying to make it seem unimportant and abstract. Serge NKVD file, 'Prisoner Questionnaire and Record of Interrogation', Orenburg, 7 March 1933.

and a cold tile floor. His cellmates had been arrested for far-fetched offences: one for 'hearing a counter-revolutionary leaflet read out among some friends without denouncing everybody immediately'.[4] In the same prison the agronomists Wolfe, Konar and Kovarsky were awaiting execution.

From there Serge was escorted to the 'prison of prisons' of 'noiseless, cell-divided secrecy' where Serge was 'in the void, enveloped in a quite astonishing silence'.[5] He spent eighty-five days in total solitude, interrupted only by six interrogations. To withstand the tension Serge slept as much as possible and worked diligently. He wrote a play, short stories, poems – all in his head, since he was not allowed writing or reading materials. He gave himself courses, and admitted that his inner life was 'most intense and rich'. He was constantly hungry, except on 1 May, International Working-man's Day, when he was given a full meal, cigarettes and matches.

The interrogations were a throwback to Tsarist traditions – nocturnal and relentless. In an aggressive mood at his first session, Serge congratulated his interrogator, Magistrate Bogen, for resuming this Tsarist ritual. Serge's account of this interrogation reveals the way in which the regime set traps for the Oppositionists, using as bait their sense of Party loyalty.

Bogen's strategy was to get to Serge as a fellow comrade, who should serve the Party by admitting the authority of the Central Committee. Serge understood the trap immediately and retorted that as an expelled member, he was no longer bound by Party discipline. Bogen then accused Serge of communicating with Oppositionists and keeping Opposition documents. He tried to link Serge to someone he did not know, a certain 'Solovian'. Serge was also asked about his meeting with Sobolevsky (also known as Sobolevich) and whether Serge had sent Anita Russakova to Sobolevich to give him the address of Solovian, who was supposedly underground. Serge rejected the accusations, denying any political activity of any kind, and declared he did not send Anita to meet with anyone.[6]

Abram Sobolevicius, or 'Sobolevich', also known as Jack Soble or Senine, was a GPU *agent-provocateur* in the German section of the Left Opposition.*

---

* Sobolevicius was a Lithuanian Jew who, with his brother Ruven (who also went under the names of Roman Well and Robert Soblen), was a leading GPU spy in Europe. Abram/Jack met with Trotsky in Prinkipo and Copenhagen, was instrumental in the collapse of the German Trotskyist section in 1933, and later expanded his scope of operations against the US government, creating a Soviet spy network in the US. He was arrested in 1957 for espionage; Robert Soblen was implicated in the Rosenberg case in 1950. See, *inter alia*, Serge's letter to Trotsky of 23 May 1936 and Serge's 'Obituary: Leon Sedov', in D.J. Cotterill (ed.), *The Serge–Trotsky Papers*, London, Pluto Press, 1994, pp. 56, 203–4; *Hearing before the Subcommittee to Investigate the Administration of the Internal Security Act*, US Senate, 21 Nov. 1947, pp. 4875–6; Georges Vereeken, *The GPU in the Trotskyist Movement*, London, New Park Publishing, 1976, pp. 29–31, 345; Harvey Klehr, John Earl Haynes and Fridrikh Igorevich Firsov, *The Secret World of American Communism*, New Haven, Yale University Press, 1995, p. 142.

Serge admitted meeting him to talk about a possible German translation of *Year One*. Clearly that meeting was a GPU provocation to set up a basis for accusations against Serge.

Subsequent interrogations proceeded along the same path, with Serge alert to pitfalls from which he would be unable to escape. On the night that Konar, Wolfe and the other agronomists were executed, they passed down the same corridors as Serge, and he sensed great danger. The next day he was summoned for interrogation by Rutkovsky, the examining magistrate for 'Serious Oppositional' cases, personal aide to the Head of the Department and a member of the secret Collegium.* Serge recalled being terrified by Rutkovsky's vicious line of questioning.[7] Rutkovsky told Serge this was his last chance to cooperate, and that if he refused he would face long years of confinement. Rutkovsky presented Serge with a fantastic document containing wild assertions extracted from Serge's young, apolitical sister-in-law Anita Russakova.† At least that is what Serge believed and wrote in the *Memoirs*.

Serge's experience in the Lubianka, followed by three years of deportation in Orenburg, helped him understand how the great trials were orchestrated, how confessions were fabricated, and how the accused were 'ripened' by ten years of persecution, demoralization, solitary confinement and torture until they were ready to sign the baseless documents. The charges against Serge, like others, were based on false testimony. Serge went to his death believing Rutkovsky's 'evidence' had been extracted by torturing his sister-in-law. In 1989 it was discovered that the entire document had been concocted, without the help of Anita Russakova.‡

---

* The account of Serge's arrest and interrogations can be found in the *Memoirs*, pp. 285–96. His criminal file, Archive-investigatory file No P–3567 in the Central Archive of the Federal Security Service, Moscow, contains the record of Serge's interrogation by Bogen (Bogin in the *Memoirs*) and Rutkovsky.

† Anita Russakova, Liuba Kibalchich's young sister, had at times been Serge's secretary, taking dictation of his translation work. Serge described her as an 'unpolitical girl whose only interest was in music, innocent in all things as a newborn baby' (Serge, *Memoirs*, p. 294). Serge refused to confirm the lies he was told were extorted from Anita under torture and demanded to see her to prove the confession was baseless. According to Serge in the *Memoirs*, his persistence led the GPU to drop the case and release Anita, but she was rearrested in April 1936, just as Serge was released (to prevent their meeting and exposing the lies which had failed against Serge), and spent twenty-five years in the gulag. Her life was ruined simply because she was related to Serge. Serge, *Memoirs*, pp. 293–6, *Russia Twenty Years After*, p. 112, Victor Serge, *From Lenin to Stalin*, New York, Monad Press, 1973, pp. 77–8, and interview with Vlady, Mexico City, May 1987.

‡ Vlady and I went to Moscow in March 1989 and made telephone contact with Anita, but were unable to procure the proper visa to visit her in Leningrad. In September 1989 two English film makers, Les Smith and Roy Battersby, met

The prepared charges were pure 'ravings' and it was clear a trap had been set. Serge knew that one bit of wavering would ensure his doom. He felt utterly alone, he said, and strangled in the dark. He understood that his captors intended to shoot him. Feeling all was lost fortified him. He decided to have nothing to do with their lies, never to give in, never abandon his Communist thought, never worship the gravedigger of the Revolution, never approve the rebirth of privilege nor the boundless misery of workers and peasants.[8]

Serge's refusal to cooperate was more than a passive silence during interrogation. He took the offensive and every day demanded that Rutkovsky allow him to confront Anita so that he could expose the lies of the GPU. In so doing, Serge put his inquisitors on trial. It was a daring gamble, but it worked. Rutkovsky ended the investigation on condition that Serge understand the GPU attached no importance to Anita's evidence (which they had manufactured). Serge was then immediately granted books, an hour's exercise each day, news of his family, and a package from the Political Red Cross. The Political Red Cross package signalled to Serge that his disappearance was known to the international community and that friends abroad must be active on his behalf.* Probably more than Serge's aggressive behaviour, the international attention drawn to his case influenced the GPU's decision to deport rather than shoot Serge. Although Serge's case was not typical – a Russian Oppositionist would most likely have disappeared forever – we can still learn a great deal about the purges from his experience.

Serge's comportment under interrogation was remarkable, but not unique. One aspect of the 'show trials' during the great purge of 1936–38 was that the interrogation process appeared infallible. The GPU, it seemed, could get anyone to confess anything. Indeed, Deputy People's Commissar of Internal Affairs Zakovsky, a former criminal who had been convicted of

---

Anita who told them she was never arrested in 1933 as written in the *Memoirs*. She therefore could not have signed the supposed denunciation presented to Serge – she had not even seen it. However, she recounted that when she was arrested in 1936, her interrogation by Rutkovsky was based on the contents of this document! (Anita Russakova, interview with Les Smith and Roy Battersby, Leningrad, Sept. 1989). In a letter Anita Russakova wrote to Vlady in summer 1990 (undated), Anita described how she told Rutkovsky he was a liar when he presented her with the baseless documents.

* In fact his comrades acted immediately upon hearing of his arrest to set up a Comité Victor-Serge to campaign for his release and raise money to support him while in deportation. Jacques Mesnil and Magdeleine Paz especially worked tirelessly for years on this issue, writing in *La Révolution prolétarienne* and other Left journals, attending meetings, badgering human rights committees, progressive lawyers in the Association Juridique Internationale, the Congress of Writers, and so forth. The material relating to the campaign is voluminous. See *La Révolution prolétarienne*, 1933–36.

murder before the Revolution, boasted that he would have been able to make Marx himself confess to working for Bismarck.[9] Yet contrary to Zakovsky and Orwell, who said a torture can be found to break anyone, some were able to resist despite the worst physical and psychological torture. For example, the protocols of the Piatakov-Radek trial show that thirty-six cases were prepared, but only nineteen people were tried – the nineteen who 'broke'.[10] The remaining seventeen defendants would not confess.

From the Lubianka Serge was taken to the old Butyrki jail, where he was left alone for several days with books. There he was presented with a paper to sign: 'Counter-revolutionary conspiracy. Condemned by the Special Collegium to three years' deportation at Orenburg'.[11] This was not a confession, but merely to acknowledge his charge and sentence. Serge, angry because he had no choice, signed and was glad to be able to look forward to a life in the open air.[12]

There was an ironic postscript to Serge's interrogations. While waiting to be deported Serge ran into the mysterious 'Solovian' – the figure his interrogator had tried to link to Serge in some conspiracy. Solovian introduced himself with the assurance that he was not in any Opposition but supported the 'General Line'. Serge wished him luck.[13] Anton Ciliga also ran into Artun Solovian, and stated he had 'irrefutable proof' that he was an *agent-provocateur* sent by the GPU.*

Orenburg

Serge's journey to his destination was something of a wonder, especially compared to his stay in the Lubianka. He met other Oppositionists in transit and shared news. He was thrilled to be outdoors. In his novel about the Orenburg experience, *Midnight in the Century*, Serge explained how Left Oppositionist ideas were carried across borders, in trains leading to deportation and prison sites.[14]

Orenburg sits on the line between Europe and Asia, between Russia and Kazakhstan. Serge assigned it to Asia. Built as a fortress against the Kazakhs, Serge described it as a 'metropolis of the steppes' which had flourished as a wealthy market city. But when Serge arrived in June 1933 the town was in ruin, ravaged by famine.

In place of the lively bazaars of yesterday, Orenburg now featured mostly empty state retail stores. Serge reported that in his three years there, no shoes arrived in Orenburg.[15] Serge's conditions of deportation were that he could not leave the town, except to walk in the woods. He found a job and lodgings, was to be issued a bread-card, and joined the hungry Kirghizians

---

* Anton Ciliga, *The Russian Enigma*, London, The Labour Book Service, 1940, pp. 563–5. Solovian's brother Moucheg Solovian was an active Oppositionist who was exiled in 1928 and shot in 1937.

and Kazakhs of Orenburg, remaining hungry until his expulsion from the Soviet Union.

Orenburg was a privileged place for deportation, reserved for leading figures. Sixteen thousand people, or one-tenth of the population, were deportees. When Serge arrived there were fifteen political deportees, among them leading Mensheviks, anarchists, SRs, Zionists and Oppositional capitulators.[16] Later the Oppositionist community swelled. Serge thought the GPU had allowed a certain homogeneity of political deportees to gather together in exile so that in the course of intellectual and political discourse, differences would arise, dividing the Opposition. It would then be easier for the GPU to separate the most irreconcilable and transfer them to worse climes and prisons.[17]

The deportee belonged to a special class unto itself. Every Soviet citizen depended on the state for survival, but this especially was true for the deportee. He or she had to report frequently to the GPU, remained completely at the mercy of a few officials for such basics as mail, work and medical care. The interrogations did not stop and the pressure to capitulate never let up. The deportee could not fraternize with Party members and was ostracized by the local population, who feared contact would jeopardize their own security.[18]

No one would hire Serge (or any deportee) unless he proclaimed support for the 'general line'.* Serge refused to capitulate, and thus got no work. He depended entirely on food parcels from his wife, and more importantly money from the sale of his books in Paris. His first three novels, *Men in Prison*, *Conquered City*, and *Birth of Our Power*, as well as his history *Year One of the Russian Revolution* were now on sale in France. When the mail got through, Serge received 300 francs† (about fifteen rubles) per month to buy

---

* If the deportee was a worker, 'responsible employment' was denied him; if he was an intellectual, he was not allowed to teach or continue his studies. Any work of adequate compensation was also forbidden. His mail was often confiscated, and in general the deportee was deprived of civil rights. He was subject to arbitrary arrest and raids, living under the constant threat of the Secret Service (Serge, *Russia Twenty Years After*, pp. 75–6). The deportee was destitute, spied on, deprived of private life, and transferred from one remote region to another, usually without any knowledge of charges. Conditions in deportation, however terrible, were better than prison. Many memoirs corroborate and elaborate Serge's testimony: e.g. Ciliga, *The Russian Enigma*; Valentin Gonzalez and Julian Gorkín, *El Campesino: Life and Death in Soviet Russia*, New York, G.P. Putnam's Sons, 1952; Nicholas Prychodko, *One of the Fifteen Million*, Boston, Little Brown, 1952; Alexander Weissberg, *The Accused*, New York, Simon and Schuster, 1951.

† The Comité Victor-Serge in Paris raised money for Serge through the journal *La Révolution prolétarienne*. The subscriptions obtained were published in each issue with the name of the contributor and amount donated. See *La Révolution prolétarienne*, 'Souscription pour Victor Serge', no. 122–2, 1933, p. 2.

food at the local *Torgsin* shop, which even at the height of famine sold food in exchange for foreign currency. Serge was able to support some of his comrades as well. For a while, Serge also received food parcels from Magdeleine Paz in Paris – packages of rice, sugar, flour and olives. Vlady told Richard Greeman that he once divided a single olive among a group of schoolmates, who had never seen one.

In the winter of 1934, Serge's wife Liuba and son Vlady joined him in Orenburg, bringing with them Serge's typewriter and books. Liuba's mental health was not strong enough to bear the terrible instability of life in deportation, however, and Serge finally decided that her presence would jeopardize the whole family's survival and sent her back to Leningrad. Vlady remained with Serge throughout his period of exile, and he remembers the time as one of tranquillity and study, but also of fierce struggle to withstand starvation and exposure during the harsh winter,* and hunger and disease during the extremely hot summer.[19]

Apart from Vlady, Serge's 'family circle' in Orenburg consisted of ten deported Oppositionists, whose characters and travails are captured in Serge's novel of the Orenburg years, *Midnight in the Century*.[20] The men and women who shared internal exile with Serge, most of them civil-war veterans, 'incarnated an epoch' and Serge wrote that 'most probably' they all perished.† They are described in detail in both the *Memoirs* and *Russia Twenty Years After*. The intensity of their experience bound these comrades together, and Serge felt strongly it was his duty to campaign ceaselessly for their lives once he was released, and to memorialize their struggles in his written works. Serge stressed that these men and women, 'journeying . . . from prison to prison, from exile to exile, tormented by privation . . . kept their revolutionary faith, their good spirits, their sparkling political intelligence',[21] which in retrospect seems remarkable.

Serge's fiction portrays the struggles, hopes, goals and tragedies of his generation of revolutionaries, whose life experience was unique. His writing is largely autobiographical, but it is also a work of the imagination. Serge used the novel as his vehicle to get at the inner truth of the tumultuous political struggles in which he and his comrades participated. His fiction communicates that truth in a way that his histories could not.

---

* In order to keep warm, the townspeople abandoned the well-made large houses which were in any case requisitioned by the GPU. They then built smaller, inferior homes, leaving the larger ones to rot. When the condition of the larger homes reached a certain stage of deterioration, permission would be granted to demolish them and sell the timber for firewood. In this way Serge and the other inhabitants were able to keep warm, while the housing stock diminished and the population increased. See Serge, *Memoirs*, pp. 306–7, and *Midnight in the Century*, translated by Richard Greeman, London, Writers and Readers, 1982.

† Serge, *Memoirs*, p. 309. In Moscow in 1989 Vlady and I learned that Lisa Senyatskaya, Vassily Pankratov's wife, had survived.

Midnight in the Century, while fictional, illustrates the thoughts, feelings and discussions of his comrades. The novel depicts many meetings and discussions of the Left Oppositionists in exile.* It is a work of optimism despite grim conditions. In a central scene the old Bolshevik Elkin and the young worker Rodion discuss the joy of sunshine – feeling they could be whisked into a cellar that evening. Asked what had become of thought in the period of the 'huge falsehood', Elkin answers Rodion: 'Right now it's something of a midnight sun piercing the skull. Glacial. What's to be done, if it is midnight in the century?' Young Rodion, Serge's hope, replies 'Midnight's where we have to live then'.[22]

Even in the worst conditions, while revolutionaries were stabbed in the back by their own Party, while fascism reared its ugly head and capitalism, gripped by depression, plunged toward war, Serge's novel reaffirmed the revolutionary spirit and bright political intelligence of his comrades. Even though it *was* midnight in the century, Serge showed morning dawning with the escape of young Rodion, who represented the new revolutionary worker.

It has been suggested that Koestler's famous novel of the purges, *Darkness at Noon*, was influenced by Serge's *Midnight in the Century*. Although the content is more frequently compared with *The Case of Comrade Tulayev*, the titles themselves have been the subject of an interesting analysis by Bill Marshall. While the titles seem to parallel each other, Marshall points to a subtle, but significant difference – in Serge's novel light triumphs over dark, while Koestler, taking his title from Milton's *Samson Agonistes*, emphasizes darkness obliterating light.[23]

Serge's characters were composites of imprisoned revolutionists.† *Midnight in the Century* reveals that their morale was excellent, despite terrible conditions; that they were able to receive information from Trotsky and the

---

* For example, by the river the group held discussions on the nature of the Soviet state and on Hegel and dialectics: pp. 67–71. Pages 71–2 discuss the report on the Left Oppositionists in the Verkhne-Uralsk Isolator and Central Prison in late 1933. On pp. 75–6 they discuss the situation in Germany and the need for a United Front, and the question of whether or not the time has come to form a new Party in the USSR. This develops into a general theoretical discussion on the congruencies between Stalin and Hitler: 'These grave-diggers were born to understand each other. Enemies and brothers. In Germany, one is burying an aborted democracy, the child of an aborted revolution. In Russia, the other is burying a victorious revolution born of a weak proletariat and left on its own by the rest of the world. Both of them are leading those they serve – the bourgeoisie in Germany, the bureaucracy here at home – toward a catastrophe.' There are many more useful discussions, including very useful portrayals of the interrogations and how some Oppositionists fought back and others caved in (pp. 41–50, 165–7, 169–71).

† Among them, Boris Mikhailovich Eltsin, the old Bolshevik comrade of Lenin, whose son Victor Borisovich Eltsin was Trotsky's assistant; Lisa Senyatskaya, pregnant wife of Vassily Pankratov, revolutionary leader in the Verkhne-Uralsk

Oppositionists in the other prisons and camps, though certainly without regularity; how they were all Oppositionists, but nevertheless held various positions.

Serge was careful to show how in discussion the Opposition maintained the revolutionary Bolshevik tradition of expressing sharp and conflicting views, in an attempt to achieve clarity. The Oppositionists were wholly different from the servile yes-men of Stalin's Party; they were thinking revolutionaries accustomed to debate.* Boris Eltsin confessed that what held them together was the GPU: 'Our unity is the work of the GPU: in fact we have as many tendencies as there are militants. I do not find this at all objectionable.'[24]

Where was Victor Serge in this mélange of Oppositionists? He stood on the left of the Trotskyists, sympathetic to the concerns of the extreme left-wing, but loyal to the ideas of the Old Man, with the outstanding difference that Serge proclaimed the death of the Bolshevik Party much earlier than Trotsky.† As a former anarchist, it was easier for Serge to break with the counter-revolutionary practices of Stalin's Party than for many of the early Bolsheviks.‡

Isolator; Lydia Svalova, young worker from Perm who had spent her youth in deportation; Fanya Epstein, Odessa intellectual and militant; Vassily Chernykh, former head of Ural Cheka, a 'revisionist' who thought all ideas now needed rethinking; the history professor Yakov Belenky, the worker Ivan Byk who had been a member of the Workers' Opposition; the proletarian from the Putilov works, Alexei Santalov, arrested for calling Stalin the 'gravedigger of the Revolution' in a bar. These comrades became, in Serge's *Midnight in the Century*, the characters Ryzhik (who Vlady insisted represented Serge himself in the novels), Elkin, Varvara, Avelii, Kostrov and Rodion.

* The Opposition was divided between capitulators (in three drafts), the democratic centralists (led by V. Smirnov and T. Sapronov), revisionists, and doctrinaires, who were subdivided into orthodox, extreme Left, and State Capitalists. Anton Ciliga and Isaac Deutscher also confirmed that the Opposition had moderate and far left currents. Anton Ciliga belonged to the 'extreme Left-wing Opposition' which distinguished itself from the Trotskyists in calling the Soviet Union a new exploitative class society, as opposed to Trotsky's characterization of the USSR as a degenerated workers' state. Ciliga belonged to the camp of Oppositionists which included 'democratic Centralism', 'workers' Opposition', 'workers' group'. They shared a concern that Trotsky was battling Stalin over the Party and that the proletariat and its condition was but a passive object in the struggle. See Ciliga, *The Russian Enigma*, especially book III, chapter VIII, pp. 261–74.

† Serge never defined the class nature of the Soviet Union as state capitalist as did many of the extreme left-wingers. His own conclusions about the class character of the Soviet state are taken up in the chapter on his final writings below.

‡ The so-called 'Right' Opposition only discovered the dangers of the one-Party anti-democratic system when it turned against them. In 1927, Bukharin wrote:

The crossroads

During the terrible winter of 1934 Serge fell deathly ill. In the country at large the famine was ending. The ruble had stabilized, pegged to a kilo of bread. But Serge had no work, and the GPU cut off his mail, his only source of food. Serge surmised the GPU was choking him off because of the clamour raised by the international campaign for his release. This knowledge boosted his morale, but it did not save his health. Yet Serge continued to give talks in the surrounding woods about the Spanish revolution and its impact on the West and the Soviet Union.

News of Rakovsky's capitulation did not dampen the exiles' morale, since they made allowance for Rakovsky's age and condition, and knew the GPU had tricked him with 'secret documents' about impending war. Ivan Byk confirmed this.

Without money or food, Serge and Vlady nearly starved to death.* In a conversation in Mexico in May 1987 Vlady recalled his experience in Orenburg: the worst was the isolation, the horrible hunger they suffered, and having to witness children 'dying like flies'. Yet he remembers the wonder and tranquility, the political discussions, the freezing nights. He felt like a young monk with his father – his teacher – in Spartan surroundings like a monastery. Vlady sketched, and managed to send Trotsky a picture. He said of Serge:

> My father was very sad, and deathly hungry, though he never lost his senses. He had a firm character and worked incessantly. Even in Orenburg he always managed to wear a clean shirt and to keep clean and dignified. I sketched, read dictionaries and studied the history of Greece and Russia. We cooked together, more often than not it was a soup made of cabbage, water and salt. We always sat down to eat, and after 'dinner' we read poetry, even my father's verses. Then my father went back to work.[25]

Serge was plagued by boils, which began to abscess, leading to an infected tumour in his left breast. No medical treatment was allowed until the 'GPU woke up, since they had to answer for us to the Central Collegium'.[26] Serge was finally taken to hospital, probably in late December 1934, just after Kirov's assassination. Serge wondered if this hospitalization saved him from being rearrested for Kirov's assassination, like his comrades Pevzner

---

'Under the dictatorship of the proletariat, two, three or four parties may exist, but on the single condition that one of them is in power and the others in prison' (*Trud*, 13 Nov. 1927). Serge commented: 'the corollary of this monstrous theory is: a single opinion in the single Party and it soon becomes the opinion of a single one'.

* Serge and Vlady survived on a little black bread and a soup made of sorrel and one egg that had to last two days. Serge, *Memoirs*, p. 311.

and Pankratov. However, Pevzner was every bit as ill as Serge; he was taken to the same hospital with scarlet fever. Perhaps the international attention Serge's case had attracted spared him.

According to Serge, the conditions in the Orenburg hospital could have come right out of some medieval hell. Serge was saved when the GPU allowed him to receive one dispatch, containing money from the sale of his books, which made it possible to buy food.

Serge received word from Pankratov, newly interned at Verkhne-Uralsk with Kamenev and Zinoviev, reporting that the new terror was far worse than before, and warning Serge and his comrades to prepare themselves.[27] Both of Serge's Orenburg comrades Pankratov and Pevzner were charged with new terms of five years' imprisonment for Kirov's assassination.

The assassination took them all by surprise, since Serge and his comrades were convinced just before Kirov's murder that the situation had begun to achieve a degree of normality. The famine was ending, the *kolkhoz* system had been modified to allow private plots and the Soviet Union was trying to present an improved world image in order to impress the League of Nations.

Serge's perceptive powers did not fail him. The Soviet Union was at a crossroads at the end of 1934. Stalin could have retreated and revived NEP in modified form, wound down the concentration camps, increased real wages, and given the peasants more breathing space – all of which would have immeasurably increased his popularity. Serge wrote that Bukharin's work on the Constitution also seemed to indicate that Stalin would choose that road.[28] Having thus analysed the situation, the Oppositionists at Orenburg spent the next year (1935) in illusive serenity, while the Politburo was torn between 'contrary inclinations'.

Underestimating the fire of the dragon

The assassination of Kirov on 1 December 1934* has rightly been called the 'keystone of the entire edifice of terror'.[29] The assassination 'ushered in an era of panic and savagery'[30] beginning with the immediate execution of 128 people, the arrest and imprisonment of the entire Zinoviev and

---

* Sergei Kirov was shot in the back by a young embittered communist, Leonid Nikolayev, at the Smolny in Leningrad. When questioned by Stalin, Nikolayev pointed to the NKVD guards and confessed they 'made me do it' and had given him four months of target practice. Witness Filipp Medved, head of Leningrad NKVD, told his friends in the camps about the scene of Nikolayev's questioning, in which he stressed Nikolayev's cry: 'They kept at me for four months. They said it was necessary for the Party.' Anton Antonov-Ovseyenko, *The Time of Stalin: Portrait of a Tyranny*, New York, Harper/Colophon Books, 1981, pp. 90–93. The full story of Kirov's assassination is also recounted in Roy Medvedev, *Let History Judge*, New York, Vintage Books, 1973, pp. 157–66.

Kamenev tendency (Serge estimated 3,000 people), the mass deportation of tens of thousands of Leningraders,* arrests among the deportees and secret trials in the prisons. In many cases Oppositionists charged with the killing of Kirov had already been in prison two years when the assassination took place. Kirov's assassination, the starting point for the 'great terror' is also the centrepiece of Serge's novel, *The Case of Comrade Tulayev* (Tulayev is Serge's fictional Kirov).

The Kirov assassination has been the subject of historical controversy.†

---

* Serge estimated that up to 100,000 people were deported from Leningrad to the Volga, the Urals, Central Asia and Siberia. He quoted Berger, a French technician living in Leningrad, who wrote about the deportations in 'USSR 1935', *La Révolution prolétarienne*, 25 Sept. 1935. Serge confirmed that between 1,200 and 1,500 of the deported Leningraders came to Orenburg, among them many women, children and elderly. *Russia Twenty Years After*, pp. 200–201. In *From Lenin to Stalin*, p. 81, Serge added that the 100,000 Leningraders were deported in a single year, 1935, the year of economic recovery.

† Alexander Orlov first implicated Stalin in his book *The Secret History of Stalin's Crimes*, New York, Random House, 1953, and his version was corroborated by Boris Nicolaevsky's 1956 essays, compiled in his *Power and the Soviet Elite: 'The Letter of an Old Bolshevik' and Other Essays*, New York, Praeger, 1965. Alexander Barmine concurred, and wrote that Stalin alone profited from Kirov's death (*One Who Survived: The Life Story of a Russian under the Soviets*, New York, G.P. Putnam's Sons, 1945, pp. 251–3). Khrushchev provided many of the facts during the Twenty-second Party Congress, later confirmed and elaborated by Roy Medvedev in *Let History Judge*, and Anton Antonov-Ovseyenko in *The Time of Stalin*. The Gorbachev years generated new controversy and interest in the Kirov affair: see Robert Conquest's *Stalin and the Kirov Murder*, New York and Oxford, Oxford University Press, 1989, and Adam Ulam's novel *The Kirov Affair*, San Diego, Harcourt Brace, 1988. J. Arch Getty insists that the evidence implicating Stalin is biased and writes that Nikolayev acted possibly in concert with the police, but without the involvement of higher-ups, including Stalin (*Origins of the Great Purges*, Cambridge, Cambridge University Press, 1985). Ulam and Getty both reject the sources implicating Stalin's role in ordering Kirov's murder. Getty restricts himself to official sources, which in the Soviet context have to be treated carefully given that the practice of falsification was institutionalized. Getty also rejects memoirs and personal accounts as source material. The subject opened in the Soviet Union with Anatoli Rybakov's *Deti Arbata* and the February 1988 *Nedelya* article charging Genrik Yagoda with being 'one of the central figures in arranging the assassination of S.M. Kirov' and the publication of previously suppressed sections of the memoirs of Anastas I. Mikoyan in the December 1987 *Ogonyok* which described how Kirov almost replaced Stalin as General Secretary in 1934. Then the playwright Mikhail F. Shatrov's '*Onward . . . Onward . . . Onward*' accused Stalin of plotting Kirov's murder. There was widespread interest in discovering the facts about the assassination because it was a turning point in Soviet history, marking the arbitrary point of departure for massive repression. A CPSU Politburo Commission headed by Mikhail Solomentsev created a special sub-commission to examine

Although at the time the assassination had been blamed on the Zinoviev-Kamenev and the Left Oppositionists, Khrushchev's official investigation, soon suppressed, implicated Stalin. Trotsky, in exile, wrote in the *Bulletin of the Opposition* that the GPU was involved and that communists of the Zinoviev, Kamenev and Trotskyist stamp rejected individual terror.[31]

Kirov had replaced Zinoviev as the head of the Leningrad Party organization. He was widely popular because he led the opposition to the execution of Ryutin in 1932.[32] At the Seventeenth Party Congress in late January 1934, the so-called 'Congress of Victors', there was a move to replace Stalin with Kirov, and in the vote for the Central Committee, Stalin received fewer votes than any other candidate. Significantly, only three votes were cast against Kirov, while 292 votes were cast against Stalin.* Boris Nicolaevsky has shown that in the official documents of the Congress the phrase (in use since the Thirteenth Party Congress) 'confirmation' by the Plenum of Stalin's appointment as General Secretary was missing. Nicolaevsky took its absence to mean that Stalin ceased to be General Secretary of the Central Committee after the Seventeenth Congress.[33]

Stalin had to remove this new threat to his power. Kirov's death proved very handy for Stalin. It eliminated a serious rival and provided a pretext for repression against those he regarded as a threat to his power. Nikolayev fired the shot that killed Kirov, but the NKVD allowed his access to the Smolny and promptly executed him afterwards. Inconvenient witnesses such as Borisov were shot or killed in traffic 'accidents'. Stalin quickly decreed 'The Law of 1 December 1934' mandating that cases be concluded in less than ten days, and that the indictment be handed to the accused only one day before the trial.[34] The accused were not allowed defence lawyers, and the death sentences were executed immediately after the verdict. This modification of penal procedure was applied retroactively to 114 people who were quickly liquidated for the crime.[35] Yezhov replaced Kirov in the Secretariat, and Zhdanov replaced him in Leningrad.

Victor Serge was convinced that Nikolayev's act was 'almost certainly an

---

the Kirov case (*Pravda*, 19 Aug. 1988). Not surprisingly, it exonerated Stalin, since to blame him would reveal the bankruptcy of the regime, and indeed the Soviet Union. In 1999, Amy Knight published *Who Killed Kirov?* (New York, Hill and Wang). Using newly declassified archival documents (though some key sources are still classified), Knight uncovers much of what has long been suspected – that Stalin engineered Kirov's murder.

* Antonov-Ovseyenko, *The Time of Stalin*, p. 80. Two hundred and ninety-two votes equal one-fourth of the Congress delegates. Antonov-Ovseyenko's source was the records of the elections commission of the Seventeenth Party Congress, which had been locked away until 1957, when a special commission of the Politburo was established after the Twentieth Party Congress to examine the archives. Roy Medvedev, in reporting the same incident, counted twenty-two fewer votes against Stalin. Medvedev, *Let History Judge*, pp. 154–7.

individual act committed by an enraged young Communist'.* Serge's intimate association with the Leningrad Party organization and the Leningrad Oppositionists, both Trotskyists and Zinovievists, led him to reject as impossible their role in the assassination. In fact, the only Left Oppositionist remaining in Leningrad in 1934 was Alexandra Bronstein. Serge affirmed that the Oppositionists in 1934 were still partisans of 'Soviet Reform' and 'reform excluded any appeal to violence'. Serge wrote that the murder confronted the Politburo with a problem: 'Not only their own responsibility for the years of darkness, but also the existence of a reserve team of government in the persecuted Opposition who, for all the abuse directed so incessantly against them, were more popular among the informed sections of the population than the leaders of the State'.[36] Serge saw Nikolayev aiming his bullet at a Party leader to express outrage at Stalin's policies. Serge did not see Stalin behind Nikolayev.

The Case of Comrade Tulayev, Serge's novel about the purges, revolves around the lone assassin whose act created a vortex of repressions. The book was serialized in the provincial literary journal *Ural*, published in Sverdlovsk in 1989.[37] At that time the commission of inquiry had not yet presented its findings. Ironically Serge's lone assassin thesis played into the hands of the Stalinists, who wished to absolve Stalin of complicity in the murder, according to Sergei Zavarotnyi of *Komsomolskaya Pravda*.[38]

Unlike Serge, Trotsky smelled the hands of the GPU in the assassination. Serge believed that the assassination was the work of 'an isolated individual', but among his two or three closest comrades was an acknowledged GPU informer.[39] Neither Serge nor Trotsky realized just how far Stalin was willing to go to achieve his ends.

However naive the Oppositionists may have been about Stalin's role in

---

* Serge, *Memoirs*, p. 314. Other writers shared Serge's view that Nikolayev acted alone: Hryhory Kostiuk and Victor Kravchenko both wrote that Nikolayev was a lone assassin and that his act was not political, but the result of jealous rage. Rumour had it that Kirov had an affair with Nikolayev's wife (Hryhory Kostiuk, *Stalinist Rule in the Ukraine*, New York, Praeger, 1960). Kravchenko repeated the same love triangle murder motive, but added that students in Leningrad were filled with romantic hope that the assassination was an expression of terror by a new popular movement. The students began to disappear from his institute, and Kravchenko wrote that thousands of students were arrested and hundreds shot following the Kirov murder (Victor Kravchenko, *I Chose Freedom*, New York, Scribner's, 1946, pp. 168–9). As to workers' reactions, Andrew Smith wrote that in the Electrazavod factory where he worked, the news of the Kirov assassination shocked the workers, but some 'smiled significantly to each other, when they were sure they were not being observed by the propagandists ... A machine hand named Vassily even went so far as to say to me, "It would have been much better if it had been Stalin instead of Kirov"' (Andrew Smith, *I Was a Soviet Worker*, New York, E.P. Dutton, 1936, p. 265).

the affair, the profound significance of the assassination was not lost on them. Serge wrote that the *attentat* revealed an 'inward-driven crisis' that showed

> the blind alley into which led the tactic of disavowal and apostasy, adopted more out of cynicism than cowardice by the oppositional elements readmitted into the Party after Zinoviev and Kamenev . . . Woe to those who forget that the proletariat cannot be served by cowardly manoeuvres, by abdications of conscience, by mental reservations, by capitulations and impostures. Let us not be astonished that a youth should reach the point, in this suffocating atmosphere, of despairing of everything save his own despair. Let us not be astonished, either, that the bureaucracy should seize upon this occasion to rid itself of its hidden adversaries. The madness and the cruelty which make it lose all sense of moderation are amazing as a confession of tremendous moral weakness; but the political calculations, which result in the measures taken against the Zinoviev tendency, are wretchedly, sordidly correct. Such an opportunity to bury these men will not present itself again.*

The assassination of Kirov on 1 December 1934 was the prelude to the 'great terror' but it took two years to pick up steam. In the interim, the inner circles of the Party were battling over their course.† Serge wrote that in 1935 the Politburo was 'torn between contrary inclinations, towards normalization on the one hand, towards terror on the other'.[40] It appeared that the stabilizing tendency would win: the abolition of bread-rationing was popular,‡ and Serge thought that Stalin was at a turning-point.[41]

Normalization meant a partial return to NEP. Whether that was still a real option was open to question, given that NEP had been a failure,

---

* Serge, *Russia Twenty Years After*, pp. 203–4. Serge credited the Stalinist bureaucracy with acting in its own self-interest, and quoted Trotsky: 'It is not Stalin who has created the bureaucratic apparatus, but the apparatus that has created Stalin in its own image'. Leon Trotsky, 'The Terrorism of Bureaucratic Self-Defence', *Bulletin of the Opposition*, Sept. 1935.

† Barmine discussed the choices as between 'conciliation' and 'totalitarian counter-revolution'. He wrote that while Stalin was destroying the ruling elite, a measure of conciliation was achieved in the country at large in the form of withdrawal of bread-cards and an improved food situation. Barmine saw the Stalin cult and the improved food situation as Stalin's manoeuvring for support by the 'politically unconscious masses' while he unleashed his terror. Barmine, *One Who Survived*, pp. 249–55.

‡ Serge also observed that the pegging of the ruble to a kilo of bread, an immense relief to the workers, had another effect: the 'rebirth of Soviet trading in the form of stores opened by the state in increasing number, and an activization of the free market'. Serge noted further, 'Where are the mysteries of the exploitation of labour? At one stroke you perceive one of the great advantages of the bureaucratic mechanism and of managed economy: exploitation there is visible at first glance'. Serge, *Russia Twenty Years After*, p. 193.

accomplishing no measurable gains in industrialization and leading to a grain crisis in agriculture.

Stalin did not go for normalization nor was he able to, because his industrial and agricultural policies, and the class relations these engendered, set in motion an inexorable descent into reliance on terror. To get the masses of workers and peasants to comply with impossible demands, their collective will had to be broken. Terror was the tool. In 1934 Serge thought the regime could choose between more authoritarian, brutal discipline or a partial retreat. With the murder of Kirov, Stalin eliminated the 'normalizing' alternative. The savage dynamic of Stalin's system would become clear to Serge in the next two hellish years.

Writings to nowhere: paid

Serge was able to support himself and his son, and occasionally other comrades, with income from his writings, and with donations gathered by the Comité Victor-Serge in Paris. Serge took advantage of the relative tranquillity deportation afforded to write. Despite the hunger, cold, isolation and uncertainty, Serge persevered and produced four books.

The arrangement Serge managed to make with Romain Rolland kept him in food. He made several copies of his manuscripts and sent them to Rolland in Paris, who then forwarded them to publishers. Rolland was not sympathetic to Serge's politics, but opposed repression in the USSR and agreed to be the intermediary for Serge.[42] Despite the precautions Serge took, including registering the manuscripts with the GPU and sending them by registered post, the first four packages were lost. Serge complained to the head of the secret police, who used the event to declare sabotage in the postal service and justify more repression. Serge gave him another set of manuscripts to send to Rolland, which also went astray, as did the next.*

---

* Among Yagoda's papers published in 1997, it states that the NKVD confiscated the first three copies of the novel about the French anarchist movement, and after a fourth copy was lost the NKVD in Orenburg informed the NKVD in Moscow that the book was lost. Genrikh Iagoda, *Narkom vnutrennikh del SSSR, General'nyi komissar gosudarstvenno bezopasnosti*, Kazan, Sbornik dokumentov, 1997, p. 431. The official permission order to send these copies to Rolland was signed by Bogrov, head of the Foreign Literature Section of *Glavlit*, and is recorded in Bogrov's registered letter of 29 Sept. 1934, #949. Serge corroborated the above in a statement of 9 June 1936, held in the Mexico archive, now in the Victor Serge Papers, Gen. MSS 238, Box 17, Folder 625, Beinecke Library, Yale University. Rolland was piqued that the Soviet authorities were blocking Serge's manuscripts, particularly since they were addressed to him. See Rolland to Jean Guéhenno, 24 Oct. 1934, in *L'Indépendance de l'ésprit, Cahiers Romain Rolland*, no. 23, Paris 1975, p. 314. In an account of his visit to the Soviet Union in 1935, Rolland wrote that he had been given a copy of Serge's novel about the pre-war

The irony was that the Post Office was required to compensate Serge for each loss, and at the rate of five per month, Serge earned 'hundreds of rubles', as much as a well-paid technician.[43]

The books Serge wrote in Orenburg included *Les Hommes perdus*, an autobiographical piece on the pre-war French Anarchists, and a sequel to *Conquered City* called *La Tourmente*, set in the year 1920, 'the zenith of the revolution'. He also wrote a collection of poems, *Résistance*, and was working on *Year Two of the Russian Revolution*. Serge said these were the only books he ever had the time to revise and polish.[44]

L'affaire Victor Serge[45]

Serge had written letters to his friends in Paris prior to exile and from Orenburg, and these letters were published in the French journal *La Révolution prolétarienne*. Supporters of Serge waged a campaign for his release which grew to such proportions that it became an embarrassment for both the French Communist Party and its fellow travellers in the intellectual community, and for the Soviet Union.

The tireless work on behalf of Serge by the Comité Victor-Serge, and especially Magdeleine Paz, Charles Plisnier and Jacques Mesnil, turned Serge's case into a *cause célèbre*. Communist Party front organizations of lawyers (L'Association juridique internationale), the Socialist Lawyers Group, and other writers' organizations such as the prestigious Congress of Writers became involved in protesting Serge's plight. Serge's case was a perfect example of the choking of free thought. A writer's life was in mortal danger, as well as the lives of his immediate family, simply because he dared to exhibit independent thought. This is the stuff human rights campaigns are made of. Paz, Mesnil, Léon Werth, Marcel Martinet, Georges Duhamel, Charles Víldrac, Maurice Parijanine, Boris Souvarine and others raised the issue constantly. Their demand was simple: free Victor Serge! Subscriptions were pouring into *La Révolution prolétarienne*,[46] not only from individuals, but from organizations and trade unions such as the United Teachers' Federation. The appeal spread to Holland (Henriette Roland-Holst), Belgium (Charles Plisnier) and Switzerland (Fritz Brupbacher.) At their annual conference, the French Teachers' Union demanded Serge's release or some justification for his imprisonment: they alerted the Soviet teachers' delegation

French anarchist movement (*Les Hommes perdus*), which Rolland had to read in one night. Yagoda had given him the copy that had been intercepted by *Gosplit* which he was to return to Yagoda. Rolland, *Voyage de Moscou, Cahiers Romain Rolland*, p. 196. In a letter to Genrikh Iagoda (18 July 1935) Rolland tried to persuade Iagoda that it would serve Soviet interests to let him take the manuscript to France. Iagoda, *Narkom vnutrennikh del SSSR*, pp. 428–9.

to the case. The League for the Rights of Man published Magdeleine Paz's documentation in *La Révolution prolétarienne*, after prodigious prodding on her part. The case splashed across the pages of other French journals such as *L'Ecole émancipée*, *Le Combat marxiste*, *Les Humbles*.[47]

The affair reached its zenith in the 1935 Communist Party organized International Congress of Writers for the Defence of Culture sponsored officially by André Malraux, André Gide, Henri Barbusse, Victor Margueritte, Romain Rolland, Elie Faure, and Alain, noted leftists of various persuasions. The Comité Victor-Serge were there in force, seeking an audience,* to the chagrin of prominent French intellectuals. Serge noted that Gide was particularly embarrassed and insisted the matter be heard,† at which point Malraux agreed to let Paz speak. She was supported by Plisnier and Henry Poulaille. A delegation of Soviet writers including Boris Pasternak, Nikolai Tikhonov, the official journalist Mikhail Koltsov,‡ Ehrenberg and others was present. They were colleagues of Serge and knew him well. Yet only Pasternak kept in the background, while the others

> fulfilled instructions and declared without a blink that they knew nothing of the writer Victor Serge – these, my good colleagues of the Soviet Writer's Union! All they knew of was a 'Soviet citizen, a confessed counter-revolutionary, who had been a member of the conspiracy which had ended in the murder of Kirov'.[48]

These writers were repressed themselves in the Great Terror of 1936–39. The appalling statement that linked Serge to Kirov's murder aroused André Gide who went straight to the Soviet Ambassador on behalf of Serge, to no avail.§

The event was to be a formative one for Gide, who changed his thinking about the Soviet Union as a result. The treatment of the Victor Serge affair

---

* Except André Breton, who 'elegantly skirted' the issue. The Comité included Salvemini, Magdeleine Paz, Henri Poulaille, and Plisnier. Victor Serge, *Carnets*, Paris, Julliard, 1952, p. 31.

† Serge had written to André Gide from Orenburg in January 1935 about their shared conceptions of pluralism and freedom in literature. It was this contact that led to Gide's insistence that Paz and Plisnier be allowed to address the Congress on the Serge affair. The letter was published in *Esprit*, 45 (June 1936), pp. 435–40.

‡ Serge says he was a man noted for his 'pliant docility' (*Memoirs*, p. 318).

§ Gide was particularly angry at the behaviour of the Soviet delegation who tried to stifle discussion of the Serge case at the Congress. William Marshall, 'Ideology and Literary Expression in the Works of Victor Serge', D.Phil. thesis, Oxford University, 1984, pp. 228–9, noted that Mme de van Rysselberghe later wrote that Gide's intervention with the Soviet Ambassador figured importantly in Serge's eventual release. M. de van Rysselberghe, *Les Cahiers de la petite dame 1929–1937*, *Cahiers André Gide* no. 5, Paris, Gallimard, 1974, pp. 462–71.

at the Congress made it evident that the Congress was 'entirely controlled, with perfect dishonesty, by the agents of the CP. He felt used, saw the moral ugliness of it.'[49] Gide later visited the Soviet Union where his moral reservations were confirmed by ugly reality.

Rolland finally interceded on Serge's behalf when he went to the Soviet Union in 1935. He was not the first to press the Serge case in Moscow. Earlier a delegation from the organization Serge belonged to in his youth, the Jeunes Gardes Socialistes of Belgium, had raised the issue in the Soviet Union and were told that Serge was in Orenburg translating and living very well.[50]

Rolland had no particular affinity with Serge's politics, but was spurred to action by the persecution of Serge as a writer.* Rolland met with Stalin, and simply asked that the Victor Serge affair be resolved one way or another, as it had become an impediment to the work of 'friends of the Soviet Union' in France.[51] André Gide and André Malraux also made similar requests.

In 1988, *Moscow News* published an account of Rolland's meeting with Stalin. This article contains the first public mention of Victor Serge's name in the Soviet press in more than fifty years.

> During the three weeks Rolland spent in the Soviet Union he met with Stalin and talked to him frankly. He expressed his concern about the repressions and tried to show how detrimental they were to the Soviet Union's prestige abroad. In reply Stalin painted a sinister picture: conspirators against Soviet power everywhere, new plots being constantly exposed . . . Rolland could neither disbelieve what he was told, nor suppress his doubts. The only concession he managed to get as a result of that conversation was Stalin's consent to allow *the exiled French anarchist Victor Serge* [my emphasis] to leave the country. Rolland did not sympathize with Serge at all, incidentally.[52]

In 1992, the transcript of Rolland's meeting with Stalin appeared in his Moscow diary, published by *Cahiers Romain Rolland*.[53]

Miraculously, the Serge case was resolved. Stalin called Yagoda to find out what Serge had confessed to, and found that Serge had not confessed, and therefore had not agreed to be complicit in anything. Stalin assured Rolland that Serge and his family would be able to leave the Soviet

---

* Serge also had mixed feelings about Rolland: he detested Rolland's writings on Gandhi because they 'contained the most exact, the most prophetic insights on the stifling character of dictatorship – all the while misunderstanding the terrible reality of a spontaneous revolution alive only by virtue of unceasing miracles of implacable activity'. Nevertheless, Serge recognized that Rolland intervened for Francesco Ghezzi in Suzdal, and 'moderately for me' (*Carnets*, published in English as 'The Tragedy of Romain Rolland, From the Diary of Victor Serge – Part IV', in *New International*, May–June 1950, p. 177).

Union.* Rolland's entreaties to Yagoda were followed to the letter: he had written to Yagoda on 18 July 1935 and told him that 'for the USSR it would be much better to send Serge to the West, because the harm he would do there would be much less than the harm done by leaving him in Orenburg'. Further, Rolland told Yagoda that if Serge was unaware of any government secrets, the best policy would be to get rid of him by expelling him from the USSR – even waiting until after Serge served his sentence.†

Expulsion and theft

On 9 April 1936 the GPU gave Serge orders to leave Orenburg in three days for Moscow, where he was to report to the GPU and then be sent on to an unknown destination. Serge entertained the notion that this meant his first term of exile was finished and another would be added on, as was generally the case. He thought, 'I only know that political deportation is *never* ended because of firm convictions'.[54]

Given the possibility of leaving the USSR, Serge had to find a place to go. His friends in the West had already begun to obtain visas for Serge, should he be released. Finding a visa was not easy, however, and doors were closed to Serge in France, where he had been imprisoned twice, Holland, and Great Britain. Finally, the Ambassador of Belgium, the country of Serge's birth, came through with a visa for three years, and Ekaterina Peshkova, the director of the Political Red Cross, sent the Belgian visa forms to Serge.

His comrades in exile, Eltsin and Bobrov, debated the meaning of Serge's departure, certain that he would end up in some dark prison or cold deportation. Serge was also uncertain, but he had some grounds for optimism. He knew of the campaign in the West, thanks to a very brave Italian Bordighist/syndicalist, Francesco Ghezzi, who had dared the GPU and travelled to Orenburg to let Serge know his friends and comrades in Europe were working on his behalf. Serge had also seen the photo in *Pravda* in 1935 of Stalin shaking hands with Romain Rolland, and had told Vlady it could mean they were saved.‡

---

* At least according to Serge in his *Memoirs*, p. 319. Later Trotsky and others speculated that Stalin had let Serge go only because he thought Serge could be of use to him. See Trotsky letter to Lola Dallin, April 1936, Boris Nicolaevsky Collection, Hoover Archive, and Elizabeth (Elsa) Poretsky, *Our Own People*, Ann Arbor, University of Michigan Press, 1969, pp. 245–6.

† Iagoda, *Narkom vnutrennikh del SSSR*, p. 429. Rolland thought it best to let Serge know he would be released, and told Yagoda to allow Serge continue to write and after proper censorship controls, to allow his books to be sent abroad to avoid fanning the flames of the enemies of the USSR.

‡ Vlady said that his father's expression at seeing the photo in the newspaper remains engraved in his memory, and there was a kind of *déjà-vu* in Brussels some months later, when Serge again read the newspaper and saw the announcement of

Ghezzi was a foreigner and highly visible; he had already been imprisoned at Suzdal and was therefore likely to be watched. To travel by train from Moscow to Orenburg, a place of exile, was to court disaster. Once there he had to lie low, remaining in the house by day and only going out at night. Vlady and Serge were astonished by his bravery, and his 'madness' for risking so much.[55] Ghezzi disappeared in 1937.*

The day came to leave Orenburg: 12 April 1936. Despite the horrendous conditions of Serge's sojourn in this exile, he found it very difficult to leave, to break the bonds that had been created through solidarity in the face of repression and adversity. Serge wrote that his 'heart was ravaged'. This experience was the driving force for his tireless work on behalf of his comrades who remained once Serge was in the West. What made this parting even harder was knowing that he would never see these comrades again, as well as uncertainty about his fate and that of his family. Serge took the precaution of giving away his household belongings on the proviso that should he be sent to some other harsh clime he could reclaim them. Serge packed his books, manuscripts and some personal memorabilia, and he and Vlady set off to Moscow, with two policemen watching them from a few seats away.

In Moscow Serge and Vlady were met by Ekaterina Pavlona Peshkova, Gorky's first wife. She was a courageous woman who had founded the Political Red Cross, a relief organization for political prisoners, during the Red Terror. Both the Cheka and the GPU tolerated her organization and its work, apparently because of who she was and the connections she had. The office of the Political Red Cross was on Kuznetski bridge, just across from GPU headquarters. Serge's reminiscence of his last day in Moscow and his encounter with Peshkova, the GPU and the bureaucratic errands to be performed differs from Vlady's.[56] Vlady's story is more dramatic, while Serge characteristically minimizes the personal drama but provides more detailed information on the workings of the GPU.

---

the Moscow Trials. On both occasions, Vlady recalled, Serge uttered breathlessly: 'We have been saved!' Interview with Vlady conducted by John Eden and Les Smith, 3 June 1989, Mexico City.

* In Moscow, March 1989, Vlady and I learned from Irina Gogua, Serge's cousin, of Ghezzi's death. Ghezzi died in Viatka spent, starved and wasted. The camp director at Viatka told Serge's sister-in-law Anita Russakova, who was also at Viatka, what had happened to Ghezzi. Russakova, still alive in Leningrad after twenty-five years in camps, was the housemaid in the camp director's house. (He selected her because she was educated and spoke French.) He asked her one day if she knew Ghezzi, and she said 'Yes, he is a marvellous character'. The camp director then said that this 'marvellous character' just died of 'exhaustion and starvation'. Anita also recounted that in 1935, when she was imprisoned because of Serge, Ghezzi managed to visit her to tell her that Serge and Vlady had been deported to 'a city in the provinces' and that she should hang on because there were people who cared for her.

Serge wrote in the *Memoirs*[57] that he was met by Peshkova, that he was able to reunite with his wife and meet his infant daughter Jeannine, who was born while he was in the hospital in Orenburg. He was not able to see his sister-in-law Anita Russakova and resolve the question of her purported confessions because she had recently been arrested and exiled to Viatka for five years. Serge believed she had been rounded up precisely to keep them from meeting.

Serge recalled that he asked Peshkova to request a twenty-four-hour delay in leaving, so he could obtain an exit permit for his manuscripts from *Glavlit*, the censorship office. Peshkova returned and told Serge to leave immediately as, 'the secret police officer just told me that you were not out of the country yet, and that he was sending Yagoda a fresh memorandum about you'.[58] Although *Glavlit* had authorized the exit visa for the manuscripts, Serge had no time to pick them up, and left. The rest of his copies of the manuscripts were stolen by the GPU.

Vlady's version fills in more detail. First he says that he and his father were met by Peshkova and Julia, Serge's cousin who was Peshkova's friend, and very close to Serge. This omission is quite interesting, but not uncharacteristic of Serge, whose family is scarcely mentioned in the *Memoirs*. Vlady remembers that Julia,* a dominant personality, began to organize the day and the errands.

Peshkova could perform her work because she was Gorky's wife, and had won the confidence of Lenin. Julia was protected by her friendship with Stalin's wife, Nadezhda Alliluyeva,[59] and perhaps because she herself had been the object of Stalin's affection in Baku in 1902.[60]

These two women met Serge and Vlady and were preoccupied with the task ahead. Serge had an order to present himself to the GPU in Moscow, and Julia and Ekaterina wanted at all costs to avoid this meeting. They were worried that should Serge be obliged to speak he would speak honestly about his political analysis and very likely not be allowed to leave.

---

* Serge finally mentions 'Julie' in connection with Peshkova in the 'Pages of his Diary', part III, *New International*, March–April 1950 in the section 'In a Time of Duplicity', p. 119. In fact what Serge said is quite misleading – he mentions Julie and Ekaterina as old friends of Gorky. That is correct, but Peshkova was also Gorky's wife. Julie, or Julia Kolberg-Gogua, was Serge's cousin on his mother's side, Irina's mother. His mother was Vera Paderevskaya of the Paderewski family, Polish gentry from Nizhni-Novgorod. Julia went to Paris in 1910 to meet Serge, who was already translating Russian writers. When she returned she told Irina Gogua that Serge's spoken Russian was poor. Conversation with Vlady and Irina Gogua, 10 March 1989, Moscow. Thanks to Richard Greeman, whose interview with Georgine Hervenz in Belgium, cousin of Victor Serge, corrected both Irina and Vlady's mistaken notion that Julia was an older half-sister, rather than a cousin of Victor Serge. (The confusion resulted from the complex terminology originally related to the extended family.)

But how could Serge miss this meeting and still comply with his expulsion order? They had his passport, his suitcases, and his visa ready. They knew that if Serge went to the GPU all would be lost. The two women cooked up a plan. Peshkova called the GPU on the telephone. With Julia listening next to her as she spoke, and Vlady and Serge listening on the extension earpiece, Ekaterina Peshkova spoke directly to Yagoda, the head of the NKVD. Peshkova said, 'Genrikh, Victor Lvovich's wife is having a nervous crisis, so Victor Lvovich wants permission to spend the night here in Moscow and leave tomorrow'. Yagoda answered, 'Tell Victor Lvovich to leave immediately! But *im-mediately*! (*nemyedlenno*!)' It was an order. They hung up, and Peshkova said, 'Well, you do not have to present yourself to the GPU. If you are asked, say that Yagoda gave you an order to leave immediately.'

Before going to the Russakovs' apartment – where Serge and Vlady were reunited with Liuba and met Serge's infant daughter Jeannine – they had time to go to *Glavlit*, and to try to sell some of Serge's expensive books.* Without mentioning the uniquely Soviet situation of having an exit visa for the person but not his works, Vlady recalls the trip to the censorship office (*Glavlit*) where Serge took his manuscripts to be censored so they could be taken with him out of the country. The woman they encountered at *Glavlit* took the manuscripts and did not give them back. Serge had seen her before various times, and Vlady also remembered her: her name was Zvyeryeva and she appears in several of the novels. In Serge's *The Case of Comrade Tulayev* she was the GPU examiner in charge of Ryzhik,† the character representing Serge himself. Vlady interjected that in Russian her name comes from *Zvernyi*, which means 'beastly, brutal, atrocious'. When she took the manuscripts from Serge, she said, 'Huh! Viktor Lvovich, so you're leaving – in order to betray . . . you are betraying us!' Serge answered, 'I do not know who is betraying, I do not believe it is me. I am continuing. One should know who is betraying. Goodbye. I hope all goes well with you.' Vlady never forgot this acrimonious meeting, and Zvyeryeva's bitterness.

Serge was given a receipt for the completed manuscript copies of his *Les Hommes perdus*, *La Tourmente*, *Résistance* and *L'An II de la révolution russe*, and told to come back the next day. The receipt is still in Vlady's possession.

---

* In the bookstore, Serge and Vlady ran into Dr Nikolayenko, an old anarchist who had travelled to Russia from France with Serge in 1919. Since then he had survived by living far from the capital, and occasionally visited the Serge family, bringing exquisite animal skins and other treasures to Liuba from his geographical expeditions. Vlady remembers this encounter as the big episode of the day. Since Serge had been unable to sell his valuable books he had saved for twenty years, he was able to present his old friend with a gift, a remembrance.

† Zvyeryeva appears in both *Conquered City*, pp. 103–5, and *The Case of Comrade Tulayev*, London, Penguin Books, 1968, pp. 245–6. Vlady remembered seeing her at various times in his childhood, and said she was just like the novelistic Zvyeryeva who judged Ryzhik in *The Case of Comrade Tulayev*.

Then, according to Vlady, Serge entrusted to Peshkova copies of his manuscripts, documents, notes, photographs and memorabilia so that she could pick up the exit visa and send them on to Serge.

That evening Serge and his family met at the station to say their good-byes and leave the Soviet Union. Liuba's mother (Vlady's grandmother Russakova) and Francesco Ghezzi were both there. Vlady remembers the tearful farewell:

> My grandmother was crying, my mother was in a crisis. My baby sister, swad-dled in my mother's yellow and green sweater, was in my mother's arms. It was 14 April 1936 – springtime. Ghezzi accompanied us to the station and our last intimate words were with this dear friend. He asked us to do everything to get him out, once we were in the West.[61]

Serge had multiple copies of the work he had completed in Orenburg.[62] He had at least eight copies of *Les Hommes perdus*, at least five copies of *La Tourmente*, and unknown quantities of the historical *L'An II de la révolution russe* and the poetry collection *Résistance*. Serge deposited the manuscript copies with the Censor of the People's Commissariat for Public Education; the Assistant Director of the Foreign Literature Section of *Glavlit*; the Political Red Cross Director Peshkova; Francesco Ghezzi. These copies were in addi-tion to the ones Serge sent to Romain Rolland that were seized in the post. He kept the rest of the copies to take with him out of the country.

The final episode in Serge's sojourn of seventeen years in the Soviet 'vic-torious revolution' is climactic. At the last station on the Soviet frontier, Negoreloye, Serge and his family were made to disembark for a final 'search'. Liuba and baby Jeannine (fourteen months old) were led off in one direction, Serge and Vlady in another. They were ordered to undress for a strip search. Vlady recalled that he was still in his underwear, with his trousers around his boots. The GPU agent prodded him to hurry and asked what was he was hiding in his socks? Vlady retorted, 'a submarine!' At that moment the whistle blew and the train started to pull away from the station. Serge and Vlady broke into a run, pulling their clothes up at the same time. They could not see Liuba and Jeannine, and Serge was horrified, thinking they would be left behind. Vlady jumped on the train and caught sight of his mother and sister. Serge was screaming 'Mama, mama, I won't leave without you!' and Vlady shouted to him, 'They're here, see for your-self!' Just before it was too late, Serge saw Liuba and jumped on the moving train. He looked back and saw the GPU agents pointing to Serge's suit-cases, containing his manuscripts, photos and personal belongings. Gone forever. Stolen by the GPU?

When the train passed the Soviet border, Vlady remembers his father going into the corridor and sighing with relief. Then he was tranquil.

Was this final humiliation simply harassment, a memento of his years in the USSR, or was this the last act of an elaborate scheme to prevent the sur-vival of Serge's writings – which began with the thrice 'lost in the mail' manuscripts? Was the GPU covering its tracks so that the state could declare it had complied, that the loss of the manuscripts was inexplicable, or even unavoidable, but they had fulfilled their obligations, the manuscripts had an exit visa, and Serge had been compensated for those lost in the post?

The hunt for the missing manuscripts

Serge was permitted to leave, but not his writings. Once in Belgium, Serge received a letter from Peshkova, in mid-May 1936, stating that permission to send the manuscripts had been granted, but that she was still awaiting formal authorization.

André Gide went to the Soviet Union in 1936. Prior to his departure, Serge wrote him an open letter, published in *La Révolution prolétarienne*, in which he thanked Gide for his role in the International Congress of Writers on Serge's behalf.[63] He then wrote of the actual conditions in the Soviet Union and implored Gide to keep his eyes wide open while there. Magdeleine Paz, who was very impressed with the letter, nonetheless felt it was a mistake to publish it openly, since it seemed 'like an ultimatum'.[64] Serge said he had too much regard for Gide not to publish it. Upon his return, Gide told Serge he had tried to obtain his manuscripts, but that it was futile.[65]

Since 1936 there have been several efforts to retrieve the manuscripts. Of the four, Serge was only able to reproduce the collection of poems which he had committed to memory. They were published in 1938 by Cahiers les Humbles, and translated into English in 1989.[66] The novels and the history remain 'lost'. In 1945 and 1946 George Orwell tried to find an English publisher for Serge's *Memoirs* and expressed interest in the missing manuscripts.[67] In 1972 the French publisher François Maspero wrote to Brezhnev respectfully requesting that Serge's papers be returned to his family. The letter was never answered.

In October 1986 I began a new campaign to retrieve the manuscripts. The time was right. Mikhail Gorbachev's policy of *glasnost* had as a specific plank the re-examination of the hidden history of the USSR. Gorbachev himself declared there should be no blank pages in Soviet history. I wrote to Gorbachev, then tried to enlist the help of prominent Soviet writers. Andrei Vosnessensky (interviewed in March 1987) curiously professed ignorance of Victor Serge, though Vlady reported that he and Vosnessensky had stayed up all night reading *The Case of Comrade Tulayev* aloud in Russian at Vlady's house in Mexico. Yevgeny Yevtushenko (interviewed in April 1987) was very helpful, urging contact with the new Soviet Foundation of Culture, set up to deal with hidden and lost treasures of the Stalin period.[68] Vladimir Karpov (interviewed May 1987), then head of the Soviet Union of Writers and a man close to Gorbachev, personally expressed great interest, because he was born in Orenburg and had never heard of Serge, and he knew I had asked Yevtushenko for help and apparently wanted to 'one-up' him, or so his translator told me.

On 22 September 1988 the Soviet Foundation of Culture responded. Encouraged, letters went to other prominent Soviet writers, historians, film-makers and influential journals and newspapers. In Mexico, Vlady made contact with Soviet journalists, diplomats and visiting *literati*. The near universal response to our efforts was 'very interesting, but who was Victor Serge?' It was time to go to the Soviet Union and press the case.

In March 1989 Vlady and I went to Moscow to generate interest in Victor Serge among writers, film-makers, activists and historians. Unbeknownst to us, interest had already been aroused. The Supreme Soviet issued a decree to rehabilitate Serge on 16 January 1989, which was carried out on 14 May 1989.*

Sergei Zavarotnyi, who had published an article about Serge and Vlady in *Komsomolskaya Pravda* in November 1988, had come into contact with Irina Gogua and, through her, Anita Russakova. Vlady, Sergei and I tried to map the trail of lost manuscripts. With Ghezzi's death, we could only hope for access to the KGB archive, or Peshkova's papers. We began with the latter.

When Peshkova died, her personal papers became a part of the Gorky Museum in Moscow. Her granddaughter Marfa Peshkova was the curator of the museum's Gorky archive. Soon after Peshkova's papers were deposited in the museum, the Central Committee had sent someone to look through them and had removed a large portion of the papers. Another archivist at the museum remembered seeing 'papers written in French'.[69]

In 1990 Sergei Zavarotnyi found Oppositionist Vassily Pankratov's wife Lisa Senyatskaya, whose grandson Vassily Pankratov wanted to help find the manuscripts. John Eden, an English film-maker, went to Orenburg with Sergei Zavarotnyi in 1990 to search for leads.[70] *Komsomolskaya Pravda* was persuaded to fund Vassily Pankratov, who knew Peshkova's granddaughter Marfa Peshkova. She led Pankratov to the closed archive of Ekaterina Peshkova's Political Red Cross. The manuscripts were not there, but there was the letter Serge wrote to Peshkova from Warsaw, dated 16 April 1936, and Peshkova's letter to the NKVD requesting the return of the manuscripts and permission to despatch them abroad.[71]

Since the initial search for Serge's 'lost' manuscripts Vlady and I undertook in 1989, the International Victor Serge Association was formed and John Eden, Richard Greeman and Alexei Gusev have visited more than seven archives. The missing manuscripts have not surfaced, though more of Serge's correspondence and photographs have been found, as well as his

---

* Neither Vlady nor I were told of this *ukaz* even though we were in Moscow between the issuing and implementation of the decree. It is reported in a note in Yagoda's papers, *Narkom vnutrennikh del SSSR*, p. 431.

criminal file and the report of his interrogation in Orenburg by the local NKVD. Subsequent requests have been made to have Serge's files released to his family, without luck.[72] At RGASPI (formerly the Central Party Archive) in 1999, I came across a note in Yagoda's papers that asserts that a search for the confiscated copies of Serge's novel about pre-war France was undertaken in the KGB-FSB archive, and nothing was found.[73] The search continues . . .

Part II

Another exile and two more:
the final years

Introduction

> Row, Vassili, row. Let's pull together
> we are brothers
> in defeat and hard times –
> our defeat is prouder and greater
> than their lying victory . . .
> It's good to go up the rivers
> as long as your back's not broken . . .
> We'll hold on as long as we can.*

This poem speaks to the state of mind of the defeated Oppositionists, who managed to retain their socialist optimism in spite of unspeakable suffering and betrayal. This conviction was based on the certainty that future progress belonged to the working class, despite fascism, despite Stalinism. Serge's political voyage brought him face to face with war, political isolation and defeat. Near its end, when Serge was exiled to Mexico, he devoted himself to intense writing and reflection. Isolated by geography, language and politics, Serge expressed his deepest thoughts about the fate of socialism in the wake of Stalin's crimes in its name.

During his final exile, Serge's former comrades in the Fourth International[1] rejected him, deluded by the GPU and blinded by their own sectarianism.[2] Although there were some political differences, they were exacerbated by intrigue. Trotskyists and social democrats alike claimed that Serge had abandoned Marxism and had become a professional anti-Stalinist of the *New Leader* type (an American right-Menshevik publication which frequently carried his byline). Trotsky himself told James Cannon[3]

---

* Excerpted from 'Boat on the Ural River', a poem Serge wrote in Orenburg on 20 May 1935 about a boat ride that he took with five other deported Communists. It is from the collection *Resistance* (pp. 25–7), poems by Victor Serge written in Orenburg, confiscated by the GPU and reconstructed from memory in the West. First published in 1938 by Cahiers Les Humbles, and translated into English by James Brooks, published by City Lights Books, San Francisco, 1989.

that Serge held absolute Menshevik ideas on Spain. But Serge, just weeks before he died, affirmed his stance in a letter to Hryhory Kostiuk:

> I remain – intransigently – a socialist, a partisan of socialist democracy. The system against which I fought and continue to fight – you know from experience – I view as a kind of totalitarianism, i.e. as something *new*, but extremely inhuman and anti-socialist.[4]

Serge's numerous essays from his final exile address his mature thinking about socialism, anarchism, the political economy and social structure of the USSR and its impact on the international political struggle. He developed his understanding of World War II and its aftermath, the new cold war and the nuclear age, the role of the vanguard Party, and questions of art, anthropology, psychology, philosophy and politics.

He was active for a time in a political group (Socialismo y Libertad) which published a few issues of *Mundo* and then split. Serge was a fish out of water in Mexico: he wrote in French for an audience in Europe and North America. He had difficulty publishing his work, was very poor and often hungry. He had problems with his young wife Laurette Séjourné. His son Vlady, attempting to stand on his own politically, often opposed Serge in the group, trying to be free of Serge's influence.[5]

Mexico had changed since it opened its doors to Trotsky in 1937. The government of Lázaro Cárdenas, which Trotsky had characterized in a letter to Alfred Rosmer as 'the only honest government in the world' was gone, and Trotsky's assassination on Mexican soil had deeply affected Mexican politics.* The assassination was a direct affront to Cárdenas, who wrote that the Stalinist thugs had violated Mexico's sanctity and betrayed Mexico's hospitality and its ideals. Mexico continued to give refuge to those escaping the Nazis, but the country's internal atmosphere changed during the government of Ávila Camacho. Serge and Vlady arrived in September 1941 among many refugees from the Spanish Civil War.[6]

Serge's command of Spanish was less than adequate, especially for a man who earned his living by writing. He was dizzy from the defeats he had survived, and the pain caused by the murder of his comrades – at the hands of Stalin in Spain and the USSR, and the Gestapo throughout Europe. Serge found Mexico exotic and fascinating, but he was truly isolated and desperately poor.†

---

* Cárdenas' son Cuauhtemoc quoted his father: 'The blood of Trotsky fertilized the soil of our country.' Cuauhtemoc Cárdenas, Inaugural remarks at Colloquium, 'Trotsky, revelador político del Mexico Cardenista', Mexico City, 18 May 1987.

† Dwight and Nancy Macdonald continued to send occasional financial support to Serge, until Laurette could get work and Serge could publish a few articles in American left journals. See various letters and cablegrams detailing sending and receiving of monies, Macdonald Papers, Yale University Library.

There was one other person in Mexico Serge could relate to – Natalia Sedova, Trotsky's widow. Vlady remembered the day he and Serge first went to visit Natalia, approaching Calle Viena by Rio Churubusco in Coyoacán. They had just arrived in Mexico, a miracle in itself, and Serge was eager to see Natalia. He had last seen Trotsky in 1927; though they corresponded while they were both in exile in Europe their paths never crossed again. Having lived most of his adult political life in 'the tail of the comet of Trotsky'* and having arrived finally in the place where Trotsky's life ended, Serge immediately gravitated toward Calle Viena. Walking along Rio Churubusco, Vlady recounted, 'my father saw the wall around Trotsky's house, where the Old Man was killed. He began to weep, and then broke into sobs'.† It was the first time Vlady had seen Serge really lose his composure. Inside, Serge and Natalia greeted each other with affection, and immediately established a rapport. Later Serge was to write that he and Natalia were the only ones left 'who knew what the Russian Revolution was really like, what the Bolsheviks were really like'.[7] They were the last survivors of the revolutionary generation of Bolshevik Left Oppositionists.‡

No one else understood this international revolutionary who was at once Belgian and Russian, an anarcho-Bolshevik and committed anti-Stalinist. Gradually he associated with the Spanish and European exile community, including Julian Gorkín§ who had been instrumental in getting Serge his Mexican visa, the French socialist leader Marceau Pivert,** Gustav Regler, a political commissar with the International Brigades in Spain, the French novelist Jean Malaquais,†† Herbert Lenhof, a psychoanalyst of the Freudian school with whom Serge had fascinating discussions about the human social psyche, and others. Manuel Alvarado, an orthodox Trotskyist, lived near Serge and stopped by frequently to discuss politics. Alvarado was a full-time militant in the Mexican section of the Fourth International with a keen interest in political economy. They had disagreements on the nature

---

* The phrase is Vlady's.

† Private conversation with Vlady in Coyoacán, 20 Aug. 1990. Vlady and I took the same walk that he and his father had in 1941.

‡ In 1988 other survivors in the Soviet Union came forward, like Nadezhda Joffe, who spent the years 1929–57 in Kolyma for her participation in the Left Opposition. Her stepmother Maria Joffe also survived and lived in Israel until her death.

§ Former International Secretary of the Spanish Partido Obrero Unificado Marxista (POUM), author of books on Spain and Trotsky's assassination.

** Leader of the pre-war French Parti Socialiste Ouvrier et Paysan (PSOP) whom Trotsky had polemicized against in 1939 as centrist, an associate of Léon Blum in the Popular Front.

†† The French author of *Planet Without a Visa* and other works, with whom Serge had a falling out, see *inter alia* Victor Serge, 'Malaquais, 17 Oct. 44', in *Carnets*, Paris, Julliard, 1952, p. 133.

of fascism: Alvarado felt Serge made too much of fascism's similarities with Stalinism.*

An important source about this period of Serge's life has been the declassified FBI documents available through the Freedom of Information Act.† The FBI kept close tabs on all the exiles in Mexico, and Serge was an unwitting but important source for them. Serge kept abreast of the activities of the various exile communities, writing details to American friends in letters (and articles to American left periodicals) that were intercepted by the FBI.[8]

Serge was not spared persecution in his final exile. Mexico had been a hotbed of GPU activity during Trotsky's stay. The Mexican Communist Party had allowed itself to be used in Stalin's service in 1940 in the first attempt on Trotsky's life led by the muralist David Alfaro Siqueiros. Laurette Séjourné recalled that Serge was sometimes followed,[9] and Vlady remembered that one day when he was walking with his father in Coyoacán, a car suddenly appeared and gunmen inside opened fire. Serge grabbed Vlady and pushed him behind a tree.[10]

As Mexican correspondent of the *New Leader*, Serge reported on the GPU's terror tactics aimed against himself and his associates. Paul Castelar, writing in the *New Leader* of 24 January 1942, noted that the 'strong-arm squad' turned on Serge, Gorkín and Pivert, trying to get them expelled from Mexico and repatriated to their various countries where they would be shot.[11]

Serge and Gorkín were slandered, maligned and boycotted. They were called Nazi agents, *sinarquistas* (Mexican fascists), Trotskyites, enemies of the United Nations. In one press dispatch picked up in the United States, Serge was named as an instigator of the railway strikes in Mexico.[12] The organizer of the slander campaign was a man who represented himself as a French journalist named André Simon. However, an article in the British *New Leader*‡ revealed Simon's true identity: he was Otto Katz, an OGPU agent assigned to

> stir up public sentiment against Regler, Serge, Pivert, Gorkín and Muniz. Having started an inflammatory press attack upon them, Katz has now organized

---

* Interviews with Manuel Alvarado in Mexico City, May 1987 and Aug. 1990. Vlady remembers Manuel as a 'rigid, dogmatic Trotskyist, but with a theoretical rigour'. After Trotsky's assassination, he worked as an economist in Mexico's banking system.

† These files, scattered through various intelligence agencies and offices, are still heavily censored. Other important sources for this period include interviews with survivors, material from Serge's archive in Mexico, and his articles in the *New Leader* and *Politics*.

‡ The newspaper of the British Independent Labour Party (ILP). This is a different paper from the American one of the same name.

'vigilante committees' to deal with these men, whom he calls 'the leaders of the Nazi Fifth Column in Latin America'.*

Mexican publications closed their doors to Serge. Miguel Alemán, future president of the republic, admitted there was intense Soviet pressure to deny Serge any means of public expression.[13] Orchestrated in Moscow, the smear campaign made use of Communist Parties in various countries, as well as the international press. Serge, Pivert, Gorkín, Regler and Muniz were labelled 'fifth columnists'. Once launched, the vicious lie was repeated in the Mexican and American Communist press. Each story used the others for confirmation which lent apparent authority to the falsehood and thus helped spread the libel to liberal and conservative papers. Initiated by the Mexican Communist Paper *Mundo Obrero*, the smear was then published several times in the American *Daily Worker*. Following this, Mexican papers cited reports in 'the American Press' that Serge and the others were Nazi agents.

To defend the victims of this libel, 170 prominent North Americans signed a letter to Ávila Camacho, President of Mexico. Among the signatories were Roger Baldwin, John Dewey, John Dos Passos, David Dubinsky, Freda Kirchwey, James T. Farrell, Sidney Hook, Quincy Howe, Reinhold Niebuhr and Adam Clayton Powell Jr. The letter asked Camacho to protect these anti-fascists from the 'reign of terror against refugees whose only crime is that they have been more intransigent [sic] and more consistent enemies of totalitarianism than their accusers'.[14]

The affair was by no means finished. After Serge, Gorkín and Pivert published a letter in *The Nation* (7 February 1942), a mysterious 'Washington dispatch' appeared headed 'Labor Conjunta Contra Espías' (Common Labour Against Spies) in the conservative Mexico City daily *Excelsior*. The dispatch made it appear that the 'American police' and FBI were interested in the suppression of the fifth columnists, thereby implicating the Secret Service and the State Department.[15] The article described Serge thus:

> One Balkisti, nicknamed Victor Serge, who is the direct successor of Leon Trotzky. This individual . . . was involved in the celebrated trial of the band of apaches of Bonnot in 1909, in France. He managed to flee from French justice and later took refuge in Russia, where he was convicted of common crimes; finally he appeared in Paris at the service of Otto Abetz in 1938, when this German was the chief of the secret agents of Hitler, which enabled him to become today Hitler's ambassador in Paris.[16]

---

* 'OGPU Threatens French and Spanish Socialists' and 'The OGPU in Mexico' (unsigned articles), *New Leader*, Saturday, 27 Feb. 1943, pp. 4–5. Otto Katz was notorious for hunting down and helping to assassinate key Soviet intelligence defectors in Europe. See Allen Weinstein and Alexander Vassiliev, *The Haunted Wood*, New York, Random House, 1999, p. 46.

At this point the American FBI was used as a source, and interest in the affair grew. Then it was picked up by the *New Masses*,[17] in a 'background' article chiding *The Nation* for its defence of the fifth columnists. On 28 February *The Nation* published a letter by seven Mexican Deputies, plus Lombardo Toledano, Ludwig Renn and Pablo Neruda (the last three known Stalinists) who 'restated the feeling of the Mexican people about the Trotskyists in their midst'. As a result, *The Nation*'s editors retreated from their earlier defence of Serge and his comrades.[18]

In the US, Dwight Macdonald continued to campaign on behalf of Serge and the others, and *The New York Times* published an account of the campaign of vilification (February 1942). A number of the signatories of the appeal to Camacho brought the matter to the attention of the State Department. Macdonald told Serge 'the State Department takes the view that the attack . . . confuses the issue of attacking the real fifth columnists and so Roosevelt has asked his personal representative in Mexico to intervene with Camacho and ask that the attacks cease, the request being of course unofficial'.[19]

Instead, the GPU offensive escalated, culminating when 200 armed thugs violently attacked an April 1943 memorial meeting for Henryk Erlich, Victor Alter and Carlo Tresca.* In this assault Julian Gorkín was stabbed and some seventy others were injured, twenty-two of them seriously. The FBI reported the attack (which it called a brawl), noting that Gorkín was wounded, that Serge was not, and that Vlady had courageously kept his cool.[20] Jeannine Kibalchich, also at the meeting, remembered that the thugs entered just as Serge was speaking. Serge shouted for her to take cover and Enrique Gironella grabbed her, protecting her with his body. She felt warm blood from a knife wound sustained by Gironella flowing onto her hair, and she was frightened into silence.† The *Militant* also carried an account of the meeting, quoting from Victor Serge:

---

* Viktor Alter and Henrik Ehrlich, leaders of the Jewish Bund socialists in Poland, fell into Russian hands in Sept. 1939. They were condemned to death, but later granted amnesty in order to organize a Jewish anti-fascist committee. They were then executed by the Soviets for 'trying to persuade Soviet troops to cease contesting the advance of the German armies'. The FBI gets part of the story right, but misses significantly. In FBI Record no. SA 153916, 4/6/43, the FBI examiner states 'Victor Alter and Heinrich Ehrlich are said to be Polish socialists, executed in Russia shortly after proposing a Jewish International Committee to fight Nazism'. Carlo Tresca was an Italian anarchist, editor of the New York Italian newspaper *Il Martello*. He was mysteriously murdered in New York in January 1943. The assassination appears to have been the work of the GPU.

† Jeannine Kibalchich, 'My Father', in Susan Weissman (ed.), *Victor Serge: A Life as a Work of Art*, Glasgow, Critique Books, 1997, p. 14. Laurette also was present, having arrived in the midst of the fray. In FBI file SA 153916, the agent commented that 'Writer [presumably Serge] continues that one of the assailants made a rather curious remark to Laurette . . . saying that the [deleted] was inside'. Was the assailant known to Laurette?

At eight o'clock, says Serge, the company of about one hundred Communists laid siege to the hall, broke down the iron door and burst into the centre looking for the speakers to beat them up. Armed with clubs of bits of broken furniture, as well as knives and guns, they formed a strong-arm squad, evidently recruited off the streets, probably hired, and led by some Communist Party militants who kept shouting, 'They are Germans, enemies of Mexico' . . . The thugs were led by Antonio Mije, Juan Comorera, Julian Carillo and Carlos Contreras. Contreras is a notorious Stalin GPU hatchet-man who was an active leader in the terror against anti-Stalinist workers in Spain during the civil war.*

Although Serge survived without injury, he was clearly marked as a target by the GPU – no longer merely for slander, but now for murder. Juan Austrich, who saved Serge from the line of fire of the Communist thugs brandishing machine guns and pistols, told Pino Cacucci that Victor Serge was the real objective of the assault.[21]

Once World War II was under way and the Soviet Union was touted as the 'bulwark' against fascism, anti-Stalinist views became less palatable in the progressive press. All over Europe and the Americas Trotskyists lost much of their public. For a maverick like Serge, an audience was even more elusive. Serge was an ardent anti-Stalinist and anti-capitalist, but he was also out of favour with the Trotskyists who considered him a centrist on his way to becoming a social democrat.†

Serge became unpublishable. One publishing house was ruined after publishing his book *Hitler Contra Stalin*.[22] Politically isolated and deprived of a livelihood, Serge wrote mostly for the desk drawer, producing some of his best work: *Memoirs of a Revolutionary* (written from 1942 to 1943, but not published until 1951); what is arguably the finest novel about the purges, *The Case of Comrade Tulayev* (1940–42, published in 1948); his novel of the fall of France *The Long Dusk* (1943–45, published in Canada in 1946); and his novel about the experience of defeat and exile called *Les Années sans pardon* (1946, published in 1971). He also kept a voluminous and fascinating journal, later published in France as *Carnets* (1952). His booklets included *La GPU prepara un nuevo crimen!* signed by Serge, Gorkín, Pivert and Regler, published first in the journal *Analisis* in 1942, another by the same four entitled *Los Problemas del socialismo en nuestro tiempo* (1944, first published in *Mundo*), *La Tragedie des écrivains soviétiques* (1947), *La Nouvel*

---

* FBI file, NY 100–31551 (declassified on 1 Aug. 1973), carrying page 13. Carlos Contreras was an Italian Communist from Trieste named Vittorio Vidali who had operated in sinister fashion in the United States under the name Enea Sormenti; Antonio Mije and Juan Comorera were also active Communists in Spain. See, *inter alia*, Victor Alba and Stephen Schwartz, *Spanish Marxism versus Soviet Communism: A History of the POUM*, New Brunswick and Oxford, Transaction Books, 1988.

† This view of Serge persisted fifty years later: see Cathy Nugent, 'Victor Serge was a revolutionary . . . but', *Workers Liberty*, no. 25, Oct. 1995, pp. 32–3.

Imperialisme russe (1947), *Vie et mort de Leon Trotski* (with Natalia Sedova, published in 1951). Serge wrote a large collection of essays, correspondence and articles on the war, the Jewish question, psychology, literature, the future of socialism, Mexican archaeology, and the evolution and nature of the Soviet system. He was preoccupied with the character of the world that would emerge from the war, which he thought was transformative and would give rise to new collectivist societies with a technocratic elite in power, and worried about the totalitarian tendencies of these new formations. Should Stalin survive the war, Serge feared he would start World War III.

The end of the war found Serge in a weakened physical condition, his head brimming with writing projects. Vlady encouraged him to return to France, where he could write and *publish*. His marriage was on the rocks, and Serge despaired of finding an audience for his ideas in his lifetime. Vlady urged him to write to André Malraux, the 'infamous' letter which Malraux excerpted and published to imply that Serge supported Gaullism.* Vlady explained the letter as a friendly attempt to renew relations with Malraux who might help Serge get back to France.[23] Serge never wrote a line publicly supporting the RPF; and as much as he feared the potential role of the Stalinists in France, he never supported Gaullism, Christianity, nor imperialism, and recognized the primacy of defending the working class, even alongside the Communists.[24] The letter to Malraux shocked left circles and became infamous because it appeared that Serge had changed sides in his final hour. He had not.

Six days after writing to Malraux, before any concrete plans were made to return to France, Serge was stopped by a fatal heart attack. It was 17 November 1947.[25] He died just after hailing a taxi, before he could tell the driver where to go. His clothes were threadbare, he had holes in his shoes;† the driver thought he had picked up a pauper. Later, Laurette, Vlady and Isabel were summoned to the morgue to identify Serge's body. Jeannine was not told for several days. Serge was buried in a cemetery for Spanish exiles,

---

* *Le Rassemblement*, 31 Jan. 1948. Serge told Malraux that he would be among those socialists in France who supported an alliance with the RPF (Rassemblement du peuple français). Both Peter Sedgwick (Appendix to Victor Serge, *Memoirs of a Revolutionary*, London, Oxford University Press, 1963, pp. 383–5) and William Marshall (*Victor Serge: The Uses of Dissent*, New York and Oxford, Berg, 1992, pp. 28–9) sufficiently explain Serge's position. Malraux opportunistically excerpted the lines from Serge's letter, and Serge died without being able to defend his intent.

† Vlady later captured the moment of Serge's death in the second of the trilogy he painted on the assassination of Trotsky. In the famous study of Trotsky's, where he was felled with an icepick, there is a pair of shoes floating overhead, with holes in them, over the open pages of a book.

in an unmarked grave. Forty-five years after his death, Serge's daughter-in-law Isabel Diaz put a headstone on his grave.

Pino Cacucci, Italian biographer of Tina Modotti, raised the possibility that Serge did not die of natural causes, but had been poisoned by the GPU with something that would make it appear that he had suffered a heart attack.[26] Juan Austrich, Cacucci's source, maintained that he had proof Serge was murdered, but his widow was unable to provide the documentation given the state of his papers following his death.[27] Others who believe that Serge was assassinated maintain that the taxi drivers' union was controlled by the Communist Party, who used the taxis in their murderous expeditions as 'killer gangs'.[28] Vlady believed it was possible that Serge was poisoned, and raised concern about Laurette, who appeared out of nowhere in the thirties to become Serge's companion. Apparently Laurette was never emotionally committed to Serge, and months after his death married a prominent Mexican Communist, and joined the Communist Party herself. In an interview with Laurette Séjourné in September 1990, I asked her if Serge could have been poisoned: she thought it possible, but did not believe it so. She considered her marriage to him 'an error', that she had been too young, and his life too full of tragedy and darkness for her to understand. She took on the task of supporting Serge, typing his manuscripts in the morning before going to work, returning in the evening to study for a degree in anthropology.[29]

The final decade of Serge's life was one of the century's most tumultuous and barbaric. From the time of Serge's release from Orenburg in April 1936 until his death in Mexico in 1947 millions were to die in Stalin's labour camps and prison basements. Millions more died in Hitler's death camps, and even more in the total war which destroyed Europe's cities and soaked her countryside in blood. A hideous postscript to the slaughter was written by the United States with the dropping of 'fat man' and 'little boy'* over Hiroshima and Nagasaki in August 1945 – the final act of World War II, and the first of the Cold War. Serge experienced first-hand Stalinism and Nazism and most of the major struggles and catastrophes of the first half of the twentieth century.

Serge died without an estate, but he left behind his written work, a lifetime of struggle, a commitment to the truth no matter how uncomfortable, 'a victorious revolution and massacres in so great a number as to inspire a certain dizziness', and a confidence, born of his critical intelligence, in the possibilities of the future.

Serge's final years were in many respects like the earlier ones: filled with writing, politics, danger, hunger, and political and personal struggle. Serge's life experience was integral to the development of his political thought. He commented: 'Events continued to overwhelm us. Even where

---

* Code names for the atomic bombs used at the end of World War II.

they took place at a distance I find it hard to separate them from my personal memories.'[30] Serge was not simply a writer or an observer – he was engaged, and his writings reflect his experiences in an immediate sense, in all the literary forms he used to express his ideas: fiction, poetry, history, political essays. Serge did not write in a customary 'scientific' style, but in a literary-autobiographical-political one that transcends the boundaries of both traditional social science and conventional literature.

6

Out of Russia,
cornered in Europe

Spring 1936: Belgian socialists are fat

Serge experienced profound culture shock upon his return to the West after more than a decade of severe deprivation in 'our Russia of revolutions'. He summed it up describing the ample meal he shared with an unemployed syndicalist militant – 'Back home over there, this is the kind of meal that a high Party official would eat!'[1] – and the observation on a May Day demonstration that Belgian workers were both well dressed and fat. Serge had seen it before, though it had receded in his memory, but the whole scene was astonishing to young Vlady, who had real difficulty understanding the concept of private property. How could all this be *owned* by one man? And for what purpose? Serge noted Vlady's incredulity and remarked, 'it all seemed mad to my Soviet adolescent'.[2]

Serge became politically active immediately, even though he was restricted through the terms of his visa from open political activity. The unfolding events in the USSR with their repercussions in Europe and Spain prevented him from sitting back, simply relieved to be 'free'.

Serge began to write about what he had just experienced and witnessed in the Soviet Union. He was surprised that many of his West European political friends, with the exception of Boris Souvarine, preferred he remain silent. For them 'Russia was still an unsullied star' and Serge was 'too bitter' after his experience.[3] He did not refrain from writing the truth in the face of what Souvarine called 'an epidemic of highly dangerous stupidity!'[4] Suddenly the reverberations of the purges beginning in Moscow hit Serge in Belgium: a rain of denunciations began, inspired by the Belgian Communist Party which led the authorities to revoke Serge's and his family's passports. More was to come. Letters went missing,* agents approached Serge in

---

* A letter from Sedov to Serge, warning him about Sobel, never arrived. See Serge to Sedov, 'Piatnitsa, 1936', 231:63, Nicolaevsky Collection, Hoover Archive.

the street, and Serge had to give up his 'well-paid work on Leon Blum's *Le Populaire* because of pressures influencing the editorial staff'.[5] Communist Party influence in journals and publishing houses made it practically impossible for Serge to publish, and where he had already published Serge found his books put on the back shelf, and the titles deleted from the catalogues. Earning a living became nearly impossible. The GPU, later to reach Sedov in Paris, Reiss in Lausanne, the POUM in Spain and Trotsky in Mexico, was stretching its tentacles toward Serge.

Stalin soon realized that Serge's release, like Trotsky's forced expulsion, was a mistake. It was more difficult to silence their voices in the West. Still, pressure could be brought to bear. On 11 July 1936, Serge was stripped of his passport and Soviet nationality.* On 13 July 1936 Serge wrote to Leon Sedov, Trotsky's son, that he had been informed by the Soviet Embassy that a decree of the *VTsIK* revoked his passport.[6] Serge was the victim of police harassment provoked by GPU-inspired denunciations. He was accused of agitation among striking miners, hiding arms for the Spanish republicans, and preparing to assassinate the King of Belgium. In the Soviet Union Serge's relatives were arrested and disappeared; most of them were never heard from again.†

The Belgian communist press demanded Serge's expulsion from the country, and Serge's former friend Jacques Sadoul began a campaign of despicable libel against him. In two articles published in *L'Humanité*, Sadoul called Serge a 'common criminal', the 'brains behind the Bonnot gang of 1911' . . . 'a valet of the pen' who having used his pen to defend the Bonnot gang, was now likewise using it 'to camouflage his complicity in the crimes of Trotsky and the defendants at the Moscow Trial'.[7] Sadoul pressed for a boycott of Serge, and met with considerable success. His invective was so vile that it led Trotsky to write to Serge at a time when

---

* From Uccles, Belgium, Serge wrote to Sedov in Paris on 1 July 1936, that he had a French visa. (Serge to Sedov, 11 July 1936, Nicolaevsky Collection, Hoover Archive). A French visa was not a travel document, however. Soviet consular officials in Belgium would not let Serge know of his changed status, and made it impossible for him to obtain travel documents (letter from Victor Serge to Leon Trotsky, 10 Aug. 1936) so he could not go to Paris, where his political activities on behalf of his comrades left behind in the Soviet Union would have been more effective.

† Serge's family in the USSR consisted of his older sister, mother-in-law, two sisters-in-law and two brothers-in-law, their offspring, and cousins. They were all apolitical. Other Oppositionists' families suffered similarly. Serge wrote of the fate of wives and children of Oppositionists who disappeared into the gulag in his personal diary, *Carnets* (Paris, Julliard, 1952). In his diary entry for 6 July 1946, he recounted the fate of Kamenev's wife (Trotsky's sister), and Rakovsky's daughter, both of whom disappeared into the most wretched of the camps. See Victor Serge, 'Pages from a Journal', *New International*, vol. 5, no. 5, Nov./Dec. 1950, p. 369.

their relations were strained by their differences on the nature of the POUM:

> To pick up a copy of *l'Humanité* is always to injure one's own feelings. My young friends drew my attention to Jacques Sadoul's article against you, an exceptional article even for that prostituted publication . . . Jacques Sadoul judges you and excommunicates you in the name of the revolution . . . He places himself between you and Lenin as Lenin's right-hand man . . . How could I not feel it necessary to express my sympathy and solidarity with you, and at the same time say to the French workers: *Jacques Sadoul is lying!* . . . But the slanderer reached the depth of ignominy in the lines where he speaks of your careerism, of your concern for 'material advantages', and where he, Jacques Sadoul, calls you, Victor Serge, a literary servant of others. Nothing is more repugnant than a servile philistine who has been told by powerful masters: 'You can do anything'. Victor Serge, you remained in the ranks of the Opposition without wavering, in the midst of an unprecedented repression, when less steadfast persons were capitulating one after the other. In prison and in exile, you belonged to the band of those whom the Thermidorean hangmen could not break. You chose, my dear friend, a very bad route to ensure your 'career and material advantages'. Why did you not follow Jacques Sadoul's example? He moved around the Soviet revolution until he could return to France, where he became a correspondent for *Izvestia*. From Paris, he sent insipid scribblings, dictated by GPU agents. What a courageous, valorous heroic post! . . . Dear Victor Serge! We know how to have contempt for these people, as you do . . . A single article by Sadoul permits an infallible diagnosis: *'Stalinism is the syphilis of the labour movement'*. The Comintern is doomed to destruction. The Sadouls will desert the sinking ship like rats. They will betray the Soviet Union five minutes before serious danger. So let us teach the youth to have contempt for this human fungus. A few more years and the vanguard of the proletariat will pass over not only the servants but also their masters. You will be among those whose names will be linked to the revival of the liberation struggle of the working class![8]

Serge left Brussels for Paris on 26 October 1936 ostensibly for two weeks, but apparently remained longer.[9] Thanks to Sadoul and the Soviets, Serge had no access to the mainstream Parisian press.

Certain Oppositionists were distrustful of Serge upon his release, reasoning that Stalin would only have let him go if he thought Serge would be of use to him.* Yet once in exile Serge set to work protesting publicly against the Moscow Trials and campaign of terror. The campaign of libel emanating from the Communist Party press against Serge effectively cut his access to the so-called Left, and pressure from Moscow accomplished the same with the mainstream press. Only the Belgian daily *La Wallonie* and far-Left journals with a tiny circulation carried his articles.

---

* Ignace Reiss, whose real name was Walter Poretsky, was wary of Serge, as was Walter Krivitsky. See Poretsky's wife Elsa's remarkable memoir, *Our Own People*, Ann Arbor, University of Michigan Press, 1970, pp. 244–6.

Despite the boycott, Serge began the nightmarish task of unravelling the labyrinth of these tragedies. Working with Trotsky, Sedov, Fritz Adler, Boris Nicolaevsky and others, Serge combed the Soviet press and took the testimony of Ciliga, Reiss, Krivitsky and Barmine.* In Belgium, France and later Mexico, Serge and a few others waged a long battle for the truth. In dozens of articles published from 1936 to 1939 Serge exposed the lies behind the charges in the Moscow Trials.[10] He set up a 'Committee for Inquiry into the Moscow Trials and the Defence of Free Opinion in the Revolution' in Paris, including many French intellectuals and artists.[11] Serge himself testified on conditions in Russian prisons and the situation of the families of the victims.[12]

Reunion of Left Oppositionist exiles:
spring and summer 1936

The summer of 1936 was dramatic: in June the Popular Front of Léon Blum was elected in France, and there was an immediate general strike; July saw the beginning of the Spanish Civil War, followed by the earth-shaking bombshell of August – the trial of the Sixteen in Moscow.† All of these struggles were fervently discussed and evaluated by the exiled Left Oppositionists in Europe.

The Left Oppositionists in question were groups of expelled Communists and young recruits to the politics of Leon Trotsky in most of the countries of Western Europe. Trotsky and Sedov were the only Russians, and now Serge joined them in the West. Serge and Trotsky had not seen each other since 1927, and were now free to correspond, hopefully to meet again. That these two survived at all was serendipitous, that they now had the chance to work together simply incredible.

Serge began his correspondence with both Trotsky and his son Lev Lvovich Sedov as soon as he arrived in Belgium. His first letter to Sedov was written three days after his arrival, his first to Trotsky on his fourth day in Belgium. They corresponded frequently throughout the summer of 1936, despite the interference of the secret police and subsequent loss and delay of letters.[13] Much of the Trotsky–Serge correspondence was published in French in 1977,[14] but the correspondence between Serge and Sedov was undiscovered until the summer of 1988.[15]

The correspondence in 1936 is introductory in character, a very warm and enthusiastic reunion of Left Oppositionist comrades who had survived

---

* Serge ghosted Barmine's book.

† Serge's original working title for his novel of the show trials and purges, *The Case of Comrade Tulayev*, was 'The Earth Was Beginning to Shake' (*La Terre commençait à trembler*). His undated manuscript of the same title which serves as the author's prospectus can be found in the Serge archive, Mexico City.

Stalin's terror only because they were expelled from the Soviet Union and who now in exile had the opportunity to begin a rich collaboration. The tone of the correspondence is sympathetic and the letters are informative and full of concern.

Serge wrote first to Sedov to establish contact, to find out how to write to Trotsky without the letters being 'intercepted by some intelligence service'.[16] He asked Sedov to send 'affectionate and loyal fraternal greetings to Lev Davidovich' and to bring the sad news of Lev Solntsev's death from hunger strike. He also warned them about Senin/Sobolevicius,* and cautioned: 'I've acquired the conviction that *agents provocateurs* have penetrated the circles of communist opposition in the West very deeply, even in Lev Davidovich's immediate circle in 1932 and 1933'.†

The next day Serge wrote his first letter to Trotsky. He had a mass of information to get to him – news of his situation, of comrades left behind in the gulag. First he extended a 'fraternal salute, the warmest, truest and sincerest possible, from a handful of deported and imprisoned comrades who are heroes and whose entire thought is still tender towards you – you of whom for years we have known almost *nothing*'.[17] He informed Trotsky of

---

* Although Serge already suspected Senin as indicated in the letter, Sedov wrote a letter warning about Senin to Serge which Serge never received (Victor Serge, *Memoirs of a Revolutionary*, London, Oxford University Press, 1963, p. 328). Adolph Senin and Roman Well were the pseudonyms of the brothers Abraham and Ruvin Sobolevicius, born in Lithuania. Senin visited Trotsky in Copenhagen in 1932, shortly before he and his brother split some members away from the German section of the Left Opposition and led them into the German Communist Party. Senin/Sobolevicius was tried as a Soviet spy in the United States and admitted that he and his brother had been operating as GPU agents since 1931. In 1940 Senin was sent to the United States, and adopted the name Jack Soblen. His first job was 'to investigate and report on the Trotskyites, and on Jewish and Zionist organizations'. He was told there were three 'Trotskyite' groups in New York and a Russian agent was planted in each. Later he was put in charge of supervising and recruiting espionage agents. See 'Exhibit No. 528' (entered as testimony) by Jack Soblen, written with Jack Lotto, 'How I Spied on US for the Reds', (*Journal-American*, 10–20 Nov. 1957), United States Senate, *Scope of Soviet Activity in the United States*, Hearing before the Subcommittee to Investigate the Administration of the Internal Security Act and Other Internal Security Laws of the Committee on the Judiciary, Eighty-Fourth and Eighty-Fifth Congresses, 1956–57, pp. 4875–91.

† Serge to Sedov, 21 April 1936. In a later letter to Sedov, dated only 'Piatnitsa' (1936), Serge elaborated on Senin: 'About Senin, personally, my mind isn't made up: whether he's an agent provocateur or a capitulator (under arrest) entirely tricked by provocateurs. *What happened to him?* It might be possible to inform on him, *but do not mention me.* They wrote me from Siberia that he's a provocateur, with a pretty convincing argument.' Serge to Sedov, 'Piatnitsa' 1936, 231:63, Nicolaevsky Collection, Hoover Archive.

Solntsev's death in Novosibirsk of hunger strike, and of Dumbadze's grave situation in Sarapul. He passed on heartfelt greetings from Boris Eltsin who had been with Serge in Orenburg, and his son Victor Eltsin in Archangel.

Serge told Trotsky how in deportation our 'thoughts turned constantly to you from the abyss of these black years'. The authorities tried everything to destroy Trotsky's influence, including officially leaked rumours and falsehoods to demoralize and confuse Trotsky's supporters. Serge wrote to Trotsky:

> at the time of Rakovsky's capitulation, the NKVD officers in private 'chats' with followers of the 'general line' put out the rumour that LD had applied or was going to apply for permission to return to the USSR on certain conditions.*

The NKVD ploy had no success whatsoever. The subtext was to communicate to Trotsky the importance of his continued principled struggle abroad, news of which reached the prisoners sporadically. It boosted their morale and kept them on course. Interestingly this even affected those who had capitulated and now regretted it, like the figure of Kostrov Serge portrayed in *Midnight in the Century*. To convey to Trotsky the mood of these comrades, Serge related how

> joyfully the comrades who remained under the GPU's heel saw me off . . . The mere thought that someone was going to give their fraternal greetings to you meant so much to them. Deportation and prison have already steeled remarkably dedicated and staunch revolutionaries, who face their systematic suffocation with extraordinary fortitude. All the comrades I've mentioned are like that.[18]

This account is unique and in marked contrast to other prison memoirs like Evgenia Ginzburg's or Maria Joffe's, whose portraits of isolation, confusion and despair heavily overshadow the occasional tiny glimpses of human solidarity, human kindness, conviction and fortitude that Serge emphasizes. Most likely this is due to the time under consideration: both Ginzburg in Kolyma and Joffe in Vorkuta deal with the general terror of 1937 and after, and had little comfort of political solidarity. Serge was relatively privileged to be confined in exile with other Left Oppositionists, arrested and deported before the mass terror of 1936–39. Those arrested before Kirov's assassination were committed politicos; after 1936 anyone could be arrested, on the slightest pretext.

Serge eagerly read the published copies of the *Bulletin of the Left Opposition* once he arrived in the West, and was relieved to find he was in broad

---

* Serge to Trotsky, in Russian, 29 April 1936. (Most of Serge's letters were in French, Trotsky's in Russian.) D.J. Cotterill (ed.), *The Serge–Trotsky Papers*, London, Pluto Press, 1994, letter 6, pp. 47–9.

agreement. Serge had worried that 'we in deportation, cut off from the comrades who can breathe freely, might accumulate considerable disagreements with them',[19] but was pleased to find virtually no differences with what he read in the January 1935 *Bulletin*, no. 42.

Serge also told Trotsky about his own arrests and deportation, which Trotsky published in the *Bulletin*, repeating the story Serge believed was true about his young sister-in-law: that the NKVD attempted to base their charge against Serge on '*false* testimony extracted from his young sister-in-law Anita Russakova'. In fact this concocted confession became the basis for Anita's arrest three years later.

The first letters from Trotsky to Serge are very solicitous, with Trotsky particularly concerned with the state of Liuba's mental health and Serge's precarious political situation. Trotsky wrote he was 'deeply affected by the news of Solntsev's death',[20] one more in a long line of close associates who died or were killed. Trotsky implored Serge for detailed information, even if brief, and for Serge to write in the *Bulletin* (under a pseudonym or unsigned to protect him from the GPU). Trotsky promised to be an 'indefatigable letter-writer' to Serge.

He also offered to help Serge materially by citing Serge's work a few times in the long introduction Trotsky was preparing for the second edition of *The History of the Russian Revolution*, which would help publicize Serge's name.* Trotsky encouraged Serge to write, in fact to consider writing his political work, and to publish in America, where compensation was the most generous. Trotsky was trying to convince Serge that writing was a way to get around the political restrictions imposed on Serge by the conditions of his stay in Belgium,† and that the writing itself was a way to put bread on his table. Further, Trotsky added, 'If you write a book with the talent that is yours and that I only discovered while abroad, you will be more useful to the movement than in any other way'.[21] Trotsky also asked Serge for news of his son Seryozha,[22] his first wife Alexandra Lvovna, her sister Maria Lvovna Sokolovskaya and his grandchildren in their care.[23]

Serge's letter to Trotsky of 25 April 1936 was published in part in the *Bulletin of the Left Opposition* (Paris), no. 50, May 1936. Serge's was the first live information from the gulag, and it was not pleasant. The news was of

---

* Trotsky to Serge, 8 May 1936, Cotterill, *Serge–Trotsky Papers*, letter 8, p. 52. Trotsky then wrote a dispatch to Associated Press on the Stalin constitution and the treatment of the Oppositionists 'Political Persecution in the USSR', 22 May 1936 (found in L.D. Trotsky, *Writings, 1935–1936*, New York, Pathfinder Press, 1973, pp. 324–8). He used Serge's material *in toto*, without mentioning Serge's name, in order to protect him politically. The dispatch was sent to thousands of American papers. Trotsky to Serge, postscript 20 May 1936 in letter of 19 May 1936. Cotterill, *Serge–Trotsky Papers*, letter 10, pp. 54–5.

† Especially if Serge published in French publications while living in Belgium. Trotsky to Serge, 8 May 1936. Cotterill, *Serge–Trotsky Papers*, letter 8, p. 52.

imprisoned Oppositionists, defiant, combative, and in good spirits, but whose physical condition was critical.*

Serge became Trotsky's French translator, working on *Revolution Betrayed*. This work was important for Serge in both a political and material sense, and Trotsky trusted Serge's translations without checking.† Once Trotsky was in Norway the conditions of his house arrest interrupted his correspondence. At this point Lev (Lyova) L. Sedov became the most trustworthy conduit of information between Trotsky and Serge. Any problem Serge had with Trotsky's translations, including suggestions to make the text stronger were written to Sedov, who then passed the information to Trotsky.‡

Serge translated very quickly and was generally pleased with Trotsky's '*wonderful* and useful book. I'm happy that in many places, my conclusions completely coincide with his, while overall both books shoot in exactly the same direction!'§ At the same time as Trotsky was writing *Revolution*

---

* For example, Dumbadze, in Sarapul, was paralysed in both arms, unable to even dress himself, with no medical attention, trying to exist on 30 rubles per month.

† Trotsky happily wrote to Serge, 'I cannot dream of a more qualified translator than you.' Trotsky to Serge, 3 June 1936. Later Trotsky told Serge: 'Your comments about the translation of my book prove that you are extremely conscientious about this task. You are such a good stylist that there is no need at all for you to check with me on the "freeness" of your translation; I fully endorse your formulations in advance.' Trotsky to Serge, 18 Aug. 1936. This letter appears in a slightly different translation in Cotterill, *Serge–Trotsky Papers*, dated 19 Aug. 1936, letter 29, p. 95.

‡ For example, Serge to Sedov (undated letter, partially typed in French with handwritten note on bottom of page in Russian, Nicolaevsky Collection 231:21, Hoover Archive), also Serge to Sedov, 13 July 1936 and 31 July 1936 (231:78; 231:80). Serge was paid for the translations, greatly alleviating his material condition. Serge was both translator and editor at times. He wrote to Lyova Sedov (no date other than 'mercredi' with text in Russian) that he has shortened the text of the Hippodrome speech which Serge feels really should not be included in the book as it is repetitive. Serge criticizes the structure of the book which is simply a collection of speeches and notes, and its repetitiveness, which he said would kill the book. Sedov's letters to Serge echo Trotsky's sentiments that Serge's translation and added notes improve the book and make it more effective. Sedov to Serge, 19 June 1937, and 20 July 1937 (231:92, 231:93, Nicolaevsky Collection, Hoover Archive).

§ Serge to Sedov, 18 Aug. 1936, postscript. The collaboration between Serge and Trotsky in their dangerous exile in 1936 was comradely. For a fuller discussion of the correspondence between them over the translation of Trotsky's work see Susan Weissman, 'Predannaya Revoliutsia L. Trotskovo i Cyd'ba Revoliutsiii V. Serzha', in M. Voyeikov (ed.), *Kniga L.D. Trotzkovo Predannaya Revoliutsia: 60 Let Spustia*, Moscow, 1997. Dimitri Volkogonov, the Russian biographer of Stalin, Lenin and Trotsky, who had unparalleled access to secret police files, has quoted a letter in the secret police archive from Serge to Sedov describing Trotsky's book as 'cumbersome, hastily written and of *small* [my emphasis] literary value'.

Betrayed, Serge was writing *Destiny of a Revolution*, which Trotsky said he was 'impatiently awaiting'. Clearly the two Oppositionists were on the same wavelength and responded similarly to the new world conjuncture; it was not the first time. Earlier examples include: Serge's *Year One of the Russian Revolution* and Trotsky's *History of the Russian Revolution*; both wrote books entitled *Literature and Revolution*; both wrote biographies of Stalin in 1940; both wrote biographies of Lenin; and both wrote memoirs.

Trotsky tried to orient Serge politically to Western Europe, and specifically to the various groups and individuals with whom Serge was in contact. Trotsky warned Serge about the Paz couple; he said Magdeleine's work to gain Serge's release was 'the only praiseworthy thing she has done in her life', and he found her husband to be 'a bourgeois conservative, harsh, narrow-minded and profoundly repulsive'.[24] He characterized Boris Souvarine as 'a journalist not a revolutionary', with 'a purely analytical intellect', 'negative' with a character that makes him poisonous in a group but also incapable of independent work.* Trotsky discussed these mutual friends and comrades in the context of the role of the Mensheviks in the USSR, who were now accommodating to the Stalinist regime and thus aiding the persecution of 'our friends'. Trotsky believed that social democrats internationally were drawing closer to the Stalinists, and hence the line between the social democrats and themselves must be clearly drawn. Trotsky wrote that their problem was not how to protect those Mensheviks who were suffering from the Stalinist regime, but how to 'protect our own selves from low blows by Menshevism and Stalinism internationally, while conducting a pitiless campaign to unmask them'. In that light Trotsky attacked the Menshevik 'deviations' of both Anton Ciliga and Boris Souvarine. Of all the comrades they knew in common, Trotsky wrote approvingly only of Alfred and Marguerite Rosmer, who despite disagreements, 'remain in esteem and sympathy'.

Trotsky's evaluations were harsh, and Serge defended his associations, stressing the importance of getting to as wide an audience as possible. Trotsky was obviously quite determined to bring Serge firmly within the framework of the International Left Opposition, and its conceptions about what kind of work and with whom it was to be done in Europe.

The correspondence in the summer of 1936 was comradely, while clarifying points of agreement and departure. Disagreement began over individuals,

---

The Nicolaevsky Collection of Serge–Sedov correspondence shows no such letter, but there is one in which Serge tells Sedov he considers the work of *fundamental* value. Either the secret archive has a letter which Sedov never saw, or the quote from it is a mistake at best or a fabrication at worst. D. Volkogonov, *Trotsky: The Eternal Revolutionary*, New York, Free Press, 1996, p. 364.

* Trotsky to Serge, 29 April 1936. Cotterill, *Serge–Trotsky Papers*, pp. 44–7. Trotsky wrote that Souvarine's book on Stalin, which he only skimmed, is 'from a theoretical and political point of view . . . worthless'.

many of whom Trotsky felt would end up on the other side of the important battles. Serge believed he owed a personal debt to his friends who had struggled for his release, and he was not ready to consign them to the dustbin of reformism or reaction.* Serge stressed to Trotsky in a letter of 23 May 1936 that he was *not* a syndicalist, but thought revolutionary syndicalists could be considered allies and that an 'amicable and non-sectarian debate' should be carried out with them. Trotsky wrote in response that he was glad of Serge's efforts to influence these comrades, but the Old Man did not change his own assessment of them.

Dismayed by the way in which internal squabbling impeded the effectiveness of political work, Serge wrote to his friend Marcel Martinet on 15 May 1936 about his distaste for the divisions in the French Left and how he hoped his work could bring them together again 'by a sort of disarmament of antipathies'. Serge was pained by what he considered petty divisions among those who should be working in concert – all the more since he felt he was obliged to all of them for their work to free him. Serge worried that

> I'll end up full of resentment or sectarian hostility or all ready for an action that's flashy but defendable after all . . . I'm in reality a curious mixture of moderation and austerity; it's not my fault if austerity tends to prevail right now. In short I refuse all action that's loud or sectarian.[25]

Serge's correspondence with Trotsky suggests that Trotsky very much wanted Serge as a close political ally. Still Trotsky harboured some suspicions about Serge's release, as did other Soviet exiles. While writing to Serge with consideration and camaraderie, at the same time he wrote to Lola Dallin and warned her to be wary of Serge.† Elsa Poretsky also wrote this in her memoir, *Our Own People*.‡ Trotsky did not believe Serge's release

---

* According to Trotsky's biographer, Pierre Broué, Trotsky was indignant that Serge had written in *La Révolution prolétarienne*, because its editors believed that Stalinism was the continuation of Bolshevism. Trotsky would have preferred Serge to collaborate with the bourgeois press. The editors of *La Révolution prolétarienne* in this period were Monatte and Louzon, not the same figures who had struggled for Serge's release. Interview with Pierre Broué, 22 May 1987, Mexico City.

† Leon D. Trotsky to Lola Dallin, May 1936, Nicolaevsky Collection, Hoover Archive. Trotsky warned Dallin to watch Serge very closely: watch his body language, his style, any suggestion that he was acting as an agent.

‡ Poretsky doubted that the campaign or even Gorky's intervention was responsible for Serge's release, and raised the possibility that the Soviets may have instigated the campaign themselves. She remembered sitting with her husband and Krivitsky at the Café des Deux Magots when they read of Serge's release. At first she took it to mean a turn for the better in the Soviet Union, but both Ludwik and Krivitsky told her that 'no one leaves the Soviet Union unless the NKVD can use him', and Ludwik thought Serge's contacts with opposition groups would be invaluable to Moscow. Poretsky, *Our Own People*, p. 245.

1 Victor Serge in the early 1920s

2 Serge, Vlady and Liuba following his release from prison, 1928

3 Anita Russakova, Serge's sister-in-law

4 Serge's uncle Nikolai Kibalchich, executed for his role in the assassination of Tsar Alexander II

5 The house at 33 Cavalry Street, Orenburg, where Serge and Vlady spent three years in exile. Painting by Vlady

6 Vlady's sketch of Serge in Orenburg, signed V.V. Serge, Orenburg, 20 March 1936. Vlady was sixteen at the time

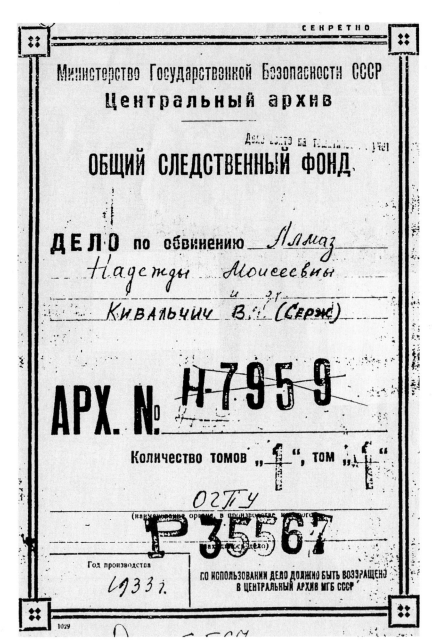

7 Serge's NKVD file from Orenburg

8 Boris Mikhailovich Eltsin, leading Left Oppositionist and former chairman of the Soviet in Ekaterinburg, who was in Orenburg with Serge. Painting by Vlady

9 Vlady's sketch of a memorial to Stalin's victims

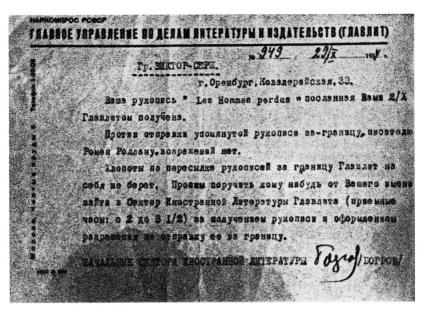

10 Receipt from the Department of Censorship, dated 29 October 1934 for *Les Hommes perdus*, Serge's confiscated novel about pre-war France

11 Serge and Vlady, about 1936

12 Liuba, Jeannine, Serge and Vlady, Brussels, 1936
[Jeannine Kibalchich]

13 Liuba with Jeannine, France [Jeannine Kibalchich]

MINISTÈRE
DE LA DÉFENSE NATIONALE
ET DE LA GUERRE

Bureau Central Militaire
de la Circulation

N° 2576/C

SAUF-CONDUIT COLLECTIF

A L L E R

Valable du VINGT HUIT MAI 1940

(¹) **au** VINGT HUIT JUIN 1940

Signature du titulaire :

CHEF DU DÉTACHEMENT

Nom : Monsieur KIBALTCHICHE

Prénoms : Victor, Napoléon

Nationalité : indéterminée

Né le 30/12/1890 a BRUXELLES

Domicile PRE St GERVAIS, I place Séverine

Profession Ecrivain

Pièce d'identité : nature récépissé de C.I

Numéros N° 76, I85807 C.L 5I0432

par P.P. valable au 20 Février I94I

Est autorisé à se rendre de Paris à PAU (Basses-

Pyrénées) - : - : - : - : - : - : - : - : - : - : - : - :

- : - : - : - : - : - : - : - : - : - : - : - : - : - : - : - : -

Mode de locomotion : tous transports publics

Motif du déplacement : Evacuation

M. KIBALTCHICHE est chef du détachement composé des

personnes indiquées d'autre part et dont il a la responsabilité.

Pʳ le Général chef du B. C. M. C.

LE CHEF d'ETAT-MAJOR

(1) Le présent sauf-conduit est à viser à l'arrivée à la Gendarmerie qui indiquera la date de
retour en fin de mission. Le titulaire devra au retour le remettre à l'autorité militaire qui l'a délivré.

14 Safe conduct for Victor Serge and his party, issued by the French
government, 1940. Note that Serge's nationality is given as 'indeterminate'

15 Laurette Séjourné
[Jeannine Kibalchich]

16 Sketches of Serge in
Marseilles, 1940, by Vlady

17 Charles Wolff, Victor Serge, Benjamin Péret and André Breton, standing in front of Villa Air-Bel, spring 1941 [Chambon Foundation]

18 Varian Fry standing in the pond at the Villa Air-Bel, watched by Victor Serge and André Breton (standing), an unidentified woman, and Jean Gemahling (with a stick). Vlady has his back to the camera. November 1940 [Chambon Foundation]

19 Victor Serge, probably on board the *Presidente Trujillo* sailing from Martinique to Santo Domingo [Chambon Foundation]

20 Victor Serge in
Mexico, 1944

21 Laurette Séjourné
in Mexico
[Jeannine Kibalchich]

22 Leon Trotsky, Coyoacán, Mexico, 1940 [photograph A.H. Buchman]

23 Victor Serge in Mexico. Photo scratched, perhaps in anger?

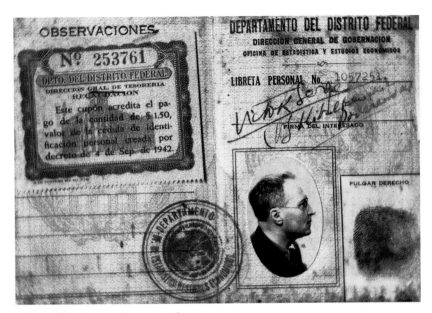

24 Serge's Mexican identity card

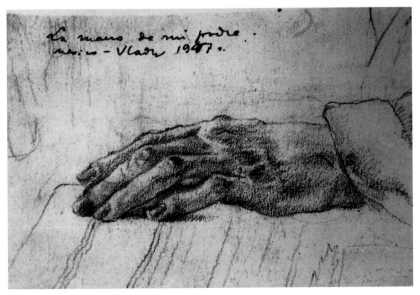

25 'My father's hand, Mexico, 1947', sketch by Vlady

26 Jeannine Kibalchich
Roussakova in 1982
[Jeannine Kibalchich]

27 Vlady and Irina Gogua, Moscow, 1989; their first reunion in fifty-seven years
[photograph Susan Weissman]

had resulted from pressure exerted at the International Writers' Congress,[26] but came about because Stalin felt he could use Serge. Trotsky feared perhaps a deal had been made.

Contrary to Trotskyist suspicions, Serge was incorruptible, and eager to reveal the truth about the Stalinist counter-revolution. Perhaps more than anyone else in Europe Serge's chief occupation became to campaign for his comrades left behind, and to expose the lies of the trials. Sedov was also entirely preoccupied in this effort, but because of the split in the French section and the internal squabbling between Trotsky and the Belgians and the two groups in France, much time was devoted to internal matters, leaving less for the necessary public campaign which Serge picked up. So Serge laid out the broad outlines of what he thought would be effective political campaigning in Europe on behalf of those languishing in the gulag and, equally important, 'to raise in a particular manner the issue of proletarian democracy – in the shape of freedom for Socialist opinion in the Soviet Union'. Serge added that 'to be a success, our campaigning must avoid being sectarian' and in this vein Serge disagreed with Trotsky on the Mensheviks today – whereas in the civil war they were counter-revolutionaries, today, seventeen years later,

> there is no other question of public emergency except that of making up our minds whether we, in the midst of persecution and imprisonment, are going to deny to our cell mates the rights of speech and thought which the bureaucracy is denying to all of us. Any such attitude of denial would be indefensible, and amount to our political suicide. Alternatively, while recanting none of the traditions of October, we can and must engage in a practical rediscovery of what workers' democracy means, proving that we fear neither debate nor rivalry and that we are not in any way the kind of people who build an enormous prison for anyone who disagrees with us. I'm writing all this to you because I've been told that you oppose collaboration with all parties and groupings in this particular matter.[27]

It appeared that Trotsky politically attacked all those who did not join him in the project to found the Fourth International. In fact, Trotsky became indignant when Serge wrote for *La Révolution prolétarienne*. Trotsky considered this an act hostile to the Fourth International. Trotsky had hoped Serge would play a leading role in the young International, as an older comrade with Russian experience. Serge's contributions to non-Fourth-International journals were, in Trotsky's eyes, betrayals.* Serge was never

---

* Trotsky saw a letter Serge had written to the editors of *La Révolution prolétarienne* in the 16 May 1936 issue of *L'Action socialiste-révolutionnaire*. In his letter to Serge of 19 May 1936 he admitted it bothered him that Serge wrote *exclusively* to a syndicalist group and added: 'If you feel you are politically closer to syndicalism than Marxism, then it remains only for me to take note of this profound difference between us.'

hostile to Trotsky. He was principally concerned with publishing wherever he could in order to raise the issue of the imprisoned revolutionary generation in the Soviet Union.

Trotsky told Serge that he (Serge) did not yet have a feel for 'the real mechanics of the struggle as it has been carried out these last few years'. He warned that the crowd around *La Révolution prolétarienne* and the Pazes have 'acted like *liberals*', whereas 'our' own comrades have done real work. Trotsky cited the work of their comrades during Bukharin's famous visit to Paris in 1936:

> the Bolshevik-Leninists burst into his conference and launched an appeal on behalf of the political prisoners of the USSR. Of course they were thrown out of the hall. It is only because of this kind of revolutionary action that the liberals could score a certain victory: 'reforms' (such as your release) are always a *by-product* of revolutionary struggle.[28]

What is rather strange about this demonstration of 'revolutionary struggle' on the part of the Trotskyist 'Bolshevik-Leninists' which Trotsky implied was more effective than the struggle around Serge's release, is that it was *no different* from the struggle Magdeleine Paz and the *Révolution prolétarienne* group waged to secure Serge's freedom.*

Trotsky continued in the same vein on the *Révolution prolétarienne* group; he wrote that they were on excellent terms with the reformist faction of the trade-union bureaucracy, which in turn was allied to the Stalinists. He called them 'a conservative sect, not at all combative, and lacking any political significance . . . The revolutionary spirit left them a long time ago.'[29] While there was most likely some truth to what Trotsky was saying, he arrogantly implied that everyone else's work was worthless compared to the political intervention of his own comrades, whose work was doing more for the liberation of prisoners.

Serge's appreciation of the work of the French comrades in the Fourth International was less sanguine. He was often frustrated that their squabbles kept them from doing the vital public work that must be done. In a letter to Lev Lyovich Sedov on 5 August 1936 he complained:

> Our French comrades' inability to work distresses me extremely and inclines me toward a rather pessimistic estimation of their perspectives. That's no way to build an organization, it'll never win over the authorities, assemble a cadre, or achieve lasting influence. Such feeble and bungling shortsightedness will hardly get you anywhere. I write this after reading the newspapers and bulletins (in French). There's not even the least desire to address the comrades with criticism, until it appears useless, with so little time left for useful work.

---

* The only difference between the actions was that Magdeleine Paz and her associates constantly interrupted the Congress from *within* the hall, while Trotsky's group *burst in* to interrupt Bukharin's conference.

I won't write more about it – and I won't return to all that again – I'll distance myself in literary work. Such infernal squabbling and unhelpful agitation! The younger comrades are both sympathetic and valuable, but in that atmosphere nothing will come of them. Forgive me for these pronouncements; you're closer to it and already know all this.[30]

There is an interruption in the correspondence after September 1936 due to Trotsky's house arrest in Norway, and the letters continue sporadically through 1939. The correspondence reveals what Adolfo Gilly described as Trotsky's universalism;[31] Trotsky was very warm and generous with potential co-thinkers, but with his political collaborators he was sharp and did not mince words. This pattern is evident throughout Trotsky's correspondence with Andrés Nin, Boris Souvarine and Victor Serge.

Unravelling the labyrinth (of madness): Victor Serge and the purges

Two events hit like thunderbolts during the summer of Serge's expulsion to the West. European skies were darkening with impending fascism and war, when suddenly revolution erupted in Spain with the July days in Barcelona. Scarcely a month later the bombshell dropped in Moscow with the first of the Moscow show trials. Vlady remembers Serge's reaction to the news that August morning. He gasped, 'We have been saved!'[32] The realization that he had got out in the nick of time impressed him greatly, and made him feel his duty to his still-imprisoned comrades more acutely.

Serge began to write incessantly. His output on the purges alone is staggering: dozens of journalistic articles published in the Belgian daily *La Wallonie*, far Left journals in France and the United States, the books *Seize fusillés: où va la révolution russe?* (September 1936); *From Lenin to Stalin* (December 1936); *Vingt-neuf fusillés et la fin de Iagoda* (April 1937); *Pour la vérité sur le procès de Moscou! 18 questions – 18 réponses* (Paris brochure, 1937). He also wrote books on Soviet political developments and the workings of the GPU, biographies, memoirs and novels reporting, analysing and describing the establishment of the Stalinist system and its significance, such as *Destiny of a Revolution* (July 1937), *L'Assassinat d'Ignace Reiss* (April 1938), *Portrait de Staline* (February 1940), *Pages de Journal 1936–38, 1945–47*, his *Memoirs of a Revolutionary*, and his two novels of the purges, *Midnight in the Century* (1936–38), and *The Case of Comrade Tulayev* (1940–42).

While undertaking this monumental task of untangling the lies spewing forth from Moscow, Serge's domestic problems were acute: his wife's sanity was in constant peril and they had no money and no work. Serge was faced with earning their daily bread, maintaining the home, taking care of baby Jeannine and sickly Liuba (along with Vlady), and writing and campaigning for his comrades left behind, now certain to die.

Despite his tremendous personal difficulties, Serge was not silenced. In

Mexico, Trotsky defended himself against the most colossal calumnies,[33] while in Europe, Serge became the chief lawyer for the falsely accused.* Their audience was limited, their reach – the world community. The task of defending the truth fell to these few voices. At a time when all of Europe was in danger of being crushed, Stalin blamed all social ills on Trotsky, his son Lev Sedov, and their fellow Oppositionists. Those who upheld the ideals of October were now accused of being behind everything that had gone wrong! Serge noted wryly, in a letter to Dwight Macdonald, that the Soviet press 'has never published a line against the Nazi-fascists and anti-Semitism'.[34]

Serge and Sedov's committee in Paris and Trotsky's Dewey Commission in Mexico managed, with precious few resources, to publish unassailable refutations of the lies trumpeted at the three show trials. Twenty years before Khrushchev's secret speech about Stalin's crimes Victor Serge tried to alert the world to what Stalin was doing in Russia. His words fell largely on deaf ears in a Europe where preoccupation with fascism and impending war blinded many communists to what was happening in the Soviet Union. Fifty years later Gorbachev's Commission of Inquiry had to admit that the trials were rigged, the charges fabricated and the accused innocent. In 1936 Victor Serge foretold the elimination of the revolutionary generation, though he felt his foresight 'was absolutely worthless'.[35] Julian Gorkín wrote that this was probably the most bitter period of Serge's life, when 'at liberty [Serge] felt the tragic agony of his comrades and his brothers. And he felt that the revolution, which had constituted a great hope, was devouring itself.'[36]

---

* Serge wrote to Lyova Sedov in a letter of 4 Sept. 1936 that they must set up every-where (Paris, Amsterdam, Brussels) a 'commission for a permanent fight against repressions (save our own!) with the anarchists, *Révolution prolétarienne*, left social-ists (Pivert), various others and ours'. Serge also called on Sedov to help immedi-ately establish a parallel non-partisan commission for the investigation of the Moscow Trials, recommending prominent intellectuals for the French Commis-sion (Serge to Sedov, 4 Sept. 1936, Nicolaevsky Collection 231:85, Hoover Archive). This became the Paris Committee for Inquiry into the Moscow Trials and Defence of Free Opinion in the Revolution, with the participation of French intellectuals such as André Breton, Félicien Challaye, Marcel Martinet, Magdeleine Paz, André Philip, Henry Poulaille, Jean Galtier-Bossière, Pierre Monatte, Alfred Rosmer, Georges Pioch, Maurice Wullens. Serge recommended that other French intellectuals participate, such as Malraux, Gide, etc., but they would not. The long title of the committee was insisted upon by Serge so that they would also have the task of 'defending, within the Spanish revolution, those whom Soviet totalitarianism would attempt to liquidate in Madrid and Barcelona by the same methods of lying and murder' (Serge, *Memoirs*, p. 331). Sedov wrote to Serge on 14 Feb. 1937 that the French committee doesn't work as well as the American and Mexican committees (367:90 Nicolaevsky Collection, Hoover Archive).

Stalin's revenge: the role of terror

To choose the victim, to prepare the blow with care, to sate an implacable vengeance, and then to go to bed . . . There is nothing sweeter in the world!*

Gorkín wrote that Stalin probably regretted letting Serge go just four months before his Moscow show trials.[37] A threatening voice had slipped from his grip, and now would require more effort to silence abroad.

Serge's voice was heard by a restricted public, but he was not silenced. He sought not simply to refute the lies, but to understand and explain the need for the lies. This meant understanding the role of terror in the creation of Stalin's system of rule. Writing at the time, Serge was not able to precisely discern the social, economic and political system still taking shape. But Serge realized that the purges could only be understood in the context of the new social relations being created.

Serge wrote in the pamphlet *Seize fusillés* that the first trial marked the beginning of the extermination of the revolutionary generation. In *La Révolution prolétarienne* Serge wrote that the massacre was needed to wipe out all reserve teams of government on the eve of war.[38] By 1937 the threat of a reserve team was not really credible, since most of the old guard were already dead, in prison, or in exile. Many others had capitulated. Furthermore, the newer Bukharinist challenges to Stalin (Ryutin in 1932 and Kirov in 1934) had also been largely eliminated. It was still necessary from Stalin's standpoint to eliminate any resonance of the old guard. This need helps explain the fantastic nature of the outrageous charges. One cannot blame Serge, writing in 1937, for failing to form a precise picture of what was unfolding in the Soviet Union. Serge was closer to the mark when he wrote that Stalin needed to eliminate all witnesses to his betrayal of the revolution – even silently critical witnesses like the old Bolsheviks locked away in prison.

Serge was convinced that the purges were not planned far in advance, although they were prepared and rehearsed; his own release was living proof. Serge had left the USSR in mid-April 1936 when the accused were already in prison; he had worked closely with Zinoviev and Trotsky, and was a close acquaintance of many others who later disappeared or were shot. He had been a leader of the Left Opposition in Leningrad and one of its spokesmen abroad, and had never capitulated. His skill and renown as a writer combined with his having been a witness to Stalin's crimes made Serge too dangerous to be allowed to escape, unless the trials had not yet been prepared. Serge believed he was not accused during the trials because,

---

* Stalin to Dzerzhinski and Kamenev one summer night, 1923. Cited by Serge in *Portrait de Staline*, Paris, Grasset, 1940, p. 177. Serge noted in a footnote that Souvarine also cited it on p. 446 of his own biography of Stalin, and that Trotsky also cited it in several writings, and it was often repeated by the old Bolsheviks.

except in the case of Trotsky, lies were only spread about those who had no means to defend themselves.*

Making sense of the terror several years later Serge was compelled to also make sense of the man behind it, recognizing that 'in a tyranny, too many things depend on the tyrant'.[39] He wrote a biography of Stalin in 1940, and then *The Case of Comrade Tulayev*, in which Stalin appears as a thoroughly human character, albeit committing monstrous acts. The point Serge stressed about Stalin was that the man was formed by the policies he practised, reacting and conforming to the mandates and logic of the situation. He became the tool of the rising bureaucracy 'going from one expedient to another, receiving failures as a boxer receives blows: without blinking, but humiliated in his heart of hearts, returning with fury against his instruments'.[40] Serge added, 'Stalinism incarnates the bureaucracy, is beginning to suffocate it . . . It is defined by fear . . . by a frenetic determination to endure.'[41]

Stalin and his group destroyed the old intelligentsia, wiped out the revolutionary generation, and subjected the new elite to terror. Stalin first embodied the elite and then reformed it to become the ruling layer. Serge understood that Stalin's betrayal was unconscious,[42] proceeding step by step.

The confessions: why?

Much has been written about how Rakovsky, Bukharin and Zinoviev could have confessed to the preposterous crimes with which they were charged. Serge had not one answer but many. Exhausted revolutionaries had succumbed to twisted logic, perverted ideals, misdirected loyalty, fear, and torture. Serge addressed the 'enigma' of confession in various forms: essays, articles, polemics, fiction and poetry.† In his poem 'Confessions' Serge

---

* Serge, *Memoirs*, pp. 330–31. Although Serge described the unplanned nature of the purges in the *Memoirs*, in his pamphlet *Seize fusillés*, Serge discussed the premeditated nature of the show trials, that their outcome was decided in advance, prepared and rehearsed. *Seize fusillés: où va la révolution russe?*, Paris, Spartacus Cahiers Mensuels, Série Nouvelle, no. 1, 1936, pp. 4–5.

† This is quite unlike Koestler's approach in *Darkness at Noon*, where the thought processes leading to confession are seen through the mental gymnastics of Rubashov, the single character who discovers the single truth that indeed the Party cannot make mistakes, and that he must comply by confessing, since that is what the Party requires. Koestler's view is monolithic, falling entirely in line with the stance adopted by the cold warriors that equates Marxism, Leninism, Bolshevism and Stalinism. In this view, lacking nuance and subtlety, Communism is anti-human: it is the Party versus the people, there is no thinking, only obedience, revolutionaries are incapable of compassion, etc. It is easy to see why Koestler, once he rejected the Soviet Union, became one of the 'god that failed' anti-communists. His book is a pure statement of Stalinist thinking. Koestler comes across as quite limited when contrasted to the richness of the voices in Serge's *The Case of Comrade Tulayev*.

portrays the misery of men who gave everything to the Party; not only their lives, but their integrity and dignity:

We have never been what we are,
the faces of our lives are not our own,
the voices that you hear, the voices that have spoken so loudly above the storm
are not our own,
nothing you have seen is true,
nothing we have done is true,
we are entirely different.

We have never thought our thoughts,
believed our faith,
willed our will,
today our only truth is despair,
this confession of a mad degeneration,
this fall into blackness
where faith is renounced and recovered one last time.

We have neither faces nor names, neither strength nor past
– for everything is over and done with
We should never have existed
– for everything is devastated
And it is we who are the guilty, we the unforgivable,
we the most miserable, we the most ruined,
it is we . . . know that
– and be saved!

Believe our confessions, join in our vow
of complete obedience: scorn our disavowals.
Once put down, the old revolt is nothing but obedience.

May those who are less devoted be proud,
may those who have forgiven themselves be proud,
may those who are more devoted be proud,
may those who have not given up be proud.

If we roused the peoples and made the continents quake,
shot the powerful, destroyed the old armies, the old cities, the old ideas,
began to make everything anew with these dirty old stones,
these tired hands, and the meagre souls that were left us,
it was not in order to haggle with you now,
sad revolution, our mother, our child, our flesh,
our decapitated dawn, our night with its stars askew,
with its inexplicable Milky Way torn to pieces.

If you betray yourself, what can we do but betray ourselves with you?
After lives such as these, what possible death could there be, if not, in this
betrayal, to die for you?

What more could we have done than kneel before you
in this shame and agony,
if in serving you we have called down upon you such darkness?

If others find in your heart stabbed a thousand times
the means to live on and to resist you in order to save you in twenty years,
a hundred years,
blessed are they by we who have never believed in benedictions,
blessed are they in our secret hearts
by we who can do nothing more.

We no longer belong to the future, we belong entirely to this age:
it is bloody and vile in its love for mankind,
we are bloody and vile like the men of this time.

Trample on us, insult us, spit on us,
vomit us,
massacre us,
our love is greater than this humiliation,
this suffering,
this massacre,
your iniquitous mouths are just, your mouths are our mouths,
we are in you,
your bullets are ours, and our mortal agony, our death, our infamy are yours,
and your vast life on these fields worked for centuries is forever ours!

Paris, 12 October 1938[43]

The purge trials were based on confessions obtained under mental and physical duress. Serge knew many of the accused intimately; he was able to interpret their published confessions because he knew how these people had behaved in other circumstances, how they viewed the Party and what they believed politically. Because of Serge's descriptive skills he was able to make comprehensible how and why the accused agreed to participate in slandering themselves. Serge said the confessions were only an enigma in the West; for anyone who knew the psychology of the Old Bolsheviks, it was no mystery.[44]

Confessing to complicity with the Gestapo or to Kirov's murder differed only in degree from the earlier capitulations made by many Oppositionists: both capitulation and confession were required by the Party. The confessions, said Serge, were made out of utter devotion. Serge quoted Smilga, an Oppositionist capitulator, who said 'We must retreat, surrender for the present, and when the masses awaken, we shall put ourselves at their head', and Zinoviev, who often said, 'We must remain within the Party, even flat on our belly in the mud, in order to be there on the day of the great awakening of the working masses.'

They were done in, Serge commented, by 'Party patriotism'. Their error, according to Serge, was that their attachment to the past prevented them from seeing the counter-revolution *within* their beloved Party, and that 'no longer with it, but in spite of it and against it – the toiling masses will one day awaken and renew the fight for socialism'.[45] Serge, a newcomer to the Party in 1919 with an anarchist past, held no institution so sacred in such a timeless fashion. The lies depended on the defendants' consent to sacrifice their consciences and their dignity. Besides, as Krivitsky pointed out, the interrogators used the magic words 'socialist', 'proletarian', and 'revolutionary', words that evoked concepts to which these men had devoted their lives.[46] These men were led to believe that their confessions would help the concepts behind the words come to fruition, even out of Stalin's bloody tyranny. But not everyone consented, and Serge pointed out that the trials selected from a larger number of accused only those who were compliant, who would sacrifice themselves at the Party's instructions. Serge held no rancour for those who dishonoured themselves, as they were Stalin's victims, and his poetic ode to them in 'Confessions' is characterized by a generous attitude of disapproving understanding.* But he remembered those who died rather than give in, sketching them in his books and articles, preserving their memory.

The revolution in reaction

Serge's analysis of the significance of Stalin's purges, written at the time and without the benefit of hindsight, connects Stalin's terror to his chaotic industrial and agrarian policy. He wrote his most complete analysis of Stalin's rule in 1936 and 1937 in the book *Destiny of a Revolution*, published as *Russia Twenty Years After* in the United States. The books, pamphlets and articles which he poured out in the period up to 1940 extended his basic analysis but did not contradict his earlier work, except on the question of planning, where Serge vacillated. *Russia Twenty Years After*, written in his most Trotskyist period, redeemed the plan as the one element proving the superiority of the system to capitalism. Later, after Trotsky's death, Serge continued to grapple with the difficult theoretical problems thrown up by the continuing evolution of Soviet society. Writing as a solitary Left Oppositionist correcting the record and upholding the principles of the revolution, Serge was often better able to evoke the atmosphere of Soviet society than to systematically and consistently define it theoretically.

Serge's ideas can be summarized: the purges, while unplanned and proceeding from an internal dynamic set in motion by Stalin's methods of industrialization and rule, created new social relations and a new, unstable

---

* In an article published in *La Wallonie*, 'Complots en URSS', 20 March 1938, Serge spoke of the great attachment to 'socialism in march' by men who would 'step over their own corpses' in order to serve their Party, which still represented to them, however distorted, the vision of socialism.

society based on coercion and terror. None of the basic problems of the society were resolved at the end of the purges, but millions paid with their lives. A needlessly costly and wasteful industrial infrastructure was constructed, with the help of massive slave labour in the camps. All forms of collective resistance were broken and any residual resistance was atomized, as the weary population concerned itself with survival, not politics.

What Serge called the ten dark years, from 1927 to 1937, represented the struggle of the revolutionary generation against totalitarianism. The struggle was uneven and the regime was able to use them one against the other, all the more efficiently since 'it had a hold on their souls'[47] through Party patriotism. Yet the 'resistance of the revolutionary generation headed by the old socialist Bolsheviks was so tenacious that from 1936 to 1938 it was necessary for the entire generation to be eliminated so that the new regime could consolidate itself'.[48]

Serge viewed Stalin's accession to power as a counter-revolution, a betrayal of everything the revolution stood for, and one of the bloodiest in history, at that. In order to maintain power Stalin had to change the regime, eliminating entirely the revolutionary generation of Bolshevik militants. The Old Bolsheviks, after all, were not managers of production, but critics and revolutionaries. The new conditions required organizers and controllers, men who could repress, not think independently. Listen to Serge's character Rublev's final thoughts before being shot:

> We were an exceptional human accomplishment, and that is why we are going under. A half century unique in history was required to form our generation. Just as a great creative mind is a unique biological and social accomplishment, caused by innumerable interferences, the formation of our few thousand minds is to be explained by interferences that were unique . . . We grew up amid struggle, escaping two profound captivities, that of the old 'Holy Russia', and that of the bourgeois West . . . We perpetually questioned ourselves about the meaning of life and we worked to transform the world . . . We acquired a degree of lucidity and disinterestedness which made both the old and the new interests uneasy. *It was impossible for us to adapt ourselves to a phase of reaction* [emphasis added]; and as we were in power, surrounded by a legend that was true, born of our deeds, we were so dangerous that we had to be destroyed beyond physical destruction, our corpses had to be surrounded by legend of treachery.[49]

Stalin broke resistance through starvation, super-exploitation, slave labour camps, and political persecution of any real or imagined protest. The new society, dubbed a 'concentration-camp universe' by Serge, had the following social structure: a 'sub-proletariat in rags' of about 15 per cent of the adult population in the camps, and a new privileged elite representing about 7 to 8 per cent of the adult population.[50] Serge repeated these new facts throughout his works, as traits pointing to the *anti-socialist* nature of the new society.

The process was unconscious, but launched forces that eluded control.

Serge attributed this partially to Stalin's lack of real contact with the situation and, thus, his inclination to panic.[51]

Serge explained in *From Lenin to Stalin* that the consequences of a policy cannot be evaded: Stalin found himself in a blind alley with the peasants because he rejected the suggestions for early and gradual industrialization. When the peasant refused to sell his grain under disadvantageous conditions Stalin resorted to taking it from him by force. This provoked peasant resistance which led to forced collectivization, expropriation and deportation of millions of peasant families. Collectivization changed and distorted the plan for industrialization. Hungry workers laboured inefficiently and left work in search of food; draconian laws were passed to discipline workers. The fifth year of the plan found the country ravaged by famine. The point of Serge's analysis was to show, step by step, how policy was reactive, unplanned and improvised, producing a system that had to rely on terror.

Serge's works begin and end with the conditions of life for the masses of people affected by Stalin's policies. He describes how the methods employed in industrialization caused the workers to resist in ways that were to shape the character of Soviet production. Workers produced poorly due to the frantic pace, their weakened physical state, and political alienation. Repression was the ultimate incentive. The conditions Serge portrayed in the first five-year plan became permanent features of Soviet economic life; workers responded to the cruel conditions with hostile resistance but in an atomized way as individuals.[52] Serge described the new working class in formation and the new elite who through force gained political control over the population, but not over economic events. Serge continually returned to the bureaucracy's self-interest as the only logic of the system.[53]

While examining the effects of Stalin's policies on both town and country, Serge evoked the daily life of the masses, contrasting it to the privileges enjoyed by the parvenus. Economic growth was accompanied by pilfering, sabotage, misery, famine, passport laws, repression and terror.

Terror and misery left the population with nothing to think about but their own survival, their own self-interest. In 1937 Serge wrote:

> The inexorable logic that necessitates the disappearance of those who hold the worst State secrets places the gifted leader in a blind alley . . . He himself feels sure of nobody . . . The Party is destroyed, governmental circles decimated, the political police decimated, the army decapitated . . . purgings everywhere . . . repressions in sphere of production . . . There is disorder, panic, terror, mute reproval, passive resistance, atomic as it were. Not being sure of the morrow nobody dares to assume responsibility. All the statistics, all the balances, all the figures are false because nobody ever dares tell the truth . . . Every text is falsified . . . The problem is to repeat the words of yesterday while killing yesterday's ideas.[54]

From Stalin's vantage point he could only see sabotage and hence continually tightened the screws in order to gain better control of the economic mechanism which paradoxically eluded the reins of control. The sabotage Stalin saw everywhere was inadvertent, as his directives were often humanly impossible to meet. In this atmosphere the demand from the top was to get everyone to knuckle under, and thus the denunciations began, in order to uncover the 'saboteurs'. Again in Serge's fiction Stalin appears to explain:

> Everyone lies and lies and lies! From top to bottom they all lie, it's diabolical . . . nauseating . . . I live on the summit of an edifice of lies – do you know that? The statistics lie, of course. They are the sum total of the stupidities of the little officials at the base, the intrigues of the middle stratum of administrators, the imaginings, the servility, the sabotage, the immense stupidity of our leading cadres . . . The plans lie, because nine times out of ten they are based on false data; the Plan executives lie because they haven't the courage to say what they can do and what they cannot do; the most expert economists lie because they live in the moon, they're lunatics, I tell you . . . Old Russia is a swamp – the farther you go, the more the ground gives . . . And the human rubbish! . . . To remake the hopeless human animal will take centuries. I haven't got centuries to work with, not I.[55]

What happened to the ordinary 'human rubbish' in these times, as Stalin sought to accomplish in a few short years what would normally take decades, if not centuries? Serge described the life of the individual in these circumstances:

> Hemmed in by police, by poverty, by lies . . . [the] worker is preoccupied with obtaining, stamping, checking and re-registering a bread card which is refused half the workers on various pretexts; his wife runs from one empty store to another, registering in a queue at doors of fishstalls in the evening in order to wrangle the next morning over a ration of salt fish . . . exposed to spying in the shop . . . coming home to tell who was arrested last night.[56]

Politically Stalin needed to blame and punish someone else for the difficulties of life caused by his own policies. Behind every obstacle could be found a conspiracy, someone Stalin could blame and execute. The dynamic of denunciation in an atmosphere of fear was like a snowball rolling downhill. In Serge's dialectical novel of the purges, *The Case of Comrade Tulayev*, one character after another fell victim to the terror which spread from the shot that killed his fictional Kirov.* To find the guilty, an order went out to the GPU who arrest and obtain confessions, followed by deportations and executions. Suppression of freedom of expression, criticism, initiative and

---

* William Marshall, in his *Victor Serge: The Uses of Dissent*, Oxford, Berg, 1992, likened it to 'a series of concentric circles, radiating outward from the cataclysm of the shot . . . like the circles of Hell, or those of a pond when disturbed' (p. 144).

popular control increased the costs of Stalinist 'planning' horribly and often led to major failures and a kind of involuntary sabotage against which the regime had no remedy except a reign of terror.[57] It was a vicious circle. Such seemingly mad methods pointed to a 'tremendous moral weakness' and revealed an 'inward-driven crisis'.[58]

Intellectual impotence, moral complicity: the role of communists and fellow travellers in the west

The purges were not confined to the Soviet Union. International Communists were lured into the web, either as victims or co-conspirators. Communists from Poland, Germany, Hungary, Finland, Iran, China, France, Czechoslovakia, Holland, Spain, Italy and the Balkans were drawn into Stalin's constellation of camps, and Soviet agents abroad dreaded the ominous recall to Moscow.[59] They knew that 'recall' was synonymous with arrest, arrest synonymous, for the most part, with death. The infamous activities of the NKVD spread to Spain and beyond: international revolutionaries sympathetic to Trotsky began to 'disappear' – until their bodies surfaced. This was the fate of Rudolf Klement in France, Ignace Reiss in Switzerland, and Georgi Agabekov* in Belgium. In Spain, Andrés Nin, Marc Rhein (the Russian Menshevik Rafael Abramovich's son), Kurt Landau, Erwin Wolf,† and Tioli were among the victims we know about.[60] Even the suspicious suicide of Walter Krivitsky in the United States has been attributed to the work of the NKVD.[61] Before the US Senate Hearings

---

* Agabekov was a top functionary of the secret service of the NKVD in Turkey who broke with Moscow in 1929, and published a book that Serge called 'a very extraordinary document of betrayal and informing' in 1935. He had belonged to the Opposition in 1923. He was murdered in Belgium, and according to Orlov was one of those who 'were liquidated in silence on the basis of a mere suspicion that they intended to break with Stalin's dictatorship and remain abroad'. His assassination passed unnoticed, quite unlike that of Reiss and Krivitsky, until an alarm was raised. His case showed that it did not matter 'how much time had elapsed since the refusal of an NKVD officer to return to the USSR, Stalin's men would sooner or later catch up with him and destroy him'. Alexander Orlov, *The Secret History of Stalin's Crimes*, New York, Random House, 1953, pp. 227–8, and Serge, 'The Diary of Victor Serge' entry for 20 Feb. 1938, in *The New International*, Jan.–Feb., 1950, pp. 54–5.

† Erwin Wolf was one of Trotsky's secretaries in Norway. He had visited Serge in Brussels just prior to going to Spain. He told Serge he could not bear studying Marxism in comfort while a revolution was fighting for its life. Serge warned him he would be murdered. Wolf went anyway (according to Serge: 'he had all the pugnacious confidence of youth'), was arrested, released and then kidnapped off the streets and disappeared. Serge, *Memoirs*, p. 337, and Victor Serge and Natalia Sedova Trotsky, *The Life and Death of Leon Trotsky*, New York, Basic Books, 1975, p. 225.

in 1957, during which both Zborowski and Orlov testified to the hand of the NKVD in Krivitsky's demise, Serge wrote a diary entry for 31 March 1944 entitled 'GUEPEOU' that

> X arrived from NY assures me in confidence that the name of the OGPU agent who murdered *Walter Krivitsky* in a Washington hotel (winter 1940–41) is known as well as all the details of the affair . . . The 'suicide' version however remains quasi-official.*

The role of the Comintern, the Communist Parties and their press, and fellow travellers in this period is notorious. For most of the people in and around the Communist Parties, the official line on the purges emanating from Moscow became an article of faith: the camps did not exist, only counter-revolutionaries were being killed, the Moscow Trials were not fabrications, Trotsky and the Oppositionists really were counter-revolutionary agents† of the Gestapo, the Mikado, the OVRA, the Okhrana, labelled 'super-Judas', 'lubricious viper', 'bloodthirsty dogs'[62] and worse. Krivitsky wrote that the 'Western world never quite realized that Soviet show trials were not trials at all, but only weapons of political warfare'.[63] Serge nonetheless undertook with Sedov the task of refutation. He commented that he and Sedov 'often felt like voices crying in the wilderness'.[64] Prominent intellectual leftists who had access to the truth chose to ignore it: Serge wrote to Romain Rolland, who had interceded on his behalf just months before. Rolland had promised Serge he would intervene if blood were shed, yet he chose to remain silent, as did Georges Duhamel and Henri Sellier.[65] These same men asked Serge to explain the mystery of the confession, and Serge shouted back,

> You then, give me an explanation of the *conscience* shown by the famous intellectuals and Western Party-leaders who swallow it all – the killing, the nonsense, the cult of the Leader, the democratic constitution whose authors are promptly shot![66]

Serge visited André Gide after he returned from his famous visit to Russia, to discuss the current situation and the fate of socialism. Before Gide went to Russia, Serge published an open letter addressed to Gide in *La Révolution prolétarienne* (May 1936),which was an appeal for Gide to keep his eyes wide open in Moscow.[67] This open letter had caused a lot of consternation in France.

---

* Victor Serge, *Carnets*, Paris, Julliard, 1952, p. 89. Elsa Poretsky, on the other hand, believed Krivitsky committed suicide (interview with her son, Roman Bernaut, Paris, May 1999).

† Serge quoted a telegraph communication from old Chinese workers in China declaring, 'Trotsky is a dog! . . . We love great Stalin as our first-born, as our dear father, wipe out these monsters!' Serge, *Seize fusillés*, p. 24.

Gide was profoundly saddened by what he saw in the Soviet Union and somewhat cast adrift politically. He was no longer the man who appeased Malraux at the International Writers' Congress in Paris in 1935, speaking of the importance of demonstrating confidence and love for the Soviet Union and making its security the most important task for European intellectuals.[68] Serge wrote in his diary (entry for end of November 1936) after his visit with Gide that he had just learned that his sister, sister-in-law and brother-in-law were arrested on 6 September, the day after the execution of Zinoviev, Kamenev and Smirnov. Serge believed they were arrested because of his writings, especially his open letters. Serge discussed the meaning of the wave of terror in the Soviet Union with Gide, and the 'impotence of intellectuals'. He stressed: 'A person can free himself, however, from moral complicity.'* Few did.

As the wave of terror intensified in Moscow and spread to Spain, the 'progressive' press outdid itself in doublespeak and outright calumny. Serge watched his Spanish comrades being shot in the back as they faced Franco's army, while the Communist press denounced the POUMistas as 'Trotskyists, spies, agents of Franco-Hitler-Mussolini, enemies of the people'. How was it possible? According to Serge:

> The average man, who cannot conceive that lying on this scale is possible, is taken unawares by stupendous, unexpected assertions. Outrageous language intimidates him and goes some way to excuse his deception: reeling under the shock, he is tempted to tell himself that there must, after all, be some justification of a higher order passing his own understanding. Success is possible for these techniques, it seems clear, only in epochs of confusion, and only if the brave minorities who embody the critical spirit are effectively gagged or reduced to impotence through reasons of State and their own lack of material resources.
>
> In any case, *it was not a matter of persuasion: it was, fundamentally, a matter of murder* [emphasis added]. One of the intentions behind the campaign of drivel initiated in the Moscow Trials was to make any discussion between official and oppositional Communists quite impossible. Totalitarianism has no more dangerous enemy than the spirit of criticism, which it bends every effort to exterminate. Any reasonable objection is bundled away with shouts, and the objector himself, if he persists . . . to the mortuary. I have met my assailants face to face in public meetings, offering to answer any question they raised. Instead they always strove to drown my voice in storms of insults, delivered at the tops of their voices. My books, rigorously documented, and written with the sole passionate aim of uncovering the truth, have been translated for publication in

---

* 'Pages from the Diary of Victor Serge', in *The New International*, vol. 15, no. 10, Sept. 1949, pp. 214–16. As to the relatives Serge mentioned, his brother-in-law Paul Marcel spent six years in prison, and his sister-in-law Esther Russakova died in a camp (interview with Irina Gogua, Moscow, March 1989). Nothing is known about his sister Vera Vladimirovna Frolova.

Poland, Britain, the US, Argentina, Chile, and Spain. In none of these places has a single line ever been contested, or a single argument adduced in reply: only abuse, denunciation and threats. Both in Paris and in Mexico there were moments when in certain cafés people discussed my forthcoming assassination quite as a matter of course.[69]

Talk of Serge's assassination was not idle chatter. Etienne (Marc Zborowski), the NKVD agent in Paris Left Opposition circles who was complicit in the deaths of Trotskyists in Europe, also had plans for Serge that were interrupted by the war.*

The tentacles of the NKVD in Europe extend the web of blackness

By 1937, the 'Great Terror' was in full force and a truly enormous witch-hunt engulfed the Soviet Union. The atmosphere of sheer terror spread beyond the borders and reached a fanatical intensity in the circles of Soviet agents abroad, as well as in Oppositionist circles. Elsa Poretsky captured the atmosphere in Moscow 1937 in the chilling account of her winter visit. All real contact with friends and neighbours was reduced to a superficial minimum, to avoid possible denunciation from others recently repressed. Whenever the phone rang, everyone froze. People took myriad precautions to avoid attention and association with others whose position, marital connections or former political experience marked them for repression. Poretsky wrote that 'Stalin had succeeded in doing something the Tsars had never done. The terror had destroyed the bonds of humanity and had made those who were directly affected go on living in a void, accept this void, and create it around themselves.'[70]

The atmosphere of anxiety and dread, of distrust and fear is captured only too well in both Serge's and Walter Krivitsky's accounts. Serge wrote, 'Black was the spring of 1937 . . . The tragedies of Russia once more cast their peculiar stupor over the world.'[71] Agents were everywhere, and even agents were in danger. Both Krivitsky and Ignace Reiss (Elsa Poretsky's husband, 'Ludwik')[72] belonged to a group of dedicated Communist NKVD agents, who were sickened by the murders and crimes committed in the name of socialism.[73] Reiss resolved to break with the NKVD and tried to

---

* Victor Alba and Stephen Schwartz, *The Communist Party in Spain*, New Brunswick, NJ, Transaction Books, 1983, p. 221. Schwartz wrote a series of controversial articles in the *New York Review of Books* and elsewhere on 'Stalin's Killerati' stating he found evidence that there was an NKVD 'hit list' and that after Sedov's name were those of Sneevliet and Serge. Interview with Stephen Schwartz, April 1989, San Francisco. Hendricus or Henk Sneevliet was killed by the Nazis in 1942. Serge's son Vlady still questions the 'natural causes' that took his father at age 57.

convince his boyhood friend Krivitsky to break with him. The NKVD decided to test Krivitsky's loyalty: knowing in advance of Reiss's defection, they assigned to Krivitsky the liquidation of his close friend. Krivitsky refused and was from that day forward a marked man.

Reiss had been mulling over the break for some time. He 'clung to his job, the only one he considered worth doing, of supplying republican Spain with weapons'.[74] He met his friend Louis Fischer, and told him of his revulsion for the Stalinist regime which was destroying the old revolutionists and with them, the revolution.[75] He tried to warn the Oppositionists in Paris that their actions were being monitored and that they were in danger. Reiss let them know that 'a decision to use terror against the opposition abroad – against us – has been taken'.[76] Serge published the 'Ludwik Warning' in an article of the same name. At the same time, Sneevliet, Serge and Sedov wanted a public statement from Reiss that would 'permit us to have confidence in him and [would] put him under the protection of public opinion'.*

Krivitsky met with Reiss, and surreptitiously let him know that his new mission, the reason he was allowed to leave Moscow, was to bring Reiss back. Reiss decided it was time to break, but was not able to persuade Krivitsky to break with him. Reiss contacted Sneevliet, because according to Elsa Poretsky he could trust him completely. They arranged to meet, in order to prepare the publicity for Reiss's break. Sneevliet tried to persuade him to make his break public, before letting the Soviets know, but Reiss believed he should first notify the Central Committee of the CPSU. This proved to be his downfall, because it gave the NKVD time to assassinate him before the story broke in the West. The Trotskyists were right that Reiss's only protection would be to ask the police for protection, and to seek maximum publicity.† Nonetheless he delayed making public his

---

* Victor Serge, 'Reiss, Krivitsky, Bastich and Others', Dec. 1937, in 'The Diary of Victor Serge', *The New International*, Jan.–Feb. 1950, p. 51. Henk Sneevliet had been an MP and leader of the railway workers' union. He founded the Indonesian Communist Party, was instrumental in the birth of the Chinese Communist Party in 1920. He represented the Javanese Socialist Party at the Second Congress of the Comintern under the name 'Maring'. In 1927 he left the Dutch Communist Party and formed the RSAP (Dutch Revolutionary Socialist Workers Party) in 1929. Sneevliet stood with the Left Opposition from 1933 to 1938. He was arrested by the Gestapo in 1942 and shot.

† Later Trotsky would write that Reiss's death was 'not only a loss, but a lesson': Reiss should have gone public, but so too should the Left Oppositionists in Europe have established connections with him in time so that Reiss would not have had to break alone against Stalin's enormous spy apparatus. Trotsky again stressed that 'the sole serious defence against the hired murderers of Stalin is complete *publicity*'. Leon Trotsky, 'A Tragic Lesson', 21 Sept. 1937, in *Writings 1936–1937*, pp. 448–51.

open letter for one week. He ended his letter by declaring for the Fourth International.*

Poretsky's wife insisted in her book that Sneevliet told Reiss he would meet him alone. Serge wrote in his *Memoirs* that Reiss 'asked to see us . . . we arranged to meet him in Rheims on 5 September 1937'.[77] In his diary entry for December 1937 Serge wrote that at first the meeting was to be between Reiss, Sneevliet, Sedov and Serge. Sedov was sick and could not attend the meeting. Serge and Sneevliet went to Rheims on the appointed day, waited at the station buffet, but Reiss did not appear. They wandered through the town, still did not find Reiss, and after two days decided to return to Paris. Waiting for the return train, Serge read in a newspaper that the previous day the bullet-ridden body of a Czech by the name of Eberhard had been picked up on the road to Chamblandes; in the pocket was a railway ticket to Rheims.† He had a clump of grey hair in his hands, belonging to the pathetic Gertrude Schildbach, a woman Ludwik had befriended and recruited, and who was now used by the NKVD to murder 'the only friend she ever had, a man she worshipped, respected and obeyed',[78] 'the only human being who had shown her consideration'.[79]

Serge and Sneevliet immediately understood that Eberhard was Reiss, and drew up a press release giving his real identity. The French press chose to remain silent. The story was finally published after Serge paid a visit to Gaston Bergery[80] of *La Fleche*, who broke the story.[81] Reiss's murder was subsequently splashed all over the European press. Krivitsky wrote that 'it had become a celebrated case in Europe and reverberated in the press of America and throughout the world'.[82] The Swiss and French investigation team were assisted by Sneevliet, Serge and Elsa Poretsky. Renata Steiner, a Swiss NKVD agent who had earlier infiltrated the Left Oppositionist circle in Paris, also gave the French police all the information needed to investigate Reiss's death.

The record of the investigation was published by Pierre Tisné in Paris in a book entitled *L'Assassinat d'Ignace Reiss*. The authors were Victor Serge, Maurice Wullens and Alfred Rosmer.[83] The identity of the assassins was finally established. The assistant chief of the Foreign Division of the OGPU-NKVD, Mikhail Spiegelglass, had organized the crime, assisted by Beletsky, Grozovsky and Lydia Grozovskaya, all members of the Soviet commercial mission in Paris.[84] The GPU agents operating in the Russian émigré society had been spying on Leon Sedov and the Left Oppositionists

---

* Reiss sent his open letter to the Central Committee of the Communist Party of the Soviet Union via the Soviet Embassy in Paris. The letter was wrapped in the Order of the Red Banner he had earned in 1927. Of course one does not resign from the Soviet secret police, as he well knew.

† One of the identities Reiss used in Europe was of the Czech Hans Eberhard. Poretsky, *Our Own People*, pp. 235–6.

in Paris, and had twice attempted to snare Sedov. One of their agents, a man named Semirensky, had taken a room next to Sedov's and was working with Renata Steiner to trap Trotsky's son and collaborator.[85]

The investigation of Reiss's murder lasted many months and led to the arrest of Renata Steiner, Etienne Martignat and Abbiate-Rossi (Roland L. Abbiate, aka François Rossi, aka Vladimir S. Pravdin), all Paris agents of the NKVD.[86] All the assassins, in a rather bizarre incongruity, were connected through an organization founded by former Tsarist officers and other white Russian émigrés as a centre for its espionage activity in Europe.* That group was the Union of Repatriation of Russians Abroad, and it was to this group that Mordka Marc Zborowski, a young Polish medical student at Grenoble, was recruited.

Zborowski, alias 'Etienne', turned out to be the 'other' agent in the Paris Left Oppositionist circle who knew that Sneevliet and Serge were going to meet Reiss in Rheims. He notified the NKVD who used the information to circumvent the meeting by killing Reiss. They recruited Gertrude Schild-bach, Renata Steiner *et al.* to lure Reiss to his death in Lausanne, while a second team of assassins was reserved for Rheims in case the first team failed.[87] His family was also meant to be killed, but at the last minute Schild-bach proved incapable of giving strychnine-laced chocolates to Poretsky's child.[88] The box of poisoned candy was later found in the Lausanne hotel room occupied by Schildbach and her companion Rossi.

Reiss left behind notes that Serge analysed in the book he co-authored with Rosmer and Wullens on the assassination. The important pieces of information, which also later showed up in Krivitsky's book, were that Stalin had been attempting secret negotiations with Hitler since at least 1934, and while pursuing an agreement with Hitler Stalin executed his general staff in June 1937. This included seventy-five out of eighty members of the Council of War and 35,000 members of the officer corps. Reiss also found evidence that despite the defeat of the Left Opposition and the ascent of Stalin's murderous policies, Leningrad communists had gone to their death shouting 'Long Live Leon Davidovich!',[89] and that Stalin was attempting to get a trial against Trotsky going in Western Europe (the

---

* General Alexander Orlov's secret letter to Trotsky warning him of the spy Zborowski in the Paris Left Opposition circle, reprinted *in toto* in Orlov's sworn testimony at the *Hearings before the Subcommittee to Investigate the Administration of the Internal Security Act and other Internal Security Laws of the Committee on the Judiciary*, US Senate, Eighty-Fifth Congress, First Session on Scope of Soviet Activity in the United States, 14–15 Feb. 1957, part 51, pp. 3425–6. Poretsky described the White Russian emigration as consisting of several groups who quarrelled among themselves but were united in their aim of overthrowing Communism in Russia. It was an easy group for the NKVD to recruit from, and all the White Russian groups were delighted with Stalin's 'liquidation of the revolution'. Poretsky, *Our Own People*, pp. 237–8.

attempted Grylewicz frame-up in Czechoslovakia)* and yet another in North America.†

A few weeks after Reiss's death two more agents came out of the closet: Alexander Barmine and Walter Krivitsky. Zborowski was assigned to report on both of them to the NKVD.[90] Barmine was an NKVD agent stationed in Athens. He had fought in the civil war and belonged to the revolutionary generation of Bolsheviks. While he was in Moscow Barmine had been married to Irina Gogua, the daughter of Serge's half-sister Julia.‡

Like Reiss and Krivitsky, Barmine was utterly sickened by Stalin's murderous activities. He handed in his resignation from the NKVD, and

---

* Anton Grylewicz was a former Reichstag deputy who set up a committee in Prague to investigate the Moscow Trials. After a GPU intrigue in which Stalin is reported to have taken a personal interest, Grylewicz, a political refugee from Nazi Germany, was arrested and deported from Czechoslovakia as an undesirable alien. Victor Serge and Natalia Sedova Trotsky, *The Life and Death of Leon Trotsky*, New York, Basic Books, 1975, p. 220.

† Victor Serge, Maurice Wullens, Alfred Rosmer, *L'Assassinat d'Ignace Reiss*, Les Humbles, Paris, April 1938. Serge's findings, based on Reiss's notes, were confirmed in Krivitsky's book *I Was Stalin's Agent*, pp. 151, 168–73. Krivitsky had heard about the Grylewicz affair as part of an attempt by the GPU to convince the world of the truth of the Moscow trials by getting similar trials going in Spain, Czechoslovakia and the United States. The idea was to link the POUM in Spain, and Grylewicz (a Trotskyist) in Czechoslovakia, to Franco and Hitler. The attempt failed. In New York the OGPU laid plans for a 'Trotskyist-Fascist' trial through an intrigue that would prove American anti-Stalinists were agents of Hitler's Gestapo. This effort led to the disappearance of American Communist Juliette Stuart Poyntz and the arrest of the American Soviet agents Donald Robinson-Rubens and his wife in Moscow, but the effort fell flat, and not much more is known (Krivitsky, ibid.). The whole story will not emerge until the KGB archives are opened, but there is an account of Poyntz's disappearance in Hugo Dewar's *Assassins at Large*, London, Wingate, 1951, pp. 97–110, and Allen Weinstein and Alexander Vassiliev, in *The Haunted Wood* (New York, Random House, 1999), identify Juliette Stuart Poyntz as a clandestine agent and Party member who disappeared in New York in June 1937 (pp. 88–9). Other agents assume she was murdered on Moscow's instruction.

‡ Interview with Irina Gogua, March 1989, Moscow. Gogua's mother Julia had been the object of Stalin's affection in 1902 in Georgia, and later married Kalistrat Gogua, a prominent Menshevik and early friend of Djugashvili. Irina was Barmine's first wife, and they remained friends until Irina's arrest in 1934. Barmine described Irina, Julia, and Gorky's wife Ekaterina Peshkova (Julia's best friend – see chapter 5), but failed to admit he married Irina and only described the women as close friends. Was he trying to protect her in the gulag? (Alexander Barmine, *One Who Survived: The Life Story of a Russian under the Soviets*, New York, G.P. Putnam's Sons, 1945, pp. 265–6.) He lost contact with her after her arrest; she learned of his death in 1987 from me in Moscow, March 1989. Irina Gogua died over New Year 1989–90, in Moscow.

ironically it arrived in Moscow in the same post as Reiss's open letter. Thus, according to Barmine, the GPU agents in Europe were

> simultaneously confronted with a double job of 'liquidation'. They could not find me, and so they dealt with the Reiss case first, an accident that probably saved my life. For their organization was now temporarily disrupted, and they were compelled to send the compromised agents into hiding and assemble a new gang.[91]

Barmine was still pursued but managed to survive. In fact, he was the only NKVD agent in Europe to openly break with Stalin who died a natural death, in the United States in 1987.* His book, aptly titled *One Who Survived*, is a remarkable memoir, which Max Eastman described as 'the most important that could be written on the socialist experiment in Russia'.[92]

The book was actually ghost-written by Victor Serge. Every night Serge met Barmine at the police-guarded home of the French socialist Marceau Pivert and took down his story. There is no indication in the published version that it was in fact written by Serge, but Serge's son Vlady has confirmed it, and was present for some of the sessions. Barmine dictated his experience, and Serge gave it literary form.[93] Serge reviewed the book in an article entitled 'Le témoignage d'Alexandre Barmine' published in *La Wallonie*, 4–5 March 1939. In this review Serge proclaimed that 'there is no man in the world who will stand up and say: "This is not true".'[94] Barmine later confessed to Max Eastman that during these writing sessions he felt as though he were 'walking in a graveyard. All my friends and life associates have been shot. It seems to be some kind of a mistake that I am alive.'[95]

What is also incredible is how small the circle of the surviving revolutionary generation really was. Serge knew all of them in the Soviet Union and abroad, and wrote their remarkable stories in his book on Reiss, and Barmine's memoir. That he was also related by marriage to Barmine, that at meetings in Paris Krivitsky and Elsa Poretsky could remember meetings with Serge in Moscow, attests to the small size of what Joseph Berger called the 'shipwrecked generation'.

---

* His obituary appeared in the *New York Times*. Barmine lived in Connecticut, and had worked for the CIA in the 1950s and 1960s. Alexander Orlov, another NKVD agent marked for 'recall' eluded his executioners and made it to the US, where he wrote a letter to Stalin detailing all Stalin's crimes and telling Stalin that if he (Orlov) were murdered, his lawyer would publish Orlov's testimony. Although Orlov was pursued for fourteen years, he survived and died naturally in 1973. Zborowski was a European NKVD agent who died a natural death in 1990, but he never broke with Stalin, though he asserted that after 1945 he took no assignments from the NKVD. See Orlov, *The Secret History of Stalin's Crimes*, pp.x–xvi, and Zborowski's testimony to the Senate Committee on the Scope of Soviet Activities in the United States, 29 Feb. 1956, part 4.

The other agent to break was Walter Krivitsky and it is here that we pick up the story of Serge, Sneevliet, Sedov, Poretsky, Krivitsky and Etienne/ Zborowski. After her husband's murder, Elsa Poretsky went to Amsterdam to stay with the Sneevliets. She travelled with them to Paris, where Sneevliet had arranged several interviews with her. When Serge came to interview Poretsky, Sneevliet told her she would be glad to meet him. She wrote that 'Serge was the last person in the world I wanted to see' and worse, he did not come alone. He brought a young friend of Sedov's with him, who introduced himself as Friedman, but who in reality was Marc Zborowski. Zborowski was known as 'Etienne' to the Trotskyists and was Sedov's secretary and assistant. According to Poretsky, Sneevliet was furious with Serge, and Serge was 'visibly embarrassed'. Poretsky wrote:

> The fact that [Serge] had passed on to Etienne the highly confidential word that I was in Paris, and worse, had brought Etienne with him to the hotel, gave Sneevliet a shock that never wore off . . . Serge's natural curiosity had made him keep seeing all kinds of people, Party members, ex-Party members, former anar-chists, every kind of Oppositionist, until the very day he was arrested, in Leningrad in 1933. Some considered this showed courage, others irresponsibil-ity. It was probably a bit of both, but carrying on as he did exposed others as well as himself to danger . . . More baffling still was the fact that Serge had managed to come out of the Soviet Union in 1936 . . . We continued to have doubts about him.[96]

Poretsky noted that Serge's account of this meeting was different from her own. Her explanation was that Serge 'was not a professional conspirator, he was essentially a writer'. She also quoted Serge out of context about Soviet 'writers in uniform' implying that Serge was describing himself:

> Poets and novelists are not political beings, because they are not essentially rational . . . The artist . . . is always delving for his raw material in the subcon-scious . . . If the novelist's characters are truly alive . . . they eventually take their author by surprise.[97]

Serge was to commit one further error, in Elsa Poretsky's mind, to cement her impression of him as a careless, if courageous, non-professional. This involved a letter she received in October 1937 signed 'Krusia', and there-after known as the 'Krusia letter'. Krusia was the name of a woman both Reiss and Krivitsky had known in their young days as Bolshevik revolu-tionaries. Elsa Poretsky immediately knew that this meant Krivitsky had broken with the NKVD and was trying to reach her. Elsa did not want to meet or help Krivitsky, as she felt 'Ludwik's [Reiss's] blood' was between them now. But Sneevliet persuaded her that Krivitsky was important and she was the link to their meeting him.

According to Poretsky, the meeting took place at Gérard Rosenthal's office (he was Trotsky's French lawyer and author of *Avocat de Trotsky*) with Poretsky, Krivitsky, Sedov, Sneevliet, Rosenthal and Pierre Naville. Serge was not there according to Poretsky, though in the *Memoirs* and his diary, *Carnets*, Serge placed himself at the meeting which he described as taking place on 11 November at Gerard's law office, which adjoined Gerard's father the doctor's office near the Gare St Lazare. Serge named himself, Sneevliet, Elsa Poretsky, Sedov, Gérard Rosenthal and Krivitsky at the meeting, but not Naville.

During the meeting Krivitsky repeated Reiss's warning to Sedov, Sneevliet and Serge that there was an agent in their midst and assassinations were planned. He would not name the agent, which infuriated Sneevliet. He did cast suspicion on Victor Serge, and later, in a report drawn up for Trotsky, Krivitsky flatly accused Serge of being the agent,[98] while Poretsky reported to Trotsky that she believed Serge had acted irresponsibly and had been used by an agent. The accusation that Serge was the agent led Isaac Deutscher to write:

> No one was, of course, less suited to act such a part than Serge. He was one of Trotsky's early adherents, a gifted and generous, though politically ingenuous, man of letters. The worst that might be said of him was that he had a foible for vainglorious chatter and that this was a grave fault in a member of an organization which had to guard its secrets from the GPU. In any case suspicion began to cling indiscriminately to anyone, even to Lyova himself, while the actual *agent provocateur* went on collecting and reading Trotsky's mail, shared all of Lyova's secrets, and used his wiles to keep his own reputation clear by casting distrust upon others.[99]

Sneevliet was enraged that Krivitsky refused to name the agent in their midst, certain that Krivitsky was lying when he insisted he did not know the agent's name. It is probable that Krivitsky spoke the truth about not knowing the agent's name because, as Zborowski himself later attested, 'an agent is never told about another unless they are supposed to work together'.[100] After the meeting Krivitsky was assigned a bodyguard by Sedov, none other than Marc Zborowski.[101] Had he known Zborowski was the agent, Krivitsky would most likely have exposed him then and there, to save his own skin. Krivitsky went on meeting Sedov nearly every day,[102] and met Serge several times as well.

At the meeting held in Gérard Rosenthal's office Krivitsky told Elsa Poretsky that the 'Krusia letter' which he had sent her care of Rosenthal, had been shown him by the NKVD who had it in their hands before it reached Amsterdam. This convinced Krivitsky that there was a dangerous agent in Sedov's circle, and that Krivitsky had to go into hiding. When Krivitsky then demanded to know how this letter got into the hands of the NKVD, Rosenthal answered, 'I gave it to Victor Serge to post to Amsterdam'.[103] Krivitsky could not understand why Rosenthal would show this letter to Serge, and Elsa Poretsky could not understand why Serge would have shown it to someone else before posting it. Poretsky believed that Sneevliet went straight from that meeting and confronted Serge with showing the 'Krusia letter' to someone else, and that is how Serge was able to so vividly describe the meeting, as if he were there. Serge's account mentions nothing of the 'Krusia letter'.

For Sneevliet, this discovery confirmed in his mind that Sedov's right-hand man Etienne/Zborowski – 'that little Polish Jew' – was the agent. Although suspicion was now cast on Zborowski, it took another twenty years for him to be exposed. Poretsky also believed that Sneevliet did not mention Serge's indiscretion further in order to shield him, and to protect himself from Trotsky's ire, no doubt because he was thinking of 'the things he had told Serge and the careless way Serge bandied everything about'.[104] Sneevliet and the other Dutch Trotskyists, as well as Serge, were already moving away from Trotsky and the French Trotskyists, and this too probably prevented his pressing the investigation of Etienne/Zborowski.

According to Zborowski, Serge thought the agent in their midst was Sedov's female secretary Lola Dallin,* and Zborowski himself threatened to break Serge's neck if he did not stop spreading that rumour, even though it deflected attention from himself.† Zborowski informed Serge that the French Left Oppositionists refused to discuss the substance of the allegations against Lola, and from then on Serge was practically excluded from the group.

Serge was not the only one to raise the possibility that Lola Dallin was an agent. The FBI file I obtained on Victor Serge through the FOIA has appended to it several pages on Lola Dallin, Marc Zborowski, and Boris Nicolaevsky, as if to say the FBI connects them to Serge. So much is deleted from the files that it is not clear why they are appended, though in the case of Lola Dallin, the FBI has only partially deleted a section entitled 'Suspicions Directed Towards Subject as Possible NKVD Agent'.[105]

Further, General Alexander Orlov tried to warn Trotsky through a letter he wrote pretending to be a Russian Jew with a close relative in the GPU. He sent the letter on 28 December 1938, warning Trotsky of the agent in their circle in Paris, whose name was Marc. He gave other details that unmistakably identified Zborowski.[106] Lola Dallin was visiting Trotsky in

---

*   Lola or Lilia Dallin, was born Ginzburg and married first Samuel Estrine and then David Dallin. She also went under the pseudonyms of Paulsen and Yakovlev. She appears in the documents under various combinations of these names; the Hoover Archive calls her Lilia Iakovlena Estrina. Her friends knew her as Lola Dallin which is the name I have chosen to use here.

†   Poretsky, *Our Own People*, p. 274. Serge himself did not write of his suspicions. Deutscher, wrote that following Klement's death Serge openly voiced his suspicion of Etienne as the NKVD agent in their midst, and Etienne worriedly asked Trotsky what to do about it. Trotsky replied that Serge and Sneevliet should lay their charges before a competent commission, but Deutscher continued, Trotsky himself did not believe the accusation (Isaac Deutscher, *The Prophet Outcast: Trotsky 1929–1940*, Oxford, Oxford University Press, 1963, p. 408).

Mexico when he received Orlov's unsigned letter, and she was made uncomfortable by the wealth of unpleasant detail in the letter. She told Trotsky,

> 'That is certainly a definitely dirty job of the NKVD, who wants to deprive you of your few collaborators that you have in France.' And at the same time, he had another letter from another unnamed agent, telling him that a woman, meaning me, is coming to visit him, and will poison him. So we both decided, 'See how they work? They want that you shall break with the only people that are left, over in France, Russians, let us say, in France in Paris.' And we decided that it isn't to be taken seriously, but it was a hoax of the NKVD.

And, Lola Dallin added, the first thing she did upon her return to Paris was to tell Zborowski everything.[107] Trotsky wrote a highly confidential letter to the Paris comrades repeating Orlov's allegations, and demanding that they investige the allegations and shadow the 'stool pigeon's' movements.* Trotsky did hypothesize that the letter he received could have been planted by the GPU to 'spread demoralization' through their ranks.[108] Did Lola Dallin circumvent the investigation by what she told Zborowski and the comrades? Finally, when Sedov was taken ill, it was Lola Dallin who suggested he go to the Mirabeau clinic run by White Russian émigrés, as she had a sister-in-law physician working there.[109] It is apparent from the evidence on Lola Dallin, including the recently decoded Venona traffic, that she was not an agent, and was in fact an ardent anti-Stalinist. But she was a loyal friend to the agent Zborowski – until he was unmasked in 1954. She never believed the allegations against him and thus protected him from exposure.

The atmosphere of suspicion was such that it provoked even more divisiveness among groups that were already rife with political discord. It was not paranoid to be on guard for agents, since they were actually being infiltrated, and comrades were being murdered. However, agent-baiting in a small organization could be just as ruinous to political effectiveness as any agent. This was an added boon for Stalin. The result was that the Left Opposition in Paris was so divided and so consumed with internal problems that their political influence was compromised.

Even though Krivitsky believed Serge was the agent, he continued to meet him in Paris, and Serge noted how nervous, shrivelled and frightened he was. Others also described Krivitsky in similar terms, and he was probably especially tense in Serge's presence. Serge was also nervous: he wrote that whenever Krivitsky put his hand in his pocket to get a cigarette, Serge likewise put his hand in his own pocket.[110]

---

* There is no evidence this inquiry was ever carried out, and Georges Vereeken, a Belgian Trotskyist close to Sneevliet and Serge at the time, has since written a book attacking the Fourth International for not having carried out the investigation, which could have unmasked Zborowski before he completed his murderous work. See Georges Vereeken, *The GPU in the Trotskyist Movement*, London, New Park Publications, 1976.

There has never been any confirmation that Serge shared the 'Krusia letter' with Zborowski. Poretsky asked Zborowski in 1954 if Serge had showed it to him, and he simply shrugged his shoulders, neither confirmation nor denial. I repeatedly tried to ask Zborowski that question, by letter, by telephone, and on a personal visit, in the years 1986 to 1988, without any success.[111] I did ask Pierre Broué, who knew Elsa Bernaut (Poretsky) and who was responsible for convincing her to write her memoir, why she was so hard on Serge. He answered that as an agent herself she was naturally suspicious of Serge, who tended to be open and generous, and as an embittered woman, she was probably offended by Serge's manner.[112] The truth may never be known. The available evidence from Soviet intelligence files on Stalin's most precious agent, Marc Zborowski, shed no new light on this subject.[113] Nor do FBI and American Intelligence agencies' files, obtained through the Freedom of Information Act, containing nearly 4,000 pages on Zborowski.

This whole affair made the relations between Serge and Sedov more strained, while Zborowski continued his deadly work. Three months later, on 16 February 1938, Lyova Sedov died in Paris just eight days short of his thirty-second birthday. The official cause of death was peritonitis following the removal of his appendix. He was taken to hospital by Zborowski and the whereabouts were kept secret. The hospital was run by White Russians; the surgeon, a former Chekist, had a record of several fatalities after relatively simple operations.[114]

The circumstances of Sedov's death suggest ample opportunity for foul play. The inquest did not yield any evidence, however, and attributed Sedov's death to post-operative complications. The family demanded a new inquest, but could not prove Sedov was killed by the GPU, which they all assumed. Right after calling the ambulance, Zborowski informed the GPU which hospital Sedov was going to,* meaning the only ones who knew were the GPU, Zborowski, Lola Dallin, and Jeanne Martin, Sedov's wife.

Stephen Schwartz, the author of a controversial set of articles published in *The New York Times Book Review*, *The New York Review of Books*, *Commentary* and elsewhere on Stalin's 'killerati', has attempted to trace the links between the NKVD assassins and prominent European intellectuals. Schwartz reported that a CIA agent told him 'strictly off the record' that they had information that Sedov had been given a poisoned orange by Zborowski.[115] Another American intelligence officer, Guenther Reinhardt, FBI covert agent involved in the 'red stealth' secret mission to uncover Soviet work in the US, also wrote that the GPU 'poisoned Sedov in Paris' in

---

* Ibid., pp. 396–7. In Zborowski's testimony to the US Senate, he remembered informing the GPU, but was uncertain he had called the ambulance. He stated that there were mysterious circumstances surrounding Sedov's death but he concurred with the final autopsy and post-mortem, which gave the cause of death as peritonitis. Zborowski testimony to the Committee on the Scope of Soviet Activities, 29 Feb. 1956, part 4.

his book *Crime Without Punishment*.[116] Dimitri Volkogonov wrote that while there is no direct evidence in the NKVD archive of Sedov being assassinated, the NKVD had a special section for developing poisons difficult to detect.[117]

In 1993, John Costello and Oleg Tsarev published the Orlov Dossier and included verbatim text of Orlov's 1965 CIA debriefing, which revealed that 'Lidya [sic] Dallin had brought Sedov an orange'.[118] When Orlov confronted the Dallins with this detail, she finally accepted as true the allegation that her friend Zborowski was indeed the agent in their midst. Tsarev, who has read the entire KGB file on Zborowski, denies the poisoned orange theory, but asserts that Sedov died of natural causes.[119] Nonetheless the NKVD took credit for doing away with Sedov,[120] and the full story has yet to be told.

Sedov's death was a terrible blow to the Trotskyist movement. Serge described the circumstances yet thought it possible he died of 'culpable negligence'.[121] He wrote an elegy to Sedov, the third of Trotsky's children to die – the fourth had disappeared in the gulag – in *La Wallonie*, 'Mort d'un ami' (26 February 1938), in which he described Sedov's funeral, where the French Trotskyists, still divided, stood apart under separate banners. In the *Memoirs*, Serge sketched Sedov thus:

> Young, energetic, of a temperament at once gentle and resolute, he had lived a hellish life. From his father he inherited an eager intelligence, an absolute faith in revolution, and the utilitarian, intolerant political mentality of the Bolshevik generation that was now disappearing. More than once we had lingered until dawn in the streets of Montparnasse, labouring together to comb out the mad tangle of the Moscow Trials, pausing from time to time under a street lamp for one or other of us to exclaim aloud: 'We are in a labyrinth of utter madness!' Overworked, penniless, anxious for his father, he passed his whole life in that labyrinth.[122]

Serge remembered shaking Rudolf Klement's hand at the funeral. Klement was a fanatically dedicated secretary of the Fourth International. Five months later, on 13 July 1938, he became the next victim of the NKVD. He was kidnapped from his apartment in Paris, with his meal still on the table.[123] Klement's decapitated torso was fished out of the Seine at Meulan, his body cut up to prevent recognition.[124]

The NKVD sponsored killings did not stop there, but grew monstrously in Spain during the civil war. Serge knew from Krivitsky and Reiss that the NKVD considered Spain their territory where they could act with impunity. Along with his old friends and Trotskyist comrades from the Dutch section, Serge mobilized to prevent the coming bloodbath, 'scattering my futile warnings in the left-wing Socialist press, as far as the United States itself'.[125] When his friend Andrés Nin fell into Soviet hands, Serge and the others did all they could to rescue him. A delegation of Serge's Spanish committee went to Spain to find Nin and were able to trace his last days before he was kidnapped by the GPU. The trail grew cold at an isolated villa next to an airfield occupied by Soviet planes.[126]

Etienne, Serge and Trotsky:
between two Left Oppositionists, the NKVD?

Etienne, or Zborowski, was assigned to spy on the Trotskyists in the West.* He gained Sedov's confidence to the point that he collected and read his mail, and was sometimes editor of the *Bulletin of the Left Opposition*. He was often the mediator of communications between Trotsky and Sedov, and between Trotsky and Serge. Since his objective was also to diminish the effectiveness of the Oppositionists, any divisions which he could foster or deepen would serve the interests of his employer. Etienne performed his tasks so well, that he became Stalin's most precious agent, and Stalin personally read all his reports.[127]

The Left Opposition in exile was in constant, real danger of physical liquidation. But this was not their only problem. While their comrades in the USSR were all being killed, the French Trotskyists worked in a milieu of suspicion, demoralization and despair. This led to unhealthy internal discord, and division. The role of the NKVD cannot be overlooked in this regard, though it would be equally incorrect to overstate their influence since real political differences emerged in an atmosphere that was not always conducive to the free expression of critical thought, especially unorthodox thought.

This was particularly discouraging to Serge, who was wrestling with the contradictions he had begun to consider inherent in 'guided organizations'. He often quoted Rosa Luxemburg that 'liberty is the liberty of the man who thinks otherwise', a principle more easily expressed than practised in the far Left, which brought together 'the best-disposed men, professing in principle respect for free thought, the critical mind, objective analysis . . . [who] in reality do not know how to tolerate thought which is different from their own'.[128] From Paris to Mexico Serge continually associated with refugee revolutionaries who embodied intolerance, with all the concomitant consequences of expulsions and inquisitions. More than simply discouraged, Serge sought to understand the problem which surely undermined their effectiveness. He also noted that back in the USSR the bureaucracy knew how to mobilize these feelings against the Opposition, and yet the Opposition itself exhibited the same intolerant qualities.

---

* In his testimony to the US Senate, Zborowski reported that among his assignments he was to inform the NKVD of the activities of the French Trotskyists, to get close to Sedov and lure him to a place where the NKVD would kidnap him (with Zborowski) and send them both back to Russia, to plant documents on the Trotskyists, to get information on their connection with Hitler, and later, as Krivitsky's bodyguard, to witness anything that might happen to him.

The problem, Serge wrote, lay in the inability to reconcile intransigence, a necessary quality of being, with respect for the different being. In Russia, socialist politics failed because the social struggles led to socialists treating Marxism as a 'faith, then a regime, a double intolerance in consequence'.[129] Serge's solution to the dilemma was 'fighting intransigence, controlled by as objective a rigour as possible and by an absolute rule of respect for others, respect for the enemy even'.[130] These are noble sentiments, but challenged even Serge in practice. In a letter written in the final year of his life he remarked that he remained 'intransigently socialist'.[131] Always aware of the difficulty, Serge remarked, 'Respect for the enemy, the totalitarians make it difficult, if not impossible'.[132]

Though Serge himself fell victim to the dirty divisive work done by agents, he was conscious that political differences and organizational practices were also responsible for his worsening relations with Trotsky from 1937 on. Serge and Trotsky began to disagree with each other in late 1936, and this grew to a practical rupture by 1939. While Kronstadt and Serge's support of the POUM were the public issues of contention, what angered Trotsky most was Serge's attitude to the Fourth International.

On 2 December 1938, Trotsky wrote a short piece that was published in January 1939 in the *Byulleten' Oppozitsii*, entitled '*Viktor Serzh i IV Internatsional*' which stated that Serge, now a member of the centrist Partido Obrero de Unificación Marxista (POUM), was an opponent to the Fourth International.[133] Serge wrote to Trotsky on 18 March 1939:

> I've decided not to react at all to the article in the *Bulletin*. You are too inaccurate, too unjust and unnecessarily offensive. I do not know who keeps you informed and how, but sadly believe me, there exists a whole nest of intrigues here (which has played its part in the death of Lev Lvovich, and before that, in the death of Reiss, as well as in the failure of the whole Fourth International movement in France).[134]

In a postscript to this letter Serge told Trotsky that his rupture with the French Bolshevik-Leninists occurred because he had been told by a 'comrade' that there were serious suspicions about Lola Dallin. Serge thought this should be investigated and confided to Rosmer, Wullens and Elsa Poretsky. Elsa told the group, who 'refused to look into *the substance* of the affair, or so I was informed through comrade Etienne. Instead – it "brought an action" against me'. While it appears that Lola was not the NKVD agent, she protected and vouched for the reliability of Etienne/Zborowski, the real agent. Zborowski was apparently successful in turning Serge into a pariah for the group. Trotsky fell right in and subjected Serge to a horrendous offensive of vitriolic prose. Many political issues were involved, but one of the worst was over Serge's translation of Trotsky's *Their Morals and Ours* and the prospectus that accompanied its French publication.

The 'Prière d'Insérer': who wrote it and to what end?

Serge translated no fewer than six of Trotsky's books into French, and, as already noted, Trotsky was very pleased to have the use of such a talent as Serge's to bring his work to French readers. Serge's translation of Trotsky's polemic on means and ends, *Their Morals and Ours* (February 1938), brought unwarranted controversy to their relationship. Unfortunately the controversy was not over the content of the book, which Serge thought contained 'many fine pages at the end'.

The book was subtitled 'Marxist Versus Liberal Views on Morality' and provoked a debate between Trotsky and John Dewey among others. Trotsky was at his polemical best in this book, brandishing wit and colourful language like an épée to skewer his opponents' ideas. He set out to distinguish revolutionary morality, which is rooted in concrete historical circumstances and aims at the liberation of humankind, from the abstract *a priori* morality advocated by liberals, social democrats and others. The 'fine pages at the end' of Trotsky's book that Serge referred to contain a discussion of the 'Dialectic Interdependence of End and Means'. Here Trotsky insisted that base means lead to base ends, that 'organically the means are subordinated to the end'[135] or, in other words, the product could only be as pure as the process.

Serge chose not to reply to Trotsky's work, as he explained in a letter to Marcel Martinet on 30 March 1939:

> I send you the transl. of *'Notre Morale et la Leur'* [sic] of L.T. that I have done. It is dynamic and well thought out from a narrow-minded point of view, historically obsolete, and falsifies everything, fanatically. I think that I will not – at least at this time – treat this subject and respond to the Old Man, or if so, only minimally, in order not to play dead to his attacks . . . his intransigence has become deadly dull, tediously overbearing.[136]

In any case the dispute with Trotsky was not over Serge's translation, or any unspoken disagreements about the ideas Trotsky expressed, but over the promotional prospectus in the French edition, which crudely attacked Trotsky. Without checking with the publisher, Trotsky assumed Serge wrote this invective:

> For Trotsky, there is no such thing as morality *per se*, no ideal or eternal morality. Morals are relative to each society, to each epoch, relative especially to the interests of social classes . . . True morality must defend the interests of humanity itself, represented by the proletariat. Trotsky thinks that his Party, once in power, today in the opposition, always represented the real proletariat; and he himself, the real morality. From this he concludes, . . . that shooting hostages takes on different meanings depending on whether the order is given by Stalin or by Trotsky or by the bourgeoisie . . . Trotsky, basing himself on Lenin, declares that *the end justifies the means* (on condition that the means are effective: for example, individual terrorism is generally ineffective). There is no cynicism in

this attitude, declares the author, merely a statement of the facts. And it is to these facts that Trotsky says he owes his acute conscience, which constitutes his *moral sense.*[137]

It is inconceivable that Serge could have penned or inspired these thoughts, so out of character with the body of his published work. Trotsky immediately presumed he had, however. Instead of verifying the facts with Serge or Les Éditions du Sagittaire, Trotsky lifted his pen and wrote a furious addendum to *Their Morals and Ours* on 9 June 1939, the essay called 'The Moralists and Sycophants against Marxism: Peddlers of Indulgences and Their Socialist Allies, or the Cuckoo in a Strange Nest'. He wrote,

> Some 'friend' . . . contrived to slip into a strange nest and deposit there his little egg – oh! it is of course a very tiny egg, an almost virginal egg. Who is the author of this prospectus? Victor Serge, who is at the same time its severest critic, can easily supply the information. I should not be surprised if it turned out that the prospectus was written . . . naturally not by Victor Serge but by one of his disciples who imitates both his master's ideas and his style. But, maybe after all, it is the master himself, that is, Victor Serge in his capacity of 'friend' of the author?[138]

The piece exudes Trotsky's vexation with the 'independents' loosely associated with the Left Opposition. One can detect his obvious frustration at being an ocean away from the discussion, an ocean away from reining in the dissidence. The essay is devoted to a scathing attack against Victor Serge (the moralist) and Boris Souvarine (the sycophant) in language memorable for its viciousness. Trotsky sustained some seven pages of tirade, accusing Serge of 'Hottentot morality', of publicly becoming a member of the POUM, of being a 'petty bourgeois moralist' who 'thinks episodically, in fragments, in clumps', of wanting 'to purge human history of civil war'. Further, Trotsky berated Serge for dating the degeneration of the revolution from the moment the Cheka began secret trials. Trotsky wrote 'Serge plays with the concept of revolution, writes poems about it, but is incapable of understanding it as it is'. Apparently one of Serge's worst attributes was that he wrote lyrically, even poetically about revolution; Trotsky returned to this in several articles.* More to the point, Trotsky wrote:

---

* In a particularly vicious attack on Serge, Trotsky replied to Serge's letter criticizing the creation of the Fourth International: 'When the Fourth International becomes "worthy of the name" in the eyes of Messrs. Literatteurs, Dilettantes, and Sceptics, then it will not be difficult to adhere to it. A Victor Serge (this one, or another) will then write a book in which he will prove (with lyricism and with tears!) that the best, the most heroic period of the Fourth International was the time, when bereft of forces, it waged a struggle against innumerable enemies, including petty-bourgeois sceptics.' (Leon Trotsky, '"Trotskyism" and the PSOP', *Writings of Leon Trotsky (1938–39)*, New York, Merit Publishers, 1969, p. 134.)

> When we evaluate from the Marxian standpoint the vacillations of a disillu-
> sioned petty-bourgeois intellectual, that seems to him an assault upon his indi-
> viduality. He then enters into an alliance with all the confusionists for a crusade
> against our despotism and our sectarianism . . . Victor Serge demanded of the
> Fourth International that it give freedom of action to all confusionists, sectari-
> ans and centrists of the POUM, Vereeken, Marceau Pivert types, to conservative
> bureaucrats of the Sneevliet type or mere adventurers of the R. Molinier type.
> On the other hand, Victor Serge has systematically helped centrist organizations
> drive from their ranks the partisans of the Fourth International.[139]

He ended his diatribe with 'the moralism of V. Serge and his compeers is a
bridge from revolution to reaction'.[140] The essay seeks to lump Serge with
other anti-Bolsheviks and anti-Leninists, those who see Stalin as the heir to
Lenin. It is remarkable for its obvious ignorance of Serge's writings.

How did Serge react to this vicious onslaught of *ad hominem* attack? He
was heartbroken. In the *Memoirs* Serge lamented:

> Deplorably misinformed by his acolytes, he wrote a long polemical essay against
> me – imputing to me an article of which I was not the author and which was
> totally at variance with my frequently expressed opinions. The Trotskyist jour-
> nals refused to publish my corrections. In the hearts of the persecuted I encoun-
> tered the same attitudes as in their persecutors . . . Trotskyism was displaying
> symptoms of an outlook in harmony with that of the very Stalinism against
> which it had taken its stand, and by which it was being ground into powder . . .
> I was heartbroken by it all, because it is my firm belief that the tenacity and will
> power of some men can, despite all odds, break with the traditions that suffo-
> cate, and withstand the contagions that bring death. It is painful, it is difficult,
> but it *must* be possible. I abstained from any counter-polemic.[141]

Serge was denied access to Trotskyist journals, but nonetheless attempted to
refute the charges internally, to clear the air and his name. Publicly Serge
refused to break solidarity with Trotsky. Serge wrote to Dwight Macdonald:

> In his recent attacks on me Leon Davidovich has so abused me that I'm almost
> glad I no longer have the means to answer him. He began by criticizing me
> without having read what I wrote, and continues to attribute to me an article
> that I did not write in a journal with which I have no association. His entire
> article entitled 'Moralists and Sycophants' is thus entirely falsely based, since he
> ascribes ideas and arguments to me that were never mine. However, I have
> written a great deal in the last twenty years on these subjects and he should
> know this! He would also do well to find out who wrote the article he attributes
> to me without so much as a care. All this is terribly sad. I sent *The New Interna-
> tional* and LD himself some corrections, the fate of which are unknown. In
> Europe the publications that attacked me in this way never published my
> replies. So I stopped replying. I am adamant.[142]

Serge then penned a reply to Trotsky which he did not publish. It was
discovered among Serge's papers by Peter Sedgwick, who translated and

published it in *Peace News*, 27 December 1963 (page 5) under the title 'Secrecy and Revolution: A Reply to Trotsky'. In a letter Serge wrote to Angelica Balabanova on 23 October 1941, he explained why he refrained from a public debate with the Old Man, who was engaged in a resolute fight against Stalinism, and whose ideas Serge still deeply respected:

> In all this painful argument with the Old Man, I kept such esteem and affection for him that, even though he wrote a long polemical attack accusing me of writing an article which was never mine and of advocating ideas which were never mine, I first sent a powerful rebuttal to the printers of *La Révolution prolé-tarienne* (Paris) and then took it back from them, preferring to suffer this unjust attack in silence. And I still think I was quite right: truth can work its way out in different ways than by offensive polemics.[143]

Serge also wrote to Trotsky on 9 August 1939 denying any connection to the odious prospectus. Trotsky replied on 7 September 1939 in *Byulleten' Oppozitsii 79–80*, 'Ocherednoe Oproverzhenie Viktora Serzha',[144] that he 'willingly accept[ed] his declaration', and then proceeded to attack Serge for having 'a confused mood of uncertainty, disillusionment, dissatisfaction, and repulsion from Marxism and proletarian revolution'. As to the authorship of the prospectus, Trotsky wrote,

> If not he personally, then one of his disciples or co-thinkers. The supposition that the prospectus was written by Victor Serge occurred to various comrades, independently of one another. And not by chance: the blurb constitutes a simple résumé of Victor Serge's latest sermonizings.[145]

Which comrades? Etienne? Pierre Frank? Whether or not Etienne directly raised the issue with Trotsky, or incited others to do so, he could be justly proud of accomplishing his objective, of dividing the two surviving Left Oppositionists and occupying them with incessant internal intrigue. Yet Trotsky seemed to dismiss the possibility of the hand of the NKVD. In a letter to Serge published in the *Writings* as 'Victor Serge's Crisis' Trotsky wrote:

> You are passing through a protracted ideological crisis and . . . you are turning your dissatisfaction with yourself into dissatisfaction with others. You write about intrigues, false information, etc. I do not know about any of that . . . I do not lose the hope of seeing you return to the road of the Fourth International. But at present you are an adversary, and a hostile one at that, who demands nonetheless to be treated as a political friend.[146]

Serge asserted categorically that he 'never published a single line concerning that work [*Their Morals and Ours*] of his, in any publication or in any shape or form'.[147] Serge continued, 'I am not the author of this prospectus: I have had no part, direct or indirect, in composing it: I have no idea who its author is: and I do not care either. Is that clear enough?'[148] The real author of the prospectus is still unknown. Vlady believes Zborowski wrote it,[149] and I put that question to him several times, without ever being graced with a reply.[150] Pierre Broué believes an editor wrote it,[151] possibly under Zborowski's guidance. Zborowski's NKVD file (partially released in 1999) reveals that he became a master of 'insertions' and rewrites to subtly change the meaning of articles.[152]

Despite Serge's denial, the issue of his authorship refused to die. Pierre Frank rehashed the rumour that Serge had written the prospectus in the introduction to the second French edition of *Leur morale et la nôtre* in 1966, three years *after* Peter Sedgwick published Serge's refutation in *Peace News*, nineteen years after Serge's death. In his introduction, Frank not only repeated that Serge wrote the prospectus, he grouped Serge with Max Eastman and Sidney Hook, two former Marxists turned Cold Warriors. How was it possible to ignore both Serge's refutation and Trotsky's acknowledgement of Serge's denial? It appears that Pierre Frank held Serge in particular contempt and had considerable influence over official Trotskyist thought about Serge.* In 1977 Michel Dreyfus published, under Pierre Broué's direction, the Serge–Trotsky correspondence *La Lutte contre le Stalinisme*.[153] Dreyfus repeated the assertion that Serge was the author of the prospectus, not even acknowledging that Serge had refuted that charge.

The rupture over the prospectus was really the culmination of disagreements over several issues, specifically Serge's support of the POUM and his attitude to the Fourth International. Trotsky was offended by this 'defection', and the intransigent and excessive tone of his polemic reflected his anger.

Defection notwithstanding, Serge still functioned in the orbit of Trotskyism and held the Old Man in great esteem; and he was considered a 'Trotskyist' by the larger political public. He later wrote in his diary:

> I went on translating the Old Man's books, *La Révolution trahie*, *Les Crimes de Staline*, *Leur Morale et la Nôtre* and to defend him. I remained in the eyes of the general public the best-known 'Trotskyist' writer – while the 'B-Ls' disparaged me as far as they could. I had become for them a 'petit-bourgeois intellectual' of whom they had to 'make use of the influence' and the 'questionable sympathy'. – The sense of possession of the truth, the intolerance and the aggressiveness devoid of critical sense of *Leur Morale* made me furious although there are fine, worthwhile pages at the end of this essay. I said so to some Trotskyists who wrote

---

* In 1974 leading members of the British section of the Fourth International told me that Serge was a 'centrist', implying he was not worth reading. Ernest Mandel, the recognized international leader of the Fourth International in Mexico in Aug. 1990 told me that he 'would drop a bomb' at the Serge Centenary Colloquium by publicly clearing Serge's name. At the Colloquium in Brussels in March 1991 Mandel praised Serge as a revolutionary journalist, but did not address Serge's dispute with Trotsky and the Fourth International.

and told the Old Man and that at once brought fresh attacks upon me. The saddest thing was that they were always insulting and always based on inaccurate data. It would have been so simple to state: We're at considerable variance on such and such a point – but the Old Man and his followers had become completely incapable of holding such a straightforward dialogue. The frightening atmosphere of persecution in which they lived – like me – made them inclined to a persecution complex and to the practice of persecution.[154]

The Fourth International, Kronstadt debate, the POUM

Trotsky's mission, once the Great Purge was under way in the Soviet Union and the Stalinists were killing the Left in Spain, was to create a world Party of revolution, a revolutionary pole of attraction for workers the world over who were repulsed by Stalinism and disgusted by the parliamentary reformism of the social democrats. He devoted most of his energy to the Fourth International, and naturally wanted all revolutionary Marxists to share his vision of this world revolutionary organization. Victor Serge, as an exiled Russian Left Oppositionist with intellectual standing in Europe, would have been an asset to the Fourth International.

Trotsky sent Serge a draft which was adopted by the July 1936 Conference for the Fourth International, entitled 'The New Revolutionary Upsurge and the tasks of the Fourth International'.[155] Serge dispatched his comments to Trotsky on 19 July 1936, titled 'A New Revolutionary Upturn?' Serge disagreed with Trotsky's assessment of the readiness of the workers in Europe for revolutionary struggle. Trotsky viewed the French Popular Front and the Spanish Civil War as signs that the revolutionary upsurge was beginning. Serge countered that workers were just 'emerging, awakening out of a long period of depression; it is the beginning of a process', that was a product of ten years of exhaustion brought on by the war and the post-war defeats.

As to the Second International, Serge wrote that it was wrong to consider it homogeneous, and 'our criticism and pressure . . . [can] help them in a more positive direction'. Their differing perceptions of the nature of the conjuncture also led to different attitudes toward the Popular Front, which Serge thought of as an arena of struggle for revolutionary working-class demands. Their task, according to Serge, was to 'exert enough pressure on the Popular Front . . . [It could] be a useful transitional form which will allow the workers to enter later phases of the struggle with greater possibilities'. Serge's slogan was 'transform the Popular Front from an instrument of class-collaboration into an instrument of class-struggle', which obviously implied a split with 'bourgeois and bourgeois-dominated elements and the re-grouping of the working class forces around a revolutionary programme which can assure them of the support of the middle classes'.[156]

A.J. Muste, an American minister whose American Workers' Party fused with the Communist League to form the American section of the Fourth

International (the Socialist Workers Party),* visited Serge in Brussels in late July 1936 on behalf of Trotsky and the Bureau for the Fourth International, in order 'to convey Leon Davidovich's proposal that I join this Bureau as a co-opted member. I accepted.'[157]

After his conversation with Muste, Serge wrote a letter to Trotsky (27 July 1936) in which he put forward his ideas on how the organization could reach and recruit as many people as possible. Serge envisioned a broad revolutionary Party with a truly professional, quality press that encouraged open debate in a fraternal style. 'Our ideological intransigence must be expressed and developed in an atmosphere of free collaboration, without anxiety about secondary differences.'[158] Serge emphasized that the organization, while being ideologically firm, remain open and non-sectarian, trying to unify non-Stalinist forces. He also wrote that the question of the 'nature of the Soviet State and of the defence of the USSR – matters on which enormous confusion reigns among the rank and file', be left open, since it was an important educational question but not one of principle.

Trotsky replied to Serge on 30 July 1936, stating that he could not agree, and moreover criticized Serge for his 'artistic and psychological' approach which was insufficiently political.[159] Trotsky was more concrete than Serge and indicated that in practice some people would not be suitable to the organization since they were 'petty bourgeois through and through; their little houses, little gardens and cars are a thousand times dearer to them than the fate of the proletariat'. Serge simply did not share Trotsky's view of these anti-Stalinist activists.

By mid-1937 Serge and Trotsky began to have serious disagreements. In 1938 Serge entered into a polemic over Kronstadt which was splashed across the pages of *The New International*, *Lutte Ouvrière*, *La Révolution prolétarienne*, *Byulleten Oppozitsii* and elsewhere. The Kronstadt debate came in the wake of the Spanish Civil War, and had everything to do with the role of the anarchists and POUM. Serge wrote in his diary:

> About this time, I had a correspondence with Trotsky on the subject of the Spanish anarchists whom Leon Sedov dismissed as 'destined to stab the Revolution in the heart'. I thought they would play a key role in the civil war and advised Trotsky and the Fourth International to publish a declaration of sympathy with them, in which the revolutionary Marxists would pledge themselves to struggle for liberty. L.D. said I was right and promised that something on these lines would be done, but it never was.
>
> In January 1937, I attended an international conference of the Fourth in Amsterdam . . . Already the Trotskyists were directing all their fire at the POUM. I took the floor to justify the POUM's participation in the Catalan Generalitat, on the grounds of the need to control and influence the Government

---

* For an insider's account of this process, see James P. Cannon, *The History of American Trotskyism*, New York, Pathfinder Press, 1972.

from within and to facilitate the arming of the masses. With Vereeken and Sneevliet, I proposed a resolution of solidarity with the POUM, which ended with an appeal to the Spanish militants to preserve the unity of their Party. Pierre Naville, Gérard Rosenthal and Rudolf Klement protested against these formulations: it became obvious that even while addressing diplomatic compliments to the POUM, they were organizing a split in its ranks. Two English delegates to Amsterdam told me that the movement of the Fourth International numbered less than a hundred members in England – and split into two rival organizations, as in France.

I came back from Amsterdam sore at heart: the impression of a sectarian movement, controlled by manoeuvres from on high, afflicted by all the mental depravities which we had struggled against in Russia: authoritarianism, factionalism, intrigues, schemes, narrow-mindedness, intolerance. Sneevliet and his Party had enough, finding the atmosphere unbreathable; they were honest, sober Dutch proletarians, used to fraternal norms of conduct. Vereeken, who idolized the Old Man, said to me: 'I give you less than six months to fall out with him. He doesn't tolerate any opposition.'[160]

Serge took part in the Fourth International, including its founding conference, and worked with its members until he developed disagreements with them over their attitude to the POUM, the stifling internal atmosphere and his conviction that within the Fourth International he

> could not detect the hope of the Left Opposition in Russia for a renewal of the ideology, morals and institutions of Socialism. In the countries I knew at first hand, Belgium, Holland, France and Spain, the tiny parties of the 'Fourth International', ravaged by frequent splits and, in Paris, by deplorable feuding, amounted only to a feeble and sectarian movement out of which, I judged, no fresh thinking could emerge. The life of these groups was maintained by nothing but the prestige of the Old Man and his great, unceasing efforts; and both his prestige and the quality of his efforts deteriorated in the process. The very idea of starting an International at the moment when all international socialist organizations were dying, when reaction was in full flood, and without support of any kind, seemed quite senseless to me.[161]

In the Fourth International Serge found a crude caricature of Trotsky's intransigence, here translated into simple inflexibility. Their shallow dogmatic and sectarian thinking was all very discouraging to Serge.

Further, Serge came to believe that the timing was all wrong: the creation of a Party of world revolution during a period of defeat (fascism, war, Soviet totalitarianism) was futile, if not pretentious. Thus the correspondence between Serge and Trotsky reveals a conflict of objectives: Trotsky wanted Serge to play a leading role in the Fourth International, and Serge was dubious of the project from the start.

Serge thought the Trotskyist Left

> spent most of their strength and . . . their time in intriguing against each other and in running each other down in whole books. I reproached them bitterly for

squandering their resources like this when no publicity was being given to our imprisoned comrades in Russia. I refused to listen to . . . their contemptible bickerings, saying to Rous: 'if I was a member of one of your two groups, this atmosphere would make me resign at once. You are sick sectarians.'[162]

Serge cut himself off from the Fourth International in 1937, tried to avoid controversy, and 'made every effort to do the militants and LD all the good turns I could'.[163] Serge did not refrain, in 1938, from writing his polemic with Trotsky over Kronstadt and other vital issues. After all, there was an entire generation of political militants who would benefit from an airing of the issues surrounding the suppression of the Kronstadt rebels. He was subjected to a torrent of abuse from Trotsky's pen in this same period. Yet even as Trotsky attacked Serge publicly, he privately wrote him: 'I am still ready to do everything to create conditions for collaboration . . . but only on one condition: if you yourself decide that you belong to the camp of the Fourth International and not to the camp of its adversaries.'[164] In a letter to Trotsky in Russian, datelined Paris, 18 March 1939, Serge defended his activities and once again laid bare his differences with the Old Man on the question of the International:

I can assure you personally that I took no part in any groupings 'opposed to the Fourth'. Of course I feel closer to comrade-heretics, because I believe they are right: it's time to follow a new road, not to stick to the well-trodden paths of the late Comintern. Nevertheless, not only did I not participate in any 'factional activities' but tried whenever I could to soften the inevitable split. You will hardly find another person in existing groups as alien to any kind of 'intrigue' as myself. But enough about that. The same thing all over again: one cannot say honestly, calmly and with dignity, 'Yes, we have serious disagreements' – one must always discredit or even slightly slander the other side.

Our disagreements are very great indeed . . . I am convinced that one cannot build an international while there are no *parties* . . . One should not play with the words 'Party' and 'International'. But there are no parties here. It is a dead end. Only small groups manage to hold out somehow in this deadlock, but they have no dynamism, no influence, nor even a common language with the working-class movement. One cannot build an international organization on intolerance and the Bolshevik-Leninist doctrine, for in the whole world there are no more than two hundred people (except the surviving inmates of Stalin, perhaps) who are in a position to understand what Bolshevism-Leninism is . . . For the time being, no one in the Fourth International groups thinks except through your head.

What should be done? The solution, I believe, lies in an alliance with all the left-wing currents of the workers' movement (its platform: the class struggle and internationalism); in free, comradely discussion of every issue, without abuse and mutual recriminations; in the creation of an International Bureau of committees and similar bodies – such a Bureau to be composed of the representatives of local movements and to work towards concrete goals; one must abandon the idea of Bolshevist-Leninist hegemony in the left-wing workers' movement and create an international alliance, which would reflect the real ideological tendencies of the most advanced sections of the working class (I am convinced that in such an alliance the Bolshevik-Leninists would have a greater influence than in their own high and mighty International).[165]

Serge's attitude to the POUM, the French Popular Front, and the Fourth International were based on his concern that the revolutionary Marxists not be cut off from the political arena that held the attention of the working class. He viewed the Trotskyists' position – in principled opposition to centrists and 'class collaborationists'– as one of purist intransigence. Serge was neither a centrist (between reform and revolution) nor a class collaborationist, but he strongly felt that the Bolshevik-Leninists could have a positive influence on these groupings which in both cases had boosted the confidence and increased the combativity of the working class. Trotsky's position of no class collaboration led him to counterpose the United Front to the Popular Front, which was correct in principle, but simply not on the agenda in either Spain or France, in Serge's view, and therefore cut the Trotskyists from the main arena of struggle. Though Serge was perhaps overly enthusiastic about what could be achieved with the Popular Front* and the POUM, he also believed that the Trotskyists would be seen as sectarian, which would lead to their isolation in a struggle too important not to have some influence over. Furthermore, the behaviour of the Fourth International over the Spanish events was disturbing: Serge wrote to Sedov that they 'consider themselves called from above to lead the revolution in another country, and they see their one path in the creation of factions *à la Comintern* and in a schismatic perspective. This path will obviously lead nowhere, if not to the discredit of the Fourth.'[166] Serge's disdain for the Fourth International's tactics in Spain and his insistence on solidarity with the POUM were seen as capitulation to reformism by the Trotskyists. Serge was forevermore labelled a centrist.

The stamp 'moralist' resulted from Serge's renewal of the debate on Kronstadt. This debate took place in 1937 and 1938 in journals in Europe and America.[167] In 'dredging up' this ignominious chapter in Bolshevik history, Serge had not changed his position of siding with the Party, but wanted the Party to understand how they came to be in the position of executing workers. The libertarians and anarchists in Europe were quick to point to the similarities between the Moscow trials and the suppression of

---

* But Serge's enthusiasm was less than Trotsky's in 1936 when Trotsky wrote to Serge in envy that Serge would be off to Paris where the 'birth-pangs of the French Revolution' had begun with a massive strike. Trotsky to Serge [in Russian], 9 June 1936. Serge replied with a cautionary note, 'The wonderful strikes in France and here show clearly that the working class is recovering after its phase of depression and extreme fatigue, and is entering a new period of struggle. In such a situation one may hope for anything, so long as one does not expect an *immediate* all-round upsurge'. Serge to Trotsky [in Russian], Brussels, 16 June 1936. Cotterill, *The Serge–Trotsky Papers*, letters 17 and 18, pp. 69–75.

the Kronstadt rebellion. While the anarchists and POUMistas were being betrayed by the Communists in Spain, the Kronstadt debate served as a foil for the larger question of whether Stalinism was the natural outgrowth of Leninism or a deviation from it.

Serge did not share this view, nor was it his purpose in intervening in the debate about Kronstadt. Trotsky saw Serge's intervention as a way of 'man-ufactur[ing] a sort of synthesis of anarchism, POUMism and Marxism',[168] which was not far off the mark. Nonetheless there was more to Serge's thinking than that. At the same time that he argued with Trotsky over Kronstadt, he defended the Party against Anton Ciliga in the same pages of the *New International*. To Trotsky Serge maintained it was a lie that the Kronstadters wanted privileges:* they wanted to end War Communism, restore Soviet democracy and trade, which is what the NEP set out to do. Serge insisted it was not only healthy to look back at what happened, and how it could have been avoided, but that this was essential to draw the lessons. Trotsky agreed that it was 'necessary to learn and think' but that advice was very easy to give after the event.[169] For his part Trotsky revealed that he did not personally 'participate in the suppression of the rebellion nor in the repressions following the suppression'. However, as a member of the government Trotsky 'considered the quelling of the rebellion necessary and therefore [I] bear responsibility for the suppression'.[170]

Trotsky aimed his fire at the 'moralists' like Souvarine and Ciliga, who were interested in the question of his personal responsibility. Serge also entered the fray, in order to defend the ideals of October from those, like Ciliga, who 'judged [the revolution] in the light of Stalinism alone' and who directed personal attacks 'against Trotsky out of bad faith, ignorance and sectarian spirit'.[171] Serge took on Anton Ciliga's ahistorical critique, stating,

> What greater injustice can be imagined towards the Russian Revolution than to judge it in the light of Stalinism alone? . . . It is often said that 'the germ of all Stalinism was in Bolshevism at its beginning'. Well, I have no objection. Only, Bolshevism also contained many other germs, a mass of other germs and those who lived through the enthusiasm of the first years of the first victorious socialist revolution ought not to forget it. To judge the living man by the death germs which the autopsy reveals in a corpse – and which he may have carried in him

---

* Trotsky had said that 'The Kronstadters had demanded privileges' and Serge countered that he had been in Petrograd with Zinoviev at the time and followed events at close hand. The country was starving and the Kronstadters demanded 'freely elected soviets' and the abolition of the militias' barricades (*zagraditelnye otriady*), which stopped the population from looking for food on their own in the countryside. Moreover, Serge insisted, both the uprisings and the repression could have been avoided had the Central Committee listened to the Kron-stadters' grievances. Victor Serge, 'Les Ecrits et les faits; Kronstadt', *La Révolution prolétarienne*, no. 254, 10 Sept. 1937.

since his birth – is that very sensible? . . . A little direct contact with the people was enough to get an idea of the drama which, in the Revolution, separated the Communist Party (and with it the dust of the other revolutionary groups) from the masses. At no time did the revolutionary workers form more than a trifling percentage of the masses themselves. In 1920–21, all that was energetic, militant, ever-so-little socialistic in the labour population and among the advanced elements of the countryside had already been drained by the Communist Party, which did not, for four years of civil war, stop its constant mobilization of the willing – down to the most vacillating . . . Eloquence of chronology: it is the non-Party workers of this epoch, joining the Party to the number of 2,000,000 in 1924, upon the death of Lenin, who assure the victory of its bureaucracy. I assure you, Ciliga, that these people never thought of the Third International. Many of the insurgents of Kronstadt did think of it; but they constituted an undeniable elite and, duped by their own passion, they opened in spite of themselves the doors to a frightful counter-revolution. The firmness of the Bolshevik Party, on the other hand, sick as it was, delayed Thermidor by five to ten years.[172]

Clearly Serge and Trotsky had much in common. It was not Serge who dredged up the debate but Trotsky, in the course of defending his record against the calumny of the Soviet state.[173] Trotsky's tone, in all of his replies, was one of exasperation. He seemed most angered by the debates Serge raised. When Serge published in *Partisan Review* an article entitled 'Marxism in Our Time',[174] Trotsky replied without any evidence of having read Serge's piece. Trotsky's disagreements with Serge here turn into *ad hominem* attack:

> The ranks of the disillusioned include not only Stalinists but also the temporary fellow travellers of Bolshevism. Victor Serge – to cite an instance – has recently announced that Bolshevism is passing through a crisis which presages in turn the 'crisis of Marxism'. In his theoretical innocence, Serge imagines himself the first to have made this discovery. Yet, in every epoch of reaction, scores and hundreds of unstable revolutionists have risen to announce the 'crisis of Marxism' – the final, the crucial, the mortal crisis.
>
> That the old Bolshevik Party has spent itself, has degenerated and perished – that much is beyond controversy . . . This does not at all invalidate Marxism, which is the algebra of revolution. That Victor Serge himself is passing through a 'crisis', i.e. has become hopelessly confused like thousands of other intellectuals – is clear enough. But Victor Serge in crisis is not the crisis of Marxism.[175]

In a fragment found among Trotsky's papers in Mexico, written sometime in 1939, he reached, perhaps, the peak of his animosity:

> Victor Serge claims that his enunciations, statements and corrections, always revolving around his own personality, must without exception be printed by the workers' publications. Why? On what basis? What does Victor Serge represent today in the workers' movement? An ulcer of his own doubts, of his own confusion and nothing more . . . What do people of the Victor Serge type represent? Our conclusion is simple: these verbose, coquettish moralists, capable of

bringing only trouble and decay, must be kept out of the revolutionary organi-zation, even by cannon fire if necessary.[176]

With this fragment Trotsky stepped over the line between viciousness and deadliness. It was as if all his frustrations at being physically prevented from playing a leading role in the struggle in the USSR and Europe were vented in his literary tantrums against comrades like Serge. His own son, Lev Lyovich Sedov, a frequent subject of Trotsky's anger, recognized the deleterious effects of this kind of outburst:

> I think that all Dad's deficiencies have not diminished as he grew older, but under the influence of his isolation, very difficult, unprecedentedly difficult, gotten worse. His lack of tolerance, hot temper, inconsistency, even rudeness, his desire to humiliate, offend and even destroy have increased. It is not 'per-sonal,' it is a method and hardly good in organization of work.*

The rupture between Serge and Trotsky was never really completed, and had the character of a quarrel with room for conciliation. Even when Trotsky spewed out the worst venom, he always left the door open for cooperation. For Serge the pain of Trotsky's invective was severe but did not deflect from his essential appreciation of Trotsky's 'greatness' whose 'traits were those of several generations, developed to a very high degree of individual perfec-tion'.[177] In an essay Serge wrote to the memory of Trotsky, he described him as

> a doer, but one who brought to everything he did a lyrical touch . . . His absolute conviction that he knew the truth made him impervious to argument toward the end and detracted from his scientific spirit. He was authoritarian, because in our time of barbaric struggles thought turned into action must of necessity become authoritarian. When power was within his reach in 1924 and 1925, he refused to seize it because he felt that a socialist regime could not be run by decree . . .
>
> The end of his life was played out in loneliness. He often paced up and down in his study in Coyoacán talking to himself . . . He would engage in discussions with Kamenev who had been shot long before; he was often heard addressing him by name. Although he was still at the height of his intellectual powers, what he wrote towards the end did not approach his earlier work in quality. People often forget that intelligence does not exist in a vacuum. What would Beethoven have been had he been exiled among the deaf? A man's intelligence needs to breathe. The Old Man's intellectual greatness was a product of his generation's. He

---

* Lev Lyovich Sedov to his mother, Natalia Sedova, 16 April 1936. Having vented his own frustration at his father's inconsistent meddling with the French Trot-skyists, Sedov never sent this letter, and remained publicly his father's most ardent supporter. The letter was found in the Nicolaevsky Collection, series 231. It was also cited by Dale Reed and Michael Jakobson in 'Trotsky Papers at the Hoover Institution: One Chapter of an Archival Mystery Story', *The Ameri-can Historical Review*, vol. 92, no. 2, April 1987, p. 366.

needed direct contact with men of the same spiritual stamp as himself, men who could understand his unspoken thoughts and could argue on his level. He needed a Bukharin, a Piatakov, a Preobrazhensky, a Rakovsky and an Ivan Smirnov; he needed Lenin to be fully himself. Even among us, who were younger but included such fine men as Eltsin, Solntsev, Yakovin, Dingelstedt and Pankratov . . . he could find no equal; they lacked the advantage of his ten unique years of experience and thought.[178]

All the more tragic, then, that Serge and Trotsky were not able to work together in those dark years, that Serge's generous, comradely attitude to Trotsky was not reciprocated.

Worse for Serge was the destructive behaviour of the Trotskyists. It is clear that Serge did not think Trotsky a Trotskyist in this sense. Trotsky's inflexibility could be understood, wrote Serge, because he was 'the last survivor of a generation of giants'. For the present generation and the future, however, Serge was convinced that

> Socialism too had to renew itself in the world of today, and that this must take place through the jettisoning of the authoritarian, intolerant tradition of turn-of-the-century Russian Marxism. I recalled, for use against Trotsky himself, a sentence of astounding vision which he had written in 1914 I think: 'Bolshevism may very well be an excellent instrument for the conquest of power, but after that it will reveal its counter-revolutionary aspects' . . . Our Oppositional movement in Russia had not been Trotskyist, since we had no intention of attaching it to a personality, rebels as we ourselves were against the cult of the Leader. We regarded the Old Man only as one of our greatest comrades, an elder member of the family over whose ideas we argued freely . . .
>
> I came to the conclusion that our Opposition had simultaneously contained two opposing lines of significance. For the great majority . . . it meant resistance to totalitarianism in the name of the democratic ideals expressed at the beginning of the Revolution; for a number of our Old Bolshevik leaders it meant, on the contrary, the defence of doctrinal orthodoxy which, while not excluding a certain tendency towards democracy, was authoritarian through and through. These two mingled strains had, between 1923 and 1928 surrounded Trotsky's vigorous personality with a tremendous aura. If, in his exile from the USSR, he had made himself the ideologist of a renewed socialism, critical in outlook and fearing diversity less than dogmatism, perhaps he would have attained a new greatness. But he was the prisoner of his own orthodoxy, the more so since his lapses into unorthodoxy were being denounced as treason. He saw his role as that of one carrying into the world at large a movement which was not only Russian but extinct in Russia itself, killed twice over, both by the bullets of its executioners and by changes in human mentality.*

---

* Serge, *Memoirs*, pp. 348–50. These thoughts were echoed in a letter Serge wrote to Trotsky on 27 May 1936. In discussing the strands of thought in the Left Opposition, Serge quoted Eltsin who admitted that the 'GPU created any unity we have'.

7

From Paris to Marseilles, Marseilles to Mexico: the long, last journey from nightmare to refuge*

When Paris ends, the world ends . . .

Serge fled Paris in June of 1940 just as the Nazis entered the city gates. The war was on, but Serge commented that the French bourgeoisie was less than enthusiastic about fighting the fascists; they preferred them to the Popular Front of Léon Blum.[1] So the 'phony war' – barely fought – ended with France's surrender and division between occupied France and the collaborationist, Vichy regime in the unoccupied south.† As the German Army advanced, the roads to the south filled with refugees not only from the occupied sector but also from defeated republican Spain and Nazi Germany.

Europe's difficult situation only magnified Serge's own already precarious political and personal predicament. The second edition of his *L'An I* was postponed and the publicity for his just published *Portrait de Stalin* was

---

* This chapter in Serge's life is very well documented. He wrote about it in *Memoirs of a Revolutionary* (London, Oxford University Press, 1963), carried on a voluminous correspondence with Dwight and Nancy Macdonald in New York in search of material assistance and a visa for himself, his family, and other refugees in dire circumstances, and the experience is memorialized in the books of Mary Jayne Gold, Varian Fry and Daniel Bénédite, all of whom were with Serge in Marseilles in Villa Air-Bel. Nancy Macdonald also wrote of her experience with her 'first refugee', Victor Serge, in her account of the committee to rescue Spanish exiles.

† The first year of World War II was called the 'phony war' because it was uneventful and led to France's rapid capitulation. Mary Jayne Gold described it as 'rather a bore . . . [because] nothing much happened on the military fronts and there was nothing much to do in the rear'. Mary Jayne Gold, *Crossroads Marseilles 1940*, New York, Doubleday, 1980, p. viii. Jean Malaquais wrote to Serge that the troops at the front were utterly passive, talking only of women and booze (Serge, *Memoirs*, p. 354).

cancelled. He now lived with Laurette Séjourné,* Vlady and Jeannine. Serge watched the bombs, knew it was time to leave, yet clung to Paris in the vain hope that the situation would turn. He commented: 'When Paris ends the world ends; useless to see the truth, how could one bear to acknowledge it?'[2] He was not the only one, and many waited longer before taking to the south. Serge simply lacked the money to plan his future. That he waited until the last possible moment to escape conforms to his character and his past – he had to be there, to witness the cataclysms, to participate. In the *Memoirs* Serge wrote that he was writing some pages of a novel, not out of a love for literature, but because 'this age must be witnessed'.[3]

The sense of history

Serge's escape during the fall of France is charted in his novel *The Long Dusk*. Several passages give glimpses of his state of mind, sardonic reflections on the role of intelligence in a Europe taken over by barbaric totalitarianisms, one fascist, the other Stalinist. His characters Tullio Gaetani and Dr Ardatov (an older, more weary incarnation of Serge) reflect on their situation, and Gaetani remembers a simpler time, when the antinomies were clearer:

> Against us, reaction, and we stood for progress, liberty, the republic, socialism . . . Do you remember the radical magazines with a picture on the cover of an athlete breaking his chains, and behind him the sun rising with straight lines for rays . . . representing the dawning day? . . . We wrote good books, we created ideological fireworks on mountains of statistics, observations, scientific findings – and we did not suspect that we were passing through the magic gates of hell. Until history descended on us with rains of shrapnel, with dictatorships, propaganda, castor oil, socialist inquisitions, liberating revolutions transformed into tyrannies, abject tyrannies affirming by decree the genius of rational organization, an anti-socialist national socialism, a Bolshevism that exterminated the Bolsheviks. I understand that people should lose their heads and come to believe in chaos, in the perverse nature of man. I say: complexity, maelstrom, and man is in it . . . a prisoner of the machines he has built, crushed by the facility of destroying and being destroyed . . . It takes centuries and generations to build a cathedral and a single bomb pulverizes it by mistake in thirty seconds. Do not you regret the good old days, Simon?

---

* Serge's second wife Liuba Russakova's mental illness finally got the better of her and Serge had to leave her behind in a sanatorium in the South of France, where she remained until her death in 1985. He met Laurette, a French actress who had worked in Italy, in Paris. Laurette was described by Mary Jayne Gold as a 'very young-looking thirty-year-old' who resembled a 'Luini Madonna' (Gold, *Crossroads Marseilles*, p. 245). Laurette Séjourné married Arnoldo Orfila after Serge's death and still resides in Mexico City. Orfila died in 1998. She has published several anthropological works.

Serge (here Ardatov) wants to respond with Spinoza's statement on the function of intelligence, not to deplore but to understand. He comments instead that this would only be true if we were disembodied minds or we understood intelligence. But Ardatov does respond:

> Perhaps it's no more difficult to invent a human order, though it's more difficult to bring it about. We were not insane. I agree that we lacked a sense of complexity, that we borrowed an infantile determinism from mechanics and a blind optimism from the prosperous bourgeoisie. Our apparent error was to be neither devious nor sceptical. We anticipated too much, we thought in terms of diagrams, and our diagrams were muddled by the daubs and splotches of reality. From the point of view of Sirius, we were right and the events were wrong. Our mistakes were honourable. And even from a point of view less absurdly exalted, we were not so wrong. There is more falsification of ideas now than real confusion, and it is our own discoveries that are falsified. I feel humiliated only for the people who despair because we have been defeated. What is more natural and inevitable than to be beaten, to fail a hundred times, a thousand times, before succeeding? How many times does a child fall before he learns to walk? How many unknown navigators were lost at sea before a Columbus, guided by a magnificent error, could discover new continents? He followed an immense and correct intuition, he groped his way, he was right. If his nerves had weakened like those of his crew, twelve hours or twenty minutes before the discovery, he would have sailed back over the pitiful safe route of true defeat and oblivion. Others would have succeeded at a later date, can we doubt it? – The main thing is to have strong nerves, everything depends on that. And lucidity.[4]

The Nazis entered Paris on 14 June, and Serge left that very day with Vlady, Laurette Séjourné, and a Spaniard, Narciso Molins.* Their experience is paralleled in the fictional escape of the Russian Revolutionary refugee Dr Simon Ardatov, the German revolutionary refugee Hilda, the Spanish Civil War refugee José Ortiga and the slightly deranged deserter Laurent Justinien in Serge's novel *Les Derniers Temps*. Serge, his family and Narciso left on foot, until 'a providential taxi' appeared and took them through the Fontainebleau woods, underneath a barrage of shells.

With Europe collapsing behind them, Serge felt a certain relief: he wrote of his 'sense of release bordering . . . on gaiety'.[5] Serge's isolation and historical marginality could be swept away with this new cataclysm. His journey through Vichy France, Marseilles and on to the 'New World' was solitary, in the sense that he was alone in the world with his sense of history and his

---

* Narciso, mentioned by first name only in the *Memoirs*, is described by Danny Bénédite (Serge's comrade in Marseilles) as an ex-member of the Executive Committee of the POUM, and a friend of Vlady's. Daniel Bénédite, *La Filière marseillaise: un chemin vers la liberté sous l'occupation*, Paris, Editions Clancier Guénaud, 1984, p. 97.

revolutionary past, alone a vanquished refugee of the revolutionary generation, cast adrift in a Europe where the Gestapo and the GPU hunted him,
and the social democrats glanced askance.

The crew of four were in need of sanctuary and Serge remembered his
'socialist' friends who had visited him in Paris and offered to reciprocate
should the situation in Paris get too 'disagreeable'. However, as Serge
blithely noted, Laurette was 'hounded, "ever so politely", out of a chateau'
of a well-to-do anarchist on a day of torrential rain[6] and when the group
entered an abandoned farm in the woods owned by a socialist journalist
friend, he begged them to be off, for surely the Nazis would be right behind
them.* This so-called socialist journalist friend, Serge related in his
Memoirs, had been converted to collaboration with the fascists. Still seeking
sanctuary, Serge tried the house of a pacifist author, Jean Giono, who had
promised him refuge, only to find 'the door . . . shut and well-guarded'.[7]

The situation was appalling in a moral sense, since some of those who
closed their doors were once refugees themselves. Some of the Spanish Civil
War refugees had even become bandits. The concern for personal survival,
material comfort and money was, to Serge, another aspect of the defeat.†
Serge noted that with the far Left remained the task of survival; the survival
of thought, and the survival of solidarity.

Even worse than the defeat was the knowledge that what was left of the
Left was shrinking:

> I realized suddenly that we political refugees, we hunted revolutionists, were
> doubly, triply, beaten at the moment, for many of us were no longer 'of us',
> having been defeated and demoralized in the depths of our souls. We had begun
> to fight among ourselves for a place on the last boat. The extremity of our defeat
> was this *sauve qui peut*. The end of solidarity means the finish of socialism and the
> workers movement.

Yet even as some of the Left jealously guarded for themselves the last few
ways out of the nightmare there were others who offered their last morsel to
share. It is this complex vision of defeat and yet survival of solidarity that
Serge evokes in some of his finest writings, in the *Memoirs*, the novel *The
Long Dusk*, and later in *Les Années sans pardon*. It is the knowledge that the

---

* Serge spoke of this friend 'who had been a socialist journalist the day before yesterday . . . now in favour of a strong military government' in 'On the Eve', *Partisan Review*, vol. 9, no. 1, Jan.–Feb. 1942, p. 23.

† This sentiment is developed in the article 'On the Eve', a fragment of the
Memoirs translated by Jean Connolly in *Partisan Review*, Jan.–Feb. 1942. When
the *Memoirs* were finally published in France in 1951 and translated into English
in 1963, this fragment was changed. Gone was the longer reflection on the
'triple' defeat, the demoralization, and at the same time, the confident hope of
being 'on the eve' (pp. 23–33).

immediate defeat is not a final one, that what is essential is understanding – the 'superabundance of consciousness and will'. Serge chose to describe this as 'the sense of history'.

The sense of history is vital if the world is to be transformed and it is that very sense, that political-historical consciousness, that threatened the survival of those who held it. The revolutionary generation faced defeat on three fronts: mind, spirit, body. The political defeat was accompanied by a moral defeat, and by a physical one, either death or deprivation. Serge's novel *The Long Dusk* reflects this giant struggle: not simply the defeat inflicted by the twin totalitarianisms on a collective scale, but the toll it took on individuals who dared to hold on to their sense of history and their dignity.

As in Serge's novels, so in his life. Now on the run, Serge was in dire financial difficulty. The pressure to survive, not only to write, but simply to eat was magnified. Serge noticed, in *The Long Dusk*, that there are those who participate in history, think and take risks, while 'people who have nothing to do surround themselves with lots of comfort. They take care of themselves.'[8] Those who think, unfortunately, cannot sustain their bodies simply by thought, nor even by writing or participation in history. Dr Ardatov echoes these sentiments:

> a good deal of physical weakness can be overcome by clear thinking, by the will to hold firm, by the sense of history that will bring us revenge, by stubbornness in clinging to one's opinions – yet there are some weaknesses that cannot be overcome. Perhaps the hardest struggle is that between the mind and the (undernourished) flesh which nourishes the mind, exalts it above the flesh and sometimes suddenly debases it.[9]

In the *Memoirs* Serge comments on the *sense of history*, which is also the title of an article he wrote for *La Wallonie* (7 August 1937), and an entry in his *Carnets* (5 January 1944). Indeed this 'sense' is part of what sets this generation of vanquished revolutionaries apart, and prevents them from dissolving into ordinary life. It is not just that members of this rapidly depleting generation 'have caught a glimpse of man resolving his own history':[10] the old world is disintegrating and new barbarisms arise amid a terrible apathy and resignation. Well then, perhaps at least this dreadful destruction will seed a renewal – which is what Serge insinuates:

> Now it is all over: the rotten tooth has been pulled out, the leap into the unknown has been made. It will be black and terrible, but those who survive will see a new world born. There are very few people who have this new sense which modern man is so painfully developing: the sense of history.[11]

Serge returned again and again to this theme. He said he learned from the Russian intelligentsia that the 'only meaning of life lies in the conscious participation in the making of history.'* The old Russian Revolutionary exiles who Serge grew up with also taught him to 'have faith in mankind and to wait steadfastly for the necessary cataclysms'.[12] This patience and sense of history became a kind of leitmotif running through all his writing and thinking. It reflected the maturity of his thought, his personal testament, but simultaneously included a measure of despair over his intellectual and political isolation and his general optimism on the human condition on its rocky road to a collective, socialist, democratic future. Serge's 'sense of history' became a kind of dialectical expression of the historical crossroads of humanity at the near half-point of the twentieth century. In the novel on the fall of France the twin dangers of fascism and Stalinism have the Left cornered, pondering their historic and yet personal significance:

We are grains of sand in the dune. Sometimes we have a glimmer of consciousness, which is essential but which may well be inefficacious. The dune has curves in its surface, caused by the wind. The consciousness of the thinking grains of sand can do nothing to change them ... we must foresee that it [the world] is moving toward the object of our hopes, passing over our bodies and our skulls on the way. Neither revolutionary rhetoric nor the spirit of sacrifice can compensate for our impotence. The Spanish Revolution was lost in advance ... the Popular Front betrayed itself in advance, the European democracies, tender mother of fascism, were defeated in advance by the totalitarian machines; and these last are equally defeated, defeated by the defeated and by the industrial machines of America and Russia, which in spite of themselves will take over the acquisitions of the Nazis, adapting them to the mentality of the Anglo-Saxon democracy and to the spirit, as yet unforeseeable, of an immense revolution seething with contradiction.

In all this, the conscious grains are precious; let us not underestimate ourselves. What counts is always the rise or fall of man. This may be pride, but it sustains us, provided of course, that it be a pride without self-complacency and without concern for appearances. A number of precious grains will be crushed or inexplicably buried. However, a century will not pass before Europe, Euramerica, Eurasia see the birth of a rational, balanced, intelligent organization capable of re-conceiving history and guiding it, and at last attacking seriously the problems of the structure of matter-energy and its galaxies. Human destiny will brighten – [13]

The novel is about more than the fall of France and symbolically the defeat of the struggles ushered in by the October Revolution and the fate of the 'shipwrecked' generation. Significantly, it is about the birth of the resistance,

---

* Serge, *Memoirs*, p. 374. Recall also Serge's earlier description of the sense of history, which could also be described as a clear political consciousness, during the age of revolution, in the now far-off twenties: 'All we lived for was activity integrated into history; we were interchangeable' (p. 177).

portrayed in the final chapter. The sense of history is not simply the knowledge that the old generation carries with them, but it is also the will to hang on, to struggle, to be the link between the defeated past and the expectant future.

The mature Serge returned to the theme of the sense of history in a diary entry for January of 1944, musing, 'Men would need a sense of history comparable to the sense of direction of migratory birds.'[14] Serge wrote that the 'enormous spiritual magnetism of Marx's work' is explicable by this 'revelation of historical sense'. In this later work Serge defined the sense of history as 'the consciousness of participation in the collective destiny, in the constant development of mankind; it involves knowledge, tradition, choice and hence, conviction, it commands a duty . . . we must live (act) according to this sudden awareness'.[15]

Those who carry this historical consciousness become dangerous men, wrote Serge, and thus the sense of history carries a psychological burden: the conflict between instinct and reason can give rise to panic. This happened in the Moscow trials. Serge had developed his understanding of Freud and psychological studies in these later years in Mexico (when he was writing *Carnets*) which is reflected in this essay. Consciousness comes into conflict with a sense of fear or primordial anguish, which then expresses the failure of the sense of history. Serge used Trotsky as an example of an individual endowed with this sense, whose personal courage allowed him not only to overcome fear, but to continue fighting, unfortunately 'with arms which had become inadequate'. Trotsky, wrote Serge, was characteristic of a 'man who endeavours to be integrated to history in order to live and whose spirit is constantly subordinated to the sense of history. He expresses this well in the last pages of *My Life*.'*

In 'Marxism in Our Time', an essay published in 1938 that became a bone of contention in the difficult relationship between Serge and Trotsky,[16] Serge noted Marxism's many contributions:

> Marxism, finally, gives us what I call the 'historical sense' it makes us conscious that we live in a world which is in process of changing; it enlightens us as to our possible function – and our limitations – in this continual struggle and creation; it teaches us to integrate ourselves, with all our will, all our talents, to bring about those historical processes that are, as the case may be, necessary, inevitable, or desirable. And it is thus that it allows us to confer on our isolated lives a high

---

* Victor Serge, *Carnets*, Paris, Julliard, 1952. Serge believed Trotsky carried this 'historical sense', could 'look with clear eyes on the worst tragedies, and even in the midst of the greatest defeats he feels himself enlarged by his ability to understand, his will to act and to resist' (Serge, *Partisan Review*, vol. V, no. 3, 1938, p. 27). There is a certain irony in Serge's exemplifying Trotsky as the consciously awakened historical instrument because in his dispute with Trotsky over Kronstadt Serge was pleading for Trotsky to use his historical sense.

significance, by tying them, through a consciousness which heightens and enriches the spiritual life, to that life – collective, innumerable, and permanent – of which history is only the record.[17]

The Macdonalds and Marseilles:
a shipwreck with too few lifebelts, and too many castaways

Serge came into contact with Dwight Macdonald through the American left literary journal *Partisan Review*, which Macdonald edited and to which Serge contributed. Serge's contributions to *PR* span the years 1938 to 1947. He was paid for his articles, alleviating somewhat his financial distress. In November 1939 Dwight Macdonald sent Serge a cheque for $38 and remarked: 'In these tragic times, I often think of you and wonder about your life in France. You can be sure you still have many friends (unknown to you) and admirers in this country.'[18] From Fenlac in the Dordogne, Serge remembered this, and wrote to the Macdonalds for help:

> By some luck I managed to flee Paris at the very last minute. We have been trav-elling in freight trains, spending nights in the fields . . . in the Loire country we were so tired that we lay down behind some stones and slept through an entire bombardment. Nowhere, in this completely chaotic world, were we able to find any asylum. Finally the roads were barred and we were stranded in the small village in the south from which I am writing you. I do not think I will be able to remain here since I know no one and have neither roof nor money nor chance of earning anything.
>
> Of all I once owned – clothes, books, writings – I was able to save only what my friends and I could carry away on our backs in knapsacks. It is very little, but fortunately includes the manuscripts which I have already begun. This letter is a sort of SOS which I hope that you will also communicate to my known and unknown friends in America. I have no money for stamps; I will be able to send off perhaps one or two letters, but that is all. I must ask you to immediately undertake some action of material aid for me. I have scarcely a hundred francs left: we are eating only one meal a day and it is a very poor one at that. I do not at all know how we are going to hold out.[19]

The Macdonalds answered this appeal by setting up the *Partisan Review* Fund for European Writers and Artists. This was the beginning of Nancy Macdonald's lifelong commitment to the 'real heroes and heroines of modern times, who have been victims of both communist and fascist total-itarianism'.[20] Victor Serge was the first refugee she helped, and by 1953 she had set up Spanish Refugee Aid, a committee that raised and distrib-uted money among 13,000 mainly political refugees of the Spanish Civil War.

On 20 July 1940 Nancy Macdonald first wrote to the American consul in Marseilles to invite Serge and his family to come to the United States to live with the Macdonalds in New York.[21] From 1940 well into 1942 the

Macdonalds were Serge's lifeline. They corresponded regularly, sent him money, and interceded on his behalf with the State Department in an attempt to get Serge first an American visa and then simply an American transit visa after his Mexican visa was obtained through the efforts of Julian Gorkín. After Serge and Vlady left France in March 1941, the Macdonalds continued to help Serge financially, and continued their efforts on behalf of Laurette Séjourné and Jeannine Kibalchich until they were also able to leave France to join Serge in Mexico in March 1942. The extensive correspondence, collected at Yale University Library, is a testament to political and human solidarity. In the *Memoirs* Serge said a letter he had received from Dwight Macdonald, whom Serge had never met, seemed 'to clasp my hands in the dark, I can hardly believe it. So then, let us hold on.'[22] Holding on was the main task.

This was Serge's fourth exile, and seventh flight in twenty years. Serge and his entourage successfully navigated the congested roads to Marseilles, only to find that they were too late. There were no more lifeboats out. Marseilles was teeming with refugees from all of beleaguered Europe. There was a surfeit of talent and brains, all at the 'limit of their nervous resources'. The Jews suffered their own particular hell. They all lived, trying to maintain a shred of human dignity, in a 'twilight zone of illegality',[23] hunted, harassed and ignored. Being a man of the far Left, Serge was shunned and excluded, marginalized and exposed. He commented:

> In drawing up visa-lists, both in America and here, the leading figures of the old exiled parties were, it seems, determined to exclude the militants of the far Left . . . Everybody is making their escape through the political family-network: groupings are of use now only for that purpose. So much the worse for the man of no Party who has dared to think only in terms of Socialism in all its vastness! All of my Party, all of it, has been shot or murdered; and so I am alone, a curiously disturbing figure.[24]

And to the Macdonalds on 14 August 1940, Serge added:

> Here is what I must ask of my known and unknown friends in America in order to survive. At present, it is impossible for me to find work or help (and I am a little handicapped by my forty-nine years). Therefore the necessity for material aid. The best thing might be for me to collaborate with some one or use some unpublished works which would seem to be of interest to various publics . . . Help is needed urgently. I understand that there are certain organizations which help political refugees, only I am outside the old well known groups and they jealously guard for their own people their connections and resources. Being alone and an independent, I have not benefited by any of these supports and I am not on the lists of the old Russian socialists which have been, I know it, drawn up in America, for help and visas (they include only Mensheviks, social-revolutionaries and Jews). For me there will have to be a separate personal appeal.

And on 22 August:

> The situation becomes more and more difficult . . . almost untenable: no place of refuge, no resources, no help and difficulties of every kind. I must hold out and again I will make every effort to hold out.[25]

Serge also contacted the Mexican Embassy in search of a Mexican visa, and Jewish organizations for help for himself and his comrades and friends.*

Serge was left to fend for himself in the summer months of 1940, trying to find refuge in Marseilles, dashing off letters to America and beyond. In *The Long Dusk*, Serge described the Left, far Left and intellectuals

> who would have remained famous if only they had had an orchestra, a hospital, a magazine or a Party to direct. But having only their brains overloaded with memories and superfluous knowledge, they were less competent at living than the pimps and Sudanese longshoremen, the pretty streetwalkers, the unemployed seaman, the Balkan racketeers.[26]

In the *Memoirs*, Serge described the exiles in Marseilles as

> a beggar's alley gathering the remnants of revolutions, democracies, and crushed intellects . . . Those with the most scars take the shock best. These are the young revolutionary workers or semi-intellectuals who have passed through countless prisons and concentration camps.[27]

Serge was a professional at being a refugee on the run: it was his main life experience. Others were far less suited. Mary Jayne Gold, an American heiress living in Europe, described the travails of Franz Werfel and his wife, Alma.† The Werfels, talented and refined, old and used to comfort, were physically ill-prepared for flight and horrified by the discomfort of retreat. Serge, on the other hand, had spent so much of his life without security that he learned to become almost indifferent to the creature comforts provided by material goods.[28]

While Serge was in Marseilles Trotsky was murdered in Mexico on 20 August 1940. Serge recalled in the *Memoirs* seeing the news and feeling that

---

* FBI file on Victor Kibalchich alias Victor Serge, Item 2–293 dated 5 Jan. 1940 and Item 2–259, 13 Aug. 1940. Here the FBI has obviously made a mistake on dates, since both items are datelined Marseilles, but in January 1940 Serge was still in Paris. It is possible he sought a Mexican visa in Paris in January, though there is no evidence for it.

† Alma had been married to three of Germany's most gifted men: Gustav Mahler, the composer; Walter Gropius, founder of the Bauhaus school of architecture, and Werfel, novelist and playwright (Gold, *Crossroads Marseilles*, pp. 180–81). Notwithstanding Gold's observation, it should be noted that Mahler was Austrian, not German.

this was an appropriate time for the Old Man to go, 'the blackest hour for the working classes: just as their keenest hour saw his highest ascendancy'.[29] Serge wrote to Fritz Brupbacher on 23 August:

> The thought of the tragic event in Mexico City and of that great mind which has just been extinguished, horribly . . . When I think of the man's high-minded intelligence, of the extraordinary rectitude of his soul, of his rich vitality, all our discords vanish, nothing remains of the quarrels over ideas that divided us, I am stunned, devastated . . . Trotsky's disappearance leaves me in a singularly per-ilous position since now I am alone, the last *free* witness – more or less – of a whole era of the Russian Revolution – and the last representative of the men who, beginning in 1923–1926, defended its essence against Stalin.[30]

Serge wrote to the Macdonalds on 22 August of having received the terrible news from Mexico and asked for information about the assassin, and again on 30 August, discreetly asking them if they had any news of 'L'affaire de Mexico'. In another letter on 26 August, Serge connected the Reiss murder, the first *attentat* on Trotsky and the final act. He asked for a photo of the assassin, and also asked the Macdonalds to express to Natalia 'all the despair-ing affection that she inspires in a handful of dispersed, but nevertheless trusted friends despite their different political views'. Serge also mentioned how badly affected Vlady had been by the assassination, and told the Mac-donalds that he thought Krivitsky could be very useful in helping them sort out the affair because of his 'experience and intuition'.[31] The Macdonalds tried to help save Trotsky as soon as they heard he had been mortally wounded. They made arrangements to send a fine 'brain specialist' to Mexico City, but it was 'too late'. Trotsky died within twenty-four hours.[32]

The death of Trotsky, followed a few months later by the death of Krivit-sky in suspicious circumstances, suddenly made Serge's situation* even more dangerous, as he intimated in his letter to Brupbacher. Mary Jayne Gold noted that no one talked any more of Serge's paranoia. In fact, Serge was on the GPU's hit list, as we noted earlier. Zborowski (Etienne), Stalin's trusted agent in the Left Opposition circle in Paris, operated in the larger NKVD French network headed by Sergei Efron and his wife, the Russian poet Maria Tsvetayeva. Efron coordinated plans to 'hit' Henrik Sneevliet and Victor Serge, but was unable to accomplish the task.[33]

The need to get out of Europe was ever more urgent. Serge wrote to the Macdonalds that he received a letter from Julian Gomez Gorkín who said he could obtain a Mexican visa for Serge (26 August), but that Serge pre-ferred to go to the United States. Serge was also adamant that he would not go unless Vlady also got a visa as Vlady had no passport. After the death of the Old Man, Serge continued,

---

* Serge and Natalia Sedova were the only Russian Left Oppositionists still alive outside the USSR.

I feel – by simple logic – noticeably more threatened than before, which is one reason to hasten our departure, it is a reason also to avoid the risks (of leaving in bad conditions), it is also a reason to prefer the US to Mexico – if one has the choice.[34]

The emergency rescue committee

In the summer of 1940, following the June invasion of France, a group of American citizens was shocked to learn that a clause in the armistice signed with Germany provided for the 'surrender on demand' of refugees. France had always been a haven for exiles, whose lives were now threatened. They put together the Emergency Rescue Committee (ERC), whose 'sole purpose was to bring the political and intellectual refugees out of France before the Gestapo and the OVRA and the Seguridad got them.'* The committee drafted Varian Fry, a Harvard graduate who had been shocked by what he saw in Germany in 1935, to move to Marseilles to get them out.

Fry linked up with Danny Bénédite, his British wife Theo, and Jean Gemahling in Marseilles. Bénédite was a left-wing socialist working in the Police Prefecture in 1936 who had helped Serge get a residence permit.[35] In 1940, he and Jean Gemahling were demobilized from the British division of the Allies and sent to unoccupied France. There they began to work in the French office of the ERC, known as Centre Américain de Secours (CAS). Their work essentially constituted the humble beginnings of the *Maquis*, or Resistance.† A family friend of the Bénédites, Mary Jayne Gold, became involved in the work of the committee and quietly financed much of its operations.‡

From August 1940 until September 1941, when Fry was forced to leave France, the ERC/CAS was in the business of rescuing, under the nose of the Gestapo, by legal and illegal means, hundreds of anti-Nazi refugees, the endangered species of talent and intellect, Jewish and non-Jewish, political and otherwise. The committee, active until June 1942, handled 2,000 cases, some 4,000 endangered people. They rescued artists, journalists, scientists, philosophers and political militants, among them Victor Serge.

---

* The secret police of Nazi Germany, fascist Italy and Francoist Spain. See Varian Fry, *Surrender on Demand*, Random House, New York, 1945, pp. ix–x.

† Indeed, in a letter Serge wrote to Danny Bénédite from Mexico on 22 June 1946, Serge commented, 'It was a beautiful beginning! It was in truth the very first Resistance, well before the word had appeared.' Victor Serge to Danny Bénédite, 22 June 1946, published in *Carnets*, Paris, Julliard, pp. 157–63.

‡ Serge's novel of the fall of France is drawn from the people and experiences in Marseilles. Danny and Theo Bénédite's experiences in the Resistance are represented in the final chapter of *The Long Dusk*, and both Varian Fry and Mary Jayne make an appearance on page 250 where Serge describes the work of Jacob Kaaden and the 'aid committee'. Kaaden was in the business of obtaining visas and met 'a blonde young de Gaullist' who was negotiating to buy a boat to get refugees out.

Serge had written that 'if it had not been for Varian Fry's American Relief Committee, a goodly number of refugees would have had no reasonable recourse open to them but to jump into the sea'.[36] As it turned out some did commit suicide, including Walter Benjamin, and possibly Rudolf Hilferding, a client of the Committee. The Committee had secured Hilferding and Rudolf Breitscheid visas and passage on a boat, but on their way out they were arrested and then turned over by Vichy officials to the Nazis. Hilferding was found hanging in the Santé prison the day he was to be turned over to the Germans. The Nazis killed Breitscheid in 1944.[37] The anti-Nazi lawyer Alfred Apfel had worked on Hilferding's and Breitsheid's cases and came to Fry's office when he heard of Breitscheid and Hilferding's arrest. Fry warned Apfel himself to be careful, and then Apfel had a fatal heart attack. Fry felt responsible and had nightmares for weeks.[38]

Villa Air-Bel – Château Espère-visa

In the Indian summer of October 1940, Mary Jayne Gold found a villa just outside Marseilles as a place of refuge from the overwhelming pressure of the Committee's work. It was originally intended to be a home for Mary Jayne, Danny and Theo Bénédite and their son Pierre. Varian Fry also needed respite from the tremendous pressure, however, and so did Jean Gemahling. Villa Air-Bel, as it was known, was huge and yet 'dirt cheap',[39] a marvellous early-nineteenth-century bourgeois eighteen-room estate, with an intelligently stocked library, grounds with a garden, and a cow for milk – ready, in Mary Jayne's words, for a large 'Victorian family' to move right in. A 'large political family' was about to.

Like most of the other refugees in Marseilles, Serge had been living in one hotel after another.[40] When Danny Bénédite invited Serge to join them at Air-Bel, he accepted with joy, but warned he was not alone – Laurette and Vlady were with him. Serge also pressed Danny to include André Breton, the dean of Surrealism, his wife Jacqueline and their young daughter Aube. Despite Breton's reputation for being difficult, Serge assured Danny that 'he's a charming man whose company is truly enriching'.[41]

This concern for the fate of other refugees permeates Serge's correspondence. He was preoccupied by the intolerable situation of the Spanish refugees, and wrote to the Macdonalds that something must be done for the POUMistas Juan Andrade,* Wilebaldo Solano,† and Narciso Molins, who

---

* Serge wrote to Nancy Macdonald that Andrade was suffering from tuberculosis in the prison of Montauban in Vichy-ruled France. Serge fictionalized Andrade's predicament in *The Long Dusk*. See correspondence, 7 Oct. 1940, and Nancy Macdonald, *Homage to the Spanish Exiles*, New York, Insight Books, 1987, p. 45.
† Leader of the POUM Youth during the Spanish Civil War, and POUM General Secretary from 1947–63. Solano visited Serge in Paris in 1937.

were in danger. Serge was particularly concerned for the safety of Elsa Poretsky, Ignace Reiss's widow, after the GPU murdered Reiss in Switzerland in 1938.*

Villa Air-Bel became a 'wonderful haven'[42] for those waiting for visas. Mary Jayne Gold, the Bénédites, Jean Gemahling, Varian Fry and others from the ERC† were now joined in the villa by Serge, Laurette Séjourné and Vlady. Serge's young daughter Jeannine was already ensconced with friends in Pontarlier (near the Swiss border).[43] She visited Air-Bel, but was not able to live with her father for nearly two years.

Serge renamed Villa Air-Bel 'Château Espère-visa',‡ 'for that was the precious commodity in which the Secours Américain dealt and for which so many hoped and waited'.[44] They stayed five months, in a pleasant atmosphere of camaraderie, work, political discussions and surrealist games, which brought the famous French surrealists of the Parisian 'Deux Magots' crowd to Château Espère-visa on Sunday afternoons. The residents also enjoyed police surveillance and food and fuel rationing.

Three of the residents of Villa Air-Bel have memorialized the experience, each providing a rare portrait of Serge. Varian Fry, who published *Surrender on Demand* in 1945 and an entirely rewritten version entitled *Assignment: Rescue* in 1968, described Serge as

---

* Macdonald–Serge correspondence, Yale University: Serge to Macdonald, 30 Aug. 1940; Nancy Macdonald to Serge, 9 Sept. 1940 and 30 Oct. 1940. When Serge first wrote to the Macdonalds nothing had yet been done about Elsa Reiss-Poretsky, but by 7 Oct. 1940, Serge was able to write to the Macdonalds that Elsa was in Lisbon on her way to the US. The Mensheviks had been active helping her, though without much success. Serge wrote that Poretsky was 'very bitter, weary of it all . . . [but] she could come alive again and show such intelligence and courage that in contact with the least useful comrades, she recaptures hope'. Serge to Macdonalds, 7 Oct. 1940.

† Such as Miriam Davenport, Monsieur Maurice and Gussie. Maurice was the name adopted by the young Romanian doctor Marcel Verzeanu. He was brought on staff at the ERC because so many of 'our intellectual customers were having nervous breakdowns' that Fry thought it wise to have a doctor on staff to treat them (Fry, *Surrender on Demand*, p. 103). In June 1997, Dr Marcel Verzeanu was honoured with the first Varian Fry award by the Committee of Concerned Christians, a committee of Christian and Jewish Clergy founded in 1992 to fight anti-Semitism, determined to keep Varian Fry's name alive. *LA Times*, 5 June 1997, B3. 'Gussie' was a fifteen-year-old boy from Danzig who became the 'office boy' at the Emergency Rescue Committee. His real name was Justus Rosenberg. He later participated in the Resistance, was arrested several times but escaped, ended up in the American Army, was twice wounded and given several military citations for gallantry in action. He is presently professor of Foreign Languages and Literature at Bard College.

‡ *Espère-visa* means hope for a visa.

a dyspeptic but keen-minded old Bolshevik . . . During his long career, he had evolved from an extreme revolutionary to a moderate democrat. At the house he talked for hours about his experiences in Russian prisons, recalled conversations with Trotsky, or discussed the ramifications and inter-relations of the European secret police, a subject on which he had a vast store of knowledge. Listening to him was like reading a Russian novel.*

Mary Jayne Gold wrote 'When Danny brought Victor Serge to the château I was thrilled to meet a real Marxist – after all that talk.'[45] In an interview with John Eden in July 1989 Mary Jayne recalled 'it was quite exciting to hear Victor speak about his life in Russia'. He had 'the manners of a prince', he 'walked and moved like a gentleman' and 'yet he had been a communist, a revolutionary since birth'. In her memoir, Mary Jayne wrote that both Breton and Serge 'had almost courtly old-school manners, so that when I asked Danny how it happened that our two revolutionaries were so *ancien régime*, he simply replied that they liked ladies of goodwill'.[46] She remembered how considerate Serge was, and was particularly impressed with what he said on a number of occasions when asked if he were Jewish: with 'his innate sense of delicacy and comprehension', he would say, 'It happens that I am not.'[47] As to Serge's physical appearance, Mary Jayne wrote

> He was about fifty years old, with finely drawn features surmounted by a bristling crew cut. He wore a dark gray flannel jacket, loosely fitting, which buttoned, Russian fashion, up close to the chin. When Victor told us his stories in the evening as we all huddled around the porcelain stove in the library, his face took on another expression because he spoke of a time when the future direction of the revolution was being played out. On such occasions he held us all in respectful silence.[48]

Mary Jayne was surprised to meet Serge's companion Laurette Séjourné, after Serge had told her he was expecting 'someone who is very dear to me'. Mary Jayne told John Eden that she anticipated 'some comrade or some such, and this beautiful little woman arrives' who looked like a 'Luini Madonna'. Laurette was twenty years younger than Serge, and very beautiful. Fry described her in contrast to Jacqueline Breton:

> Laurette Séjouren [sic], Victor Serge's friend, was a woman as unlike Jacqueline [Breton] as Jacqueline was unlike everybody else. She was dark and quiet and very reserved. Although she generally stayed in her room during meals, professing not to be interested in food, the servants reported a large consumption of leftovers between meals.[49]

Jacqueline Breton was blonde, vivacious, sexy and outgoing, while Laurette was reserved and quiet. Still, Mary Jayne recalled problems between Serge

---

* The quote is a composite from the two editions of Fry: *Surrender on Demand*, p. 115, and *Assignment: Rescue* (New York, Four Winds Press, 1968), p. 120.

and Laurette, who was much younger and flirtatious, and thought that Serge was jealous. They often stayed in their room for dinner.

Danny Bénédite recalled that even with the tension that existed at Air-Bel, due to their dangerous situation and their personal and political conflicts, the atmosphere was relaxing. He and Serge explored the gardens, counting forty-five different trees and bushes, André Breton collected insects, which he sometimes used in his games, and Varian Fry observed the birds. Everyone used the library. They all spent time in their respective rooms working. Serge was writing *The Case of Comrade Tulayev*, Breton was writing *Fata Morgana*. Vlady spent much of his time sketching on the terrace. At night they gathered to listen to Serge or Breton read the pages they had written, to have political discussions or to play games. Both Serge and Breton circulated their books, which were read by all.[50]

When the food situation became worse in December and meals were particularly sparse Serge would recite his various prison adventures. They had political discussions all the time. Jean Gemahling was the only Gaullist, the rest were leftists, the two Americans an audience. Mary Jayne Gold remembers it was Vlady who first aroused her curiosity about Marxism.* Danny recalled Serge and Vlady arguing over the character of the Vichy regime, which Vlady insisted was 'simply fascist'. Serge corrected him, saying that

> It hasn't any of the positive elements (I hesitate to use the word) of fascism. This is a mélange of monarchist, clerical and militarist tendencies, the expression of a dying society decaying in disgrace and masochism.[51]

Serge had a major political influence on Danny Bénédite, who described him:

> In his fiftieth year, [he] was the affectionately respected elder statesman. He had finely-chiselled features, soft grey hair growing out of a high forehead, steel-framed glasses, a soft voice and measured gestures. His physical appearance and his distinguished manners were those of a well-bred Anglo-Saxon clergyman, but I have never been tempted to see in this former comrade of Lenin 'a scrupulous old maid' as Claude Lévi-Strauss later described him . . . For some of us, this

---

* Vlady was a passionate and fanatical Marxist, Gold wrote, but he was adept in the ways of survival as well (remember he had been with Serge in Orenburg). When food became quite scarce Vlady collected dried fruits and nuts and made them into rolls and sold them. Mary Jayne wrote: 'Our Marxist theoretician was openly engaged in a small private enterprise. In a period of near famine his fruit rolls stand out in my memory as a gastronomic delight' (Gold, *Crossroads Marseilles*, pp. 308–9). Vlady remembers making these rolls with Modigliani (the painter's brother) in an apartment converted to a workshop. The story of the 'croque-fruits' is told by Alain Paire in 'Octobre 1940–Décembre 42, Sylvain Itkine et les "croque-fruits": imagination sociale, théatre et résistance'. (Thanks to Pierre Sauvage for this unpublished article.)

man [who summed up all the tendencies of the turn-of-the century workers movement,] incarnated the Revolution and its prestige; for others he personified a humanist socialism fiercely opposed to the socialism that Stalin had compromised, perverted and depraved. I met Victor four years ago, when he arrived in Paris, the last Oppositionist let out of the USSR after an international campaign of protest before the first Moscow trial . . . Serge was caught in the crossfire between the men of the right who made use of his revolutionary antecedents and the communists for whom he was an abominable 'trotsko-fascist.' This man, constantly slandered, often threatened, who revealed an astonishing even-temperedness in these trials and accepted the insults that were hurled at him with great dignity, had become one of my best friends.[52]

Bénédite wrote that Serge and Breton were the stars[53] at Air-Bel, and though they were both 'more or less Trotskyists' according to Mary Jayne Gold, there were tensions between them. Danny Bénédite was less enthused with Breton as he did not think much of the surrealist movement, but Serge had recommended Breton be with them, and that was enough. Danny wrote: 'Serge was our conscience, Breton would be our animator.'[54]

On Sundays the Air-Bel was transformed with the arrival of Breton's surrealist friends. The Parisian cafés seemed to be reconstituted at the château. The visitors included Oscar Dominguez, Herold-Blamer, Victor Brainier, Wilfredo Lam, Max Ernst, Georges Dumas, Boris Voline (the Russian anarchist), Pierre Herbart, André Gide, Jean Malaquais and others. The games, which drew these artists to the château, had a history in surrealist circles as a technique to 'reach the inner and lost realities and to liberate the mind from the bonds of occidental logic. The games also achieved that curious juxtaposition of incongruities in which the surrealists detected profound and unexpected meanings.'[55] In Air-Bel, the games were mainly a distraction from trouble and danger. Serge joined in, but evidently did not think much of this side of Breton. According to Mary Jayne:

Although Breton and Serge had publicly supported each other politically there was often considerable tension between them. Both were revolutionaries, but Victor had lived through the revolution in the streets of Moscow and Leningrad, not Paris. From a literary point of view they were incompatible. Victor wrote in a sensitive, realistic style that to André was meaningless, and he was intolerant of what he considered to be André's flirtation with the Beyond . . . Victor Serge was the only one of the boarders to whom this present adventure was a way of life . . . To me his books are much more moving and poignant than those of Solzhenitsyn because Victor Serge had been with them. He was of them.

Victor had somehow managed to live through what he hoped would change life on this planet. Since his early days he had seen his friends and comrades executed or assassinated or diplomatically commit suicide. Perhaps he had reason to be irritable and dyspeptic at times. Those who disliked him called him paranoid. After Trotsky's assassination there was less talk of paranoia.

One day when he and Laurette and I were crossing over the port . . . halfway over he glanced back furtively once or twice. Then he turned to me and said apologetically, 'you will have to excuse me, I have been followed so often . . . It's an old Bolshevik habit, a habit one does not lose easily' . . . at the café he chose the last table and sat with his back to the protecting wall.[56]

Even at Air-Bel suspicions arose amid the terrible atmosphere of an 'expiring bourgeois world'. Rumours were rife, and one day Miriam told Mary Jayne that a prominent Menshevik, also a client of the Committee, 'has told me that Victor Serge is a Stalinist agent. You will have to tell Varian.' Mary Jayne wrote that neither of them believed the rumour, but 'we had both learned recently from Serge himself that Stalinists were capable of anything and that in a revolutionary situation only the cause mattered'. Mary Jayne told Varian about the rumour, and he said, with a guffaw, 'My God, how these Russians intrigue!'*

The heightened GPU work outside the Soviet Union began to mortally threaten Serge. Varian Fry's relationship with the French authorities and the American Embassy become strained as the French Communist Party took advantage of the 'French government's inherent fear of revolutionaries' and mounted a campaign of slander, accusing Fry of Trotskyism. Serge's presence at Air-Bel finally compromised the work of the committee, as Varian Fry and the ERC were being labelled Trotskyist. Mary Jayne Gold admits 'they thought of themselves as Trotskyists' but this label was a liability in an agency dealing with the State Department. Fry eventually had to ask Serge to leave the villa. Serge scarcely mentioned this in his *Memoirs*, but Mary Jayne was quick to point out the evil Stalinist hand behind this ugly slander. Mary Jayne's gangster boyfriend Killer, who hated all the intellectuals at the villa except Serge, was devastated. He said, 'I'm just as good as any of your friends, but next to a guy like Serge I'm a shit. Just a shit.'†

Serge was shattered that he had to leave. Thanks to the work of Julian Gorkín in Mexico and the Macdonalds in New York, his Mexican visa had just come through, but no visa was yet obtained for Vlady or Laurette and Jeannine, nor was it clear if he could travel through Spain, Portugal and Cuba.[57] Serge wrote to the Macdonalds on 5 January 1941 from a hotel in Marseilles:

> Note our new address. On the personal side, everything has become distressingly much more complicated for me. We had rented with some good friends, among them André, an abandoned villa on the outskirts of town; of the friends

---

* Gold, *Crossroads Marseilles*, pp. 246–7. Although Gold never names the prominent Menshevik, it could have been Boris Nicolaevsky, who had been with Serge in Paris, where doubts about him also surfaced from Elsa Reiss Poretsky, and Lola Dallin, a close associate of Nicolaevsky.

† Serge had told Killer of his exploits and prison sentence with the Bonnot gang, which endeared him to Killer for all time. Serge told Mary Jayne he liked Killer because 'he reminds me of myself when I was young' (Gold, *Crossroads Marseilles*, p. 286). Killer later become the model for Serge's character Laurent Justinien in his novel *The Long Dusk*.

living there with us were the collaborators of Mr F, but a whole plot has been woven in order to force us to separate, on the pretext that the co-workers of the Emergency Rescue Committee could be compromised by their close relations with me! The enormity in all of this, is that despite the clarity of the scheme and the profound esteem that unites us all, it worked – as a result of the atmosphere. I am once again faced with the housing problem, and it is tied to many others . . . You follow without doubt better than us the events that complicate again our personal problems. But in this regard, I am not at all a pessimist.[58]

Despite the extremely difficult new circumstances – a particularly severe winter amid food and fuel shortages on top of a lack of funds – Serge did not allow pessimism to overtake him. Mary Jayne informed Miriam Davenport of Serge and Séjourné's departure in a cryptic letter dated 30 January 1941, stating 'There was a terrific Committee crisis at the villa last week. Laurette, Victor and Vlady had to leave as they were considered not *tout à fait, au fait*, Social Standing you know.'[59]

Prior to Serge's 'expulsion' from the château one incident at Air-Bel is worth relating. The police arrived at the villa at the time of Marechal Pétain's visit to Marseilles with search warrants. They confiscated Serge's pearl-handled revolver, 'A delicate instrument but efficient enough to pierce Victor's brain if the OGPU got too close',[60] and his typewriter and one of his books, which Serge said they would now use to 'try and match the letters of my machine with the Stalinist tracts I am supposed to be writing'.[61] Bénédite wrote that the police were aggressive and arrogant and had information about all of the inhabitants. They turned to Serge and addressed him as Monsieur Serge, or 'Would you prefer Mr Kibalchich? It is your real name, no?'[62] Having searched the villa, the police arrested the lot of them. In fact the police had asked the Air-Bel occupants to come to the police station, as a formality. Serge advised his co-habitants that the police always say that. His experiences taught him that a few hours could last days, weeks or even years. Fry said, 'Good, at least you are always the optimist!'[63] They were first interrogated, then interned on board the SS *Sinaia*, along with some 600 other unfortunate souls suspected of possibly causing a disturbance during the Marechal's visit. Some 20,000 were arrested for the four-day duration of Marechal Pétain's visit to Marseilles. It was December 1940.[64]

The men were taken to the hold, the women given third-class cabins. Mary Jayne was given a cabin with Laurette and Serge, who 'on account of age and a heart condition, was accorded this special privilege'. Mary Jayne related that Serge thought they were doing very well, but nonetheless instructed them on how to be prepared. He took out his handkerchief and showed them how to fold it and place it under the chin so that the skin never touched the dirty wool of the blankets handed out. 'Furthermore', went on the old professional, 'it is wise to bring something to read. Takes your mind off your troubles.' He pulled out a volume from his pocket. '*Merde*. It's my own. Here, Mary Jayne. You can have it.' It was *Les Hommes* *dans la prison.* 'Re-merde, alors,' she said. 'Thanks.'* Varian Fry ended up with the book in his pocket, with a dedication from Serge 'In memory of our common captivity on the Sinaia, and in complete sympathy'.[65]

A few days before Serge and Vlady and the Bretons finally boarded the *Capitaine Paul Lemerle* for Mexico, Fry informed them that André Malraux was in Marseilles and asked if Malraux could join them for dinner. Bénédite recalled that Serge answered: 'Why not? I would rather like to tell him what I think of his collusion with the Stalinists in Spain.'[66] Serge, Fry and the Bénédites dined with Malraux on 19 March 1941 at Le Dantesque restaurant in Marseilles. Bénédite related that at the meal Malraux listened attentively to Serge's reproaches and agreed that 'many mistakes were made during the repression in Catalonia in May 1937'.†

On 25 March 1941 Serge finally left Europe aboard a ship that he described to Danny as 'A tin of sardines on which a fag-end has been stuck!'[67] On board with Serge were the Bretons, Claude Levi-Strauss, and the painter Wilfredo Lam.

From Marseilles to Martinique to Mexico: the visa hunt, the FBI and Serge

Serge was a difficult case. His membership in the CPSU and his work with the Comintern meant he would never get past the State Department's application of the reactionary Smith Act, preventing the issue of even a US transit visa.

Fry and Gold portray the work of the European Rescue Committee as exhaustive and exhausting. Serge admitted they were 'overwhelmed by work and the appeals from concentration camps, and in constant peril themselves . . . this was a shipwreck with too many castaways'.[68] Another picture emerges of the American Rescue Committee from the Macdonald papers. Dwight and Nancy Macdonald in New York worked continually on behalf of Serge and his family. They report a less than cordial reception from the American office of the Rescue Committee, made up of democrats and liberals more inclined to save their own than a well-known former Bolshevik such as Serge. While it is clear from the various sources that Varian Fry's

---

* Gold, *Crossroads Marseilles*, pp. 273–6. Serge also helped Mary Jayne cope with the 'evil-looking' food they received aboard, which she had trouble eating: Serge insisted 'that in prison one must eat anything and everything one can get down, and moreover one must hold it down. "You must keep up your strength. You never know how long you will be held."'

† Bénédite, *La Filière marseillaise*. This was the last time Serge saw Malraux, and it was not a pleasant evening. In 1947, Serge turned to Malraux for help in leaving Mexico, and Malraux published part of Serge's letter to him to make it appear Serge had become a Gaullist. Perhaps he was getting back at Serge for this evening of reproaches. Serge's letter to Malraux is excerpted in his FBI file.

group in Marseilles was doing everything humanly possible, the New York committee dragged their heels in tandem with the State Department. This outraged the Macdonalds, who dashed off letters to Freda Kirchwey,* editor of *The Nation*, Eugene Lyons, editor of *The American Mercury* and anyone else they could pressure to help. On 24 September 1940 Dwight Macdonald received a letter from the New York ERC saying they could no longer do anything on the case of 'Vladimir Kibaltschiche (Victor Serge)' [sic] because of 'Serge's previous Communist affiliations'.[69] Macdonald resubmitted the case and got letters of support from John Dewey, Eugene Lyons, Sidney Hook, Margaret Marshall (literary editor of *The Nation*), Meyer Schapiro, Reverend Frederick Reustle, Max Eastman,† and James Farrell. Macdonald insisted that Serge's anti-totalitarian views and writings, his years in Stalin's gulag and his great danger in France should be sufficient reason to give him immediate entry into the US.[70] The rest of the Macdonald correspondence is filled with more of the same: urgent cables to Serge, cheques sent, letters lost, bureaucratic barriers, endless paper trails.

The desperate need for immediate action was frustrated by the sluggish pace of bureaucratic committees,‡ whether they belonged to the State or to

---

* On 12 Sept. 1940 Dwight Macdonald wrote to Freda Kirchwey complaining about the New York ERC's 'scandalous laxness' in dealing with Serge's 'life and death' need for a visa, and suggested that perhaps the ERC was negligent because Serge was both 'a left wing anti-fascist and anti-Stalinist'. On 18 Sept. 1940 Kirchwey replied that the ERC was overworked, but was doing everything it could. She indicated that politics 'had nothing to do with the delay' in the ERC handling of the Serge case, but that Serge may be refused a US visa because he is 'a Communist', even if 'an anti-Stalinist Communist.' Macdonald Papers, Yale University Library.

† There is a separate correspondence between Serge and Eastman which found its way into the FBI files released to this author. The letter from Serge to Eastman, dateline Marseilles, 14 Aug. 1940, appeals to Eastman for material aid and help with a visa for Serge and Vlady. Serge stated that he was 'one of the last refugees of the Russian Revolution' and expressed the conviction that 'a better time is coming after the dark period we are in'. Item 2–257, declassified Victor Kibalchich alias Victor Serge memorandum for Mr Foxworth, signed P.J. Wacks, Washington, DC, 23 Sept. 1941.

‡ For example, the ERC in New York was provided with the necessary affidavits and papers by the Macdonalds, yet these documents needed to pass through various internal committees and subsequent delays before being passed on to the Solicitor General's office in an official visa request. Dwight Macdonald, in frustration, bypassed the committee and went to a lawyer who wrote to the Solicitor General directly. See letters of Sept. and Oct. 1940 in Yale collection of Macdonald papers. In 1941 the Macdonald's refugee committee merged with the International Rescue Association (IRA), which concentrated exclusively on left-wing refugees, while the Emergency Rescue Committee focused more on intellectuals and artists.

the resistance. Serge's case could only be considered when committees met, which was not daily, whereas every day he was in danger. Once the Mexican visa was finally procured, it came in the wrong name, made out to the pseudonym 'Serge', not 'Kibalchich' (a problem for Serge's son Vlady Kibalchich),* and listed Serge's nationality as 'Spanish' rather than 'Russian'. Worse, the visa could expire before it made it back and forth across the Atlantic to be corrected. In the meantime, the Macdonalds paid for Serge's passage from Lisbon, which meant Serge had to get to Portugal through Spain. Since the Franco government did not recognize Mexican documents,[71] Serge would require an exit permit from France plus Portuguese and Spanish transit visas. The paper chase became a labyrinth. Yet the Macdonald correspondence demonstrates their dogged persistence in getting through the tangled document web.† In the end, a transit visa was granted six days *after* Serge managed to board the *Paul Lemerle* for Mexico.

The visa application process, in the meantime, made Victor Serge known to American intelligence services. While seemingly endless red tape dangerously delayed his departure, Serge was being investigated.[72] His FBI file indicated that the US Army, Navy, FBI, State Department, Justice Department, and Military Intelligence had all been spying on Serge. The correspondence between Serge, the Macdonalds and official agencies in France[73] was photographed by the FBI and all the names mentioned were investigated, no matter if the correspondence was sent through the mail, by clipper, telephone or American Express, rendering the Macdonalds' efforts and Aesopian language fruitless.

Ironically, once the Macdonalds succeeded in getting Serge a temporary transit visa his bags were marked USA. The belongings got in, but not

---

* Vlady did not get a visa with Serge right away. Serge wrote to the Macdonalds in a letter of 16 Sept. 1940 that if Vlady could not accompany him, even though the situation was extremely dangerous, he would not go. Serge explained that Vlady at twenty was at a dangerous age to be in Europe because of the war. On the other hand, Jeannine, who was nearly six, was safe in a house in Pontarlier and could come later, but 'she is the only joy of my life' and Serge had not seen her in a year. Serge implored the Macdonalds to get a visa for Laurette, who could bring Jeannine with her. Macdonald Papers, Yale University Library. See also, Jeannine Kibalchich, 'Victor Serge, mi padre', published as 'My Father', in Susan Weissman (ed.), *The Ideas of Victor Serge: A Life as a Work of Art*, Glasgow, Critique Books, 1997.

† Dwight Macdonald wrote to Serge on 2 June 1941 that Serge could only get a US transit visa if he agreed to testify before the Dies Committee. The Dies Committee preceded the House Un-American Activities Committee (HUAC), which made an investigation in 1940 of Communist activity following the Stalin–Hitler pact. In order to get Serge to consider testifying, Macdonald mentioned that the Old Man had been willing to testify. (Trotsky had considered testifying to clear his name from the Stalinist slander.)

their owner! The Immigration Department confiscated Serge's two suit-cases from the SS *Boringen*, and the FBI assigned special agents to photograph the contents and translators to translate the documents 'which were written in foreign languages'.[74] The documents were then summarized for the attention of J. Edgar Hoover.

While Dwight and Nancy Macdonald were actively engaged on Serge's behalf in New York, the FBI was similarly busy paying translators to make Serge's words comprehensible to intelligence agents – in order to discover legal grounds to deny Serge a simple transit visa through the US.*

Meanwhile, Serge and Vlady sailed out of the nightmare to a new world and an uncertain future, in a cargo boat converted 'into an ersatz concentration-camp of the sea'.[75] Reflecting on the world he was leaving, Serge wrote that he was able to faintly grasp the essential:

> We have not lost after all . . . only for the moment. In the struggles of society we contributed a superabundance of consciousness and will, which greatly exceeded the forces at our command. We have spoken in the name of the working classes, whose aspirations and needs we have tried to make clear. But they most often . . . could not understand us, could not wake up to themselves . . . All of us have behind us a certain number of mistakes and failings, for creative thought of any kind can proceed only with hesitating, stumbling steps. The first of these is intolerance towards our own comrades . . . Our salvation lies in a tolerant intran-sigence which recognizes in each other the right to error, that most human of rights, and each other's right to *think otherwise* . . . We have caught a glimpse of man resolving his own history. And we have known how to win, we must never forget that . . . This experiment of ours will not be wasted. Beaten yes, but our spirit is strong. We are on the eve of *tomorrow*.[76]

Vlady remembered reading Bukharin and Preobrazhensky's *ABC of Communism* on deck, when Serge approached somewhat angrily. Serge grabbed the book, and said, 'This is not the time' and tossed the book into the sea. He added, 'You should be studying a Spanish primer, that's what's important now'.[77]

They docked first in Martinique, where Vlady recalled Vichy officials making the rounds, asking which passengers were Jewish. Serge's reply was, 'I do not have that honour'.[78] In a letter to Mary Jayne Gold, Serge described Martinique as French in form only, but more like 'a kind of Gestapo'. There they were jailed and robbed. When Serge complained that the role of the police should not be to rob travellers, they were threatened with deportation to the Sahara. Detained for weeks in a concentration camp at Fort de France, Serge wrote of the primitive conditions of their incarceration: no running water, charged twenty-five francs a day for 'indescribably nasty' food.[79]

---

* Serge never got the transit visa but the FBI's case on Serge remained open and he was subjected to intense scrutiny for the rest of his life.

The boat sailed from Martinique to Ciudad Trujillo, Dominican Republic, where Serge was visited by US Naval Attaché John A. Butler, Captain
of the US Marine Corps, who filed a confidential intelligence report.[80] The
summary discussion in the report contains the kinds of political inaccura-
cies that someone unfamiliar with the revolutionary movement would
make. After the agent left Vlady recalled Serge's laughing at the kinds of
questions put to him.[81]

Butler reported that Serge was a member of the 'Red General Staff'
(Serge's civil war rank, from his Soviet passport), that Serge was a 'socialist
democrat' who stated that 'Trotsky's Party disappeared with Trotsky's
death'. Serge was reported to have said that Stalin's government would be
replaced by a Popular Front government, that the 'Red General staff
emphasized bacterial warfare' and 'built more submarines than publicly
admitted'. The agent remarked that Serge was 'a brilliant, well-trained
observer, whose first thoughts are against Stalin, although he is for democracies'. Serge reportedly named Lucien Vogel as a 'Communist agent in the
US'. Vogel, according to the report, was one of the Communist agents who
were active in the Popular Front, who subsequently escaped to the US at
the time of the German invasion.[82]

Serge also told the agent that 'Without doubt Krivitsky was killed by
the OGPU', and that Alexander Barmine and Boris Nicolaevsky could both
advise on Russian questions.* Finally agent Butler admitted that Serge was
waiting in the Dominican Republic for a transit visa through Cuba en route
to Mexico. The Macdonalds were still trying to get Serge temporary transit
to New York, the safest way from the Dominican Republic to Mexico.†

In the tropical August sun at Ciudad Trujillo, Serge set to work. He
completed *Hitler contra Stalin* in four weeks for a Mexican public, and complained he could not sleep for worry about the nightmare sweeping over

---

* This is not the indiscretion it appears to be, as both Barmine and Nicolaevsky
  had already themselves been contacted by American intelligence. Barmine went
  on to work for the CIA (as an advisor on Soviet affairs) after he served in the
  American army in World War II, and Nicolaevsky accompanied American
  Intelligence to Germany in 1945 to retrieve his stolen archive.
† The correspondence with Dwight and Nancy Macdonald throughout this ordeal
  is a testament to their generosity and solidarity. They sustained a frustrating
  and expensive campaign to assure Serge and other refugees safe passage out of
  Nazi Europe and never allowed pessimism to take hold. Nancy Macdonald's
  letters are a delightful mixture of political astuteness and American innocence,
  encouraging and always sympathetic. Serge and Vlady were penniless, hungry,
  anxious for their safety and worried sick about Laurette, Jeannine, and their
  many friends still in Europe. While Nancy was remarkably efficient in arranging their support and defence, sending money and passage as needed, her letters
  intersperse political discussion with attending to her son's tonsillitis, and stories
  of weekends spent on Long Island playing piano, swimming and going to clam-
  bakes.

Russia. The book was subtitled *La fase decisiva de la guerra mundial* and was dedicated to the combatants and builders of the Mexican revolution. Ediciones Quetzal, the small house that brought it out, was ruined after publishing such an uncompromising anti-Stalinist and anti-capitalist analysis of World War II.

Macdonald and Serge's correspondence also had a theoretical dimension, on issues such as the economic nature of fascism. By 1941 Macdonald took the 'unpopular' view that fascism was 'decisively different, economically, from capitalism' and required 'wholesale revisions of hitherto blindly accepted' theory.* Serge disagreed, pointing to Daniel Guérin's analysis, however simplified, which shows how 'big capital gives birth to fascism, which creates an economy that finally is turned over to big capital – itself a lovely straight jacket'.[83] Serge concluded that war resulted because of the bankruptcy of German capitalism and the weakness of German socialism.

Five months after leaving Europe, Serge finally received a letter from Mary Jayne Gold. In his reply[84] Serge described his situation as still 'complicated and dangerous': his travel visa had expired, leaving him with no documents to go to Mexico. The State Department 'had stabbed the anti-fascist emigration in the back', so that only the pro-fascists with their dollars could travel to the Americas. Serge wrote that the committees were sleeping, satisfied with their work. His American transit visa was granted but then denied.

Dismayed by the American inaction with the refugees, Serge told Mary Jayne he was surprised by how soon the war had turned into a Nazi–Soviet conflict. This meant that the Nazis could not afford to wait until the end of winter to 'flatten' Russia. Serge believed the Russians could defeat the Nazis because 'the Russians still have energy in reserve' but he was worried by Hoover's speech following the Nazi invasion of the USSR, which revealed the 'reactionary spirit' of the Americans and their allies who 'seemed to be more afraid of a new Europe than a Nazi Europe'.

Serge described to Mary Jayne Gold how he and Vlady adapted themselves to the hot sun in Ciudad Trujillo by working from dawn to lunch – Serge writing, and Vlady drawing 'spectacularly'. Serge told Mary Jayne that his 'typewriter doesn't rest', nor did he, kept up at nights with anxious preoccupation for Laurette, Jeannine, and his comrades left behind in the gulag. Serge confided that he was uncomfortable about his total dependence on the Macdonalds for survival, and that he hated the single life without Laurette, complaining that the Mexican comrades did not seem to pay attention to how important it was for a couple to be together. Serge had

---

* Macdonald to Serge, 14 June 1941, Macdonald Archive, Yale University. Macdonald's view had obviously changed since 1938, when he wrote the introduction to Daniel Guérin's book, *Fascism and Big Business* (New York, Pioneer, 1939), applying the analysis of the book to the American scene in 1938.

even suggested at one point to Nancy Macdonald that if the visas for Laurette and Jeannine did not come together, that Laurette should come first, then Jeannine with Laurette's son René.*

It took Serge and Vlady six harrowing months to get from Marseilles to Mexico. They were detained in Martinique, suffered tropical heat and insecurity in the Dominican Republic, were denounced and turned away in Haiti, and detained again in Cuba at the Tescornia concentration camp. For Serge, detention was a way of life. Vlady remembered that in Tescornia Serge could easily spot which refugees were 'our own people' and told Vlady to offer them cigarettes. The Macdonalds got Freda Kirchwey of *The Nation* to cable Cuban immigration, vouching for the anti-fascist integrity of both Serge and Vlady, to no avail. In the end they were bailed out by a Salvadoran political activist who had read Serge's poems in French.[85]

On 4 September 1941 Serge and Vlady finally arrived in Mexico, the last exile. Flying for the first time, Serge reflected on the 'new vision of the world'[86] flight afforded. It was appropriate that his new life in a new world begin with a new method of transport. Yet he could not help note that it was reserved for the 'unenthusiastic rich' and was also a machine of death and destruction.

---

* Serge to Nancy and Dwight Macdonald, 7 June 1941. Nancy Macdonald replied on 12 June 1941 that the visas for Laurette, Jeannine and René had come through. Laurette's son René, in fact, never made the journey, as the war made it too dangerous for Laurette to collect him in Italy. He was left in Italy and raised by his grandmother. He finally came to Mexico as an adult, full of hostility for his mother for having 'abandoned him'. Interviews with Jeannine Kibalchich, Mexico, Sept. 1990, and Aug. 1996.

8

From Mexico, whither the USSR, the world?

In Mexico Serge wrote in profusion, considered new ideas and new directions, became involved politically with the group Socialismo y Libertad, which first published *Analysis*, and then *Mundo*. Socialismo y Libertad was a diverse collection of exiles from Russia, France, Spain and Germany, each bringing their own experiences, traditions and defeats. Serge and Vlady became political antagonists in this group, which later split due to internal divisions.*

The GPU's (NKVD)† persecution escalated from vicious slander of Serge to an imminent threat against his life.[1] After NKVD and Communist Party thugs physically attacked Serge and the others, Serge, Pivert, Gorkín and Regler wrote a book to publicize their situation, and thus help protect themselves. Appended to their book, *La GPU prepara un nuevo crimen!* is a remarkable collection of letters of solidarity signed by hundreds of intellectuals.‡ In

---

* According to Vlady, the antagonism was primarily the immature rebellion of a son trying to carve his own path against the wisdom and experience of his father (interview, Aug. 1990). The other divisive element in the exile group was Jean Malaquais, the French novelist, who incorporated this experience into his novel *World Without Visa*, New York, Doubleday, 1948.

† The Soviet secret police was still popularly known as the GPU, though its name changed to NKVD in 1934.

‡ The last section of the book was filled with documents demonstrating the solidarity that individuals and organizations expressed with these exiled revolutionaries. The American progressive press, including *The Nation*, *Partisan Review*, *The Militant*, *The New Leader*, and *The Call* all came to their support. Norman Thomas dedicated his half-hour radio programme to them, the Israeli newspapers of New York assumed their defence, as did many other newspapers and magazines, including *The New York Times*. Only the *Daily Worker* and *New Masses*, both Communist organs, attacked them. Hundreds of prominent American intellectuals addressed a letter to President Avila Camacho which was included in *La GPU prepara un nuevo crimen!* (pp. 54–7). Signatories to the appeal

the initial statement Serge and his comrades answered charges that they were 'Trotskyites'. They declared that while they admired the great revolutionary,[2] none of them, except Serge, had ever belonged to the Trotskyist movement. Each of them had separated from Trotsky, they wrote, over questions of philosophy, history and organization.

While Gorkín, Pivert and Regler refuted the charges by denying their links with Trotskyism, Serge instead stressed his record of obstinate resistance to lies, falsehoods and despotism, from Petrograd to Orenburg to Rheims to Mexico and the terrible consequences he suffered in the form of years of captivity. He ended on a hopeful note, declaring, 'I continue in the service of mankind, liberty, and the Russian Revolution which fights once more for the liberty of the world. I firmly hope that it will be renewed and liberated from totalitarianism, with the right to a great future.'[3]

In this final exile, Serge was very poor, and 'indescribably lonely'.[4] In an entry in his personal diary, Serge lamented his political and literary isolation, writing 'for the drawer at over fifty', aware that the present dark world situation might outlast his lifetime. He noted that in 'this free land of America' he was writing as the Russians did around 1930, and that he had 'reached the stage of asking myself if my name alone will be an obstacle to publication'.[5] While his novels and *Memoirs* (except for *The Long Dusk*) did not see publication before his death, Serge did publish much of his journalism in small reviews in the US and France. Nevertheless, many worthwhile pieces remain in Serge's archive which have never been published.

In the US Serge was read and promoted by Dwight Macdonald and his journal, *Politics*, as well as *Partisan Review*, and by Daniel Bell and David Dallin* at the *New Leader*, for which Serge was the Mexican correspondent. He was also listed as an international contributor to *Modern Review*, a journal largely financed by the International Ladies Garment Workers' Union. His articles also appeared in the *New International*, especially after Max Shachtman's Workers' Party took it over in the 1940 split in the American Socialist Workers' Party. The *New International* printed excerpts of Serge's *Memoirs*, *Year One*, and seven excerpts from his diary, or *Vieux Carnets*.[6] Serge was also published in *Socialist Call*, *Horizons*, *España Libre* (New York), and in Mexico in *Analysis*, *Mundo*, *Rumbo*, *La Nación*, *Excelsior*, *El Informador*, and others. In Cuba Serge was the subject of a long article in *Bohemia*.[7] Serge also carried on a rich correspondence with the Macdonalds, Sidney Hook, William Phillips and others, including George

---

included the Governor of the State of California, and from Great Britain, three Labour ministers, three independent ministers, and many well-known writers, trade unionists, and the leadership of the Independent Labour Party.

* David Dallin, leading Menshevik and author of numerous books on the USSR, including *The Real Soviet Russia* (New Haven, Yale University Press, 1944) and with Boris Nicolaevsky, *Forced Labor in Soviet Russia* (New Haven, Yale University Press, 1947), married to Lola Dallin.

Orwell, who tried to get Serge's *Memoirs* published with Secker and Warburg.*

Serge wrote about varied themes, analysing the current situation, expressing interest in psychology and anthropology, and concern for the prospects of struggle for genuine socialism. In Mexico, Serge's wife passionately embraced early Mexican culture, Serge formed a friendship with the German psychologist Herbert Lenhof, and he engaged in rich discussions among European revolutionary exiles.

The Mexican group Socialismo y Libertad wrote another book together which was the product of their discussions on the nature of the present period. The book was written throughout 1942 and 1943, and published in January 1944 as *Los Problemas del socialismo en nuestro tiempo*, by Serge, Gorkín, Pivert and Paul Chevalier.[8] Serge's contribution, 'War of Social Transformation'[9] outlined his position on the character of World War II, which he saw as fundamentally different from World War I. Serge's conception of the global conflict was that it was a war taking place in a transitional epoch, and would usher in new social formations which would be characterized by a tendency toward totalitarian collectivist command economies.

Serge described the existence of a duality of power in Germany between the capitalist class and the Nazi bureaucracy. Citing Hilferding's 1910 work on the relationship between economic and political power and Franz Neumann's study of Nazi Germany as 'totalitarian monopoly capitalism', Serge wrote that he thought James Burnham's and Dwight Macdonald's newer and more expressive formulation of 'bureaucratic collectivism' better described this social formation. To emphasize his point, Serge quoted something Trotsky wrote in 1939, a year before his death:

> The Soviet regime, fascism, Nazism, and the New Deal undeniably share common traits determined in the last instance by the collectivist tendencies of the modern economy . . . As a consequence of the exhaustion of the working class, these tendencies take on the form of bureaucratic collectivism.[10]

Serge wrote widely on this issue: the same ideas and even the same citations permeate his unpublished essays, his review articles and his diary entries.

The Mexican political group enlarged their contacts and continued their discussions of the character of the world throughout 1944. They tried to hammer out a new manifesto, which Serge thought both inappropriate and

---

* Serge was so poor that he had only one copy of the *Memoirs*, which he was naturally reluctant to trust to the overseas post. Much of his correspondence with Orwell deals with how Serge could safely get his copy to Orwell. See George Orwell to Dwight Macdonald, London, 4 April 1945. Dwight Macdonald was similarly attempting to find an American publisher for the *Memoirs*. This did not happen until Oxford University Press published Peter Sedgwick's translation in 1963.

imperious. In his diary entry of 13 September 1944, Serge severely criticized the document, which he indicated was formulated by Marceau Pivert,
Enrique Gironella and 'W.S.' Serge tended to question every thesis put
forward by these independent socialists, which he considered nothing but
'old stock phrases'.[11] His frustration was evident, as Serge was grappling
with new uncertainties while they were repeating old formulae.

The Trotskyists in their various organizations, following the Old Man's
theoretical lead, had forecast that Stalin would not survive World War II,
that the war would give way to a new revolutionary upsurge. As it turned
out, Stalin defeated Hitler and embarked on a new enslavement of returning soldiers, and a vast, forced reconstruction programme. In Western
Europe, the revolutionary upsurge failed to gather sufficient force and was
successfully 'contained'. The new conjuncture did not conform to their preconceptions, nor to Trotsky's predictions. With Trotsky's death, the Trotskyists were bereft of his authoritative theoretical pre-eminence. As Serge
had said, the Trotskyists found it difficult to think outside Trotsky's head,
valiant though they were as militants. Many prewar activists left politics
after the war, discouraged by political differences, or failed realizations.

The anti-Stalinist Left organizations Serge had wanted to group together
in International Committees suffered similarly. Nor was Serge's group in
Mexico, Socialismo y Libertad, immune to internal division and isolation
from real political struggle. Much of what Serge wrote about the Fourth
International turned out to be equally true of other non-Stalinist groups,
including syndicalists, libertarian socialists, left Mensheviks, and Trotskyists. Political militants in the forties were hampered not just by the war, but
also by the failure of their predictions about the Soviet Union. Stalinism survived, and fascism inflicted horrible wounds on the working class. Working
alone, Serge grappled with these questions in a creative political way.

Stalinism, the emergence of the technocracy and 'totalitarian collectivism'

Serge's writings in this last period revealed his fresh thinking, and active,
agile mind. He erred, mistaking tendencies for trajectories, but nonetheless
went farther than Trotsky had, without abandoning socialism like so many
others whose 'god had failed'. Regarding socialists who had not abandoned
Marxism, Serge bemoaned the fact that most seemed to view history
through a timeworn framework, as if it were still 1917 or even 1871.[12]

For Serge the struggle was no longer simply between capitalism and
socialism. Stalinism itself was now an obstacle to socialism. In response to
reading an Independent Labour Party bulletin from England, Serge wrote
in his diary that there are no longer just two adversaries facing each other,
revolution and reaction. Now there are three: conservatism, socialism and
Stalinist totalitarianism, locked in mortal conflict.[13] Presciently, Serge
wrote in 1944: 'I'm inclined to think that the fate of Europe will not be

decided until Stalinist totalitarianism is restricted or destroyed by the new conflicts which of necessity it brings forth.'[14]

Stalinism exerted a negative influence on all current struggles. Serge insisted, for example, that the colonial revolution had been limited by the Kremlin to an anti-imperialist struggle rather than one for socialism. This view was unpopular on the left, a point reiterated by Laurette Séjourné.[15] She said Serge did not support independence in India, nor did he support Ho Chi Minh. In *Partisan Review*, *La Wallonie*, and *La Révolution prolétari-enne* Serge wrote that the struggle for socialism remained in Europe, that national liberation struggles would lead to an extension of Soviet totalitar-ianism, ultimately anti-socialist and anti-human.

Having said that, Serge noted in a later diary entry that Hilferding saw better than Trotsky the present conflict from the point of view of the incredible power of the totalitarian state:

> This power is so great that the USSR is in a position to dominate, channel, crush the revolutionary movements of Western Europe, Asia and to a certain extent Latin America. She can nip in the bud the ones that would embarrass her and support, promote, arm effectively the others. LT's proposition [that the salva-tion of the Russian Revolution would come from the revolutionary transforma-tions in Western Europe, the contagiousness of which the totalitarian Russian apparatus would not be able to resist] could only come true if the Russian total-itarian state were to weaken, spent from inside by extraordinary efforts.[16]

In the same vein, Serge criticized Dwight Macdonald's ingenuousness in *Politics* for imagining the Communist parties could be reformed.[17] Serge thought Macdonald lived in too free a country to understand! The new type of leader who would emerge was the type of Mao and Tito, 'cynical and *con-vinced*, who will be "revolutionary" or counter-revolutionary – or both at the same time – according to the orders they receive and capable of a turn-about from one day to the next'.[18] In fact, Serge wrote that when Mao Tse-tung was in Moscow in 1926–27, he 'sympathized deeply with the Opposition, but he ended up by adopting the cynically pragmatic formula: Who can give us arms and money?'*

Serge was quite clear on the nature of the Communist parties, but he did not have a viable organizational strategy. In a conversation with Narciso Molins, Serge said the worst thing a genuine socialist Left could do would be to remain a tiny sect. Far better, wrote Serge, to enter the old Socialist parties, where democratic practices would make it possible to have some influence. Molins was sceptical of the 'old opportunists' who 'would calmly

---

* Serge, *Politics*, Feb. 1945, p. 62. Serge was wrong about Mao being in Moscow in this period. This journal of politics and popular culture was edited by Dwight Macdonald after he left *Partisan Review* on his journey from Trotskyism to anar-chism. The journal lasted from 1944 to 1949.

let us be murdered by the Stalinists'.[19] Serge did not disagree, but had no other prescription. Yet in 1947 Serge would write in *Partisan Review* that 'the old reformism is no less outmoded than insurrection. Socialist action is by definition, neither exceptionally timid nor exceptionally violent, but it seems that it has to be both transformer and liberator, or else disintegrate'.[20] In the same article, Serge stressed that Stalinism and social democracy were inching toward each other, and that the blindness of the social democrats towards 'this darkest of despotisms' was unforgivable ('They have not seen the Kazakh die of famine'). In an evident clarity of purpose that Serge had not demonstrated in his conversation with Narciso Molins, Serge stated, 'If socialism . . . does not proclaim itself as the Party of human dignity, obviously it will only be crushed between the reactionaries and the totalitarians'.[21] Now more than ever, Serge told the readers of *Politics*, we must reconstruct 'a conscious and energetic socialist movement that will not allow itself to be manipulated by the CP'.[22]

Stalin's barbarity was matched if not outdone by Hitler's extermination of the Jews. Serge was horrified by the Nazi atrocity, deciding this made World War II more than simply an imperialist war. The anti-Semitism unleashed by the war gave it a peculiar character. Serge wrote in his diary on 12 November 1944 that the unspeakable horror of the Nazi attempt to annihilate the Jews, with so little opposition even from Jews abroad, was beyond comprehension. Serge declared 'I am lost' when trying to understand – the Nazis reversed the trend of human evolution* and destroyed the achievements of thousands of years of history. It is no wonder that in a conversation with an unnamed Polish socialist in December 1944 Serge agreed that 'since dignity and hope alone remain to be saved, we are advocates of absolute uncompromisingness'.[23]

Serge's intransigence and commitment to socialist democracy were demonstrated in the numerous essays he left unpublished in Mexico. Contemplating the scenarios for the future and seeing hope for vast socialist movements in Europe, Serge wrote:

> Socialism has only been able to grow within bourgeois democracy (of which it was to a large extent the creator). If by unawareness, lack of educated, energetic leaders, various corruptibilities, it is taken in tow by 'revolutionary' Stalinism (revolutionary, insofar as the planned economy still is in comparison with traditional capitalism – and it's a slight extent, considering the evolution of the whole of capitalism towards planning-control-collectivisation), it abdicates and succumbs, inevitably crushed and disgraced. Its only chance of life and victory is in intransigence vis-à-vis Stalinist totalitarianism, by the upholding of beliefs in democracy and humanism (excluding controlled thought) and vis-à-vis capitalist conservatism, in the fight for the restoration of the traditional democratic liberties, become revolutionary.[24]

---

* The evolution from animality to humanism.

This passage contains the germ of what preoccupied Serge for the short remainder of his life. He was able to detect the germ but not able to see what organism would grow from it. In the end, Serge left hundreds of essays, all of which deserve publication. His thoughts expressed throughout were broadly similar:* the USSR was neither capitalist nor socialist;[25] the regime operated out of fear and in permanent conflict with its own people, using a mighty totalitarian state machine against them; the new world order was one which would change the social structure of the world. Serge perceptively noted the postwar nationalizations were accommodations to the reality of the socialist revolution and its consequences, however degraded. Serge saw the collectivization of production as the foundation of a new social structure, but he understood that the concentrated control of production could encourage totalitarianism. At the same time, Serge noted that the poverty of traditional socialist thought collided with the immense revolutionary crisis of the modern world, which forcefully put socialism on the agenda.[26]

Serge's thinking about the world during and immediately after the war is intimately connected to his analysis of the character of Stalinism. In an essay 'L'URSS a-t-elle un régime socialiste?'[27] Serge stated that few socialist theorists had the time to develop their theoretical vision of the future, and were 'unable to see beyond the limited horizons of the concrete present'.†

In this essay Serge came very close to adopting a bureaucratic collectivist analysis of the USSR,‡ a 'third solution' which was neither capitalist nor socialist but was defined by 'bureaucratic planning based on the obliteration, degradation or abolition of private property'. Serge was influenced by Franz Neumann's *Behemoth*,§ which defined the social structure of Nazi

---

* In fact, Serge was often repetitive, using the same examples and the same phrases.

† Nor did theorists integrate their vision of the future into the living philosophy of the socialist movement.

‡ The bureaucratic collectivist analysis, best put forward by the Italian Bruno Rizzi and the American Max Shachtman, sees Stalinism as representing a new social order that is neither socialist nor capitalist, and constitutes a unique form of class exploitation and oppression. The new ruling class, in this theory, derives its power not from ownership of the means of production, but 'ownership' of the state which rules the economy through the Communist Party. This form of totalitarian political power cannot concede any form of popular political control, even as exists under capitalism where the roots of social power lie in property ownership. See Max Shachtman, *The Bureaucratic Revolution: The Rise of the Stalinist State*, New York, The Donald Press, 1962, and Bruno Rizzi, *The Bureaucratization of the World*, 1939, first English edition introduced by Adam Westoby, New York, The Free Press, 1985.

§ Franz Neumann, *Behemoth: The Structure and Practice of National Socialism 1933–1944*, Oxford, Oxford University Press, 1942, 1944. Franz Neumann, a member of the Frankfurt School, wrote this classic account of Nazi Germany in 1944. Neumann identifies the economic and political roots of totalitarianism in

Germany, and was struck by its similarities to Stalinism. James Burnham, Dwight Macdonald and Sidney Hook also reached the conclusion that the totalitarian states bore great resemblance. Trotsky too, following Marx, wrote (in August 1939) of the collectivist tendencies of the modern economy.

Serge took Trotsky's intuitive glimpse further and showed how, although Nazism was based on capital and supported by capital, the source of privileges in Nazi society depended more on compliance with the political regime than ownership of the means of production.* Serge was struggling here to define the future based on present tendencies. *Laissez-faire* would be limited by controls that in practice would abolish the free market. The economic collectivism he thought was synonymous with socialism when he was young now represented a new and terrible form of exploitation. This collectivism had no connection to the goals of socialism, 'the realization of a rational economy and the liberation of mankind, the realization of a human destiny that achieves a new dignity'.[28] Instead it actually worsened the human condition and was, consequently, anti-socialist.

Serge examined the Soviet Union in the light of this new world form. While recognizing new distinct social categories in the USSR, Serge did not want to enter into the discussion of whether they should be called 'classes, castes, social layers or something else'.[29] This distinguishes him from both orthodox Trotskyist analysis and the new class analysts of the state capitalist or bureaucratic collectivist tendencies. Serge examined instead what he called the 'facts' of Soviet social structure, in which as much as 15 per cent of the population comprised a penal workforce, enslaved, exploited and constantly renewed (the 'special reserve of labour'), 7 per cent of the Soviet social hierarchy corresponded to the privileged layers, and the remaining 78 per cent were exploited, impoverished workers.[30]

Soviet totalitarianism, according to Serge, was established from 1936 to 1938 through a bloody counter-revolution. The experience of Stalinism proved that the abolition of private property, collectivization and 'planning' could lead to a powerful, terrorist economic machinery and the most

---

industrial capitalism, while paying attention to the specific historical conditions of Germany. He noted that 'National Socialism is out to create a uniformly sadomasochistic character, a type of man determined by his isolation and insignificance, who is driven by this very fact into a collective body.' The atomization of the working class, the suspension of legal and democratic norms and the centrality of anti-Semitism are all understood by Neumann as the outcome of the centralization of capital.

* Serge, 'L'URSS a-t-elle un régime socialiste?', six pages, Mexico 1946, Serge archive, Mexico, p. 2. In fact, Serge went way out on a limb in July 1943, in a letter sent to the editor of *Mundo*, rhetorically titled 'Es capitalista la economía Nazi?' a question he danced around without directly answering. Serge to Camarade directeur de *Mundo*, July 1943, Serge archive, Mexico.

inhumane anti-socialism. In an unpublished fragment Serge left behind in Mexico, he characterized the USSR as a 'bureaucratic totalitarian state' and, reaffirming the programme of the Left Opposition, insisted that had 'democratic planning' as opposed to 'Stalinist planning' been in place industrialization would have 'been slower but less exhausting and more fertile'.[31]

In a longer essay, 'Economie dirigée et démocratie'[32] Serge again characterized the Soviet totalitarian state as one under siege, with a directed (or command) economy, rationing, state control over labour, a monopoly of power, thought control, and terror. Serge traced the administration of the economy to the 'war time socialism' introduced in the capitalist economies during World War I, refined in the Soviet state with a one-Party system, which Serge wrote, was no longer a political Party but a bureaucratic-military apparatus.[33] While in the Soviet case the aim was socialist and in the fascist anti-socialist, Serge wrote they both accomplished 'collectivization and planification of production within a national framework . . . which is autarchic'.[34]

Serge here stressed the essential difference between Stalinism and Nazism. The former rested on the annihilation of the old privileged classes, the collectivization of production and a new governing class of parvenus from the working class that rules in contradiction with itself because it must preserve the psychological tradition of socialism. The Nazi regime relied on capital for its creation and support, resulting in a limited kind of dual power between the trusts and the Party bureaucracy. This duality made the Nazi regime less homogeneous, according to Serge.

Serge thought the social transformations of Europe in the coming postwar world would include federations like the United States rather than traditional nineteenth-century nation states; that the reconstruction would require continent-wide planification. Serge thought the new Europe would be totalitarian and fascistic.

As for the USSR, Serge described its continued anti-socialist course without even conceding a minimum of democratic reform. Brute force and the 'complete absence of ideology . . . translates simply as *fear of thought and ideas*'.[35] Under these conditions, Serge wrote, neither Soviets nor Bolsheviks nor Bolshevik parties could reemerge. He continued: 'The Soviet experience shows us [in the implementation of the five year plans] what horrible waste, what involuntary sabotage and what unnamed sufferings the totalitarian regime imposed on the people in their own name.'[36]

What Serge turned to here and in three other unpublished essays was the increased importance and privilege of the administrators and functionaries and technicians in the controlled economies. Examining the nature of *collectivisation planifiée* Serge feared the creation of a technocracy to run the planning commissions would become the real governing power and replace the state. The problem for the working class would then be how to control the technocrats. Serge is here the precursor of the kind of thinking exemplified by the East Europeans Georgy Konrad and Ivan Szelenyi, who identified the class power of the intelligentsia, whose teleological knowledge of production put them in a position of power in Soviet-type societies.[37]

Serge wrote that this form of economic organization created a passive obedience, horror of initiative and responsibility, individual massive resistance, involuntary sabotage, and enormous waste. The directed economy substitutes a minimal economic security for the insecurity of economic liberty. But freedom from unemployment is not real liberation unless there is also freedom of opinion. 'If instead of fearing unemployment and hunger one has now to fear repression for one's thoughts, then a new captivity has emerged, maybe heavier and more regressive than the old.'[38]

Serge wrote in an earlier article published in *Partisan Review*, 'What Is Fascism?', that he found broad agreement with James Burnham on the role of the managers,* that

> The next European revolution will be fought on the terrain of planned economy – no longer for or against strangled capitalism . . . but over the question of management – for whom? To whose benefit? . . . The category of managers will tend to crystallize into a class and to monopolize power.[39]

Thus Serge thought that Burnham's theory was not incompatible with Marxism and that

> Capitalist economy is going under, yielding to new types of transitional planned economies: capitalism is so hopeless that we see the counter-revolutions it incited now forced to strangle their begetter, as in Germany and Italy and tomorrow elsewhere perhaps under other forms. But this does not do away with the problem of socialism. It remains in the very heart of the planned economies, because of the clash of interests (material and immaterial) between the rulers and the masses. Nor should we neglect the factors of psychology and tradition. From this standpoint, the struggle bears quite different aspects, according to whether the new managerial class is the product of an anti-working class and anti-Marxist counter-revolution, respectful (in theory) of private property, wedded to the principles of authority and hierarchy, as is the case in Germany and Italy – or whether it is a class of usurpers who still invoke an ideology and tradition conflicting with its usurpation and standing for the democracy of work and the complete liberation of man. I emphasize this in order to emphasize that even from the viewpoint of the 'managerial revolution' deep antagonisms exist between Nazism and Stalinism. In every case, finally, when confronted with a planned economy, we should pose the question: 'Planned by whom?

---

* Though the first pages of this essay are a sustained attack on Burnham's abandonment of the Marxist method, his vulgar Marxism, and his facile equation of Bolshevism and Stalinism. His critique of Burnham's politics continued in another unpublished essay in the Mexico Archives called 'Lenin's Heir?' and in a letter to Sidney Hook in 1943.

Planned for whom? Planned for what end?' It is on this front that socialists will fight in the future, side by side with the masses.[40]

Though Serge was sometimes ambiguous in his use of the term 'planned economy', the above passage makes it clear that he did not consider it Marxist planning, but for want of a better word often settled on 'planning'. Yet the questions he asked, 'planning for whom, by whom?' demonstrated that for Serge the essential issue was that of democratic self-organization versus totalitarian control.

As for the role of the technocrats or managers, Serge was not the first to draw attention to the growth of this group.* Serge noticed that this stratum ran across social formations and concluded, at least partially, that there was a form of convergence, or that one social formation would result. This did not turn out to be the case. Both Burnham and Serge perceived that the world was in transition from capitalism and that the transition had transitional forms. Serge also pointed out the role that the first socialist revolution played in influencing this transition.

The first socialist revolution influenced the modern development of the world, both capitalist and non-capitalist. In the absence of workers' democracy in the Soviet Union, administrators make the deliberate decisions that direct the economy, while in the advanced capitalist world the administrator-managers also increase their controlling role in production. If one looks at the immediate postwar world as the beginning of a standoff between capitalism and socialism, that is between capitalists and workers, a lacuna leading somewhere as yet undetermined – then Serge's essays from this period appear all the more farsighted, even though he could not see how it would end. Rather than seeing the increasing role of managers and controllers of production as a product of the failure of socialism, he saw these managerial forms as steps on a necessary ladder.

While Serge could note the tendencies, he died just as the Cold War was beginning and so was not able to see the actual contours of the postwar world. The world was not going collectivist, fascism remained capitalist though in a desperate form, and postwar capitalism remained capitalism, though it also adopted new forms.† In much of Serge's work there is a fundamentally correct perception which is very suggestive, without being sufficiently penetrative. These insights also show Serge to be miles ahead of

---

* Serge's observation that managers gradually play a greater role in capitalist production was noted by Marx, who spoke of 'the joint stock firm making the capitalist otiose'.

† Serge, on the other hand, wrote to the editors of *Partisan Review* that it was wrong to call fascism a 'new order' since there was 'nothing new in despotism . . . Nazism brings an order new only in relation to capitalism, made up of old things that we hate, a really phenomenal retrogression, war being the oldest thing in the world.' *Partisan Review*, Sept.–Oct. 1941, p. 422.

his cohorts, a thinker of the present time grappling with real problems instead of old postulates.*

Serge was certain socialism would ultimately win, and that it would come first to Europe, because Stalinism was inherently a weak system, even though he considered it more powerful and more dangerous than capitalism. Stalinism became more and more dangerous because of its weakness and, Serge wrote, because of the resistance of the working class, which would ultimately have the last word.

In an undated and unpublished essay from Mexico, Serge explored the lacuna mentioned above, in which the class struggle continues amidst a decomposing capitalism – because of the influence of the Russian Revolution – all the while making an enormous effort to break the resistance of the working class. This essay repeats many of the tendencies Serge discussed elsewhere, but succinctly. He saw the defeats of the working class in Germany and Spain as a sign of the decline of the working class, because of Stalinism and unemployment due to the rationalization of production. Serge wrote that the war was ultimately between totalitarian collectivism and the possibility of historically conscious collectivism. If the former wins then it is the end of socialism for a whole era – but Serge did not think it would win.[41]

In this unpublished essay Serge again wrote of the tendency in modern capitalism toward a planned collectivization which marked the end of 'liberal' free-market capitalism. The collectivization of production would come into conflict with the privileges of the owning minorities, and would give rise to new privileged minorities – the administrators and technicians – who the big capitalists would seek to integrate. In the new collectivism, the planning commissions would wield enormous power, like the old capitalist/financial oligarchies of earlier capitalism. There would also be enormous tension in the 'directed economy' between the privileged minorities, who would resort to totalitarian methods to repress the masses, and the need for freedom for scientific investigation – essential for technical progress – and freedom of criticism and freedom of initiative for the workers, essential for efficiently functioning factories. Thus Serge saw industrial democracy as indispensable to the collectivization of production. Finally, Serge asserted that the class struggle will continue and socialism will be the natural and perfect culmination of these collectivist societies.

These last essays written from Serge's lonely Mexican exile show how much the Soviet Union continued to occupy centre stage in Serge's thinking, and how deeply affected he was by the turbulent events in Europe

---

* In this sense Serge went farther than Trotsky, who was clearly capable and should have begun to consider these problems, but was still too wedded to defending the nationalized property forms in the Soviet Union to actually analyse the content of these property forms.

before and during the war. He was haunted by the twin fears of the spread of totalitarian collectivism and the possibility of a new war, which he thought Stalin was preparing, and worried that Stalin might use nuclear weapons. This preoccupation weighed heavily upon Serge who thought the Soviet Union was inherently unstable and weak, with Stalin ruling through brute force alone. He came to believe that change had to come from within, but this was nearly impossible to accomplish.

In 1945 Serge wrote an article in English which stated that the democratic aspirations of the Soviet workers must be encouraged from the outside. He even laid out a programme for the 'Great Soviet reform' which he saw as the only guarantee against a new war. Serge was troubled by his vision of totalitarian collectivisms strangling human rights on a world scale and understood that only class struggle and mass action could counteract this perspective, the very actions most difficult to undertake in a totalitarian society. This article is uncharacteristic for Serge, because it seems to promote a democracy very similar to bourgeois democracy.*

Serge struggled with these questions as a Marxist with the experience of Stalinism foremost in his mind, and having just gone through fascism. The mature Serge was no less Marxist for going beyond the orthodoxies, nor had he reverted to anarchism, moralism, centrism or Menshevism. He was constantly developing, incorporating new ideas: in 1943, he wrote to Dwight Macdonald that modern psychology must be integrated with Marxism, which would be enriched by this body of knowledge. After all, he told Macdonald, 'Man is a conscious animal!'[42] In May 1947, Serge published an article 'Socialism and Psychology', in which he argued forcefully that 'to meet the exigencies of our day, socialism must enrich itself with the newly-acquired knowledge of the motivating factors determining human conduct'.†

Serge, then, was engaged in a renewal of Marxist thought, in which no shibboleth was too sacred to leave unscrutinized. Even the revolution of 1917, which Serge defended just as strongly as he defended its early years, the time of Lenin, was worthy of new reflection. Serge wrote that thirty years later one could not expect 1917 to repeat itself in a transformed global situation with new actors on the scene. There was still much to learn

---

* The lack of precision may have been due to Serge's English. Unpublished MS, 'On the Russian Problem' 1945, eight pages, Serge archives, Mexico.

† Serge, 'Socialism and Psychology', in *Modern Review*, vol. 1, no. 3, May 1947, p. 195. Serge had read both Bruno Bettelheim's 'Behavior in Extreme Situations', published in *Politics*, 1945, and Erich Fromm's 1941 *Escape from Freedom* (New York, Rinehart, 1941), and found both these studies revealing. They confirmed his own observations and helped understand 'men under totalitarianism', and the socio-psychological seeds of totalitarianism present in the soil of all modern societies. Serge was not arguing for a 'behaviouralist' approach, but noted that the existing socialist literature oversimplified the human personality.

from the experience of the first proletarian revolution, but surely one essential lesson was that new revolutions must be 'socialist – in the humanist sense of the word – and more precisely, *socializing*, through democratic, libertarian means'.[43] Another important lesson regarded organization, which Serge recognized as necessary, though he cautioned against 'centralization, discipline, [and] guided ideology'.

Finally, Serge, ever the optimist in spite of the darkness, reminded his readers that even though the first socialist revolution led to the 'concentration camp universe' of Stalinism, its 'high degree of development attained by state-controlled production' along with the advent of capitalist nationalizations in Europe would again create imperatives that would 'combine with the desire for social justice and a new found freedom to once again place the economy at the service of the community'.[44]

Serge drew on the essential humanism of Marxism and its scientific spirit of open inquiry, while attacking those like Sidney Hook[45] and James Burnham, who separated the class struggle from socialism and saw Stalinism as the same as Bolshevism, Stalinist planning as Marxist planning. Serge was full of hope for the future, despite living through terrible defeats and persecution so severe that he acknowledged that 'critical intelligence' itself was dangerous to survival.[46] Foreseeing totalitarian collectivist societies that were fundamentally anti-democratic and anti-socialist, Serge affirmed that the citizens of these states would 'soon demand control over the elaboration and application of plans, choosing of managers and leaders, and the liberties which this control requires'.[47]

Conclusion

Victor Serge's political trajectory, his writings and his life experience were unique in the revolutionary movement. His revolutionary integrity and dedication to humanity were not negotiable, were in fact beyond compromise. In an obituary for Serge that appeared in the January 1948 edition of *Modern Review*, the editors proclaimed, 'His *chef d'œuvre* was his own life'.[48] In a *New Left Review* article Nicholas Krasso wrote that Serge's life was most remarkable as a 'corrective' to Stalinism.[49] Serge was an intransigent socialist who believed at the same time that intransigence was necessary and dangerous: he was a Leninist whose support of the Russian Revolution and its ideals was unwavering, and who, while contributing to Menshevik journals, nonetheless took them to task for identifying Leninism with Stalinism; and at the same time, Serge criticized certain of Lenin's practices for leaving the door open for a Stalin. Serge was a Trotskyist who was spurned by the Trotskyists, who called him a centrist for his nonconformist views. Serge differed from the Trotskyists because he held that the revolution began to degenerate with the establishment of the Cheka and the death penalty, and slid down the road to totalitarianism as early as 1921 with Kronstadt and NEP. He even dared to suggest that the Marxist project as interpreted by too many 'Marxists' was totalitarian,[50] though the aspiration and struggle for social justice was profoundly democratic.

Serge angered all his political associates by publishing wherever he could; Trotsky was enraged to see his articles in *La Révolution prolétarienne*, which he considered a journal of 'petty bourgeois syndicalists', and Dwight Macdonald and others worried about Serge's association with the Menshevik *New Leader* in New York. In the former case Serge disagreed with Trotsky and published with the sole aim of gaining as wide an audience as he could, and with the latter, Serge was also trying to make a living and so published where he could with pay. Macdonald, who befriended, supported and published Serge, worried that Serge was becoming a professional anti-Stalinist like the others around the *New Leader* such as Max Eastman and Sidney Hook. Alan Wald reiterates this point in his article 'Victor Serge and the New York Anti-Stalinist Left, 1937–47',[51] where he is certain that Serge was on the same path as these ex-Marxists.

Serge confounded his comrades by his associations, as he always had from the earliest days when he associated in the USSR with the theosophists, the Bolsheviks and the anarchists, in France with the revolutionary syndicalists, socialists and Trotskyists, with the POUM in Spain and the Fourth Internationalists in Belgium and France. It was no different in Mexico, where Serge took up with psychologists, revolutionists, syndicalists and social democrats. Serge was, in sum, always a maverick. He was universally denounced and maligned, by the Right (as a unrepentant Marxist revolutionary), by the Stalinists (who called him a fascist-Trotskyite fifth columnist), and by the Trotskyists (who called him a centrist or a petty-bourgeois intellectual moralist). The social democrats considered him an ex-Marxist, and the various anti-Stalinists on the Left, when they were not attacking him, were claiming him as their own.

Throughout this study we have tried to show where Serge stood, and what his ideas were in relation to the course of Soviet historical and political development. It is because his writings are so varied in his final years, and so suggestive – often taking ambiguous directions – that he could easily be claimed or disowned by any of the anti-Stalinist tendencies. What distinguishes his writing, apart from its poetic expressiveness, is that it is rich, varied and questioning.

Even in defeat, Serge sought to reaffirm his Marxism, noting that socialists

> should not be too discouraged if we see clearly why and how we have been beaten. After all, we are used to it, we know that we must be the defeated for a long time in order no longer to be so one day. And we have, in spite of everything, enough victories behind us to keep us going, provided we do not renounce the compass Marx has left to us.[52]

Serge was unable to satisfactorily resolve the lives of his characters in *The Long Dusk*[53] and so considered the work inferior. It was history that offered no resolution, but this novel, like Serge's work in general, was one of great insight and evocation, and also of hope, not naïve hope, but of a far more profound hope based on a deep understanding of human history and social processes. This hope that Serge's work expresses was a victory in itself.

Serge's ideas consigned him to a life of poverty and obscurity: his rejection of both the Soviet state and the capitalist West assured his marginality. He paid dearly: he has been ignored or poorly understood, his books have disappeared, been confiscated, or gone unpublished even though they establish him as a man of the contemporary world whose ideas are increasingly relevant.

The last word should go to Serge, who insisted that 'The course is set on hope':

André who was killed in Riga,
Dario who was killed in Spain,
Boris whose wounds I dressed,
Boris whose eyes I closed.

David, my bunk mate
dead without knowing why
in a quiet orchard in France –
– six bullets for a 20-year-old heart . . .

Karl, whose nails I recognized
when you had already turned to earth,
you, with your high brow and lofty thoughts,
what was death doing with you!
Dark, tough human vine.

The North, the waves, the ocean
capsize the boat, the Four, now pallid,
drink deeply of anguish,
farewell to Paris, farewell to you all,
farewell to life, God damn it!

Vassili, throughout our sleepless midnights
you had the soul of a combatant
from Shanghai,
and the wind effaces your tomb
in the cornfields of Armavir.

Hong Kong lights up, hour of tall buildings,
the palm resembles the scimitar,
the square resembles the cemetery,
the evening is sweltering and you are dying,
Nguyên, in your prison bed.

And you, my decapitated brothers,
the lost ones, the unforgiven

the massacred, René, Raymond,
guilty but not denied.

O rain of stars in the darkness,
constellation of dead brothers!

I owe you my blackest silence,
my resolve, my indulgence
for all these empty-seeming days,
and whatever is left me of pride
for a blaze in the desert

But let there be silence
on these lofty figureheads!
The ardent voyage continues,
the course is set on hope.

When will it be your turn, when mine?

The course is set on hope.[54]

Notes

Preface to the Paperback Edition

1 Susan Weissman (ed.), *The Ideas of Victor Serge, A Life as a Work of Art*, London, Merlin Press, 1997.
2 In France, Pierre Broué published *Notes d'Allemagne 1923* (La Brèche-PEC, 1990), Jean Riere published *Pour un Brasier Dans un Désert* (Type-Type Plein Chant, 1998); Jean Riere and Jil Silberstein published *Victor Serge, Memoires d'un Revolutionnaire et autres ecrits politiques 1908–1947* (Bouquins, 2001), and the publisher La Découverte brought out Serge's *Tropique du Nord,* and *Vie et mort de Leon Trotsky* in 2003. In Italy, Attilio Chitarin published *Victor Serge: Socialismo e Totalitarismo, Scritti 1933–1947* (Prospettiva, 1997). In English, Serge's *Resistance, Poems* (City Lights, 1989), *Year One of the Russian Revolution* (Writers & Readers, 1992), *Russia Twenty Years After* (Humanities, 1996), *Revolution in Danger* (Redwords, 1997), *Witness to the German Revolution* (Bookmarks, 2000), *Memoirs of a Revolutionary* (The Iowa Series, 2002), *The Case of Comrade Tulayev* (New York Review Books Classics, 2004), *Victor Serge, Collected Writings on Literature and Revolution* (Francis Boutle Publishers, 2004), *What Every Radical Should Know About State Repression* (Ocean Press, 2005), *Unforgiving Years* (New York Review Books, 2008), *Conquered City* (New York Review Books, 2011), and an unabridged new edition of *Memoirs of a Revolutionary*, translated by Peter Sedgwick with George Paizis (New York Review Books Classics, 2012), were republished, as well several works on Serge. In Russia, Serge's *Polnoch' Veka* and *Delo Tulaeva* (Ural'skoe Izdatel'stvo, 1991), *Ot revolutsii k totalitarizmu: Vospominaniya Revolutsionera* (Praksis, 2001), and *Zavoevann'ii Gorod* (Praksis 2002) were published.
3 Walter Lacqueur, 'The Case of Victor Serge', *Partisan Review*, vol. LXX, no. 1, 2003.
4 Christopher Hitchens, 'The Case of Comrade Serge', *Los Angeles Times*, Book Review, 10 Feb. 2002.
5 Yevgeny Yevtushenko, June 2001.
6 Victor Serge, *Memoirs of a Revolutionary*, New York, New York Review Books Classics, 2012, p. 74.
7 He used the term 'collectivist' to describe a 'more or less mixed collectivization of [the means of] production'. See Victor Serge, 'L'URSS a-t-elle une régime socialiste?', *Masses*, Paris, 1947, and *Spartacus*, Série B, no. 50, Oct.-Nov. 1972.
8 Victor Serge, 'Necesidad de una renovación del Socialismo', *Mundo, Libertad y Socialismo*, Mexico, June 1945.
9 Victor Serge, 'Pour un Renouvellement du Socialisme', *Masses/Socialisme et Liberté*, no. 3, June 1946, pp. 12–14. (Victor Serge, *Mémoires d'un Révolutionnaire et autres écrits politiques 1908–1947*, Paris, Bouquins, 2001, pp. 838–47.)

10 Serge, 'L'URSS a-t-elle une régime socialiste?'
11 Serge, 'Necesidad de una renovación del Socialismo', p. 18.
12 Serge, 'Pour un Renouvellement du Socialisme'.
13 Ibid.
14 Victor Serge to Dwight Macdonald, 10 March 1945, Macdonald Papers, Yale University Library.
15 Ibid.
16 Workers' individual rights have improved, winning protection from discrimination at work, but at the expense of union rights and protections – which have been eroded and often exist in name only. For a nuanced discussion of the relationship of the rights consciousness to the labour movement (in the US) see Nelson Lichtenstein, *State of the Union: A Century of American Labor*, Princeton, NJ, Princeton University Press, 2002, chapter 5.
17 As we have seen in the continued so-called coloured revolutions ousting leaders who cheated their way to power in fraudulent elections.

Preface and Acknowledgments

1 Serge's Mexico archive has now found a home at Yale University's Beinecke Rare Book and Manuscript Library.
2 I also obtained Marc Zborowski's files, hoping in vain to find evidence of his role in the Trotsky–Serge rupture.
3 Rossiiskii gosudarstvennyi arkhiv sotsial'no-politicheskoi istorii, formerly RTsKhIDNI, the Russian Center for the Preservation and Study of Documents of Most Recent History.

Part I In the orbit of revolution: Introduction

1 Victor Serge to Sidney Hook, 10 July 1943.
2 See for example the works of D. Filtzer, D. Mandel, D. Koenker, W. Chase, A. Rabinowitch, L. Siegelbaum, R. Suny, among many others.
3 Serge, April 1942, in the 'Joint Declaration', in Victor Serge, Julian Gorkín, Marceau Pivert and Gustav Regler, *La GPU prepara un nuevo crimen!* Mexico DF, Edición de 'Analysis' (Revista de Hechos e Ideas), 1942.
4 William Marshall, *Victor Serge: The Uses of Dissent*, Oxford, Berg, 1992; Susan Weissman (ed.), *The Ideas of Victor Serge: A Life as a Work of Art*, Glasgow, Critique Books, 1997; David Cotterill (ed.), *The Serge–Trotsky Papers*, London, Pluto Press, 1994; 'Victor Serge: The Century of the Unexpected', *Revolutionary History*, vol. 5, no. 3, autumn 1994.
5 See Serge's discussion on emergent totalitarianism in chapter 1 and on bureaucratic totalitarian collectivism in chapter 8 of the present work. The bureaucratic collectivist school of thought is best expressed by the works of Max Shachtman in the United States and Bruno Rizzi in Italy.
6 See the works of Arch Getty, Sheila Fitzpatrick and Lynn Viola among others.
7 V. Serge to S. Hook, 'Marxisme et démocratie', 10 July 1943.

1 In the service of the Revolution: 1917–21

1 Victor Serge, *From Lenin to Stalin*, New York, Monad Press, 1973, p. 13. First French edition published in 1937.

2 Victor Serge, *Lenin: 1917*, Mexico, Ediciones Transición, 1977, pp. 19–20. First published in Paris as *Lénine, 1917*, Librairie du Travail, 1925, and reprinted with a new preface as *Vingt ans après*, Paris, Cahiers Spartacus, 1937.

3 Victor Serge, *Memoirs of a Revolutionary*, London, Writers and Readers, 1984, p. 67. First published as *Mémoires d'un révolutionnaire*, Paris, Editions du Seuil, 1951.

4 Serge's account of this encounter is in *La Ville en danger: l'an II de la révolution russe*, Paris, Librairie du Travail, 1924. A slightly different version is found in the *Memoirs*, p. 66. Published in English in 1997 as *Revolution in Danger*, London, Redwords, translated by Ian Birchall.

5 Serge, *La Ville en danger*, p. 86. These 'tommies' affected Serge deeply; he also wrote of this encounter in the *Memoirs* (see note 4 above) and in *Birth of Our Power*, London, Writers and Readers, 1967, p. 244. Here we see how Serge's novels blur the lines between fact and fiction.

6 One letter Serge wrote from Precigne survives. On 30 April 1918, Serge wrote to the Minister of the Interior in Paris, volunteering to fight in the French Army and the Légion étrangère. He was refused. (Thanks to Pierre Broué for this letter.) Serge's description of his experiences at Precigne form the middle section of his second novel, *Birth of Our Power*, and is also described in the *Memoirs*, pp. 63–9. Pierre Pascal, a French Communist living in Moscow who married Serge's sister-in-law, later wrote a four-part memoir called *Mon Journal de Russie*, Lausanne, L'Age d'Homme. In the second volume Pascal described Serge's study group in Precigne, p. 107.

7 Serge, *Memoirs*, pp. 63–4.

8 Victor Serge, 'Trente ans après la révolution russe', first published in Nov. 1947 in the tiny French left-wing publication *La Révolution prolétarienne*, directed by the French syndicalist Alfred Rosmer. This retrospective was published in the month of Serge's death.

9 Serge, *Memoirs*, p. 71.

10 Ibid., p. 69.

11 Ibid., pp. 70–71.

12 Ibid., pp. 71–2.

13 Ibid., p. 74.

14 Ibid.

15 Ibid., p. 11.

16 Ibid., p. 9.

17 Sources on this period include Richard Parry; *The Bonnot Gang*, London, Rebel Press, 1987; Ezra Brett Mell, *The Truth about the Bonnot Gang*, London, Coptic Press, 1968; Luc Nemeth, 'On Anarchism', in Susan Weissman (ed.), *The Ideas of Victor Serge*, Glasgow, Critique Books, 1997; Emile Becker, *La 'Bande à Bonnot'*, Paris, Les Nouvelles Editions Debresse, 1968; Bernard Thomas, *La Bande à Bonnot*, Paris, Claude Tchou, 1968; Kibalchich–Serge files in the Archives of the Prefecture of Police in Paris, and Serge's writings in *L'Anarchie* (*Anarchy*).

18 Le Rétif, 'Note on Belgium', *Bulletin of the Anarchist International*, no. 7, Nov. 1908, p. 5.

19 Quoted in Parry, *The Bonnot Gang*, p. 50.

20 Le Rétif, 'The Unlawful', *Le Communiste*, no. 14, 10 June 1908.

21 Nemeth, 'On Anarchism', p. 125. The office at rue Fessart was also Serge and Rirette's home.

22 Mell, *The Truth*, p. 13.

23 Parry, *The Bonnot Gang*, p. 156.

24 Ibid., p. 153.

25 Victor Serge, *Men in Prison*, Paris, 1931; London, Writers and Readers, 1977, p. 250.

26 Serge, *Memoirs*, p. 36.

27 Ibid., p. 47.

28 Ibid., pp. 27–31.

29 Ibid.

30 Serge's Party documents are in Fond 495, opis 19, RGASPI, Moscow.

31 Serge, *Memoirs*, p. 151.

32 Serge wrote, 'I am with the bandits', in 'Les Bandits' in the 4 Jan. 1912 edition of *L'Anarchie*.

33 See *inter alia*, Serge, *Les Anarchistes et l'expérience de la révolution russe*, Paris, Cahiers du Travail, 1921; *Memoirs, From Lenin to Stalin*, his numerous articles in *Bulletin Communiste*, and *Clarté*; also Paul Avrich, *Anarchists in the Russian Revolution*, London, Thames and Hudson, 1973; Leon Trotsky, *History of the Russian Revolution*, London, Sphere Books, 1967; Alfred Rosmer, *Moscow under Lenin*, New York, Monthly Review Press, 1971, pp. 97–101, among numerous other works.

34 Serge, 'La Pensée anarchiste', in *L'Anarchie* and *Le Crapouillot*, special issue, 1938, p. 12.

35 Serge, 'L'Anarchisme', unpublished essay written in the forties (no date provided), Serge archives, Mexico.

36 Peter Sedgwick, 'The Unhappy Elitist: Victor Serge's Early Bolshevism', published posthumously in *History Workshop Journal*, vol. 17, spring 1984, pp. 150–56.

37 Ibid., p. 151.

38 Sedgwick quotes from Guerin's book on anarchism, in which Serge apparently told Gaston Leval that the Communists were establishing a 'dictatorship *over* the proletariat' while publishing pro-regime journalism abroad. See Sedgwick, 'Unhappy Elitist', p. 152, and p. 156n.

39 Recorded conversation with Vlady in Mexico City, Feb. 1986.

40 'Marxism et démocratie', letter from Serge to Sidney Hook, May 1943. Serge archives, Mexico.

41 Written before the banning of Party factions. Sedgwick intimates that the factions banned had positions which closely corresponded to Serge's. See Peter Sedgwick, introduction to Serge's *Memoirs*, p. xii.

42 *L'Anarchisme*, unpublished typescript, no date, Mexico, archives.

43 Serge explained this apparent paradox in 'Meditation sur l'anarchie', published in *Esprit*, March 1937, Paris.

44 Serge, *Les Anarchistes et l'expérience de la révolution russe*, p. 29. The quotation cited demonstrates how Serge was very careful in his analysis of the Russian Revolution and its subsequent degeneration, to distinguish the avoidable from the unavoidable aspects – and shows how Serge's analysis was rooted in concrete circumstances.

45 Serge, *Memoirs*, p. 104.

46 Serge, *Les Anarchistes et l'expérience de la révolution russe*, pp. 81–119.

47 Serge, ibid., p. 44.

48 Serge, *Memoirs*, pp. 71–2.

49 Ibid., p. 73.

50 Ibid., p. 76.

51 Ibid., p. 77.

52 Leon Trotsky, 'Manifesto of the Communist Internationale to the Proletarians of the World', March 1919.

53 Serge, *Memoirs*, p. 89. Rosmer, in his *Moscow under Lenin* (pp. 35–6) describes Serge as 'the best possible guide' because of his political background, his knowledge of languages, his experiences in the labour movement in various European countries, and his curiosity about what exactly was happening in the Western democracies and his desire to show the visiting delegates of the Comintern the Russian Revolution from the inside.

54 Serge, *Memoirs*, p. 83.

55 Interview recorded with Vlady Kibalchich, Mexico City, May 1987.

56 Serge, *Memoirs*, p. 88.

57 Greeman, pp. 181–200. James Hulse notes, in *The Forming of the Communist International* (Stanford, Calif., Stanford University Press, 1964), that Serge and Mazin, 'who were virtually conscripted for their assignments with the Comintern, found it ironical that they should have been singled out to organize and plan the world revolution' (p. 26). Hulse's book on the Comintern is almost singular in mentioning Serge's role in its early history, and his sources are Serge himself (the *Memoirs*), and his early articles for *L'Internationale Communiste* 7/8, Nov.–Dec. 1919, Stockholm reprint. It is curious that there are no other authoritative sources that corroborate Serge's *Memoirs* (and Hulse's book) on a subject of such significance as the formation of the Communist International.

58 Hulse, *The Forming of the Communist International*, pp. 24–9.

59 Moscow's Comintern archive, Fond 495 of RGASPI, has documents showing Serge joined the Petrograd Bureau of the Comintern on 7 June 1919, and later in 1921 notes that Serge could work in French, English, Spanish, Russian, Polish and German.

60 Serge, *From Lenin to Stalin*, p. 35.

61 Serge, *Memoirs*, p. 90

62 A pirate edition of this book was reissued by the French police as an internal education document for the use of their 'employees' during the 1960s. See Jean Riere's note to English edition, 1978.

63 Ibid.

64 Serge, *Memoirs*, p. 92.

65 See his letter to Anton Ciliga in *New International*, Feb. 1939, p. 54.

66 Victor Serge, from the Foreword, *Year One of the Russian Revolution*, New York, Holt, Rinehart and Winston, 1972, p. 18. Reprinted in a joint edition published by Bookmarks and Pluto Press in London and Writers and Readers in New York in 1992. First published as *L'An I de la révolution russe*, Paris, 1930.

67 Serge, *Year One of the Russian Revolution*, author's foreword, p. 19.

68 In Stalinist historiography Trotsky switched roles with Stalin and became the one who opposed the seizure of power. This was popularized in Eisenstein's widely acclaimed film, *October*. See also *Year One*, p. 380n and p. 67.

69 Ibid., p. 56.

70 Ibid., pp. 56–61.

71 *Bulletin Communiste*, vol. II, nos 36–37 (double issue), pp. 612–20.

72 Serge, *From Lenin to Stalin*, p. 23.

73 Ibid., p. 15.

74 See Serge's biography of Lenin, *Lenine, 1917*, Paris, 1925. Published in English translation (by Al Richardson) as 'Lenin in 1917', in *Victor Serge: The Century of the Unexpected: Essays on Revolution and Counter-Revolution, Revolutionary History*, vol. 5, no. 3, autumn 1994, pp. 3–53.

75 With the publication of Richard Pipes's massive *The Russian Revolution* (New York, Knopf) in 1990, this idea was resurrected.

76 Serge, 'Trente ans après la révolution russe', pp. 3–4. Published in English in Susan Weissman (ed.), *Victor Serge: Russia Twenty Years After*, Atlantic Highlands, NJ, Humanities Press, 1996, p. 302.

77 Serge, *Year One*, pp. 88 and 381n.

78 Ibid., p. 100.

79 Serge, *Memoirs*, p. 245.

80 Tamara Deutscher, book review of *Year One*, in *Critique* 1, spring 1973, p. 95.

81 Serge, *Memoirs*, p. 349. Tamara Deutscher also points out this contradiction in her review of Serge's book which appeared in *Critique* 1. She answers Serge with Serge: 'Serge's own truthful and despairing narrative provides all the evidence that in the 'Year One' there was no chance, no possibility to translate into practice his – and the Bolsheviks' – high aspirations and hopes' (p. 95).

82 Leon Trotsky, *Between Red and White: Social Democracy and the Wars of Intervention in Russia, 1918–1921*, London, New Park Publications, 1975. First published in 1922 as *Mezhdu Imperializmom i Revolyutsiei*, Moscow, State Publishing House.

83 See for example, Robert V. Daniels, *The Conscience of the Revolution*, New York, Simon and Schuster, 1960, and the minutes of the Central Committee of the Bolshevik Party from August 1917 to February 1918, reproduced in English *The Bolsheviks and the October Revolution*, London, Pluto Press, 1974. Parts are also included in R.V. Daniels's *A Documentary History of Communism*, vol. 1, Hanover, NH, University Press of New England, 1984.

84 Serge, *Russia Twenty Years After*.

85 Marcel Liebman, 'Was Lenin a Stalinist?', in Tariq Ali (ed.), *The Stalinist Legacy*, Harmondsworth, Penguin Books, 1984, p. 140.

86 Serge, *Russia Twenty Years After*, p. 305.

87 See 'Theses of the Left Communists (1918)' published in the first number of the Moscow-produced journal *Kommunist* on 20 April 1918, translated and published by *Critique* in 1977. Half of the 'Theses' are translated in Daniels's collection, *A Documentary History of Communism*, vol. 1, pp. 98–102.

88 See *The Bolsheviks and the October Revolution: Central Committee Minutes of the Russian Social-Democratic Labour Party (Bolsheviks) August 1917 to February 1918*, London, Pluto Press, 1974. The minutes pertaining to the Brest-Litovsk terms of peace, in particular, show how deep the divisions in the Bolsheviks were. Reading this volume is a corrective to the notion of Bolshevik monolithism in the early period.

89 Serge, *Year One*, p. 169.

90 Ibid., p. 172.

91 Serge was writing *Year One* in the years 1928–30.

92 Serge, *Year One*, p. 175.

93 Serge, *Year One*, p. 224.

94 Ibid., pp. 220–26.

95 Leonard Schapiro, *The Russian Revolutions of 1917*, New York, Basic Books, 1984, p. 170. Serge's figures, which he got from Karl Radek's report to the First All-Russian Congress of Economic Councils, give an even larger picture of the 'burden of Brest-Litovsk': The Soviet Republic, he wrote, lost 40 per cent of its industrial proletariat, 45 per cent of its fuel production, 90 per cent of its sugar production, 64–70 per cent of its metal industry, 55 per cent of its wheat. *Year One*, p. 199.

96 Serge, *Memoirs*, p. 68.

97 Seppo Hentilä, 'Finland Becomes Independent', in O. Jussila, S. Hentilä and J. Nevakivi (eds), *From Grand Duchy to a Modern State*, London, Hurst, 1995, p. 103.

98 Ibid., p. 105.

99 E.H. Carr, *The Bolshevik Revolution, 1917–1923*, vol. 1, London, Macmillan, 1953, pp. 287–9.

100 Ibid., p. 105.

101 Carl Erik Knoellinger, *Labor in Finland*, Harvard University Press, 1960, p. 46.

102 Ibid., pp. 47–50.

103 Serge, *Year One.*

104 Hentilä, 'Finland Becomes Independent', pp. 110–12.

105 Serge's discussion on the events in Finland can be found in *Year One*, pp. 182–91.

106 Serge also wrote an article in *Clarté* on the Finnish experience: 'Une Grande Experience oubliée: La Commune finlandaise de 1918', *Clarté*, vol. XVI, no. 8, 1926–27, pp. 237–41.

107 All his writings on the civil war are similar.

108 Serge, *Portrait de Staline*, Paris, Editions Bernard Grasset, 1940, pp. 57–8.

109 Serge, *Memoirs*, p. 80.

110 Serge, *Russia Twenty Years After*, p. 310.

111 Serge, *What Everyone Should Know about State Repression*, London, New Park Publications, 1979, p. 62.

112 Serge, *Memoirs*, p. 118.

113 Serge, *Russia Twenty Years After*, p. 307.

114 James Petras discusses the problem of the relationship of repression and democracy in the transition period in 'Authoritarianism, Democracy and the Transition to Socialism', in *Socialist Register* 1986.

115 Richard Greeman, in his foreword to the English translation of the novel, wrote that Serge answered the difficult question presented by the need for revolutionary repression in the form of this tragic novel, which poses the irony of victory in defeat and defeat in victory. *Conquered City*, London, Writers and Readers, 1978, pp. xiv–xv.

116 Isaac Deutscher, *The Prophet Armed, Trotsky 1879–1921*, Oxford, Oxford University Press, 1970, p. 465.

117 Serge, *Memoirs*, p. 108.

118 Stalin's exploits are discussed by Serge in *Portrait de Staline*, Paris, Editions Bernard Grasset, 1940, pp. 49–56, by Boris Souvarine in *Stalin: A Critical Survey of Bolshevism*, New York, Longman, Green, 1939, pp. 222–53, by

Trotsky in *My Life*, Harmondsworth, Pelican Books, 1975, and by Isaac Deutscher in his biography *Stalin: A Political Biography*, Harmondsworth, Penguin Books, 1966.

119 Serge, *Memoirs*, pp. 108–9.

120 Serge, *From Lenin to Stalin*, pp. 33–4, *Russia Twenty Years After*, pp. 12–13, and *Memoirs*, pp. 108–9.

121 Serge, *Memoirs*.

122 Ibid., p. 112.

123 See also footnote 36 above.

124 Ibid., p. 113.

125 Serge, *Russia Twenty Years After*, p. 312.

126 Lenin, cited by Maurice Dobb in *Soviet Economic Development*, London, Routledge and Kegan Paul, 1966, p. 123.

127 Serge, *Memoirs*, pp. 115–18.

128 Ibid., p. 117.

129 Ibid., p. 118.

130 Quoted in *Year One*, pp. 357 and 410–11n. It came from Kritsman's *Geroicheskii Period Velikoi Russkoi Revoliutsii*, Moscow, 1926, which Serge called 'remarkable' and 'the only book which undertakes a serious analysis of War Communism'.

131 Serge, *Year One*, p. 360.

132 Ibid.

133 Ibid., pp. 368–71.

134 Ibid., p. 118.

135 Serge wrote on Kronstadt in the *Memoirs*, pp. 124–32 (reprinted by Solidarity Press, London, 1967); 'Once More: Kronstadt', in *New International*, July 1938, pp. 211–12 (reprinted in V.I. Lenin and L.D. Trotsky, *Kronstadt*, New York, Monad Press, 1979); 'A Letter and Some Notes', in *New International*, Feb. 1939, pp. 53–4; 'La tragique d'une révolution', in *La Vie Ouvrière*, no. 152, 31 March 1922; 'Le problème de la dictature', in *La Vie Ouvrière*, no. 159, 19 May, 1922; 'Dictature et contre-révolution économique', in *La Vie Ouvrière*, no 182, 3 Nov. 1922. Also, see the articles published in *La Révolution prolétarienne*: nos 254 and 257, 10 Sept. 1937 and 25 Oct. 1937 under the title 'La Vie et les faits'; no. 277, 25 Aug. 1938, 'Sur Cronstadt 1921 et quelques autre sujets'; and no. 281, 25 Oct. 1938, 'Cronstadt 1921: Defence de Trotsky, réponse à Trotsky' (under the title 'La Vie et les faits'); Nov. 1947, 'Trente ans après la révolution russe'; in *Portrait de Staline*, p. 55; and in *The Life and Death of Leon Trotsky*, written in collaboration with Natalia Sedova Trotsky, New York, Basic Books, 1975, 106–8.

136 'What We Are Fighting For' (*Za Chto my boremsia*), the statement of the Kronstadt revolutionary committee, 8 March 1921, published in *Pravda o Kronshtadte* (pp. 82–4), translated by Paul Avrich and published as an appendix in *Kronstadt 1921*, Princeton University Press, 1970, pp. 241–3.

137 Serge, 'Fiction and Fact: Kronstadt', in *La Revolutión prolétarienne*, no. 254, 10 Sept. 1937, pp. 702–3.

138 Avrich, *Kronstadt*, p. 4.

139 Ibid., pp. 95–116.

140 Serge, *Russia Twenty Years After*, p. 313.

141 Ibid., p. 313.

142 Serge, 'Once More: Kronstadt', *New International*, July 1938, p. 211.

143 Serge, 'Fiction and Fact: Kronstadt', *La Révolution prolétarienne*, no. 254, 10 Sept. 1937, p. 703. In D.J. Cotterill (ed.), *The Serge–Trotsky Papers*, London, Pluto Press, 1994, p. 165.

144 Serge, *Memoirs*, pp. 125–6.

145 Ibid., pp. 128–9.

146 Serge, *Russia Twenty Years After*, p. 314.

147 Serge, *Memoirs*, p. 135.

148 Serge, *Russia Twenty Years After*, p. 314. Although Serge was upholding the right to voice and organize around critical viewpoints, he also admitted elsewhere that by 1921 all revolutionaries were already inside the Bolshevik Party, as the other parties had proved their bankruptcy in the course of the Revolution and civil war. Serge nevertheless criticized the effects of the growing siege mentality within the Party.

149 Serge thought Thermidor was reached on November 1927, ironically, on the tenth anniversary of the October Revolution. This coincided with the defeat of the Opposition within the Party and the subsequent expulsion, arrest and deportation of its members; and the sacrificing of the Chinese proletariat for the prestige and power of Stalin. Serge, *Memoirs*, pp. 213–25.

150 Serge, *Memoirs*, p. 131.

151 Ibid., p. 132.

152 Typescript, 'Définition du socialisme', unpublished, no date, Serge archives, Mexico. The Mexican Serge archive was transferred in Sept. 1996 to Yale University's Beinecke Rare Book and Manuscript Library. This typescript is in the Victor Serge Papers, Box 5, Folder 276.

153 Serge, *Memoirs*, p. 134.

154 Ibid.

155 Ibid., p. 147.

156 Ibid.

157 Ibid., pp. 147–8.

158 Ernest Mandel, 'In Defence of Socialist Planning', in *New Left Review* 159, Sept.–Oct. 1986, pp. 22–32.

159 See chapters 4 and 6.

160 Serge, *Memoirs*, p. 148.

161 Ibid., pp. 138 and 146.

162 Ibid., p. 150.

163 Serge, *Memoirs*, pp. 155–6.

164 *Inprekorr* is an acronym of International Press Correspondence.

2 Blockaded in Berlin; neutralized in Vienna; and into the Soviet fray

1 His family consisted of his wife Liuba, and son Vlady.

2 Victor Serge, *Memoirs of a Revolutionary*, London, Oxford University Press, 1963, pp. 157–8.

3 Ibid.

4 Serge was often imprecise about dates in the *Memoirs*. He wrote of his activities in the USSR in autumn 1921 and began his discussion of Germany with the events of 1922. In his *Clarté* article of 1 Dec. 1923, Serge said he arrived 'at the end of 1921'.

5 Serge, *Memoirs*, pp. 159–60.

6 R. Albert, 'Devant la révolution allemande: les riches contre la nation', *Clarté*, no. 46 (1 Nov. 1923), p. 428.

7 Serge, *Memoirs*, p. 160.

8 Ibid., p. 159.

9 Ibid., p. 162.

10 The Comintern had various publications, usually published simultaneously in several languages. *Kommunisticheskii Internatsional* (beginning in 1919) was published in Russian, German, French and English, with the Russian edition coming out most regularly; *Internationale Presse-Korrespondenz* (beginning in Sept. 1921) was published in German, English and French, the English and French being less full than the German; Serge edited the French edition, called *La Correspondance Internationale*. For a description of these journals, see E.H. Carr, *The Bolshevik Revolution 1917–1923;* vol. 3, Bibliography, pp. 580–82; and Franz Borkenau, *World Communism: A History of the Communist International*, Ann Arbor, University of Michigan Press, 1962, bibliographical notes, pp. 430–31.

11 According to Julian Gorkín, Serge's close associate in Mexico, in an interview conducted by Richard Greeman in Paris in 1964. Cited in Greeman, 'Victor Serge: The Making of a Novelist, 1880–1928', Unpublished Ph.D. thesis, Columbia University, 1968, p. 286.

12 His articles are listed in the bibliography. Pierre Broué, Trotsky's biographer, edited and annotated a collection of Serge's articles in Germany, published for the first time in Serge's name in 1990 in the centenary year of Serge's birth. Pierre Broué, *Victor Serge: Notes d'Allemagne (1923)*, Montreuil, La Breche, 1990.

13 Serge, *Memoirs*, p. 161.

14 Alexei Berlovsky was a former Russian prisoner-of-war in Germany. Serge, *Memoirs*, p. 161.

15 Serge, *Memoirs*, p. 158.

16 The name given by its enemies to the International Working Union of Socialist Parties, popularly known as the 'Vienna Union'; Serge thought it an appropriate name for the centrist groups 'conglomerated midway between the reformists and the Bolsheviks'. See E.H. Carr, *The Bolshevik Revolution*, vol. 3, pp. 407–8, and Serge, *Memoirs*, pp. 163–4.

17 Ibid.

18 Victor Serge, *Year One of the Russian Revolution*, New York, Holt, Rinehart and Winston, 1972, chapter 10: 'The German Revolution', pp. 312–49.

19 Ibid.

20 *Theses Resolutions and Manifestos of The First Four Congresses of the Third International*, p. 462n.

21 Serge, *Memoirs*, p. 168.

22 Alfred Rosmer, *Moscow under Lenin*, New York, Monthly Review Press, 1971, pp. 167–72, and *Theses Resolutions and Manifestos of the First Four Congresses of the Third International*, pp. 309–436.

23 Rosmer, *Moscow under Lenin*, p. 196.

24 Serge, *Memoirs*, pp. 147–8.

25 Victor Serge, *From Lenin to Stalin*, New York, Monad Press, 1973, p. 40.

26 Serge, *Memoirs*, p. 165.

27 Ibid.

28 See Rosmer, *Moscow under Lenin*, pp. 196–8.

29 See E.H. Carr, *The Interregnum, 1923–1924*, London, Macmillan, 1954, pp. 174–85, and Helmut Gruber, *International Communism in the Era of Lenin: A Documentary History*, Greenwich, Conn., Fawcett Publications, 1967, p. 437. Serge mentions the 'Schlageter line' which Radek pushed through in the *Memoirs*, though not in conjunction with the meeting he (Serge) had attended. Serge, *Memoirs*, p. 169.

30 Serge, *Memoirs*, p. 169.

31 See R. Albert, 'L'Allemagne en 1923: l'Inflation catastrophique', *La Vie Ouvrière*, Dec. 1925–June 1926, nos 310–70, and R. Albert, 'Notes d'Allemagne', *La Correspondance Internationale*, July–Nov. 1923.

32 Serge, *Memoirs*, p. 169.

33 Ibid.

34 R. Albert, *Clarté*, nos 52 and 53, 1 and 15 Feb., 1924.

35 Serge, *Memoirs*, p. 169.

36 Carr, *The Interregnum*, p. 174.

37 The article appears in Leon Trotsky, *The First Five Years of the Communist International*, vol. 2, New York, Monad Press, 1972, pp. 347–54.

38 Serge, *Memoirs*, p. 170.

39 Carr, *Interregnum*, p. 218, and Isaac Deutscher, *The Prophet Unarmed, Trotsky 1921–1929*, Oxford, Oxford University Press, 1959, pp. 142–5.

40 Serge, *Memoirs*, p. 171.

41 Ibid., p. 172.

42 Ibid., p. 174.

43 Deutscher, *The Prophet Unarmed*, pp. 142–4, Borkenau, *World Communism*, pp. 247–8, Gruber, *International Communism*, p. 441, Carr, *Interregnum*, pp. 210–15.

44 Gruber, *International Communism*, p. 442n.

45 Ibid.

46 See articles signed 'R. Albert' in *LCI*, no. 61 (31 July 1923), no. 63 (7 Aug. 1923), no. 77 (28 Sept. 1923), no. 78 (2 Oct. 1923), no. 89 (9 Nov. 1923), no. 90 (13 Nov. 1923); and in *BC*, no. 41 (11 Oct. 1923) and no. 47 (22 Nov. 1923).

47 R. Albert, *La Vie Ouvrière*, no. 60, 1926.

48 He had already consolidated his power base in the provincial Party apparatus, but not the Party as a whole.

49 'Greetings to *La Vérité*, *Writings of Leon Trotsky, 1930*. Quoted in Trotsky, *The Challenge of the Left Opposition (1923–1925)*, New York, Pathfinder Press, 1975, p. 163.

50 This account is to be found in Rosmer's excellent book, *Moscow under Lenin*, pp. 208–9.

51 Serge, *Memoirs*, pp. 174–5.

52 Serge, ibid., Gruber, *International Communism*, p. 441.

53 Trinadtsataya Konferentsiya Rossiisskoi Kommunisticheskoi Partii (Bol'shevikov) (1924), p. 173, cited in Carr, *Interregnum*, p. 236.

54 Serge wrote to the Comintern executive in early 1924 of his plans to work in Vienna on the Editorial Board of *Inprekorr*. Fond 495, Op. 19, D. 25, 1.5, RGASPI, Moscow.

55 Serge, *Memoirs*, p. 177.

56 Ibid., p. 181.

57 Ibid., p. 182.

58 Ibid., p. 194.

59 Ibid., p. 187.

60 Ibid., pp. 188–9.

61 Referring to the 'Lenin levy'. Serge, *Memoirs*, p. 186.

62 Victor Serge, 'Le Fascisme en Autriche', *La Vie ouvrière*, Oct. –Nov. 1925.

63 Serge, *Memoirs*, p. 190.

64 Ibid.

65 Serge later was allowed to continue his translations of Lenin in the Lenin Institute, closely supervised for 'possible sabotage'. Serge, *Memoirs*, p. 273.

66 According to Serge's son Vlady, interviewed in Mexico City, Jan. 1986.

67 Serge, *Memoirs*, p. 176.

68 Ibid.

69 Richard Greeman calls it 'pedestrian' but says the pedestrian quality points to Serge's objective position (indeed that of the entire Left Opposition) as a loyal member under the yoke of the Party. Greeman, 'Victor Serge: The Making of a Novelist', p. 308.

70 Victor Serge, *Lenin 1917*, originally published by Librairie de Travail, Paris, 1925; quotes here from Spanish edition, Ediciones Transición, Mexico, 1977, p. 26. Published in English as 'Lenin in 1917', in 'Victor Serge: Century of the Unexpected', in *Revolutionary History*, vol. 5, no 3, autumn 1994, pp. 3–53.

71 Serge, 'Lenin 1917', p. 24.

72 V.I. Lenin, *Marxism and Insurrection, Selected Works*, Moscow, Progress Publishers, p. 380. Serge's quote on p. 60 of 'Lenine 1917' slightly abridges the original. Emphasis is Lenin's.

73 See chapter 1, p. 19.

74 A. Bely, 'Christ est ressuscité', *Clarté*, no. 27, 1923, p. 77, translator Victor Serge.

75 'Les Ecrivains russes et la révolution', *Clarté*, 1922, p. 388.

76 'Le Nouvel écrivain et la nouvelle littérature', *Clarté*, 1923, p. 160.

77 Ibid.

78 These writers were profiled in *Clarté*, no. 36, 1923 ('Boris Pilniak'); no. 56, 1924 ('"La Semaine"' de I. Libedinsky'); no. 74, 1925 ('Vsevolod Ivanov') and vol. 1925 ('La Littérature épique de la révolution: N. Tikhonov et Serafimovitch').

79 Victor Serge, 'Mayakovsky', *Clarté*, vol. 1924, pp. 504–8.

80 Victor Serge, 'Is a Proletarian Literature Possible?' translated from *Clarté* 12, 1 March 1925, and published in *Yale French Studies*, 1967, pp. 138–9.

81 *Krasnaia nov'*, no. 4, 1925, pp. 271–2, quoted in Stephen Cohen, *Bukharin and the Bolshevik Revolution*, Oxford University Press, 1973, p. 205.

82 Cohen, *Bukharin*. MAPP (Moscow Proletarian Association) and VAPP, the writers' organization for Bolshevik partisans of proletarian literature called for a dictatorship of the Party in the field of literature.

83 Serge, 'Is a Proletarian Literature Possible?', pp. 142–3.

84 Serge, *Clarté* 12, 1 March 1925, p. 144 (English translation).

85 See Evgenii Preobrazhensky, *O Morali*, quoted in Donald Filtzer, *Soviet Workers and Stalinist Industrialization: The Formation of Modern Soviet Production Relations 1928–1941*, New York, M.E. Sharpe, 1986, pp. 18, 276n.

86 See ibid., pp. 18–19.

87 Serge, *From Lenin to Stalin*, pp. 40–42.
88 A. Podshchekoldin, '*1922 god: fabriki – rabochim privilegii – partapparatu*', *Argumenti i fakti*, no. 27, 1990.
89 Serge, *Memoirs*, p. 190.
90 Ibid., p. 191.
91 Ibid., p. 192.
92 Ibid.

3 Back in the USSR – the Left Opposition struggles 1926–28

1 Victor Serge, *Memoirs of a Revolutionary*, London, Oxford University Press, 1963, p. 193.
2 Ibid., p. 199.
3 Ibid., p. 205.
4 Ibid., p. 199.
5 Ibid., p. 195.
6 Ibid.
7 Victor Serge, 'Trente ans après la révolution russe', published in English in Susan Weissman (ed.), *Victor Serge: Russia Twenty Years After*, Atlantic Highlands, NJ, Humanities Press, 1996, p. 314.
8 Ibid., p. 315.
9 Ibid., p. 24.
10 Ibid., p. 25.
11 Cited in Geoffrey Hosking, *The First Socialist Society: A History of the Soviet Union From Within*, Cambridge, Mass., Harvard University Press, 1985, p. 140.
12 Victor Serge, *Retrato de Stalin*, Mexico, Ediciones Libres, 1940, p. 71.
13 See Boris Souvarine, *Stalin: A Critical Survey of Bolshevism*, New York, Longman, Green, 1939, p. 432, and all of chapter IX.
14 Robert Daniels, *The Conscience of the Revolution*, Cambridge, Mass., Harvard University Press, 1960, p. 233.
15 Isaac Deutscher, *The Prophet Unarmed, Trotsky 1921–1929*, Oxford, Oxford University Press, 1959, p. 132.
16 Ibid., pp. 75–7.
17 Serge, *Russia Twenty Years After*, p. 153.
18 Referring here not to Bukharin, Zinoviev and Kamenev with whom Trotsky could engage in theoretical debate, but to Stalin's cohorts Kalinin, Voroshilov and like 'mediocrities' as Serge called them.
19 Trotsky explained that he did not partake in social 'amusements' with other members of the leading stratum, in order to avoid boredom; moreover, when he did appear, group conversations would stop, and those in conversation would look either bitterly or shamefacedly toward Trotsky. Leon Trotsky, *My Life*, Harmondsworth, Pelican Books, 1975, p. 525.
20 The phrase is Sieva Volkov's (Trotsky's grandson). Private conversation, Mexico City, May 1987.
21 Trotsky, *My Life*, p. 532.
22 Ibid., p. 534.
23 Ibid.
24 Deutscher, *The Prophet Unarmed*, p. 241.
25 Ibid., p. 242.

26 Trotsky's declaration at the Thirteenth Party Congress, 1924. Quoted in Deutscher, *The Prophet Unarmed*, p. 161.

27 Serge, *Russia Twenty Years After*, pp. 155–6.

28 Ibid., p. 150.

29 G. Hoskings, *The First Socialist Society: A History of the Soviet Union from Within*, Cambridge, Mass., Harvard University Press, 1985, p. 143.

30 Serge, *Russia Twenty Years After*, p. 151.

31 Victor Serge, letter to Jacques Mesnil, quoted in *Russia Twenty Years After*, pp. 151–2n.

32 Serge, *Russia Twenty Years After*, pp. 147–8.

33 Ibid.

34 Here his position, written in 1936, is less nuanced than in 1923–25 and tallies exactly with Trotsky's. Ibid., p. 148.

35 Victor Serge, 'Reply to Ciliga', *New International*, Feb. 1939, p. 54.

36 Serge, *Russia Twenty Years After*, pp. 278–9.

37 Grigory Sokolnikov was a leader of the Zinoviev group with Kamenev and Krupskaya at the Fourteenth Party Congress. As Finance Minister he espoused 'rightist' economic policies, encouraging private enterprise; but he stood with the Left on the issues of Party democracy, political reform, the struggle against bureaucracy and Stalin's growing power. See Deutscher, *The Prophet Unarmed*, p. 247; Daniels, *The Conscience of the Revolution*, p. 291, and E.H. Carr, *Socialism in One Country*, London, Macmillan, 1958, part two, pp. 73–4.

38 See Donald Filtzer, *Soviet Workers and Stalinist Industrialization: The Formation of Modern Soviet Production Relations 1928–1929*, New York, M.E. Sharpe, 1986, pp. 13–15.

39 Victor Serge, *From Lenin to Stalin*, New York, Monad Press, 1973, p. 40. See also Carr, *Socialism*, pp. 59–74, and Deutscher, *The Prophet Unarmed*, p. 244.

40 Victor Serge, 'Vers l'industrialisation', part II, *Clarté* XVI–10, 29 Nov. 1927, p. 486.

41 Ibid.

42 Ibid., p. 488. In this section of Serge's article he quoted from the Counter-Thesis of the Opposition (counter to the Thesis approved by the Central Committee, written by Rykov and Kr'ijanovski) written by Zinoviev, Trotsky, Kamenev, Rakovsky, Piatakov, Smilga and others and published in the discussion documents of *Pravda* of 17 Nov. 1927.

43 Serge, *From Lenin to Stalin*, p. 41.

44 Deutscher discusses the differences between Trotsky and Preobrazhensky in *The Prophet Unarmed*, pp. 237–8.

45 Preobrazhensky admitted that a part of the surplus product was captured by private capital in the form of merchant's profit, due in large part to the inadequate state of the system of distribution in the young Soviet state. He also conceded that the NEP men were profiting on internal loans; but he did not go as far as Serge did in terms of the scale of wealth obtained by the new bourgeoisie. See Evgeny Preobrazhensky, *The New Economics*, Oxford, Oxford University Press, 1965 pp. 189–90.

46 Serge, 'Vers l'industrialisation', quoting Kondoruchkin, *Le Capital privé devant la justice soviétique*, Librairie de l'état, 1927.

47 Serge, 'Vers l'industrialisation', part I, *Clarté* XV–8, p. 440, 20 Oct. 1927.

48 Ibid., p. 441.

49 Upon his return to the USSR Serge noted when meeting people he had not seen since 1921: 'We did not create the Revolution to come to this.'

50 Leon Trotsky, *Writings*, New York, Pathfinder Press, 1973, Supplement to 1929–33, p. 70.

51 In a private conversation in Mexico City, May 1987.

52 Serge, *Memoirs*, p. 207.

53 See Trotsky, *My Life*, p. 111.

54 Serge, *Memoirs*, p. 208.

55 Ibid.

56 Ibid., p. 212.

57 Ibid.

58 Ibid., p. 213.

59 Ibid.

60 Ibid., p. 214.

61 Ibid., p. 215.

62 Ibid., p. 218.

63 Ibid., p. 219.

64 Ibid., p. 220.

65 Ibid., p. 221.

66 Ibid., p. 220.

67 Ibid., pp. 220–21.

68 Ibid., p. 222.

69 Ibid., p. 225.

70 In *Russia Twenty Years After*.

71 Deutscher discusses this demonstration in *The Prophet Unarmed*, pp. 372–6.

72 Serge, *Memoirs*, p. 226.

73 Ibid.

74 Louis Fischer, *Men and Politics, An Autobiography*, London, Jonathan Cape, 1941, pp. 91–2.

75 See, for example, Victor Serge, *From Lenin to Stalin*, p. 86; *Portrait de Staline*, Paris, Editions Bernard Grasset, 1940, chapter XXI; 'The Third Moscow Trial', in *La Révolution prolétarienne*, March 1938; *Seize fusillés*, Paris, Spartacus Cahiers Mensuels, 1936, pp. 19, 31–4; *Life and Death of Leon Trotsky* (with Natalia Sedova), New York, Basic Books, 1975, p. 181; *Memoirs*, pp. 333–4.

76 Serge, *Memoirs*, p. 227.

77 Ibid., p. 228.

78 Fischer, *Men and Politics*, pp. 92–3.

79 Deutscher, *The Prophet Unarmed*, pp. 381–4. Fischer also describes the funeral and the crowd protecting Trotsky in his autobiography, *Men and Politics*, p. 93.

80 Serge quoted Bukharin in *Memoirs*, p. 231.

81 Ibid., p. 232.

82 Ibid.

83 Ibid., pp. 234–5.

84 Ibid., p. 235.

85 See Trotsky, *My Life*, pp. 562–71.

86 Serge, *Memoirs*, p. 233.

87 The title came from a phrase of Lenin. The journal staunchly defended the Opposition against the campaign of persecution. The Paz circle in France later grew and a new bi-monthly journal called *La Révolution prolétarienne* took the

place of *Contre le Courant*. Its contributors were mainly revolutionary syndicalists and literary figures including Georges Duhamel, Charles Víldrac, Georges
Pioch, Leon Werth, Marcel Martinet and Henri Poulaille. These French intellectuals later waged an international campaign to secure Serge's release from
Stalin's prison camps.

88 Serge, *Memoirs*, p. 234. Serge did not reach Paris for another nine years, three
of which he spent in captivity.

89 Alfred Rosmer, *Moscow under Lenin*, New York and London, Monthly Review
Press, 1971, pp. 35–7.

90 Rosenthal (1903–92) became Trotsky's lawyer, and Naville remained a Trotskyist activist his entire life in France.

91 Serge, *Memoirs*, p. 231.

92 *Clarté*, part I, no. 15, Nov. 1927, pp. 436–42, and part II, no. 16, Dec. 1927,
pp. 485–91.

93 There were seven articles in all. Six appeared in *Clarté*, the first 'Le Bolshevisme
et l'Asie', *Clarté*, New Series, no. 7, 15 March 1927, pp. 195–9; then the five
part series entitled 'La lutte des classes dans la révolution chinoise' appearing in
Clarté, New Series, no. 9, 15 May 1927, pp. 259–66; no. 11, 15 July 1927,
pp. 323–9; no. 12, 15 Aug. 1927, pp. 356–62; no. 13, 15 Sept. 1927,
pp. 382–92; no. 14, 15 Oct. 1927, pp. 406–12; and the last article 'Canton',
appeared in *La Lutte des classes*, no. 1, Feb.–March 1928. *Clarté* was a Marxist
and Communist journal, independent of the Communist Party, but controlled
by it. The two editors, Marcel Fourier and Pierre Naville, both belonged to the
Party.

94 Pierre Naville, in his preface to the French and Spanish recompilation of
Serge's *Clarté* articles, wrote that throughout 1926 any articles in *Clarté* on
China simply reflected the Comintern line uncritically. That changed when
the writings of Trotsky and Zinoviev began to filter out of the USSR, and with
the appearance of Serge's articles, which 'established the real characteristics of
the "class struggle in the Chinese revolution"' and 'notably clarified the errors
of the Comintern'. Naville commented that Serge's articles made *Clarté* realize
it had committed a series of errors, and turned the attention of the French leftists to the Chinese revolution. Pierre Naville, Preface to Victor Serge, *La Revolución China 1926–1928*, Mexico, Editorial Domes, 1984, pp. 8–10.

95 Published in France as *La Révolution chinoise, 1927–29*, Paris, Savelli, 1977; and
in Mexico by Vlady, as *La Revolución China 1926–1928*, Mexico, Editorial
Domes SA., 1984. The Italian edition was published by Samonà e Savelli,
1971, and the German edition was published by Verlag Neue Kritik, 1975.
The English translation appeared as 'The Class Struggle in the Chinese Revolution' in *Revolutionary History*, vol. 5, no 3, autumn 1994: *Victor Serge: The Century
of the Unexpected, Essays on Revolution and Counter-Revolution*, pp. 55–141, translated by Gregor Benton.

96 Naville, who later wrote extensively on China, wrote the preface to the French
and Spanish editions of the collection of Serge's articles on China.

97 Serge, *Memoirs*, p. 220.

98 'Le Bolshevisme et l'Asie', *Clarté*, New Series, no. 7, 14 March 1927. Serge
also had access to the publications of the Communist International, and to the
French Communist journal, *L'Humanité*.

99 Victor Serge, *Clarté*, no. 12, 15 Aug. 1927, p. 105 of the Spanish recompilation.

Serge stressed, quoting Lenin, that Communism should not be subordinated to Sunyatsenism, nor the Communist Party to the Kuomintang.

100 Serge, *La Revolución China*, p. 141, Spanish edition.

101 Ibid., pp. 141–5.

102 Ibid., p. 147.

103 Mao Tse-tung, 'Analysis of Classes in Chinese Society' (March 1926) and 'Internal Information on an Investigation of the Peasant Movement of Hunan' (March 1927).

104 Mao Tse-tung, quoted in Serge, 'La Lutte des classes dans la Révolution chinoise', *Clarté*, no. 12, 15 Aug. 1927, p. 358. Author's translation.

105 Ibid.

106 Serge, *Memoirs* p. 216.

107 Serge, *From Lenin to Stalin*, p. 45.

108 Serge, *Russia Twenty Years After*, p. 256.

109 Serge, *From Lenin to Stalin*, p. 45.

110 Serge, *Russia Twenty Years After*, p. 256.

111 Serge, *Memoirs*, p. 217.

112 *Writings of Leon Trotsky 1938–1939*, Pathfinder Press, New York, 1969, pp. 261–4.

113 Souvarine, *Stalin*, p. 471.

114 Serge, *Russia Twenty Years After*, pp. 159–60.

115 Trotsky, *My Life*, p. 552.

116 *Writings of Leon Trotsky*, p. 262.

117 Ibid., p. 263.

118 Trotsky, *My Life*, p. 553.

119 Souvarine, *Stalin*, p. 472.

120 Ibid., p. 474.

121 Serge, *Russia Twenty Years After*, p. 162n.

122 Serge, *Memoirs*, p. 239.

123 Serge, *Russia Twenty Years After*, p. 160n.

124 Serge, *Memoirs*, pp. 239–40.

125 Ibid., pp. 242–3.

126 The stories of the fate of these Oppositionists is found in Serge's *Russia Twenty Years After*, pp. 94–114.

127 RGASPI, F. 495, Op. 2, D. 83 (Moscow) contains data on Serge's first Soviet arrest.

128 Taped interview with Vlady, Mexico City, May 1987.

129 Serge, *Memoirs*, p. 240.

130 See 'Victor Serge en prison', *Clarté*, vol. 1928, no. 4, pp. 89–90. The editorial is quoted in full in Richard Greeman, 'Victor Serge: the Making of a Novelist, 1890–1928', unpublished Ph.D. thesis, Columbia University, 1968, pp. 400–401.

131 Serge, *Memoirs*, p. 238.

4 Stalinization 1928–33: the bureaucratic counter-revolution, solitary struggles in precarious freedom

1 Victor Serge, *Memoirs of a Revolutionary*, London, Writers and Readers, 1984, p. 244.

2 Ibid., p. 161.

3 Ibid., pp. 263–4.

4 Ibid.

5 Ibid.

6 Ibid.

7 Ibid.

8 As told to Serge by Ilya Yonov, an old friend, former Zinovievite Opposition-ist, at that time the head of the literary publishing house of the State Press. Serge, *Memoirs*, p. 262.

9 Although *Men in Prison* was translated, proofread and made into pages, *ibid*. In 1989, some of Serge's fiction finally began to appear in Soviet provincial liter-ary journals, and in 1991 *The Case of Comrade Tulayev* and *Midnight in the Century* were published in a single volume in Russia: Viktor Serzh, *Polnoch' Veka, Delo Tulayeva*, Cheliabinsk, Yuzhno-Ural'skoi Izdatel'stvo, translators Vladimir Babintsev, Ellen Grey.

10 'The Conscience of the Writer' reprinted from *Now* in David Craig's anthology *Marxists on Literature*, Harmondsworth, Penguin Books, 1973, p. 439. The original French article was published as the supplement to *Masses* Jan. 1947, no. 6, in *Les Egaux*, p. 7.

11 Serge, *Memoirs*, p. 272.

12 Ibid., p. 173.

13 A useful discussion of the chain of events set in motion by the general crisis in NEP in 1927–28, leading to the wholesale and ruthless collectivization of the peasants in 1929–30 can be found in Moshe Lewin's book *Russian Peasants and Soviet Power: A Study of Collectivization*, Evanston, Northwestern University Press, 1968.

14 Panaït Istrati (ghosted by Serge), *Soviets 1929*, Paris, Rieder, 1929, pp. 22–3.

15 Victor Serge, 'Trente ans après la révolution russe', published in English in Susan Weissman (ed.), *Victor Serge: Russia Twenty Years After*, Atlantic High-lands, NJ, Humanities Press, 1996, p. 163.

16 Serge, *Memoirs*, p. 246.

17 Lewin, *Russian Peasants and Soviet Power*, pp. 217–18, 532.

18 Serge, *Russia Twenty Years After*, p. 163.

19 Serge, *Memoirs*, p. 257.

20 Victor Serge, *From Lenin to Stalin*, New York, Pioneer Publishers, 1937, p. 58.

21 Ibid., p. 167.

22 Ibid.

23 Serge, *Russia Twenty Years After*, p. 168.

24 J. Stalin, '*Golovokruzhenie ot uspekhov. K voprosam kolkhoznogo dvizheniia*', *Sochi-neniia* 12, pp. 191–9. The article 'Dizzy with Success' appeared in *Pravda*, 2 March 1930.

25 Serge, *From Lenin to Stalin*, p. 64.

26 Serge, *Russia Twenty Years After*, p. 169.

27 Ibid., p. 170. See also Bohdan Krawchenko, 'The Famine in the Ukraine in 1933', *Critique* 17, 1986, pp. 137–47, and Robert Conquest, *Harvest of Sorrow*, Oxford, Oxford University Press, 1986.

28 Serge, *Russia Twenty Years After*, p. 163.

29 Ibid.

30 Ibid., p. 244.

31 Serge, *From Lenin to Stalin*, p. 53.
32 Trotsky to Rakovsky, 13 July 1928. Quoted in Isaac Deutscher, *The Prophet Unarmed, Trotsky 1921–1929*, Oxford, Oxford University Press, 1959, p. 447n.
33 Anton Ciliga, *The Russian Enigma*, London, The Labour Book Service, 1940, pp. 84–5.
34 Serge, *From Lenin to Stalin*, pp. 53–4.
35 Vlady recalled that Kazantzakis lived with them for six months in 1927–28. Taped interview, Mexico City, May 1987.
36 Panaït Istrati, *Vers l'autre flamme: Après seize mois dans L'U.R.S.S 1927–1928*, Paris, Union Générale d'Editions, 1980, pp. 113–14. Also in Serge, *Memoirs*, p. 277.
37 Serge, *Memoirs*, p. 279.
38 He had been in the Soviet Union twice: the first tour lasted three months until December 1927; then he and Kazantzakis went to Athens, and after two months returned to tour the Soviet Union for a year. They went to Bykovo in the beginning of May 1928. Istrati left the USSR for France on 15 Feb. 1929. See Marcel Mermoz, 'Introduction', *Vers l'autre flamme*, Fondation Panaït Istrati, 10/18, Union Générale d'Editions, Paris, 1980, p. 11, and Istrati, *Vers l'autre flamme*, pp. 199–202.
39 Victor Alba, 'Boris Souvarine: Logic and Indignation', *Journal of Contemporary Studies*, vol. VIII, no. 4, fall/winter 1985, though appearing in spring 1986.
40 Mermoz, 'Introduction', pp. 23–4. Richard Greeman, in his article 'Victor Serge: Writer and Witness', *New Politics*, vol. 1, no. 2 (New Series), winter 1987, p. 214, confirms the story of Bilili carrying the manuscript in her bodice and cites Monique Jutrin-Klener, *Panaït Istrati*, Paris, 1970, p. 9.
41 Anton Antonov-Ovseyenko, *The Time of Stalin: Portrait of a Tyranny*, Harper Colophon Books, 1981, p. 56.
42 Istrati, *Soviets 1929*, p. 139.
43 Ibid., p. 203.
44 Ibid., p. 209.
45 Ibid., pp. 205–7.
46 Victor Serge and Natalia Sedova Trotsky, *The Life and Death of Leon Trotsky*, New York, Basic Books, 1975, p. 167.
47 Ibid., pp. 47, 59.
48 Istrati, *Soviets 1929*, p. 55.
49 Ibid., pp. 47–9.
50 Ibid., p. 51.
51 Ibid., p. 56.
52 Ibid., pp. 54–5.
53 See Christian Rakovsky, 'The Five Year Plan in Crisis', *Critique* 13, 1981, pp. 13–53.
54 This theoretical current is discussed in Donald Filtzer's afterword to Rakovsky's article, 'The Five Year Plan in Crisis'. Rakovsky's article *'Na s'ezde i v strane'* was originally published in *Byulleten' oppozitsii* 25/26, 1931, pp. 9–32.
55 The Soviets began describing the command system during the Gorbachev years. Hillel H. Ticktin described the hierarchically administered economy in 'The Contradictions of Soviet Society and Professor Bettelheim', *Critique* 6, 1976, pp. 17–44.

56 Serge, *Russia Twenty Years After*, p. 13.

57 Serge referred to conditions in 1936. Ibid., p. 14.

58 Ibid., p. 8.

59 Ibid., p. 166.

60 See *Russia Twenty Years After*, part II, chapter 3, 'Industrialization and Collectivization (1928–1934)', pp. 163–77, and chapter 4, 'The Great Wretchedness (1931–1934)', pp. 174–85.

61 Ibid., p. 172.

62 Ibid., chapter 2.

63 Ibid., p. 18.

64 Ibid., pp. 15–16. *Sotsialisticheskii Vestnik* places this strike in April–May 1932, not 1931.

65 Ibid., p. 178.

66 Christian Rakovsky, 'The "Professional Dangers" of Power' (letter to Valentinov), collected in Rakovsky, *Selected Writings on Opposition in the USSR 1923–30*, London, Allison and Busby, 1980, p. 128.

67 Serge, *Memoirs*, p. 248.

68 Ibid.

69 Ibid.

70 Serge, *Russia Twenty Years After*, p. 174.

71 Robert Conquest, *The Great Terror*, Harmondsworth, Penguin Books, 1968, p. 733.

72 Academician Tarle, according to Serge, the 'only non-Marxist Soviet historian of repute, spent long months in prison and was deported to Alma-Ata; today [1942] he is the most official of all historians in the Soviet Union'. Serge, *Memoirs* p. 250.

73 See G. Hosking's brief summary in *The First Socialist Society: A History of the Soviet Union from Within*, Cambridge, Mass., Harvard University Press, 1985, chapter 6, esp. pp. 149–53 and 172–4.

74 Serge, *Memoirs*, p. 249.

75 Hosking, *The First Socialist Society*, p. 151.

76 Serge, *Russia Twenty Years After*, p. 173.

77 Serge, *Memoirs*, p. 248.

78 Ibid.

79 Ibid., pp. 248–9.

80 Ibid., pp. 250–52.

81 Ibid. Serge was wrong about the date of Ryazanov's death which was 1938.

82 *Victor Serge: Russia Twenty Years After*, including Serge's *Thirty Years After*, edited and introduced by Susan Weissman, Atlantic Highlands, NJ, Humanities Press, 1996, p. 320.

83 Stalin, *Sochineniia*, XI, p. 287, quoted in Roy Medvedev, *Let History Judge*, New York, Vintage Books, 1973, p. 68.

84 Serge, *Memoirs*, p. 258. The Opposition published the two documents (Kamenev's confidential résumé of his meeting with Bukharin, and Kamenev's notes for Zinoviev) abroad and illegally in Moscow in 1928. Serge quoted the essential passages in *From Lenin to Stalin*, with comments, pp. 95–100.

85 Serge, *Russia Twenty Years After*, pp. 320–21.

86 Ibid.

87 Serge, *Memoirs*, p. 258.

88 The Ryutin affair is discussed widely in the literature: see Ciliga, Serge, Trotsky, Deutscher, Conquest, Hosking, Getty, etc. Ciliga summarizes the programme, in his *Russian Enigma*, pp. 279–80. Ciliga's information is based on the members of Ryutin's group who were sent to the Verkhne-Uralsk Isolator where Ciliga was imprisoned.

89 Ciliga, ibid.

90 Serge, *Memoirs*, p. 254.

91 Ibid., p. 257. Hopefully this book survived.

92 Isaac Deutscher presents an account of Blumkin's life and the episode which brought him the death sentence in *The Prophet Outcast, Trotsky 1929–1940*, Oxford, Oxford University Press, 1963, pp. 84–91. Although he quoted Serge's account, it is different from Serge's on several counts. See Serge, *Memoirs*, pp. 255–7.

93 Ibid., p. 260.

94 Deutscher, *The Prophet Outcast*, p. 163. Naum Jasny, who dedicated his *Soviet Industrialization 1928–1952*, Chicago, Chicago University Press, 1961, to Vladimir Gustavovich Groman, confirmed in a reminiscence of Groman that he had backed Stalin and Bukharin until 1928, opposing Trotsky on industrialization. When Stalin made his 'left turn' the Mensheviks were brought to trial.

95 Serge, *Memoirs*, p. 260.

96 To be more precise: *From Lenin to Stalin*, which detailed the fate and last words of Trotsky's closest collaborators and of the Zinovievists, was written with the passion of a committed journalist and historian whose facts must stand up to scrutiny, and with the prose of a poet whose words sear the consciousness of the reader. The book is filled with long quotes from letters Serge received, while it was still possible to correspond. Later, Serge quoted from reports smuggled out of the prisons and camps. The contrasting character of many of the revolution's *literati* was revealed by Serge, who knew them all or had access to others who did. How else would we know Blumkin wrote a memoir, or how Solnstsev died, or that Muralov refused capitulation to the very end? *Russia Twenty Years After* gives case histories of A. Tarov, Trotskyist, the SRs Abraham Gortz and Leo Gerstein, Boris Chernov, and Volkenstein; Social Democrats George Kuchin, Sommer, Goldenberg, Ramishvili, Eva Broido, Braunstein, Lieber and Zederbaum (Martov's brother); Anarchists Nicolas Rogdayev, Aaron Baron, Vladimir Barmash, Gerassimchik, Albert Inaun, Sandomirsky, Zeinl Mühsam, the Tuscan syndicalist Otello Gaggi and others. Oppositionists Albert Heinrichsen, Vassily Chadev, Georg Butov, Yakov Blumkin, Silov, Rabinovich, Yoselevich, Blumenfeld, Sosnovsky, Leon Papermeister, Helen Tsulukidze, Old Bolshevik Kote Tsintsadze, Eleazar Solntsev, Trotsky, Alexandra Bronstein, Gregory Yakovin, Vassily Pankratov, Shanan Pevzner, Socrates Gayvorkian, Dvinsky, Man Nevelson (married to Trotsky's daughter Nina), Grinstein, Nicolas Gorlov, Aaron, Paul and Samuel Papermeister, Anna Yankovskaya, Marie Ivanovna, Ida Lemelman, Boris Mikhailovich Eltsin, Victor Eltsin, Maria Mikhailovna Yoffe, Lado Dumbadze, Lado Yenukidze, Joseph Krasskin, Vladimir Kossior, Mikhail Andreyevich Polevoy, Trukhanov, Nicolai Muralov, Mikhail Bodrov, Dora Zack, Ida Shumskaya, Boris Ilych Lakhovitsky, Alexis Semenovich Santalov, Lyda

Svalova, Yakov Belenky, Yakov Byk, Fanya Upstein, Leonid Girchek, Vassily Mikhailovich Chernykh; Sheva Ghenkina, Nadyezhda Almaz, Anita Russakova; the democratic centralist Oppositionists Vladimir Smirnov and Timothey Sapronov, the capitulators Zinoviev, Kamenev, Ivan Smirnov, Eismont, Tolmachev, Red Professors Sliepkov, Astrov, Maretsky, Eikhenwald, Worker-Bolshevik Kayurov, Worker Oppositionist Shliapnikov and Medvedyev, and many more . . .

97 Serge, *Russia Twenty Years After*.

98 Vlady, private conversation, 3 July 1988.

99 Serge mentioned conditions in his communal flat in various writings: see *Memoirs*, his article 'Complots en URSS', *La Wallonie*, and *Russia Twenty Years After*, where Serge wrote that his in-laws (the Russakovs) lived in the same communal flat.

100 Serge, *Memoirs*, p. 274.

101 The story about Serge's family is found in the *Memoirs*, pp. 277–8, 294–5, 322; *Russia Twenty Years After*, pp. 111–14, Attilio Chitarin, 'Una Voce dal gulag: lettere inedite di Victor Serge', *Revista di Storia Contemporanea*, no. 3, 1978, pp. 426–45, Panaït Istrati, *Vers l'autre flamme*, pp. 149–94, and Pierre Pascal, *Mon Journal de Russie*, vol. III and vol. IV, Lausanne, L'Age d'Homme, 1922–27.

102 Serge, *Memoirs*, pp. 279–80.

103 Titled 'La Profession de foi de Victor-Serge', *La Révolution prolétarienne*, vol. 1933, no. 152, p. 193. Reprinted in Serge's *Seize fusillés, où va la révolution russe?* Paris, Cahiers Spartacus, no. 1, serie nouvelle, 1936.

104 Serge, '1933, Tout est mis en question', in *Seize fusillés*, p. 47.

5 Orenburg 1933–36, interrogation and deportation: digging the graves of the Revolution

1 Victor Serge, *From Lenin to Stalin*, New York, Pioneer Publishers, 1937, pp. 68–9.

2 Victor Serge, *Memoirs of a Revolutionary*, London, Writers and Readers, 1984, p. 286.

3 Ibid.

4 Serge, *Memoirs*, p. 288.

5 Ibid., p. 190.

6 Serge's criminal file, P–3567, Central Archive of Federal Security Service, Moscow, summary by Alexei Gusev.

7 M. Rutkovsky later became Marc Zborowski's boss in Moscow. See Dimitri Volkogonov, *Trotsky: The Eternal Revolutionary*, New York, The Free Press, 1996, p. 334.

8 Serge, *Memoirs*, pp. 284–96, *From Lenin to Stalin*, pp. 77–8. Serge's characters Ryzhik and Elkin, in his novel *Midnight in the Century* (London, Writers and Readers, 1982), act in a similarly bold, forthright and almost reckless manner, attacking Stalin's politics from the year 1907 on, denouncing his crimes and his role as gravedigger. We assume this was Serge's stance during his interrogation. See *Midnight in the Century*, pp. 65, 143, and especially pp. 165–7, 169–71.

9 Yevgeny Ambartsumov, 'A Venomous Fog Lifts: Victims of the Moscow Trials Have Been Rehabilitated', *Moscovskiye novosti*, 19 June 1988, p. 10. Appeared

in the English edition of *Moscow News*, no. 25, 26 June to 3 July 1988, as 'The Poisonous Mist Disperses', p. 10.

10 Ibid.

11 Serge, *Memoirs*, pp. 296–7. See also 'Extract from the minutes of Special Consultation of OGPU Collegium', 28 May 1933, in Serge's criminal file.

12 Ibid.

13 Ibid.

14 Serge, *Midnight in the Century*, p. 102.

15 Serge, *Memoirs*, p. 299.

16 Ibid., p. 303.

17 Ibid.

18 Susan Weissman (ed.), *Victor Serge: Russia Twenty Years After*, Atlantic Highlands, NJ, Humanities Press, 1996, p. 75.

19 Information supplied by Vlady, interview in Mexico City, May 1987.

20 Translated by Richard Greeman and published by Writers and Readers.

21 Ibid., p. 307.

22 Serge, *Midnight in the Century*, pp. 117–18.

23 W.J. Marshall, *Victor Serge: The Uses of Dissent*, New York and Oxford, Berg, 1992, pp. 140–41.

24 Serge, *Memoirs*, p. 307.

25 Taped interview with Vlady in Mexico, May 1987.

26 Serge, *Memoirs*, p. 311.

27 Ibid., p. 312.

28 Ibid., p. 315.

29 Robert Conquest, *The Great Terror*, Harmondsworth, Penguin Books, 1968, p. 73.

30 Serge, *Memoirs*, p. 313.

31 *Byulleten Oppozitzii*, no. 41, Jan. 1935.

32 Boris Nicolaevsky, 'The Murder of Kirov', *Sotsialistichesky Vestnik*, May, Oct. and Dec. 1956, collected in the same author's *Power and the Soviet Elite*, New York, Praeger, 1965, p. 71.

33 Nicolaevsky, 'Murder of Kirov', p. 92. Nicolaevsky indicated that his analysis of the Seventeenth Party Congress was shared by Bukharin, and later by L.S. Shaumian in an article in *Pravda* of 7 Feb. 1964.

34 Roy Medvedev, *Let History Judge*, New York, Vintage Books, 1973, pp. 159–60.

35 Serge, *Russia Twenty Years After*, p. 197.

36 Ibid., p. 314.

37 *Ural*, nos 1–3, 1989. The novel was then published, along with Serge's *Midnight in the Century* in 1991. See *Polnoch' Veka; Dyelo Tulayeva*, Chelyabinsk: Iuzhnno-Urals'skoe Knizhnoe Izdatel'stvo, 1991, translated and with an introduction by Vladimir Babintsev. The translation of *The Case of Comrade Tulayev* is by Ellen Gray.

38 Interview with Sergei Zavarotnyi, Moscow, March 1989.

39 Serge, *Russia Twenty Years After*, p. 203.

40 Serge, *Memoirs*, p. 315.

41 Ibid.

42 The arrangement was explained in a letter Magdeleine Paz wrote to Marcel Willard of the Association Juridique Internationale, 19 Nov. 1934, published in *La Révolution prolétarienne*, Nov. 1934, pp. 12–13.

43 Serge, *Memoirs*, pp. 313–14.

44 Ibid., p. 315.

45 The events surrounding the Victor Serge affair and the 1935 Congress of Writers are discussed, *inter alia*, in the *Memoirs*, pp. 317–19, William Marshall, 'Ideology and Literary Expression in the Works of Victor Serge', D.Phil. thesis, Oxford University, 1984, pp. 228–9, and twenty-six articles published in *La Révolution prolétarienne* from 1933 to 1936. Two letters to Magdeleine Paz datelined Brussels, May 1936, were also published in *Seize fusillés, où va la révolution russe?* Paris, Spartacus Cahiers Mensuels, no. 1, 1936, 1972, pp. 51–8, and Jacques Mesnil published 'Pour Victor Serge' in *Les Nouvelles Littéraires*, 22 July 1933, where Magdeleine Paz also published a response. The affair is also treated in Herbert R. Lottman, *The Left Bank: Writers, Artists, and Politics from the Popular Front to the Cold War*, London, Heinemann, 1982 and Richard Greeman, 'The Victor Serge Affair and the French Literary Left', in *Victor Serge: The Century of the Unexpected, Revolutionary History*, vol. 5, no 3, autumn 1994, pp. 142–74.

46 See for example the list of contributors in *La Révolution prolétarienne*, no. 122–2, 1933.

47 Serge, *Memoirs*, p. 317.

48 Ibid.

49 Victor Serge, *Carnets*, Paris, Julliard, 1952.

50 Jacques Mesnil, 'Au Pays de la dictature bureaucratique: Les menteurs officiels contre Victor Serge', in *La Révolution prolétarienne*, no. 184, 1934, and Magdeleine Paz, 'L'Affair Victor Serge n'interesse pas l'Association juridique internationale', in *La Révolution prolétarienne*, 1934, pp. 12–13.

51 Serge wrote in *Pages of a Diary*: 'He came to see Stalin in 1935 and asked that a period be put to "l'affaire Victor Serge," that I be either sentenced or freed. Stalin said he was "not up on the matter" and promised my liberty if it was at all possible. It was to this request in particular that I owe my life, it seems to me.' Serge, *New International*, May–June 1950, 'The Tragedy of Romain Rolland: Pages from the Diary of Victor Serge IV', p. 178.

52 Tamara Motylyova, 'Romain Rolland: I am defending the USSR, not Stalin', *Moscow News* weekly no. 13, 1988, 22 March 1988, p. 16.

53 Romain Rolland, *Voyage de Moscou, Cahiers Romain Rolland*, no. 29, Paris, Albin Michel, 1992. See also Richard Greeman, 'The Victor Serge Affair', pp. 142–74.

54 Victor Serge, *Memoirs d'un révolutionnaire 1901–1941*, Editions du Seuil, Paris, 1951, p. 337. This particular passage is not in the English edition, which is shorter than the original by an eighth.

55 Taped interview with Vlady, Moscow, March 1989.

56 Both accounts are presented here.

57 Serge's account of his last days in the USSR can be found on pp. 321–2.

58 Ibid., p. 322.

59 Interview with Vlady, March 1989.

60 According to her cousin Irina Gogua. Interview, 10 March 1989, Moscow.

61 As told to John Eden and Les Smith, Mexico City, 3 June 1989.

62 This account used the following sources: Serge's writings, Richard Greeman's unpublished paper 'Liberation', and Vlady's recollection.

63 'Lettre à André Gide', Brussels, May 1936, *La Révolution prolétarienne*, 13–157, 14–158.

64 Serge, *Carnets*, p. 21.

65 Ibid.

66 The first English translation of Serge's poems, *Resistance* was published by City Lights Books, San Francisco, translated by James Brook, 1989.

67 George Orwell to Dwight Macdonald, 4 April 1945 and 14 Feb. 1946. Thanks to David Cotterill for sending me these letters.

68 Yevtushenko to Weissman, 18 June 1987.

69 Telephone conversation between Vlady and archivist, Moscow, March 1989.

70 The story of Eden's search for Serge's manuscripts and the establishment of the Victor Serge museum in Orenburg is in 'The Search for Victor Serge', in Susan Weissman (ed.) *The Ideas of Victor Serge: A Life as a Work of Art*, Glasgow, Critique Books, 1997, pp. 27–33.

71 Both letters were printed in the *Victor Serge Centenary Group Newsletter*, Jan. 1991, p. 9. See also Murray Armstrong, 'The Searchers', *The Guardian Weekly*, Saturday–Sunday, 22–23 Sept. 1990, for an account of the search.

72 Requests were made in person by this author in 1993, 1996, 1997 and 1999; by Richard Greeman in 1992 and 1994; by John Eden in 1993. Alexei Gusev in Moscow has continued the search with limited access to FSB files.

73 Genrikh Iagoda, *Narkom vutrennikh del SSSR*, Kazan, Sbornik dokumentov, 1997, p. 431.

Part II Introduction

1 The Fourth International was founded by Trotsky and his co-thinkers in 1938 as a world organization of revolutionary Marxism. They believed the Comintern had been thoroughly Stalinized, was unreformable, and would never be in the forefront of revolution anywhere.

2 See *inter alia*, Leon Trotsky, 'Victor Serge and the Fourth International', 2 Dec. 1938, 'Intellectual Ex-Radicals and World Reaction', 17 February 1939, in L.D. Trotsky, *Writings 1938–39*, New York, Merit Publishers, 1969; Pierre Frank, Introduction to *Kronstadt* by V.I. Lenin and L.D. Trotsky, New York, Monad Press, 1979, and in the journal *Quatrième Internationale*, Nov.–Dec. 1947, Paris, an obituary for Serge stated: 'Serge soutint la politique centriste . . . on regrettera que ce militant révolutionnaire . . . dégagé de son experience personnel du stalinisme, certes cruelle et deprimante, que des doutes sans fondements serieux sur le marxisme révolutionnaire.'

3 Trotsky to Cannon, 24 Dec. 1937, 'Les "leçons d'Espagne" et le Menchevisme dans les rangs des Partisans de la IV Internationale.' This letter, found in the Serge archives in Mexico, was not printed in the English edition of Trotsky's *Writings*.

4 Victor Serge to Podoliak (pseudonym for Hryhory Kostiuk), 22 June 1947. Pseudonym established by Kostiuk, who gave me this letter, during an interview in November 1985. The original read: '*Ya ostaius – neopokolebimo – sotsialistom, storonnikom demokraticheskogo sotsializma. Sistemu protiv kotorii ya borolsya i borius – i kot. {sic} vui znaete po opuitu, – ya rassmatrivuyo kak raznovidnost totalitarisma t.d. nechto novoe, po kraine beschelovechnoe i antisotsialisticheskoe*'.

5 Taped interviews with Vlady, 20 Aug. 1990, and 7 Aug. 1996, and with Laurette Séjourné, 6 Sept. 1990, Mexico.

6 Laurette and Jeannine joined them in March 1942. RCA radiogram to Nancy

Macdonald, 6 March 1942, from Laura [sic] and Victor Serge, announcing arrival in Veracruz of 'Laura' and Jeannine. Macdonald Papers, Yale University Library.

7 Victor Serge, *Carnets*, Paris, Julliard, 1952, 15 Jan. 1944. Serge's daughter Jeannine Kibalchich also fondly remembered the weekly visits with her father to Natalia Trotsky's house. Jeannine Kibalchich, 'My Father', in Susan Weissman (ed.), *Victor Serge: A Life as a Work of Art*, Glasgow, Critique Books, 1997, p. 13.

8 The FOIA files have deleted the addressee and most of the names (at least of those who are still living) but have left in Serge's name and address as writer of the various letters. FOIA, Office of Censorship, USA, Registered no. 125, Serial no. 5967, letter postmarked 2 April 1943 (unphotographed, but distributed to stations ONI, SDC, MID, DR, examined on date 5 April 1943, three pages; letter from Serge to (deleted), postmarked 16 March 1944 and intercepted and examined 20 March 1944, entitled (by FBI) 'Russian Author in Mexico Discusses European Political Emigrations to Mexico', four pages). In this document we learn that the Russian emigration consisted of Natalia Sedova, Serge, and the widow of Andrés Nin, that the Bund (a Jewish workers' party and Russia's first mass Marxist party) was active in the Jewish emigration, that the Romanian and Czech emigration was actively promoting democracy and anti-antisemitic ideas, and of the activities of the representatives of the Comintern in Mexico. As a result of these communications J. Edgar Hoover addressed a letter to Birch D. O'Neal at the American Embassy in Mexico (25 May 1944, FBI file 100–36676–20), about Serge, a.k.a. 'Victor Napoleon Kibaltchiche, Victor Napoleon Lvovitch, Victor Kibaltchiche, Victor Serge, V. Paderewski [Serge's mother's maiden name] – Espionage-R.'

9 Interview with Laurette Séjourné, 6 Sept. 1990, Mexico City.

10 Interview with Vlady, Coyoacán, Aug. 1990. Vlady recounted the incident as we walked past the same tree he and his father hid behind that day.

11 See Paul Castelar, 'GPU Terror Starts in Mexico, Former Agent Killed, Opponents in Peril', *New Leader*. 24 Jan. 1942, p. 1.

12 Owen, Roche (ALN), 'Mexico Trotzkyites Peril Rail Transport', datelined Mexico City. This article appeared in the FBI file on Serge, document file 100–36676 (Victor Serge) indexed 21 May 1944, declassified 1 June 1984. Unfortunately the FBI deleted the published source of this article. The clipping appears to be from page 3, section 1 of the *Worker*, though deletions make the exact source unclear.

13 Macdonald Papers, 1942, Yale Collection.

14 Copy of letter to Ávila Camacho. See also Dwight Macdonald to Serge, 10 Feb. 1942, Yale Collection.

15 FBI Memorandum 57958, 1 Feb. 1942.

16 FBI Memorandum 57955.

17 *New Masses*, 24 March 1942, p. 15.

18 *New Masses*, 24 March 1942, reprinted in FBI file 161–9182–1, 16 April 1942.

19 Nancy Macdonald to Victor Serge, 6 March 1942, Macdonald Papers, Yale University Library.

20 FBI file, Record no. SA 153916, Serial no. 5967, 3 pp. Declassified 6/1/84.

21 Pino Cacucci, *Tina Modotti*, Barcelona, Circe Bolsillo, 1995 (published in English as *Tina Modotti: A Life*, New York, St Martin's Press, 1999; the page numbers cited refer to the Spanish edition), p. 281.

22 Julian Gorkín, biographical sketch of Serge, Mexico archive.

23 Interview, Mexico, Jan. 1986.

24 See, for example, *Seize fusillés à Moscou; où va la révolution russe?*, Paris, Spartacus Cahiers Mensuels, 1936, p. 125.

25 Cacucci, *Tina Modotti*, pp. 281–2.

26 Ibid.

27 Interview with Austrich's widow, Mexico City, Aug. 1996. Her husband had died just months before I spoke with her.

28 Cacucci, *Tina Modotti*, p. 282.

29 Laurette Séjourné later became a renowned Mexican anthropologist.

30 Victor Serge, *Memoirs of a Revolutionary*, London, Oxford University Press, 1963, p. 177.

6 Out of Russia, cornered in Europe

1 Victor Serge, *Memoirs of a Revolutionary*, London, Oxford University Press, 1963, p. 324.

2 Ibid.

3 Ibid., p. 326.

4 Ibid.

5 Ibid., p. 328.

6 'Vuikhozhy iz Sov. Posol'stva; Tam mne soobshchili shto na postan ovleniem VTSiK'a, ya lishon Sov. Grazhdanstva.' Serge to Sedov, Uccles to Paris, 13 July 1936, Series 231: 78, Nicolaevsky Collection, Hoover Archive, Stanford University.

7 *L'Humanité*, 2 and 14 Feb. 1937. Discussed in the correspondence between Serge and Trotsky: D.J. Cotterill (ed.), *The Serge–Trotsky Papers*, London, Pluto Press, 1994, pp. 33, 102.

8 Lev Davidovich Trotsky to Victor Serge, 'On the Subject of Jacques Sadoul', 5 March 1937, first published in Pierre Broué (ed.), *Le Mouvement Communiste en France (1919–1939)*, Paris, Editions du Minuit, 1967. In *Writings of Leon Trotsky (1936–1937)*, New York, Pathfinder Press, 1979, pp. 218–20.

9 Serge to Sedov, 18 Oct. 1936: 'I'll be there [Paris] on the 26th [Budu 26vo I khotel bui vas bidet v gorode 27vo ili 28vo nepremenno.] 231:18, Nicolaevsky Collection, Hoover Archive.

10 In *La Wallonie, Socialist Call, Révolution prolétarienne*, etc.

11 Serge, *Memoirs*, p. 331.

12 *The Case of Leon Trotsky*, New York, Merit Publishers, 1937, pp. 43–4. See also Serge's entries in *Carnets*, Paris, Julliard, 1952, for the fate of prominent Bolshevik relatives, such as Kamenev's wife Olga (Trotsky's sister), Rakovsky's family, etc.

13 There are sixteen letters from Serge to Trotsky, sixteen letters from Trotsky to Serge, twenty-five letters from Serge to Sedov, and seven from Sedov to Serge for 1936.

14 M. Dreyfus, *La Lutte contre le Stalinisme*, Paris, Maspero, 1977. A fuller volume appeared in English in 1994: edited and introduced by David Cotterill with introductions by Philip Spencer and Susan Weissman, *The Serge–Trotsky*

Papers: Correspondence and Other Writings Between Victor Serge and Leon Trotsky, London, Pluto Press.

15 The Hoover Institution of Stanford University announced in 1988 that they had discovered a previously unknown collection of Trotsky's papers within the Boris Nicolaevsky collection which was sealed until 1982. Jean Van Heijenoort and Pierre Broué were allowed access to the collection, and Broué informed me of some Serge letters he had seen in the collection. With the generous assistance of Dr Elena Danielson and Dr Carole Leadenham, I was able to retrieve photocopies of Serge and Sedov's correspondence of 1936–37. I am very grateful to Robert E. Wahl and Michel Vale for transcriptions and translation assistance of the poor photostatic copies.

16 Serge to Sedov, in French, Brussels, 21 April 1936.

17 Serge to Trotsky, 22 April 1936. Letter 1 in Cotterill, *Serge–Trotsky Papers*, pp. 40–41.

18 Ibid.

19 Serge to Trotsky, 29 April 1936. Letter 6 in Cotterill, *Serge–Trotsky Papers*, p. 49.

20 Trotsky to Serge, 24 April 1936 (in Russian).

21 Trotsky to Serge, 3 June 1936. Letter 13 in Cotterill, *Serge–Trotsky Papers*, p. 62.

22 Trotsky to Serge, 24 April 1936, Letter 2 in Cotterill, *Serge–Trotsky Papers*, pp. 41–2.

23 Trotsky to Serge, 29 April 1936. Eleven of the letters Trotsky wrote to Serge are collected in *Writings of Leon Trotsky: Supplement (1934–1940)*, New York, Pathfinder Press, pp. 657–83. Trotsky's grandchildren left in Alexandra's care were Zina's daughter, Nina's two children, and Lyova's son (Liulik). See Pierre Broué, *Trotsky*, Paris, Librairie Artheme Fayard, 1988, pp. 551, 691, 804.

24 Trotsky to Serge, 29 April 1936. Yet a year later Sedov wrote Serge that Magdeleine Paz, despite being very busy, had kindly been helping their comrade Tarov to get a work permit. Sedov to Serge, 4 June 1937 (367:19, Nicolaevsky Collection, Hoover Archive).

25 Serge to Marcel Martinet, 15 May 1936, in Dreyfus, *La Lutte contre le Stalinisme*, pp. 157–9.

26 See chapter 5.

27 Serge to Trotsky, Brussels, 27 May 1936. Letter 12, in Cotterill, *Serge–Trotsky Papers*, pp. 59–60.

28 Trotsky to Serge, 19 May 1936.

29 Ibid.

30 Serge to Sedov, in Russian, 5 Aug. 1936. 231:82, Nicolaevsky Collection, Hoover Archive.

31 Adolfo Gilly, 'El Jefe de la IV Internacional: Apuntes y Reflexiones', conference paper in 'Trotsky: revelador Politico del Mexico Cardenista (1937–87)', 22 May 1987, UNAM, Mexico City. The same point about Trotsky's treatment of his daily political collaborators compared to potential comrades, workers, was made to the author by Pierre Broué in conversation at the same conference.

32 Interview with Vlady, June 1989, conducted by John Eden and Les Smith.

33 See *The Case of Leon Trotsky*, Merit Publishers, New York, 1937. Trotsky proposed Serge as a witness, to testify in Paris, p. 43.

34 Victor Serge to Dwight Macdonald, 16 Jan. 1940, Macdonald Papers, Yale University Library.

35 Serge, *Memoirs*, p. 333.

36 Julian Gorkín, 'Adios a Victor Serge', in *Mundo*, no. 15, Jan.–Feb. 1948, Santiago de Chile, p. 6.

37 Ibid.

38 *La Révolution prolétarienne*, March 1937.

39 Serge, unpublished manuscript, 'Le dernier livre de Trotsky: Staline', 1946, Serge archive, Mexico City.

40 Victor Serge, *Portrait de Staline*, Paris, Editions Bernard Grasset, p. 175.

41 Victor Serge, 'Trente ans après la révolution russe', published in English in Susan Weissman (ed.), *Victor Serge: Russia Twenty Years After*, Atlantic Highlands, NJ, Humanities Press, 1996, pp. 297–8.

42 In an article Serge wrote in Mexico, published in *Rumbo*, titled 'Balance de la Reacción Staliniana', Oct. and Nov. 1941, pp. 9 and 30.

43 This is the third section, called 'Confessions', of Serge's long poem, 'The History of Russia', collected in *Résistance*, pp. 18–24.

44 Serge explained the enigma of the confession in various writings: *From Lenin to Stalin*, p. 86; *Portrait de Staline*, chapter XXI; 'Le Troisième procès de Moscou', in *La Révolution prolétarienne*, 10 March 1938; *Seize fusillés*, pp. 19, 31–4; *Life and Death of Leon Trotsky* (with Natalia Sedova), New York, Basic Books, 1975, pp. 233–9; *Memoirs*, pp. 333–4.

45 Serge, *From Lenin to Stalin*, p. 86.

46 Walter Krivitsky, *In Stalin's Secret Service*, New York and London, Harper Brothers, 1939, p. 190.

47 Serge, *Russia Twenty Years After*, p. 321.

48 Ibid.

49 Victor Serge, *The Case of Comrade Tulayev*, London, Penguin Books, 1968, pp. 360–61.

50 Serge, *Carnets*, entry for 15 Nov. 1946.

51 Serge, *Russia Twenty Years After*, part III, chapter 7.

52 Serge discussed this in *Soviets 29*, Paris, Rieder, 1925; *Russia Twenty Years After*, and in essays from the Mexico archive.

53 See, *inter alia*, Serge, *Soviets 1929*, *Russia Twenty Years After*, and *From Lenin to Stalin*. Serge also wrote extensively on the effects of Stalin's policies on science, art and literature.

54 Serge, *Russia Twenty Years After*, pp. 297–8.

55 Victor Serge, *The Case of Comrade Tulayev*, Harmondsworth, Penguin Books, 1968, pp. 167–8.

56 Serge, *Russia Twenty Years After*, p. 185.

57 Victor Serge, 'Russia', unpublished manuscript, no date, Serge archives, Mexico.

58 Serge, *Russia Twenty Years After*, p. 204.

59 See Elizabeth Poretsky, *Our Own People*; Ann Arbor, University of Michigan Press, 1969; Walter Krivitsky, *In Stalin's Secret Service*, New York and London, Harper Brothers, 1939, on the fate of Soviets abroad and his own narrow escape from being 'recalled'; and Roy Medvedev, *Let History Judge*, New York, Vintage Books, 1973, on the repression of foreign communists. Alexander Orlov, in *The Secret History of Stalin's Crimes*, New York, Random House, 1953,

wrote that forty agents were recalled during the summer of 1937, out of which only five refused to return.

60 An excellent account of the murderous role of the NKVD in Spain can be found in Victor Alba and Stephen Schwartz, *Spanish Marxism versus Soviet Communism: A History of the POUM*, New Brunswick and Oxford, Transaction Books, 1988, especially chapters 6 and 7.

61 See Marc Zborowski's (Etienne's) testimony before Senator Eastland's 'Scope of Soviet Activity in the United States' Hearings before the Subcommittee on Internal Security of the Committee on the Judiciary of the United States Senate, 85th Congress, in the Session held 14 and 15 Feb. 1957, part 51, and Alexander Orlov's testimony before the same committee, especially p. 3464.

62 No charge was too fantastic for *Izvestia* or *Pravda* to print, and these were duly repeated in Communist Party organs in the West. In a long article 'La Troisième procès de Moscou', Serge listed the charges against Trotsky and the Oppositionists, and the reaction to these by the Stalinists in France. Published in *La Révolution prolétarienne*, 10 March 1938.

63 Krivitsky, *Stalin's Secret Service*, pp. 187–8.

64 Serge, *Memoirs*, p. 331.

65 Ibid., pp. 333–4.

66 Ibid.

67 Also published as 'Pismo Viktora Serzha Andre Zhidu', in *Byulleten' Oppozitzii*, no. 51, 1936, pp. 9–11.

68 The account of Gide's actions at the Congress can be found in Herbert Lottman, *The Left Bank: Writers, Artists, and Politics from the Popular Front to the Cold War*, London, Heinemann, 1982, p. 95.

69 Serge, *Memoirs*, p. 338.

70 Poretsky, *Our Own People*, pp. 183–203.

71 Serge, *Memoirs*, p. 340.

72 Ignace S. Poretsky's pseudonym was Ludwik. Reiss was a remote family name he used once he broke with the NKVD because his wife Elsa was certain the name was unknown in Moscow. She and Sneevliet then decided to use the name Reiss for the body of 'Hans Eberhard', the cover name he was using when he was assassinated, and it is by this name that Ignace Poretsky has since been known. Poretsky, *Our Own People*, p. 241.

73 Their stories are well documented in Poretsky, *Our Own People*; Krivitsky, *Stalin's Secret Service*; Isaac Deutscher, *The Prophet Outcast, Trotsky: 1929–1940*, Oxford, Oxford University Press; Serge, *Memoirs*, *Carnets* (with Maurice Wullens and Alfred Rosmer), *L'Assassinat d'Ignace Reiss*, Paris, Editions Pierre Tisné, 1938; Alba and Schwartz, *Spanish Marxism*; Pierre Broué, *Trotsky*, pp. 868–82, testimony of Zborowski, Lola Dallin and Alexander Orlov to the US Senate, 'Scope of Soviet Activity in the US' Hearings; Kyril Khenkin (Soviet agent in Paris and Spain), author of *L'Espionnage soviétique*, Paris, 1981; Hede Massing, *This Deception*, New York, Duell, Sloan and Pearce, 1951; and in fiction by Tariq Ali, *Fear of Mirrors*, London, Arcadia Books, 1999.

74 Poretsky, *Our Own People*, p. 210.

75 Louis Fischer, *Men and Politics: An Autobiography*, London, Jonathan Cape, 1941, pp. 479–82.

76 Serge, 'Reiss, Krivitsky, Bastich and Others', Dec. 1937, in 'The Diary of Victor Serge', *The New International*, Jan.–Feb. 1950, p. 51.

77 Serge, *Memoirs*, p. 342.

78 Poretsky, *Our Own People*, p. 241.

79 Ibid., p. 236.

80 Serge, *Memoirs*, p. 343.

81 Serge, Diary entry, *The New International*, Jan.–Feb. 1950, p. 52.

82 Krivitsky, *Stalin's Secret Service*, p. 261.

83 Serge, Wullens and Rosmer, 'L'Assassinat d'Ignace Reiss', *Les Humbles*, April 1938.

84 Serge and Sedova, *Life and Death*, p. 226.

85 Ibid.

86 Thanks to Loic Damilaville for sharing French police files on the Reiss affair. Dossier Ignace Reiss: Archives de la Prefecture de Police, no. E.246–731 – Police judiciare – et E.133.740.

87 Lola Dallin's testimony to the Hearing before the Subcommittee to Investigate the Administration of the Internal Security Act and other Internal Security Laws of the Committee on the Judiciary, US Senate, 84th Congress, Second Session on Scope of Soviet Activity in the US, 29 Feb. 1956, part 4. Mrs Dallin cited as her source the French and Swiss police reports.

88 Poretsky, *Our Own People*, p. 234.

89 Serge, Wullens, Rosmer, 'L'Assassinat d'Ignace Reiss', p. 19.

90 Zborowski's testimony on the Scope of Soviet Activity in the US, 2 March 1956, Washington DC, US Senate, Subcommittee to Investigate the Administration of the Internal Security Act. Zborowski was accompanied by his attorney, Herman A. Greenberg, and this was the first question he answered in this session.

91 Alexander Barmine, *One Who Survived: The Life Story of a Russian under the Soviets*, New York, G.P. Putnam's Sons, 1945.

92 Max Eastman, 'Introduction' to Barmine, *One Who Survived*, p. xi.

93 The French edition of the book credits Victor Serge with the French translation. Alexandre Barmine, *Vingt ans au service de l'U.R.S.S. Souvenirs d'un diplomate soviétique*, traduction français de Victor Serge, Paris: Editions Albin Michel, 1939.

94 Serge, 'Le témoignage d'Alexandre Barmine', *La Wallonie*, 4–5 March 1939, p. 14. Barmine's book was first published in France and Britain under the title *Memoirs of a Soviet Diplomat*.

95 Eastman, 'Introduction', p. xi.

96 Poretsky, *Our Own People*, pp. 244–6.

97 Ibid., p. 246, quoting from Serge, *Memoirs*, p. 265.

98 Krivitsky to Nicolaevsky, Paris 25 Oct. 1938; thanks to Gary Kern for the text, which he translated.

99 Deutscher, *The Prophet Outcast*, pp. 391–2. Deutscher cited Lyova's letters to his father of 19 Nov. 1937 and Trotsky's letter to Lyova of 22 Jan. 1938, and Etienne's correspondence to Trotsky in the Harvard Archives.

100 Poretsky, *Our Own People*, p. 274.

101 Zborowski's testimony to Senator Eastland's Committee on the Scope of Soviet Activities in the US, 29 Feb. 1956, part 4.

102 Krivitsky, *Stalin's Secret Service*, p. 267.

103 Poretsky, *Our Own People*, pp. 252–4.

104 Ibid., p. 255.

105 FBI Secret Files, Internal Security Act of 1950, titled 'Lydia [sic] Dallin, a.k.a.: Mrs. David J. Dallin, née Lilia Ginzberg, was: Lilia Estrin, Lilly Estrin, Lola Estrin, Mrs. Samuel Estrin', 23 May 1956, three pages, no. 240, 376. She was called Lola Paulsen or Lola Yakovlev in the movement; born Lilia Ginzburg and first married the Menshevik Samuel Estrin, then the Menshevik David Dallin. See Broué, *Trotsky*, pp. 1051–2.

106 Orlov's Testimony to Senate Committee on Scope of Soviet Activities, pp. 3423–9.

107 Testimony of Lola Dallin, Senator Eastland's Subcommittee on the Scope of Soviet Activities in the US, 29 Feb. 1956, part 4.

108 Leon Trotsky, 'A GPU Stool Pigeon in Paris', 1 Jan. 1939, signed 'Van', in Leon Trotsky, *Writings*, Supplement 1934–40, New York, Pathfinder Press, 1979, pp. 818–19.

109 Broué, *Trotsky*, p. 876.

110 Serge described his meetings with Krivitsky in the *Memoirs*, pp. 343–5, *Carnet*, entry for Dec. 1937, in *The New International*, Jan.–Feb. 1950, pp. 51–5.

111 Weissman to Zborowski, 22 Oct. 1986, 26 July 1987, 2 April 1988; numerous phone calls from January 1986 through September 1988. He never spoke more than three words to me, and then hung up. I went to his house in San Francisco on 19 March 1988 and was not allowed in. His wife Regina Zborowski was more cordial, and encouraged me to keep trying. According to Stephen Schwartz, however, she 'watched over Zborowski carefully, and prevented him from speaking to anyone' (interview, Oct. 1989). Zborowski died 30 April 1990 at the age of 81.

112 Interviews with Pierre Broué, Mexico City, May 1987, and Los Angeles, Oct. 1989.

113 Dimitri Volkogonov donated his portion of Zborowski's NKVD file to the Library of Congress.

114 The surgeon's name was Dr Boris Girmunsky (Broué, *Trotsky*, p. 876). See also Lequenne, Krivine and Kahn in *Cahiers Leon Trotsky*, no. 13, March 1983, pp. 25–55 for a discussion of the circumstances of Sedov's death and the agent-surgeon Girmunsky.

115 Interview with Stephen Schwartz, Oct. 1989, San Francisco. The same information is cited in Alba and Schwartz, *Spanish Marxism versus Soviet Communism*, p. 221.

116 Guenther Reinhardt, *Crime without Punishment: The Secret Soviet Terror against America*, New York, Hermitage House, 1952, p. 58n. Pierre Broué, in his biography of Trotsky, repeats the 'poisoned orange' account. Pierre Broué, *Trotsky*, p. 876.

117 Dimitri Volkogonov, *Trotsky, The Eternal Revolutionary*, New York, The Free Press, 1996, pp. 359–60.

118 John Costello and Oleg Tsarev, *Deadly Illusions: The KGB Orlov Dossier*, New York, Crown Publishers, 1993, appendix III, pp. 406–11.

119 Interview with Oleg Tsarev, Moscow, 4 June 1999.

120 Costello and Tsarev, *Deadly Illusions*, pp. 469–70.

121 Serge, *Memoirs*, p. 345.

122 Ibid., p. 344.

123 Serge, *Carnets*, p. 44.

124 Pierre Broué described Klement's disappearance in his *Trotsky*, p. 878. Georges Vereeken raised the possibility that Klement was killed because he knew who the agent was, or perhaps was an agent himself. See Georges Vereeken, *The GPU in the Trotskyist Movement*, London, New Park Publications, 1976, chapter 17, 'Rudolf Klement: An Agent? Certainly a Coward', pp. 238–318.

125 Serge, *Memoirs*, p. 336.

126 Ibid., p. 337.

127 Zborowski testimony, US Senate Hearings, 29 Feb. 1956, part 4, pp. 88–9.

128 Serge, *Carnets*, 2 Oct. 1944 entry titled 'Intransigence, Intolerance, Conflicts', p. 145.

129 Ibid., p. 146.

130 Ibid.

131 Serge to Kostiuk, 22 June 1947.

132 Serge, *Carnets*, p. 146.

133 *Byulleten' Oppozitsii*, no. 73, Jan. 1939, p. 16.

134 Serge to Trotsky (in Russian), Paris, 18 March 1939. Letter 39 in Cotterill, *Serge–Trotsky Papers*, pp. 108–10.

135 Leon Trotsky, *Their Morals and Ours*, New York, Merit Publishers, 1969, p. 37.

136 Serge to Marcel Martinet on 30 March 1939.

137 'Prière d'Insérer', 1939 edition of *Leur morale et la nôtre (Their Morals and Ours)*, Paris, Editions du Sagittaire; appendix C of (English) 1969 edition, New York, Merit Publishers, 1969.

138 Leon Trotsky, 'The Moralists and Sycophants against Marxism', in *Their Morals and Ours*, p. 41.

139 Ibid., p. 45.

140 Ibid., p. 50.

141 Serge, *Memoirs*, p. 349.

142 Serge to Macdonald (in French), 22 Oct. 1939, Macdonald Papers, Yale University Library.

143 Victor Serge to Angelica Balabanova, 23 Oct. 1941, Serge archive, Mexico.

144 L.D. Trotsky, *Byulleten Oppozitsii*, no. 79–80, Aug.–Sept., 1939, p. 31. The English translation, 'Another Refutation by Victor Serge', is published as appendix B in the Merit edition of *Their Morals and Ours*.

145 Trotsky, *Byulleten Oppozitsii*, no. 79–80, p. 31.

146 Trotsky to Serge, 6 May 1939. Published in *Writings of Leon Trotsky: Supplement 1934–1940*, p. 836.

147 Victor Serge, 'Secrecy and Revolution – A Reply to Trotsky', *Peace News*, London, 27 Dec. 1963, p. 5.

148 Ibid.

149 Private conversation, Mexico City, Jan. 1986.

150 See p. 222 and note 111 above.

151 Private conversation, Los Angeles, Oct. 1989.

152 NKVD File 104, 19.4.37, from Oleg-Petr, the codename of S.M. Glinsky, aka V. Smirnov, the Paris resident who ran Zborowski (known in the NKVD as Tulip).

153 Broué proclaimed dissatisfaction with the result. Interviews with Pierre Broué, Mexico 1987 and Los Angeles 1989.

154 Serge, 'Ma rupture avec Trotski' July 1936, *Carnets*, pp. 44–7.

155 Published in Trotsky, *Writings 1935–1936*, New York, Pathfinder Press, 1973, pp. 32–5.

156 Victor Serge: 'Observations on the Theses of the July Conference of the Fourth International, Sections 1, 5, and 9', 19 July 1936, Serge archives.

157 Serge, 'Ma rupture avec Trotski', p. 44.

158 Serge to Trotsky, Brussels, 27 July 1936. Letter 24 in Cotterill, *Serge–Trotsky Papers*, p. 83.

159 Trotsky to Serge, 30 July 1936. Letter 25 in Cotterill, *Serge–Trotsky Papers*, pp. 86–90.

160 Serge, 'Ma rupture avec Trotski', pp. 44–7.

161 Serge, *Memoirs*, p. 348.

162 Serge, 'Ma rupture avec Trotski', p. 48.

163 Ibid.

164 Trotsky to Serge (in Russian, 15 April 1938. Letter 38 in Cotterill, *Serge–Trotsky Papers*, pp. 107–8.

165 Serge to Trotsky, 18 March 1939. Letter 39 in Cotterill, *Serge–Trotsky Papers*, pp. 108–10.

166 Serge to Sedov, 21 Jan. 1937, 231:100, Nicolaevsky Collection, Hoover Archive.

167 The following articles comprised the main part of the debate: Trotsky: 'On Makhno and Kronstadt (6 July 1937); Serge: 'Fiction and Fact, Kronstadt' (*La Révolution prolétarienne*, 10 Sept. 1937); Serge, 'Kronstadt 1921, Against Sectarianism, Bolshevism and Anarchism' (*La Révolution prolétarienne*, no. 257, 25 Oct. 1937); Trotsky: 'Hue and Cry Over Kronstadt', 15 Jan. 1938 (*The New International*, April 1938); Serge, 'Once More: Kronstadt' 28 April 1938 (*The New International*, July 1938); Trotsky, 'Again on the Kronstadt Repression', 6 July 1938; Serge, 'A Letter and Some Notes', Feb. 1939; Serge 'More on the Suppression of Kronstadt', 6 July 1938 (*The New International*, Aug. 1938).

168 Trotsky, 'Hue and Cry over Kronstadt'.

169 Ibid.

170 Ibid.

171 Serge, 'A Letter and Some Notes', p. 53.

172 Victor Serge, 'Reply to Ciliga', *The New International*, Feb. 1939.

173 The subject came up during the Dewey Commission on the Moscow Trials.

174 Victor Serge, 'Marxism in Our Time', *Partisan Review*, vol. V, no. 3, Aug.–Sept. 1939, pp. 26–32.

175 Trotsky, 'Intellectual Ex-Radicals and World Reaction', 17 Feb. 1939, published in *Writings 1938–1939*, pp. 194–6.

176 Trotsky, *Writings*, Supplement *1934–40*, p. 872.

177 Serge, 'The Old Man', 1 Aug. 1942, written in Mexico, 'to the memory of Leon Davidovich Trotsky' and published in Serge and Sedova, *The Life and Death of Leon Trotsky*, p. 4.

178 Serge and Sedova, *Life and Death*, pp. 2–5.

7 From Paris to Marseilles, Marseilles to Mexico: the long, last journey from nightmare to refuge

1 Victor Serge, *Memoirs of a Revolutionary*, London, Oxford University Press, 1963, p. 352.

2 Ibid., p. 356.

3 Ibid., p. 364.

4 Victor Serge, *The Long Dusk*, New York, Dial Press, 1946, translated from the French original *Les Dernier Temps* by Ralph Manheim, pp. 317–18.

5 Serge, *Memoirs*, p. 357.

6 Ibid., p. 359.

7 Ibid.

8 Serge, *The Long Dusk*, p. 356.

9 Ibid., pp. 61–2.

10 Serge, *Memoirs*, 366–7.

11 Ibid., pp. 357–8.

12 Ibid., p. 358.

13 Serge, *The Long Dusk*, pp. 72–3.

14 Victor Serge, *Carnets*, Paris, Julliard, 1952 and Avignon, Actes Sud, 1985, p. 53.

15 Ibid.

16 See chapter 6.

17 Victor Serge, 'Marxism in Our Time', *Partisan Review*, vol. V, no. 3, Aug.–Sept. 1938, p. 27.

18 Dwight Macdonald to Victor Serge, 14 Nov. 1939, Macdonald Papers, Yale University Library.

19 Victor Serge to Nancy and Dwight Macdonald, published in Nancy Macdonald, *Homage to the Spanish Exiles*, New York, Insight Books, 1987, p. 55.

20 Ibid., p. 15.

21 Nancy Macdonald to American Consul, 20 July 1940, Macdonald Papers, Yale University Library.

22 Serge, *Memoirs*, p. 360.

23 Mary Jayne Gold, *Crossroads Marseilles 1940*, New York, Doubleday, 1980, p. 169.

24 Serge, *Memoirs*, p. 361. The visa lists drawn up in France that Serge refers to were not the visa lists of Varian Fry's Emergency Rescue Committee, but of Frank Bohn who was a right-wing socialist and the AFL representative in Marseilles. He worked with the ERC, was in fact Fry's first contact, and Fry took over and greatly expanded the work after Bohn returned to the US. See Serge's letters of 19 Aug., 30 Aug., 7 Sept. and 8 Oct. 1940 to the Macdonalds (Yale Collection); Varian Fry *Surrender on Demand*, New York, Random House, 1945, pp. 7–12, 51–9, 93.

25 These letters to 'Cher Amis' – the Macdonalds, gave Serge's address as care of Madame Sosnovski, 123 rue Horace Bertin, Marseilles.

26 Serge, *The Long Dusk*, p. 307.

27 Serge, *Memoirs*, p. 362.

28 Fry, *Surrender*, pp. 5–6 and 168–71; Gold, *Crossroads Marseilles*, pp. 178–99; and Serge, *Memoirs*, pp. 371–2.

29 Serge, *Memoirs*, p. 365.

30 Serge to Brupbacher, Brupbacher papers, Zurich. Cited in Richard Greeman, 'Victor Serge y Leon Trotsky (1936–1940)', *Vuelta* vol. 6, no. 63, Feb. 1982, p. 31.

31 Serge to the Macdonalds, 26 Aug. 1940, Macdonald Papers, Yale University Library.

32 Nancy Macdonald to Victor Serge, 30 Sept. 1940. This letter was written in a cryptic style, but apparently did not reach Serge, at least this copy. (The letter was sent in duplicate to Marseilles and Lisbon.) It was returned to the Macdonalds from Lisbon in December of 1940.

33 See, *inter alia*, Victor Alba and Stephen Schwartz, *Spanish Marxism versus Soviet Communism: A History of the POUM*, New Brunswick, NJ, Transaction Books, 1988. pp. 220–21.

34 Serge to Macdonalds, 7 Oct. 1940 (Macdonald papers, Yale University Library).

35 Daniel Bénédite, *La Filière marseillaise: Un Chemin vers la liberté sous l'occupation*, Paris, Editions Clancier Guénaud, 1984, pp. 1–2.

36 Serge, *Memoirs*, p. 362.

37 For the accounts of their fate, see Gold, *Crossroads Marseilles*, pp. 302–5, Serge, *Memoirs* p. 364, and Fry, *Surrender*, pp. 170–78.

38 Fry, *Surrender*, pp. 176–7; Serge, *Memoirs*, p. 365; Gold, *Crossroads Marseilles*, p. 305.

39 Gold, *Crossroads Marseilles*, p. 242.

40 Bénédite, *La Filière*, p. 54.

41 Ibid., p. 58.

42 Fry, *Surrender*, pp. 113–22.

43 Jeannine Kibalchich, letter to Susan Weissman, 21 Sept. 1990.

44 Gold, *Crossroads Marseilles*, p. 244.

45 Ibid., p. 247.

46 Ibid., p. 248.

47 Interview with Mary Jayne Gold conducted by John Eden, July 1989.

48 Gold, *Crossroads Marseilles*, pp. 254–5.

49 Fry, *Surrender*, p. 121.

50 Bénédite, *La Filière*, pp. 116–28.

51 Ibid., p. 128.

52 Ibid., pp. 116–17.

53 Ibid., p. 116

54 Ibid., p. 118.

55 Gold, *Crossroads Marseilles*, p. 251. Fry also described the games, *Surrender*, pp. 125–6.

56 Gold, *Crossroads Marseilles*, pp. 253–5.

57 Nancy Macdonald to Laurette Séjourné, 6 Dec. 1940, and throughout December 1940. (Macdonald Papers, Yale University Library.)

58 Serge to Macdonalds, 5 Jan. 1941.

59 Gold, *Crossroads Marseilles*, p. 307.

60 Ibid., p. 266.

61 Ibid., pp. 266–7.

62 Bénédite, *La Filière*, p. 143.

63 Fry's account is in his book, *Surrender*, pp. 136–49.

64 Bénédite, *La Filière*, pp. 145–7.

65 Fry, *Surrender*, p. 146.

66 Bénédite, *La Filière*, p. 214.

67 Ibid., p. 191.

68 Serge, *Memoirs*, p. 364.

69 Mildred Adams, Executive Secretary of New York Emergency Rescue

Committee, to Dwight Macdonald, 24 Sept. 1940. Macdonald Papers, Yale University Library.

70 Macdonald to Mr Warren, 30 Sept. 1940, Macdonald Papers, Yale University Library. See also Serge's FBI file.

71 This is all documented in the Macdonald collection of papers at Yale, and fairly faithfully recorded in Serge's FBI file.

72 From 1987 to 1996 Serge's FBI file was slowly released to this author after years of correspondence with the FOIA Appeals Office. Files on Victor Serge were found in the archives of these branches of American intelligence: 1. Dept of State, Visa Services; 2. Diplomatic Security Service of Dept of State, agent Walter S. Pedigo, investigating in Mexico City from April to May 1954 reports Serge – dead seven years – as a famous painter living in Mexico; 3. Dept of Army, US Army Intelligence and Security Command; 4. HQ Southern Defense Command, Fort Sam Houston. Includes subversive annex on magazine *Politics* 'a Trotskyite organ' mentioning Serge's Mexican group, dated 6–13 Dec. 1946; contains names and addresses of Serge and all his associates in Mexico with short biographies, plus information on Dwight Macdonald; 6. Defense Intelligence Agency; 7. US Dept of Justice, FBI; 8. US Army Intelligence and Security Command; 9. Office of Legal Policy, FBI; 10. New York FBI; 11. Washington FBI; 12. Dept of Navy, Naval Intelligence Command, Aug. and Sept. 1941, Naval Attaché in Ciudad Trujillo, Dominican Republic, reports on 'political forces, foreign penetration'; Intelligence Report 63215 24 Jan. 1946, Mexico on *Mundo*, Serge, Movimiento socialismo y libertad; 13. Central Intelligence Agency has four memoranda from 1950 to 1975, denied access; 14. Immigration and Naturalization Service; 15. War Department, Military Intelligence Service, Washington; 16. US Dept of Justice, Office of the Solicitor General.

73 For example, see Item 2–344, letter to Minister of Public Health from Minister of Interior of French Republic dated Feb. 1937.

74 Item 65–8336, FBI file on Victor Serge.

75 Serge, *Memoirs*, p. 366.

76 'On the Eve', *Partisan Review*, vol. 9, no. 1, Jan.–Feb. 1942, pp. 30–31. An abbreviated version is in the *Memoirs*, pp. 366–7.

77 Interview with Vlady, Jan. 1986, Mexico City.

78 Ibid.

79 Serge to Mary Jayne Gold, Ciudad Trujillo, 1 Aug. 1941, 8 pp., Serge archive, Mexico City.

80 Department of the Navy, Naval Intelligence Command, released to author through FOIA request. The file contained intelligence reports from agents in Chile, Colombia, Cuba, the Dominican Republic, Peru, and the 'Fifteenth Naval District'. The document, filed 14 Aug. 1941, was marked 'confidential', serial no. 0871716, Document #100–36676–5, dated 30 Sept. 1941.

81 Interview with Vlady Kibalchich, Mexico City, May 1987.

82 Confidential Intelligence Report, Naval Intelligence, Serial R–194–41, Ciudad Trujillo, 14 Aug. 1941.

83 Serge to Dwight Macdonald, 18 June 1941, Macdonald Papers, Yale University Library.

84 Serge to Mary Jayne Gold, 10 Aug. 1941, from Ciudad Trujillo. Serge archive, Mexico.

85 Interview with Vlady Kibalchich, Cuernavaca, Mexico, Aug. 1996.
86 Serge, *Memoirs*, p. 369.

8 From Mexico, whither the USSR, the world?

1 See above, 'Another Exile and Two More: The Final Years', pp. 180–81.
2 Victor Serge, Julian Gorkín, Marceau Pivert and Gustav Regler, *La GPU prepara un nuevo crimen!*, Serie 'Documentos', Edición de 'Analysis', Revista de Hechos e Ideas, Mexico DF, 1942, p. 16.
3 Ibid., p. 21.
4 Serge to Marcel Martinet, no date, Serge archive.
5 Victor Serge, 'Difficulty in Writing, Russian Writers', 10 Sept. 1944, in *Carnets*, Paris, Julliard, 1952, p. 134.
6 These were the only extracts published in English, until 1980–81, when eleven extracts were published in the Scottish journal of international literature, arts and affairs, *Cencrastus*, translated by John Manson. Manson's English translations of Serge's 1944 diary entries are posted on http://www.victorserge.net.
7 *Bohemia*, La Habana, 7 Sept. 1941, vol. 33, no. 36, written by Gilberto Gonzalez y Contreras.
8 Victor Serge, Julian Gorkín, Marceau Pivert and Paul Chevalier, *Los Problemas del socialismo en nuestro tiempo*, Mexico, Ediciones Ibero-Americanas, 1944.
9 Ibid., pp. 11–41.
10 Ibid., pp. 19–20.
11 Serge, 'Ideological Discussions', 13 Sept. 1944, in *Carnets*, pp. 117–20.
12 Serge, 'Socialist Problems', entry for 25 Nov. 1944, in *Carnets*, p. 168.
13 Ibid.
14 Ibid., p. 170.
15 Interview with Laurette Séjourné, 6 Sept. 1990, Mexico City.
16 Serge, *Carnets*, p. 181.
17 'Stalinism and the Resistance – A Letter from Victor Serge', *Politics*, Feb. 1945, pp. 61–2. In this letter Serge tried to alert the American Left to the totalitarian nature of the Communist Parties, which would brook no dissidence.
18 Serge, *Carnets*, p. 171.
19 Ibid.
20 Serge, 'The Socialist Imperative', in *Partisan Review* discussion, 'The Future of Socialism: V', Sept.–Oct. 1947, vol. XIV, no. 5, p. 515.
21 Serge, *Partisan Review*, Sept.–Oct. 1947, p. 516.
22 Serge, *Politics*, Feb. 1945, p. 62.
23 Serge, *Carnets*, 10 Dec. 1944, p. 177.
24 Ibid., p. 182.
25 Serge, 'Necesidad de una renovación del Socialismo', *Mundo*, Libertad y Socialismo, June 1945 (but written in April 1943), p. 18.
26 Ibid.
27 Dated 1946, Serge archive, Mexico. Published in *Masses*, Paris, 1947.
28 Ibid.
29 Ibid.

30 Ibid.

31 Victor Serge, unpublished typescript, no date, no title, Serge archive, Mexico. (This fragment appears to have been written just after the war.)

32 Victor Serge, 'Economie dirigée et démocratie', thirty-six pages, no date, Serge archive, Mexico. Published in *Revolutionary History*, vol. 5, no 3, autumn 1994, pp. 177–98.

33 Ibid., p. 4.

34 Ibid.

35 Ibid., p. 12n.

36 Ibid., p. 15.

37 See Georgy Konrad and Ivan Szelenyi, *The Intelligentsia on the Road to Class Power*, New York, Harcourt, Brace Jovanovich, 1979.

38 Serge, 'Economie dirigée', pp. 21–2.

39 Victor Serge, 'What Is Fascism?', *Partisan Review*, vol. VIII, no. 5, Sept.–Oct. 1941, p. 420.

40 Ibid., pp. 420–21.

41 This is a loose summary of Serge's unpublished typescript, no date, no title, two pages, found in the Mexico archive. Many of the same points were raised in Serge's letter to Dwight Macdonald of 10 Sept. 1943.

42 Serge to Macdonald, Mexico, 7 Sept. 1943. (Macdonald Papers, Yale University Library).

43 Susan Weissman (ed.), *Victor Serge: Russia Twenty Years After*, Atlantic Highlands, NJ, Humanities Press, 1996, p. 326.

44 Ibid., p. 328.

45 Serge to Sidney Hook, 'Marxism et démocratie', 10 July 1943.

46 Serge, *Memoirs*, p. 376.

47 Typescript, no title, no date, Serge Archives, two pages.

48 'In Memoriam: Victor Serge', *Modern Review*, vol. II, no. 1, Jan. 1948, pp. 6–7.

49 Nicholas Krasso, 'Revolutionary Romanticism', *New Left Review*, no. 21, Sept.–Oct. 1963, pp. 107–11.

50 'Définition du socialisme', unpublished manuscript, no date, Serge archive, Mexico. Also, Box 5, Folders 276–8, Serge Papers. Yale University Beinecke Library.

51 Susan Weissman (ed.), *Victor Serge: A Life as a Work of Art*, Glasgow, Critique Books 1997, pp. 99–118.

52 Serge, 'What Is Fascism?', *Partisan Review*, vol. VII, no. 5, Sept.–Oct. 1941.

53 Diary entry for 4 Dec. 1944, 'On the Ending of the Novel', *Carnets*, p. 173.

54 'Constellation of Dead Brothers' (1935), Orenburg, published in *Resistance*, San Francisco, City Light Books, 1989, pp. 34–5.

Glossary

Abramovich, Raphael (known as *A. Rein*) (1880–1963): Leading member of the Bund, RSDLP Central Committee member, Menshevik Internationalist in World War I, member of the Central Executive Committee of Soviets 1917–18. He co-founded the Menshevik's émigré journal, *Sotsialisticheskii Vestnik*, left the USSR in 1920, and eventually settled in New York in 1940, where he contributed to the Yiddish press *Forvarts* (*Jewish Daily Forward*). He is also the author of *Soviet Revolution* (1962).

Alter, Victor (1890–1943): Polish socialist and leader of the Bund, refugee from Hitler in the USSR in 1939. He was executed along with Henrik Erlich in 1941. A memorial and protest meeting organized in Mexico by Serge and his comrades in 1943 (when the executions were made known) was violently attacked by the Stalinists.

Alvarado, Manuel (1913–2005): Founding member of the Mexican Left Opposition, originally from Guanajuato, who organized to bring Serge to Mexico. As a young, orthodox Trotskyist, Alvarado criticized Serge for saying that fascism and Stalinism bore important similarities, but Alvarado insisted that Serge became more Trotskyist while in Mexico, and more critical of the POUM.

Analysis: Journal, successor to *Mundo*, published by the exile group Socialismo y Libertad in Mexico.

Andrade, Juan (1897–1981): Leader of the Juventud Socialista in Spain, which eventually became the Partido Comunista Español (PCE) in 1921 with Andrade on its Executive Committee, editing its journal *La Antorcha*. Expelled in 1927 as a Trotskyist sympathizer, Andrade led the Izquierda Comunista until it dissolved in 1934, fusing with the BOC to form the POUM in 1935 with Andrade in the leadership. He was arrested in 1937 and tried as a 'Trotsky Fascist', but was released in 1938 and exiled to France. In 1940 Andrade was imprisoned by the Gestapo along with Wilebaldo Solano and others for organizing resistance.

Antonov-Ovseenko, Vladimir (1884–1938): Russian army Officer and Menshevik supporter, Antonov-Ovseenko mutinied and was condemned to death in 1906. After the February Revolution, he joined the Bolsheviks, was appointed to the Party's Central Committee and led the Red Guards who seized the Winter Palace in the October Revolution. He became one of the leaders of the Left Opposition, but capitulated in 1928 and was later Soviet Consul General in Barcelona during the Spanish Civil War. Stalin was convinced that Antonov-Ovseenko was plotting against him and recalled him to the Soviet Union in August 1937, where he was arrested and shot without trial in 1938.

Austrich, Juan (?–1996): POUM militant exiled to Mexico who saved Serge from the line of fire when the Mexican CP, fortified by GPU agents, laid siege to an April 1943 memorial meeting for militants assassinated by the NKVD. Austrich insisted Serge was the target of the assault. Years later Austrich maintained that he had proof that Serge was murdered by the GPU with some kind of poison. This has not been independently confirmed.

Babel, Isaac (1884–1940): Russian language writer from Odessa, Babel was a Bolshevik in 1917 and political commissar during the civil war. He published *Red Cavalry* in 1926 and *Odessa Tales* in 1927. As a critic of the regime, he had great difficulties getting published. In 1934, he declared at the Union of Soviet Writers that he had 'invented a new genre; silence'. Arrested in 1939, his works were confiscated.

Balabanova, Angelica (1878–1965): Russian who emigrated to Italy, where she was a militant member of the Socialist Party from 1900, writing for *Avanti*. She taught Marxism to the young, insecure socialist journalist (at the time) Benito Mussolini. Balabanova returned to Russia as a Zimmerwaldist, joining the Bolsheviks in 1917, and becoming Moscow Secretary of the Comintern. She broke with the Bolsheviks in 1922 and left the USSR. Expelled from the Party in 1924, she joined with the Italian Maximalists, emigrated first to Switzerland, living sometimes in Vienna where Serge met with her, then Paris and later the US.

Baldwin, Roger (1884–1981): A Pacifist who joined with A.J. Muste, Norman Thomas, Scott Nearing and Oswald Garrison Villard to form the Fellowship of Reconciliation (FOR), then with Jane Addams, Lillian Wald and others formed the American Union Against Militarism (AUAM) during World War I. Imprisoned for two years as a conscientious objector in 1918; in 1919 Baldwin joined the Industrial Workers of the World (IWW). In 1920 he helped found the American Civil Liberties Union (ACLU) and directed it for thirty-five years, campaigning against the persecution of the left and fighting against racism and poverty. He signed a letter to the president of Mexico demanding the protection of Serge and others and protesting the reign of terror against anti-Stalinist refugees.

Barbusse, Henri (1873–1935): Pacifist writer, author of *Le Feu* (Under Fire) in 1916, which won the Prix Goncourt. Barbusse went to Moscow in 1918 and joined the Bolsheviks. He founded the periodical *Clarté* (1919) and joined the French Communist Party in 1923. He was editor of the weekly *Monde*. He wrote *Stalin: un monde nouveau à travers un homme* (Stalin: A New World Seen Through the Man) (1935). Subsequently, Barbusse led a violent press campaign against his former friend Panaït Istrati and was harshly criticized as a hypocrite by Serge (whom he met in September 1927). Serge noted that Barbusse dedicated a book to Trotsky but then denounced him as traitor once Stalin won power.

Barmine, Alexander (1899–1987): Born in Byelorussia (now Belarus), Barmine joined the Red Army and participated in the civil war, and became an intelligence officer and diplomat posted to Athens. He 'resigned' from the NKVD after the arrest of Marshal Tukhachevsky and fled first to Paris in 1937, then the US in 1940 with his Greek wife Mari. In Paris he dictated his story to Serge, published as *Vingt Ans Au Service de L'URSS: Souvenirs d'un Diplomate Sovietique* (French translation by Victor Serge). Barmine was briefly married to Irena Gogua, Serge's niece, in Russia. He was a private in the US Army in World War II and worked in the Office of Strategic Studies (OSS) in 1943–44. In 1948 Barmine joined *Voice of America*, serving for sixteen years as chief of its Russian branch. He was married to Edith Kermit Roosevelt from 1948 to 1952.

Bell, Daniel (1919–2011): A member of the Young People's Socialist League (YPSL) from the age of thirteen, editor of *Common Sense* and *The New Leader*, and co-founder of the magazine *The Public Interest*. Bell is an influential sociologist and social theorist. Among his many books are *The End of Ideology* and *The Cultural Contradictions of Capitalism*. Bell published some two dozen of Serge's articles in *The New Leader* from 1942 to 1947 and helped organize the Committee for the defence of Victor Serge, Julian Gorkín and Marceau Pivert.

Bely, Andrei (1880–1934): Pen name of Boris Nikolaevich Bugaev, the Russian symbolist poet and author of the symbolist novel *Petersburg* (1916; 1922), considered his masterpiece. He was the leading light of *Volfila* (Free Philosophic Society), a group in Moscow in the early 1920s that organized big public debates. Serge was also a member, and translated Bely's poem 'Christ est ressuscité' (Christ Is Risen) into French.

Bénédite, Daniel (1912–1990): Militant in the Socialist Youth, and member of Marceau Pivert's *Gauche revolutionnaire* and, later, the PSOP (Workers and Peasants' Socialist Party). He became friends with Serge in 1936 in Paris. In 1940 Bénédite worked with Varian Fry and others at the French Emergency Rescue Committee (ERC) to get political and intellectual refugees from Marseilles to destinations abroad, including Serge and André Breton. Daniel and his wife Theo were with Serge,

Breton, Mary Jayne Gold et al. at Villa Air-Bel. Bénédite was an early figure in the French Resistance against the Nazis. After World War II he worked as a freelance journalist.

Berkman, Alexander (1870–1936): Russian American anarchist who emigrated to New York at the age of eighteen. Berkman served fourteen years in prison for the attempted assassination of Pittsburgh capitalist Henry Clay Frick during the Homestead strike of 1892, and wrote *Prison Memoirs of an Anarchist*. Lover and collaborator of Emma Goldman, they were arrested in 1917 for opposing the draft and deported to the Soviet Union in 1919. Berkman and Goldman (along with Serge and his father-in-law Russakov) attempted conciliation between the Kronstadt sailors and the Bolsheviks in 1921.

Blok, Alexander (1880–1921): Russian lyrical poet who took part in the 1905 Revolution and enthusiastically greeted the 1917 October Revolution. This was reflected in his poem about the Red Guards, 'The Twelve', considered his most important literary work, which Serge translated into French. Blok was a symbolist, like Bely. He died in August 1921 of 'debility', which Serge said was the same as starvation, brought about by the food shortages in Russia during the civil war.

Blumkin, Iakov G. (1899–1929): Left social-revolutionary, member of the Cheka who murdered the German ambassador on the order of his Party, which was opposed to the treaty of Brest-Litovsk. He was a dear friend of Serge's since 1919. Arrested, pardoned, member of the Soviet intelligence services, partisan of the Left Opposition, he risked a visit to Trotsky in 1929 and was shot on his return to Moscow. According to Serge, he managed to write his memoirs, but the manuscript was confiscated by the GPU. It has never been found.

Body, Marcel (1894–1984): Body was in the French army's military mission in Russia at the time of the October Revolution, but he refused orders to fight against it and joined the French Communist group in Moscow. He worked with Serge as a translator in the early years of the Comintern, editing the French periodical *Troisième International* in Moscow, and was part of the French commune at Lake Ladoga in 1921 with Serge. He was sent to Christiania, Norway, as a special secretary to the Supreme Soviet in 1921 and was a diplomat in Norway alongside Alexandra Kollontai. Body was a member of the Executive of the Comintern in 1926. He refused to stay in the diplomatic service and returned to France in 1927, where he was expelled from the French Communist Party in 1928 for recommending the electorate vote for a socialist candidate. He founded *La Vérité* and gathered the oppositional circle Union des Travailleurs Révolutionnaires around this periodical, and was involved in the syndicalist movement. His memoirs are published in three volumes.

La Bohemia: Newspaper published in Havana, Cuba. On 7 September 1941 (Año 33, vol. 33, no. 36) Gilberto González y Contreras published a long article about Serge entitled 'Victor Serge: El Ultimo Evadido de Europa'.

Bordiga, Amadeo (1889–1971): Engineer from Naples who played a prominent role in the 'maximalist' wing of the Italian Socialist Party. He was a founder, along with Antonio Gramsci, of the Italian Communist Party, and was the best-known figure of the Italian Left Faction, also known as the Promoteo Group. He rejected the United Front tactic and broke with the Comintern in 1929. The Bordigists worked with the Left Opposition until the end of 1932. Serge met him at the Second Congress of the Comintern in Moscow, and again in 1922 (also in Moscow), finding him a man of 'penetrating intellect' and 'dark forecasts', gloomy and quarrelsome.

Brandler, Heinrich (1881–1967): German revolutionary activist, Brandler was a member of the SPD who was expelled in 1915. He was one of the founders of the Spartakus group and co-founder of the German CP (KPD). He became its leader at the (illegal) Jena Congress in September 1921, replacing Paul Levi. Brandler was in Moscow to help prepare the October 1923 German insurrection. Zinoviev held him responsible for its disastrous failure. Branded a Trotskyist, he was sent to Kazakhstan until 1926. Expelled from the KPD in 1928, Brandler founded the KPO (Communist Party – Opposition), the first national section of the so-called 'International Right Opposition', which elaborated a Marxist analysis of fascism. Brandler emigrated to France in 1933, and to Cuba in 1941, then returned in 1949 to the RFA and headed the group *Arbeiterpolitik.*

Breitsheid, Rudolf (1874–1944): Social-Democratic Minister of the Interior of the German Republic in 1918, president of the German Social-Democratic Party.

Breton, André (1896–1966): Writer, artist and poet, member of the PCF from 1927 until his expulsion in 1933. Breton was the co-founder of the surrealist movement, writing its signature document, the *Surrealist Manifesto* (1924), as well as *Nadja, Fata Morgana,* and other works. He visited Trotsky in Mexico in 1938, where he and Trotsky wrote the *Manifesto: Towards a Free Revolutionary Art: André Breton and Leon Trotsky* (1938), calling for 'complete freedom of art' – increasingly difficult with the world situation of the time. The Manifesto was formulated by Breton and Trotsky with Diego Rivera as a signatory. Breton returned to France, but escaped during the Vichy regime to Marseilles where he joined Serge at Villa Air-Bel. They boarded the boat to Mexico together with their families, arriving in 1941.

Bronstein, Alexandra Lvovna Sokolovskaya (1872–1938?): She won Trotsky to Marxism, and they married and had two daughters (Zinaida and Nina) while in prison and Siberian exile from 1900 to 1902. Sokolovskaya was an educator and was close to Lenin's widow, Nadezhda Krupskaya, in the early 1930s. Serge reports that she was (along with him) the only other Left Oppositionist at large in Leningrad in 1929, and that she was arrested in 1935 and deported to Tobolsk after having taken care of Trotsky's grandchildren. She was last seen in a Kolyma labour camp by Nadezhda Joffe, Adolph Joffe's daughter.

Brupbacher, Fritz (1874–1945): Socialist Swiss physician practising in workers' quarters. He was a pioneer of the left socialists, and a libertarian internationalist influenced by French revolutionary syndicalism. He founded the socialist monthly *Polis* (1906–08) with his friend Max Tobler, contributed to *La Vie ouvrière* and French syndicalist papers, and was expelled from the Party in 1914 because of his anarchist leanings. He campaigned on behalf of his friend Victor Serge in the Comité Victor-Serge.

Bulletin communiste: Organ of the Committee of the Third International.

Burnham, James (1905–87): Professor of Philosophy at New York University, he, Max Shachtman and James P. Cannon were the leaders of the Trotskyist movement in the US. Burnham co-edited the Trotskyist theoretical journal *The New International* and published numerous articles and pamphlets. He began to disagree with certain aspects of Marxism, disagreements that he considered secondary until the start of World War II, when the polemic on the position to take toward the USSR erupted. In 1941, he published *The Managerial Revolution*. Serge wrote about Burnham's theory in *Partisan Review* and in correspondence with Sidney Hook. Burnham later turned to the right, supported the American intervention in Vietnam, and became a regular contributor to the conservative *National Review.*

Butov, Georgi V. (?–1928): Head of Trotsky's cabinet during the civil war. Arrested and deported in 1928, died after a fifty-five-day hunger strike at Butyrka.

Byk, Ivan (?–1937): Worker and tanner who fought in the Ukraine, then joined the Opposition. He was deported to Orenburg.

Cacucci, Pino (1955–): Italian journalist and author of numerous books, including *Tina Modotti: A Life*, in which he suggests that Serge was poisoned by the GPU with a substance that would make it appear Serge had suffered a heart attack.

The Call: The official organ of the Socialist Party, founded as *The New York Call* in 1908. Early contributors included Agnes Smedley, Margaret Sanger, Eugene Debs and Elizabeth Gurley Flynn. During the Red Scare of 1919 its offices were raided and wrecked. Norman Thomas, future leader of the Socialist Party of America, was editor until the journal disappeared in 1923. It re-emerged as *The Socialist Call* in 1930 and was published continuously up to the 1950s. Upton Sinclair and Sidney Hook were among its contributors. Serge published one article in the journal in May 1943: 'The War and the Resurgence of Socialism – An Optimistic Approach'.

Callemin, Raymond (c.1889–1913): Serge's boyhood friend from

Brussels, who was with him in an anarchist commune in Belgium, then moved to France, where he was the brains behind the illegalist Bonnot Gang. Serge solidarized with his friend but opposed their use of violence as a tactic. Callemin was Serge's co-defendant in the 1913 trial of the Bonnot Gang; he was sentenced to death and sent to the guillotine.

Cannon, James (1890–1974): One of two central leaders of American Trotskyism. An educated worker and excellent organizer, Cannon began in the Socialist Party, was active in the IWW, joined the John Reed wing of the Communist Labor Party, and was an early leader of the Workers Party of America. He was a delegate to the Comintern in 1922, where he likely first met Serge. Cannon joined the International Left Opposition and started the *Militant* in 1928. He saw Serge again at the founding conference of the Fourth International in 1938. His books include *The Struggle for a Proletarian Party*, *Notebook of an Agitator* and *The First Ten Years of American Trotskyism*. Cannon allied with Trotsky in 1939–40 against Max Shachtman over the 'Russian question': the character of the USSR. In 1941, Cannon and others were indicted for conspiring to overthrow the US government and sentenced to prison from 1943 to 1945.

Cárdenas, Lazaro (1895–1970): General, president of Mexico from 1934 to 1940. His government was the only one in the world to grant Trotsky political asylum. He also opened Mexico to Victor Serge, and to Spanish exiles.

Chadayev, Vassily Nikiforovich (?–1928): Serge's comrade who appears under the name Vassilii in Serge's poem 'Constellation of Dead Brothers'. Serge reports that Chadayev was the first to raise the question of a second Party. Editor of *Krasnaya Gazeta*, organizer of the central area cell of the Leningrad Left Opposition with Serge, Chadayev was expelled from the Party with Serge in 1927. He was arrested but did not recant. Sent on a journalistic assignment to Kuban to investigate the kolkhozes, Chadayev was murdered by bandits on 26 August 1928 on a road on the steppe near a market town.

Chicherin, Georgi Vassilievich (1872–1936): Menshevik, later Bolshevik in 1918, People's Commissar of Foreign Affairs from 1921 to 1930. He lived next to Serge's friend Iakov Blumkin at the Metropole. Serge described him as a foreign affairs specialist who rarely emerged from his archives.

Ciliga, Ante (1898–1992): Yugoslav Communist who spent ten years in the USSR, nearly six of them in captivity. Arrested for sympathizing with the Left Opposition in 1930, he was deported to Verkhne-Uralsk, a camp known as an 'isolator'. Freed in 1935, he was expelled from the USSR, saved by his Italian nationality. Serge saw him in Paris in 1938, again saved by his Italian passport, this time from the Yugoslav fascists. Ciliga wrote a caustic critique of Stalinist society and its repression of workers and peasants as well as an account of its left critics in *Dix ans au pays du mensonge déconcertant* (Paris, 1938), titled *The Russian Enigma* in English. Serge and Trotsky discussed Ciliga's views in their correspondence.

Clarté: Founded by Henri Barbusse in 1919, organ of the *Mouvement international de la pensée* that ceased publication in 1926 but was revived the same year by Pierre Naville and others. It took up the defence of the Left Opposition and, in 1928, became *La Lutte de classes*, which was published until June 1935 as the theoretical journal of the Communist Left Opposition and later of the Communist League.

Contre le courant: Journal founded in 1927 by Maurice Paz. The title had its origins in a phrase of Lenin's. The journal resolutely defended the theses of the Opposition in a climate of persecution.

Dallin, David (1889–1962): RSDLP member, militant internationalist Menshevik leader and a member of the Moscow Soviet who was arrested and exiled in 1921. He was a co-editor of *Sotsialisticheskii Vestnik* from 1923 to 1933 and wrote twelve books on Russia, including *The Real Soviet Russia* and *Forced Labor in Soviet Russia* (with Boris Nikolayevsky). His second wife was Left Oppositionist Lola Dallin. David Dallin collaborated with Daniel Bell to promote Serge in the US and to defend him from attack by the Stalinists. He was a prolific columnist for *The New Leader*, where he exposed Marc Zborowski, Stalin's spy in the Left Opposition. The Dallins had helped Zborowski in numerous ways until he was unmasked. Zborowski had rewarded his friends (the Dallins) by spying on them.

Dallin, Lola (1898–1981): Née Iilia Laklovlena Ginzberg in Latvia, she was married first to the Menshevik Samuel Estrin (they later both became Left Oppositionists) and then to David Dallin. She was also known as Lydia or Lilia and had the pseudonyms Paulsen, P, and Yakovlev. She left the USSR in 1923 for Berlin and moved to Paris in 1933, where she worked as secretary to Boris Nikolayevsky at the International Institute of Social History. In 1935 Lola began working with Lev Sedov on the *Bulletin of the Left Opposition*, handling his correspondence with Trotsky and the leaders of Trotskyist groups in Europe and America. She stored fifteen bundles of LDT's archive in her apartment, later transferring them to the Institute, from where they were stolen in November 1936. She worked closely with Mark Zborowski, was a leader of the Russian Section of the Fourth International, and collected many of the testimonies presented in the Dewey Commission in Mexico. When Lev Sedov fell gravely ill in 1938, Lola Dallin and Zborowski took him to the Mirabeau clinic in Paris on the advice of her sister-in-law, a physician at the clinic. Sedov died there under mysterious circumstances in February 1938. In 1939 Lola visited Trotsky in Mexico at the time that he received a warning from General Orlov that there was an NKVD agent in the Paris Left Opposition circle, a Polish Jew named Mark. Lola vouched for Zborowski, convincing Trotsky that this was an NKVD hoax to create panic and disrupt the work of the organization. The American FBI and CIA suspected that Lola Dallin was an NKVD agent, paired with Zborowski. Serge also had suspicions about her. The evidence is slim, but she clearly covered for Zborowski, preventing earlier discovery. The Dallins helped bring Zborowski to the US, and later helped Victor Kravchenko defect from the Soviets in Washington, DC, in 1944. From 1954 to 1956 Lola Dallin cooperated fully with the FBI in providing testimony about Zborowski, the NKVD agent in the Left Opposition in Paris (and the US).

Davenport, Miriam (1915–99): American who lived in France from 1935 to 1941 and worked closely with Varian Fry and Mary-Jayne Gold in Marseilles, helping to save many endangered artists, intellectuals and anti-Nazi political refugees through the ERC. Among her clients were Serge and André Breton.

Dewey, John (1859–1952): American philosopher and educator who served at age seventy-eight as chairman of the commission investigating the Moscow Trials. Instrumentalist and pragmatist, known as *the* philosopher of democracy, Dewey was also an important public intellectual, a controversial educational reformer, and an outspoken supporter of the labour movement and other progressive causes. At the request of Dwight and Nancy Macdonald, Dewey wrote a letter to the U.S. consul in Cindad Trujillo to solicit a visa for Serge.

Dingelstedt, Fyodor (1890–1937): Social Democrat in 1910. After the revolution, he rose to become the head of the Institute of Red Professors, later the Director of the Institute of Leningrad Forests and official of the Left Opposition. He was deported to Vorkuta, where he was a member of the Strike Committee during the hunger strikes in 1936. He was sent to Solovietskii, where he fought for improvements in detention conditions, then disappeared.

Dos Passos, John (1896–1970): American 'committed' novelist who Serge admitted was the only writer who influenced his own literary work. Dos Passos was a signatory to the letter to the president of Mexico defending Serge and his comrades. Author of *U.S.A.*, Dos Passos was critical of the vulgar consumerism and social indifference of American culture. Radicalized in the 1920s, Dos Passos moved from sympathy for the Communist Party to staunch anti-Stalinism by the late 1930s and moved to the libertarian right by the 1940s.

Dubinsky, David (1892–1982): President of the International Ladies' Garment Workers' Union (ILGWU) from 1932 to 1966. Dubinsky was an authoritarian giant who dominated the world of Jewish labour and socialism while supporting the conservative factions in American labour. An anti-communist social democrat, Dubinsky signed the appeal to the president of Mexico in defence of Serge and his comrades.

Duhamel, Georges (1884–1936): French physician and writer who supported the free Victor Serge campaign from 1933 to 1936 in France and became Serge's friend after 1936.

Dumbadze, Lado (?–1937): Typographer and chairman of the first Bolshevik Soviet in Tiflis. He was a member of the Left Opposition but was so badly shocked in the civil war that he couldn't feed or dress himself. He was arrested and sent from prison to prison and then deported to Sarapul.

Dzerzhinsky, Felix (1877–1926): Polish revolutionary of bourgeois origin who became a Marxist at eighteen and was close to Rosa Luxemburg. He was imprisoned five times, deported and escaped three times. He served five years of forced labour but was liberated by the February Revolution. He was a member of the Petrograd MRC, which organized the insurrection of 1917, then chairman of the Cheka and later the GPU. Serge described him as a man of ascetic honesty, unbreakable self-possession and amazing capacity for work, who 'devoted his life, with a poet's ardour, to the transformation of man and of life'.

Eastman, Max (1883–1969): Prolific writer, poet, radical editor, translator and author. Eastman edited *The Masses* from 1912 to 1917, moving it to the left. He was a friend and comrade of John Reed. When *The Masses* was suspended during the trials of several of its editors for violating the Espionage Act, Eastman started *The Liberator*. He lived in the USSR from 1922 to 1924 and released Lenin's last testament to the world press in 1927. He was a supporter, and biographer, of Trotsky, and translated his works into English, including *The History of the Russian Revolution*. Eastman began to question Marxism, equated Stalinism with Leninism, and moved to the right (with Sidney Hook) beginning in the 1940s. Serge corresponded with Eastman and appealed for his material help and aid in getting a visa out of Europe in 1940.

L'École émancipée: Political and educational periodical founded in 1910 for militant revolutionaries in education. Serge published an article in its issue of 14 February 1926, under the title 'Pourquoi la France n'a pas d'intellectuels revolutionnaires'. *L'École émancipée* participated in the campaign for his release and its militants helped him get to Marseille in 1940.

Efron, Sergei (1893–1941): Russian poet and White Army officer who was recruited as an NKVD assassin while in France. He headed one network spying on the Left Opposition in Paris but was unable to get two on his hit list: Sneevliet and Serge. Efron's wife, the poet Marina Tsvetaeva, committed suicide after Efron returned to Russia and was executed.

Ehrenburg, Ilya (1891–1967): Prolific Soviet writer, journalist, translator, World War II propagandist and cultural figure. Ehrenburg participated in the 1905 Revolution, alongside Nikolai Bukharin, his close friend. Later, as a war reporter in Paris, Ehrenburg was able to maintain a measure of independence while being submissive to Stalin. He knew

Serge well, yet feigned ignorance during the 'Victor Serge Affair' at the 1935 Paris Congress for the Defence of Culture.

Eltsin, Boris Mikhailovich (1879–1937): Old Bolshevik, member of the executive committee of the Soviets in 1917, head of the clandestine centre of the Opposition in 1928. He was put in solitary confinement in Suzdal prison in 1929 then deported to Orenburg, where Serge was also in exile. Serge portrayed him in the character of Elkine in *Midnight in the Century*.

Eltsin, Victor Borisovich (1899–1937): Son of Boris Mikhailovich Eltsin, and himself a Bolshevik, political commissar during the civil war and editor of the Russian edition of Trotsky's *Complete Works*. He was a member of the Left Opposition in Moscow, one of Trotsky's gifted secretaries who spent five years in prison and was then deported in 1928 to Archangel. There is no trace of him after 1936.

Erlich, Henryk (1882–1942): Activist of the socialist Bund, member of the Petrograd Soviet, Warsaw City Council and the executive committee of the Second International. He was arrested by the NKVD in 1939 and condemned to death, but he was released in 1942 and joined the newly formed (Soviet) Jewish Anti-Fascist Committee. After Erlich (together with Victor Alter) was arrested by the NKVD in Kuybyshev and shot in December 1942, a wave of protests among socialist circles in the West followed. Serge and his comrades organized a memorial protest in Mexico that was violently attacked by Stalinists.

España Libre: A broad-based bilingual periodical published in New York by the Confederated Spanish Societies. It was devoted to news of struggles in Spain as well as of the widely scattered exile community who had gained political asylum in the US after 1939, when Franco's fascism triumphed in the civil war. Serge published several articles in *España Libre*.

Excelsior: Conservative, establishment Mexican daily newspaper that accused Serge of being in the service of the Gestapo in Paris in an article quoting a mysterious 'Washington Dispatch', but which was a classic piece of Stalinist vilification.

Farrell, James T. (1904–79): American writer who published more than twenty-five novels, best known for his *Studs Lonigan* trilogy. Farrell was a member of the Communist Party in the 1930s but became disaffected with Stalinism and joined the Socialist Workers Party, leaving in 1946 to join the Workers Party. He was a signatory to the letter to the president of Mexico defending Serge and his comrades.

Ferrer, Francisco (1859–1909): Spanish anarcho-syndicalist and educational reformer who opened the Escuela Moderna (Modern School) to teach radical social values. He was arrested in 1906 but released uncharged over a year later. His school failed and closed while he was incarcerated. After his release in 1908, he wrote *The Origins and Ideals of the Modern School*. He also founded the journal *Solidaridad Obrera*.

Following the declaration of martial law in 1909 during the Catalan worker's uprising, Ferrer was arrested and blamed for the popular revolt. He was executed by firing squad at Montjuïc Castle in Barcelona on 13 October, sparking an international wave of protest. His execution radicalized the young Victor Serge, who took part in the protest demonstration in Paris.

Figner, Vera (1852–1942): A leader of Narodnaya Volya (People's Will), the Russian populist group responsible for the assassination of Tsar Alexander II – which she helped plan. Serge's parents were also in the group and as a result went into exile to escape repression. Figner was sentenced to death, but the sentence was eventually commuted to life imprisonment in Siberia, where she spent six years and then another twenty years at Shlüsselburg prison. She was released in 1904. Serge translated her *Memoirs of a Revolutionist* into French, working alongside this 'exemplary character'.

Fischer, Louis (1896–1970): Louis Fischer was the *New York Evening Post* European correspondent in Germany from 1921, then Moscow in 1922. He began writing for *The Nation* in 1923 but left in 1945 after a dispute with editor Freda Kirchwey over the journal's sympathetic reporting of Stalin. While in the USSR Fischer published *Oil Imperialism: The International Struggle for Petroleum* (1926) and *The Soviets in World Affairs* (1930). He covered the last open demonstration of the Left Opposition, Adolf Joffe's funeral in Moscow in 1927. He reported on the Spanish Civil War and joined the International Brigade fighting Franco. He later wrote for *The Progressive*, wrote his autobiography, *Men and Politics* (1941), and biographies of *Gandhi* (1950), *Stalin* (1952) and *Lenin* (1964).

La Flèche: Organ of the *Front commun* (Common Front) against fascism and the war and for social justice, founded in 1934. The paper was edited by Gaston Bergery, who broke the story of the assassination of Ignace Reiss after Serge visited Bergery at the offices of the newspaper. The rest of the French press remained silent.

Frank, Pierre (1905–84): Pierre Frank, a chemical engineer, joined the Left Opposition in France in 1928 and worked with surrealist Pierre Naville and syndicalist Alfred Rosmer, later serving as Trotsky's secretary in Prinkipo from 1930 to 1933. Frank led the Marxist wing of the Ligue Communiste with R. Molinier and became a central leader of the Fourth International and LCR in France. He wrote *The Long March of the Trotskyists* and *Histoire de l'Internationale communiste (1919–43)*. In the introduction to the second French edition of Trotsky's *Leur morale et la nôtre* in 1966, Frank repeated the false rumour that Serge wrote the prospectus to the first edition, attacking Trotsky.

Fry, Varian (1907–67): Harvard-educated classicist and editor from New York City, Fry helped save thousands of endangered refugees who were caught in the Vichy French zone, arranging their escape from Nazi terror during World War II, including Marc Chagall, Franz Werfel, Alma Mahler, Hannah Arendt, Victor Brauner, Wifredo Lam and Victor Serge. He lived in Villa Air-Bel outside Marseilles with Serge, Vlady, André Breton, Mary Jane Gold and others, while continuing the ERC work. Known as 'the American Schindler', Fry died in obscurity, having been reprimanded by the US government for his actions. His book *Surrender on Demand*, published in 1945 and entirely rewritten as *Assignment: Rescue* in 1968, memorializes the experience.

Gemähling, Jean (1912–2003): Liaison agent with British expeditionary Corps in 1940, Gemahling worked with Varian Fry in the ERC in 1940–41 and lived with Serge, Fry and others at Villa Air-Bel. He helped create the resistance network 'Combat' after having made contact with Henri Fresnay through Serge. Gemahling was arrested by the Gestapo twice but managed to escape.

Ghezzi, Francisco (1894–1942): Italian anarcho-syndicalist, delegate to the Congress of the Red Trade Unions International in Moscow where he met and became close friends with Serge. He was arrested in Berlin on his way home. Serge was in Germany and campaigned for Ghezzi's release. Ghezzi was granted asylum in the USSR in 1922, working there for the rest of his life. When Serge was arrested and deported to Orenburg in 1933, Ghezzi helped his family. Ghezzi courageously accompanied Serge to the train station when Serge was expelled from the country in 1936 and then took charge of Serge's manuscripts. He was arrested in 1937 and sent to Vorkuta where he died in 1942.

Gide, Andre (1869–1951): Winner of the Nobel Prize for literature in 1947. A pre-eminent figure at the International Congress of Writers for the Defence of Culture (21–25 June 1935), he took up the case of Victor Serge. It was thanks to his intervention that Magdeleine Paz and Charles Plisnier were able to take the floor at the Congress. He later intervened with the Soviet ambassador in Paris.

Gironella, Enrique (Enrique Pascual Adroher) (1908–87): Gironella was a member of the POUM Executive Committee who was arrested in 1937 as a 'Trotsky Fascist'. He emigrated to Mexico, where he collaborated with Serge and Vlady in the group Socialismo y Libertad, and was stabbed during the violent attack of the public meeting they organized to protest the execution of Erlich and Alter. Gironella edited *Mundo* with Serge, Pivert, Gorkín and others.

Glazman Mikhaïl S. (?–1924): Trotsky's secretary during the civil war. Glazman participated in the editing and publication of several volumes of Trotsky's *Complete Works*.

Gogua, Irina (1905–90?): Serge's relative (her mother, Julia Nikolayeva Kolberg, was Serge's cousin, and her father was the Georgian Menshevik Kalistrat Gogua). Irina was a childhood friend of Nadezhda Alliluyeva, Stalin's wife. She worked at the Kremlin with Avel Yenukidze. She was also married, for a time, to Alexander Barmine. Gogua survived twenty-one years in Ukhta, a camp for 'goners'.

Gold, Mary Jayne (1909–97): A Chicago heiress who lived in Marseilles in 1940, where she worked with Varian Fry and Miriam Davenport in the ERC, which Fry had formed to aid the thousands of refugees waiting in Marseilles for a visa out of Europe. Gold bankrolled the work of the ERC and paid for the chateau Serge dubbed 'Espere Visa' where they (Fry, Gold, Serge, Breton and others) lived before leaving France in 1941. Gold's memoirs *Crossroads Marseilles 1940* (Doubleday, 1980) and *Marseilles Année 40* (Phebus, 2001) tell the story.

Goldman, Emma (1869–1940): Militant American libertarian and feminist born in the Russian empire, dubbed 'one of the most dangerous women in America'. She and Alexander Berkman were deported to the USSR in 1919, where they attempted to mediate in the events of Kronstadt, meeting at the apartment of Serge's father-in-law, Alexander Russakov. Goldman wrote *My Disillusionment with Russia* (1923). Serge described her 'organizing flair', her 'narrow but generous prejudices, and her self-importance, typical of American women devoted to social work'.

Gorkín, Julián (1901–87): Born J. García Gómez-Ribera, Gorkín was a Spanish revolutionary, member of the POUM executive and editor of *Batalla*. Gorkín was arrested by a Stalinist militia in Spain in 1937 and tried as a 'Trotskyist Fascist' along with Andrade and Arquer. Serge campaigned for an investigation into the trumped-up charges and his release. Gorkín emigrated to Mexico and in 1941 worked to secure a visa (along with Dwight and Nancy Macdonald) for Serge, still in Vichy France. In 1943 Gorkín took a bullet meant for Serge during a violent attack at a public meeting protesting the execution of Polish socialists Erlich and Alter.

Gorky, Maxim (1868–1936): Born Alexei Maximovich Peshkov, in Nizhni-Novgorod, where he knew Serge's mother's family. Gorky was a Russian writer and friend of Lenin who became critical of the Bolsheviks' political and cultural censorship and growing authoritarianism. He invited Serge to join him in editing his journal *Novaya Zhizn* in 1919. Gorky quietly interceded with Stalin to allow Serge to leave the USSR in 1936, and in return publicly supported some of Stalin's policies, whitewashing Stalin's forced labour camps in poems. Serge thought Gorky would 'explode', and he did, finally breaking with Stalin shortly before his death in 1936.

Gramsci, Antonio (1891–1937): Italian writer, political theorist and revolutionary leader, a socialist and editor of the weekly *L'Ordine Nuovo*, promoting workers' councils and workers' education. In 1921 Gramsci was a founding member of the Italian Communist Party and went to Moscow in 1922–23 and from there to Vienna in 1924, where he met Serge. His books include *The Prison Notebooks*, *Letters from Prison* and *The Modern Prince and Other Writings*.

Gussie (1921–): Nickname of Justus Rosenberg, the youngest member of the team led by Varian Fry that rescued some of Europe's most famous artists, writers and intellectuals during World War II. Born in Dantzig, 'Gussie' was, at age fifteen, the errand boy for the ERC. Later he joined the Resistance, but ended the war in the US Army. He teaches at Bard College and the New School.

Hilferding, Rudolf (1877–1941): German Social Democrat, editor in chief of the SPD daily, *Vorwärts* (1907–15), and author of *Finance Capital* (1910). He was Minister of Finances in 1923 (when Serge was in Germany) and 1928, and MP from 1924 to 1933. He emigrated to France in 1933 and was handed over by the Vichy government to the Gestapo. Hilferding was executed in 1941.

Hook, Sidney (1902–89): One of America's most controversial public philosophers and an important New York intellectual. Hook was a Marxist in his early life, publishing the influential *Towards the Understanding of Karl Marx* (1933). He was a leading disciple of John Dewey and went from being an anti-Stalinist Communist to a pragmatic Social Democrat, later drifting rightwards to become a partisan of the Cold War and supporter of Ronald Reagan. Hook maintained an intellectually rich correspondence with Serge and was one of the many American intellectuals who came to Serge's defence when he was under attack in Mexico.

Horizons: The premiere British 'modernist' literary magazine edited by Cyril Connolly during World War II, when literary culture had to be actively defended against its many opponents. Its contributors included Orwell, Auden, Eliot, Miller, Sartre, Waugh, Thomas and many others. Serge published his 'Letter from Mexico' in its January 1947 issue.

Howe, Quincy (1900–77): Author, wartime correspondent and well-known broadcast journalist with CBS and ABC news who was a signatory to the letter to Mexican President Ávila Camacho in 1942, asking for protection for Serge and his comrades.

Independent Labour Party: Founded in 1893 and led by Keir Hardie. The ILP played a key role in the founding of the British Labour Party in 1906, but split away in 1932 as a revolutionary socialist organization that was more centrist in practice.

El Informador: Mexican daily published in Guadalajara since 1916.

International Ladies' Garment Workers' Union (ILGWU): At the height of its power during the 1930s and 1940s, the ILGWU was one of the most important progressive unions in the US. It was founded in 1900 as an organization dominated by Jewish and Italian immigrants. Serge was listed as an international contributor to the ILGWU-financed monthly *Modern Review*, which published his article 'Socialism and Psychology' in May 1947 and an obituary notice of Serge in January 1948.

Istrati, Panaït (1884–1935): Romanian author who wrote in French and was nicknamed the 'Maxim Gorky of the Balkans'. Istrati lived in the USSR from 1927 to 1929. Serge was his political guide, friend and collaborator. Heartbroken by his experiences in the USSR, Istrati wrote a trilogy about them, *Vers l'autre flamme*. He used his name in the second volume, though it was written by Serge, still in Leningrad at the time.

Joffe, Adolf Abramovich (1883–1927): Veteran of the Russian workers' movement, personal friend of Trotsky and member with him of the Mezhduraionnyi (Internationalist) organization before October 1917. Joffe became a diplomat, was the Soviet ambassador to Berlin (he was expelled from Germany on the eve of the 1918 German Revolution for 'Bolshevik agitation') and China after the Revolution. Gravely ill, he committed suicide in 1927, just after the Left Opposition was expelled from the Party, investing his act with the character of a protest against Stalin's regime.

Joffe, Maria Mikhailovna (1900–88): Second wife of leading Bolshevik Adolf Joffe and a prominent member of the Trotskyist opposition to Stalinism. She survived twenty-nine years in prison camps in the Soviet Union and was freed in 1957. She lived in Israel from 1975 until her death. See her autobiography, *One Long Night* (London, New Park Publications, 1977).

Kalinin, Mikhaïl Ivanovich (1875–1946): member of the RSDLP in 1898, Bolshevik in 1903, organiser of a strike at the Putilov factories at Petrograd in 1905 and nominal head of the Soviet state in 1919. In 1921 Kalinin was sent to Kronstadt to negotiate with the rebels but reported to the Party that they were led by a White General, a fabrication. Initially a Bukharinist, on Lenin's death he followed the majority of the Politburo to swing to Stalin.

Kazantzakis, Nikos (1838–1957): Greek writer (*Zorba the Greek*, 1946). Kazantzakis visited the USSR in 1927 on the occasion of the tenth anniversary of the Revolution. He toured the USSR with Panaït Istrati, with Serge as their political guide. Kazantzakis admired Serge and urged him to be a writer, first and foremost.

Kibalchich, Vladimir Viktorvich, 'Vlady' (1920–2005): Son of Victor Serge, named after Vladimir Mazin, Serge's comrade in the civil war and Comintern. Born in Petrograd, Vlady spent his youth in Petrograd, Berlin, Vienna, Leningrad, Orenburg, Brussels, Paris and Marseilles, his life paralleling the development and degeneration of the Soviet Union, from the civil war to deportation and exile. He turned to the arts when very young, skipping school to pass hours at the Hermitage in Petrograd, where he found refuge from the growing insanity of his mother and the detention of his father. Vlady was a prolific painter, muralist and lithographer. He rebelled against the nationalist realism of the New Mexican Muralist Movement that led to the 'movement of rupture' in art. His murals and paintings are in Mexico and Managua, and 4,600 of his works have been given to the National Institute of Fine Arts of Mexico and to the 'Centro Vlady', associated with the Universidad Autónoma de Mexico. Vlady was a militant revolutionary, a self-taught polyglot and writer. He accompanied his father in deportation to Orenburg from 1933 to 1936. Together with his father he joined the POUM in Paris. Vlady's resourceful spirit helped to feed his family, a surrealist group and other refugees at the Villa Air-Bel, outside Marseilles. Escaping Europe during the war was difficult and dangerous, because Serge was a former Bolshevik and Vlady was Jewish on his mother's side. Serge and Vlady were imprisoned in Martinique, Santo Domingo and Cuba. After finally making it to Mexico in 1941, he married Isabel Diaz Fabela in 1947. In Mexico, he was a member of the group Socialismo y Libertad and the illustrator of its journal *Mundo* (1943–45). Vlady published and illustrated many of Serge's numerous writings, and remained his entire life in Trotsky's orbit. Some of his work can be seen at www.vlady.org.

Kibalchich-Vidal, Jeannine (1935–2012): Serge's daughter, who he first met upon his release in 1936 in Moscow when she was just over a year old. In Paris her mother, Liuba Russakova, was increasingly psychologically unstable and was interned in a mental institution in the south of France. Jeannine was cared for in Pontarlier by friends while Serge battled for a visa out of Europe during the war. Laurette Séjourné, Serge's third wife, brought Jeannine to Mexico in 1942. Jeannine married and had four sons, and worked as an executive administrator at UNAM (Autonomous University of Mexico). See her 'Victor Serge, My Father', in Susan Weissman (ed.), *The Ideas of Victor Serge*, Glasgow, Critique Books, 1997.

Kirchwey, Freda (1893–1976): Managing editor, literary editor, editor and publisher of *The Nation* from 1918 to 1955, when she was fired for her increasingly anti-Stalinist views. Kirchwey focused on large political and international issues – the Spanish Civil War, democracy versus fascism and Nazism, pacifism and collective security, the plight of refugees and Zionism, McCarthyism and censorship. Kirchwey was pro-Soviet until some of her political friends were executed during Stalin's purges. She was one of the signatories of the letter to the president of Mexico defending Serge, and the Macdonalds turned to her for help getting Serge passage and documents from France to Mexico.

Klement, Rudolf (1910–38): Trotsky's secretary in Turkey and a dedicated secretary of the Fourth International who was murdered by the NKVD in Paris in July 1938, just as he was preparing for the founding conference of the Fourth International, and compiling a dossier investigating Sedov's death and the role of 'Etienne' aka Marc Zborowski. Before he could deliver these documents, Klement was kidnapped from his apartment in Paris. His decapitated torso was fished out of the Seine at Meulan, his body cut up to prevent recognition. Serge knew him in

Brussels and Paris, thought of him as a 'young doctrinaire' who worked at a 'fanatical pitch'.

Kollontai, Alexandra (1872–1952): Russian revolutionary, Kollontai was a militant activist in the international women's movement, a Menshevik until 1914, a member of the Bolshevik Central Committee in 1917, and People's Commissar for Social Affairs. Together with Bukharin she founded the Left Communist fraction and opposed the peace of Brest-Litovsk. She led the Workers Opposition and was later an ambassador to Mexico, Norway and Sweden. Kollontai sympathized with the Left Opposition but later 'conformed'. She defended free love and published *Marxism and the Sexual Revolution.* She was the only member of Lenin's Central Committee to escape Stalin's purges.

Kostiuk, Hryhory (1902–2002): Pseudonym 'Podoliak'. Literary scholar and publicist who spent five years in different Soviet prison camps. He founded various Ukrainian literary organizations and wrote several books, including *Stalinist Rule in Ukraine.* He corresponded with Serge and published Serge in Ukrainian journals.

Kotziubinsky, Yuri Mikhailovich (1897–1937): Member of the Left Opposition in 1923 and later the United Opposition. He refused to capitulate or make false confessions, and was expelled from the Party and shot without trial.

Kritsman, Lev Natanovich (1890–1938): Bolshevik economist, one of the first heads of the VSNKh (Vysshyii Sovet Narodnogo Khozyaistva), the Supreme Soviet of the Economy.

Krivitsky, Walter (1899–1941): Born Samuel Ginzburg in Galicia (now Ukraine), Krivitsky joined the Bolsheviks, was sent to Germany for the 1923 revolution, then became Chief of Soviet military intelligence in Europe. He criticized Stalin's policy in Spain and broke with Moscow after the assassination of his childhood friend and comrade Ignace Reiss. In Paris (in hiding), Krivitsky and Reiss's widow Elsa Poretsky were suspicious of Serge, believing Stalin wouldn't have allowed him to leave the USSR unless he could be of service to Stalin. Krivitsky met with Serge several times in Paris. Ironically, the Stalinist agent Zborowski was assigned as Krivitsky's bodyguard in Paris. At the end of 1938, he sailed to the US, where, with the assistance of Isaac Don Levine, he wrote *In Stalin's Secret Service*, published in 1939. That same year, he testified before the Dies Committee (later to become the House Un-American Activities Committee) and was debriefed by the Department of State. On 10 February 1941, Krivitsky was found dead in the Bellevue Hotel in Washington, DC. His death was officially declared a suicide, though there are allegations that he was murdered by Soviet intelligence. His biographer, Gary Kern, calls it 'the impossible suicide'.

Kropotkin, Peter (1842–1921): Russian anarcho-communist, writer, geographer, philosopher and evolutionary theorist, Kropotkin's father was a Russian prince, and Kropotkin spent his early life as an Imperial

Cadet and later a cavalry officer. His funeral in 1921 marked the last time anarchists were permitted to freely gather in Soviet Russia. Serge had not visited Kropotkin because of their 'painful' political differences, but remarked at the funeral that he was the only Party member accepted in anarchist circles. Kropotkin's books include *The Conquest of Bread, Fields, Factories and Workshops, Mutual Aid: A Factor of Evolution* and *Memoirs of a Revolutionary*.

Kun, Béla (1886–1937): Founder of the Hungarian Communist Party in 1918 and leader of the short-lived Soviet Republic of Hungary in 1919. Kun represented the Comintern in Germany (1921), where he led many disastrous initiatives. He remained a Comintern official, was arrested in 1937 and shot for 'Trotskyism'.

Landau, Kurt (1903–37): Austrian Communist Party member who rallied to the Left Opposition in 1930 in Berlin. He broke with Trotsky over the POUM and departed for Spain, where he worked with the POUM journal *La Batalla*. Landau was 'disappeared' in September 1937, probably by the GPU. His precise fate is unknown – some accounts have him tortured to death in Barcelona in the offices of the PSUC (Unified Socialist Party of Catalonia, Stalinist), though his wife Katia does not exclude the possibility that he was taken back to the USSR and killed. Serge wrote telegrams of protest to President Negrín when the GPU accused Landau of having acted as an agent of the Gestapo.

Herbert Lenhof (?–?): Psychoanalyst of the Freudian school and refugee from Nazi Germany who was a good friend of Serge's in Mexico. His correspondence with Serge from New York from 1945–47, some eighty letters in less than two years, analyses the psychological aspects of totalitarianism, the political situation in Mexico and the future of European culture.

Libertad, Albert (1875–1908): French anarcho-individualist and crippled street fighter who used his crutches as weapons. Founder of *Causeries populaires* (1902) and the journal *L'Anarchie*, which Serge later edited. His true name remains unknown.

Lominadze, Vissarion Vissarionovich (Beso) (1897–1935): A former head of the Communist Youth, loyal to Stalin, who was his cousin. He was sent to China with Neumann in charge of the preparations for the insurrection of Canton (1927), which ended in a bloodbath. After the Chinese events, Lominadze became an Oppositionist and formed the anti-Bukharinist group known as the Young Stalinist Left, also called the 'rightist-leftist bloc', in 1929, along with Jan Sten and Sergei Syrtsov. He committed suicide in Sverdlovsk in 1935 on the eve of his arrest.

Lukács, György (Georg) (1885–1971): Hungarian Communist philosopher and literary critic, author of *History and Class Consciousness* (1923) and *Lenin: A Study in the Unity of His Thought* (1924), who fled to Vienna after the short-lived Hungarian Soviet Republic in 1919, where he worked with Serge, Adolf Joffe and Antonio Gramsci in *Inprekorr*.

Lutovinov, Luri (1887–1924): Member of Workers Opposition who committed suicide after the defeat of the Opposition.

La Lutte des classes: The journal *Clarté*, sympathetic to the ideas of the Left Opposition, changed its name to *La Lutte des classes* in the spring of 1928.

Lyons, Eugene (1898–1985): Radical journalist, editor of *The American Mercury*, who worked with Dwight Macdonald in trying to help Serge get a US visa. After some collaboration with the Trotskyists, he moved rightward, becoming a conservative anti-communist journalist.

Macdonald, Dwight (1906–82): Editor, combative journalist, essayist, literary and film critic, who went from Trotskyism to anarchism – and was the 'most fiery' of the New York intellectuals on the editorial board of *Partisan Review*. He left *PR* in 1943 and started *Politics* in 1944. Macdonald read and promoted Serge, helped him financially and worked to secure him a visa out of France. He and his wife Nancy left a large correspondence with Serge, the Macdonald Papers at Yale University Library.

Macdonald, Nancy Gardiner Rodman (1910–96): Granddaughter of the president of the New York Stock Exchange, she married Dwight Macdonald and contributed to his radicalization. She turned their apartment into a political and literary centre, and was manager of *Politics* in the 1940s. In 1941 she started the Partisan Review Fund for European Writers and Artists, then, in the 1950s, the Spanish Refugee Aid, which proclaimed solidarity with the anti-fascist and anti-Stalinist exiles. Serge was the first to receive her support and aid. This activity is abundantly documented in her voluminous correspondence, kept in the Dwight Macdonald Papers of Yale University Library. She wrote *Homage to the Spanish Exiles: Voices from the Spanish Civil War* (Human Science, 1987).

Maîtrejean, Rirette (1887–1968): Pseudonym of Anna Estorges, individualist anarchist and feminist militant, who was Serge's first wife. She met Serge at Lille in 1909, and they lived together in Paris and co-edited *L'Anarchie*. They were co-defendants in the infamous Bonnot Gang trial of anarchist 'bandits' in 1913. She was acquitted and married Serge in prison in 1915 so they could have the right to visit and correspond. They were briefly reunited in Barcelona in 1917.

Malaquais, Jean (Vladimir Malecki) (1908–98): Polish novelist and Marxist who emigrated to France in 1930 and later fought in the Spanish Civil War. He gravitated to the anti-Stalinist far left in France and later in exile in Mexico, where he participated in the Socialismo y Libertad group with Serge, Gironella, Pivert, Gorkín and others. He and Serge had bitter political arguments and fell out with each other. Malaquais' 1939 novel about immigrant miners in France, *Les Javanais*, won the Prix Renaudot. Serge was a character in his *Planet sans visa*, about anti-fascist exiles in Marseilles.

Malraux, André (1901–76): French novelist, art theorist and Minister for Cultural Affairs, Malraux won the Prix Goncourt in 1933 for *La Condition Humaine*. He was one of the official sponsors of the International Congress of Writers for the Defence of Culture organized by the French Communist Party in 1935 and was chairing the proceedings when the Victor Serge Affair confronted the participants with Stalin's repression of writers and persecution of Serge. Malraux joined Republican forces in Spain during the Civil War. Serge met with him in Marseilles in 1941, chiding him for his collusion with the Stalinists in Spain. Malraux was appointed Minister of Information (1945–46) by President Charles de Gaulle, and then became France's first Minister of Cultural Affairs (1959–69). In 1947 Serge turned to Malraux for help in leaving Mexico. Malraux published an excerpt of Serge's letter to him, making it appear that Serge had become a Gaullist like Malraux.

MAPP (Moscow Association of Proletarian Writers) and **VAPP** (All-Russian Association of Proletarian Writers): Associations of writers favourable to a dictatorship of the Party – in favour, in other words, of placing literature under Party control.

Marshall, Margaret (1900–74): Worked at *The Nation* from 1928 to 1953 in various capacities. She was literary editor from 1937 on and is credited with raising its standard of criticism and bringing well-known authors to its pages. Marshall wrote a letter of support on Serge's behalf to the State Department in 1940 in an effort to get him to the US. She was fired in 1953 for her anti-communist views.

Martinet, Marcel (1887–1944): Revolutionary French poet, Communist and pacifist who opposed World War I as an internationalist. He was close to Trotsky from World War I until Trotsky's death. Martinet was literary editor of *L'Humanité* in 1918–19 but resigned with the rise of Stalinism. He defended Serge from 1933 in *Où va la Révolution russe? L'Affaire Victor Serge*. In 1935 Martinet intervened against Romain Rolland, who had taken up the accusations of Moscow against Zinoviev and Kamenev in *La Revolution proletarienne*. There is a substantial correspondence with Serge, and Martinet's series *Les Cahiers du Travail* (Labour Notebooks) published pamphlets by Serge.

Maurice, 'Monsieur' (Marcel Verzeano) (1911–2006): Young Romanian doctor who joined the ERC. He was with Serge and Vlady at Villa Air-Bel outside Marseilles. Verzeano left in October 1941 with a phony passport, travelling to the US on a Portuguese ship, where he became Associate Professor of Biophysics at UCLA Medical School and then a Professor of Neurobiology at UC Irvine.

Maurín, Joaquín (1896–1973): Spanish revolutionary and activist in the teachers union. He met Serge in Moscow as a CNT delegate in 1921. Maurín married Souvarine's sister, founded the Catalonian Communist Party and the journal *La Batalla*. After imprisonment in Montjuïc for four years under Primo de Rivera and exile in Paris, Maurín returned to Barcelona where he founded the workers' and peasants', party Bloque

Obrero y Campesino (BOC). In 1935 he merged the BOC with Nin's Left Communists to form the POUM. During the civil war, Maurín was captured by the Falangist police, condemned to death and jailed in a series of prisons, ending in Barcelona. Released in 1946 after ten years in prison, Maurín went into exile in New York City. There he established the American Literary Agency (ALA) promoting Latin American writers and wrote several books of history and sociology. His correspondence with Serge is held at Stanford University's Hoover Archive.

Mazin, Vladimir (1882–1919): Born Vladimir Ossipovich Lichtenstadt, Mazin was a revolutionary intellectual and Serge's collaborator in creating the Comintern press services. He participated in the 1905 Revolution, was a 'maximalist' involved in bombing actions and spent ten years in Schlüsselburg prison (outside Petrograd), where he translated Kant and Baudelaire, wrote *Goethe and the Philosophy of Nature*, and became a Marxist. He was liberated from the prison in the February Revolution and was installed as president of the Soviet of Shlüsselburg. Mazin joined the Bolsheviks in early 1919 and influenced Serge to join the Party in May 1919. In the civil war Mazin insisted on being sent to the front and tried to stop White General Yudenich's offensive against Petrograd. Mazin, with his small band of 'determined comrades' fighting the White cavalry, was killed in October 1919. Serge loved him like a brother and named his son Vladimir in his memory.

Mesnil, Jacques (Jean-Jacques Duelshauvers) (1872–1940): Journalist, art critic and anarchist who evolved in the direction of Communism. He and his wife Clara were close friends of Serge. They worked with Romain Rolland during World War I and collaborated with Serge in the early days of the Comintern. Mesnil worked with *La Vie ouvrière* and *L'Humanité* and later *La Revolution proletarienne*.

The Militant: Weekly newspaper of the Communist League of America (1928–36) and later of the Socialist Workers Party, the American section of the Fourth International. In 1942 *The Militant* came to the vigorous defence of Serge. It is still published today.

Molins y Fabrega, Narciso (1910–64): Spanish revolutionary journalist, editor of *La Batalla* and close collaborator of Andreu Nin, who joined the POUM with the Communist Left. He was on the Executive Committee of the POUM and escaped death because he was in Paris coordinating the POUM's international solidarity network. Serge actively collaborated in this work. Narciso Molins y Fabrega was a close friend of Vlady's and accompanied Serge and Vlady from Paris to Marseilles. Later in Mexican exile, Molins y Fabrega worked with Serge and Vlady politically.

Monatte, Pierre (1881–1960): Anarcho-syndicalist organizer and journalist, revolutionary trade unionist, founder of the syndicalist weekly *La Vie ouvrière* in 1909 and in 1925 of *La Revolution proletarienne*, which Serge contributed to frequently. Although disagreeing with Trotsky, he defended the persecuted Trotskyists and published numerous articles on the Spanish revolution and the crimes and repression of Stalinists against the POUM and the CNT.

Monde: Weekly newspaper edited by Henri Barbusse that appeared from 1928 to 1935. Serge wrote some articles for it.

Mundo: Monthly published by the Socialismo y Libertad group in Mexico. The first issue appeared in June 1943, with production and illustrations by Vlady. Serge published 'Necesidad de una renovación del Socialismo' (Necessity of a Renewal of Socialism) in the first issue and later 'A Donde Va Stalin?' (Where Is Stalin Headed?) in the October–November 1943 issue. Serge broke with *Mundo* in May 1944.

Munis, Grandizo (1912–89): Spanish Left Oppositionist who opposed the liquidation of the Spanish Trotskyists into the POUM. In 1936, Munis founded the Trotskyist group *La Voz Leninista*, which was infiltrated by the GPU spy Leon Narvich, who was killed by the POUM revenging the death of Nin. Munis was imprisoned and tortured by the Stalinists in 1938, but escaped and fled to Mexico, where he led the Spanish Trotskyists in exile, participated in the Emergency Conference of the Fourth International (1940) and was a close collaborator of Natalia Sedova Trotsky. He wrote a state capitalist analysis of the Soviet Union, *Parti-Etat, Stalinismo, Revolution*, and an account of the Spanish Civil War, *Jalones de Derrota: Promesa de Victoria*.

Muste, Abraham J. (1885–1967): Dutch-born American clergyman and political activist, Muste worked in the labour, pacifist and US civil rights movements. In 1929 he founded the Committee for Progressive Labor Action that became the American Workers Party, which in 1934 merged with the Communist League (the Left Opposition group in the US) to form the Socialist Workers Party. Muste met with Trotsky in Norway in 1936, and also met Serge in Brussels in July (1936) to get him to join the Bureau for the Fourth International. When he returned to the US that year Muste became a Christian pacifist. The correspondence between Muste and Serge shows the high regard they had for each other.

La Nación: Argentine periodical that published Serge's article 'Hitler contra Stalin; el III Reich, agonizante' (Hitler Against Stalin, the Agony of the Third Reich) in its 11 July 1941 issue.

The Nation: The New York–based independent leftist weekly journal of news, opinion and culture that published a letter from Serge, Gorkín and Pivert in February 1942, when they were the target of attacks by the Stalinists in the US and in Mexico.

Naville, Pierre (1904–93): Naville was the very last of the original Parisian surrealists who launched the movement in the 1920s. He was co-editor (with Benjamin Péret) of the first three numbers of the journal *La Révolution surrealiste*, then organized and co-edited the journal *Clarté*. Naville went to Moscow in 1927 with Gerard Rosenthal – Serge was their political guide. He took them to meet Trotsky, and they both joined the Left Opposition. Naville rapidly became one of its principal international leaders. In 1928, he published Serge's account of events in Russia in *Clarté*, which led to both their expulsions, Serge from the Soviet Party, and Naville from the French. Naville played an important role in the founding of the Fourth International in 1938. He left the Fourth International during the war and was later a militant activist in Socialist organizations in France. He became a sociologist of repute, writing on labour and on China. Naville's books include *Les Reines de la main gauche* (1924), *La Révolution et les Intellectuels* (1926 and 1975) and *Trotsky vivant* (1962).

Neruda, Pablo (1904–73): Chilean poet, diplomat, winner of the 1972 Nobel Prize for Literature, and loyal member of the Communist Party of Chile. As Consul General in Mexico in 1939, Neruda hid the artist David Alfaro Siqueiros after the May 1940 failed attempt to assassinate Leon Trotsky (in exile in Mexico), and then arranged a Chilean passport for Siqueiros, enabling him to flee the country. In 1942 Neruda published a letter in *The Nation* along with seven Mexican Deputies, and two other Stalinists, chiding *The Nation* for defending Serge and his comrades, 'fifth columnists'.

Neumann, Franz (1900–54): German left-wing political activist, Marxist theorist and labour lawyer, best known for his classic theoretical analysis of Nazi Germany, *Behemoth: The Structure and Practice of National Socialism, 1933–1944*. After imprisonment by the Nazis in April 1933, he escaped to England, joining the Frankfurt School in 1936. In the US Neumann became deputy chief of the Central European Section of the Office of Strategic Services (OSS). Serge was influenced by Neumann's analysis and was struck by its similarities to Stalinism. Neumann identified the economic and political roots of totalitarianism in industrial capitalism, while paying attention to the specific historical conditions of Germany. He saw the atomization of the working class, the centrality of anti-Semitism, and the suspension of democratic and legal norms as the outcome of the centralization of capital.

Neumann, Heinz (1902–37): German Communist initially associated with Fischer-Maslow, later rallying to Thälmann and the Stalinists. Neumann was sent to China as an agent of the Comintern (1927), where he was an organizer of the Canton Communist uprising. Serge's article on this Stalinist disaster got him expelled from the Party. Neumann returned to Germany and edited the *Rote Fahne*. As a Communist member of the Reichstag, he promoted Stalin's disastrous 'social fascists' line, which opened the door to Hitler. Neumann disappeared in the purges of 1937 after having taken refuge in the Soviet Union from the Nazis.

The New International: Journal of the Communist League of America, then, from 1938 onward, of the Socialist Workers Party and finally, from Spring 1940, of its minority, which formed the Workers Party. The magazine was founded and edited by Martin Abern and Max Shachtman.

Serge published nearly two dozen articles in the journal both before and after the 1940 split.

The New Leader: Newsweekly of the Socialist Party and later of the Social Democratic Federation, edited by Daniel Bell in the 1930s. This anti-Stalinist newspaper carried articles about Serge, Pivert and Gorkín, who were under attack in 1942–43, as well as information about the committee formed to defend them. From 1943 to 1947 Serge contributed more than twenty articles and was considered its Mexican correspondent.

The New Masses: *The New Masses* began as *The Masses*, which was shut down by the US government in 1917 because of its neutral stance on World War I and its critical cartoons and articles that the government decided violated the Espionage Act. It was brought back under editor Max Eastman as *The Liberator*. Contributors included Roger Baldwin, Norman Thomas, John Reed, Louise Bryant, Bertrand Russell, Dorothy Day, Helen Keller, Louis Untermeyer and others. It was taken over by the Communist Party in 1922, displeasing many of its writers, who started their own journal, *The New Masses*, in 1926. Most of the well-known left-wing writers and artists produced reportage, fiction, poetry and art for the magazine, including Max Eastman, Eugene O'Neill, Upton Sinclair, Richard Wright, James Agee, Sherwood Anderson, Alvah Bessie, Erskine Caldwell, John Dos Passos, Theodore Dreiser, Ralph Ellison, Waldo Frank, Ernest Hemingway, Josephine Herbst, Langston Hughes, Carl Sandburg, and satirists Art Young and William Gropper. *The New Masses* ceased publication in 1948.

Nicolaevsky, Boris Ivanovich (1887–1966): Historian, archivist, Bolshevik turned Menshevik leader who was on the commission investigating the Okhrana (Tsarist Secret Police) files. He served as director of the History of the Revolutionary Movement Archive in Moscow, representative of the Moscow Marx-Engels Institute, and Paris representative of the International Institute for Social History (IISH) in Amsterdam. The failed negotiations over the Soviet offer to purchase the Marx-Engels Archive and the politically motivated theft from Nicolaevsky's office of Leon Trotsky's archives in 1936 affected him greatly. Nicolaevsky fled to New York at the end of 1940. In 1945 he accompanied American intelligence to Germany to retrieve his stolen archive. His collection is housed at the Hoover Institution Archive at Stanford University.

Niebuhr, Reinhold (1892–1971): Professor of Christian social ethics who was vice-chairman of the Socialist Party in the 1920s, dropped much of his social radicalism after World War II and preached 'conservative realism', and was the best-known Cold War Liberal. He helped found the Americans for Democratic Action (ADA) in 1947 with Eleanor Roosevelt, John Kenneth Galbraith, Walter Reuther, Arthur Schlesinger and Hubert Humphrey. Niebuhr signed the letter to President Camacho of Mexico asking for protection for Serge and his comrades.

Nin, Andreu (1892–1937): Catalan revolutionary, syndicalist militant of the CNT in Barcelona, and CNT Delegate to the Comintern. Nin lived in the USSR from 1921 to 1930, working for the Comintern. He was Secretary of the Red International of Unions (Profitern). He became a close friend of Serge in Leningrad. Serge said Nin enjoyed life and was a model revolutionary. In the USSR Nin translated Pilnyak and Dostoevsky into Catalan. He was a member of the Left Opposition but managed to leave the USSR in 1930 with his Russian wife and two daughters. In Spain he led the Catalan Left Opposition, became a leader of the POUM, was arrested in 1937 and disappeared, tortured to death. Nin was a syndicalist who became an ardent anti-Stalinist, yet argued with Trotsky over the POUM and its support for the Popular Front.

Orlov, Alexander (Lev L. Feldbine) (1895–1973): Bolshevik, NKVD agent who was sent to Spain in 1936 as head of espionage during the civil war, tasked with arresting and executing left opponents of the PCE. Orlov organized the secret transport of the entire gold reserve of the Spanish Republic to the USSR. He was recalled to Moscow in 1938 but refused to return, realizing he would be executed, and fled to the US, going underground. It was Orlov who tried to warn Trotsky about the presence of an NKVD agent named Marc within the Opposition circle in Paris. To protect himself, Orlov wrote a letter to Stalin, detailing all Stalin's crimes, promising to keep all the secrets he knew if Stalin spared him and his family. If he were murdered, Orlov told Stalin, his lawyer would publish Orlov's testimony. Though he was pursued for fourteen years, Orlov kept his word and published his memoirs, *The Secret History of Stalin's Crimes*, only after the death of Stalin in March 1953, fifteen years after his own flight.

Orwell, George (1903–50): Author of *Nineteen Eighty-Four*, *Animal Farm* and *Homage to Catalonia*, an account of his experiences in the Spanish Civil War as a member of the POUM. Orwell corresponded with Serge and tried to get Serge's *Memoirs of a Revolutionary* published with Secker and Warburg in London.

Pankratov, Vassili F. (1893–1938): Bolshevik, organiser of the Kronstadt sailors' rebellion in 1917. Pankratov was jailed in 1929 and was a revolutionary leader in the Verkhne-Uralsk Isolator. He was arrested in deportation, accused of having created a clandestine centre of the Opposition with Solnstsev. His wife Lisa Senyatskaya was in Orenburg with Serge.

Parijanine, Maurice (known as Maurice Donzel) (1885–1937): Writer, poet and editor of *Les Humbles*. Parijanine was the French translator of Leon Trotsky's autobiography, *My Life*. He collaborated with Serge in the translation work of the Comintern Executive and participated in the free Victor Serge campaign in 1933–36. Serge wrote a memorable portrait of him in *Deux recontres*.

Partisan Review: Founded by William Phillips and Philip Rahv in 1934, *Partisan Review* was originally a cultural and literary journal of the

Communist Party's John Reed Club, and an alternative to *The New Masses*. Critical of the Party line on culture and politics by 1936, the founders relaunched *PR* as an independent journal of 'the modern sensibility in literature and the arts and a radical consciousness in social and political matters'. It became a mainstay of the anti-Stalinist left and the forum for the brilliant and contentious stable of writers who became known as the 'New York Intellectuals'. Edited by Dwight Macdonald from 1937 to 1943, *PR* published and paid Serge for his articles in the years 1938 to 1947, the year he died.

Pascal, Pierre (1890–1983): As part of the French military mission in Russia from 1916, Pascal opposed the French anti-Soviet intervention and was close to the Bolsheviks and Lenin, calling himself the 'catholic Bolshevik'. Pascal joined the French Communist Group in Russia along with Serge, Marcel Body and Jacques Sadoul. He married Jenny Russakov, the sister of Serge's wife Liuba. Pascal returned to France in 1933, became a French translator of Russian literature, and wrote a multi-volume memoir/history of his years in Russia (*Mon journal de Russie*).

Pasternak, Boris (1890–1960): Nobel Prize winner for literature and author of *Doctor Zhivago*, Pasternak was a colleague of Serge and was in Paris in 1935 at the Congress for the Defence of Culture, where the campaign to free Victor Serge was raised. Pasternak stayed in the background while the other Soviet writers – also Serge's colleagues – feigned ignorance of Serge but affirmed that he was a 'confessed counter-revolutionary' and more. Pasternak was silent but not complicit, and Serge noted his courage elsewhere in complaining to Stalin about censoring other Soviet writers.

Paz, Magdeleine (1889–1973): French anti-Stalinist journalist, activist and novelist married to Maurice Paz (1896–1985), a lawyer, early leader of the French CP and Trotskyist. They had collaborated with (and befriended) Serge in Paris on the publication of *Contre le courant*, the journal of the Communist opposition founded by Paz. They kept up a correspondence with Serge through both his arrests in the Soviet Union, sending him food parcels in Orenburg and leading the successful 'free Serge' campaign from 1933 to 1936 in Paris.

Paz, Octavio (1914–98): Mexican poet, writer and diplomat who received the Nobel Prize for Literature in 1990. Paz fought with the Republicans in Spain, became disgusted with Stalinism, and rejected the left when the Cold War began. In 1942 he met Serge in Mexico, along with Benjamin Péret and Jean Malaquais. He considered Serge an important influence on the evolution of his political ideas.

Peshkova, Ekaterina Pavlona (1876–1965): Soviet human rights activist, humanitarian, and Maxim Gorky's first wife. She was a major organiser of the Moscow Committee of the Political Red Cross, created in 1918 to help political prisoners and dissolved in 1938. Serge entrusted some manuscripts to her before he was expelled from the USSR in 1936. Peshkova was often the only person who actually helped the political prisoners during the years of Stalin's repressions, passing on letters and parcels of food, and advocating amnesties and the shortening of jail terms. Thousands of Soviet intellectuals owed their lives to her.

Pestaña, Angel (1886–1937): Spanish anarcho-syndicalist and later syndicalist leader. Pestaña was a watchmaker, and one of the main leaders of the CNT in 1917. He represented the CNT at the Second Congress of the Comintern in 1922 in Moscow, where he met Serge, as well as Lenin, Trotsky, Zinoviev and other Bolshevik leaders.

Phillips, William (1907–2002): Co-founder and long-time editor of *Partisan Review*. Phillips published and defended Serge, and in 1946 wrote a blistering editorial against *The New Republic* and *The Nation*, calling them Stalin's bootlickers. During the McCarthy era, Lillian Hellman confronted Phillips for not defending her and other writers when they were attacked by the House Un-American Activities Committee. Phillips replied that whereas *Partisan Review* had effectively opposed McCarthyism in several editorials, Hellman and others did not deserve to be defended because they were silent when countless Soviet intellectuals were arrested, tortured and repressed by Stalin.

Piatakov, Yuri (1890–1937): An Old Bolshevik who became People's Commissar for the Ukraine, spokesman of the Opposition of 1923 and the 'Platform of the 46'. Serge cautioned that Piatakov was a pessimist who stayed with the Opposition out of principle and his personal attachment to Trotsky. He 'capitulated' in 1928 and was re-elected to the Central Committee (1930 and 1934). His name is mentioned by Lenin in his will. Arrested in 1936, he was the principal defendant of the second Moscow Trial in January 1937, was condemned to death and shot on 1 February 1937.

Pilnyak, Boris (1894–1938): Soviet 'anti-urbanist' novelist of *The Naked Year*, *Mahogany* and *The Volga Falls into the Caspian Sea*. Pilnyak was a close friend of Serge. He courageously went to the GPU to protest Serge's arrest. Pilnyak himself was arrested in 1937 for Trotskyism and espionage, and disappeared without a trace.

Pivert, Marceau (1895–1958): Pivert was a teachers union activist and leading militant on the left of the French Socialist Party. Expelled from the SFIO, Pivert founded the anti-authoritarian, Marxist Left Workers and Peasants' Socialist Party (PSOP) in 1938, but it was outlawed in 1940. Pivert went into exile in Mexico and was active with Serge, Vlady, Gorkín, Gironella, Malaquais and others in the Socialismo y Libertad group.

Plisnier, Charles (1896–1952): Lawyer, writer and founder of the Belgian Communist Party. Plisnier was expelled in 1928 with the Left Opposition. He participated in the defence of Serge (mentioned in his

Faux passeports ou les Memoires d'un agitateur) and tried to get him a Belgian visa in 1936.

Poulaille, Henry (1896–1980): Libertarian, novelist and literary editor at Editions Grasset and the journal *Le nouvel âge littéraire*, where he promoted and published proletarian authors. He was a signatory to the 1925 Manifesto 'Rififi sur le rif' that appeared in *L'Humanité*, signed by the surrealists, workers and intellectual groups including Barbusse, Serge, Breton, Péret, Lefebvre, Rolland and others. Poulaille participated in the defence of Serge, who described him as 'a true son of the workers' suburbs who did not mince his words'. Serge and Poulaille had planned to publish a weekly in 1940 called *Last Days*, but couldn't as they had to flee the advancing Nazis.

Powell, Adam Clayton Jr (1908–72): Eminent leader of the civil rights movement in the 1950s and 1960s, and member of Congress from Harlem from 1945 to 1971. Powell fought for racial desegregation in the schools and in the army. He expanded access to higher education, extended the minimum wage to include retail workers, and worked for equal pay for women. Powell was a signatory of the letter to the president of Mexico in defence of Serge and his comrades.

Preobrazhensky, Evgeny (1886–1937): Old Bolshevik, economist and secretary of the Party in 1919. He was widely known as the 'economist of the Left Opposition' and was the author of the *New Economics* (1926), outlining the theory of 'primitive socialist accumulation'. Preobrazhensky and Smilga were sent to meet with Serge in 1926 to unify the two Leningrad oppositions. He was arrested and exiled to Uralsk in 1928. Preobrazhensky capitulated in 1929 but later became a member of a clandestine opposition group with Smirnov. Serge met him again in 1932 and sensed he was 'a doomed man'. Preobrazhensky was executed without trial.

Radek, Karl Bernardovich (1885–1939): Karl Radek grew up in the socialist movements of Galicia, Poland, Germany and Russia, was a sparkling writer (according to Serge) with a flair for synthesis and sarcasm. He joined Lenin in Zurich in 1914, and in 1918 was a Left Communist opposing the terms of the Treaty of Brest-Litovsk and demanding nationalization of large-scale industry in the new Soviet Union. Radek was in Germany with the Comintern at the same time as Serge and played a role in the failed 1923 German Revolution. Radek was a leader of the Left Opposition, was expelled from the Party in 1927 and deported to Ishim. He capitulated in 1929 and was readmitted in 1930. He was tried for treason at the second Moscow Trial of the Seventeen in 1937, confessed (implicating others) and was spared execution. Radek was murdered by the NKVD in a labour camp.

Rakovsky, Christian (1873–1941): Bulgarian socialist revolutionary, Bolshevik and Soviet diplomat; journalist, physician and essayist. His essay 'The Professional Dangers of Power' (August 1928) is a lucid critique of Stalinist 'bureaucratic centrism'. Rakovsky was active in the Balkans, lived in France and Russia, held Romanian citizenship and was a leader of the Second International, the Bulgarian Social Democratic Union and the Romanian Socialist Party. He founded more than ten periodicals. Rakovsky was a lifelong collaborator and close friend of Trotsky. He was an original member of the Comintern, served as head of government in the Ukrainian SSR and, after Trotsky's expulsion, was the core of the opposition within the USSR. Though he himself 'repented' before Stalin in 1934, he was executed, on Stalin's orders, with 150 imprisoned oppositionists in 1941, during the first months of the German army's attack on the USSR.

Reed, John (1887–1920): American journalist, revolutionary political activist, and writer of the classic account of the Russian Revolution, *Ten Days that Shook the World*, for which Lenin wrote the preface. John Reed witnessed and chronicled both the Mexican and Russian revolutions. Serge knew him in Petrograd and helped organize Reed's clandestine departure through Finland, brought to life in Warren Beatty's film of Reed, *Reds*. While on Comintern tour to the Far East in 1920, Reed caught typhus and died. He was given a state funeral and is the only American to be buried in the Kremlin Wall.

Regler, Gustav (1898–1963): Author of *The Great Crusade* and *The Owl of Minerva*, Regler was a member of the German Communist Party who fled Germany after the Nazi victory. In Paris in 1935, Regler raised the issue of persecuted German intellectuals at the International Congress in Defence of Culture. He fought in Spain with the international Brigades, but he was purged and left the CP. He was Serge's companion and comrade in exile in Mexico, but Serge broke with him in 1944, though he wrote that Regler, who was a 'poet by temperament, like Rilke', was a man of genuine intellectual and moral 'worth'. Regler co-authored the book *La GPU prepara un nuevo crimen* with Serge, Pivert and Gorkín.

Rein, Marc (1909–37): Russian socialist engineer, son of Menshevik leader Rafael Abramovich, and a journalist for several socialist papers. He went to Spain as a foreign correspondent to support the anti-fascist forces but disappeared in April 1937 from the Hotel Continental in Barcelona and was never found. Serge believed that he had been taken to Russia to blackmail his father. The GPU in fact kidnapped him and took him to Russia to be used in the Third Moscow Trial in 1938, to connect the accused with the exiled Menshevik leadership. The kidnapping was apparently organized by Orlov, who supervised the kidnapping and execution of left-wing opponents of Stalin in Spain during the civil war and later defected to the US. In spite of frantic efforts by Rafael Abramovich and Western socialist supporters, he was never seen alive again and is thought to have been murdered by the GPU (NKVD).

Reiss, Ignacy (1899–1937): Born Nathan Markovich Poreckil Poretsky in Galicia, Poretsky-Reiss was a militant socialist who joined the Polish Communist Party in 1919 and worked for the Soviet secret services in Europe under the pseudonym of Ludwig. He broke with Moscow in July 1937 and announced his realignment with the Fourth International. Known as 'Ignace Poretsky', 'Ignatz Reiss', 'Ludwig', 'Ludwik', 'Hans Eberhardt', 'Steff Brandt' and 'Nathan Poreckij'. Serge went to meet him in Switzerland with Henk Sneevliet, but the NKVD got there first. Serge investigated the murder and wrote *L'Assassinat d'Ignace Reiss*, with Maurice Wullens and Alfred Rosmer. His wife, Elsa Bernant Poretsky (1898–1976), an NKVD agent and author of *Our Own People*, suspected Serge was also an agent.

Renn, Ludwig (1889–1979): German writer who wrote under the pen name Arnold Friedrich Vieth von Golsseneau. Renn joined the KPD in 1928, fought in Spain with the International Brigades, lived in Mexico from 1940 to 1948, then returned to Berlin, where he lived out his life. He was a known Stalinist, according to Serge, and signed a letter published in *The Nation* (28 February 1942) denouncing the journal for defending the Trotskyists in Mexico – i.e. Serge and his comrades.

Reustle, Frederick (1915–96?): At the request of Dwight Macdonald in 1940, Reverend Frederick Reustle, German anti-Fascist refugee, wrote letters on behalf of Serge to the State Department to grant Serge a visa.

La Révolution prolétarienne: French revolutionary syndicalist journal edited by Pierre Monatte and Robert Louzon, who campaigned for Serge's release from the USSR and published dozens of his articles from 1928 to 1947.

Roland-Holst, Henriette (1869–1952): Dutch writer, member of the Social-Democratic left in 1898, internationalist during World War I and associate of Rosa Luxemburg. She was a co-founder of the Left Social-Democratic Party and of the journal *Tribune*. She participated in the campaign in support of Serge.

Rolland, Romain (1866–1944): French dramatist, novelist, essayist, art historian and pacifist who was awarded the Nobel Prize for Literature in 1915. He was initially hostile to the Russian Revolution but later became a supporter and fellow traveller of Stalin's USSR, giving his support to the Moscow Trials. From deportation in Orenburg, Serge got official permission to send copies of his novels to Rolland in Paris, who had agreed to handle Serge's publications in France. The NKVD nonetheless prevented them from actually being sent. In 1935, Rolland was in Moscow on the invitation of Maxim Gorki and met with Stalin. Though he had no affinity with Serge's politics, he interceded (successfully) on Serge's behalf. Yagoda (head of the NKVD) gave Rolland a copy of Serge's novel *Les Hommes perdus* to be read and returned in one night. Rolland failed to persuade Yagoda to allow him to take the manuscript to France.

Rosenthal, Gerard (1903–92): One of the original French surrealists, along with his close friend Pierre Naville, Rosenthal edited the surrealist publication *Oeuf dur*, and later *Clarté*. He and Naville were in Moscow as French Communist Party delegates to the tenth anniversary celebration of the Revolution. Their political guide was Victor Serge, who took them to visit Trotsky and Zinoviev. Both later became prominent Trotskyists in France – Rosenthal headed the French section of the Left Opposition and later the Fourth International. He was Trotsky's lawyer in France and was the author of *Avocat de Trotsky* (1975).

Rosmer, Alfred (1877–1964): Rosmer was a close, lifelong friend of Trotsky, whom he met during the war in France. He was in Moscow in 1920, where Serge served as his political guide and became his friend. Rosmer was a member of the Executive Committee of the Comintern and became a leading figure of the Communist Party before his expulsion in 1924 for having shown solidarity with Trotsky and opposing Stalin. Rosmer devoted himself to denouncing the crimes of Stalinism and was a member of the Dewey Commission, which cleared Trotsky of all charges made during the Moscow Trials. His books include *Lenin's Moscow* and *Trotsky and the Origins of Trotskyism*.

Rumbo: Mexican journal where Serge published 'Balance of the Stalinist Reaction' ('Balance de la reacción staliniana') in October–November 1941.

Russakov, Alexander Ivanovich (1874–1934): Serge's father-in-law, and an anarchist who fought at Rostov during the 1905 Revolution. He was secretary of the Trade Union of Russian Seamen at Marseille but was expelled from France in 1918 for having organized a strike on a boat loaded with ordnance for the Whites. Serge and the Russakovs reached the USSR in the same boat in 1918. Serge married Liuba, Russakov's daughter, and French Left Oppositionist Pierre Pascal married his other daughter, Jenny. In the Soviet Union Russakov worked in a dyeworks. The attempts to mediate the Kronstadt conflict in 1921 took place in his apartment. Russakov was the target of an anti-Semitic persecution campaign in 1929, and in 1932 was denied a bread-card. He died of the privations. Panaït Istrati wrote about it in *The Russakov Affair*, published in Paris.

Russakova, Anita (1906–93): Anita was Serge's sister-in-law, the younger sister of Liuba. At times she served as Serge's secretary. She was arrested in 1933 and used as bait to get Serge to confess. Anita was released, but the concocted confession, purportedly wrung from her in 1933, served as the basis for her to be rearrested in 1936, probably to prevent her from meeting Serge, who had just been released. Anita Russakov spent twenty-five years in the gulag.

Russakova, Liuba (1898–1984): Bilingual typist and Lenin's stenographer, Liuba met Serge en route to the USSR from France in 1919. They lived in the Astoria hotel and worked at the Smolny. Their son Vladimir Kibalchich was born in 1920. By 1928 Serge was arrested and the entire

Russakov family was indicted, tormented and persecuted. This went on for nine years, and it drove Liuba mad. In 1934 she joined Serge and Vlady in deportation in Orenburg but relapsed and was sent back, hiding her pregnancy from Serge. Their daughter Jeannine Kibalchich was born in 1935. Serge was expelled from the USSR with Liuba, Vlady and baby Jeannine. In exile in Belgium and France, Liuba's mental instability continued, and she was committed to a mental hospital in the south of France, where she remained until her death at age 85.

Riazanov, David Borisovich (1870–1938): Born David Borisovich Goldendakh, Ryazanov was an independent Marxist revolutionary and archivist, who was quoted as saying 'I am neither a Bolshevik nor a Menshevik, I am a Marxist.' He is best remembered as the founder of the Marx-Engels Institute and editor of the first large-scale effort to publish their collected works. Arrested in 1937 as a purported member of a 'right-opportunist Trotskyist organization', the Military Collegium of the USSR Supreme Court condemned Ryazanov to death and he was executed later that same day.

Sadoul, Jacques (1881–1956): Sadoul was a lawyer, reserve officer and military attaché to the French Embassy at Moscow in 1917, who went over to the Bolsheviks and was in the civil war. He was a Comintern delegate and worked for the Executive. Serge worked with him in Moscow and Berlin, appreciated his 'mocking intelligence' and 'political adroitness', but back in France in 1936 Sadoul wrote slanderous articles about his former friend Serge, urging a boycott of his work. Trotsky came to Serge's defence, expressing his solidarity with him at a time when their own relations were strained.

Schapiro, Meyer (1904–96): Professor Emeritus at Columbia University, multi-disciplinary critic and historian, lifelong radical and for more than fifty years a pre-eminent figure in the intellectual life of New York. Schapiro joined YPSL while in high school, had ties to the Communist Party in the 1920s, but worked in the anti-Stalinist left from 1936 on. Schapiro became a contributor to *The Marxist Quarterly*, *The New Masses*, *The Nation* and *Partisan Review*. He was a classical Marxist and a genuine independent, shifting from revolutionary socialism to left social democracy in the 1950s. He wrote letters on behalf of Serge in his quest to get entry to the US in 1940.

Sedov, Lev Lvovich (1906–38): Eldest son of Trotsky and Natalia Sedova, member of the Left Opposition in USSR, and leader of the international Left Opposition in the West from his exile in Paris, where he published the *Bulletin of the Left Opposition*. Serge and Sedov worked tirelessly together to refute the charges of the Moscow Trials. A substantial correspondence between Sedov and Serge is held at Stanford University's Hoover Archive. Sedov's *The Red Book on the Moscow Trials* (1936) analyzed and discredited the verdicts of the trials. Serge described him as 'overworked, penniless, anxious for his father', an energetic, even-tempered, intelligent young man who spent his entire life in the 'labyrinth of utter madness'. Sedov died in mysterious circumstances in Paris on 16 February 1938, eight days before his thirty-second birthday.

Seguí, Salvador (1887–1923): Catalan anarcho-syndicalist leader of the 1917 general strike and insurrection in Barcelona, and the first General Secretary of the CNT in Spain. He was known as 'sugar boy' for the sugar cubes he ate while drinking his coffee. He was Serge's friend when in Spain and was depicted as 'Dario' in Serge's novel *Birth of Our Power*. Seguí was murdered in 1923 by killers in the service of the industrial elite.

Séjourné, Laurette (1911–2003): Born in Perugia, Italy, Laura Valentini Corsa (aka Laura Bianchi) married a Frenchman, Séjourné, and associated with cultural and cinematic circles in Paris, meeting André Breton, Jean Cocteau and Serge in 1937. Strongly politicized, Laurette divorced Séjourné and married Serge, accompanying him to Marseilles (and Villa Air-Bel). She joined Serge and Vlady in Mexico in 1942, bringing with her Serge's daughter Jeannine, who considered Laurette her second mother. There Séjourné worked to support Serge while studying anthropology and Mexican archaeology. Shortly after Serge died in 1947, Laurette married Arnaldo Orfila, the director of the Fondo de Cultura Economica and founder of Siglo XXI Editores. With Orfila, Laurette moved in Communist Party circles, but maintained a close friendship with Natalia Sedova, Trotsky's widow. During the 1950s, Séjourné did anthropological fieldwork in Oaxaca, but then changed to archaeology, excavating at the pre-Spanish metropolis of Teotihuacan. She is best known for her theories concerning the Mesoamerican cultural hero Quetzalcoatl and her 1957 publication on the cosmology and religion of the Toltecs and Aztecs, translated into English as *Burning Water: Thought and Religion in Ancient Mexico*.

Shachtman, Max (1904–72): Max Shachtman was an author, translator, editor and militant leader of the early Communist, Socialist and Trotskyist movements in the US. A Polish immigrant, Shachtman was expelled from the Party in 1928 after adopting Trotsky's views. In 1929 Shachtman, James Cannon, Martin Abern and other Trotskyists formed the Communist League of America (CLA). Shachtman worked as Trotsky's secretary in France in 1933, edited *The New International*, wrote *Behind the Moscow Trial* and translated Trotsky's *The Stalin School of Falsification*. He also corresponded with Serge and translated his book *Destin d'une Revolution*, which appeared in English in 1937 under the title *Russia Twenty Years After*. *The Bureaucratic Revolution: The Rise of the Stalinist State* is probably his best-known book. In the 1960s, Shachtman was a leading anti-Stalinist and worked with Bayard Rustin in the civil rights movement. He ended up supporting the American intervention in Vietnam, weakening the American left.

Shatov, Bill (Vladimir Sergeevich) (1887–1938): Russian revolutionary anarcho-syndicalist, RSDLP member who emigrated to New York in 1907. He regularly contributed to and edited the anarchist journal *Golos Truda* (Voice of Labor). A militant organizer and agitator, Shatov joined the Wobblies (IWW) and led its Russian section. He returned to Russia after the February Revolution in the summer of 1917 with Voline, John Reed and Louise Berger. Though an anarchist, he fought with the Bolsheviks in the civil war, was a member of the Military-Revolutionary Committee, and was chief of security in Petrograd. In 1919, he became what Serge called the virtual leader of the Tenth Red Army. Shatov was appointed Minister of Transportation in the Far East (Siberia) in 1920, where he worked on the Turkestan-Siberia railways. Exiled to Siberia in 1937, Shatov was executed the following year.

Shliapnikov, Alexander Gavrilovich (1887–1937): Bolshevik from 1903, metal worker and leader of the Petrograd Soviet during the February Revolution, and People's Commissar of the first Soviet government. Shliapnikov co-founded the Workers Opposition with Alexandra Kollantai in 1920. He was expelled from the Party in 1933, arrested in 1935 and shot in 1937.

Smilga, Ivar Tenisovich (1892–1938): A Bolshevik and leader of the Left Opposition, who allied with Lenin in 1917 on the question of insurrection and participated in the Finnish Commune as Chairman of the Regional Committee of the Soviets in Finland. He led the Seventh Army on the march to Warsaw in 1920. He was a leader of the Left Opposition, was expelled from the Party and deported in 1927, capitulated in 1929, was arrested in 1932 and again in 1935. Smilga was executed in 1938.

Smirnov, Ivan Nikitich (1881–1936): Old Bolshevik and member of the Central Committee in 1920, who was People's Commissar for Posts and Telegraphs from 1923 to 1927, where Serge would visit him. Smirnov was a leader of the Left Opposition from its beginning in 1923. He capitulated in 1929, was reinstated in the Party in 1930 but then led a clandestine group of Trotskyists. He was sentenced to death and executed during the first Moscow Trial in 1936.

Sneevliet, Hendricus Josephus Franciscus Marie (Henk) (1883–1942): An MP and leader of the railway workers' union in Holland, Sneevliet founded the Indonesian Communist Party and was instrumental in the birth of the Chinese Communist Party in 1920. He represented the Javanese Socialist Party at the Second Congress of the Comintern under the name 'Maring'. In 1927 he left the Dutch Communist Party and formed the RSAP (Dutch Revolutionary Socialist Workers Party) in 1929. Sneevliet stood with the Left Opposition from 1933 to 1938. He was very close to Serge in Paris in the late 1930s, especially after 1937. The two went to Rheims intending to meet Ignace Reiss, killed the previous day by the GPU. Sneevliet was suspicious of Etienne (Marc Zborowski) and defended Serge when Elsa Poretsky (Reiss's widow) and

Krivitsky intimated that Serge could be an agent. Both Sneevliet and Serge were isolated by the French Trotskyists because they voiced their concerns. Sneevliet took part in the resistance against the German occupation of the Netherlands during World War II, was heavily involved in the February Strike of 1941, and had to go into hiding. He founded the MLL Front (Marx-Lenin-Luxemburg Front) that engaged in socialist propaganda opposing the Nazi occupation. In April 1942 the Nazis finally arrested him and the rest of the MLL Front leadership. They were executed on 12 April 1942, reportedly singing *The Internationale* as they went to their deaths.

Socialismo y Libertad: Political Circle formed in Mexico by anti-Stalinist, Russian, French, German and Spanish exiles. They published *Mundo*, *Libertad y Socialismo* and later *Analysis*. Serge and Vlady participated in the group and its journal, which Vlady illustrated. The group gathered anti-Stalinist intellectuals, who engaged in discussion on a wide area of theoretical, political and cultural issues that were often later published as articles in the journal. The group's internal differences led eventually to a split.

Socialist Call: See *The Call*.

Socialist Party (USA): Founded in 1901, the ecumenical organization of American radicals, compromising between reform and revolution. Led by Eugene Debs, the Party received a million votes in 1912 and 1920 (with Debs as its presidential candidate). The revolutionaries led by John Reed split in 1919. Norman Thomas became the Party's leader from 1928.

Socialist Workers Party: American section of the Fourth International first formed as the Communist League of America after being expelled from the US Communist Party in 1929. In 1934, the CLA merged with A.J. Muste's American Workers Party, and in 1936 entered the US Socialist Party. In 1938 the Fourth International was founded and the American Trotskyists, led by James Cannon, got themselves expelled from the Socialist Party and founded the Socialist Workers Party. Serge published numerous articles in the theoretical journal of the SWP, *The New International*, both before and after the split in 1940 – when Shachtman took the publication with him to the Workers Party.

Sokolnikov, Grigori Yakovlevich (1888–1939): Economist and Old Bolshevik from 1905, exiled to Paris until 1917, Sokolnikov worked with Trotsky on the editorial board of *Nace Slovo* during World War I. Member of the Central Committee from 1919 to 1937 and ambassador to London from 1929 to 1932, Sokolnikov played an important part in the civil war and was Commissar of Finance from 1922 to 1926. A leading member of the Leningrad Opposition, he defined the Soviet state as 'state capitalist' and criticized its inability to make the economic system function efficiently. Sokolnikov coincided with the Left Opposition politically on the questions of bureaucracy and the need for Party democracy, but with the right opposition on economic policy. He was condemned to ten years in 1937 and executed at the end of the second Moscow Trial.

Solano, Wilebaldo (1916–2010): General Secretary of the Juventud Comunista Ibérica, the POUM's Communist Youth during the Spanish Civil War in 1936 and founder of the weekly *El Comunista*. Jailed in 1938, Solano managed to escape and cross the Pyrenees into France, where a group of militants from the PSOP (led by Daniel Guerín and organized by the POUM in Paris with Marceau Pivert and Victor Serge) awaited them. He later described the drama of this meeting and the warm solidarity he and his comrades felt. Serge had a huge influence on them. Detained again in 1941 and sentenced to twenty years, Solano was liberated by French Resistance fighters in 1941. In 1947 he was named General Secretary of the POUM while in exile in France and held this post until 1963. From exile in France he directed *La Batalla*, wrote a biography of Andreu Nin, articles on Serge and many other books. He collaborated in Ken Loach's film *Tierra y Libertad* (Land and Freedom) which brought the Spanish revolution of 1936 to life for younger generations. In 1987 Solano was a founder of the Fundación Andreu Nin and its president.

Solntsev, Eleazar B. (1900–36): A member of the Left Opposition, Solntsev was a revolutionary from his high school years. He graduated from the Institute of Red Professors in History and Economics and was one of the most outstanding members of his generation in the Left Opposition; Trotsky described him as brilliant. He was attached to the Soviet Commercial Mission in Berlin and was secretly an adviser to the German Opposition, but also the organizer of the international opposition in Europe before going to the US, where he was a Soviet trade attaché in New York. Deported to the Verkhne-Uralsk isolator for a five-year term in 1928, and sentenced to a second five-year term in 1935, Solntsev refused to capitulate, declared a hunger strike and died after eighteen days, just as he was being transferred to exile. When Serge was released and expelled from the USSR in 1936, he informed Trotsky of Solntsev's death.

Sosnovsky, Lev Semyanovich (1886–1937): Old Bolshevik who took part in the 1905 Revolution and who Trotsky described as an 'incomparable publicist and social commentator'. He became a journalist after the October Revolution, editing the newspaper *Bednota*, aimed at the broad mass of peasant readers. He was popular for his critiques of the 'bureaucratic mind'. A leader of the Left Opposition, he was expelled from the Party, arrested and deported, but he was one of the last to capitulate in 1934. Sosnovsky was executed (without trial) in 1937.

Sotsialisticheskii Vestnik (Socialist Courier): Newspaper of the Mensheviks in exile, published from 1921 to 1965, in Berlin until 1933, then in Paris until 1940 and thereafter in New York.

Souvarine, Boris Lifschitz (1895–1984): Journalist at *Le Populaire* in 1917, the Kiev-born Souvarine was a founder and leader of the French Communist Party (PCF) and a member of the Comintern Executive from 1919. He opposed the rise of Stalin and published Trotsky's *New Course* in France. After his expulsion from the Party in 1924, Souvarine became close to anti-Stalinist figures in Paris (including Marcel Body, Christian Rakovsky and Panaït Istrati), relaunched the *Bulletin Communiste* in 1925 and organized the Marx-Lenin Communist Circle, later called the Democratic Communist Circle, which published *La Critique Sociale*. His growing break with Trotsky was over his view that, by 1927, the Soviet Union was 'state capitalist', against Trotsky's analysis of it as a 'degenerated workers' state'. Souvarine defended Serge when he was arrested in 1928. In 1936 Souvarine encouraged the newly exiled Serge to write the 'naked truth', 'undiluted and brutal', about the USSR. Serge was influenced by Souvarine's book on Stalin, which Trotsky dismissed as 'worthless'. Though critical of Souvarine, Serge defended him. In later years Souvarine moved rightward, becoming fiercely anti-communist and hostile to Serge.

Thomas, Norman (1884–1968): Member of the Socialist Party, candidate for governor of New York in 1924. After the death of Eugene Debs, Thomas became the Party's candidate for president in every election from 1928 to 1948. A strong critic of the Soviet Union, Thomas also denounced rearmament and the development of the Cold War. When Serge, Gorkín and others were attacked by the NKVD and the CP in Mexico in 1942, Thomas dedicated his half-hour radio programme to them.

Toledano, Lombardo (1894–1968): Mexican labour leader, head of the CTM from 1934 to 1940. Strongly supported by the USSR, though not a formal member of the Mexican Communist Party, Toledano later distanced himself from the Communists and in 1948 founded the Partido Popular (now the PPS, Popular Socialist Party). In 1942 he joined seven Mexican Deputies, Pablo Neruda and Ludwig Renn in writing a letter to *The Nation* protesting their defence of Serge and his comrades.

Tukhachevsky, Mikhaïl Nikolayevich (1893–1937): Russian officer who rallied to the revolution and became Commandant-in-chief of the Red Army, defending Moscow in 1918 in the civil war. Trotsky gave Tukhachevsky command of the Fifth Army in 1919, and he captured Siberia from Kolchak and helped defeat General Denikin in the Crimea in 1920. Stalin was supposed to provide support to Tukhachevsky in Poland in 1920 but instead marched to Lvov, where he was defeated. Tukhachevsky and Trotsky strongly criticized Stalin's actions there, which Stalin never forgot. In 1921 he commanded the Seventh Army during the suppression of the Kronstadt rebellion. In June 1937, Tukhachevsky and seven other top commanders were arrested, charged with conspiracy with Germany, found guilty and immediately executed.

Two-and-a-half International: International Working Union of Socialist Parties (Union of Vienna), created in 1921 by ten European Socialist Parties (including the German USPD, British ILP, French SFIO, Italian Maximalists, etc.) that refused to join the reorganized Second International and did not accept the twenty-one conditions for becoming part of the Comintern (Third International), and decided instead to form the Two-and-a-half International. They proclaimed the necessity of defending Soviet Russia and instituting a general action against the imperialist excesses of the Entente, but thought it would only be possible for the international proletariat to achieve if it organized itself on the basis of the principles of revolutionary socialism, gathering all its forces together into a mighty international organization.

Vaillant-Couturier, Paul (1892–1937): Pseudonym of Paul Charles Couturier, Communist French writer and journalist, editor in chief of *L'Humanité*. Once Serge's comrade, he worked against him after Serge's first arrest in 1928. An editorial in *Lutte de classes* campaigned for Serge's release, but Vaillant-Couturier wrote in *L'Humanité* that Serge had been well treated by the Soviet regime.

La Wallonie: Belgium publication that published more than 200 articles written by Serge from 1936 to 1940. The editor was Isidore Delvigne. *La Wallonie* published 131 issues, ceasing publication in May 1940.

Werfel, Franz (1890–1945): Czech (Austrian-Bohemian) writer, best known for *The Forty Days of Musa Dagh*. Hunted by the Gestapo for his anti-Nazi writings, Werfel and his wife were rescued by Varian Fry and the ERC, making it safely to the US. His wife Alma had been married to the composer Gustav Mahler and Bauhaus school of architecture founder Walter Gropius. Alma was the subject of Klimt's famous painting *The Kiss*.

Werth, Leon (1878–1955): French journalist, art critic, novelist and friend of Serge in the late 1930s. Werth was a supporter of the Left Opposition and wrote the preface to Serge's novel *L'Affaire Tulaev*.

Wolf, Erwin (1902–37): Czech-German born in the Sudetenland, who joined the Left Opposition in Berlin in 1932, then was politically active in Paris before taking Jan Frankel's place in 1935 as one of Trotsky's secretaries in Norway. Wolf volunteered to go to Spain during the Spanish Civil War. He visited Serge in Brussels and told him he couldn't study Marxism in Europe while a revolution was struggling for survival. Serge tried to dissuade him, to no avail. Wolf was last seen in a Barcelona prison in 1937, though it is unknown if he was secretly transferred to the USSR and killed or whether he was murdered in Spain.

Workers Party: Formed in 1940 by Max Shachtman and James Burnham after the split with the Socialist Workers Party over the class nature of the USSR, which the new organization characterized as a type of bureaucratic collectivism. In 1949 it became the Independent Socialist League (ISL), which officially dissolved in 1958.

Wullens, Maurice (1894–1945): Left journalist and editor of the journal *Les Humbles* to which Serge contributed several articles. Wullens fought in the free Victor Serge campaign, participated in the Commission for Enquiry into the Moscow Trials and for the defence of freedom of opinion in the revolution.

Yagoda, Genrikh Grigorievich (1891–1938): Director of the NKVD from 1934 to 1936. He supervised the arrest, show trial and execution of the Old Bolsheviks Lev Kamenev and Grigory Zinoviev. When Romain Rolland interceded on Serge's behalf with Stalin, Stalin phoned Yagoda to see if Serge had confessed to anything – and Yagoda reported that he hadn't. In 1997 Yagoda's papers were published, revealing officially that the NKVD confiscated three copies of Serge's novel about the pre-war French anarchist movement, written while Serge was in Orenburg. These were the copies that should have been sent to Romain Rolland. Yagoda was ultimately a victim of the purge himself. He was replaced by Nikolai Yezhov as head of the NKVD in 1936 and arrested in 1937. Charged with wrecking, espionage, Trotskyism and conspiracy, Yagoda was a defendant at the Trial of the Twenty-One, the last of the major Soviet show trials of the 1930s. He confessed, was found guilty and shot.

Yakovin, Grigori Yaklovlevich (1896–1938?): Historian of Germany, graduate of the Institute of Red Professors and militant from Leningrad, member of the Opposition in 1923 and the United Opposition. Serge met regularly with him in the clandestine Leningrad Opposition circle and considered him to be one of two Marxist theoreticians of genuine worth. Yakovin was arrested and made the rounds of the jails, disappearing in 1937.

Zborowski, Mark Grigorievich (1908–90): Known as Etienne in the Trotskyist movement, Zborowski joined the Polish Communist Party in 1926, and was arrested for strike activity and sentenced to four years. He was recruited to the NKVD while in France in 1932 and instructed to infiltrate the Paris Left Opposition circle and get close to Trotsky's son Lev Sedov. Zborowski gained his confidence, becoming joint editor of the *Bulletin of the Opposition* with Sedov and Lola Dallin. Though never a killer, Zborowski made it possible for Trotsky's archive to be stolen, for prominent oppositionists to be targeted for elimination, and he sowed discord within the opposition, including between Trotsky and Serge, and between Serge and the French Trotskyists. In the US Zborowski also made a name for himself in the fields of medical anthropology and Jewish studies. He was unmasked in the US in 1954, perjured himself and was sentenced to five years imprisonment, and served nearly half before resuming his successful academic career in San Francisco at Mount Zion Medical Center and UCSF.

Bibliography

I Works by Victor Serge

These are presented by category, and for the most part in chronological order. This is not a record of Serge's total literary output, but reflects the material I have read and used for this study. Serge's Mexican archive was acquired by Yale University's Beinecke Rare Book and Manuscript Library in 1996.

A *Works on history, literature and politics, including published books and pamphlets*

1 *Contre la faim*, Paris, *L'Anarchie*, 1911. A pamphlet signed 'Le Rétif', Serge's first pseudonym.

2 'Esbozo crítico sobre Nietzsche' (written 1917), with an essay by Juan Garzon entitled 'El Nietzsche de Serge', in *Casa del Tiempo*, vol. I, no. 3, Nov. 1980. This article, translated into Spanish by Costa-Iscar, first appeared in *Tierra y libertad* in 1917.

3 *Pendant la guerre civile: Petrograd mai–juin 1919*, Paris, Bibliothèque du Travail, 1921.

4 *Les Anarchistes et l'expérience de la révolution russe*, Paris, Cahiers du Travail, 1921, reprinted as *Les Anarchistes dans la révolution russe*, Paris, Editions de la Tête de Feuilles, 1973.

5 *La Ville en danger: l'an II de la révolution*, Paris, Librairie du Travail, 1924. Also published as *La Defensa de Petrogrado: Año Segundo de la revolución Rusa*, Mexico, Ediciones Transición, 1977. *Pendant la guerre civile, Les Anarchistes et l'expérience de la révolution russe* and *La Ville en danger* were published in English as *Revolution in Danger, Victor Serge, Writings from Russia 1919–1921*, translated by Ian Birchall, London, Redwords, 1997.

6 *Lénine, 1917*, Paris, Librairie du Travail, 1925. Reprinted with a new preface as *Vingt ans après*, Paris, Cahiers Spartacus, 1937. Also published as *Lenin: 1917*, Mexico, Ediciones Transición, 1977. Published in *Victor Serge: The Century of the Unexpected, Revolutionary History*, vol. 5, no. 3, autumn 1994.

7 *Les Coulisses d'une sûreté générale: l'Okhrana*, Paris, Librairie du Travail, 1925. Reissued as *Ce que tout révolutionnaire doit savoir de la repression*, Paris, Maspero, 1970. English translation by Judith White, *What Everyone Should Know about State Repression*, London, New Park Publications, 1979.

8 *La Lutte des classes dans la révolution chinoise*, published in *Clarté* throughout 1927, reprinted as *La révolution chinoise*, Paris, Editions Savelli, 1977, and as *La revolución*

china 1926–1928, Mexico, Editorial Domes, 1984. Published in *Revolutionary History*, vol. 5, no. 3, autumn 1994.

9 *Soviets 1929*, Paris, Rieder, 1929 (published under the name Panaït Istrati as the third volume of his trilogy *Vers l'autre flamme*).

10 *Vie des révolutionnaires*, Paris, Librairie du Travail, 1930.

11 *L'An I de la révolution russe*, Paris, Librairie du Travail, 1930, reprinted by Maspero in 1971. English translation by Peter Sedgwick, *Year One of the Russian Revolution*, New York, Holt, Rinehart and Winston, 1972, and London, Allen Lane, 1972. Published in Spanish as *El Año I de la revolución rusa*, 1931, and reprinted in Mexico by Siglo XXI, 1967.

12 *Littérature et révolution*, Paris, Editions de la Librairie Valois, 1932, reprinted by Maspero in 1976 and 1978. Published in Spanish as *Literatura y revolución*, Barcelona, Editorial Fontamara, 1978.

13 *Seize fusillés: où va la révolution russe?*, Paris, Spartacus Cahiers Mensuels, Serie Nouvelle, no. 1, 1936, 1972.

14 'De Lénine à Staline', *Le Crapouillot*, special issue, Paris, Jan. 1937. English translation by Ralph Manheim, *From Lenin to Stalin*, New York, Pioneer Publishers, 1937, London, Secker and Warburg, 1937, and New York, Monad Press, 1973, 1992.

15 *Vingt-neuf fusillés et la fin de Iagoda*, special issue of *Lectures prolétariennes*, no. 3, April 1937.

16 *Pour la vérité sur le procès de Moscou! 18 questions – 18 réponses*, Paris, 1937 (brochure edited by Committee for the Inquiry into the Moscow Trials and the Defence of Free Opinion in the Revolution).

17 *Destin d'une révolution: URSS 1917–1937*, Paris, Grasset, 1937. English translation by Max Schachtman, *Russia Twenty Years After*, New York, Pioneer Publishers, 1937, and *Destiny of a Revolution*, London, Jarrolds, 1937. Republished in 1996 in New York by Humanities Press as *Victor Serge: Russia Twenty Years After*, prepared by Susan Weissman.

18 'Méditation sur l'anarchie', revue *Esprit*, no. 55, Paris, April 1937.

19 'La Pensée anarchiste', in *L'Anarchie* and *Le Crapouillot*, special issue, Paris, 1938.

20 *L'Assassinat d'Ignace Reiss*, with Maurice Wullens and Alfred Rosmer, Paris, Editions Pierre Tisné, 1938, and in *Les Humbles*, cahier no. 4, vingt-troisième série, April 1938, Paris.

21 'La Révolution russe: février-octobre 1917', chapter six in *Histoire des révolutions de Cromwell à Franco*, Paris, Editions Gallimard, 1938.

22 'Vie d'un révolutionnaire', preface to Joaquin Maurin, *Révolution et Contre-révolution en Espagne*, Paris, Rieder, 1938.

23 'Deux rencontres' in *Les Humbles*, Cahiers 8–12, Aug.–Dec. 1938, special issue à Maurice Parijanine, also in *Témoins*, Zurich, 1960. English translation by Peter Sedgwick published as 'Twice Met' in *International Socialism*, no. 20, spring 1965.

24 *Portrait de Staline*, Paris, Editions Bernard Grasset, 1940. Spanish edition, *Retrato de Stalin*, Mexico, Ediciones Libres, 1940.

25 *Hitler contra Stalin*, Mexico City, Ediciones Quetzales, 1941.

26 *La GPU prepara un nuevo crimen!* by Victor Serge, Julian Gorkín, Marceau Pivert and Gustav Regler, Serie 'Documentos', Mexico DF, Edición de 'Analysis' (Revista de Hechos e Ideas), 1942.

27 *Los Problemas del socialismo en nuestro tiempo*, by Victor Serge, Julian Gorkín, Marceau Pivert and Paul Chevalier, Mexico City, Ediciones Ibero Americanas, *Mundo*, 1944.

28 *La Tragédie des écrivains soviétiques (Conscience de l'écrivain)*, Paris, Editions René Lefeuvre, coll. 'Les Egaux', supplement to *Masses*, Jan. 1947, no. 6. Published in English as 'The Writer's Conscience' in *Now*, no. 7, 1947, and reprinted in David Craig's anthology *Marxists on Literature*, Harmondsworth, Penguin Books, 1973.

29 *Le Nouvel impérialisme russe*, Paris, Cahiers Spartacus, 1947, reprinted with four articles by Serge as *Hommage à Victor Serge, Le Nouvel impérialisme russe*, Paris, Cahiers Spartacus, Série B, no. 50, 1972.

30 *Pages de journal (1936–1938)* and *1945–1947* in *Les Temps Modernes*, nos 44 and 45, June and July 1949.

31 *Vie et mort de Léon Trotski*, written in collaboration with Natalia Sedova Trotsky, Paris, Amiot-Dumont, 1951. English translation by Arnold Pomerans, *The Life and Death of Leon Trotsky*, New York, Basic Books, 1975, and London, Wildwood House, 1975.

32 *Le Tournant obscur*, Paris, Les Iles d'Or, 1951 (this is a fragment of the *Memoirs*, published separately in error).

33 *Mémoires d'un révolutionnaire 1901–1941*, Paris, Editions du Seuil, 1951. English translation by Peter Sedgwick, *Memoirs of a Revolutionary*, London, Oxford University Press, 1963 and Writers and Readers, 1984.

34 *Carnets*, Julliard, Paris, 1952, reprinted Avignon, Actes Sud, 1985. Part of Serge's diary was published in *New International*, New York, Sept. 1949 – Nov.–Dec. 1950, translated by James Fenwick. Another eleven extracts were published in the Scottish journal of international literature, arts and affairs, *Cencrastus*, winter 1980–81. An English translation by John Manson can be found at: http://www.victor serge.net/Carnets/index.htm.

35 *Kronstadt*, reprinted by Solidarity Press, London, 1967.

36 *Victor Serge et Leon Trotsky: La Lutte contre le stalinisme*, texts from 1936–49, edited by Michel Dreyfus, Paris, Maspero, 1977. Published as *The Serge–Trotsky Papers*, edited by D.J. Cotterill, London, Pluto Press, 1994, translated by Peter Sedgwick with introductory material by D.J. Cotterill, Philip Spencer and Susan Weissman.

37 *Cuadernos, Cahiers, Tetradi, Victor Serge*: edited by Vladimir Kibalchich, Mexico City, Marzo 1984. This contains correspondence between Serge and Mounier, Simone Weil, Andrés Nin, 'Retrato de Lenin', a fragment of Serge's unfinished novel about Mexico, *Anacleto*, and various articles from *Carnets* and elsewhere, richly illustrated by Vlady.

38 *Notes d'Allemagne (1923)*, edited and introduced by Pierre Broué, Montreuil, La Breche, 1990.

39 'Dossier', *Diaris i Revistes*, no. 5, *Centenari Victor Serge 1890–1990*, Barcelona, Fundació Andreu Nin, 1990.

B *Novels and short stories*

1 *Les Hommes dans la prison*, Paris, Rieder, 1930. English translation by Richard Greeman, *Men in Prison*, New York, Doubleday, 1969; London, Gollancz, 1970; London, Writers and Readers, 1978.

2 *Naissance de notre force*, Paris, Rieder, 1931. English translation by Richard Greeman, *Birth of Our Power*, New York, Doubleday, 1967; London, Writers and Readers, 1978.

3 *Ville Conquise*, Paris, Rieder, 1932. English translation by Richard Greeman, *Conquered City*, New York, Doubleday, 1975; London, Gollancz, 1976; London, Writers and Readers, 1978.

4 *Mer Blanche*, published in *Les Feuillets bleus*, no. 295, May 1935; Paris, Maspero 1972.

5 *L'Impasse Saint-Barnabé*, published in *Esprit* nos 43 and 44, Apr.–May 1936.

6 *S'il est minuit dans le siècle*, Paris, Grasset, 1939, reprinted by Le Livre de Poche, 1976. English translation by Richard Greeman, *Midnight in the Century*, London, Writers and Readers, 1982.

7 *Les Dernier temps*, Montreal, Editions de l'Arbre, 1946; Paris, Bernard Grasset,

1951. English translation by Ralph Manheim, *The Long Dusk*, New York, The Dial Press, 1946.

8   *L'Affaire Toulaev*, Paris, Editions du Seuil, 1948. English translation by Willard R. Trask, *The Case of Comrade Tulayev*, New York, Doubleday, 1950; London, Hamish Hamilton, 1951; Penguin Books, 1968; Journeyman Press/Pluto Press, 1992.

9   *La Folie de Iouriev*, published in *Preuves*, no. 24, Feb. 1953. Published as *L'Hôpital de Leningrad*, Paris, Maspero, 1972.

10 *Les Années sans pardon*, Paris, Maspero, 1971.

11 *Le Tropique et le Nord* (includes the short stories in titles 4, 5 and 9 above, plus *Le Seisme*), Paris, Maspero, 1972.

C *Poetry*

1   *Résistance*, poems written in Orenburg and confiscated, then reconstituted in Europe and published in Paris, Cahiers Les Humbles, 1938. Republished as *Pour un brasier dans un desert*, Paris, Maspero, 1972. English translation by James Brook, *Resistance*, San Francisco, City Light Books, 1989.

2   Various poems published in *Les Feuillets bleus*, 295, May 1935, *Lettres françaises*, Buenos Aires, April 1940, *Contemporains*, April 1951, and *Témoins*, Zurich, Feb. 1959.

3   Poems found in Serge archive, Mexico:
    'Un Américain' à John Reed (Petrograd, 1921)
    No title, 1912
    'Le tireur' à Iouri, Goggnitz, 1924
    'Berlin', 1922
    'Train rapide'
    Styrie, 15 May 1925
    'Europe' Petrograd, 1921
    'Chant de la patience'
    'Mexique (Fragments) IDYLLE' in *Contemporains*, no. 4, April 1951, pp. 501–2
    'Mains' Nov. 1947 (written the day he died).

D *Published correspondence*

There is an immense collection of correspondence. Cited here will only be correspondence I read and used for this study.

1   Correspondence with Henri Barbusse, 1928: *Les Humbles*, Paris, 1937.

2   Correspondence with Antoine Borie, 1946–47: *Témoins*, 21, Zurich, Feb. 1959.

3   Correspondence with André Gide, 1935–44: *Seize fusillés à Moscou*, Paris, Cahiers Spartacus, 1936, reprinted from *Esprit* and *La Révolution prolétarienne*.

4   Correspondence with René Lefeuvre, 1936–47: *Seize fusillés à Moscou*, Paris, Cahiers Spartacus, 1936.

5   Correspondence with Herbert Lenhof, Julian Gorkín and Danny Bénédite, 1946, published in *Carnets*, 1952.

6   Correspondence with Marcel Martinet, 1921–36. Dossier Serge, Musée Social, rue Las Cases, Paris.

7   Correspondence with Emmanuel Mounier, 1940–47, in *Cuadernos Victor Serge*, Mexico, 1984.

8   Correspondence with Magdeleine Paz and friends, 1936, *Seize fusillés à Moscou*, reprinted from *Esprit*, *Les Humbles* and *La révolution prolétarienne*.

9   *Victor Serge et Léon Trotsky: la lutte contre le stalinisme*, 1936–39, Paris, Maspero, 1977.

E *Unpublished correspondence*

1 Dwight and Nancy Macdonald, 1939–47, Macdonald Papers, Sterling Library, Yale University. (This collection contains hundreds of letters between Serge and the Macdonalds.)
2 George Orwell: Orwell Archive, University College London.
3 Leon Lyovich Sedov, 1936–38, Boris Nicolaevsky Collection, Hoover Archive of the Hoover Institution, Stanford University. This collection contains more than 100 letters between Serge and Sedov.
4 Correspondence held at the Serge archive in Mexico City, 1941–47 (number denotes how many letters):
   Audiberti (1)
   Angelica Balabanova (2 and 2 from VS)
   Daniel Bénédite (1)
   Theo Bénédite (1)
   Jean Blanzat (1 and 2 from VS)
   André Breton (2)
   James Burnham
   Theodore Dan (1)
   Eleanora Deren (1)
   John Dewey (1)
   Georges Duhamel (1)
   Max Eastman (2)
   André Fer (1)
   George Varian Fry (3 and 2 from VS)
   Fritz Fraenckel
   Michael Fraenckel
   José Gabriel (1 and 2 from VS)
   Giono (2 and 1 from VS)
   Mary Jayne Gold
   Gordon (1)
   Julian Gorkín (1)
   Eulalia Guzman (1)
   Famille Hervens (Serge's relatives in Belgium)
   Henriette Roland-Holst (1)
   Sidney Hook (1)
   Hryhory Kostiuk
   Wilfredo Lam et Helen (1)
   Harold Laski
   Lucien Laurat et Marcelle Pommera (13)
   S.M. Levitas (12)
   Monatte (1)
   Gustava Nachmann (1)
   Octavio Paz (1)
   William Philipps
   Charles Plisnier
   Raymond (1)
   Marie Louise et Gustav Regler (2)
   Gustav Regler (2)
   Jean-Paul Samson (7)
   Natalia Sedova (Trotsky) (1)
   Max Shachtman

Helene Sgourdelis (3)
Tavernest (1 and 1 from VS)
José Valades (1 and 1 from VS)
Vautheir

F *Works confiscated by the Soviet censorship*

1   *L'An II de la révolution russe*, a history of War Communism.
2   *Les Hommes perdus*, a memoir of the prewar French anarchist movement.
3   *La Tourmente*, a sequel to *Conquered City*, a novel about War Communism in Russia, 1920.
4   *Résistance*, poems written in Orenburg and confiscated, reconstituted in Europe and published.

G *Translations (Russian into French)*

1 FICTION

a   André Bely, *Christ est ressuscité* (fragments), *Clarté*, no. 27, 1923, p. 77.
b   Henriette Chaguinian, *Hydrocentrale*, Paris, Editions sociales internationales, 1933.
c   M. Cholokhov, *Terres défrichées*, published in Paris, Editions sociales internationales, 1933 and appeared in the journal *Révolution prolétarienne*, no. 175, 25 May 1934.
d   Fedor Gladkov, *Le Ciment*, Paris, Editions sociales internationales, 1928; and 1929, with Serge's name mentioned on the cover and Serge's preface inside.
e   Vladimir Mayakovsky, *26–27 février 1917* (fragments), *Nouvelle Age* no. 9, 1931.

2 HISTORY AND POLITICS

a   Vera Figner, *Mémoires d'une révolutionnaire*, Paris, Gallimard, 1930.
b   Lapidus and K. Ostrovitianov, *Précis d'économie politique (L'économie politique et la théorie de l'économie sovietique)*, Paris, Editions sociales internationales, 1929.
c   V.I. Lenin, *Œuvres complètes*, Paris, Editions sociales internationales, 1928:
    vol. 7, *Les Débuts de la première révolution russe (1904–1905)*;
    vol. 13, *Matérialisme et empiriocriticisme*;
    vol. 20, *Les Débuts de la révolution russe (March–June 1917)*.
    L'Imperialisme, derniere étape du capitalisme, Paris, Librairie de *l'Humanité*, 1923.
d   Lenin and Zinoviev, two volumes of *Contre le courant*, Paris, Bureau d'Editions, 1927 (translated with Maurice Parijanine); also Paris, Maspero, 1970.
e   Leon Trotsky, *Terrorisme et Communisme*, Paris, Librairie de *l'Humanité*, 1926.
    Lénine, Paris, Librairie du Travail, 1925 (translated with Maurice Parijanine).
    Où va l'Angleterre, Paris, Librairie de *l'Humanité*, 1926.
    Europe et Amérique, Paris, Librairie de *l'Humanité*.
    La Révolution trahie, Paris, Grasset, 1936; also Pris, Editions de Minuit, 1973.
    Les Crimes de Staline, Paris, Maspero, 1973, two vols.
    Leur Morale et la nôtre, Paris, Editions du Sagittaire, 1939.
f   Grigory Zinoviev, *Lénine*, Paris, Librairie de *l'Humanité*, 1926.
g   Alexander Barmine, *Vingt ans au service de l'URSS: souvenirs d'un diplomate*, Paris, Albin Michel, 1939.

H *Unpublished manuscripts*

It is impossible to list all of Serge's unpublished essays and manuscripts. The following is a selection of material used in this study, grouped in rough chronological order, if date provided.

'L'Anarchisme' (no date provided).

Typescript, 'A Definition of Socialism', unpublished, no date.

Two typescripts, no title, no date.

'A Definition of Socialism', unpublished manuscript, no date.

'Le Socialisme est-il scientifique?'

'Etudes', no title, five pages, no date.

Franz Kafka: *Erzahlungen und Kleine Prosa Beschreibung Ein Kampfkes*, Schoken [sic] Books, New York (a review).

Horizon, edited by C. Connolly, London (review).

Partizan Review [sic] (a review of the journal).

'Opinions et faits sur la question juive'.

to: *The Statesman and Nation*, London.

The Socialist Leader, London.

The New Leader, New York.

David Dallin and Boris Nicolaevsky: *Forced Labor in Soviet Russia*, Yale University Press (a review).

'Sur Leo Baeck'.

Leo Baeck: *The Pharisees*, Schocken Books, New York (review).

'Ecrivaines française (notices)' published in *Partisan Review*.

'Sur Leon Werth: "Déposition"'.

'Matérialisme dialectique et dogmatisme'.

'Marxisme et psychologie'.

'L'Anarchisme'.

'La Deuxième Internationale'.

'La Mentalité révolutionnaire Russe'.

'Le Trotskysme'.

'Notre bilan d'un quart de siècle' (partially typed, partially handwritten, four pages).

'Le Rapport des forces sociales (avant la IIe guerre mondiale)'.

For *The Call*, New York ('Sur les 2e et 3e guerres mondiales').

'La Francia de hoy, deslizamiento hacia la guerra civil, aborto del fascismo francés' (nine pages, in Spanish, no date).

'L'Europe de demain: neo-totalitarisme ou démocratie?'

'Russie'.

'Bilan de la réaction stalinienne'.

'Stalinisme, extermination des juifs, humanisme'.

'Le Peuple russe n'est pas totalitaire (par *Left*)'.

'Les Forces démocratiques en URSS'.

'Importance de la Mongolie'.

'Socialisme et psychologie'.

'Economie dirigeé et démocratie' (published in *Revolutionary History*, London, autumn 1994).

'Proposiciones Del Independent Labour Party (I.L.P.) de Inglaterra Relativas a Los Problemas consecuentes a Un Nuevo Movimiento Socialista Internacional, *Problemas a Considerar*' (no date, in Spanish).

'L'Avenir du socialisme'.

'Alice et Otto Ruhle sont morts'.

'Modigliani, notice nécrologique'.

'Peuples et régimes'.

'Que deviennent les réfugies italiens en URSS?'

'Sur le conflit russo-polonais et le régime de l'URSS'.

'Que la guerre economique commença ave le nazisme'.

'Es capitalista la economia nazi?'

'L'Assassinat de Trotsky. Dossier sur Jacson-Mornard'.

'Calomnie (1936–37)'.

'Thèses sur la révolution russe (1937)'.

'Puissance et limites du Marxisme' (Feb. 1938 and Oct. 1941).

'Bessarabie et Dobroudja' (9 May 1940).

Serge to Nancy and Dwight Macdonald (7 June 1941).

'Pour la démocratie soviétique' (14 Sept. 1941).

'La Guerre et la démocratie soviétique', Mexico (7 Dec. 1941).

'Avenir de l'URSS' (Dec. 1941).

'Mexico, enero de 1942: a los Ciudadanos, Presidente de los Estados Unidos Mexicanos, Presidente de la Cámara de diputados, Secretario de Gobernación' signed Serge, Gorkín, Pivert (Dossier de la Calomnie).

'Bilan provisoire de la campagne de Russie', 5 Feb. 1942 (Pour *Bohemia*).

'Une Definition de la position socialiste-révolutionnaire "traditionnelle" dévant la guerre' (May 1942).

'La Guerre et la pensée' (4 Aug. 1942).

Lettre à Maurice Wullens sur l'antisémitisme et quelques autres sujets (7 June).

'L'Extermination des juifs de Varsovie' (28 Jan. 1943).

'La Question juive, réponse à la revue "Babel"' (12 Oct.).

'Marxism et démocratie', letter from Serge to Sidney Hook (May 1943).

'La Fondation de la IIIème Internationale' (end May 1943).

'L'Organisation du Komintern' (end May 1943).

'Sur le probleme des Partis' (June 1943).

'L'Internationalisme socialiste est-il-fini?' (June 1943).

'Le Socialisme et l'avenir de l'Europe' (July 1943).

Letter to Harold Laski, 6 Aug. 1943 ('sur la collaboration de socialism européene avec l'URSS')

'Le Reformisme a-t-il un avenir?' (Sept. 1943).

Two letters to Dwight Macdonald, on socialism, psychology, the war, Spanish Civil War, etc. (7 Sept. 1943 and Oct. 1943).

'Où va Staline?' (Mexico, 4 Oct. 1943).

'Socialisme et questions coloniales' (Nov. 1943).

'Réponse au questionnaire de l'ILP concernant un nouveau mouvement Socialiste International' (Mexico, 6 Dec. 1943).

'Determinisme de la politique de l'URSS' (1943?).

No title, eight theses, 1943.

'Sur Malaquaise (Journal de Guerre)', published in *Hijo Pródigo*, Mexico, March 1944.

'Sur Jean Malaquaise (Journal de Guerre)', published in *Politics*, New York, April 1944.

'Deuil à Mexico (sur la mort de Fritz Fraenckel)', 26 June 1944 (sent to Levitas at *New Leader*, New York).

'Les Enigmes staliniennes' (Mexico, 6 Sept. 1944).

'Manœuvres dans le Komintern' (10 April 1944).

'La Pologne et l'avenir de l'Europe' (Nov. 1944).

'Vers un renouvellement du socialisme?' (Mexico, Jan. 1945).

'Le Temps du courage intellectuel' (Mexico, Jan. 1945) (for 'BABEL', Santiago de Chile).

'L'Economie planifiée et la liberté de la presse', *New Leader*, New York, 20 Feb. 1945.

'Problèmes du socialisme' (Feb. 1945).

'Lenin's Heir?' (end May 1945).

Two letters to S. Levitas of the *New Leader*, New York, 7 June 1945 and 18 June 1945, both letters in English, warning about Manouilski, Duclos and others who may be agents in the USA.

'Necessity of Free Information and discussion for the European Trade-union and Social-ist Movements' (in English, 2 June 45).

'Les Oppositions en URSS' (Mexico, July 1945).

'On the Russian Problem', twelve pages in English (Oct. 1945).

'Le Dernier livre de Trotsky: Staline' (1946).

'L'Alternative: démocratie russe' (March 1946), for *The Call*, New York.

'Existentialisme?' (April 1946), handwritten note says 'publié' New York 1946.

'Planification et liberté' (Mexico, 1946).

'El Ciudano Vichinsky' (in Spanish), 1947, three pages.

'L'Appareil central du Komintern', published in *Plain Talk*, New York, Feb. 1947.

'Crimes sur crimes' (Mexico, May 1947).

'La Substance du Komintern' (with cover letter to S.M. Levitas of the *New Leader*, New York, Mexico, 24 Oct. 1947).

'L'URSS a-t-elle un régime socialiste?' (published in *Masses* 1947 and *Acción Sociale* 1947).

'Les Causes de l'impérialisme soviétique' (Nov. 1947, for *Revista de las Americas*).

'Trente ans après la révolution russe' (Nov. 1947, published in *La Révolution prolétari-enne*, Nov. 1947 and in Susan Weissman (ed.), *Victor Serge: Russia Twenty Years After*, New York, Humanities Press, 1996.).

I *Journalism (cited by periodical)*

This is not a complete list of Serge's journalism.

L'Anarchie, 1909–12
'Les Anarchistes et la transformation sociale', no. 252 (3 Feb. 1909).

'Sur la violence', no. 297 (15 Dec. 1910).

'The Individualist and Society', no. 323 (15 June 1911), signed 'Le Rétif', in English at http://endehors.homepage.com/RETIF.HTM

'Les Bandits', no. 352 (4 Jan. 1912).

Bulletin Communiste (Organe du Parti Communiste SFIC), 1921–24
'Les Anarchistes en Russie', 1921, p. 57.

'La Révolution d'octobre à Moscou', nos 36–37, 1921, p. 612.

'Lettre de Russie', 1921, p. 723.

'Révolution-légende et révolution-réalité', 1921, p. 755.

'Les Tendances nouvelles de l'anarchisme russe', 1921, p. 808.

'Les Méthodes et les procèdes de la police russe', 1921, p. 829.

'La Confession de Bakounine', 1921, p. 941.

'Raymond Lefebvre', no. 14, 1921, p. 223.

'Lichtenstadt (Mazine)', no. 42, 1921, p. 702.

'Notes d'Allemagne', R. Albert, no. 41, 11 Oct. 1923, pp. 625–31.

'Notes d'Allemagne', R. Albert, no. 42, 18 Oct. 1923, pp. 650–52.

'Notes d'Allemagne', R. Albert, no. 43, 25 Oct. 1923, pp. 779–80.

'Notes d'Allemagne', R. Albert. no. 45, 8 Nov. 1923, pp. 808–10.

'Notes d'Allemagne', R. Albert, no. 46, 15 Nov. 1923, pp. 823–30.

'Notes d'Allemagne', R. Albert, no. 47, 22 Nov. 1923, pp. 853–5.

Byulleten oppozitsii, 1936–39
'Pis'mo Viktora Serzha André Zhidu', no. 50, May 1936.

(Serge letter to Trotsky reproduced in a report on Political Persecution in the USSR, signed 'LT') no. 51, July–Aug. 1936.

Clarté, 1922–27 (Directeur Henri Barbusse)

'Les Classes moyennes dans la révolution russe', 1922.

'Les Ecrivains russes et la révolution', no. 17, 11 July 1922, pp. 385–90.

'Le Nouvel Ecrivain et la nouvelle littérature', no. 31, 15 Feb. 1923, pp. 158–60.

'Boris Pilniak', no. 36, 20 May 1923, pp. 272–5.

'Devant la révolution allemande: les riches contre la nation', R. Albert, no. 46, 1 Nov. 1923, p. 428.

'Au Seuil d'une révolution: la "retraite d'octobre" en Allemagne', Berlin, Jan. 1924. R. Albert (à suivre), no. 52, 1 Feb. 1924. pp. 66–8.

'Au Seuil d'une révolution: le P.C. Allemand se critique lui-même'. R. Albert, no. 53, 15 Feb. 1924, pp. 96–8.

'Notations d'Espagne', no. 55, 1924, p. 140.

'"La Semaine"' de I. Libedinsky', no. 56, 1924.

'Chroniques de la vie intellectuelle en Russie: Vsevolod Ivanov', no. 56, 1 April 1924, pp. 151–4.

'Lénine 1917', no. 58, 1924, p. 203.

'Vsevolod Ivanov', no. 74, 1925.

'Un Incident (lettre à "Nakanounie")', no. 59, 1924, p. 241.

'Lénine 1917', no. 59, 1924, p. 223.

'Lénine 1917', no. 60, 1924, p. 249.

'Lénine 1917', no. 61, 1924, p. 285.

'Chroniques de la vie intellectuelle en Russie: Valère Brioussov', no. 67, 1 Nov. 1924, p. 473.

'Chroniques de la vie intellectuelle en Russie: Mayakovsky', no. 69, 1 Dec. 1924, pp. 504–8.

'La Littérature épique de la révolution: N. Tikhonov et Serafimovitch', no. 79, Dec. 1925–Jan. 1926, pp. 389–91.

'Une Fière Equipe', no. 70, 1925, p. 8.

Parijanine, 'La ville en danger, de Victor Serge' (book review), no. 70, 1925, p. 24.

'Une Littérature prolétarienne est-elle possible?' no. 72, 1925, p. 121.

'La Verité sur l'attentat de Sarajevo. La complicité de l'Etat-Major russe', no. 74, 1925, p. 205.

'Un Portrait de Lénine par Trotski', no. 75, 1925, p. 255.

'La Littérature épique de la révolution', no. 79, 1925, p. 389.

'Les Jeunes Ecrivains russes de la révolution entre le passé et l'avenir', no. 2, 1926–27, p. 50.

'Les Nouveaux Aspects du problème de la guerre', no. 3, 1926–27, p. 67.

'Au Lendemain de l'insurrection d'octobre', no. 4, 1926–27, p. 115.

'La Mariage en U.R.S.S', no. 6, 1926–27, p. 175.

'Le Bolchevisme et l'Asie, no. 7, 1926–27, p. 195.

'Grande Expérience oubliée: la commune finlandaise de 1918', no. 8, 1926–1927, pp. 237–41.

'La lutte des classes dans la révolution chinoise (I)', new series, no. 9, 15 May 1927, pp. 259–66.

'La Lutte des classes dans la révolution chinoise (II)', no. 11, 15 July 1927, pp. 323–9.

'La Lutte des classes dans la révolution chinoise (III)', no. 12, 15 Aug. 1927, pp. 356–62.

'La Lutte des classes dans la révolution chinoise (IV)', no. 13, 15 Sept. 1927, pp. 382–92.

'La Lutte des classes dans la révolution chinoise (V)', no. 14, 15 Oct. 1927, pp. 406–12.

'Vers l'industrialisation (I)', no. 15, 1927, p. 436.

'Vers l'industrialisation (II)', no. 16, 29 Nov. 1927, p. 486.

'Canton', appeared in *La Lutte des classes*, no. 1, Feb.–March 1928 (last of the series on the Chinese revolution).

La Correspondance Internationale, 1921–25 (all articles signed as R. Albert)
'Le Bilan d'une année 1922', no. 1, 3 Jan. 1923, pp. 1–2.
'L'Anniversaire du 15 Janvier: Karl Liebknecht et Rosa Luxembourg' (Berlin), no. 3, 10 Jan. 1923, pp. 1–3.
'Nouvelles d'Allemagne', no. 12, 9 Feb. 1923, p. 75.
'Notes d'Allemagne', no. 61, 31 July 1923, pp. 456–7.
'Notes d'Allemagne', no. 63, 7 Aug. 1923, pp. 471–2.
'La Grève générale en Allemagne: notes d'Allemagne', no. 64, 15 Aug. 1923, pp. 477–9.
'Notes d'Allemagne: la grande coalition a l'œuvre' (Berlin), no. 70, 5 Sept. 1923, pp. 523–8.
'Notes d'Allemagne', no. 71, 8 Sept. 1923, p. 535.
'Notes d'Allemagne', no. 72, 11 Sept. 1923, pp. 542–3.
'Notes d'Allemagne', no. 73, 14 Sept. 1923, pp. 551–2.
'La Dictature militaire en Espagne: la causes du mouvement', no. 74, 18 Sept. 1923, pp. 557–8.
'Notes d'Allemagne: vers la guerre civile', no. 77, 28 Sept. 1923, pp. 581–2.
'Notes d'Allemagne', no. 78, 2 Oct. 1923, pp. 591–2.
'Notes d'Allemagne' (Berlin), no. 79, 5 Oct. 1923, pp. 599–600.
'Notes d'Allemagne', no. 82, 16 Oct. 1923, pp. 623–4.
'Notes d'Allemagne: vers une commune allemande', no. 83, 19 Oct. 1923, pp. 630–31.
'Notes d'Allemagne', no. 84, 25 Oct. 1923, pp. 639–41.
'Notes d'Allemagne', no. 85, 26 Oct. 1923, pp. 649–51.
'Notes d'Allemagne', no. 86, 30 Oct. 1923, pp. 656–8.
'Notes d'Allemagne', no. 87, 2 Nov. 1923, pp. 662–4.
'Notes d'Allemagne' (Berlin), no. 89, 9 Nov. 1923, pp. 679–81.
'Notes d'Allemagne' (Berlin), no. 90, 13 Nov. 1923, pp. 689–92.
'Notes d'Allemagne', no. 91, 17 Nov. 1923, pp. 696–7.
'Notes d'Allemagne' (Berlin), no. 92, 20 Nov. 1923, pp. 705–6.

The Communist
'Five Years Struggle' vol. 4, May–Oct. 1923, pp. 162–4.

The Communist International
'Frame of Mind of the French Proletariat', no. 1, May 1919.
'Letter from France', no. 2, June 1919.

Le Crapouillot, 1938
'La Pensée anarchiste', número special, Jan. 1938, pp. 2–13.

L'Emancipation Paysanne
'Staline contre les paysans', 3 Feb. 1940, pp. 1–8.

l'En Dehors
'A propos de Romain Rolland', 15 Feb. 1934.

Esprit, 1936–39
'Lettres à Magdeleine Paz et à André Gide', no. 45, June 1936.
'Méditation sur l'Anarchie', no. 55, March, 1937.
'Litvinov', no. 81, June 1939.

La Flèche, 1936–7
'Ténèbres', no. 31, 19 Sept. 1936.

'Un Appel de Victor Serge à Romain Rolland', no. 52, 6 Feb. 1937.
'Analyse d'un crime', no. 78, 7 Aug. 1937.

El Hijo Pródigo (Revista Literaria)
'El Mensaje del Escritor', vol. VI, no. 21, Dec. 1944.

Horizon (A Review of Literature and Art)
'Letter from Mexico', vol. XV, no. 85, Jan. 1947, pp. 63–72.

L'Humanité, 1924–27
'La Vie intellectuelle en URSS: un nouveau livre de Maxime Gorki', 5 Aug. 1926.
'Littérature prolétarienne: la vie intellectuelle en URSS', 26 Sept. 1926.
'Littérature prolétarienne: Iouri Libedinsky', 17 Oct. 1926.
'Ecrivains prolétariens: A. Serafimovitch', 11 Dec. 1926.
'Ecrivains prolétariens: les mémorialistes de la révolution', 19 Dec. 1926.
'Les Idées de Boris Pilniak', 25 May 1927.

Les Humbles, 1936–39
'Lettres à Maurice Wullens', vol. 21, no. 5, May 1936, and no. 8, Aug. 1936.
'Lettres à Henri Barbusse', vol. 22, nos 8–9, Aug.–Sept. 1937.
'Deux rencontres', vol. 24, nos 8–12 (Aug.–Dec. 1939), published in English as 'Twice
    Met' in *International Socialism*, vol. 20, spring, 1965.

Inprekorr, Vienna
R. Albert, 26 Feb. 1925.
R. Albert, 12 Mar. 1925.

International Presse-Korrespondenz
R. Albert, vol. 1, Oct.–Dec. 1921, nos 1–20.
R. Albert, no. 103, 21 June 1923, p. 869.

International Press Correspondence (Inprecorr) (English edition)
'The Causes of the Russian Famine', vol. I, no. 3, 1921, p. 26.
'The Reality of the Famine', vol. I, no. 6, 8 Nov. 1921, p. 51.
'To the Rescue: For the Right of Political Asylum', R. Albert, vol. I, no. 6, 8 Nov.
    1921, p. 45.
'The Downfall of the Russian "Whites"', R. Albert, vol. I, no. 10, 22 Nov. 1921, p. 82.
'Intellectual Life in Russia' (Kiev), vol. 2, no. 68, 12 Aug. 1922.
'The Nobel Case' (Kiev), vol. 2, no. 69, 15 Aug. 1922.
'From Havre to Kattovitz and Vienna' (Moscow), R. Albert, vol. 2, no. 75, 1 Sept. 1922.
'Five Years . . .' (Kiev, 20 Oct. 1922), vol. 2, no. 96, 7 Nov. 1922.
'The Worst Counter-Revolution', vol. 2, no. 108, Dec. 1922.
'To the Rescue of the Spaniards', R. Albert, vol. 2, no. 2, 1922, p. 16.
'The Social Democrats and Reparations', R. Albert, vol. 3, no. 33 [15], 19 April 1923.
'From Gallifet to Mussolini', R. Albert, vol. 3, no. 34 [16], 26 April 1923.
'War: A Conversation with a Pacifist', R. Albert, vol. 3, no. 36 [18], 9 May 1923.
'French Imperialism in Poland', vol. 3, no. 41 [23], 7 June 1923.
'The Military Dictatorship in Spain', R. Albert, vol. 3, no. 62 [40], 27 Sept. 1923.
'The New Fiume Crisis', R. Albert, vol. 3, no. 64 [41], 4 Oct. 1923.
'The Museum of the Revolution in Petrograd', vol. 3, no. 54 [32], 2 Aug. 1923.
'Lenin and Imperialism' (Kiev), vol. 3, no. 60 [38], 13 Sept. 1923.
'The Bloodiest of All Democracies', R. Albert, vol. 4, no. 2, 10 Jan. 1924.

'The Third International', R. Albert, vol. 4, no. 15, 28 Feb. 1924.
'May 1st, 1924' (Paris) R. Albert, vol. 4, no. 26, 24 April 1924.
'After the French Elections', R. Albert, vol. 4, no. 30, May 1924.
'Anatole France', vol. 4, no. 73, 16 Oct. 1924.
'Five Months of the Government of the Left Block in France', R. Albert, vol. 4, no. 77, 6 Nov. 1924.
'The Ebert Slander Case', R. Albert, vol. 4, no. 86, 18 Dec. 1924.
'The Events in Spain', R. Albert, vol. 4, no. 90, 31 Dec. 1924.
'The Police Provocations in Poland', 1925, no. 64, p. 919.
'The Assassination of Todor Panitza in Vienna', R. Albert, 1925, no. 43, p. 554.
'Friedrich Ebert', R. Albert, 12 March 1925, no. 19, p. 271.
'The German Tcheka', R. Albert, no. 17, 26 Feb. 1925, p. 230.

Left
'The Basis of a New International', April 1944, pp. 94–7.
'There Are Democrats in Russia', Aug. 1946, pp. 175–8.

Modern Review
'Socialism and Psychology', vol. 1, no. 3, May 1947, pp. 194–202.
'In Memoriam: Victor Serge' (the editors), vol. 2, no. 1, Jan. 1948, pp. 6–7.

Mundo, Libertad y Socialismo
'A donde va Stalin?' Mexico, Oct.–Nov. 1943, pp. 14–15.
'Necesidad de una renovación del Socialismo', Mexico, June 1943, pp. 18–19.
'Socialismo y psicología', no. 16, Santiago de Chile, April–May 1948, pp. 10–14.
'La Tragédia de los escritores sovieticos', no. 17, Santiago de Chile, Aug.–Sept. 1948, pp. 8–12.
'Los Alemanes', no. 18, Santiago de Chile, Feb.–March 1949, pp. 10–13.

New Essays
'Escape from Freedom, by Erich Fromm', reviewed by Serge, vol. 6, no. 3, spring 1943.

The New International, 1938–39, 1942, 1949–51
'Once More: Kronstadt', July 1938, pp. 211–12.
'A Letter and Some Notes', Feb. 1939, pp. 53–4.
'Reply to Ciliga', Feb. 1939, p. 54.
'Again, Riazanov and Sneevliet', Sept. 1942, p. 255.
Excerpts from Serge's *Year One* printed in the following:
    'The October Insurrection', vol. 14, no. 3, March 1948, pp. 83–90.
    'The Counter-Revolutionary Socialists', vol. 14, no. 4, April 1948, pp. 123–6.
    'The First Flames of Civil War', vol. 14, no. 5, July 1948, pp. 155–8.
    'The Dissolution of the Constituent Assembly', vol. 14, no. 6, Aug. 1948, pp. 187–90.
    'Summary of First Months', vol. 14, no. 7, Sept. 1948, pp. 220–21.
    'The Dispute Over Brest-Litovsk', vol. 14, no. 8, Oct. 1948, pp. 252–5.
    'The Revolution in Finland', vol. 14, no. 9, Nov. 1948, pp. 282–6.
    'Left Communism and Inner-Party Conflict', vol 15, no. 1, Jan. 1949, pp. 30–33.
    'The Suppression of the Anarchists', vol. 15, no. 2, Feb. 1949, pp. 60–62.
    'Life and Culture in 1918', vol. 15, no. 7, July 1949, pp. 157–9.
Excerpts from Serge's 'Pages of a Diary' printed in the following:
    'André Gide, Arrests at Leningrad (Vera, Esther), Disappearance of Andrés Nin, Krivitsky', vol. 15, no. 10, Sept. 1949, pp. 214–18.

'Reiss, Krivitsky, Bastich, Others, Agabekov, Rossi, Anton Ciliga, The Klement Affair, Krivitsky, Brandler, Dzerzhinsky, Stalin, Semyonov', vol 16, nos 1–2, Jan.–Feb. 1950, pp. 51–7.
'The Case of Doriot, Alexis Tolstoy, Nicola Bombacci', vol. 16, nos 3–4, March–April 1950, pp. 115–21.
'The tragedy of Romain Rolland, Erongaricuaro, Justification of Duplicity', vol. 16, nos 5–6, May–June1950, pp. 177–9.
'Fedin and Gorky', vol. 16, nos 7–8, July–Aug. 1950, pp. 249–51.
'The Tomb of Coyoacán, Jacson, The Assassin', vol. 16, nos 9–10, Sept.–Oct. 1950, pp. 309–13.
'Koka, Kravchenko', vol. 16, nos 11–12, Nov.–Dec. 1950, pp. 368–71.

New Leader, 1942–47 (Serge was their Mexican correspondent)
'Letter from Victor Serge', vol. XXV, 7 Feb. 1942, p. 1.
'Gorkín stabbed as Mexican CP Wrecks Erlich, Tresca Meeting', vol. XXVI, 17 April 1943, p. 1.
'Letter from Victor Serge', vol. XXVI, 1 May 1943, pp. 1 and 7.
'The Trotsky Murder – GPU Fails to Save Jacson from 20-year Term', vol. XXVI, 8 May 1943, p. 4.
'Another Chapter in the Mystery of Mornard – Trotsky's Murderer', vol. XXVI, 20 Nov. 1943, p. 2.
'Spanish Liberation Junta in Action', vol. XXVII, 12 Feb. 1944, p. 5.
'Stalin's Plan for Germany', vol. XXVII, 11 March 1944, p. 9.
'The Spanish Junta', vol. XXVII, 8 April 1944, p. 5.
'Men in Exile', vol. XXVII, 13 May 1944, p. 7.
'Spain at the Crossroads', vol. XXVII, 10 June 1944, p. 6.
'The Fate of Italian Refugees in the USSR', vol. XXVII, 19 Aug. 1944, p. 9.
'In Defense of André Gide', vol. XXVII, 2 Dec. 1944, pp. 12–13.
'Who Will Succeed Franco, an Interview with Indalecio Prieto', vol. XXVII, 16 Dec. 1944, p. 6.
'The Death of Oumansky', vol. XXVIII, 10 Feb. 1945, p. 4.
'Spanish Communist Maneuvers', vol. XXVIII, 17 Feb. 1945, p. 7.
'Stalin's Drang Nach Osten' (Mongolia as base of Russian operations in Asia), written with Robert T. Oliver, vol. XXVIII, 18 Aug. 1945, p. 6.
'The Spanish Government in Exile', vol. XXVIII, 15 Sept. 1945, p. 3.
'Toledaño, CTAL and WFTU', vol. XXVIII, 17 Nov. 1945.
'Plebiscite for Spain?' vol. XXVIII, 22 Dec. 1945, section 1, p. 8.
'A Note on Lombardo Toledano', vol. XXIX, 9 Nov. 1946, p. 5.
'Trotsky's Murderer', vol. XXX, 5 April 1947, p. 5.
'Ukrainian Writers in DP Camps', vol. XXX, 26 April 1947.
'The NKVD in Mexico', vol. XXX, 12 July 1947, p. 2.
'Toledano's New Party', vol. XXX, 1 Nov. 1947, p. 1.
'Death of Victor Serge' (the editors), vol. XXX, 22 Nov. 1947.

Partisan Review, 1938–47
'Marxism in Our Time', vol. V, no. 3, Aug.–Sept. 1938.
'Note on Kronstadt – letter', vol. VI, no. 2, winter 1939.
'What Is Fascism?' vol. VIII, no. 5, Sept.–Oct. 1941, p. 420.
'French Writers, summer 1941', vol. VIII, no. 5, Sept.–Oct. 1941.
'On the Eve', vol. IX, no. 1, Jan.–Feb. 1942.
'In Memory: L.D. Trotsky', vol. IX, no. 5, 1942.
'French Expectations', vol. XII, no. 2, spring 1945.

'The Socialist Imperative', discussion, 'The Future of Socialism: V', vol. XIV, no. 5, Sept.–Oct. 1947.

Plain Talk
'Inside the Comintern', Feb. 1947, pp. 22–3.

Politics, 1944–47
Note on Mundo, vol. 1, no. 3, March 1944
Review of Malaquais' *War Diary*, vol. 1, no. 3, March 1944.
'The Revolution at Dead-End', vol. 1, no. 5, June 1944.
'The End of Europe', vol. 1, no. 7, Aug. 1944
'Stalinism and the Resistance: A Letter', vol. 2, no. 2, Feb. 1945.
'War Communism', vol. 2, no. 3, March 1945.
'Kronstadt', vol. 2, no. 4, April 1945.
'Vignettes of NEP', vol. 2, no. 6, June 1945.
'Letter from Victor Serge', vol. 2, no. 6, June 1945.
'The Responsibility of Peoples', vol. 2, no. 8, Aug. 1945.
'In Memory: Boris Voline', vol. 3, no. 2, Feb. 1946.
'Soviet Culture: Mandelstam', vol. 3, no. 11, Dec. 1946.
'The Communists and Viet Nam', vol. 4, no. 2, March–April 1947.

La Révolution prolétarienne, 1928–47
'La Profession de foi de Victor Serge', no. 22, 3 Nov. 1928.
'Lettre de Victor Serge au Comité Central Executif des Soviets', no. 153, 10 June 1933.
'Les Documents de l'accusation contre V. Serge: sa correspondance', no. 156, 25 July 1933, pp. 3–4.
'La Correspondance de Victor Serge', no. 158, 28 Aug. 1933.
'La Correspondance de Victor Serge', no. 160, 25 Sept. 1933, pp. 15–17.
'La Correspondance de Victor Serge', no. 163, 10 Nov. 1933, pp. 6–7.
'Quatre d'entre toutes' (poem), 1935, pp. 11–12.
'Lettre à *La Révolution prolétarienne*', no. 221, 25 April 1936.
'Lettres à Magdeleine Paz et André Gide', no. 224, 10 June 1936.
'Note de lecture "sur la brochure d'Yvon: ce qu'est devenue la révolution russe"', no. 228, 10 Aug. 1936, p. 13.
'Le Cauchemar stalinien', no. 229, 25 Aug. 1936.
'Autour d'un crime', no. 230, 10 Sept. 1936.
'Suite du cauchemar', no. 232, 10 Oct. 1936.
'Pas de témoins!' no. 233, 25 Oct. 1936.
'L'Exécution', no. 235, 25 Nov. 1936.
'Crimes en Russie, intrigues en Espagne', no. 236, 10 Dec. 1936.
'L'Intrigue stalinienne en Espagne', no. 238, 10 Jan. 1937.
'Insuite à grande tirage', no. 240, 10 Feb. 1937.
'La Fin de Yagoda', no. 244, 10 April 1937.
'La Fin des écrivains thermidoriens', no. 246, 10 May 1937.
'Victoir et defaite à Barcelone', no. 247, 25 May 1937.
'La Crise du regime stalinien', and 'Gamarnik', no. 249, 25 June 1937.
'Adieu à Andrés Nin', 'Bezymenski', no. 253, 25 Aug. 1937.
'Les Ecrits et les faits', 'Cronstadt', 'Cauchemar en URSS', 'Exécution de Mdivani, suicide de Lioubtchenko', 'Ce que Staline veut détruire', no. 254, 10 Sept. 1937.
'Les Ecrits et les faits', no. 255, 25 Sept. 1937.
'Les Ecrits et les faits', 'Barbarie' 'Karakhane' 'L'Isolateur de Yaroslavl', no. 256, 10 Oct. 1937.

'Les Ecrits et les faits', 'Cronstadt 1921', 'Contre l'esprit de secte', 'Bolchevisme et anarchisme', no. 257, 25 Oct. 1937.

'Le Stalinisme est-il une nécessité historique?' 'Antonov-Ovseenko', no. 258, 10 Nov. 1937.

'Boukharine executé?' no. 259, 25 Nov. 1937.

'Erwin Wolf', no. 260, 10 Dec. 1937.

'Chronique du sang versé', no. 262, 10 Jan. 1938, pp. 1–2.

'Leon Sedov', no. 265, 25 Feb. 1938.

'Le Troisième procès de Moscou, I', no. 266, 10 March 1938.

'Le Troisième procès de Moscou, II', no. 267, 25 March 1938.

'Le Troisième procès de Moscou, III', no. 269, 25 April 1938.

'Nouvelles d'URSS', 'Le Birobidian, republique juive', no. 276, 10 Aug. 1938.

'Adieu à Barthélémy de Liczt', no. 279, 25 Sept. 1938, p. 4.

'Sur Cronstadt 1921', no. 277, 25 Aug. 1938.

'Les Idées et les faits', no. 281, 25 Oct. 1938.

'Qu'est devenu Francesco Ghezzi?' no. 294, 10 May 1939, p. 14.

'Crimes sur crimes', no. 303, May 1947.

'Trente ans après la révolution russe', no. 309, Nov. 1947.

La Révolution prolétarienne, articles about Serge:

'Souscription pour Victor Serge', no. 122–2, 1933.

'Lettres', no. 11–155, 1933.

'Pour la libération de Victor Serge' no. 14–158, 1933.

'Au secours de Victor Serge' no. 15–55.

'Victor Serge et Rakovsky acclamés au Congress unitaire de l'Enseignement', no. 11–319, 1933.

'L'affaire Victor Serge n'interesse pas l'Association juridique internationale', no. 12–13, à Marcel Willard by Magdeleine Paz, dated 19 Nov. 1934.

'VICTOR SERGE EST LIBRE, En URSS, une foule de militants remplissent les prisons, les camps de concentration, les lieux de deportation. Ils y meurent', April 1936.

'Stalin privé Victor Serge de sa nationalité', no. 15–223, 21 July 1936.

Rumbo (Mexico)

'Balance de la reacción staliniana', Oct.–Nov. 1941, pp. 9 and 30.

Socialist Call

'The War and the Resurgence of Socialism – An Optimistic Approach', 7 May 1943, p. 2.

'Trust Anti-Fascists in Europe's Prisons', 12 May 1944, p. 8.

'The Mystery Behind Russian Policy', part 2, 8 Sept. 1944, p. 8.

'Will Stalinism Last?' 14 May 1945, p. 6.

'The Russian People Have Earned the Right to Full Democracy', 20 May 1946, p. 5.

Tierra y Libertad, 1917

'Esbozo crítico sobre Nietzsche', published in five parts: no. 369, Dec. 1917 (reprinted from no. 358 because of censorship difficulties); no. 359, 8 Aug. 1917; no. 361, 24 Oct. 1917; no. 362, 31 Oct. 1917; no. 363, 7 Nov. 1917.

La Vie Ouvrière, 1921–26

'La tragique d'une révolution', no. 152, 31 March 1922.

'Le problème de la dictature', no. 159, 19 May 1922.

'Dictature et contre-révolution économique', no. 182, 3 Nov. 1922.
'Le Fascisme en Autriche', Oct. and Nov. 1925.
'Sur Romain Rolland', April 1926.

La Wallonie, 1936–40
'L'Amer', 27–28 June 1936, p. 4.
'Souvenirs', 8 July 1936, p. 3.
'Misère d'Unamuno', 22–23 Aug. 1936, p. 4.
'Gide retour d'URSS', 21–22 Nov. 1936, p. 4.
'Le Plus Triste Voyage d'André Gide', 19–20 Dec. 1936, p. 12.
'Au dernier Congrès des Soviets', 12–13 Dec. 1936, p. 10.
'Le Souvenir de Vladimir Illitch', 23–24 Jan. 1937, p. 8.
'Le Drame russe', 30–31 Jan. 1937, p. 10.
'Pour une cause sacrée', 6–7 Feb. 1937, p. 12.
'Yagoda', 10–11 April 1937, p. 8.
'Pensée dirigée', 24–25 April 1937, p. 8.
'Le Poète de la commune', 1–2 May 1937, p. 8.
'Adieu à Gramsci', 8–9 May 1937, p. 10.
'Musée du soir', 12–13 June 1937.
'Production et démocratie', 17–18 July 1937, p. 8.
'Le Bourrage de crane', 24–25 July 1937, p. 8.
'Boris Pilniak', 31 July 1937, p. 8.
'Le Sens de l'histoire', 7 Aug. 1937, p. 8.
'Adieu à un ami', 14–15 Aug. 1937.
'Bezymenski', 21–22 Aug. 1937, p. 10.
'D'un livre sur Karl Marx', 11–12 Sept. 1937, p. 10.
'Qu'est-ce que la culture?' 18–19 Sept. 1937, p. 10.
'La Crise de l'industrie soviétique', 25–26 Sept. 1937, p. 10.
'Intellectualisme et intelligence', 9–10 Oct. 1937, p. 10.
'L'Evolution du droit penal en URSS', 16–17 Oct. 1937, p. 10.
'Il y a vingt ans', Nov. 1937, p. 10.
'Le Drame russe: Boukharine', 27–28 Nov. 1937, p. 14.
'La Confession de Bakounine', 4–5 Dec. 1937, p. 10.
'Angel Pestagna', 18–19 Dec. 1937.
'Pogrome en quatre cents pages', 8–9 Jan. 1938, p. 10.
'Francesco Ghezzi', 15 Jan. 1938.
'Meyerhold', 29–30 Jan. 1938, p. 10.
'Mort d'un ami . . . ', 26–27 Feb. 1938.
'Le Mystère des aveux', 12–13 March 1938, p. 12.
'Complots en U.R.S.S.?' 19–20 March 1938.
'Le Drame de Krestinski', 3 April 1938.
'Chaliapine', 16–17 April 1938, p. 8.
'Boreal', 23–24 April 1938, p. 11.
'Crime et criminologie', 7–8 May 1938, p. 11.
'Le Témoignage d'Anton Ciliga', 14–15 May 1938, p. 10.
'Nouvelles de Moscou . . . ', 17–18 June 1938.
'Révolutions et tyrannies', 23–24 July 1938, p. 8.
'Défense de la culture', 30 June–1 July 1938, p. 8.
'Remarques sur l'antisémitisme', 12–13 Nov. 1938, p. 10.
'Le Drame des juifs de l'Allemagne', 19–20 Nov. 1938, p. 10.
'Un Numéro des 'Izvestia'', 26–27 Nov. 1938, p. 14.
'La Crise de l'U.R.S.S . . . L'affaire Kossarev', 3–4 Dec. 1938.

'De la guerre civile à l'économie dirigée', 8 Dec. 1938.
'Les "Protocoles de Sages de Sion"', 10–11 Dec. 1938, p. 10.
'De Ejov à Beria', 17–18 Dec. 1938.
'*Les Rescapes* d'Henry Poulaille', 24–25 Dec. 1938, p. 10.
'Noire année 1938', 31 Dec. 1938, p. 12.
'Deux conceptions de l'histoire', 11–12 Feb. 1939.
'Le Témoignage d'Alexandre Barmine', 4–5 March 1939, p. 14.
'Dix-huit congrès . . .', 18–19 March 1939, p. 10.
'Lumières sur l'U.R.S.S.', 1–2 April 1939, p. 10.
'Juifs de Russie . . .', 8–9 April 1939, p. 10.
'Hérésie et orthodoxie', 6–7 May 1939, p. 10.
'Terre des hommes', 27–28 May 1939, p. 10.
'Un Empire des steppes', 10–11 June 1939, p. 8.
'Les Juifs et la révolution', 24–25 June 1939, p. 8.
'La Fin d'une grande actrice', 29–30 July 1939, p. 8.
'Marx et Bakounine', 12–13 Aug. 1939, p. 8.
'La Fin de la révolution française', 19–20 Aug. 1939, p. 8.
'Responsabilité de quelques intellectuels', 12 Sept. 1939, pp. 1–2.
'Billet a un écrivain', 7–8 Aug. 1939, pp. 1–2.
'S'il est minuit dans le siècle', 30 Jan. 1940, pp. 1 and 4.

Vaplite Literaturno-khudozhnii zhurnal (Ukrainian), 1925–26
'Peregrupyvannya revoliutsnikh Frantsuz'kikh Pic'mennikiv' (Zoshchit Pershii, Vil'na
    Akademiya Proletars'koi Literatyri) Kharkiv, 1926, pp. 77–91.
'Ideologichnii Stan Novitn'oi Frantsuz'koi Literaturi', no. 1, 1927, pp. 116–26.

II Interviews

Manuel Alvarado, Mexico City; Pierre Broué, Mexico and Los Angeles; Isabel Diaz, Mexico City; Irina Gogua, Moscow; Mary Jayne Gold (conducted by John Eden), France; Albert Glotzer, New York and Los Angeles; Richard Greeman, Connecticut; Jeannine Kibalchich, Mexico City; Vlady Kibalchich, Mexico and Moscow; Roy Medvedev, Moscow; George Novack, Mexico City; Anita Russakova (conducted by Les Smith), Leningrad; Laurette Séjourné, Mexico City; Lisa Senyatskaya (Pankratov's wife, with Serge in Orenburg, conducted by Les Smith), Leningrad; Wilebaldo Solano, Paris; Ada Voitolovskaya (conducted by Les Smith), Leningrad; Sieva Volkov, Mexico and Los Angeles; Yevgeny Yevtushenko, Los Angeles.

III Intelligence files on Victor Serge

From 1987 to 1989 some 175 pages of intelligence reports on Victor Serge were released to the author through a Freedom of Information Act request. In 1997 a further 491 pages were released. The FBI admits they have many documents which are still classified – eighty-seven pages of the documents released in 1997 (FBI letter, 29 Jan. 1997). The file begins in 1940 and ends in 1954 (seven years after Serge's death). It contains intelligence reports from agents in Chile, Colombia, Cuba, the Dominican Republic, Peru, and the Fifteenth Naval District, in Washington, New York, and San Francisco. Several branches of intelligence were involved in gathering information on Serge: the Dept of Justice and the Dept of State, Visa Services, the Diplomatic Security Service, the Defense Intelligence Agency (in Mexico), HQ Southern Defense command, Fort Sam Houston, Dept of Army, US Army Intelligence and Security Command, Dept of Navy, Naval Intelligence Command, the FBI, Naval Attaché in Ciudad Trujillo, Dominican Republic.

The reports range from biographical to 'analytical' and are filled with errors of fact and interpretation. Some of Serge's works are summarized, some are translated. Serge's correspondence and his journalism are often cited, sometimes reproduced whole. Much is still deleted. Names, addresses and dates of birth are listed for Serge, his family and his associates in Mexico, including short biographies of each.

Files were also obtained from the French Police Prefecture from the late 1930s, and in Russia from RTsKhIDNI (now RGASPI, the Comintern Archive and Central Party Archive) from 1919–28, as well as Serge's NKVD file from Orenburg in 1933.

IV Secondary sources: works on Victor Serge

A *Theses*

Greeman, Richard, 'Victor Serge: The Making of a Novelist, 1890–1928', Ph.D. dissertation, Columbia University, 1968.

Marshall, W.J., 'Ideology and Literary Expression in the Works of Victor Serge', D.Phil. thesis, Wolfson College, Oxford University, 1984.

Weissman, Susan, 'Victor Serge: Political, social and literary critic of the USSR, 1919–1947; the reflections and activities of a Belgo-Russian Revolutionary caught in the orbit of Soviet political history', Ph.D. thesis, University of Glasgow, 1991.

B *Articles, reviews and essays about Serge*

Armstrong, Murray, 'The Searchers', Weekend *Guardian*, London, 22–23 Sept. 1990, pp. 18–22. Also published as 'Zagadka rukopisei Viktora Serzha', *Kul'tura*, no. 48 (1585), 1990, p. 22.

Arnot, Bob, 'Serge forward!' *Labour Left Briefing*, Dec. 1997.

Ascherson, Neal, 'Poisoned Cities', *New York Review of Books*, vol. 9, 9 Nov. 1969, p. 29.

Bénédite, Daniel (on Serge, no title), typescript.

Bensky, Lawrence, 'Behind the Lines' (review of *Birth of Our Power*), *New York Times*, vol. 116, 19 May 1967, p. 37.

Bongiovanni, Bruno, 'Victor Serge e il Totalitarismo', unpublished article 1987.

Castelár, Paul, 'GPU Terror Starts in Mexico, Former Agent Killed, Opponents in Peril', *New Leader*, 24 Jan. 1942.

—— 'CP uses Mexican Labor News for New Attacks on Anti-Fascist Refugees', *New Leader*, 7 March 1942.

—— 'OGPU Threatens French and Spanish Socialists' and 'The OGPU in Mexico' (unsigned articles), *New Leader*, Saturday, 27 Feb. 1943, pp. 4–5.

Chitarin, Attilio, 'Una voce dal gulag: lettere inedité di Victor Serge', *Revista di Storia Contemporanea*, no. 3, 1978, pp. 426–45.

—— 'Víctor Serge y la Revolutión Rusa ¿Dónde estaba el error?' Suplemento 'El Buhu', *El Excelsior*, 24 April 1988, Mexico DF.

Deutscher, Tamara, 'Victor Serge, *Year One of the Russian Revolution*', *Critique* 1, spring 1973, pp. 93–7.

Eden, John, 'Victor' (treatment for screenplay), 1989.

—— 'In Search of the Exile', in Susan Weissman (ed.), *The Ideas of Victor Serge: A Life as a Work of Art*, Glasgow, Critique Books, 1997.

Filtzer, Don, 'The Destiny of a Revolution: Victor Serge's *Russia Twenty Years After*', *Against the Current*, vol. XIII, no. 1 (new series), March–April 1998, pp. 41–3.

Frank, Pierre, 'Introduction', V.I. Lenin and L.D. Trotsky, *Kronstadt*, New York, Monad Press 1979, and in the revue *Quatrième Internationale*, Nov.–Dec. 1947.

Frankel, Jonathan, Review of *From Lenin to Stalin*, *American Political Science Review*, vol. 71, no. 4, Dec. 1977, p. 1723.

Gerhardt, G., 'Les Hommes dans la prison par V. Serge', in *L'Humanité* 26 June 1930.

Gilberto Gonzalez y Contreras, 'Victor Serge, el último evadido de Europa', *Bohemia*, La Habana, vol. 33, no. 36, 7 Sept. 1941, pp. 8–12.

Goldthorpe, Jeff, 'The Malaise of the Left and the Odd Elation of Victor Serge', *Against the Current*, vol. 3, no. 3, winter 1985, pp. 50–51.

Goodman, Walter, 'When the Revolution was Young: *The Conquered City*', *The New York Times Book Review*, 28 Dec. 1975, p. 14.

Gorkín, Julian, 'Adiós a Victor Serge', in *Mundo* no. 15, Jan.–Feb. 1948, Santiago de Chile, p. 6.

—— 'Les Dernières années de Victor Serge, 1941–1947', Afterword to Serge's *Mémoires d'une révolutionnaire*, Paris, Club des éditeurs, 1957, pp. 377–86.

Greeman, Richard, 'Victor Serge and the Tradition of Revolutionary Literature', *Tri-Quarterly*, 8, winter 1967, pp. 39–60.

—— '"The Laws are Burning" – Literary and Revolutionary Realism in Victor Serge', *Yale French Studies*, no. 39, 1967, pp. 146–59.

—— 'Victor Serge's *The Case of Comrade Tulaev*', *Minnesota Review*, vol. 15, fall 1980, pp. 61–79.

—— 'Victor Serge y Leon Trotski (1936–1940)', *Vuelta*, vol. 6, no. 63, Feb. 1982, pp. 22–33.

—— 'Victor Serge: Writer and Witness', *New Politics*, vol. 1, no. 2 (new series), winter 1987.

—— 'The Victor Serge Affair and the French Literary Left', in *Victor Serge: The Century of the Unexpected, Revolutionary History*, vol. 5, no. 3, autumn 1994, pp. 142–74.

—— Various chapters of unpublished biography of Serge.

Hoberman, J., 'Who Is Victor Serge? (And Why Do We Have to Ask?)', *Village Voice*, no. 30, 1984.

Howe, Irving, 'Serge's Novel', in *The New International*, Jan.–Feb. 1951, pp. 56–9.

Johnson, Roy, 'Victor Serge as Revolutionary Novelist', in *Literature and History*, vol. 5, no. 1, spring 1979, pp. 58–85.

Kibalchich, Jeannine 'Victor Serge, mi padre', published as 'My Father', in Susan Weissman (ed.), *The Ideas of Victor Serge: A Life as a Work of Art*, Glasgow, Critique Books, 1997, pp. 1–19.

Kibalchich, Vlady, 'La Vida como obra de arte', in Susan Weissman (ed.), *The Ideas of Victor Serge: A Life as a Work of Art*, Glasgow, Critique Books, 1997, pp. 21–5.

Krasso, Nicholas, 'Revolutionary Romanticism', *New Left Review*, no. 21, Sept.–Oct. 1963, pp. 107–11.

Lungdahl, 'An Old Revolutionary Looks at the World', Interview with Victor Serge, *El Informador*, Mexico, 30 Dec. 1945, pp. 4 and 7.

Macdonald, D.L., 'Wallace Stevens and Victor Serge', *Dalhousie Review*, vol. 66, no. 1, spring–summer 1986, pp. 174–80.

Maitrejean, Rirette, 'De Paris à Barcelone', *Témoins*, no. 21, Feb. 1959, pp. 37–8.

MacIntyre, Alasdair, 'True Voice' (review of Serge's *Memoirs*), *New Statesman*, 30 Aug. 1963, pp. 259–60.

Manson, John, '"Les Derniers Temps" ou "Les Grandes Vacances"?' *Weighbank*, no. 14, Oct. 1981, pp. 4–7.

—— 'Notes' on *Carnets* (1944), *Cencrastus*, no. 4, winter 1980–81, pp. 16–20.

—— 'Victor Serge's Emigrations', *Southfields*, no. 2, 1996, 'Exiles and Emigrés' edition.

—— 'The Carnets', in Susan Weissman (ed.), *The Ideas of Vicor Serge: Life as a Work of Art*, Glasgow, Critique Books, 1997, pp. 223–38.

Marshall, William J., *Victor Serge: The Uses of Dissent*, New York and Oxford, Berg, 1992.

Martinet, Marcel, *Où va la révolution russe? L'affaire Victor Serge*, Paris, Librairie du Travail, 1934.

Maspero, François, 'Victor Serge, poète de la flamme', *Le Monde*, 25 Dec. 1998, p. 24.

Mesnil, Jacques: 'L'Affaire Victor Serge et l'interview de Romain Rolland', in *La Révolution prolétarienne*, 25 June 1933.

Morgan, Edwin, 'Siege Mentalities' (review of *Conquered City*), *Times Literary Supplement*, 30 July 1976, p. 951.

Motylyova, Tamara, 'Roman Rolland: I Am Defending the USSR, not Stalin', in *Moscow News* weekly no. 13, 1988, p. 16.

Mounier, Emmanuel, 'Victor Serge', *Esprit*, 16, no. 1, Jan. 1948, pp. 112–13.

Pages, Pelai, 'Victor Serge y la guerra civil española', unpublished manuscript, twenty-one pages.

Paz, Magdeleine: 'Réponse à "L'Homme qui n'adhère à rien"' *Le Monde*, 2 April 1933.

—— 'L'Affaire Victor Serge', in *Les Cahiers des Droits de l'Homme*, 10 June 1933.

—— 'Liberté pour Victor Serge! Discours de Magdeleine Paz au Congrès international des Ecrivains', *La Révolution prolétarienne*, nos 227–11, 228–12, 229–13, 1936.

—— 'La Voix de Victor Serge', preface to *Seize fusillés: où va la révolution russe?*, Paris, Spartacus, 1936.

Ross, Betty, 'El fin de totalitarismo es previsto por Victor Serge, *Excelsior*, Mexico City, 22 Oct. 1941, p. 3.

Roule, Jean, 'Un Gran Libro' (review of *Hitler contra Stalin*), *Rumbo*, Mexico, Nov. 1941, p. 8.

Rovida, Giorgio, 'Sul l'ideologia rivoluzionaria da *L'Affaire Toulaev* à *Les Années sans pardon*', unpublished manuscript, twenty pages.

Salisbury, Harrison E., 'Dawn of Darkness at Noon' (review of *Memoirs of a Revolutionary*), *Saturday Review*, 14 Dec. 1963, p. 48.

Sedgwick, Peter, 'The Unhappy Elitist: Victor Serge's Early Bolshevism', published posthumously in *History Workshop Journal*, vol. 17, spring 1984, pp. 150–56.

—— 'Doing Time' (review of *Men in Prison*), *New Society*, 30 July 1970, pp. 207–8.

—— 'Victor Serge, *From Lenin to Stalin*', *Critique 2*, autumn 1973, pp. 95–7.

—— 'Victor Serge and Socialism', *International Socialism*, no. 14, autumn 1963; reprinted in Susan Weissman (ed.), *The Ideas of Victor Serge: A Life as a Work of Art*, Glasgow, Critique Books 1997.

—— 'A Portrait of Victor Serge', *New Politics*, 1962/63.

Silone, Ignazio, 'Stalin – and Anti-Stalin' (Review of *S'il est minuit dans le siècle*), in *Correspondance*, April 1940, pp. 23–4.

—— 'Pour Victor Serge', in *Les Nouvelles Littéraires*, 22 July 1933.

Solano, Wilebaldo, 'Victor Serge, España Y el POUM', in Susan Weissman (ed.), *The Ideas of Victor Serge: A Life as a Work of Art*, Glasgow, Critique Books 1997.

Sulzberger, C.L., and Sedova, N.I., Correspondence published in *New York Times*, 14 Feb. 1948 and 9 March 1948, reprinted in 'Paranoid Politics', *Signs*, 1948, pp. 247–61.

Tavera Garcia, Susanna, 'Victor Serge y el sindicalismo catalán: Barcelona 1917, una estancia desconocida', unpublished manuscript, twenty pages.

Screenan, Dermot, 'The Bolshevik's Pet Anarchist: The Life, Times and Confessions of Victor Serge' in *Red and Black Revolution* and at http://flag.backened.net/revolt/rbr/rbr4_serge.htm 1998.

Wald, Alan, 'Victor Serge and the New York Anti-Stalinist Left, 1937–47', in Susan Weissman (ed.), *The Ideas of Victor Serge: A Life as a Work of Art*, Glasgow, Critique Books 1997.

Wilson, Edmund, 'Russia: Escape from Propaganda' (Review of *Russia Twenty Years After*), *The Nation*, no. 145, 13 Nov. 1937, pp. 532–4.

Weissman, Susan, 'Victor Serge: From Petrograd to Orenburg', *Against the Current*, vol. II, no. 6 and vol. III, no. 7 (new series) Jan.–Feb. and Mar.–April 1988, pp. 40–46.

—— 'Victor Serge's Critique of Stalinism: Bureaucracy and Planlessness', *Against the Current*, vol. III, no. 2 (new series), May–June 1988, pp. 36–40.

—— 'De Petrograd à Orenbourg: la critique du développement politique soviétique par Victor Serge', *Cahiers Leon Trotsky*, no. 37, March 1989, pp. 87–107.

—— 'Kronstadt and the Fourth International' in D.J. Cotterill, *The Serge–Trotsky Papers*, London, Pluto Press, 1994.

—— 'The Left Opposition Divided: The Trotsky–Serge Disputes', in Hillel Ticktin and Michael Cox (eds), *The Ideas of Leon Trotsky*, London, Porcupine Books, 1995.

—— 'Victor Serge, The Forgotten Marxist', in Susan Weissman (ed.), *Victor Serge: Russia Twenty Years After*, New York, Humanities Press, 1996.

—— 'Serge and Trotsky's Views: Post Theories Strengths and Limitations', *Journal of Trotsky Studies*, no. 4, 1996.

—— 'Introduction' and 'On Stalinism', in Susan Weissman (ed.), *The Ideas of Victor Serge: A Life as a Work of Art*, Glasgow, Critique Books, 1997.

—— 'Victor Serge, a Profile', *New Socialist*, June 1998.

—— 'Dossier Victor Serge: de Petrograd a Orenburgo – el mundo de Victor Serge y el nuestro', *El Rodoballo*, vol. 10, no. 10, spring 2000, pp. 53–60.

—— (ed.), *Victor Serge: Russia Twenty Years After*, New York, Humanities Press, 1996.

—— (ed.), *The Ideas of Victor Serge: A Life as a Work of Art*, Glasgow, Critique Books, 1997.

Wullens, Maurice, 'Pour Victor Serge', in *Les Humbles*, June 1933.

C Secondary sources (general)

Alba, Victor, *The Communist Party in Spain*, New Brunswick, NJ, Transaction Books, 1983.

Alba, Victor and Stephen Schwartz, *Spanish Marxism versus Soviet Communism: A History of the POUM*, New Brunswick and Oxford, Transaction Books, 1988.

Ali, Tariq, *Fear of Mirrors*, London, Arcadia Books, 1998.

—— (ed.), *The Stalinist Legacy*, Harmondsworth, Penguin Books, 1984.

Antonov-Ovseenko, Anton, *The Time of Stalin: Portrait of a Tyranny*, New York, Harper Colophon Books, 1981. First published in the USA as *Stalinshchina: Portret tirana*, Khronika Press, 1980.

Avrich, Paul (ed.), *Anarchists in the Russian Revolution*, London, Thames and Hudson, 1973.

—— *Kronstadt 1921*, New York, W.W. Norton, 1970.

Balabanova, Angelica, *My Life as a Rebel*, New York, Harper and Brothers, 1938.

Barbusse, Henri, *Stalin*, New York, Macmillan, 1935.

Barmine, Alexander, *One Who Survived: The Life Story of a Russian under the Soviets* (first published in France and Britain in 1938, under the title *Memoirs of a Soviet Diplomat*), New York, G.P. Putnam's Sons, 1945.

Beck, F., and Godin, W., *Russian Purge and the Extraction of Confession*, London, Hurst and Blackett, 1951.

Becker, Emile, *La 'Bande á Bonnot'*, Paris, Les Nouvelles Editions Debresse, 1968.

Bénédite, Daniel, *La Filière marseillaise: Un chemin vers la liberté sous l'occupation*, Paris, Editions Clancier Guénaud, 1984.

Berger, John, *The Look of Things, Selected Essays and Articles*, Harmondsworth, Penguin Books, 1972.

Bettelheim, Bruno, *The Informed Heart*, London, Thames and Hudson, 1961.

Body, Marcel, *Un Piano en bouleau de Carélie: mes années de Russie (1917–1927)*, Paris, Hachette, 1981.

Bolleten, Burnett, *The Spanish Revolution, The Left and the Struggle for Power during the Civil War*, Chapel Hill, The University of North Carolina Press, 1979.

Borkenau, Franz, *World Communism: A History of the Communist International*, Ann Arbor, University of Michigan Press, 1962.

Broué, Pierre, *Le parti Bolchevique*, Paris, Editions de Minuit, 1963.

—— *Révolution en Allemagne*, Paris, Editions de Minuit, 1971.

—— *Le révolution et la guerre d'Espagne*, Paris, Editions de Minuit, 1961.

—— *Trotsky*, Paris, Librairie Artheme Fayard, 1988.

—— *Histoire de l'Internationale Communiste*, Paris, Librairie Artheme Fayard, 1997.

—— (ed.), *La Question chinoise dans l'Internationale Communiste* (1926–27), Paris, EDI, 1976.

Burnham, James, *The Managerial Revolution*, New York, John Day, 1941.

Cacucci, Pino, *Tina Modotti*, Barcelona, Circe Bolsillo, 1995. Published in English as *Tina Modotti: A Life*, New York, St Martin's Press, 1999.

Campeanu, Pavel, *The Origins of Stalinism*, translated by Michel Vale, Armonk New York, M.E. Sharpe, 1986.

Cannon, James P., *The History of American Trotskyism*, New York, Pathfinder Press, 1972.

Carr, E.H., *The Bolshevik Revolution 1917–1923*; three volumes, London, Macmillan, 1953

—— *The Interregnum, 1923–1924: A History of Soviet Russia*, vol. IV, London, Macmillan, 1954.

—— *Socialism in One Country*, four volumes, London, Macmillan, 1958.

—— *The October Revolution*, New York, Alfred Knopf, 1969.

—— *The Comintern and the Spanish Civil War*, edited by Tamara Deutscher, New York, Pantheon Books, 1983.

Carr, E.H., and Davies, R.W., *Foundations of a Planned Economy*, two volumes, New York, Macmillan, 1969.

Central Committee Minutes: *The Bolsheviks and the October Revolution*, London, Pluto Press, 1974.

Chase, William, *Workers, Society and the Soviet State: Labor and Life in Moscow, 1918–1929*, Urbana and Chicago, University of Illinois Press, 1987.

Ciliga, Anton, *The Russian Enigma*, London, The Labour Book Service, 1940.

Claudin, Fernando, *The Communist Movement*, two volumes, New York and London, Monthly Review Press, 1975.

Cliff, Tony, *State Capitalism in Russia*, London, Pluto Press, 1974.

Cohen, Stephen F., *Bukharin and the Bolshevik Revolution*, Oxford, Oxford University Press, 1971.

Conquest, Robert, *The Great Terror*, Harmondsworth, Penguin Books, 1968.

—— *The Harvest of Sorrow*, New York and Oxford, Oxford University Press, 1986.

—— *Stalin and the Kirov Murder*, New York and Oxford, Oxford University Press, 1989.

Costello, John, and Tsarev, Oleg, *Deadly Illusions: The KGB Orlov Dossier*, New York, Crown Publishers, 1993.

Cox, Michael, 'The First Congress of the Toilers of the East documents', in *Critique* 1, spring 1973, pp. 101–2.

Craig, David (ed.), *Marxists on Literature: An Anthology*, Harmondsworth, Penguin, 1975.

Crossman, Richard (ed.), *The God that Failed*, New York, Bantam, 1952.

Dallin, David J., *The Real Soviet Russia*, New Haven, Yale University Press, 1944.

Dallin, David J., and Nicolaevsky, Boris I., *Forced Labor in Soviet Russia*, New Haven, Yale University Press, 1947.

Dallin, Lola, Testimony to United States Senate Hearing before the Subcommittee to

Investigate the Administration of the Internal Security Act and Other Internal Security Laws of the Committee on the Judiciary, Eighty-Fourth and Eighty-Fifth Congresses, 1956–57, 6 March 1956.

Daniels, Robert V., *A Documentary History of Communism*, two volumes, Hanover, NH, University Press of New England, 1984, 1988.

—— *The Conscience of the Revolution*, New York, Simon and Schuster, 1960.

—— (ed.) *The Stalin Revolution, Foundations of Soviet Totalitarianism*, Lexington, Mass., Heath, 1972.

Degras, Jane (ed.), *The Communist International 1919–1943*, Documents, three volumes, London, Frank Cass, 1970.

Deutscher, Isaac, *The Prophet Armed, Trotsky 1879–1921*, Oxford, Oxford University Press, 1954.

—— *The Prophet Unarmed, Trotsky 1921–1929*, Oxford, Oxford University Press, 1959.

—— *The Prophet Outcast, Trotsky 1929–1940*, Oxford, Oxford University Press, 1963.

—— *Stalin: A Political Biography*, revised edition, Harmondsworth, Penguin Books, 1966.

Dobb, Maurice, *Soviet Economic Development*, London, Routledge and Kegan Paul, 1966.

Eagleton, Terry, *Marxism and Literary Criticism*, London, Methuen, 1976.

Eastman, Max, *Writers in Uniform*, London, Allen and Unwin, 1934.

—— *The Young Trotsky*, London, New Park Publications, 1980, first published in 1926.

Filtzer, Donald, *Soviet Workers and Stalinist Industrialization, The Formation of Modern Soviet Production Relations 1928–1941*, New York, M.E. Sharpe, 1986.

—— Afterword to Christian Rakovsky, 'The Five Year Plan in Crisis', in *Critique* 13, 1981, pp. 13–54.

Fischer, Louis, *Men and Politics, An Autobiography*, London, Jonathan Cape, 1941.

Fischer, Ruth, *Stalin and German Communism: A Study in the Origins of the State Party*, Cambridge Mass., Harvard University Press, 1948.

Fitzpatrick, Sheila (ed.), *Cultural Revolution in Russia, 1928–1931*, Bloomington, University of Indiana Press, 1978.

Fry, Varian, *Surrender on Demand*, New York, Random House, 1945.

—— *Assignment: Rescue*, New York, Four Winds Press, 1968.

The Gelfand Case, vols I and II, Detroit, Labor Publications, 1985.

Getty, J. Arch, *Origins of the Great Purges*, Cambridge, Cambridge University Press, 1985.

—— *Stalin's Road to Terror* (with Oleg Naumov), New Haven, Yale University Press, 1999.

Gide, André, *Regreso de la URSS, seguida de retoques a mi regreso de la URSS*, Barcelona, Muchnik Editores, 1982. (Spanish translation of French original, *Retour de l'URSS, suivi de retouches à mon retour de l'URSS*, Paris, Gallimard, 1968.)

Ginzburg, Evgenia, *Into the Whirlwind*, London, Penguin Books, 1967.

—— *Within the Whirlwind*, New York and London, Harcourt Brace, Jovanovich, 1981.

Gold, Mary Jayne, *Crossroads Marseilles 1940*, New York, Doubleday, 1980.

Gonzalez, Valentin, and Gorkín, Julian, *El Campesino: Life and Death in Soviet Russia*, New York, G.P. Putnam's Sons, 1952.

Gorkín, Julian, *El revolucionario profesional*, Barcelona, Ayma S.A. Editoria, 1975.

—— *Como asesinó Stalin a Trotsky*, Barcelona, Plaza and Janes, S.A., 1965.

Gramsci, Antonio, *Selections from the Prison Notebooks*, edited by Quintin Hoare, London, Lawrence and Wishart, 1971.

Gruber, Helmut, *International Communism in the Era of Lenin: A Documentary History*, Greenwich, Conn., Fawcett Publications, 1967.

Hosking, Geoffrey, *The First Socialist Society: A History of the Soviet Union from Within*, Cambridge, Mass., Harvard University Press, 1985.

Howard, Dick (ed.), *Selected Political Writings of Rosa Luxemburg*, New York, Monthly Review Press, 1971.

Howe, Irving, *Politics and the Novel*, London, Stevens and Sons, 1961.

—— *Leon Trotsky*, New York, Viking Press, 1978.

Hulse, James, *The Forming of the Communist International*, Stanford, Calif., Stanford University Press, 1964.

Iagoda, Genrikh, *Narkom vutrennikh del SSSR, General'nyi komissar gosudarstvennoi bezopasnosti.* Kazan, Sbornik dokumentov, 1997.

Isaacs, Harold, *The Tragedy of the Chinese Revolution*, with an introduction by Leon Trotsky, London, Secker and Warburg, 1938.

Istrati, Panaït, *Vers l'autre flamme*, Paris, Rieder, 1929, republished with an introduction by Marcel Mermoz, Paris, Fondation Panaït Istrati, Union Générale D'Editions, 1980.

—— *Soviets 1929*, Paris, Les Editions Rieder, 1929.

James, C.L.R., *World Revolution: 1917–1936*, London, Martin, Secker and Warburg, 1937.

Jasny, Naum, *Soviet Industrialization 1928–1952*, Chicago, University of Chicago Press, 1961.

Joffe, Maria, *One Long Night*, London, New Park Publications, 1977.

Joffe, Nadezhda, *Back in Time: My Life, My Fate, My Epoch: The Memoirs of Nadezhda A. Joffe*, Oak Park, Michigan, Labor Publications, 1995.

—— *Moi Otyetz, Adol'f Abramovich Ioffe*, Moscow, Vozvrashchenie, 1996.

Jussila, Osmo, Hentilä, Seppo, and Nevakivi, Jukka, *From Grand Duchy to a Modern State: A Political History of Finland since 1809*, London, Hurst, 1999.

Kagarlitsky, Boris, *The Thinking Reed: Intellectuals and the Soviet State 1917 to the Present*, London, Verso, 1988.

Kaiser, Daniel H. (ed.), *The Workers Revolution in Russia 1917: The View from Below*, Cambridge, Cambridge University Press, 1987.

Kazantzakis, Helen, *Nikos Kazantzakis, A Biography Based on His Letters*, Berkeley, Calif., Creative Arts Book Co., 1983.

Klehr, Harvey, Haynes, John Earl, and Firsov, Fridrikh Igorevich, *The Secret World of American Communism*, New Haven, Yale University Press, 1995.

Knoellinger, Carl Erik, *Labor in Finland*, Cambridge, Mass., Harvard University Press, 1960.

Knight, Amy, *Who Killed Kirov?* New York, Hill and Wang, 1999.

Koenker, Diane, *Moscow Workers and the 1917 Revolution*, Princeton, NJ, Princeton University Press, 1981.

Koestler, Arthur, *Darkness at Noon*, London, Penguin 1964.

Konrad, Georgy, and Szelenyi, Ivan, *The Intelligentsia on the Road to Class Power*, New York, Harcourt Brace Jovanovich, 1979.

Kostiuk, Hryhory, *Stalinist Rule in the Ukraine*, New York, Frederick A. Praeger Publishers, 1960.

Kravchenko, Victor, *I Chose Freedom*, New York, Scribners, 1947.

Krawchenko, Bohdan, 'The Famine in the Ukraine in 1933', *Critique* 17, 1986, pp. 137–47.

Krivitsky, Walter, *In Stalin's Secret Service*, New York and London, Harper Brothers, 1939.

Lane, David, *Politics and Society in the USSR*, London, Weidenfeld and Nicolson, 1970.

Lacouture, Jean, *André Malraux*, New York, Pantheon Books, 1975.

Lenin, V.I., *Selected Works* (three volumes), Moscow, Progress Publishers, 1971.

Lenin, V.I., and Trotsky, LD, *Kronstadt*, New York, Monad Press, 1979.

Lewin, Moshe, *Russian Peasants and Soviet Power*, Evanston, Northwestern University Press, 1968.

—— *Lenin's Last Struggle*, London, Wildwood House, 1968.

—— *Political Undercurrents in Soviet Economic Debates*, London, Pluto Press, 1974.

Levine, Isaac Don, *The Mind of an Assassin*, London, Weidenfeld and Nicolson, 1959.

Lottman, Herbert, *The Left Bank: Writers, Artists and Politics from the Popular Front to the Cold War*, London, Heinemann, 1982.

Lukacs, G., *History and Class Consciousness*, London, Merlin Press, 1971.

Lukes, Steven, *Marxism and Morality*, Oxford, Oxford University Press, 1985.

Macdonald, Dwight, *Memoirs of a Revolutionist, Essays in Political Criticism*, Cleveland, Meridian, 1958.

Macdonald, Nancy, *Homage to the Spanish Exiles*, New York, Insight Books, 1987.

Madsen, Axel, *Malraux, A Biography*, New York, William Morrow, 1976.

Malaquais, Jean, *World Without Visa*, New York, Doubleday, 1948.

Malraux, André, *Anti-Memoirs*, New York, Holt, Rinehart and Winston, 1968.

Mandel, Ernest (ed.), *Fifty Years of World Revolution*, New York, Monad Press, 1968.

—— 'In Defence of Socialist Planning', in *New Left Review*, no. 159, Sept.–Oct. 1986, pp. 22–32.

Mandelstam, Nadezhda, *Hope Against Hope*, Harmondsworth, Penguin Books, 1970.

Marx, Karl, and Friedrich Engels, *The Communist Manifesto*, London, Verso, 1998.

—— *Collected Works*, New York and Moscow, International Publishers, 1975.

Massing, Hede, *This Deception*, New York, Duell, Sloan and Pearce, 1951.

Mell, Ezra Brett, *The Truth about the Bonnot Gang*, London, Coptic Press, 1968.

Medvedev, Roy A., *Let History Judge*, New York, Vintage Books, 1973.

—— *On Stalin and Stalinism*, Oxford, Oxford University Press, 1979.

—— *Nikolai Bukharin*, New York and London, W.W. Norton, 1980.

Naville, Pierre, *Trotsky Vivant*, Paris, Editions d'Aujourd'Hui, 1962, 1975.

Neumann, Franz, *Behemoth: The Structure and Practice of National Socialism 1933–1944*, Oxford, Oxford University Press, 1942, 1944.

Nicolaevsky, Boris, *Power and the Soviet Elite: 'The Letter of an Old Bolshevik' and Other Essays*, New York, Praeger, 1965.

Nove, Alec, *An Economic History of the USSR*, London, Penguin Books, 1969.

—— *Stalinism and After*, London, Unwin and Hyman, 1975, 1988.

—— *Marxism and 'Really Existing Socialism'*, London, Harwood Academic Publishers, 1986.

O'Neill, William L., *A Better World: The Great Schism: Stalinism and the American Intellectuals*, New York, Simon and Schuster, 1982.

Orlov, Alexander, *The Secret History of Stalin's Crimes*, New York, Random House, 1953.

—— Testimony to the United States Senate Hearing before the Subcommittee to Investigate the Administration of the Internal Security Act and Other Internal Security Laws of the Committee on the Judiciary, Eighty-Fourth and Eighty-Fifth Congresses, 1956–57, part 51, 14–15 Feb. 1957, pp. 3423–9.

Parry, Richard, *The Bonnot Gang*, London, Rebel Press, 1987.

Pascal, Pierre, *Mon Journal de Russie*, four vols, Lausanne, L'Age d'Homme, 1975–82.

People's Commissariat of Justice of the USSR, *Report of Court Proceedings in the Case of the Anti-Soviet 'Bloc of Rights and Trotskyites'*, Moscow, 1938.

Petras, James, 'Authoritarianism, Democracy and the Transition to Socialism', in *Socialist Register* 1986.

Phelps, Christopher, *Young Sidney Hook: Marxist and Pragmatist*, Ithaca, Cornell University Press, 1997.

Pipes, Richard, *The Russian Revolution*, New York, Knopf, 1990.

Ponomarev, B., *The Plot against the Soviet Union and World Peace, Facts and Documents*, Moscow and New York, Workers Library Publishers (no date, 1938?).

Poretsky, Elisabeth K., *Our Own People*, Ann Arbor, University of Michigan Press, 1969.

Preobrazhensky, Evgeny, *The New Economics*, Oxford, Oxford University Press, 1965.

—— *From NEP to Socialism*, London, New Park Publications, 1973.

—— *O Morali i klassovykh normakh*, Moscow, 1923.

Prychodko, Nicholas, *One of the Fifteen Million*, Boston, Little, Brown, 1952.

Rabinowitch, Alexander, *The Bolsheviks Come to Power: The Revolution of 1917 in Petrograd*, New York, W.W. Norton, 1976.

Rakovsky, Christian, *Selected Writings on Opposition in the USSR 1923–30*, London, Allison and Busby, 1980.

—— 'The Five Year Plan in Crisis', *Critique* 13, 1981, pp. 13–53. From, 'Na s'ezde i v strane', *Byulleten' oppozitsii*, no. 25/26, 1931, pp. 9–32.

Reed, Dale, and Jakobson, Michael, 'Trotsky Papers at the Hoover Institution: One Chapter of an Archival Mystery Story', *The American Historical Review*, vol. 92, no. 2, April 1987.

Reinhardt, *Crime without Punishment: The Secret Soviet Terror against America*, New York, Hermitage House, 1952.

Reissner, Larissa, *Hamburg at the Barricades*, London, Pluto Press, 1977.

Rizzi, Bruno, *La Burocratización del mundo*, Barcelona, Ediciones Peninsulá, 1977.

Rogovin, Vadim, *1937: Stalin's Year of Terror*, Oak Park, Michigan, Mehring Books, 1998.

Rosenstone, Robert A., *Romantic Revolutionary, A Biography of John Reed*, New York, Vintage Books, 1975.

Rosmer, Alfred, *Moscow under Lenin*, New York, Monthly Review Press, 1971.

Rubin, I.I., *The History of Economic Thought*, edited and translated by Donald A. Filtzer, London, Ink Links, 1979.

Samios, Eleni: *La verdadera tragedia de Panaït Istrati*, Santiago de Chile, Ediciones Ercilla, 1938.

Schapiro, Leonard *The Russian Revolutions of 1917: The Origins of Modern Communism*, New York, Basic Books, 1984.

Schwartz, Stephen, *Intellectuals and Assassins*, London, Anthem Press, 2000.

Schwarz, Solomon, *Labor in the Soviet Union*, New York, Cresset Press, 1952.

Scott, John, *Behind the Urals, An American Worker in Russia's City of Steel*, Bloomington, Indian University Press, 1942.

Shachtman, Max, *Behind the Moscow Trial*, New York, Pioneer Publishers, 1936.

—— *The Bureaucratic Revolution, The Rise of the Stalinist State*, New York, The Donald Press, 1962.

—— *Genesis of Trotskyism: The First Ten Years of the Left Opposition*, London, IMG Publications, 1973.

Sheridan, Clare, *Russian Portraits*, London, Jonathan Cape, 1921.

Siegelbaum, Lewis H., and Suny, Ronald Grigor, *Making Workers Soviet: Power, Class and Identity*, Ithaca, NY, Cornell University Press,1994.

Singer, Daniel, *Whose Millennium: Theirs or Ours?* New York, Monthly Review Press, 1999.

Smith, Andrew, *I was a Soviet Worker*, New York, E.P. Dutton, 1936.

Smith, S.A., *Red Petrograd: Revolution in the Factories 1917–1918*, Cambridge, Cambridge University Press, 1983.

Souvarine, Boris, *Una Controvérsia con Trotski*, Mexico, Universidad Autonoma de Sinaloa, 1983.

—— *Stalin: A Critical Survey of Bolshevism*, translated by C.L.R. James, New York, Longman, Green, 1939.

Suny, Ronald Grigor, *The Soviet Experiment*, New York, Oxford University Press, 1998.

Swingewood, Alan, *The Novel and Revolution*, London, Macmillan, 1975.

Thomas, Bernard, *La Bande à Bonnot*, Paris, Claude Tchou, 1968.

Ticktin, H.H., 'Towards a Political Economy of the USSR', *Critique* 1, 1973. pp. 20–41.

—— 'The Contradictions of Soviet Society and Professor Bettleheim', *Critique* 6, 1976. pp. 17–44.

—— *Origins of the Crisis in the USSR*, Armonk, New York, M.E. Sharpe, 1992.

Trotsky, Leon, *Between Red and White: Social Democracy and the Wars of Intervention in Russia, 1918–1921*, London, New Park Publications, 1975.

—— *Bolshevism and Stalinism*, New York, Pioneer Publishers, 1937.

—— *The Case of Leon Trotsky* (verbatim transcript of Trotsky's testimony before the Dewey Commission, Coyoacán, Mexico, 10–17 April 1937), New York, Merit Publishers, 1937.

—— *The Challenge of the Left Opposition (1923–1925)*, edited by Naomi Allen, New York, Pathfinder Press, 1975.

—— *The Crisis of the French Section 1935–1936*, New York, Pathfinder Press, 1977.

—— *In Defense of Marxism*, London, New Park Publications, 1971.

—— *The First Five Years of the Communist International*, two volumes, London, New Park Publications, 1973.

—— *History of the Russian Revolution*, three volumes, London, Sphere Books, 1967.

—— *On the Kirov Assassination*, New York, Pioneer Publishers, 1956.

—— *On Literature and Art*, New York, Pathfinder Press, 1970.

—— *Literature and Revolution*, Ann Arbor, Michigan University Press, 1960.

—— 'Marxism in Our Time', Merit pamphlet, New York, Pioneer Publishers, 1939.

—— *My Life*, Harmondsworth, Pelican Books, 1975.

—— *The New Course*, London, New Park Publications, 1943, 1972.

—— *The Permanent Revolution and Results and Prospects*, New York, Pathfinder Press, 1969.

—— *Problems of the Chinese Revolution*, New York, Pioneer Publishers, 1967.

—— *Revolution Betrayed*, New York, Merit Publishers, 1965.

—— 'The Moralists and Sycophants against Marxism', in *Their Morals and Ours*, New York, Merit Publishers, 1969.

—— *The Spanish Revolution 1931–1939*, New York, Pathfinder Press, 1973.

—— *Stalin's Gangsters*, London, New Park Publications, 1977.

—— *Trotsky's Diary in Exile 1935*, Cambridge, Mass., Harvard University Press, 1976.

—— *Writings*, ten volumes 1931–40, New York, Pathfinder Press, 1973.

—— *Writings of Leon Trotsky: Supplement (1934–1940)*, New York, Pathfinder Press, 1979.

Trotsky, Lev Davidovitch, and Rosmer, Alfred and Marguerite, *Correspondance 1929–1939*, Paris, Gallimard, 1982.

United States Senate, 'Scope of Soviet Activity in the United States', Hearing before the Subcommittee to Investigate the Administration of the Internal Security Act and Other Internal Security Laws of the Committee on the Judiciary, Eighty-Fourth and Eighty-Fifth Congresses, 1956–57.

Van Heijenoort, Jean, *With Trotsky in Exile, From Prinkipo to Coyoacán*, Cambridge, Mass., Harvard University Press, 1978.

van Rysselberghe, M. de, *Les Cahiers de la petite dame 1929–1937*, Cahiers André Gide no. 5, Paris, Gallimard, 1974.

Vereeken, Georges, *The GPU in the Trotskyist Movement*, London, New Park Publications, 1976.

Viola, Lynne, *The Best Sons of the Fatherland, Workers in the Vanguard of Soviet Collectivization*, New York, Oxford University Press, 1987.

Volgokonov, D., *Trotsky: The Eternal Revolutionary*, New York, Free Press, 1996.

Volin (Vsevolod Mikhailovich Eichenbaum), *La Revolución desconocida (historia del silencio bochevique)*, Mexico, Ediciones Mexicanos Unidos, 1984.

Wald, Alan M., *The New York Intellectuals: The Rise and Decline of the Anti-Stalinist Left from the 1930s to the 1980s*, Chapel Hill, University of North Carolina Press, 1987.

—— *The Revolutionary Imagination: The Poetry and Politics of John Wheelwright and Sherry Mangan*, Chapel Hill, University of North Carolina Press, 1983.

—— *The Responsibility of Intellectuals: Selected Essays on Marxist Traditions in Cultural Com-*

mitment, Atlantic Highlands, NJ, Humanities Press, 1992.

Waters, Mary-Alice (ed.), *Rosa Luxemburg Speaks*, New York, Pathfinder Press, 1969.

Weinstein, Allen, and Vassiliev, Alexander, *The Haunted Wood*, New York, Random House, 1999.

Weissberg, Alexander, *The Accused*, New York, Simon and Schuster, 1951.

Weissman, Susan, 'Back in the USSR', in Carl Finamore (ed.), *Gorbachev's USSR: Is Stalinism Dead?*, San Francisco, Walnut Press, 1989.

White, James, 'Historiography of the Russian Revolution in the Twenties', *Critique* 1, spring 1973, pp. 42–54.

—— *The Russian Revolution 1917–1921: A Short History*, London, Edward Arnold, 1994.

Winegarten, Renée, *Writers and Revolution: The Fatal Lure of Action*, New York, New Viewpoints, 1974.

Wreszin, Michael, *A Rebel in Defense of Tradition: The Life and Politics of Dwight Macdonald*, New York, Basic Books, 1994.

Zborowski, Mark, Testimony to the United States Senate Hearing before the Subcommittee to Investigate the Administration of the Internal Security Act and Other Internal Security Laws of the Committee on the Judiciary, Eighty-Fourth and Eighty-Fifth Congresses, 1956–57, 29 Feb. 1956.

Index